Fourth Edition

FAMILIES & CHANGE

This book is dedicated to Claire Elise Askeland

Born August 28, 2008

The Next Generation

Fourth Edition

FAMILIES & CHANGE

Coping With Stressful Events and Transitions

Editors

Sharon J. Price
The University of Georgia

Christine A. Price
Montclair State University

Patrick C. McKenry
The Ohio State University

Los Angeles | London | New Delhi
Singapore | Washington DC

For information:

SAGE Publications, Inc.
2455 Teller Road
Thousand Oaks, California 91320
E-mail: order@sagepub.com

SAGE Publications Ltd.
1 Oliver's Yard
55 City Road
London EC1Y 1SP
United Kingdom

SAGE Publications India Pvt. Ltd.
B 1/I 1 Mohan Cooperative Industrial Area
Mathura Road, New Delhi 110 044
India

SAGE Publications Asia-Pacific Pte. Ltd.
33 Pekin Street #02-01
Far East Square
Singapore 048763

Printed in the United States of America

Library of Congress Cataloging-in-Publication Data

Families & change: coping with stressful events and transitions / Sharon J. Price, Christine A. Price, editors; with Patrick C. McKenry.—4th ed.
    p. cm.
Includes bibliographical references and index.
ISBN 978-1-4129-6851-5 (pbk.)
    1. Families—United States. 2. Social problems—United States. 3. Social change—United States.
I. Price, Sharon J. II. Price, Christine A. III. McKenry, Patrick C. IV. Title: Families and change.

HQ536.F332 2010
306.850973—dc22   2009017680

This book is printed on acid-free paper.

    10   11   12   13   10   9   8   7   6   5   4   3

Acquisitions Editor:	Kassie Graves
Editorial Assistant:	Veronica K. Novak
Production Editor:	Astrid Virding
Copy Editor:	Cheryl Rivard
Typesetter:	C&M Digitals (P) Ltd.
Proofreader:	Ellen Brink
Indexer:	Molly Hall
Cover Designer:	Arup Giri
Marketing Manager:	Stephanie Adams

Contents _____

Preface _____

The fourth edition of *Families & Change: Coping With Stressful Events and Transitions* presents the vast literature that has emerged in recent years detailing families' responses to various transitions and stressful life events. Scholarly interest in family stressors is not new. The social and behavioral sciences evolved during the Progressive Era (1890–1920) out of an interest in social problems facing families as a result of industrialization and urbanization. The primary interest at this time was in social reform and the use of research to help in solving these problems. During the 1920s and 1930s, scholars started focusing on the internal dynamics of families. Because of the disillusionment with the effects of social reform programs and the growing depersonalization of mass society, there was an increasing interest in the well-being and personal adjustment of families and individuals. Researchers became interested in healthy lifestyles, mental health, and child development. Both family sociology and family therapy started developing at this time (Cole & Cole, 1993).

Two major societal disruptions—the Great Depression and World War II—prompted further attention on how families cope with unprecedented change. Angell (1936) and Cavan and Ranck (1938) identified various family characteristics that mediated the impact of the effects of the depression—that is, family organization, integration, and adaptability. These findings remain largely unchallenged today (Boss, 1987). Hill (1949), in his study of wartime family separations, developed a framework for assessing family crises: the ABC-X model. This framework, with its emphasis on family resources and definitions that mediate the extent of the stress or crisis response, serves today as the basis for most stress and coping theoretical models. The 1950s represented a focus on both the integrity of the American family as an institution and traditional family patterns. The social and political revolution of the 1960s, the technological changes accompanying the greater industrialization and urbanization of the 1970s, 1980s, and 1990s, resulted in a proliferation of research on families' coping and adaptation to a multitude of changes and new problems.

Between the times that the first and fourth editions of this text were published (1994–2009), our society has witnessed major and significant changes.

Technology has advanced, industrialization and urbanization have expanded, population is denser (including housing, traffic, demand on the infrastructures), and the events surrounding 9/11 and the continuing threats of terrorism have made daily life more complicated and impersonal. Based on multiple indications, the stress and change that families are experiencing appear to be increasing in intensity. Today, families often live with a constant sense of insecurity and stress. They are experiencing the consequences of a deepening economic recession, including loss of jobs; serious threats to pensions, investments, savings, and benefits; and our involvement in two wars and their aftermath. Add to these stress producers the ongoing natural disasters including hurricanes, tornadoes, storms, floods, and earthquakes, as well as the events of everyday life, accidents, and discrimination based on race, religious beliefs, gender, and sexual orientation. In addition, gender roles are blurred, families are more diverse, and the basic conceptualization of "family" has changed in response to increasing options in postmodern society. Therefore, families, which were once viewed as havens for individuals who were stressed by external problems, are increasingly challenged to meet their own needs.

It is evident, however, that many of our colleagues are involved in developing knowledge, as well as teaching classes and offering outreach programs, in areas that focus on the stressors confronting families. For example, before the development of the first edition of *Families & Change,* Pat and I conducted an extensive review of more than 400 randomly selected undergraduate and graduate college and university catalogs. These institutions ranged from small, private, liberal arts colleges to large, land-grant/research universities. We found that more than 60% offered courses that dealt with family problems, stress, and/or change. These courses were found in departments of social work, home economics/human ecology, sociology, human services, psychology, human development, family science, family relations, child and family development, health, professional studies, and criminology. We also surveyed instructors of these courses and discovered that texts representing a compilation of recent research findings in this area were almost nonexistent. For this edition, we combined this information with feedback from instructors who had used the third edition of *Families & Change,* our publisher, and students. The purpose of this fourth edition (as with the first, second, and third editions) is to provide a text appropriate for the study of various family problems, stressors, and changes in today's society.

This text represents an integration of research, theory, and application, drawing on the interdisciplinary scholarship in each topic area. It is intended to serve as a basic or supplementary text for undergraduate and introductory graduate courses on family or social problems. This edition will also be useful to professionals, novices, and those with considerable experience, especially in social work, education, and public health, who increasingly work with families who are confronting a multitude of problems.

In light of this goal, each edition has reflected transitions taking place in the larger society as well as in families. This has been achieved by including updated research findings and new topics in selected chapters. For example, in this edition, we have included chapters on homeless families (also included in the first edition), the impact of military life on individuals and families, lesbian- and gay-parent families, and African American families (included in the first and second editions). In addition, the chapters on remarriage and illness have a different approach than in past editions.

Each chapter presents an overview of our current understanding of selected family transitions and stressors, and most include possible mechanisms of intervention. However, each author was also afforded the opportunity to present his or her area of expertise in the manner that he or she viewed as appropriate.

The topics in this book represent both predictable and unpredictable problems and stressors. Predictable family problems would include those stressors that are inherently stressful even though they are foreseen. We take the position that all abrupt or disjunctive changes, although moderated or buffered by the family's coping resources, are likely to be stress producing. Such predictable or normative changes include marriage, parenting, aging, death, and dying. Other problems are potentially more traumatic because they cannot be predicted. These would include physical illness, death, mental illness, external traumas, substance abuse, war, violence, economics, divorce, and remarriage. We take the position that many of these problems are interrelated and often combine to produce stress-related responses. For example, stress related to economic issues may lead to marital problems, including violence; they may then initiate a cycle of divorce, personal and economic disorganization, and remarriage.

We also assume that family problems, change, and stress responses are not always "bad" for a family. The disequilibrium that develops requires new methods for handling problems. Out of this situation new and creative solutions may arise that are superior to those that were present when the problem occurred. This experience may enable the family to handle future crises in a superior manner, and it may result in greater individual and group satisfaction with family life.

Not all family stressors could be reviewed because of page constraints. The topics chosen represent major issues today and have received considerable social, professional, and research attention. Some family problems that met these criteria were not included as separate chapters because they are components of other chapters.

A Word of Caution

In the past editions of *Families & Change,* authors included Study Questions and Suggested Readings. In the third edition, however, and in view of the vast amount of information available on the World Wide Web, authors included Web addresses related to their specific topic. There was a very positive response, and, therefore, in this edition authors have included additional references and Internet resources. Several authors, however, included cautions about using Web pages. Because anyone can create a Web page, there are literally millions of Web sites related to the topics included in this volume. For example, a Google search revealed over 30 million Web pages related to *families* and more than 7 million Web pages related to *family stress*. It is apparent that one cannot critically review this vast volume of Web pages. In addition, many Web pages contain questionable information, present inaccurate information, or have links to Web sites that contain questionable information. Therefore, authors suggested limiting searches to Web sites from the domains of edu, gov, or those that are based on reputable community programs. These are university, government, or community Web sites, and are more likely to be reviewed by peers or governing bodies.

Overview of Chapters

We begin this text (Chapter 1) with an updated overview of the research on family problems, stressors, change, and coping. The nature and origin of the problems and changes facing families today are discussed, noting that while many of today's problems are not new, the degree of change in American society is unprecedented. The history of systematic inquiry into family problems and change is traced to individual physiological stress studies in the late 17th century; these studies of individuals have evolved in today's focus on whole-family interaction and an increased emphasis on resiliency. A social systems approach is presented as the integrating framework for studying families under stress, and views families as dynamic mechanisms, always in the process of growth and adaptation as they deal with change and stressor events.

In Chapter 2, Gary Peterson, Charles Hennon, and Terence Knox focus on parenthood as a stressor. They emphasize a "realistic" approach that integrates research on parental stress with family stress theory and recognizes that carrying for and socializing children involves challenges and hassles as well as satisfactions and fulfillment. The authors address (a) why parental stress is so common, (b) why parental stress varies within mothers and fathers, (c) why parents vary in their capacities to cope with and adapt to stress, and (d) what linkages exist between parental stress and the adjustment (or maladjustment) of parents and children. This approach helps one understand the wide range of circumstances varying from highly disruptive crises, to chronic stress, to normative challenges, and increases our understanding about how parental stress applies to both individuals and families.

Christine A. Price and Áine Humble, in Chapter 3, focus on the individual and family challenges that result from aging. The concept "aging family" pertains to family systems with emphasis on relationships, transitions, and social support networks of older family members. They describe demographic changes, the uniqueness of this population, and specific stressors in later life. The latter includes positive life events, but also loss, physical decline, and a decrease in economic and social resources. In addition, later life is often characterized by major transitional events including retirement and caregiving. Adaptive and coping strategies applied by individuals and their families in later life are also reviewed.

Colleen Murray, Katalin Toth, Barbara Larsen, and Shane Moulton discuss family experiences with death, dying, and grief in Chapter 4. These authors note that the death of a family member is widely considered the most stressful event that families face; this stress varies depending on which family member dies. Death is a normative and often predictable event, but it is not viewed as normal by society, including many researchers and clinicians. It is often treated as a problem rather than something that can result in growth and strength. Adapting to the loss of a family member is hampered by a lack of cultural support for the bereaved, a minimum of rituals surrounding death, and poorly defined roles for the chronically ill or the bereaved. A social systems perspective is used to describe family reactions, noting that the family responds as a unit to the death of a family member and that a variety of characteristics may influence the outcome for families. Gender, culture, and religion also are identified as important mediating factors in the grief process.

Jeremy B. Yorgason, in Chapter 5, discusses the characteristics of illnesses, a model for viewing illness and family resilience, and research findings related to childhood illness, spousal illness, and illness of aging parents. His discussion is based on a model linking health stressors to individual and family outcomes through adaptive processes and enduring vulnerabilities and characteristics. In addition, he emphasizes the role of resiliency in this process.

In Chapter 6, Richard Gelles discusses the incidence and etiology of various forms of violence in families and intimate relationships. Estimates suggest that it is pervasive in American society. The author goes beyond individual explanations to discuss societal factors that are related to family violence, including gender, race, socioeconomic status, stress, social isolation, age, type of relationship, and intergenerational patterns. More theoretically, models from psychology, sociology, and biology are used to provide the systems context for family violence. In addition, the author addresses the costs of violence to the larger society, and suggests preventative measures that would focus on eliminating norms that legitimize and glorify violence including reducing violence-provoking stress created by society, integrating families into a network of kin and community, changing the sexist character of our society, and breaking the cycle of violence in families.

Judith Fischer, Kevin Lyness, and Rachel Engler discuss issues involving families coping with alcohol and substance abuse in Chapter 7. These authors incorporate a biopsychosocial model, which includes biological, psychological, and social influences. The biopsychosocial model joined with the family stress and coping model acknowledges the contribution of these factors at each juncture: stressor, resource, perception, coping, and managing. In this chapter, several aspects of coping are reviewed: (a) factors that give rise to the need for coping, (b) factors that contribute to coping, and (c) the outcomes of coping efforts. There is a particular focus on the mediating and moderating effects that intervene between two variables, that is, variables that mediate or modify the associations between parent and offspring drinking.

In Chapter 8, Angie Schock-Giordano and Stephen Gavazzi discuss the experiences of individuals and their families as they cope with stressors associated with mental health. The authors review the incidence of mental illness and variations based on gender, ethnicity, and socioeconomic status. Similar to other authors, they view mental illness as a biopsychosocial phenomenon; that is, the cause, course, and outcome of all illnesses are influenced by the interaction between the biological, psychological, and social factors. A family systems perspective is adopted, which demonstrates how all family members interact as a system when coping when one or more of their members suffer from a mental disorder. Thus, questions regarding cause, assessment of family resources, and treatment options are reformulated within a family systems framework.

Suzanne Bartholomae and Jonathan Fox address the issues of economic stress and families in Chapter 9 using the Family Economic Stress Model as a framework. In this updated review, the authors emphasize that American families face a worsening economy and economic uncertainty. Families may react with fear, anger, worry, anxiety and depression. They also discuss normative, situational, and temporary stressors, as well as the economic life cycle of families. Management of resources can also be sources of stress or comfort. Stress is often related to disagreement over the use of resources and concern about their availability. The authors also examine normative economic stressors, economic demands at different stages of the life cycle, dangers of debt accumulation, and planning for retirement.

In Chapter 10, Mark Fine, Lawrence Ganong, and David Demo discuss divorce as a family process that has consequences for husbands, wives, and children. In this review, they emphasize how a risk and resiliency perspective adds to family systems theory. Although divorce is often viewed as a serious problem that results in severe long-term adjustment problems, the authors suggest that while women and children are at risk for long-term negative consequences of divorce, this assumption cannot be applied to all. Rather, recent studies of larger and more representative samples suggest moderate and short-term effects for adults and children. The authors also propose intervention strategies that may facilitate divorce adjustment.

Kay Pasley and Michelle Lee discuss remarriage as a stressor in Chapter 11. They present the issues that complicate stepfamilies by focusing on the sources of stress as well as the broader social context in which these families live. In addition, they emphasize definitions of stepfamilies and the impor- tance of including the various types of stepfamilies, and offer recommen- dations and strategies for managing these stressors and ultimately strengthening stepfamily life.

In Chapter 12, Abbie Goldberg discusses the challenges confronting lesbian- and gay-parent families. Using an ecological or systems approach, she reviews the situational and contextual forces that impact lesbian, gay, and bisexual (LGB) persons' experiences as they move through the life course. These include issues surrounding "coming out," forming and maintaining intimate relationships, barriers faced in becoming parents, relationships with their parents (i.e., grandparents), schools, and the legal system. In addition, she included implications for professionals with regard to supporting LGB parents.

In Chapter 13, Kevin Bush, Stephanie Bohon, and Hyoun Kim discuss the resources and barriers to immigrant families who are adapting to their new environments. Families are deeply involved in the immigration process from the time the decision to migrate is made to the processes involved in acculturation and adaptation. Barriers and stressors exist at the community or societal level, family level, and individual level. These often include language barriers, diminished social support networks, intergenerational conflict, marital conflict, poor housing, discrimination, inadequate public policies and programs, and lack of economic resources. The family system experiences stress that can lead to changes, and changes can result in more adaptive rules, roles, and patterns of interaction.

In Chapter 14, Pearl Stewart addresses stress and coping in African American families. She discusses common issues and stressors including the impact of changing socioeconomic status on the African American family structure as well as workplace issues for the emerging middle-class African Americans, and African American fathering. In addition, this chapter emphasizes the various methods utilized by African American families for confronting these stressors. These include relying on their extended family networks, racial socialization, and spirituality.

Elizabeth Lindsey and Christina A. Sanchez, in Chapter 15, discuss the stressors associated with being homeless. They discuss the varied definitions of "homelessness" and demographics related to this phenomenon with emphasis on homeless women and their children. Several theories that help explain why some poor people become homeless while others do not become homeless are presented. These include structural and socioeconomic factors, individual factors, and social factors. They also discuss the pathways to homelessness as well as the pathways out of homelessness.

In Chapter 16, Heather Helms, Jill Walls, and David Demo discuss everyday hassles and family stress. Specifically, they examine how daily stress and hassles are associated with family functioning, paying particular attention to the variability in family members' experiences and the invisible dimensions of family work. A stress-vulnerability-adaptation model is introduced as a way to frame the research on daily hassles and family stress, paying particular attention to the diversity that exists across and within families. In addition, the authors discuss how the existing policies and practices in the United States fail to mesh with the daily life of American families and propose policy interventions.

In Chapter 17, James Martin and Michelle Sherman present insights into the impact of military life on individuals and families, with an emphasis on available resources and interventions. They present extensive information about the unique characteristics and challenges of persons who are active members of the military and veterans and their families. In addition, they emphasize needed skills for those involved in providing services to these populations.

In Chapter 18, Melissa Herzog presents a general overview of family stress intervention using a developmental–systemic framework. Using the ABC-X model and the literature on family stress, she addresses (a) the importance of assessing and classifying types of stressor events before starting treatment or intervention, (b) family processes and characteristics most often identified as protective factors or beneficial resources in managing stress, and (c) the implications of these processes and characteristics for clinical assessment and intervention with families experiencing stress or crisis, including illustrations for applicable therapeutic strategies.

References

Angell, R. C. (1936). *The family encounters the depression.* New York: Scribner.

Boss, P. (1987). Family stress. In M. B. Sussman & S. K. Steinmetz (Eds.), *Handbook of marriage and the family* (pp. 695–724). New York: Plenum.

Cavan, R. S., & Ranck, K. H. (1938). *The family and the depression.* Chicago: University of Chicago Press.

Cole, C. L., & Cole, A. L. (1993). Family therapy theory implications for marriage and family enrichment. In P. G. Boss, W. J. Doherty, R. LaRossa, W. R. Schumm, & S. K. Steinmetz (Eds.), *Sourcebook of family theories and methods: A contextual approach* (pp. 525–530). New York: Plenum.

Hill, R. (1949). *Families under stress.* New York: Harper & Row.

Acknowledgments _____

This is the fourth edition of *Families & Change,* and you will notice that Christine A. Price has joined me as coeditor. At the time the third edition was being completed, and after we worked together for almost 30 years, Patrick McKenry died. He is greatly missed, but his thumbprint is still on this book. Because of Pat's death and when SAGE requested a fourth edition, I was hesitant because of the absence of a coeditor. However, I asked Christine A. Price (Associate Professor in the Department of Family and Child Studies at Montclair State and my niece) if she would join me in this endeavor. This is a particularly appropriate choice because Pat McKenry was a friend and mentor to her when she was on the faculty at The Ohio State University. Furthermore, although the third edition was completed under sad times, there was a great celebration while the fourth edition was being developed—Christine gave birth to Claire, her daughter and my great-niece. Let me assure you, however, that this made for a different set of challenges.

The support, advice, and encouragement we received from persons who have used the third edition in their classes and the authors who contributed to this volume are especially valued and important. The authors' quality contributions, cooperativeness, enthusiasm, timely responses, and encouragement have been invaluable. I have known some authors who contributed to this volume for two and three decades, and some have contributed to all four editions of this book (Gavazzi, Murray, Demo, Ganong, Gelles, Fox, and Bartholomae); others have contributed to two (Lindsey, Helms, Hennon, Herzog, Bush, Bohon, Kim, Schock-Giordano, Fischer, Lyness, and C. Price) and three (Peterson, Fine) volumes. Christine and I continued with the goal to involve selected younger scholars; we are very glad that "senior" authors are increasingly involving junior colleagues or students to be coauthors and some former second authors have moved into the position of senior authors. In addition, several new senior authors were asked to contribute to this edition (Yorgason, Pasley, Goldberg, Stewart, Martin). Therefore, we extend a special thank-you to all authors; your efforts and contributions are appreciated.

Sharon J. Price

The following reviewers are gratefully acknowledged:

Eboni J. Baugh
University of Florida

Joanna E. Bettmann
University of Utah

Barbara Hoglund
Metropolitan State University

Megan J. Murphy
Iowa State University

Angie M. Schock-Giordano
California State University, Northridge

1

Families Coping
With Change

A Conceptual Overview

Sharon J. Price, Christine A. Price,
and Patrick C. McKenry (Posthumously)

Cynthia and David are in their early 60s and are the parents of four adult children. Until this year they were looking forward to retirement in 2 to 3 years. However, because of the economic turndown, their savings and investments have been drastically reduced, and their private business is barely surviving. Consequently, their lives have been filled with high levels of stress, and from all indications this will increase. For multiple reasons, the courts recently awarded them custody of their 4-year-old grandson. As a consequence, they are once again involved in securing babysitters, arranging play dates, enrolling a child in preschool, and driving a child to appropriate activities. In addition to these increased demands, last week they found out that David's parents, because of a lack of resources, will be coming to live with them. His parents are in their 90s and are very frail.

Stanley and Laurie were extremely excited about their adoption of a little girl from Bulgaria. They arrived at a major U.S. airport with their new daughter after a 16-hour flight, tired but happy. All the new daughter's grandparents (three sets as a result of divorce and remarriage) met them at the airport decked out in decorated hats and shirts and carrying many balloons. Naturally, the grandparents wanted to spend time with their new granddaughter, and although they stayed at a nearby hotel, for several days they spent every waking hour at Laurie and Stanley's house. The new parents were exhausted and had minimal time to spend alone with their daughter. This was a very exciting time, and they loved having their parents participate in the wonderful events, but they were relieved when the grandparents left and they could begin to establish a schedule for their new family.

Carlin is in a state of shock. He just learned that he is to be laid off after working for the same company for more than 20 years. He is very concerned about finding a new job; he is middle-aged, unemployment rates are at an all-time high, and he is afraid his job skills may not be competitive in today's labor market. Sarah, his wife, is a teacher and her salary will probably cover most of their basic expenses, but he is still very worried, not only about finding another job but about expenses related to adequate health insurance, the new roof the house needs, and their two children in college. Carlin and Sarah know that at a minimum, they will have to cut back on their expenses significantly; and they may have to move to another location so that Carlin can secure a job.

Families increasingly experience a wide variety of stressors associated with both positive and negative events. Advances in technology, industrialization, urbanization, increased population density (including housing, traffic, and demand on the infrastructures), terrorism, and economic issues are frequently identified as making daily life more complicated and impersonal. Gender roles are blurred, and families are more diverse as a result of divorce, unwed parenthood, remarriage, immigration, and mobility. Add to these events ongoing natural disasters such as hurricanes, tornadoes, storms, floods, and earthquakes, as well as everyday stressors such as accidents and discrimination based on race, religious beliefs, gender, and sexual orientation. More recently, U.S. families are facing a constant sense of insecurity and stress due to the severe economic downturn in the global economy; a rising unemployment rate; sobering financial losses in pensions, investments, and savings accounts; disappearing benefits; and the reality of war in both Iraq and Afghanistan. When one considers the accumulation of these events, it quickly becomes apparent that stress is a part of everyday life.

Families were once viewed as havens for individuals who were stressed by external pressures, but today they are increasingly challenged to meet individual emotional needs. Complicating the matter is that many still hold the myth that happy families are (or should be) free from stress. Many believe it is acceptable to experience stress from outside families, that is, environment- and work-related stress, but not stress within families.

Families are often faced with many unique problems, not because of any identifiable crisis, event, or situation, but because of everyday societal change. For example, technology, which has facilitated an increasing life span, has also brought about a growing aged population with whom already overextended and geographically mobile families must cope. Young family members are contending with the realization that there may be fewer opportunities and resources available for them as compared to their parents and grandparents. In addition, the fluidity of family structures requires most families to deal with several family structural transitions during the life course (Price, McKenry, & Murphy, 2000; Teachman, Polonko, & Scanzoni, 1999).

All families experience stress as a result of change, whether change is "good" or "bad." The impact of change is dependent on the family's perception of the situation as well as coping ability. Boss (1988, 2002, 2006) defines *family stress* as pressure or tension on the status quo; it is a disturbance of the family's steady state. Life transitions and events often provide an essential condition for psychological development, and family stress is perceived as inevitable and normal, or even desirable since people and, therefore, families, must develop, mature, and change over time. With change comes disturbance and pressure—what is termed *stress* (Boss, 2002). Changes affecting families also occur externally (e.g., unemployment, natural disasters, war, acts of terrorism), and these also create stress in family systems. Change becomes problematic only when the degree of stress in a family system reaches a level at which family members and/or the family system become dissatisfied or show symptoms of disturbance.

The Study of Family Stress and Change

In comparison with the long history of research in the general area of stress and coping, theoretical and clinical interest in family stress, problems, and coping is a rather recent phenomenon. Research on family stress and coping evolved gradually from various disciplines that have examined stress and coping from more than an individualistic perspective.

According to the *Oxford English Dictionary,* the term *stress* can be traced back to the early 14th century when stress had several distinct meanings, including hardship, adversity, and affliction (Rutter, 1983). Even among stress researchers today, stress is variably defined as a stimulus, an inferred inner state, and an observable response to a stimulus or situation; there is also debate concerning the extent to which stress is chemical, environmental, or psychological in nature (Frankenhaeuser, 1994; Lazarus & Folkman, 1984; Sarafino, 1990).

In the late 17th century, Hooke used the term *stress* in the context of physical science, although the usage was not made systematic until the early 19th century. Stress and strain were first conceived as a basis of ill health in the 19th century (Lazarus & Folkman, 1984). In the 20th century, Cannon (1932) laid the foundation for systematic research on the effects of stress in observations of bodily changes. He showed that stimuli associated with emotional arousal (e.g., pain, hunger, cold) caused changes in basic physiological functioning (Dohrenwend & Dohrenwend, 1974). Selye (1978) was the first researcher to define and measure stress adaptations in the human body. He defined stress as an orchestrated set of bodily defenses against any form of noxious stimuli (General Adaptation Syndrome). In the 1950s, social scientists became interested in his conceptualization of stress, and even today, Selye's work accounts for much of the scholarly interest in stress and coping (Lazarus & Folkman, 1984; Lovallo, 1997).

Meyer, in the 1930s, taught that life events may be an important component in the etiology of a disorder and that the most normal and necessary life events may be potential contributors to pathology (Dohrenwend & Dohrenwend,

1974). In the 1960s, Holmes and Rahe (1967) investigated life events and their connection to the onset and progression of illness. Through their Schedule of Recent Events, which includes many family-related events, Holmes and Rahe associated the accumulation of life changes and those of greater magnitude to a higher chance of illness, disease, or death.

In the social sciences, both sociology and psychology have long histories of study related to stress and coping. Sociologists Marx, Weber, and Durkheim wrote extensively about "alienation." Alienation was conceptualized as synonymous with powerlessness, meaninglessness, and self-estrangement, clearly under the general rubric of stress (Lazarus & Folkman, 1984). In psychology, stress was implicit as an organizing framework for thinking about psychopathology, especially in the theorizing of Freud and, later, psychologically oriented writers. Freudian psychology highlighted the process of coping and established the basis for a developmental approach that considered the effect of life events on later development and gradual acquisition of resources over the life cycle. Early psychologists used anxiety to denote stress, and it was seen as a central component in psychopathology through the 1950s. The reinforcement-learning theorists (e.g., Spence, 1956) viewed anxiety as a classically conditioned response that led to unserviceable (pathological) habits of anxiety reduction. Existentialists (e.g., May, 1950) also focused on anxiety as a major barrier to self-actualization (Lazarus & Folkman, 1984). Developmentalists (e.g., Erickson, 1963) proposed various stage models that demand that a particular crisis be negotiated before an individual can cope with subsequent developmental stages. Personal coping resources accrued during the adolescent–young adult years are thought to be integrated into the self-concept and shape the process of coping throughout adulthood (Moos, 1986). Crisis theorists (e.g., Caplan, 1964) conceptualized these life changes as crises, with the assumption that disequilibrium may provide stress in the short run but can promote the development of new skills in the long run.

The study of family stress began at the University of Michigan and the University of Chicago during the 1930s and the upheavals of the Depression (Boss, 2002). Reuben Hill, referred to as the father of family stress research (Boss, 2006), was the first scholar to conceptualize family stress theory (Hill, 1949, 1971) when he developed the ABC-X model of family stress and his model of family crisis (Boss, 1988, 2002, 2006). A second generation of family stress researchers made major contributions to this basic model (e.g., Boss, 1988, 2002; Figley, 1978; McCubbin, 1979; McCubbin & McCubbin, 1988), and Boss addressed recent developments in the evolution and use of family stress theory (Boss, 2002, pp. 2–14). These include:

1. The introduction of the *mind-body-family connection*. In contrast to the measurements of life events, the emphasis is on the measurement of human reactivity during intensely stressful situations.

2. The reintroduction of *family resilience*. This is a process that implies growth within families becoming stronger for having had a stressful experience with greater emphasis on context.

3. Increased emphasis on the *role of spirituality and faith* in the management of family stress.

4. Increase in the recognition of *posttraumatic stress disorder;* increased recognition that an individual's response to an isolated event such as rape may be the same as the response to a mass catastrophe (war, torture, act of nature).

5. Increased *use of "disaster" teams* that are deployed into an arena immediately after a catastrophe; more emphasis is placed on crisis instead of stress.

6. Increased emphasis on *stress resulting from caring for an individual* with long-term illness or disability, including the elderly.

7. Recognition that the *demands created by balancing work and family* (time bind, parents and children rarely being home, overwork) result in high stress levels in many families.

8. Shift to emphasis on individuals' and families' *perceptions, interpretations, and beliefs* about stress producing situations/events.

9. Adaptation of *social constructionism* in working with stressed families. Focus is on stories and processes that guide distressed families including how they reframe, restory, and construct a new narrative that helps families manage stress.

10. Increase in use of *narrative analysis*. Distressed people tell their story, their truth, and interpretation of what they believe about their situation.

Family Stress Theory

Social Systems Perspective

Family theorists typically have used a social systems approach in their conceptualization of families under stress. As a result, families are viewed as living organisms with both symbolic and real structures. They have boundaries to maintain and a variety of instrumental and expressive functions to perform to ensure growth and survival (Boss, 1988). As with any social system, families strive to maintain a steady state. Families are the products of both subsystems (e.g., individual members, dyads) and suprasystems (e.g., community, culture, nation).

Although most general stress theories have focused on only the individual, the primary interest of family stress theory is the entire family unit. Systems theory states that the system is more than the sum of its parts (Boss, 2006; Hall & Fagan, 1968). In terms of families, this means that the collection of family members is not only a specific number of people but also an aggregate of particular relationships and shared memories, successes, failures, and aspirations (Boss, 1988, 2002). However, systems theory also involves studying the individual to more completely understand a family's response to stress.

A social systems approach allows the researcher to focus beyond the family and the individual to the wider social system (suprasystem). Families do not live in isolation; they are part of the larger social context. This external environment in which the family is embedded is referred to as the "ecosystem," according to social systems theory. This ecosystem consists of historical, cultural, economic, genetic, and developmental influences (Boss, 1988, 2002). Thus, the family's response to a stressor event is influenced by living in a particular historical period, its cultural identification, the economic conditions of society, its genetic stamina and resistance, and its stage in the family life cycle.

ABC-X Model

The foundation for a social systems model of family stress lies in Hill's (1949) classic research on war-induced separation and reunion. Although his ABC-X formulation has been expanded (Boss, 1988, 2002; Burr, Klein, & Associates, 1994; McCubbin & Patterson, 1982; Patterson, 1988), it has withstood careful assessment and is still the basis for analyzing family stress and coping (Boss, 2002, 2006). This family stress framework may be stated as follows: A (the provoking or stressor event of sufficient magnitude to result in change in a family)-interacting with B (the family's resources or strengths)-interacting with C (the definition or meaning attached to the event by the family)-produces X (stress or crisis). The main idea is that the X factor is influenced by several other moderating phenomena. Stress or crisis is not seen as inherent in the event itself, but conceptually as a function of the response of the disturbed family to the stressor (Boss, 1988, 2002, 2006; Burr, 1973; Hill, 1949). (See Figure 1.1.)

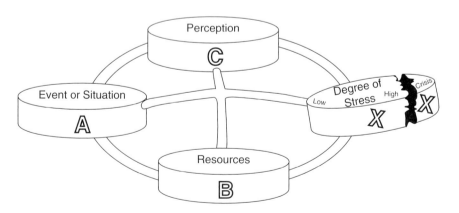

Figure 1.1   ABC-X Model of Family Crisis

SOURCE: Hill, R. (1958). Social stresses on the family: Generic features of families under stress. *Social Casework, 39*, 139–150. Reprinted with permission from *Families in Society* (www.familiesinsociety.org), published by the Alliance for Children and Families.

Stressor Events

A stressor event is an occurrence that provokes a variable amount of change in the family system. Anything that changes some aspect of the system such as the boundaries, structures, goals, processes, roles, or values can produce stress (Boss, 2002). This variable denotes something different than the routine changes within a system that are expected as part of its regular, ordinary operation. This variable is dichotomous; that is, an event either changes or does not change (Burr, 1982). The stressor event by definition has the potential to raise the family's level of stress. However, the degree of stress is dependent on the magnitude of the event as well as other moderating factors to be discussed. Also, both positive and negative events can be stressors. Life events research has clearly indicated that normal and/or positive changes can increase an individual's risk for illness. Finally, stressor events do not necessarily increase stress levels to the point of crisis; the family's stress level can be managed and the family can return to a new equilibrium.

Researchers have attempted to describe various types of stressor events (e.g., Boss, 1988, 2002; Hansen & Hill, 1964; Rees & Smyer, 1983). Lipman-Blumen (1975) has described family stressor events in terms of nine dimensions: (1) internal versus external, (2) pervasive versus bounded, (3) precipitate onset versus gradual onset, (4) intense versus mild, (5) transitory versus chronic, (6) random versus expectable, (7) natural generation versus artificial generation, (8) scarcity versus surplus, and (9) perceived solvable versus perceived insolvable. (These dimensions are defined in Table 1.1.) The type of event may be highly correlated with the family's ability to manage stress. Other researchers (e.g., McCubbin, Patterson, & Wilson, 1981; Pearlin & Schooler, 1978) have classified stressor events in terms of their intensity or hardship on the family.

One dichotomous classification that is often used by family stress researchers and clinicians is normal or predictable events versus nonnormative or unpredictable or situational events. Normal events are part of everyday life and represent transitions inherent in the family life cycle, such as the birth or death of a family member, child's school entry, and retirement. Normative stressor events by definition are of short duration. Although predictable and normal, such life cycle events have the potential of changing a family's level of stress because they disturb the system equilibrium. These events lead to crisis only if the family does not adapt to the changes brought about by these events (Carter & McGoldrick, 1989).

Nonnormative events are the product of some unique situation that could not be predicted and is not likely to be repeated. Examples of nonnormative events would include natural disasters, loss of a job, or an automobile accident. Unexpected but welcome events that are not disastrous may also be stressful for families, such as a promotion or winning the lottery. Although these events are positive, they do change or disturb the family's routine and thus have the potential of raising the family's level of stress (Boss, 1988).

There has been much recent interest in the study of isolated versus accumulated stressors. Specifically, life event scholars (e.g., Holmes & Rahe, 1967;

Table 1.1   Ten Dimensions of Family Stressor Events

(1) *Internality versus externality:* Refers to whether the source of the crisis was internal or external to the social system affected.

(2) *Pervasiveness versus boundedness:* Refers to the degree to which the crisis affects the entire system or only a limited part.

(3) *Precipitate onset versus gradual onset:* Marks the degree of suddenness with which the crisis occurred, that is, without or with warning.

(4) *Intensity versus mildness:* Involves the degree of severity of the crisis.

(5) *Transitoriness versus chronicity:* Refers to the degree to which the crisis represents a short- or long-term problem.

(6) *Randomness versus expectability:* Marks the degree to which the crisis could be expected or predicted.

(7) *Natural generation versus artificial generation:* Connotes the distinction between crises that arise from natural conditions and those that come about through technological or other human-made effects.

(8) *Scarcity versus surplus:* Refers to the degree to which the crisis represents a shortage or overabundance of vital commodities—human, material, and nonmaterial.

(9) *Perceived solvability versus perceived insolvability:* Suggests the degree to which those individuals involved in the crisis believe the crisis is open to reversal or some level of resolution.

(10) *Substantive content:* This dimension differs from the previous nine in that it subsumes a set of subject areas, each of which may be regarded as a separate continuum graded from low to high. Using this dimension, the analyst can determine whether the substantive nature of the crisis is primarily in the political, economic, moral, social, religious, health, or sexual domain or any combination thereof.

SOURCE: Adapted from Lipman-Blumen (1975).

McCubbin et al., 1981; Sarason, Johnson, & Siegel, 1978) suggest that it is the accumulation of several stressor events rather than the nature of one isolated event that determines a family's level of stress. The clustering of stressor events (normative and/or nonnormative) is termed *stress pileup*. An event rarely happens to a family in total isolation. Normal developmental changes are always taking place and nonnormative events tend to result in other stressors; for example, losing a job may result in a family having to move, or marital disruption. By focusing on only certain events or stressors, researchers may fail to capture the complexity in the range and clustering of stressors (Pearlin, 1991).

More recently, researchers have offered an alternative perspective on stressor events. Instead of assessing major life events that tend to be extreme in nature and are fairly low in base-rate occurrence (Fisher, Fagot, & Leve, 1998), researchers are focusing on daily stressors or hassles and ongoing strains and their relationship to stress outcomes. Daily hassles not only parallel major life events in their potential to engender stress, but they have an even stronger relationship than traditional life event measures in predicting physical health (Derogatics & Coons, 1993; Gruen, 1993).

Not all stressor events, however, are clear-cut. As a result, a state of ambiguity is created. Boss (1999, 2006)) addressed the issue of *ambiguous loss* resulting from incongruency between physical and psychological/emotional presence/absence. There are two major types of ambiguous loss: (1) a person being physically absent but psychologically or emotionally present (missing children, divorce, a family member in prison, soldiers missing in action, immigrants) and (2) when a person is physically present but psychologically/emotionally absent (a person that has Alzheimer's disease or a chronic mental illness, chronic substance abuse; a spouse preoccupied with work or another issue) (Boss, 1999). Ambiguous loss not only disrupts family functioning, it results in a lack of clarity regarding who is "in" and who is "outside" the family, as well as appropriate roles for family members. This type of ambiguity is the most stressful situation a person and/or family can experience. Boss attributed this high level of stress to the following factors: (a) People are unable to problem solve because they do not know whether the problem is final or temporary; (b) the ambiguity prevents people from adjusting by reorganizing their relationship with the loved one; (c) families are denied social rituals (e.g., funeral, death certificate) that usually support a clear loss; (d) friends/neighbors tend to withdraw rather than give support; and (e) ambiguous loss may continue for a long time; therefore, those who experience it become physically and emotionally exhausted (Boss, 1999, pp. 7–8).

Additional factors that could influence families' perceptions in a stressful situation include *spirituality, values and beliefs, culture,* and *stage of the family life cycle.* As earlier noted, there has been an increased emphasis on the role of spirituality, beliefs, and faith on family stress. Boss (2002, 2006) discussed several cases where a strong sense of spirituality results in a more positive attitude, hope, and optimism when families are confronted with a stressful situation. Faith can be a major coping mechanism resulting in families turning to their religious institutions and communities more than cognitive problem solving (Tix & Frazier, 1998, in Boss, 2002). Of course, spirituality can be experienced within or outside formal religious institutions. Regardless of the source, spiritual associations can bring a sense of meaning, wholeness, and connection with others. For example, religious communities provide guidelines for living and scripted ways to make major life transitions, as well as congregational support in times of need (Walsh, 2006).

The belief system and/or value orientation of families may also influence their perceptions of stressful events. For example, families with a *mastery orientation* may believe they can solve any problem and control just about anything that could happen to them. In contrast, families with a *fatalistic orientation* are more likely to believe that everything is determined by a higher power; therefore, all events are predetermined and not under their control. As a consequence, a highly fatalistic orientation could be a barrier to coping because it encourages passivity, and active coping strategies have been found to be more effective than passive strategies (Boss, 2002).

The third factor, *stage of the family life cycle*, points to the variation in structure, composition, interaction (between family members as well as between the family and the outside culture), and resources in families (Price, McKenry, & Murphy, 2000). Consequently, families at different stages of the life cycle vary in their response to stressful situations. This is particularly relevant as families move from one stage of development to another during normative transitions. It is during these periods of change (a child is born, children leave home, a family member dies) that families are likely to experience high levels of stress as they adjust rules, roles, and patterns of behavior (Aldous, 1996). This stress is also impacted by whether the transition is "on time" or "off time" as well as expected or unexpected (Rodgers & White, 1993). In general, "off time" (e.g., a child dies before a parent dies) and unexpected (a family member dies in an accident) transitions create periods of greater stress. This greater stress could, at least partially, be attributed to the family members' perception of the stressful situation as being overwhelming or unfair.

Resources

The family's resources buffer or moderate the impact of the stressor event on the family's level of stress. Hansen (1965) uses the term *vulnerability* to denote the difference in families' physical and emotional responses to stressful stimuli (Gore & Colten, 1991). This moderator denotes variation in a family's ability to prevent a stressor event or change from creating disruptiveness in the system (Burr, 1973). When family members have sufficient and appropriate resources, they are less likely to view a stressful situation as problematic. McCubbin and Patterson (1985) defined *resources* as traits, characteristics, or abilities of (a) individual family members, (b) the family system, and (c) the community that can be used to meet the demands of a stressor event. Individual or personal resources include financial (economic well-being), educational (problem solving, information), health (physical and emotional well-being), and psychological (self-esteem) resources.

The term *family system resources* refers to internal attributes of the family unit that protect the family from the impact of stressors and facilitate family adaptation during family stress and/or crisis. Family cohesion (bonds of unity) and adaptability (ability to change) (Olson, Russell, & Sprenkle, 1979, 1983) have received the most research attention. These two dimensions are the major axes of the Circumplex Model (Olson et al., 1979). This model suggests that families who function moderately along the dimensions of cohesion and adaptability are likely to make a more successful adjustment to stress (Olson, Russell, & Sprenkle, 1980). However, it should be noted that the family literature contains studies and writings that qualify or refute the curvilinear interpretation of the relationship between adaptability and cohesion and effective functioning; instead, these studies support a linear relationship between these two dimensions and effective outcomes (Anderson & Gavazzi, 1990).

Community resources refer to those capabilities of people or institutions outside the family upon which the family can draw for dealing with stress. Social support is one of the most important community resources, although it can, of course, be provided by individual family members. Social support may be viewed as information disseminated to facilitate problem solving and as the development of new social contacts who provide help and assistance. Social support offers information at an interpersonal level that provides (a) emotional support, (b) esteem support, and (c) network support (Cobb, 1976). In general, social support serves as a protector against the effects of stressors and promotes recovery from stress or crisis. Increasingly, the concept of community resources has been broadened to include the resources of cultural groups; for example, ethnic minority families are thought to be characterized by more elaborate and efficient patterns of social support (Hill, 1999; McCubbin et al., 1998).

Definition of the Event/Perceptions

The impact of the stressor event on the family's level of stress is also moderated by the definition or meaning the family gives to the event. This variable is also synonymous with family appraisal, perception, and assessment of the event. Thus, subjective definitions can vary from viewing circumstances as a challenge and an opportunity for growth to the negative view that things are hopeless, too difficult, or unmanageable (McCubbin & Patterson, 1985). Empirical findings suggest that an individual's cognitive appraisal of life events strongly influences the response (Lazarus & Launier, 1978) and may be the most important component in determining an individual's or family's response to a stressor event (Boss, 2002).

This concept has a long tradition in social psychology in terms of the self-fulfilling prophecy that if something is perceived as real, it is real in its consequences (Burr, 1982). Families who are able to redefine a stressor event more positively (i.e., reframe it) appear to be better able to cope and adapt. By redefining, families are able to (a) clarify the issues, hardships, and tasks to render them more manageable and responsive to problem-solving efforts; (b) decrease the intensity of the emotional burdens associated with stressors; and (c) encourage the family unit to carry on with its fundamental tasks of promoting individual members' social and emotional development (McCubbin & Patterson, 1985).

Lazarus and Launier (1978) discussed the impact of an individual's learned cognitive attributional style on the stress response; this work has been applied to the study of families as well (e.g., Boss, 1988). For example, a family may respond to an event in terms of "learned helplessness," thereby increasing their vulnerability due to low self-esteem and feelings of hopelessness. Such a family would react to the unemployment of a spouse by failing to look for another job or failing to support that family member in the search for another job.

It has long been thought that men and women inherently differed in their susceptibility to and reaction to stressor events, with women being more likely to experience stress from relationship-oriented events and men, from external events that threatened the family or their good-provider role (Gore & Colten, 1991). Thoits (1991) uses identity theory to suggest that men and women are more likely to experience stress when an important identity is threatened, such as one's traditional family gender role. Yet evidence has accumulated that challenges the notion of gender differences in response to stressor events. With changing gender roles, men's distress is as affected by relationships with partners as is women's, and women's distress is as affected by the quality of their job experiences as is men's (Barnett, 1993).

Stress and Crisis

According to social systems theory, stress represents a change in the family's steady state and is the response of the family to the demands experienced as a result of a stressor event. Stress is not inherently bad; it becomes problematic when the degree of stress in the family system reaches a level at which the family becomes disrupted or individual members become dissatisfied or display physical or emotional symptoms. The degree of stress ultimately depends on the family's definition of the stressor event as well as the adequacy of the family's resources to meet the demands of the change associated with the stressor event.

The terms *stress* and *crisis* have been used inconsistently in the literature. In fact, many researchers have failed to make a distinction between the two. Boss (1988, 2006) makes a useful distinction as she defines crisis as (a) a disturbance in the equilibrium that is so overwhelming, (b) pressure that is so severe, or (c) change that is so acute that the family system is blocked, immobilized, and incapacitated. When a family is in a crisis state, at least for a time, it does not function adequately. Family boundaries are no longer maintained, customary roles and tasks are no longer performed, and family members are no longer functioning at optimal physical or psychological levels. The family has thus reached a state of acute disequilibrium and is immobilized.

Family stress, on the other hand, is merely a state of changed or disturbed equilibrium. Family stress therefore is a continuous variable (degree of stress), whereas family crisis is a dichotomous variable (either in crisis or not). A crisis does not have to permanently break up the family system. It may only temporarily immobilize the family system and then lead to a different level of functioning than that experienced before the stress level escalated to the point of crisis. Many family systems, in fact, become stronger after they have experienced and recovered from crisis (Boss, 1988).

Coping

Family stress researchers have increasingly shifted their attention from crisis and family dysfunction to the process of coping. Researchers have become more interested in explaining why some families are better able to manage and endure stressor events rather than documenting the frequency and severity of such events. In terms of intervention, this represents a change from crisis intervention to prevention (Boss, 1988; McCubbin et al., 1980).

The study of family coping has drawn heavily from cognitive psychology (e.g., Lazarus, 1966, 1976; Lazarus & Folkman, 1984) as well as sociology (e.g., Pearlin & Schooler, 1978). *Cognitive coping strategies* refers to the ways in which individual family members alter their subjective perceptions of stressful events. Sociological theories of coping emphasize a wide variety of actions directed at either changing the stressful situation or alleviating distress by manipulating the social environment (McCubbin et al., 1980). Thus, family coping has been conceptualized in terms of three types of responses: (1) direct action (e.g., acquiring resources, learning new skills), (2) intrapsychic (e.g., reframing the problem), or (3) controlling the emotions generated by the stressor (e.g., social support, use of alcohol) (Boss, 1988; Lazarus & Folkman, 1984; Pearlin & Schooler, 1978). These responses can be used individually, consecutively, or, more commonly, in various combinations. Specific coping strategies are not inherently adaptive or maladaptive; they are very much situation specific. Flexible access to a range of responses appears to be more effective than the use of any one response (Moos, 1986).

Coping interacts with both family resources and perceptions as defined by the "B" and "C" factors of the ABC-X model. However, coping actions are different than resources and perceptions. Coping represents what people do, that is, their concrete efforts to deal with a stressor (Pearlin & Schooler, 1978). Having a resource or a perception of an event does not imply whether or how a family will react (Boss, 1988; Lazarus & Folkman, 1984).

Although coping is sometimes equated with adaptational success (i.e., a product), from a family systems perspective, coping is a process, not an outcome per se. Coping refers to all efforts expended to manage a stressor regardless of the effect (Lazarus & Folkman, 1984). Thus, the family strategy of coping is not instantly created but is progressively modified over time. Because the family is a system, coping behavior involves the management of various dimensions of family life simultaneously: (a) maintaining satisfactory internal conditions for communication and family organization, (b) promoting member independence and self-esteem, (c) maintaining family bonds of coherence and unity, (d) maintaining and developing social supports in transactions with the community, and (e) maintaining some efforts to control the impact of the stressor and the amount of change in the family unit (McCubbin et al., 1980). Coping is thus a process of achieving balance in the family system that facilitates organization and unity and promotes individual growth and development. This is consistent with systems theory, which suggests that the families that most effectively cope with stress are strong as a unit as well as in individual members (Buckley, 1967).

Boss (1988) cautions that coping should not be perceived as maintaining the status quo; rather, the active managing of stress should lead to progressively new levels of organization as systems are naturally inclined toward greater complexity. In fact, sometimes it is better for a family to "fail to cope" even if that precipitates a crisis. After the crisis, the family can reorganize into a better-functioning system. For example, a marital separation may be very painful for a family, but it may be necessary to allow the family to grow in a different, more productive direction.

In addition to serving as a barrier to change and growth, coping also can serve as a source of stress. There are three ways that coping itself may be a source of additional hardship (Roskies & Lazarus, 1980). One way is by indirect damage to the family system. This occurs when a family member inadvertently behaves in such a way as to put the family in a disadvantaged position. For example, a father may become ill from overwork to ease his family's economic stress. The second way that coping can serve as a source of stress is through direct damage to the family system. For example, family members may use an addictive behavior or violence to personally cope, but this will be disruptive to the family system. The third way that coping may increase family stress is by interfering with additional adaptive behaviors that could help preserve the family. For example, denial of a problem may preclude getting necessary help and otherwise addressing the stressor event (McCubbin et al., 1980).

Adaptation

Another major interest of family stress researchers in recent years has been the assessment of how families are able to "recover" from stress or crisis. Drawing from Hansen's (1965) work, Burr (1973) described this process in terms of a family's "regenerative power," denoting a family's ability to recover from stress or crisis. According to McCubbin and Patterson (1982), the purpose of postcrisis or poststress adjustment is to reduce or eliminate the disruptiveness in the family system and restore homeostasis. However, these authors also note that family disruption has the potential of maintaining family relations and stimulating desirable change. Because system theorists (e.g., Buckley, 1967) hold that all systems naturally evolve toward greater complexity, it may be inferred that family systems initiate and capitalize on externally produced change in order to grow. Therefore, reduction of stress or crisis alone is an incomplete index of a family's adjustment to crisis or stress.

McCubbin and Patterson (1982) use the term *adaptation* to describe a desirable outcome of a crisis or stressful state. *Family adaptation* is defined as the degree to which the family system alters its internal functions (behaviors, rules, roles, perceptions) and/or external reality to achieve a system (individual or family)–environment fit. Adaptation is achieved through reciprocal relationships in which (a) system demands (or needs) are met by resources from the environment and (b) environmental demands are satisfied through system resources (Hansen & Hill, 1964).

According to McCubbin and Patterson (1982), demands include normative and nonnormative stressor events as well as the needs of individuals (e.g., intimacy), families (e.g., launching of children), and social institutions and communities (e.g., governmental authority). Resources include individual (e.g., education, psychological stability), family (e.g., cohesion, adaptability), and environmental (social support, medical services) attributes. Adaptation is different than adjustment. Adjustment is a short-term response by a family that changes the situation only momentarily. Adaptation implies a change in the family system that evolves over a longer period of time or is intended to have long-term consequences involving changes in family roles, rules, patterns of interaction, and perceptions (McCubbin, Cauble, & Patterson, 1982).

McCubbin and Patterson (1982) have expanded Hill's (1949) ABC-X model by adding postcrisis/poststress factors to explain how families achieve a satisfactory adaptation to stress or crisis. Their model consists of the ABC-X model followed by their "double ABC-X" configuration. (See Figure 1.2.)

McCubbin and Patterson's (1982) "Double A" factor refers to the stressor pileup in the family system, and this includes three types of stressors. The family must deal with (1) unresolved aspects of the initial stressor event, (2) the changes and events that occur regardless of the initial stressor (e.g., changes in family membership), and (3) the consequences of the family's efforts to cope

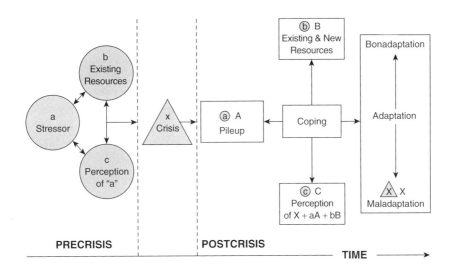

Figure 1.2   Double ABC-X Model

SOURCE: McCubbin, H. I., & Patterson, J. M. (1982). Family adaptation to crisis. In H. I. McCubbin, A. E. Cauble, & J. M. Patterson (Eds.), *Family stress, coping, and social support* (pp. 26–47). Reprinted by permission of Charles C Thomas, Publisher, Springfield, IL.

with the hardships of the situation (e.g., intrafamily role changes). The family's resources, the "Double B" factor, are of two types. The first are those resources already available to the family and that minimize the impact of the initial stressor. The second are those coping resources (personal, family, and social) that are strengthened or developed in response to the stress or crisis situation. The "Double C" factor refers to (a) the perception of the initial stressor event and (b) the perception of the stress or crisis. The perception of the stress or crisis situation includes the family's view of the stressor and related hardships and the pileup of events as well as the meaning families attach to the total family situation. The family's postcrisis/poststress perceptions involve religious beliefs, redefining (reframing) the situation, and endowing the situation with meaning.

The "Double X" factor includes the original family crisis/stress response and subsequent adaptation. Family crisis/stress is at one end of the continuum of family adjustment over time, and family adaptation is the outcome at the other end of the continuum.

Boss (1988, 2002) cautions against the use of the term *adaptation* to describe the optimal outcome of a stressful or crisis state. She contends that the family literature appears to assume that calm, serenity, orderliness, and stability are the desired ends for family life. Like Hoffman (1981), Boss maintains that systems naturally experience discontinuous change through the life cycle in the process of growth. If adaptation is valued over conflict and change, then families are limited to a perspective that promotes adjustment to the stressor event at the expense of individual or family change. Boss contends that sometimes dramatic change must occur for individual and family well-being, including breaking family rules, changing boundaries, and revolution within the system. For example, an abused wife may need to leave or at least dramatically change her family system to achieve a sense of well-being for herself and perhaps for other family members. Therefore, in order to avoid circular reasoning, Boss prefers use of the term *managing* to refer to the coping process that results from the family's reaction to stress or crisis. Specifically, "unless crisis occurs, the family is managing its level of stress. Managing high stress and being resilient are indeed the alternative outcome to falling in crisis" (Boss, 2002, p. 89).

Patterson (1988) has further revised the double ABC-X model to include the community system as well as the individual and family systems. This complex form of analysis requires that the (a) stressors, (b) resources, and (c) meanings/definitions of the individual, family, and community systems as well as their interactions be considered. Patterson's extension of the double ABC-X model is consistent with biopsychosocial systems models that attempt to deal with the complex interplay and multiplicative interactions among biological, psychological, and social phenomena regarding health and illness (McDaniel, Hepworth, & Doherty, 1992). For example, research on domestic violence has noted the role of testosterone and alcohol use as it interacts with other variables in increasing the risk of men's abuse of a female partner (Hillbrand & Pallone, 1994).

Resiliency

More recently, family scholars have begun to assess family stress outcomes from a family strengths perspective (Bonanno, 2004). Based on studies of children and families who thrive under adversity, family researchers have applied the concept of *resiliency* to family adaptation (Boss, 2006; Cowan, Cowan, & Schulz, 1996; Elder & Conger, 2000; McCubbin et al., 1998; Vandsburger, Harrigan & Biggerstaff, 2008; Walsh, 2006). In the early 1970s, scholars used the term *competence* to describe how people thrived in the face of adversity. Today, this term has been replaced by *resilience* (Boss, 2006). Resilience has its roots in family stress, and is both an individual and family phenomenon. It has been defined as "the capacity to rebound from adversity strengthened and more resourceful . . . an active process of endurance, self-righting, and growth in response to crisis and challenges (Walsh, 2006, p. 4). In addition, Boss (2006) described resiliency as the ability to stretch (like elastic) or flex (like a suspension bridge) in response to the pressures and strains of life. In general, resiliency refers to the coping strengths of those families that seem to benefit from the challenges of adversity; the ability to successfully deal with a stressor event usually results in outcomes as good or better than those that would have been obtained in the absence of the adversity (Cichetti & Garmezy, 1993; Hawley & DeHaan, 1996; Rutter, 1987). These coping strengths are thought to be characteristics acquired through repeated successful mastery of stressor events (Masten & Garmezy, 1985).

Rather than presenting a pathological view, or deficient model, of families, the emphasis is on family wellness and strengths (Hawley & DeHaan, 1996; McCubbin & McCubbin, 1988; Walsh, 2006). In contrast to Hill's (1949) model, which hypothesized that following a crisis, families would return to functioning at a level below or above their previous level, resilient families are expected to return to a level at or above their previous level.

At this point, it appears that the focus on family resilience represents a combination of family strengths and family stress literature. Perhaps the most valuable conceptual contribution has been the recognition of a family ethos, that is, a schema, worldview, and/or sense of coherence that describes a shared set of values and attitudes held by a family unit that serves as the core of the family's resilience (Hawley & DeHaan, 1996, 2003). Scholars have moved beyond viewing resiliency as a characteristic of an individual to providing a framework for viewing resiliency as a quality of families (Hawley & DeHaan, 2003).

Conclusion

Families today are being challenged with an unbelievable number of changes and problems that have the capacity to produce stress and crisis. After many years of focusing on individual stress responses, researchers have begun systematic assessments of whole-family responses, often by focusing on resiliency. The major theoretical paradigm that has been used to study family responses to stressor events has been the social systems model. Developing from Hill's (1949) work on the effect of wartime separation, various characteristics of stressor events as well as the mediating effects of perceptions and resources have been studied, suggesting that there is nothing inherent in the event per se that is stressful or crisis producing. More recently, family stress research has moved beyond the linear relationship of stressor, buffer/moderator, and response to look at coping and adaptation as a process that continues over time, that is, how families actually manage stress and/or crisis. Coping is conceptualized as an ongoing process that facilitates family organization but also promotes individual growth. Increasingly, the outcome of interest is adaptation, that is, the ability of a family to make needed changes and ultimately recover from stress and crisis. Adaptation, like coping, however, should not be perceived as a definitive end product because families are always growing and changing. Furthermore, the serenity and stability synonymous with adaptation are not always functional for family members, and for some families, the response to a stressor event may result in a higher level of functioning. Finally, emphasis on the resilience of families has received increasing attention. By acknowledging the ability of families to successfully manage stressful events, scholars are broadening our understanding of how some families thrive in the face of adversity.

Suggested Readings and Internet Resources _____

Boss, P. (2006). *Loss, trauma, and resilience: Therapeutic work with ambiguous loss.* New York: W. W. Norton and Company.

Hill, R. (1949). *Families under stress.* Westport, CT: Greenwood.

McCubbin, H., & McCubbin, M. (1988). Typology of resilient families: Emerging roles of social class and ethnicity. *Family Relations, 37,* 247–254.

eXtension (an interactive learning environment delivering research-based knowledge from land-grant universities across the United States) offers a variety of publications related to managing family stress:

Family Caregiving: http://www.extension.org/family%20caregiving

Managing Financial Stress: http://www.extension.org/pages/Managing_Stress

Disaster Preparedness: http://www.extension.org/pages/Stress_and_Decision_Making_After_a_Disaster

Loss and Grief: http://www.extension.org/pages/Loss_and_Grief

The University of Minnesota Extension Services offers a series of publications on how families can positively manage stress: http://www.extension.umn.edu/topics.html?topic=3&subtopic=85.

Michigan State University Extension offers a series of bulletins developed to assist families in family stress and coping issues: http://www.fcs.msue .msu.edu/ff/familystress.html

The University of Illinois Extension offers several factsheets on recognizing and handling family stress: http://urbanext.illinois.edu/familyworks/ stress-00.html

The Utah State University Cooperative Extension offers a series of publications to assist families in managing the effects of natural and human-caused disasters: http://extension.usu.edu/ueden/htm/family

The American Psychological Association offers publications for members and nonmembers on topics related to family stress: www.apa.org (Search: Stress).

References

Aldous, J. C. (1996). *Family careers: Rethinking the developmental perspective.* Thousand Oaks, CA: Sage.

Anderson, S. A., & Gavazzi, S. M. (1990). A test of the Olson Circumplex Model: Examining its curvilinear assumption and the presence of extreme types. *Family Process, 29,* 309–324.

Barnett, R. C. (1993). Multiple roles, gender, and psychological distress. In L. Goldberger & S. Brezitz (Eds.), *Handbook of stress: Theoretical and clinical aspects* (pp. 427–445). New York: Free Press.

Bonanno, G. A. (2004). Loss, trauma, and human resilience: Have we underestimated the human capacity to thrive after extremely aversive events? *American Psychologist, 59*(1), 20–28.

Boss, P. (1987). Family stress: Perception and context. In M. Sussman & S. Steinmetz (Eds.), *Handbook on marriage and the family* (pp. 695–723). New York: Plenum.

Boss, P. G. (1988). *Family stress management.* Newbury Park, CA: Sage.

Boss, P. G. (1999). *Ambiguous loss.* Cambridge, MA: Harvard University Press.

Boss, P. G. (2002). *Family stress management: A contextual approach* (2nd ed.). Thousand Oaks, CA: Sage.

Boss, P. (2006). *Loss, trauma, and resilience: Therapeutic work with ambiguous loss.* New York: W. W. Norton and Company.

Buckley, W. (1967). *Sociology and modern systems theory.* Englewood Cliffs, NJ: Prentice Hall.

Burr, W. R. (1973). *Theory construction and the sociology of the family.* New York: John Wiley.

Burr, W. R. (1982). Families under stress. In H. I. McCubbin, A. E. Cauble, & J. M. Patterson (Eds.), *Family stress, coping, and social support* (pp. 5–25). Springfield, IL: Charles C Thomas.

Burr, W. R., Klein, S. R., & Associates. (1994). *Reexamining family stress: New theory and research.* Thousand Oaks, CA: Sage.

Cannon, W. B. (1932). *The wisdom of the body.* New York: Norton.

Caplan, G. (1964). *Principles of preventive psychiatry.* New York: Basic Books.

Caplan, G. (1974). *Support systems and community mental health*. New York: Behavioral Publications.

Carter, B., & McGoldrick, M. (1989). Overview: The changing family life cycle: A framework for family therapy. In B. Carter & M. McGoldrick (Eds.), *The changing family life cycle: A framework for family therapy* (pp. 3–28). Boston: Allyn & Bacon.

Cichetti, D., & Garmezy, N. (1993). Prospects and promises in the study of resilience. *Developmental and Psychopathology, 5,* 497–502.

Cobb, S. (1976). Social support as a moderator of life stress. *Psychosomatic Medicine, 38,* 300–314.

Coelho, G., Hamburg, D., & Adams, J. (1974). *Coping and adaptation.* New York: Basic Books.

Cowan, R. A., Cowan, C. P., & Schulz, M. S. (1996). Thinking about risk and resilience in families. In E. M. Hetherington & E. A. Blechman (Eds.), *Stress, coping, and resiliency in children and families* (pp. 1–38). Mahwah, NJ: Lawrence Erlbaum.

Derogatis, L. R., & Coons, H. L. (1993). Self-report measures of stress. In L. Goldberger & S. Breznitz (Eds.), *Handbook of stress: Theoretical and clinical aspects* (pp. 200–233). New York: Free Press.

Dohrenwend, B. S., & Dohrenwend, B. P. (1974). *Stressful life events: Their nature and effects.* New York: John Wiley.

Elder, G. H., & Conger, R. D. (2000). *Children of the land: Adversity and success in rural America.* Chicago: University of Chicago Press.

Erikson, E. H. (1963). *Childhood and society.* New York: Norton.

Figley, C. (Ed.). (1978). *Stress disorders in Vietnam veterans.* New York: Brunner/Mazel.

Fisher, P. A., Fagot, B. I., & Leve, C. S. (1998). Assessment of family stress across low-, medium-, and high-risk samples using the Family Events Checklist. *Family Relations, 47,* 215–219.

Frankenhaeuser, M. (1994). A biopsychosocial approach to stress in women and men. In V. J. Adesso, D. M. Reddy, & R. Fleming (Eds.), *Psychological perspectives on women's health* (pp. 39–56). Philadelphia: Taylor and Francis.

Gore, S., & Colten, M. E. (1991). Gender, stress and distress: Social-relational influences. In J. Eckenrode (Ed.), *The social context of coping.* New York: Plenum.

Gruen, R. J. (1993). Stress and depression: Toward the development of integrative models. In L. Goldberger & S. Breznitz (Eds.), *Handbook of stress: Theoretical and clinical aspects* (pp. 550–569). New York: Free Press.

Hall, A. D., & Fagan, R. E. (1968). Definition of system. In W. Buckley (Ed.), *Modern systems research for the behavioral scientist* (pp. 81–92). Chicago: Aldine.

Hansen, D. A. (1965). Personal and positional influence in formal groups: Propositions and theory for research on family vulnerability to stress. *Social Forces, 44,* 202–210.

Hansen, D. A., & Hill, R. (1964). Families under stress. In H. Christensen (Ed.), *Handbook of marriage and the family* (pp. 215–295). Chicago: Rand McNally.

Hawley, D. R., & DeHaan, L. (1996). Toward a definition of family resilience: Integrating life-span and family perspectives. *Family Process, 30,* 283–298.

Hawley, D. R. & DeHaan, L. (2003). Toward a definition of family resilience: Integrating life-span and family perspectives. In P. Boss (Ed.), *Family stress: Classic and contemporary readings* (pp. 57–70). Thousand Oaks, CA: Sage.

Hill, R. (1949). *Families under stress.* Westport, CT: Greenwood.

Hill, R. (1971). *Families under stress.* Westport, CT: Greenwood. (Original work published in 1949)

Hill, R. (1999). *The strengths of African American families: Twenty-five years later.* New York: University Press of America.

Hillbrand, M., & Pallone, N. J. (1994). *The psychobiology of aggression: Engines, measurement, control.* New York: Haworth.

Hoffman, L. (1981). *Foundation of family therapy: A conceptual framework for systemic change.* New York: Basic Books.

Holmes, T. H., & Rahe, R. H. (1967). The social readjustment rating scale. *Journal of Psychosomatic Research, 11,* 213–218.

Lazarus, R. (1966). *Psychological stress and the coping process.* New York: McGraw-Hill.

Lazarus, R. (1976). *Patterns of adjustment.* New York: McGraw-Hill.

Lazarus, R. S., & Folkman, S. (1984). *Stress, appraisal, and coping.* New York: Springer.

Lazarus, R. S., & Launier, R. (1978). Stress-related transactions between person and environment. In L. A. Pervin & M. Lewis (Eds.), *Perspectives in interactional psychology* (pp. 360–392). New York: Plenum.

Lipman-Blumen, J. (1975). A crisis framework applied to macrosociological family changes: Marriage, divorce, and occupational trends associated with World War II. *Journal of Marriage and the Family, 27,* 889–902.

Lovallo, W. R. (1997). *Stress and health: Biological and psychological interaction.* Thousand Oaks, CA: Sage.

Masten, A. S., & Garmezy, N. (1985). Risk, vulnerabiity, and protective factors in developmental psychopathology. In B. B. Lahey & A. E. Kazdin (Eds.), *Advances in clinical child psychology* (Vol. 8, pp. 1–52). New York: Plenum.

May, R. (1950). *The meaning of anxiety.* New York: Ronald.

McCubbin, H. I. (1979). Integrating coping behavior in family stress theory. *Journal of Marriage and the Family, 41,* 237–244.

McCubbin, H. I., Cauble, A. E., & Patterson, J. M. (1982). *Family stress, coping, and social support.* Springfield, IL: Charles C Thomas.

McCubbin, H. I., Futrell, J. A., Thompson, E. A., & Thompson, A. I. (1998). Resilient families in an ethnic and cultural context. In H. I. McCubbin, E. A. Thompson, A. I. Thompson, & J. A. Futrell (Eds.), *Resiliency in African-American families* (pp. 329–351). Thousand Oaks, CA: Sage.

McCubbin, H. I., Joy, C. B., Cauble, A. E., Comeau, J. K., Patterson, J. M., & Needle, R. H. (1980). Family stress and coping: A decade review. *Journal of Marriage and the Family, 42,* 125–141.

McCubbin, H., & McCubbin, M. (1988). Typology of resilient families: Emerging roles of social class and ethnicity. *Family Relations, 37,* 247–254.

McCubbin, H. I., & Patterson, J. M. (1982). Family adaptation to crisis. In H. I. McCubbin, A. E. Cauble, & J. M. Patterson (Eds.), *Family stress, coping, and social support* (pp. 26–47). Springfield, IL: Charles C Thomas.

McCubbin, H. I., & Patterson, J. M. (1985). Adolescent stress, coping, and adaptation: A normative family perspective. In G. K. Leigh & G. W. Peterson (Eds.), *Adolescents in families* (pp. 256–276). Cincinnati, OH: Southwestern.

McCubbin, H. I., Patterson, J. M., & Wilson, L. (1981). *Family inventory of life events and changes (FILE): Research instrument.* St. Paul: University of Minnesota, Family Social Science.

McDaniel, S. H., Hepworth, J, & Doherty, W. J. (1992). *Medical family therapy: A biopsychosocial approach to families with health problems*. New York: Basic Books.

Moos, R. H. (1976). *Human adaptation: Coping with life crisis*. Lexington, MA: D. C. Heath.

Moos, R. H. (1986). *Coping with life crises: An integrated approach*. New York: Plenum.

Naisbitt, J., & Aburdene, P. (1990). *Megatrends 2000: Ten new directions for the 1990s*. New York: Morrow.

Olson, D. H., Russell, C. S., & Sprenkle, D. H. (1979). Circumplex model of marital and family systems cohesion and adaptability dimensions, family types, and clinical applications. *Family Process, 18*, 3–28.

Olson, D. H., Russell, C. S., & Sprenkle, D. H. (1980). Marital and family therapy: A decade review. *Journal of Marriage and the Family, 42*, 239–260.

Olson. D. H., Russell, C. S., & Sprenkle, D. H. (1983). Circumplex Model of Marital and Family Systems: VI. Theoretical update. *Family Process, 22*, 69–81.

Patterson, J. M. (1988). Families experiencing stress. *Family Systems Medicine, 6*, 202–237.

Pearlin, L. (1991). The study of coping: An overview of problems and directions. In J. Eckenrode, *The social context of coping* (pp. 261–276). New York: Plenum.

Pearlin, L., & Schooler, C. (1978). The structure of coping. *Journal of Health and Social Behavior, 19*, 2–21.

Price, S. J., McKenry, P. C., & Murphy, M. (2000). *Families across time: A life course perspective*. Los Angeles: Roxbury.

Rees, H., & Smyer, M. (1983). The dimensionalization of life events. In E. Callahan & K. McCluskey (Eds.), *Life-span developmental psychology: Non-normative life events* (pp. 328–359). New York: Academic Press.

Rodgers, R. H., & White J. M. (1993). Family developmental theory. In P. G. Boss, W. J. Doherty, R. LaRossa, W. R. Schumm, & S. K. Steinmetz (Eds.), *Sourcebook of family theories and methods: A contextual approach* (pp. 225–254). New York: Plenum.

Roskies, E., & Lazarus, R. (1980). Coping theory and the teaching of coping skills. In D. Davidson & S. Davidson (Eds.), *Behavioral medicine: Changing health lifestyles* (pp. 38–69). New York: Brunner/Mazel.

Rutter, M. (1983). Stress, coping, and development: Some issues and questions. In N. Garmezy & M. Rutter (Eds.), *Stress, coping, and development* (pp. 1–41). New York: McGraw-Hill.

Rutter, M. (1987). Psychosocial resilience and pretective mechanisms. *American Journal of Orthopsychiatry, 57*, 316–331.

Sarafino, E. P. (1990). *Health psychology: Biopsychosocial interactions*. New York: John Wiley & Sons.

Sarason, L., Johnson, J., & Siegel, J. (1978). Assessing the impact of life changes: Development of the life experiences survey. *Journal of Consulting and Clinical Psychology, 64*, 932–946.

Selye, H. (1978). *The stress of life*. New York: McGraw-Hill.

Spence, K. W. (1956). *Behavior therapy and conditioning*. New Haven, CT: Yale University Press.

Teachman, J. D., Polonko, K. A., & Scanzoni, J. (1999). Demography and families. In M. B. Sussman, S. K. Steinmetz, & G. W. Peterson (Eds.), *Handbook of marriage and the family* (pp. 39–76). New York: Plenum.

Thoits, P. A. (1991). On merging identity theory and stress research. *Social Psychology Quarterly, 54,* 101–112.

Tix, A. P., & Frazier, P. A. (1998). The use of religious coping during stressful life events: Main effects, moderation, and mediation. *Journal of Consulting and Clinical Psychology, 66*(2), 411–422.

Toffler, A. (1990). *Power shift: Knowledge, wealth, and violence at the edge of the 21st Century.* New York: Bantam.

Vandsburger, E., Harrigan, M., & Biggerstaff, M. (2008). In spite of it all, we make it: Themes of stress and resiliency as told by women in families living in poverty. *Journal of Family Social Work, 11*(1), 17–35.

Walsh, F. (2006). *Strengthening family resilience.* New York: Guilford.

2

Conceptualizing Parental Stress With Family Stress Theory

Gary W. Peterson,
Charles B. Hennon, and Terence Knox

Adults worldwide are encouraged to become parents, value and nurture their children, and experience the young as sources of happiness and life satisfaction (Hennon & Wilson, 2008). In particular, women are under pressure to consider children as the primary means of experiencing fulfillment in their lives, though some men appear to be incorporating this more extensively into their identities (Marsiglio, Roy, & Fox, 2005; Peterson, Bodman, Bush, & Madden-Derdich, 2000; Ulrich & Weatherall, 2000). Pronatalist norms, grounded in religious and secular values, provide a principal basis for most adults' preferences to become mothers and fathers.

Cultural images of parenthood often focus on the positive meanings associated with caring for and socializing children. Positive representations of parenting follow directly from beliefs that having children makes parents' lives complete. Having children is seen as a source of novelty, stimulation, and fun and as solidifying ties among parents, grandparents, and other kin. Parenthood also provides a socially defined marker of mature status, a sense of permanence, and feelings of personal efficacy (Beck & Beck-Gernsheim, 1995; Hennon & Wilson, 2008; Kwok & Wong, 2000; Radina, Wilson, & Hennon, 2008).

An alternative view is that parenthood is not inherently negative or positive, but recognizes in a more "realistic" fashion that caring for and socializing children involves both positive and negative challenges consisting of daily hassles, tension, and anxiety as well as satisfactions and fulfillment. Many aspects of parental stress are understood by currently involved parents, at a commonsense level, who face both the mundane and more dramatic challenges of their daily lives. Parents have mental models of themselves as parents, which involves evaluating the challenges and benefits experienced as they fulfill their parenting duties.

How parents appraise themselves in terms of such challenges and accomplishments is decisive in the development and maintenance of parenting stress

(Abidin, 1992). Stressful experiences occur throughout the life course, even on a daily basis—during the intense hours of childbirth, when a toddler bites a sibling, or when a teenage daughter pushes for autonomy and becomes monitored less by parents. Stress also is evident during positive experiences with children—as when a father fidgets in his seat waiting for his 13-year-old daughter's performance in the school play, knowing viscerally how nervous she is.

Many parents will feel acute stress or crisis when their 16-year-old daughter informs them that she is pregnant or when their 18-year-old son, winner of a scholarship to an elite private college, announces he no longer sees the meaning of college in his future and instead wants to do a stint in the Marines. Perhaps more difficult is the daily challenge that a parent faces from the relentlessly difficult behavior of an autistic child or by a teenager who has just been arrested for theft.

Parents also can become stressed by difficult job circumstances that compel them to spend less positive time with, be less supportive of, and use less effective discipline with their children (Kremer-Sadlik & Paugh, 2007). Stepfamilies, as part of all the new adjustments they must make, often report elevated levels of stress (Hennon, Hildenbrand, & Schedle, 2008). Ethnic minority and immigrant families often experience continuing or periodic stress, especially when confronting the challenges of balancing the demands of the dominant and minority cultures (Hennon, Peterson, Hildenbrand, & Wilson, 2008; Hennon, Peterson, Polzin, & Radina, 2007).

Grandparents are often called upon to play either supplemental or primary parenting roles to the extent that their children (who are now parents) become involved in drug use, are inadequately prepared for parenting, or demonstrate other problematic parental behaviors (e.g., criminal behavior, mental health problems) (Letiecq, Bailey, & Kurtz, 2008). The point is that some degree of parental stress is virtually a universal experience for mothers, fathers, and their surrogates, including parents, grandparents, aunts, stepparents, and others who step in to fulfill parental roles. The ubiquitous nature of these experiences underscores the importance of understanding how parental stress contributes to effective or ineffective functioning of mothers, fathers, and other caregivers (Crnic & Low, 2002; Deater-Deckard, 1998; Deater-Deckard & Scarr, 1996; Hennon, Peterson, et al., 2008; Letiecq et al., 2008; Ostberg & Hagekull, 2000).

Consistent with these ideas, the primary purpose of this chapter is to integrate the research on parental stress with concepts central to family stress theory (Hennon et al., 2009; Hennon & Peterson, 2007; Hill, 1949, 1958; McCubbin & Patterson, 1986; McKenry & Price, 2005; Patterson, 2002; Radina et al., 2008). Key concepts from family stress theory, consisting of stress and crisis, stressor event (or stressor), resources, definition of the stressor (or perception), coping, and adaptation, are used to accomplish this integration. As part of addressing the primary purpose, this chapter also addresses (a) why the experience of parental stress is so common, (b) why the degree of parental stress varies widely within the population of mothers and fathers, (c) why parents vary in their capacities to cope with and adapt to stress, (d) what linkages exist between parental stress and the adjustment (or maladjustment) of parents and children, and (e) what strategies exist for controlling and reducing adverse parental stress.

Rethinking the research literature on parental stress in terms of family stress theory provides a more systemic or family systems view of this work. Previous research and conceptualization of parental stress has been largely an outgrowth of psychological theory (Crnic & Low, 2002) by emphasizing the internal experiences of individuals (e.g., parents) who experience psychological "distress," while limited attention has been devoted to "relationship" or "systemic" conceptions. In contrast, this chapter seeks to reinterpret parental stress more extensively in terms of the family relationship or the systemic context of parent–child relationships.

Family Stress Theory and Parental Stress Applied to Parenting: The X Factor

The foundation of family stress theory is Reuben Hill's (1949, 1958) classic work on the ABC-X model, which proposes that family crisis (the X factor) results from a complex three-way interaction among the stressor event (the A factor), the resources that families bring to bear on the stressor (the B factor), and the definition or meaning that families assign to the stressor (the C factor). According to this model, stress or crisis is not simply the direct result of the event itself, but also is a product of how a family defines demanding circumstances and the extent to which the family has resources available for coping (Boss, 1992, 2002; Hennon et al., 2009; Patterson, 2002).

Hill (1949, 1958) developed family stress theory to examine the circumstances of a "crisis" in which a sudden, dramatic event occurs (e.g., a hurricane strikes a family's home or a child's diagnosis of having cancer) that immobilizes or incapacitates the family. Subsequent research using family stress theory has increasingly dealt with ordinary, normative, cumulative, and long-term changes within families, rather than focusing on only such dramatic events (Crnic, Gaze, & Hoffman, 2005; Crnic & Low, 2002; McKenry & Price, 2005). Scholars have devoted greater attention in recent years to normative transitions in the life course, such as when parents and infants form attachment bonds or when adolescents negotiate greater autonomy from parents. Another emergent focus has sought to understand how the accumulation of more than one demanding circumstance (e.g., when parents' employment stress adds to parental stress) impairs effective parental functioning and influences the daily experiences of mothers, fathers, and children (Baker et al., 2003; Kremer-Sadlik & Paugh, 2007; Shumow & Lomax, 2002). Consequently, researchers have devoted increased attention to understanding how families (and especially parents) cope with stress and are resilient in the face of demanding circumstances (Bush & Peterson, 2008). Increasingly, neither family nor parental stress has become viewed as inherently bad or good (Crnic et al., 2005; Crnic & Low, 2002; Hobfoll & Spielberger, 1992; Patterson, 2002), but rather that it becomes problematic only when family members experience dissatisfaction (or distress) (Boss, 2002). These negative experiences occur only when changes are perceived as being disruptive to the family system, particularly within the areas of child care and child socialization.

Although some debate exists about the efficacy of *change* at the systemic level (Hobfoll & Spielberger, 1992), most scholars view family systemic transitions as sources of stress, often experienced as tension within either the parent–child or the larger family system (Boss, 2002; Hennon, Peterson, et al., 2008; Patterson, 2002). Various life transitions and events provide essential ingredients for normal psychosocial development, but they do so by evoking disturbances and pressures for change (i.e., stress) in the roles and expectations faced by family members (Heinicke, 2002). Because family members and family systems are subject to developmental change, stress becomes an inevitable consequence of everyday life, both within parent–child relationships and the larger family system.

One contribution of family stress theory has been to move the construct of "stress" solely from applications at psychological levels to applications at both relationship and family systems levels of analysis (Boss, 2002; Hennon et al., 2009; McKenry & Price, 2005). At the psychological level, parental stress is defined as an aversive emotional reaction (or "distress") by an individual parent to the demands of occupying child-care and child-socialization roles (Crnic et al., 2005; Crnic & Low, 2002; Deater-Deckard, 1998). In contrast, stress at the relationship or family systems level is defined as pressure or tension within a relationship system that is synonymous with change (Boss, 2002). Such pressures for systemic change, depending on how parents view them, may contribute either to psychological distress or to positive psychological feelings at the individual level of experience. Both family stress and parental stress thus involve changes that affect either the family system or family members' personal assessments of these changes. The kinds of changes that may evoke stressful reactions include dramatic crisis events, more mundane daily hassles, and the accumulation of several difficult circumstances (i.e., strain).

From a systems perspective, parental stress also must be viewed in terms of *reciprocal* or even *multidirectional* processes (Kuczynski, 2003; Kuczynski & Parkin, 2007). As such, parental stress is both a *product* of connections with other systemic connections (e.g., relationships with coworkers or with a person's spouse/partner) and an *activator* of parental behavior and other responses that have consequences for other family members (Deater-Deckard, 1998; Hennon et al., 2009). In addition to work environments and marital conflicts as sources of stress, for example, children can be sources of parental stress that shape the responses of parents to the young in a cyclical manner (Peterson & Hann, 1999). Parental stress results, in part, from a variety of mothers' and fathers' circumstances based on their bidirectional connections with children and other individuals, both within and beyond family boundaries. Such system-based circumstances include sudden job loss, severe spousal conflict, divorce or remarriage of parents, migration, and disengagement from extended-family members.

As an activator, parental stress has consequences within the parent–child relationship by fostering changes both in the psychological experiences of parents and in their childrearing behavior, sometimes leading to dysfunctional parenting (Baker et al., 2003; Crnic & Low, 2002; Deater-Deckard, 1998; Ostberg & Hagekull, 2000). Stressful responses by parents, in turn, may have consequences for the social, emotional, and cognitive development of children (Ardelt & Eccles, 2001; Bush & Peterson, 2008; Jones & Prinz, 2005; Peterson, 2005; Peterson & Hann, 1999). For example, highly stressed parents are more inclined than less stressed parents to be anxious and emotionally reactive as well as preoccupied with adult-centered goals. They are also less likely to monitor their young and to maintain child-centered objectives in child rearing. Thus, parental stress tends to *spill over* into child rearing, contributing to parents' being less responsive and affectionate as well as to their being more neglectful, punitive (authoritarian), and abusive toward children (Bush & Peterson, 2008). These declines in the quality of parenting may lead to such negative outcomes in the young as reduced willingness to be responsive to parents' expectations or noncompliance, less effective social skills, problems with peer adjustment, feelings of rejection, lowered self-esteem, disruptive and aggressive behaviors, social withdrawal, and distressed psychological experiences (Bush & Peterson, 2008; Crnic et al., 2005; Crnic & Low, 2002; Deater-Deckard, 1998; Hastings, 2002; Peterson, 2005; Peterson & Hann, 1999). In contrast, less distressed parents tend to be more responsive, warm, rational, and moderate in the kinds of control they use with children (e.g., use of firm control, reasoning, consistent rule enforcement, and monitoring rather more punitive or intrusive forms of control) (Coleman & Karraker, 1998, 2000; Crnic & Low, 2002; Deater-Deckard, 1998; Shumow & Lomax, 2002). Child characteristics associated with such positive parental behaviors include high self-esteem, effective school achievement, competent social skills, effective peer adjustment, and the maintenance of a balance between conforming to parents and progressing toward autonomy. These characteristics of children and adolescents are key subdimensions of social competence, or what a variety of cultures view as adaptive attributes of the young (Bush & Peterson, 2008; Hennon & Wilson, 2008; Kâğitçibaşi, 1996; Peterson & Hann, 1999; Peterson, 2005; Peterson & Hennon, 2007; Peterson, Madden-Derdich, & Leonard, 2000).

Similar to other aspects of systemic relationships, the *connections* between parental stress and child characteristics are not limited to circumstances where social influence is viewed as flowing only from parent to child. Instead, children and their perceived attributes have considerable influence on the degree of stress that parents experience. The existing literature also generally supports the family systems hypothesis that relationships, such as those between spouses and parent–child, are interdependent. Consistent findings indicate, for example, that parents who report greater intimacy and communication in their marriages also tend to be less stressed as well as more responsive, affectionate, and moderately controlling with children (Bush & Peterson, 2008; Chen & George, 2005; Grych, 2002; Peterson, 2005; Stone, Buehler, & Barber, 2002). Clearly, the parent–child relationship is characterized by reciprocal or even multidirectional influences, with parental stress being both a "product" and an "activator" of changes within the family system and larger social contexts (Hennon, Peterson, et al., 2008; Kuczynski, 2003; Kuczynski & Parkin, 2007).

Stressors or Stressor Events for Parents: Factor A _____

Stressors or stressor events (the A factor) consist of those occurrences that may be of sufficient magnitude to bring about feelings of tension for parents as well as changes within parent–child relationships and the larger family system. However, because many stressful circumstances for parents do not occur as discrete events, we prefer to use the general term *stressor* because parents may be dealing with multiple stressors that can accumulate, with the overall magnitude of accumulating stressors being important for determining the overall level of parental stress. (Hennon et al., 2009; McCubbin & Patterson, 1986).

Although a stressor has the *potential* to evoke change and psychological responses, the occurrences that impinge on the parent–child relationship are not synonymous with the onset of stress. Instead, stressors threaten the status quo of families and parent–child relationships, but they are *not solely capable* of fostering stress and imposing demands on individuals and relationships. By themselves, stressors (a) do not have all the necessary ingredients (i.e., the B factor *resources* and the C factor *definitions*) for creating parental stress, (b) have no inherent positive or negative attributions, and (c) may never produce a crisis that immobilizes the parent–child relationship. Instead, stressors are best described as neutral phenomena involving pressures that may either develop quickly or unfold over a long period of time. Rather than always being sudden disruptions, many stressors are of moderate strength and accumulate as demanding circumstances "pile up" over time (McCubbin & Patterson, 1986; McKenry & Price, 2005; Patterson, 2002).

Despite the fact that stressors have no inherent meaning, scholars have developed a variety of classification systems to identify common ways that parents and families respond to these circumstances (McKenry & Price, 2005). Most such systems include three common categories: normative stressors, nonnormative stressors, and chronic stressors. Because specific stressors can sometimes fit within more than one of these categories, such classification systems often fail to be mutually exclusive.

Normative Stressors

Normative stressors are events that are either endemic to everyday life (i.e., daily hassles) or longer-term developmental transitions that are components of the typical family life course (McKenry & Price, 2005).

Daily Hassles

Daily hassles include the constant caregiving demands and pressures that arise from everyday tasks involved in dealing with children. Many everyday child-rearing experiences are sources of self-defined competence and satisfaction for parents as they engage and solve parent–child challenges (Bush & Peterson, 2008; Peterson, 2005; Peterson & Hann, 1999; Shumow & Lomax, 2002). In contrast, other parenting experiences are less positive, such as dealing with children's whining, their annoying conduct based in undeveloped self-control, endless cleaning-up activities, loss of sleep, interruptions, lack of personal time, and time-consuming errands. Some hassles are infrequent and situational, whereas others occur repeatedly as everyday features of life (Crnic et al., 2005; Crnic & Low, 2002). By itself, each hassle may have limited consequences, but the cumulative impact of daily hassles may result in substantial amounts of stress for parents (Hennon et al., 2009; Sepa, Frodi, & Ludvigsson, 2004).

Single-parent families may be particularly prone to stress resulting from daily hassles because adult partners are not available to share the everyday tasks of child rearing and help buffer the challenges and stress. The daily hassles that single parents face are complicated by economic disadvantage, employment demands, and minimal social support that many of these parents experience, which may accumulate and lead to feelings of isolation, exhaustion, depression, and distress (Kremer-Sadlik & Paugh, 2007; Ontai, Sano, Hatton, & Conger, 2008; Ostberg & Hagekull, 2000; Patterson & Hastings, 2007; Weinraub, Horvath, & Gringlas, 2002; Wood, 2003).

Many daily hassles can occur repeatedly because individuals remain in contexts that have consistent, predictable demands that structure their circumstances. Consequently, the cumulative nature of daily hassles associated with parenting may change parent–child relationships gradually in problematic directions over time (Ontai et al., 2008). As difficult daily hassles occur with regularity, parents who once were satisfied and dealt with these circumstances competently may gradually become increasingly dysfunctional and experience growing stress. These evolving circular processes eventually may produce less competent, unresponsive, and less satisfied parents, along with children who further elicit such responses by becoming more aggressive and acting out (Crnic et al., 2005; Crnic & Low, 2002).

Developmental Transitions

Developmental transitions are another source of normative stress. The developing characteristics of the young, and the changing social meanings associated with these transitions, serve to challenge parents and initiate necessary changes within parent–child relationships. Developmental transitions have the potential to result in accumulating stressors that can be perceived collectively as disruptive change and contribute to psychological distress.

One of the pivotal developmental transition periods occurs when the young are experiencing the adolescent years. A key issue that evokes stress for parents is the process of granting increased autonomy to their children (Steinberg & Silk, 2002). Normally, parents who grant autonomy engage in a gradual process of allowing adolescents greater choice and independence as relationship rules concerning power and control are renegotiated (Peterson, 2005, 2008; Peterson, Bush, & Supple, 1999). This process of "letting go" in Western, individualistic cultures, if conducted competently, is not a sudden transfer of authority. Instead, competent parents and their developing teenagers engage in lengthy mutual renegotiation processes that originate in childhood, accelerate during adolescence, and continue until the eventual transition to adulthood is accomplished (Collins & Steinberg, 2006).

This letting-go process presents many potential stressors, especially when parents are reluctant to grant their children autonomy. Some parents have difficulty accommodating these changes and resist recognizing the need to gradually conclude an important stage of life as parents of dependent children. Some scholars have found that this "distancing process" also involves heightened conflict and stress between adolescents and parents (Collins & Steinberg, 2006; Peterson, 2008; Steinberg & Silk, 2002). Consequently, an adolescent's desire for autonomy often evokes feelings of distress and separation anxiety by parents who are facing demands for relationship changes that they perceive as a loss of control (Hock, Eberly, Bartle-Haring, Ellwanger, & Widaman, 2001). Parent–adolescent conflict and, by inference, parental distress may be normative results of the letting-go process as relationship rules are renegotiated (Collins, Laursen, Mortenson, & Ferreira, 1997; Shumow & Lomax, 2002; Springs, Rosen, & Matherson, 2002). Moreover, within ethnic minority families who are recent immigrants to the United States, a process referred to as *generational dissonance* can further exacerbate the normal levels of parental stress and conflict with adolescents (Hennon & Peterson, 2007; Hennon, Peterson, et al., 2008; Radina et al., 2008). The typical pattern for this process becomes evident when the younger generation adjusts to the new culture faster than their parents, who may perceive this rapid change as a betrayal of their culture of origin. The result is that immigrant parents may experience distress resulting from differential acculturation rates across generations (Berry, 2005). Such adverse feelings, referred to as *acculturative stress*, often foster greater distance between the generations as parents experience greater stress.

Nonnormative Stressors

Parents also face stressor events that are nonnormative in the sense that they are unpredictable occurrences that are substantially disruptive to the everyday pattern of parent–child relationships (McKenry & Price, 2005). Nonnormative stressor events are often sudden, dramatic occurrences that have considerable potential to disrupt the lives of parents. Most often, these stressors are products of unique situations that are unlikely to be repeated. Examples include a natural disaster, the sudden death of a child, a severe injury to a family member, an unexpected job promotion, and winning the state lottery. All are unexpected circumstances and have the potential to evoke substantial disruptions for parents in the daily rhythms of parent–child and family relationships. Moreover, the disrupted family relationships and structural changes evoked by these occurrences have the potential to increase the psychological distress of parents (McKenry & Price, 2005). These events, however, are not inherently stressful in exactly the same way for all parents, but vary in their disruptive qualities depending on such factors as the parents' subjective interpretations and their available resources (or vulnerabilities). Off-time developments (e.g., premarital pregnancies, delayed developmental milestones in children) and the diagnosis of unexpected circumstances or the sudden awareness of changes (e.g., childhood leukemia, being laid off from work) are types of nonnormative stressors.

Off-Time Developments

People generally anticipate that certain circumstances, such as retirement, the death of an elderly family member, and the advent of grandparenthood, will occur as part of normal family transitions at expected times of the life course (Boss; 2005; Carter & McGoldrick, 1999; Hennon et al., 2009; Hennon & Peterson, 2007). However, when such normal events occur at unanticipated times, they can become sources of disruptive distress for parents. For example, during the school-age years of children, the death of a parent often is extremely traumatic for the surviving parent and the children, in part because of the off-time nature of the event. In similar fashion, parents often experience considerable upheaval when learning about their teenage daughter's pregnancy and become grandparents much earlier than anticipated. By confronting families with sudden demands to mobilize resources for coping, such off-schedule, unanticipated events can disrupt the functioning of families and affect the subjective experiences of parents and other family members (Miller, Sage, & Winward, 2005).

Initial Awareness or Diagnosis

Another type of nonnormative stressor for parents may result from acute situations involving the initial awareness or diagnosis of unexpected circumstances and deviant or abnormal child characteristics. Examples include delinquency, conduct disorders, attention deficit behavior, physical illness, poor mental health, and birth defects (Ambert, 1997; Baker et al., 2003; Hennon & Peterson, 2007; Rimmerman & Duvdevani, 1996; Ryan,

Miller-Loessi, & Nieri, 2007; Tong, Lowe, Sainsbury, & Craig, 2008). The initial diagnosis that a child has leukemia, for example, is likely to be defined as an acute stressor that disrupts the lives and psychological well-being of parents. Likewise, parents are likely to experience acute stress or crisis when their son phones home from jail stating that he has been arrested for selling drugs. Recent research indicates that when parents are initially confronted with their child's delinquency, they often experience distress, worry, edginess, and feelings of devastation (Ambert, 1997, 1999; Caldwell, Horne, Davidson, & Quinn, 2007). Parents' subsequent experience with severe, nonnormative stressors may be converted gradually into chronic stressors (see below), perhaps of more moderate strength, as the parents become more accustomed (or adapted) to these challenges.

Chronic Stressors

Chronic stressors are atypical circumstances that occur over extended periods of time, are difficult to amend, and may have debilitating effects, both for parents and for the parent–child relationship. These include such stressors as parents' daily employment demands that compete with parenting (Gottfried, Gottfried, & Bathurst, 2002; Hennon, Hildenbrand, & Schedle, 2008; Kremer-Sadlik & Paugh, 2007), poverty (Hennon et al., 2009), acculturation after migration (Berry, 2005; Hennon, Peterson, et al., 2008; Peterson & Hennon, 2007; Radina et al., 2008), and persistent marital conflict (Stone et al., 2002). The physical, financial, and emotional demands faced by parents of children who either suffer long-term illnesses or demonstrate persistent abnormal qualities are examples of chronic stressors.

Child Effects: Long-Term Demands

As an illustration of chronic stress, specific child characteristics are often identified as contributing to such stressful circumstances for parents (Ambert, 1997). This is particularly true where the shock of an initial diagnosis or recognition has passed and the realities of the long-term challenges faced by parents have set in. This conception, commonly referred to as *child effects*, underscores the impact of children's health and well-being on the social-emotional lives of parents (Ambert, 1997; Peterson & Hann, 1999; Wood, 2003). For example, children who have long-term illnesses, physical discrepancies, or problematic behavior patterns such as asthma, attention-deficit/hyperactivity disorder (ADHD), congenital birth defects, and physical handicaps can bring about stressful circumstances for parents. Moreover, children who are frequently aggressive or disruptive can confront parents with substantial demands for investments of time, energy, and emotion (Hastings, 2002; Kent & Peplar, 2003; Podolski & Nigg, 2001; Rubin & Burgess, 2002).

Of particular interest to social scientists are children with identified social-emotional problems whose attributes serve as sources of chronic demands that parents find uniquely challenging. Examples include youngsters diagnosed as demonstrating conduct disorders, delinquency, attention deficit disorders, autism, or schizophrenia (Ambert, 1997; Baker & McCal, 1995; Baker et al., 2003; Kent & Peplar, 2003; Podolski & Nigg, 2001; Rubin & Burgess, 2002; Singer, Ethridge, & Aldana, 2007). Especially when disturbed children reside with parents, these circumstances can exert highly negative influences, even throughout the parents' later years of life. Accumulating stressors include such things as treatment costs, social stigma, demanding supervision requirements, distrust of the young, and the constant need for care. These difficult circumstances create considerable potential for parents to experience anger, embarrassment, guilt, and despair (Ambert, 1997, 1999; Caldwell et al., 2007; Singer et al., 2007).

Parental Resources and Parents: Factor B

The level of disruptive change within parent–child relationships and the psychological experience of parents may be partially determined (i.e., moderated or mediated) by *resources* (the B factor). Resources are the potential strengths of individuals, families, and other systems that may act as vehicles through which parents can obtain what they value. Accounting for resources, however, must also include consideration of latent factors that may contribute to pressures for change and foster distress as well as identify potential sources of recovery (Boss, 1992, 2002; Hennon et al., 2009; Hennon et al., 2007; Hill, 1949; Patterson, 2002). Consequently, *positive resources* are the traits, qualities, characteristics, and abilities of parents, parent–child relationships, family systems, and the larger social context that have the capacity to address the demands of stressors. These individual and relationship resources (or potential sources of "regenerative power") have the *latent* capability of buffering stress by decreasing the negative effects of stressors. The concept of resources also includes *negative resources*, or the *potential* vulnerabilities of parents and parent–child relationships to stressors and crisis events. These individual and relationship resources have the latent capacity to accentuate stress by increasing the negative effects of stressors (McCubbin & Patterson, 1986; Patterson, 2002).

A distinguishing characteristic of resources (both positive and negative) is their *potential* rather than *actual* nature (Hennon et al., 2007; McCubbin & Patterson, 1986; Patterson, 2002). This is illustrated by the observation that parents with seemingly equivalent resources often vary in the extent to which they are capable of bringing these capacities to bear within the parent–child relationship. Variability in resource accessibility underscores the idea that resources are simply latent capacities and may or may not be *actualized,* or placed into action, for particular circumstances. Resources are often classified as to their origins, such as within the person, familial environment, or other social contexts.

Personal Resources of Parents

The individual or personal resources of parents include economic well-being, knowledge (e.g., of child development), interpersonal skills, and physical health. Other personal resources are those that define positive or negative mental health such as a strong sense of self-efficacy, positive self-esteem, and diminished tendencies toward psychopathology (e.g., depression) (Coleman & Karraker, 1998, 2000; Cummings, Davies, & Campbell, 2000; Kwok & Wong, 2000; Shumow & Lomax, 2002). Illustrative of individual resources are psychological and emotional qualities that are components of parents' competence or incompetence as they socialize and care for children. Parental competence, a complex array of individual resources (among other resources), is composed of such qualities as psychological maturity, empathy, warmth, secure self-image, self-efficacy, capacity to express affection, and ability to exercise firm control (Bush & Peterson, 2008; Grusec & Davidov, 2007; Peterson, 2005; Peterson & Hann, 1999; Peterson & Hennon, 2007; Teti & Candelaria, 2002). Such personal competencies function as potential resources that empower parents for marshaling their resources to manage stressful circumstances.

The inverse circumstances, or negative resources, also apply to the psychological and relationship experiences of parents. Adults who have psychological or emotional problems, such as extensive depression, anger, and anxiety, often bring personal issues into the parent–child relationship that make them vulnerable to the adverse consequences of parenting stress (Cummings et al., 2000). Parents who are self-preoccupied, depressed, highly anxious, distant, hostile, or abusers of substances are less capable of dealing effectively with stressors or crisis events (Cummings et al., 2000; Teti & Candelaria, 2002; Vondra & Belsky, 1993) and less likely to demonstrate the necessary patience, sensitivity, and responsiveness to raise children effectively (Bush & Peterson, 2008; Cole & Tan, 2007; Crnic et al., 2005; Peterson et al., 2000).

Familial and Social Resources

Parents also draw on resources and experience vulnerabilities that are situated within the family system and the larger social-ecological context (Cochran & Niego, 2002; Hennon et al., 2009; Hennon & Peterson, 2007). Concerning the larger social-ecological context, parental efficacy (or a sense of being confident as a parent) (Ontai et al., 2008) may be influenced by the quality of their neighborhoods (Shumow & Lomax, 2002). Assistance from social networks, often referred to as *social support*, has been associated with a variety of positive mental health outcomes for parents, including lower psychological distress (Pierce, Sarason, & Sarason, 1996) and better capacities to deal with stressful events (Koeske & Koeske, 1990; Ostberg & Hagekull, 2000). Supportive partners, extended kin, and aspects of larger social networks have the potential to assist parents in dealing with stressors and crises by providing advice, emotional support, material assistance, and encouragement (Melson, Windecker-Nelson, & Schwarz, 1998; Radina et al., 2008; Wood, 2003). Moreover, social networks may provide negative influences, such as when high marital conflict or emotional distance contributes to parental stress and may diminish the quality of parenting (Crnic et al., 2005; Crnic & Low, 2002; Ontai et al., 2008; Radina et al., 2008; Stone et al., 2002).

Scholars differ in the types of social support they identify, but most distinguish between *emotional support,* or behavior that communicates caring (Pierce et al., 1996), and *instrumental support,* or concrete assistance that reduces parents' tasks and responsibilities of parents (Cochran & Niego, 2002; Hennon et al., 2009; Hennon, Peterson, et al., 2008). Although conceptualized as separate phenomena for the purposes of clarification, emotional and instrumental support are not mutually exclusive. Indeed, the two types of support often overlap, as when a grandfather quickly cancels his cherished plans to play golf with buddies because his single-parent daughter needs him to babysit his grandson. This unselfish act allows his daughter to help with an emergency situation at her workplace when her son's day-care center is closed. The tangible child care provided is instrumental support, whereas this grandfather's selfless action to defer his recreational plans on short notice is illustrative of providing emotional support to his daughter.

The parents' marital relationship is another aspect of the immediate social network that is a potential source of support and may function to increase or decrease the vulnerability of parents (Boss, 2002; Grych, 2002; Ontai et al., 2008; Patterson, 2002; Peterson & Hann, 1999; Stone et al., 2002). Scholars have frequently concluded that the role of potential social support beyond family boundaries is secondary to the role of marital relationships. A key feature of these relationships that may prevent stress is the extent to which parents support each other (usually studied as fathers supporting or not supporting mothers). Research indicates that parental (usually maternal) stress is reduced when a spouse uses humor to lighten difficult moments, listens to the partner's frustrations, and shares caregiving responsibilities. Parental stress also is reduced when marital satisfaction is high, marital conflict is low, and spouses share housework responsibilities. The importance of husbands providing support to wives cannot be overstated because recent evidence indicates that mothers have more responsibility, more involvement, and experience greater parental stress from child rearing (Crnic et al., 2005; Hennon & Wilson, 2008; Parke, 2002). Marriages characterized by a lack of shared caregiving, low support from fathers, marital dissatisfaction, and high marital conflict function as negative resources that add to parental (maternal) stress (Cochran & Niego, 2002; Deater-Deckard & Scarr, 1996; Stone et al., 2002).

Social support has the potential to diminish feelings of parental depression and increase coping abilities during times of stress (Cochran & Niego, 2002;

Hennon, Peterson, et al., 2008; Koeske & Koeske, 1990; Ostberg & Hagekull, 2000). Support from outside family boundaries becomes important when parents are not married, the involvement of partners in caregiving is inadequate, or alternative significant others (e.g., siblings) are not available (Ontai et al., 2008). Moreover, social support has the potential to affect the quality of parenting indirectly by enhancing, maintaining, or impairing the emotional well-being of mothers and fathers (Pierce et al., 1996). Support that reduces parental distress encourages parents to be more nurturant and rational and to use more moderate forms of control, while avoiding harsh or rejecting forms of child rearing (Belsky & Vondra, 1989; Crnic et al., 2005; Crnic & Low, 2002).

Consistent with conceptions of resources and vulnerabilities, an important recognition is that social networks are not always supportive and may instead accentuate parental stress. This is illustrated by the stress, conflict, frustration, and disappointment that often characterize the families of unmarried teenage mothers (Miller-Johnson et al., 1999). Under these circumstances, the social support conveyed might be judgmental and restrictive and actually increase the stress of parents. For teenage mothers, effective social support involves providing assistance while also fostering autonomy in a manner that acknowledges the young parent's viewpoints, accepts the teen's feelings, and refrains from excessive control over the young person's experiences and behaviors (Miller, Sage, & Winward, 2005; Pierce et al., 1996). Such an approach reduces stress, provides short-term assistance for the daily demands of parenting, and provides encouragement for the long-term psychosocial maturity of youthful parents.

Parental Definitions: Factor C

As noted above, events or phenomena by themselves do not create the experience of stress or crisis. Instead, parents and other family members construct their own realities or impose subjective "definitions" of their circumstances (Peterson & Hennon, 2005; Peterson & Rollins, 1987). Consequently, the meanings that individuals and families attribute to phenomena (the C factor) help to determine whether they experience stressor or crisis events as positive, negative, or neutral (Boss, 2002; McCubbin & Patterson, 1986; McKenry & Price, 2005). Although each person's or family's appraisal is somewhat unique, Hennon et al. (2009) identified patterns and provided a typology of these appraisals. The typology indicates that *benign* appraisals designate that the stressor situation is not hazardous. *Challenges* are circumstances appraised as likely to be handled appropriately. Appraisals classified as *threatening* are circumstances believed to have the potential to cause harm or loss to the family, though such outcomes have not yet occurred (e.g., growing financial difficulties that may lead to bankruptcy). If managed appropriately, the threat can be avoided. However, if the threat cannot be dealt with effectively, harm can result for a family. A fourth category, *harm/loss*, represents situations appraised as having already resulted in damage within the family system (e.g., a person's health has been compromised, bankruptcy has been filed, or a person is stigmatized). The overall significance of the appraisal categories is that virtually identical events may evoke varied responses by different parents and other family members. Subjective appraisals of the circumstances either help to decrease the emotional burdens associated with stressors or lead to a sense of hopelessness, denial of reality, or simply acceptance in the face of unpredictable circumstances (Boss, 2002; Hennon et al., 2009; McCubbin & Patterson, 1986; Patterson, 2002). Variability in definitions is rooted in many sources, including differences in life experiences, diversity in ethnic or cultural norms, variations in family traditions, and resources available (Boss, 2002).

These ideas from family stress theory are reinforced by research findings concerning the subjective experiences of parents. Of special importance is the idea that parental beliefs, values, attitudes, expectations, and "developmental scenarios" provide meaning for their relationships with their children and help to determine how they will respond to the young. Specifically, parents make attributions about their children's moods, motives, intentions, responsibilities, and competencies that shape the parents' emotional responses (e.g., positive stress or distress) as well as their subsequent childrearing approaches (Sigel & McGillicuddy-De Lisi, 2002). Parents tend to hold their children accountable for negative behavior when they believe that children intend to misbehave and could choose to restrain themselves. Parents who make such attributions are more likely to be distressed and to use punitive behavior toward their children, partly because they perceive children as being able to "know better." In contrast, parents who view younger children as being immature, not yet fully competent, or lacking intention or responsibility for their actions are more inclined toward positive feelings and less inclined to be punitive or rejecting. Instead, parents who maintain such positive definitions are likely to be less stressed about their socialization roles. Diminished parental stress, in turn, often translates into the expression of greater nurturance and moderate forms of control such as reasoning, monitoring, and consistent rule enforcement (Hennon & Peterson, 2007; Peterson & Hann, 1999). Consequently, awareness of parental beliefs and subjective definitions is critical for understanding the varied intensity of both parental distress and more positive feelings as factors that influence how parents respond to their children (Deater-Deckard, 1998).

A closely related means of conceptualizing how subjective interpretations lead to parental stress is the degree to which parents view their children's characteristics as deviating from parents' expectations about what is normative (Goodnow, 2002). Parents can define their children as deviating from their expectations in either positive or negative directions, with greater deviations from the subjectively accepted norm producing greater distress for parents. A negative deviation is an adverse view of an attribute that parents perceive as being deficient in terms of contemporary social norms or cultural values (Goodnow, 2002). The most frequent parental responses to such negative deviations (e.g., aggressive or conduct disorder behavior) are (a) adverse subjective experiences (e.g., psychological distress) and (b) communicating the parent's negative feelings to children (e.g., punitive, withdrawn, or rejecting behavior). In contrast, positive deviations are those characteristics that are assigned favorable definitions, in part, because parents have come to view these attributes (e.g., successful school achievement) as either meeting or surpassing their standards that coincide with existing social norms. Some parents may experience satisfaction or positive feelings (positive stress) regarding specific developmental changes (e.g., growing autonomy during adolescence), which is viewed as affirming both their own competence and their interpretation of what constitutes culturally valued definitions of youthful competence (Springs, Rosen, & Matherson, 2002). Common responses to positive definitions include supportive behavior and moderate control strategies, such as reasoning and rule-based supervision. The specific responses of parents to children tend to be shaped not by just the children's actual characteristics but also by the parents' subjective attributions and expectations, which may or may not reflect objective standards (Goodnow, 2002; Sigel & McGillicuddy-De Lisi, 2002).

Parental Coping

The current emphasis on coping in family stress theory underscores how this perspective includes not only the experiences of crisis and dysfunction but also how families manage, endure, and recover from stressors (Patterson, 2002). Coping involves *taking direct actions* (e.g., acquiring resources, learning new skills, and asking for assistance), *altering one's interpretations* (e.g., reframing circumstances), and *managing one's emotions* (e.g., through social support or substance use). Families can use these strategies individually, successively, or, more often, in various combinations to meet demands. Specific coping strategies are not inherently adaptive or maladaptive, but are useful to a degree that depends on the precise nature of the circumstances at hand (Hennon et al., 2009; McKenry & Price, 2005; Patterson, 2002).

The process of coping interacts with both the available resources and the perceptions of parents, which means that these are conceptually different but often indistinguishable from each other in a lot of circumstances. Instead of being a potential ability, the process of coping involves *specific efforts that parents expend to manage a stressor or crisis event*. Whether active coping seeks to maintain the status quo or to achieve new levels of family organization, it involves *making actual responses to or redefining* the circumstances at hand (McKenry & Price, 2005). The kinds of coping responses that parents use can vary with the specific ethnic or cultural background of a family (Hennon et al., 2007; Hennon, Peterson, et al., 2008; Hennon & Wilson, 2008). Asian

American parents, for example, are less inclined than European American parents to seek help provided by mental health agencies (e.g., therapy or casework services) as a means of coping with stress. In Asian cultures, revealing one's personal stress to a professional clinician or caseworker tends to be stigmatized as immaturity, social disgrace, weakness, and poor self-discipline (Fong, 1998).

Several examples of coping with parental stress can be found in the literature on parent–child relationships. Cognitive coping strategies include passive approaches, such as denial or avoidance, as well as active approaches involving positive reappraisal and problem-focused strategies (Crnic et al., 2005; Crnic & Low, 2002; Ostberg & Hagekull, 2000). Research indicates that parents of children with ADHD can cope (i.e., reduce their stress) through "positive reframing"—that is, by thinking about particular circumstances as challenges that they might overcome or master rather than as overwhelming obstacles (Podolski & Nigg, 2001). Such "active" coping strategies are more successful in reducing stress and restoring constructive parental behaviors than are "passive" approaches involving acceptance as an outgrowth of fatalism.

Other coping strategies involve drawing on or orchestrating resources from the social environment, perhaps in the form of parent education, to learn more about high-quality parenting, child development, or how to manage stress (Hennon et al., 2007; Radina et al., 2008). The logic here is that by experiencing educational programming, parents who understand children better and are more informed about parenting skills will be more likely to develop realistic expectations for child development and respond more competently to the many challenges of socializing the young. Subsequently, these parents are likely to be more capable of accessing resources, managing their responses, and developing the necessary social support networks to buffer stress levels and enhance parenting skills (Cochran & Niego, 2002). Critical attributes for parental coping are the willingness and ability to take advantage of the sources of social support that are potentially available (Pierce et al., 1996). For example, a single mother who is struggling to supervise and control a delinquent teenage son might gain assistance from her social network of parents, siblings, and neighborhood friends. However, a failure to use coping capacities may occur if her feelings of pride, embarrassment, or personal responsibility prevent her from using these supports.

Parental Adaptation

Another concept that family stress theorists address is *adaptation,* or the ability of parents and other family members to recover from stress and crisis. Recovery may occur either through the elimination of disruptions in family relationships and a return to preexisting patterns or by moving to new levels of relationship organization and stability (Hennon et al., 2009; Hill, 1949, 1958; McCubbin & Patterson, 1986).

A prominent example of parental adaptation research is the work on the experiences of custodial mothers following marital separation or divorce (Hetherington & Stanley-Hagan, 2002). Stress is a common result in custodial mothers' lives as role transitions are forced on them with the loss of their marital partners and, frequently, the withdrawal of fathers from parental roles. Subsequently, many custodial mothers shoulder new responsibilities as providers, build new support networks, and incorporate aspects of the father's role into their parenting repertoires. Such changes often occur under difficult economic circumstances that contribute to psychological problems such as distress, anxiety, and depression. Subsequently, these negative mental health conditions place mothers at risk for declines in the quality of their performance as parents. Custodial mothers who experience increased irritability and stress often become (a) less capable of monitoring children, (b) more permissive, (c) more punitive, and (d) more inclined to engage in coercive exchanges with children (especially boys). Fortunately, in the majority of cases, the stressful circumstances of these mothers subside over time, and the quality of mother–child relationships often restabilizes approximately 1 to 2 years following the onset of the marital crisis (Bush & Peterson, 2008; Hetherington & Stanley-Hagan, 2002). The most frequent outcome of undergoing stress or crisis is that parents eventually manage stress, adapt to new circumstances, and restore the quality of their childrearing behavior.

Conclusion

The scholarship on parental stress can be conceptualized as an example where general constructs from family stress theory can add to our understanding of both the individual and relationship levels of family systems. The experience of parental stress or crisis is a complex product of several factors: (a) the nature of the stressor or crisis event, (b) the potential resources available to parents, (c) the subjective definitions that parents assign to the stressor events, (d) the particular coping styles that parents use, and (e) the relative abilities of parents and the parent-child relationships to adapt and recover from stress and crisis.

The application of family stress concepts to the research on parental stress helps in understanding a wide range of circumstances, varying from highly disruptive (nonnormative) crises to chronic stress and more normative challenges. A major contribution of family stress theory is the insight provided into how parental stress applies to both the individual and relationship levels of families. Although parental stress is a virtually universal phenomenon, parents' experiences of stress vary widely in intensity. Applying family stress theory concepts to the scholarship on parental stress helps to show more clearly (a) how parental stress is such a universal experience, (b) why the intensity of parental stress varies from parent to parent, (c) how parents cope with and adapt to stress differently, and (d) how parental stress influences the psychosocial well-being of the young by affecting parents' childrearing strategies.

Parental stress can function to devastate, inhibit, or energize mothers and fathers, depending on numerous individual and social-environmental factors.

Internet Resources

Parenting Special Needs: Stress Management:
http://specialchildren.about.com/od/stressmanagement/Stress_Management .htm

Stress Management for Parents:
http://www.healthyplace.com/Communities/parenting/cdi/parenting/ stress.htm
http://www.childdevelopmentinfo.com/parenting/stress.shtml

U.S Army-Stress Management for Parents (power point presentation for download):
chppm-www.apgea.army.mil/dhpw/Readiness/StressManagementFor Parents.ppt
Center for Effective Parenting: http://www.parenting-ed.org

University Extension Services

Most state university extension services offer information on parenting and/or stress in addition to information on workshops and other parenting programs. Here are three examples:

Human Development and Family Science Extension, at The Ohio State University:
http://fcs.osu.edu/hdfs

University of Missouri Extension:
http://www.outreach.missouri.edu/main/family

University of Maine Extension:
http://www.umext.maine.edu/onlinepubs/htmpubs/4186.htm

References

Abidin, R. R. (1992). The determinants of parenting behavior. *Journal of Clinical Child Psychology, 21,* 407–412.

Ambert, A. (1997). *Parents, children, and adolescents: Interactive relationships and development in context.* Binghamton, NY: Haworth.

Ambert, A. (1999). The effect of male delinquency on mothers and fathers: A heuristic study. *Sociological Inquiry, 69,* 368–384.

Ardelt, M., & Eccles, J. S. (2001). Effects of mothers' parental efficacy beliefs and promotive parenting strategies on inner-city youth. *Journal of Family Issues, 22,* 944–972.

Baker, B. L., McIntyre, L. L., Blacher, J., Crnic, K., Edelbrock, C., & Low, C. (2003). Preschool children with and without developmental delay: Behaviour problems and parenting stress over time. *Journal of Intellectual Disability Research, 47,* 217–230.

Baker, D. B., & McCal, K. (1995). Parenting stress in children with attention-deficit hyperactivity disorder and parents of children with learning disabilities. *Journal of Child and Family Studies, 4,* 57–68.

Beck, U., & Beck-Gernsheim, E. (1995). *The normal chaos of love* (M. Ritter & J. Wiebel, Trans.). Cambridge, UK: Polity.

Belsky, J., & Vondra, J. (1989). Lessons from child abuse: The determinants of parenting. In D. Cicchetti & V. Carlson (Eds.), *Child maltreatment: Theory and research on the causes and consequences of child abuse and neglect* (pp. 153–202). New York: Cambridge University Press.

Berry, J. W. (2005, June). *Acculturation: Social, cultural, and psychological change among immigrants.* Paper presented during workshop Agency and Human Development under Conditions of Social Change, Jena, Germany.

Boss, P. (2002). *Family stress management* (2nd ed.). Thousand Oaks, CA: Sage.

Boss, P. G. (1992). Primacy of perception in family stress theory and measurement. *Journal of Family Psychology, 6,* 113–119.

Bush, K. R., & Peterson, G. W. (2008). Family influences on childhood development. In T. P. Gullotta (Ed.), *Handbook of childhood behavioral issues* (pp. 43–67). New York: Taylor & Francis.

Caldwell, C. L., Horne, A. M., Davidson, B., & Quinn, W. H. (2007). Effectiveness of multiple family group intervention for juvenile first offenders in reducing parenting stress. *Journal of Child and Family Studies, 16,* 443–459.

Carter, B., & McGoldrick, M. (Eds.). (1999). *The expanded family life cycle: Individual, family, and social perspectives* (3rd ed.). Needham Heights, MA: Allyn & Bacon.

Chen, J., & George, R. A. (2005). Cultivating resilience in children from divorced families. *The Journal of Counseling and Therapy for Couples and Families, 13,* 452–455.

Cochran, M., & Niego, S. (2002). Parenting and social networks. In M. H. Bornstein (Ed.), *Handbook of parenting: Vol. 4. Social conditions and applied parenting* (2nd ed., pp. 393–418). Mahwah, NJ: Lawrence Erlbaum.

Cole, M. C., & Tan, P. Z. (2007). Emotion socialization from a cultural perspective. In J. E. Grusec & P. D. Hastings (Eds.), *Handbook of socialization: Theory and research* (pp. 516–542). New York: Guilford Press.

Coleman, P. K., & Karraker, K. H. (1998). Self-efficacy and parenting quality: Findings and future applications. *Developmental Review, 18,* 47–85.

Coleman, P. K., & Karraker, K. H. (2000). Parenting self-efficacy among mothers of school-age children: Conceptualization, measurement and correlates. *Family Relations, 49,* 13–24.

Collins, W. A., Laursen, B., Mortenson, N., & Ferreira, M. (1997). Conflict processes and transitions in parent and peer relationships: Implications for autonomy and regulation. *Journal of Adolescent Research, 12,* 178–198.

Collins, W. A., & Steinberg, L. A. (2006). Adolescent development in interpersonal context. In W. Damon & R. M. Lerner (Eds.), *Handbook of child psychology: Vol. 3. Social, emotional, and personality development* (6th ed., pp. 1003–1068). New York: Wiley.

Crnic, K., Gaze, C., & Hoffman, C. (2005). Cumulative parenting stress across the preschool period: Relations to maternal parenting and child behavior at age 5. *Infant & Child Development, 14,* 117–132.

Crnic, K., & Low, C. (2002). Everyday stresses and parenting. In M. H. Bornstein (Ed.), *Handbook of parenting: Vol. 5. Practical issues in parenting* (2nd ed., pp. 243–267). Mahwah, NJ: Lawrence Erlbaum.

Cummings, E. M., Davies, P. T., & Campbell, S. B. (2000). *Developmental psychopathology and family process.* New York: Guilford.

Deater-Deckard, K. (1998). Parenting stress and child adjustment: Some old hypotheses and new questions. *Clinical Psychology: Science and Practice, 5,* 314–333.

Deater-Deckard, K., & Scarr, S. (1996). Parenting stress among dual-earner mothers and fathers: Are there gender differences? *Journal of Family Psychology, 10,* 45–59.

Fong, T. P. (1998). *The contemporary Asian American experience: Beyond the model minority.* Upper Saddle River, NJ: Prentice Hall.

Goodnow, J. J. (2002). Parents' knowledge and expectations: Using what we know. In M. H. Bornstein (Ed.), *Handbook of parenting: Vol. 3. Being and becoming a parent* (2nd ed., pp. 305–332). Mahwah, NJ: Lawrence Erlbaum.

Gottfried, A. E., Gottfried, A. W., & Bathurst, K. (2002). Maternal and dual-earner employment status and parenting. In M. H. Bornstein (Ed.), *Handbook of parenting: Vol. 2. Biology and ecology of parenting* (2nd ed., pp. 363–388). Mahwah, NJ: Lawrence Erlbaum.

Grusec, J. E., & Davidov, M. (2007). Socialization in the family: The roles of parents. In J. E. Grusec & P. D. Hastings (Eds.), *Handbook of socialization: Theory and research* (pp. 284–308). New York: Guilford.

Grych, J. H. (2002). Marital relationships and parenting. In M. H. Bornstein (Ed.), *Handbook of parenting: Vol. 4. Social conditions and applied parenting* (2nd ed., pp. 315–333). Mahwah, NJ: Lawrence Erlbaum.

Hastings, R. P. (2002). Parental stress and behaviour problems of children with developmental disability. *Journal of Intellectual and Developmental Disability, 27,* 149–160.

Heinicke, C. M. (2002). The transition to parenting. In M. H. Bornstein (Ed.), *Handbook of parenting: Vol. 3. Being and becoming a parent* (2nd ed., pp. 363–388). Mahwah, NJ: Lawrence Erlbaum.

Hennon, C. B., Hildenbrand, B., & Schedle, A. (2008). Stepfamilies and children. In T. P. Gullotta & G. M. Blau (Eds.), *Family influences on childhood behavior and development: Evidence-based prevention and treatment approaches* (pp. 167–192). New York: Routledge.

Hennon, C. B., Newsome, W. S., Peterson, G. W., Wilson, S. M., Radina, M. E., & Hildenbrand, B. (2009). Poverty, stress, resiliency: Using the MRM Model for understanding and abating poverty-related family stress. In C. A. Broussard & A. L. Joseph (Eds.), *Family poverty in diverse contexts* (pp. 187–202). New York: Routledge.

Hennon, C. B., & Peterson, G. W. (2007). Estrés parental: Modelos teóricos y revisión de la literatura [Parenting stress: Theoretical models and a literature review]. In R. Esteinou (Ed.), *Fortalezas y desafíos de las familias en dos contextos: Estados Unidos de América y México* (pp. 167–221) [Strengths and challenges of families in two contexts: The United States of America and Mexico]. México, D. F.: Centro de Investigaciones y Estudios Superiores en Antropología Social (CIESAS) y Sistema Nacional para el Desarrollo Integral de la Familia (DIF). [Research Center and Superior Studies in Social Anthropology and National System for the Integral Development of the Family].

Hennon, C. B., Peterson, G. W., Hildenbrand, B., & Wilson, S. M. (2008). Parental stress amongst migrant and immigrant populations: The MRM and CRSRP models for interventions [Stress Parental em Populações Migrantes e Imigrantes: Os Modelos de Intervenção MRM e CRSRP]. *Pesquisas e Práticas Psicossociais, 2,* 242–257.

Hennon, C. B., Peterson, G. W., Polzin, L., & Radina, M. E. (2007). Familias de ascendencia mexicana residentes en Estados Unidos: recursos para el manejo del estrés parental [Resident families of Mexican ancestry in United States: Resources for the handling of parental stress]. In R. Esteinou (Ed.), *Fortalezas y desafíos de las familias en dos contextos: Estados Unidos de América y México* (pp. 225–282) [Strengths and challenges of families in two contexts: The United States of America and Mexico]. México, D. F.: Centro de Investigaciones y Estudios Superiores en Antropología Social (CIESAS) y Sistema Nacional para el Desarrollo Integral de la Familia (DIF).

Hennon, C. B., & Wilson, S. M. (Eds.). (2008). *Families in a global context.* New York: Routledge.

Hetherington, E. M., & Stanley-Hagan, M. (2002). Parenting in divorced and remarried families. In M. H. Bornstein (Ed.), *Handbook of parenting: Vol. 3. Being and becoming a parent* (2nd ed., pp. 287–316). Mahwah, NJ: Lawrence Erlbaum.

Hill, R. (1949). *Families under stress.* New York: Harper.

Hill, R. (1958). Generic features of families under stress. *Social Casework, 49,* 139–150.

Hobfoll, S. E., & Spielberger, C. D. (1992). Family stress: Integrating theory and measurement. *Journal of Family Psychology, 6,* 99–112.

Hock, E., Eberly, M., Bartle-Haring, S., Ellwanger, P., & Widaman, K. F. (2001). Separation anxiety in parents of adolescents: Theoretical significance and scale development. *Child Development, 72,* 284–298.

Jones, T. L., & Prinz, R. J. (2005). Potential roles of parental self-efficacy in parent and child adjustment: A review. *Clinical Psychology Review, 25,* 341–363.

Kâğitçibaşi, Ç. (1996). *Family and human development across cultures: A view from the other side.* Mahwah, NJ: Lawrence Erlbaum.

Kent, D., & Peplar, D. (2003). The aggressive child as agent in coercive family processes. In L. Kuczynski (Ed.), *Handbook of dynamics in parent-child relations* (pp. 131–144). Thousand Oaks, CA: Sage.

Koeske, G. F., & Koeske, R. D. (1990). The buffering effect of social support on parental stress. *American Journal of Orthopsychiatry, 60,* 440–451.

Kremer-Sadlik, T., & Paugh, A. L. (2007). Everyday moments—Finding "quality time" in American working families. *Time & Society, 16,* 287–308.

Kwok, S., & Wong, D. (2000). Mental health of parents with young children in Hong Kong: The roles of parenting stress and parenting self-efficacy. *Child & Family Social Work, 5,* 57–65.

Kuczynski, L. (2003). Beyond bidirectionality: Bilateral conceptual frameworks for understanding dynamics in parent-child relations. In L. Kuczynski (Ed.), *Handbook of dynamics in parent-child relations* (pp. 3–24). Thousand Oaks, CA: Sage.

Kuczinsky, L., & Parkin, C. M. (2007). Agency and bidirectionality in socialization: Interactions, transactions, and relational dialectics. In J. E. Grusec & P. D. Hastings (Eds.), *Handbook of socialization: Theory and research* (pp. 259–283). New York: Guilford.

Letiecq, B. L., Bailey, S. J., & Kurtz, M. A. (2008). Depression among rural Native American and European American grandparents rearing their grandchildren. *Journal of Family Issues, 29,* 334–356.

Marsiglio, W, Roy, K., & Fox, G. L. (2005). Situated fathering: A spatially sensitive and social approach. In W. Marsiglio, K. Roy, & G. L. Fox (Eds.), *Situated fathering: A focus on physical and social spaces* (pp. 4–30). Lanham, MD: Rowman & Littlefild.

McCubbin, H. I., & Patterson, J. M. (1986). Adolescent stress, coping, and adaptation: A normative family perspective. In G. K. Leigh & G. W. Peterson (Eds.), *Adolescents in families* (pp. 256–276). Cincinnati, OH: Southwestern.

McKenry, P. C., & Price, S. J. (2005). Families coping with problems and change: A conceptual overview. In P. C. McKenry & S. J. Price (Eds.), *Families and change: Coping with stressful events and transitions* (3rd ed., pp. 1–24). Thousand Oaks, CA: Sage.

Melson, G. F., Windecker-Nelson, E., & Schwarz, R. (1998). Support and stress in mothers and fathers of young children. *Early Education and Development, 9,* 261–281.

Miller, B. C., Sage, R., & Winward, B. (2005). Adolescent pregnancy. In T. P. Gullotta & G. R. Adams (Eds.), *Handbook on the treatment and prevention of dysfunctional behavior: Theory, practice, and prevention* (pp. 567–587). New York: Springer.

Miller-Johnson, S., Winn, D. M., Coie, J., Maumary-Gremaud, A., Hyman, C., Terry, R., et al. (1999). Motherhood during the teen years: A developmental perspective on risk factors for childbearing. *Development and Psychopathology, 11,* 85–100.

Ontai, L., Sano, Y., Hatton, H., & Conger, K. J. (2008). Low-income rural mothers' perceptions of parental confidence: The role of family health problems and partner status. *Family Relations, 57,* 324–334.

Ostberg, M., & Hagekull, B. (2000). A structural modeling approach to the understanding of parenting stress. *Journal of Clinical Child Psychology, 29,* 615–625.

Parke, R. D. (2002). Fathers and families. In M. H. Bornstein (Ed.), *Handbook of parenting: Vol. 3. Being and becoming a parent* (2nd ed., pp. 27–63). Mahwah, NJ: Lawrence Erlbaum.

Patterson, C. J., & Hastings, P. D. (2007). Socialization in the context of family diversity. In J. E. Grusec & P. D. Hastings (Eds.), *Handbook of socialization: Theory and research* (pp. 328–351). New York: Guilford.

Patterson, J. M. (2002). Integrating family resilience and family stress theory. *Journal of Marriage and Family, 64,* 349–360.

Peterson, G. W. (2005). Family influences on adolescent development. In T. P. Gullotta & G. R. Adams (Eds.), *Handbook on the treatment and prevention of dysfunctional behavior: Theory, practice, and prevention* (pp. 27–55). New York: Springer.

Peterson, G. W. (2008). Connectedness and autonomy: Tension or compatibility? In H. Reis & S. Sprecher (Eds.), *Encyclopedia of human relationships* (pp. 445–452). Thousand Oaks, CA: Sage.

Peterson, G. W., Bodman, D. A., Bush, K. R., & Madden-Derdich, D. A. (2000). Gender and parent-child relationships. In D. H. Demo, K. R. Allen, & M. A. Fine (Eds.), *Handbook of family diversity* (pp. 82–104). New York: Oxford University Press.

Peterson, G. W., Bush, K. R., & Supple, A. (1999). Predicting adolescent autonomy from parents: Relationship connectedness and restrictiveness. *Sociological Inquiry, 69,* 431–457.

Peterson, G. W., & Hann, D. (1999). Socializing children and parents in families. In M. B. Sussman, S. K. Steinmetz, & G. W. Peterson (Eds.), *Handbook of marriage and the family* (2nd ed., pp. 327–370). New York: Plenum.

Peterson, G. W., & Hennon, C. B. (2005). Conceptualizing parenting stress with family stress theory. In P. C. McKenry & S. J. Price (Eds.), *Families and change* (3rd ed., pp. 25–48). Thousand Oaks, CA: Sage.

Peterson, G. W., & Hennon, C. B. (2007). Influencias parentales en la competencia social de los adolescentes en dos culturas: una comparación conceptual entre los Estados Unidos y México [Parental influences on the social competence of adolescents in two cultures: A conceptual comparison between the United States and Mexico]. In R. Esteinou (Ed.), *Fortalezas y desafíos de las familias en dos contextos: Estados Unidos de América y México* (pp. 111–166) [Strengths and challenges of families in two contexts: The United States of America and Mexico]. México, D. F.: Centro de Investigaciones y Estudios Superiores en Antropología Social (CIESAS) y Sistema Nacional para el Desarrollo Integral de la Familia (DIF).

Peterson, G. W., Madden-Derdich, D. A., & Leonard, S. A. (2000). Parent-child relations across the life-course: Autonomy within the context of connectedness. In S. J. Price, P. C. McKenry, & M. J. Murphy (Eds.), *Families across time: A life course perspective* (pp. 187–203). Los Angeles: Roxbury.

Peterson, G. W., & Rollins, B. C. (1987). Parent-child socialization. In M. B. Sussman & S. K. Steinmetz (Eds.), *Handbook of marriage and the family* (pp. 471–507). New York: Plenum.

Pierce, G. R., Sarason, B. R., & Sarason, I. G. (Eds.). (1996). *Handbook of social support and the family.* New York: Plenum.

Podolski, C., & Nigg, J. T. (2001). Parental stress and coping in relation to child ADHD severity and associated child disruptive behavior problems. *Journal of Clinical Child Psychology, 30,* 503–513.

Radina, M. E., Wilson, S. M., & Hennon, C. B. (2008). Parental stress among U.S. Mexican heritage parents: Implications for culturally relevant family life education. In R. L. Dalla, J. Defrain, J. Johnson, & D. Abbott (Eds.), *Strengths and challenges of new immigrant families: Implications for research, policy, education, and service* (pp. 369–391). Lanham, MD: Lexington Books.

Rimmerman, A., & Duvdevani, I. (1996). Parents of children and adolescents with severe mental retardation: Stress, family resources, normalization, and their application for out-of-home placement. *Research in Developmental Disabilities, 17,* 487–494.

Rubin, K. H., & Burgess, K. B. (2002). Parents of aggressive and withdrawn children. In M. H. Bornstein (Ed.), *Handbook of parenting: Vol. 1. Children and parenting* (2nd ed., pp. 383–418). Mahwah, NJ: Lawrence Erlbaum.

Ryan, L. G., Miller-Loessi, K., & Nieri, T. (2007). Relationships with adults as predictors of substance use, gang involvement, and threats to safety among disadvantaged urban high-school adolescents. *Journal of Community Psychology, 35,* 1053–1071.

Sepa, A., Frodi, A., & Ludvigsson, J. (2004). Psychosocial correlates of parenting stress, lack of support and lack of confidence/security. *Scandinavian Journal of Psychology, 45,* 169–179.

Shumow, L., & Lomax. R. (2002). Parental efficacy: Predictor of parenting behavior and adolescent outcomes. *Parenting Science and Practice, 2,* 127–150.

Sigel, I. E., & McGillicuddy-De Lisi, A. V. (2002). Parents' knowledge and expectations: Using what we know. In M. H. Bornstein (Ed.), *Handbook of parenting: Vol. 3. Being and becoming a parent* (2nd ed., pp. 333–359). Mahwah, NJ: Lawrence Erlbaum.

Singer, G. H. S., Ethridge, B. L., & Aldana, S. I. (2007). Primary and secondary effects of parenting and stress management interventions for parents of children with developmental disabilities: A meta-analysis. *Mental Retardation and Developmental Disabilities Research Reviews, 13,* 357–369.

Springs, B., Rosen, K., & Matherson, J. (2002). How parents experience a transition to adolescence: A qualitative study. *Journal of Child and Family Studies, 11,* 411–425.

Steinberg, L., & Silk, J. S. (2002). Parenting adolescents. In M. H. Bornstein (Ed.), *Handbook of parenting: Vol. 1. Children and parenting* (2nd ed., pp. 103–133). Mahwah, NJ: Lawrence Erlbaum.

Stone, G., Buehler, C., & Barber, B. K. (2002). Interparental conflict, parental psychological control, and youth problem behavior. In B. K. Barber (Ed.), *Intrusive parenting: How psychological control affects children and adolescents* (pp. 53–95). Washington, DC: American Psychological Association.

Teti, D. M., & Candelaria, M. A. (2002). Parenting competence. In M. H. Bornstein (Ed.), *Handbook of parenting: Vol. 4. Social conditions and applied parenting* (2nd ed., pp. 149–180). Mahwah, NJ: Lawrence Erlbaum.

Tong, A., Lowe, A., Sainsbury, P., & Craig, J. (2008). Experiences of parents who have children with chronic kidney disease: A systematic review of qualitative studies. *Pediatrics, 121,* 349–360.

Ulrich, M., & Weatherall, A. (2000). Motherhood and infertility: Viewing motherhood through the lens of infertility. *Feminism and Psychology, 10,* 323–336.

Vondra, J., & Belsky, J. (1993). Developmental origins of parenting: Personality and relationship factors. In T. Luster & L. Okagaki (Eds.), *Parenting: An ecological perspective* (pp. 1–33). Hillsdale, NJ: Lawrence Erlbaum.

Weinraub, M., Horvath, D. L., & Gringlas, M. B. (2002). Single-parenthood. In M. H. Bornstein (Ed.), *Handbook of parenting: Vol. 3. Being and becoming a parent* (2nd ed., pp. 109–149). Mahwah, NJ: Lawrence Erlbaum.

Wood, D. (2003). Effect of child and family poverty on child health in the US. *Pediatrics, 112,* 707–711.

3

Stress and Coping in Later Life

Christine A. Price and Áine M. Humble

The experience of aging takes place within the context of families. Yet, until recently, aging has been viewed primarily from a human development perspective, with little recognition given to the importance of family relationships or the impact that family roles and responsibilities have on the aging process. In response to this situation, the field of *family gerontology* has emerged to draw attention to the intersection between aging and family systems. This intersection can be conceptualized from the perspective of the aging individual or from the family system, with emphasis on the experiences of older family members (Blieszner & Bedford, 1995). This bidirectional approach enables researchers and practitioners to consider the influences that family members have on individual responses to the processes of aging as well as the impacts that older adults have on families.

The terms *nuclear family* and *extended family* are familiar to most people; however, the more recently coined term *aging family* is less well known. The study of aging families pertains to entire family systems, with emphasis on relationships, transitions, and social support networks of older family members. From a family development perspective, the aging family consists of individuals who have passed the childrearing years and are now experiencing events and transitions of later life (Brubaker, 1990) such as retirement, widowhood, later-life divorce, and caregiving. Additionally, later-life marriage, sibling relations, fictive kin, and grandparenting are relationships particularly relevant to the aging family system. Not all older adults follow a traditional life course (i.e., marry, have children, launch children, retire), yet everyone ages within a family context, regardless of the size of the family or whether all members are biologically related. Because of the diversity of families and lifestyles in the United States today, scholars need to recognize the many types of families that impact older individuals and their aging experiences. Thus, for the purposes of this chapter, we employ the concept of "aging family" that includes a broad definition of family relationships, and we focus on aging family systems rather than individual aging family members.

Several factors make aging families unique and noteworthy in comparison with other families. First, as previously suggested, aging families are heterogeneous. Some have four or more living generations, whereas others have only two generations. Some have emotionally close ties and members interact on a regular basis, yet others display conflicted interaction styles or infrequent interaction because of personal reasons or geographic distance. Some aging families include couples in long-term marriages and same-sex or opposite-sex couples in cohabiting or common-law relationships, whereas others consist of single, divorced, or widowed older adults. Regardless of the differences in aging families, many face similar later-life transitions and age-related changes. It is by focusing on these similarities that scholars can better understand how aging families function.

Another factor that makes aging families different from other families is the extended-family history that members share. How the members of aging families communicate with one another and how they respond to family crises, for example, depend largely on the interaction patterns and coping strategies they have established in earlier years (Brubaker, 1990). A long family history can be a source of strength for family members or, alternatively, a painful barrier that may be difficult or impossible to overcome.

Finally, a third factor that sets aging families apart from families in earlier life stages is the likelihood that aging families will experience coinciding joyful and painful events. At no other life stage is the family system more likely to encounter growth and loss in such close proximity. For example, the loss of a spouse or partner can have a profound impact on the well-being of the surviving individual as well as challenge the stability and functioning of an entire family system. At the same time, the birth of a grandchild can be a life-altering event for a new grandparent and an opportunity for increased family cohesion. These later-life transitions can occur within a short time period and contribute to both joyful and painful emotions, making for complex and bittersweet family dynamics.

Despite what we are learning about aging families and the unique challenges they face, it is important to recognize that these families exist within a larger social and cultural context. Scholars can gain a better understanding of aging families by recognizing the many demographic changes that are currently taking place in the United States and globally. These shifting trends directly affect how aging families evolve and how they respond to the demands of later life.

Demographic Trends

Demographic changes that took place in the United States during the 20th century have had profound effects on the structure of American society. For example, the average life expectancy of an infant born in the United States increased from 47.3 years in 1900 to 76.9 years today (He, Sengupta,

Velkoff, & DeBarros, 2005; Hetzel & Smith, 2001). This is the greatest increase in longevity ever documented over the course of human history and has resulted in the rapid growth of the older adult population. In 2006, 35.5 million Americans, or 12.1% of the population, were over the age of 65 (U.S. Census Bureau, 2008). This extended adulthood is a result of medical advances, improvements in pharmacology, and improved sanitation and nutrition. In addition, the discovery of antibiotics and the widespread immunization against disease have dramatically reduced infant mortality and childhood death rates, thus resulting in more adults surviving to old age. Given these dramatic improvements, U.S. Census Bureau predictions indicate that additional growth in the older adult population will occur when the baby-boom population (born between 1946 and 1964) begins turning 65 in 2011. For instance, the older population (65+) is projected to double in number from 36 million in 2003 to 72 million in 2030. By 2050, this same population is estimated to be 86.7 million (He et al., 2005).

Age Differences

Gerontologists frequently differentiate individuals over 65 years old into three categories: *young old* (65 to 74), *middle old* (75 to 84), and *oldest old* (85 and above) (Hooyman & Kiyak, 2007). Those in the oldest-old population are the fastest-growing segment of older adults, increasing from 3.1 million in 1990 to 4.7 million in 2003 (He et al., 2005; Hetzel & Smith, 2001). This segment is more likely than younger elders to have health and/or mobility limitations, to have experienced the death of a spouse, or to require instrumental assistance.

Centenarians (living 100+ years) are another segment of the aging population demanding more attention as a result of their expansion. From an estimated 37,000 in 1990[1] to more than 84,000 in 2007, this population is a direct result of decreased mortality and access to better health care (He et al., 2005; U.S. Census Bureau, 2008). Consisting of 80% women, the centenarian population is a valuable resource for researchers investigating the intricacies of longevity.

Gender Differences

In addition to cohort differences in the older adult population, gender differences also exist. Life expectancy for a female child born today in the United States is estimated at 80 years; for a male child, it is 74 years. As a result of men's higher mortality rates across the life span and differences in ". . . attitudes, behaviors, social roles and biological risks between men and women," women outnumber men in later life (He et al., 2005, p. 36). Scholars usually calculate gender imbalance in the population by creating sex ratios that compare the number of men per 100 women. The ratio is 72 men per 100 women at age 65 but drops to 47 men per 100 women by age 85

(U.S. Census Bureau, 2008). As American women increasingly enter the work-force, experience higher stress levels, and adopt unhealthy lifestyle habits, it is expected that they will lose their longevity advantage over men (Himes, 2002).

Racial/Ethnic Differences

The older adult population in the United States is racially and ethnically diverse, and the level of diversity in this group is predicted to dramatically increase. In 2003, 83% of the aging population was non-Hispanic white; this population is expected to decrease to 61% by 2050. In comparison, the Hispanic population is expected to grow the most dramatically, increasing from 6% of the total aging population in 2003 to 11% by 2030. The African American aging population will also increase from 8% to 10% from 2003 to 2030, and Asian American elders will increase from 3% to 5% in the same time frame (He et al., 2005). Overall, members of minority groups (Hispanics, African Americans, and Asian Americans) are expected to constitute 25% of the aging population by the year 2030, an increase from 16% in 2000 (Himes, 2002).

As is evident from this discussion of demographic shifts and their numerous implications, aging families are currently in a state of change. Extended years of adulthood, the availability of supportive resources, and mobility limitations all affect how older adults perceive and cope with the stressful events of later life.

Stress in Later Life

Stress as experienced by older adults is an important area of research, parti-cularly in light of the expanding aging population and the implications of this growth. Scholars who focus on this topic emphasize the effects of stress on health and well-being (Aldwin, Yancura, & Boeninger, 2007) as well as recognize different types of stressful experiences older adults encounter, for example, chronic role strains, daily hassles, and lifetime trauma (Krause, 2007). Researchers frequently emphasize the coping strategies of individuals as they age rather than how aging families experience and adapt to later life challenges. What is important to recognize, however, is that stressors asso-ciated with later life are often experienced within the context of a family system with multiple generations being affected. Furthermore, in accordance with ecological systems theory (Bronfenbrenner, 1979), aging individuals and their families confront these issues at multiple systemic levels. At the *macrosystem* level (i.e., the cultural contexts that influence how people live), families must deal with government policies (i.e., Medicare, Social Security), economic realities, and social expectations surrounding care. Comparatively, at the *exosystem* level (i.e., the community environment), formalized health care, insurance companies, skilled- or intermediate-care facilities, and other professional agencies are involved. At the *meso-* and *microsystem* levels, respectively, aging families manage the immediate living environment, neighborhood resources, and transportation accessibility as well as renegotiate family roles and responsibilities related to caring for aging loved ones.

Knowledge about stress and aging has centered primarily on two assumptions. The first is the predominance of loss experienced in later life, for example, the loss of a spouse or partner to death, the loss of independence as a result of illness or disability, or the loss of socially respected and identified roles. Earlier in life, individuals are more likely to encounter stressors associated with growth that occur in a context of excitement and future potential such as marriage and parenthood as well as educational and professional opportunities. The critical difference between stress encountered in later life and that experienced in early or middle adulthood relates to the types of stressors encountered. Certain life events are more commonly experienced in later life than at any other time over the life span (Williamson & Dooley, 2001). These include the transition to grandparenthood, retirement, deaths of friends and family members, chronic illness, and becoming a caregiver. Seniors are likely to face decisions that are more difficult than those that younger adults must make, such as decisions regarding placing a spouse in a nursing home, moving from a family home to a retirement community, or giving up one's right to drive. Furthermore, these changes can take place within a context of physical decline and the contraction of social and family interaction patterns. Finally, developing new intimate relationships following the end of long-term relationships may be challenging (Gierveld, 2002), particularly because the relationship landscape has dramatically changed since the older individuals were first "dating" (e.g., the low but increasing risk of HIV/AIDS infection in older adults and the availability of Viagra).

The second assumption associated with stress in later life is the reduction of coping assets to assist older adults in managing the challenges of old age. The economic and social resources available to older adults are assumed to decrease with age as a result of restricted financial reserves, geographic distance from family, and limited community assistance. Nevertheless, even though many of the stressors associated with aging may be challenging, aging is not about just decline and disability. Although aging is not always easy, getting older can involve personal growth and development, a sense of satisfaction with one's accomplishments, and enthusiasm for new experiences and transitions.

There are competing perceptions of old age in terms of how much stress is experienced. For example, researchers have established that seniors encounter fewer life events and transitions than do younger adults (Aldwin et al., 2007; Stawski, Sliwinski, Almeida, & Smyth, 2008). Later life is frequently characterized as a time of fewer responsibilities than young adulthood, as well as less salient social roles, decreased time demands, and therefore greater flexibility and freedom. In contrast, aging can be considered a stressful life process (Lawrence & Schigelone, 2002). A sense of trepidation about getting older is pervasive among Americans, many of whom fear difficulties such as increased illness and disability, dependence on others for care, and the death of a spouse. From this perspective, it appears that older adults experience greater stress, and thus are more vulnerable to stress than are younger adults.

Researchers comparing whether older adults experience more stress in later life than younger cohorts have found that older adults are much less likely to rate life events as stressful when compared with younger populations (Aldwin et al., 2007; Charles & Almeida, 2007). Although most research has compared the experiences of young and middle-old adults, Stawski and colleagues (2008) examined the daily stressors of the very old and found that adults with an average age of 80 years reported lower frequency of daily stressors and less negative emotions associated with stress than did younger adults. This resilience to stressful events may be attributed to a number of factors, for example, reduced stress exposure as a result of limited mobility or lifestyle activities. Alternatively, older adults may report fewer stressful experiences as a result of their mastery of effective coping strategies or their differing perceptions of what constitutes stress as compared to younger adults (Charles & Almeida, 2007; Stawski et al., 2008).

In addition to considering the variation in stress experienced over the life span, it is important to recognize the different types of stressors that members of various older-adult age groups experience. For example, stressors encountered during the young-old years can differ significantly from those encountered during the middle-old and oldest-old years. During the young-old years, a majority of seniors are making their own decisions, engaging with family and community activities, and experiencing anticipated and normative life events (e.g., grandparenthood or retirement). These transitions can be stressful because they involve role changes and family adjustments, but they also offer opportunities for growth and development. However, as age increases, the likelihood of an individual's encountering unanticipated, nonnormative life events increases dramatically, especially with regard to physical frailty, disability, and cognitive impairment. As a result, stressors experienced in late life, especially at age 85 and beyond, are associated with greater stress in a context of increasing dependence and age-related decline. Documenting the diversity of stressors encountered in later life is more challenging due to researchers' proclivity to collapse older adults into one age group.

According to the ABC-X model of family stress, the perception of an event as stressful (the C factor) is the most powerful variable in explaining family stress (Boss, 1987). Thus, it is critical that scholars understand what older adults identify as stressful life events. Three major categories of stressors are frequently mentioned by older adults: (a) health and physical functioning, (b) personal and social problems, and (c) difficulties faced by family members (Aldwin, 1990; Aldwin, Sutton, Chiara, & Spiro, 1996). Events that appeared to cause the highest stress ratings included the death of a child, the institutionalization of a spouse, or the death of a spouse. Least stressful life events were a spouse's retirement, the individual's own retirement, and an increase in paid or volunteer responsibilities. Interestingly, inherent in most research on stress is the assumption that the circumstances individuals identify as stressful are usually circumstances that affect them directly. However, the results of Aldwin et al.'s work indicate that this may not always be the case. In fact, the older adults in their sample spent considerable amounts of time worrying about their spouses' health, children's marriages, grandchildren's life choices, and friends' and neighbors' problems. Such *nonegocentric stress* (defined as stress stemming from the circumstances of others as opposed to oneself) is congruent with Erikson's theory of generativity (Aldwin, 1990).

Transitional Events in Later Life

Theories of family stress generally depict stressors as disruptive events that precipitate change in the family system. As health limitations increase and other age-related changes take place, the aging family system must adapt to new demands and role transitions (Stephens, 1990). Specifically, family members are called on to provide assistance to older members in the form of caregiving, providing transportation, taking care of finances, and listening to fears or concerns.

Two factors that influence a family's ability to respond to stress and maintain family equilibrium are family integration and family adaptability. Derived from family stress theory (Boss, 1987), these concepts apply to the family system regardless of a family's life stage. *Family integration* refers to a sense of cohesion and unity within a family based on the members' common interests and affection for each other. *Family adaptability* refers to a family's ability to be flexible in times of change through discussion and renegotiation of family roles and responsibilities. Families best equipped to manage crisis events are those that have established cohesive ties to one another as well as the ability to respond effectively to change (Boss, 1987). Two advantages that aging families have over families in earlier life stages are established patterns of interaction and coping strategies that family members can rely on during difficult periods.

Many later-life events can test the adaptability and the coping resources of an aging family. Although some transitions involve more stress than others, all require family members to respond to change, individually and collectively. Two major transitions that aging families frequently encounter are retirement and caregiving. In the following sections, we address these potential stressors and the implications they have for the aging family system.

Retirement

Retirement is a normative event currently experienced by the majority of older adults. Historically, research on this topic focused almost exclusively on men, but this transition is increasingly common among women. According to the U.S. Department of Labor, women's employment increased from 43% in 1970 to 59% in 2006 (Chao & Rones, 2007).

Given that the greater part of adulthood is tied to employment and work identity, the loss of this salient role has been portrayed as stressful; for example, retirement has been linked to reduced psychological well-being, low morale, and strained marital relations. The evidence supporting these assertions, however, has been largely indirect and contradictory (Nuttman-Shwartz, 2004). Furthermore, there is a difference between stress associated with the retirement event (i.e., retirement transition stress) and stress resulting from living in retirement (i.e., retirement state stress) (Bossé, Aldwin, Levenson, & Workman-Daniels, 1991). Nonetheless, some studies have found that approximately one-third of retirees report retirement living as stressful, citing such issues as financial challenges and boredom (Bossé et al., 1991; Bossé, Spiro, & Kressin, 1996). This finding translates into more than 2 million Americans encountering difficulty after leaving the workforce.

In the current economic climate, it is important to recognize that stress for retirees has become increasingly tied to stock market trends and declines in the values of pension plan equities and personal retirement portfolios. From 2007 to 2008, "the value of equities in pension plans and household portfolios fell by $7.4 trillion" (Munnell & Muldoon, 2008, p. 1). This economic decline has significant implications for current retirees who depend on retirement pensions and savings to live as well as potential retirees who often have a significant proportion of their monetary assets invested in the stock market (Munnell, Aubry, & Muldoon, 2008). Contributing to the financial concerns of retirees are the consequences of a shift in pension coverage from defined benefit plans to defined contribution plans. Defined benefit plans are employer-sponsored pension plans in which benefits are based on a standard formula and investments are managed by the company. With these types of pension plans, individuals have less responsibility and experience less risk since benefits must be paid regardless of a decrease in employer pension assets. (Of course, these benefits may be considerably reduced should an employer be forced to lay off workers, freeze their pension plan [i.e., no longer offer a defined benefit plan], or declare bankruptcy.) In contrast, defined contribution plans, such as 401(k)s and IRAs (individual retirement accounts), enable individuals to invest their earnings at whatever rate they choose and to manage these investments independently, which results in bearing greater risk on potential returns. Moreover, if the stock market declines, the retirement assets of those invested in defined contribution plans are more directly affected, contributing to greater financial uncertainty.

As a result of disproportionately more defined contribution plans combined with a decline in the stock market, financial stress of current and future retirees is considerable. Those living in retirement are watching their retirement incomes decline with limited time to recuperate their losses due to their advanced age. Besides returning to work, these individuals have limited options. In comparison, individuals planning to retire may have to postpone retirement or accept retiring with fewer assets than originally planned. Fortunately, those who are farther away from their planned retirement age may have more time to recoup their losses.

In addition to financial concerns, both the timing of retirement and reasons for retiring are related to retirement stress, and this is experienced in different ways by men and women. Men who retire prior to age 65 and those who retire involuntarily or unexpectedly report high stress levels, low retirement satisfaction, a reduced sense of usefulness, and problems with interpersonal relationships (Bossé et al., 1996). Other circumstances that contribute to higher retirement stress for men include lower socioeconomic status, stressful life events, low social support in retirement, lack of financial security, and poor health (Bossé, Levenson, Spiro, Aldwin, & Mroczek, 1992; Solinge & Henkens, 2005). Preliminary studies exploring predictors of retirement stress for women have found more dissatisfaction and anxiety among retired women with lower levels of education, more financial instability, fewer social contacts, and poorer health (Bossé et al., 1992; Solinge & Henkens, 2005). Additionally, because of women's increasingly continuous work histories, their expanded identification with their work roles, their vulnerability to the social losses associated with retirement, and pressure to retire by a husband or as a result of caregiving responsibilities, they may encounter greater retirement problems than men (Zimmerman, Mitchell, Wister, & Gutman, 2000). Some of these problems include social isolation, loss of social status, reduced self-esteem, depression, lower perceived health, and economic insecurity (Marshall, Clarke, & Ballantyne, 2001; Price, 2002; Price & Joo, 2005).

Retirement can be a long-anticipated event that provides new opportunities for personal growth and development, the discovery of new interests and relationships, and a release from demanding time constraints. At the same time, it can pose unique challenges, including the loss of a work role identity, decreased social contact with peers, a reduced sense of personal achievement, and loss of economic stability (Szinovacz, 2003). Because retirement is a significant life transition, the entire aging family is affected—not only the retiring older adult but also his or her spouse, children, extended kin, and friends and neighbors (Solinge & Henkens, 2005; Szinovacz & Davey, 2005). Retirement can involve a change of residence; whether such a move is welcome or not, it usually involves the loss of a family home, the downsizing of a household and reduction of family possessions, and adjustment to new friends and a new community.

Retirement can affect marital relationships, both positively and negatively (Davey & Szinovacz, 2004; Szinovacz & Davey, 2005). For couples who jointly retire, especially those who share mutual interests and have effective communication skills, retirement can be a time of increased marital satisfaction and renewed intimacy. For other couples, however, extended free hours together with limited structure can result in greater conflict or may reveal an indisputable lack of common interests. Retirement may impact spouses differently as well, depending on the timing. When couples experience *dyssynchronized retirement*, meaning they retire at different times, retirement satisfaction can be negatively affected; this is particularly true when wives continue to be employed after their husbands retire (Davey & Szinovacz, 2004).

The retirement transition can also affect adult children and grandchildren. Those who are expecting financial assistance or child-care support from their retired parents may experience disappointment or conflict when retirees choose to spend their money on traveling and fill their time with new hobbies. Alternatively, retirees who expect adult children and grandchildren to fill their days may encounter feelings of resentment or increased emotional distance from them.

Caregiving

The term *caregiver* refers to anyone who provides assistance to someone who is physically or psychologically impaired and therefore dependent on others. Caregiving can be *informal* (i.e., provided by unpaid volunteers) or *formal* (i.e., provided by paid care workers) and can take the form of different types of assistance. *Instrumental support* (hands-on services that assist with daily functioning) and *emotional support* (actions and gestures expressing affection and encouragement) are two general types of assistance that researchers have frequently explored (Pearlin, Aneshensel, Mullan, & Whitlatch, 1996). *Care management* (e.g., arranging for paid care and seeking out information and resources) is a care activity seldom studied (Rosenthal, Martin-Matthews, & Keefe, 2007) but increasingly experienced, particularly for individuals providing assistance from a distance.

Because the risk of experiencing chronic illness and/or disability is associated with advancing age, older adults and their families frequently encounter increased caregiving responsibilities. However, estimates of the number of caregivers in the United States vary somewhat because of differing definitions of caregiving. According to the National Alliance for Caregiving and AARP (2005), 34 million individuals are providing care to an adult over age 50 who is in poor health. In fact, 23 million American households (21%) are caring for a person age 50 or older.

Family caregiving usually consists of assistance provided to an aging family member by a spouse, adult children, extended-family members, and fictive kin relations. Decisions about who will provide care depend on a variety of factors, including the potential caregivers' geographic proximity to the care recipient, gender, availability of time, work schedule flexibility, physical health, and emotional closeness with the care recipient. In addition to these considerations, most families follow a gendered family pattern called the *caregiving hierarchy* in determining caregiving responsibilities. If a spouse is available, he or she will likely become the primary caregiver. When a spouse is unable to provide care, an adult child, usually a daughter or daughter-in-law, assumes the caregiving responsibilities. In situations where no adult children are available, other family members or fictive kin, frequently women (sisters, nieces, granddaughters, neighbors), step in to provide care (Uhlenberg & Cheuk, 2008).

The motivation to provide care is what sets family caregiving apart from assistance supplied by more formal sources. Family members provide care because of feelings of love and affection, feelings of filial responsibility (Silverstein, Gans, & Yang, 2006), intergenerational solidarity (Roberts, Richards, & Bengtson, 1991), or a desire to reciprocate for earlier support. In some circumstances, care is provided because of family pressure to do so. The caregiving relationship can also be influenced by a variety of factors, including the relationship history between family members, geographic proximity, extent of disability, and availability of support resources. As a result of this multiplicity, it is difficult to generalize caregiver experiences and the stress associated with family caregiving. In fact, research that has explored the prevalence of caregiver burden (i.e., effects on psychological and physical health) compared with burden among noncaregivers has often resulted in inconsistent findings (Pinquart & Sörensen, 2003).

Providing care to an aging family member is not a simple or easy task. Caregivers often face extensive demands on their time as well as difficulties that test their physical and mental endurance. Emotions commonly associated with caregiver burden include depression, loneliness, anger, and guilt. Caregivers frequently exhibit higher levels of depression, physical fatigue, and social isolation (Johnson, 2008). Those caring for loved ones with dementia experience the most severe stress because of challenges specific to cognitive decline—that is, behavior problems, the need for constant supervision, progressive deterioration, and lack of reciprocal expressions of affection and gratitude (Pinquart & Sörensen, 2003). Another unique challenge for dementia caregivers is facing the reality of *ambiguous loss* (Boss, 1999). Persons who experience any type of dementia gradually lose their abilities to communicate, reason, and even remember the names and faces of loved ones. For their caregivers and families, persons with dementia eventually become psychologically absent even though they are still physically present. This type of partial loss can be very difficult for family members to understand and accept, particularly for the caregivers, who must witness this gradual disappearance on a daily basis.

Caregivers and their families cope with the stress associated with caregiving depending on the types of stressors they encounter, structural factors (e.g., gender, marital status, employment, and income) as well as interpersonal and socioemotional changes in the care receiver. For example, a family member may find it difficult to accept a change in the nature of his or her relationship with the care recipient because of the recipient's decreased functional capacity or cognitive decline. A family member who is not directly involved in the care of the older adult may resist believing the caregiver's description of the extent of the disability, and this can result in family conflict. Additionally, the primary caregiver, whether a spouse or an adult child, often must redefine his or her own relationship expectations and adjust his or her interactions in order to accommodate the increasing dependence of the loved one.

Negotiating the competing demands of caregiving can be another source of caregiver burden. Many caregivers are not prepared for the extensive responsibilities associated with providing care yet do so with little or no help

(Johnson, 2008). Eventually, caregivers may experience *role overload* or *caregiver burnout* by becoming physically exhausted and emotionally drained. At this stage, caregivers often must make critical decisions about turning to others for assistance or scaling back their involvement in caregiving because of their own physical illness or severe depression. Caregivers who are employed may be forced to reduce their hours or leave work entirely before they are financially and psychologically ready to do so (Johnson, 2008). Unfortunately, most caregivers wait until they are in a crisis situation before they ask for help. Furthermore, when they do request assistance, they often experience feelings of guilt, disappointment, or even failure at not being able to provide all of the care their loved one requires. In addition to caregiver burnout, the experience of *intergenerational ambivalence* is another stressful component of the aging parent–adult child relationship that can exacerbate a caregiving situation. Defined as the "simultaneous existence of positive and negative sentiments in the older parent–adult child relationship" (Pillemer, Suitor, Mock, Sabir, Pardo, & Sechrist, 2007, p. 775), feelings of ambivalence can lead to considerable psychological distress for both generations and may complicate the caregiving process.

Some caregivers experience considerable stress associated with their caregiving role, whereas others report feeling emotional closeness with the care recipient, a sense of accomplishment and satisfaction with providing care, and family cohesion resulting from members being brought together in response to a difficult situation. For the latter group, caregiving is not particularly stressful and can actually result in positive gain (Brubaker, 1990). Why do some caregivers experience more stress than others? According to Pinquart and Sörensen (2003), certain variables moderate caregivers' experience of stress, including the relationship of the caregiver to the care receiver, the age and gender of the caregiver, and the extent of the care recipient's disability. Furthermore, positive aspects of caregiving, such as increased emotional closeness and feelings of satisfaction, may counter the negative caregiving realities.

It is important to recognize that the stress associated with family caregiving goes beyond that experienced by caregivers. Recipients of care (i.e., the aging family members) encounter their own unique stressors related to their illness and increased dependence. Reduced self-esteem, frustration at their lack of autonomy, and suffering chronic and sometimes terminal illness can result in considerable stress and depression among care receivers. Furthermore, most caregiving situations are inequitable in that the care recipient receives more support than he or she is able to reciprocate. This inequity contributes to reduced well-being in the care recipient as he or she experiences feelings of being a burden to others (Brown, 2007).

Although a primary caregiver is commonly identified within a family and usually becomes responsible for assuming many responsibilities, other family members may also be called on to assist with providing care. As a result, the entire family system must make accommodations and adjustments to respond to a variety of new demands (Stephens, 1990). These adjustments often occur over time with varying levels of change taking place, which are referred to as first-order, second-order, and third-order processes (Watzlawick, Weakland, & Fisch, 1974). At the first level, a family initially attempts to make minimal adjustments to accommodate a family member's declining health. Eventually, however, the family realizes that to manage the escalating challenges associated with the situation effectively, responsibilities and interaction patterns must be restructured—which leads to second-order processes. Second-order processes consist of the adjustment of schedules, routines, and/or rules, but also may be effective for only so long. Eventually, third-level change may be necessary, involving a reformation of shared family values, worldviews, or philosophies of life (Reiss, 1981).

According to the ABC-X model of family stress, a family's response to the stress is often influenced by two significant factors: (a) the family's definition of the event and (b) the resources a family has available (e.g., support services, coping strategies, financial security). In recognition of the stress associated with caregiving, numerous agencies and organizations have developed interventions—for example, support groups, respite-care services, adult day-care services, and educational and resource information—aimed at assisting caregivers and their families. These resources can assist families with their methods of coping with stressful situations as well as provide valuable information about what federal, state, and community resources are available. Families can find out about the caregiving-related services by contacting the Eldercare Locator, a public service of the U.S. Department of Health and Human Services. They may also contact their state/provincial unit on aging or their local Area Agency on Aging, which are county-based agencies that enable older adults to remain in their homes.

Models of Coping and Adaptation

Research indicates that the most stressful events older adults encounter pertain to health, interpersonal relationships, financial strains, and/or work-related issues (Moos, Brennan, Schutte, & Moos, 2006). Older adults cope with these age-related challenges using various methods that can differentially impact their health and well-being. Most research on coping in later life focuses exclusively on individual coping strategies and their effectiveness on the health and well-being of older adults. Because older adults frequently experience multiple stressors at one time (i.e., failing health, increased dependence, and reduced social and financial resources), the coping methods they exhibit are critical to their adjustment. Because aging and coping are such individualized processes, dependent on personal lifestyle factors, resources, and environmental conditions, scholars have found it difficult to establish a universal model of coping.

The ways in which older adults manage stressful life events and the coping strategies they employ have become topics of increasing interest among gerontological researchers. Lazarus and Folkman (1984) contributed significantly to our understanding of the coping process in a variety of stress-related contexts, including later adulthood, grief and bereavement, caregiving, and, most recently, the care and subsequent loss of a partner to HIV/AIDS (Folkman, 2001). According to this stress and coping model, individuals consistently appraise their environments for potentially stressful interactions or events. A person who perceives something in the environment as threatening, challenging, or harmful often implements certain coping strategies to manage the stressful situation. These coping strategies depend on personal resources and lifestyle factors, the immediate environment, and the nature of the event itself.

Problem-focused coping, for example, occurs when an individual attempts to establish a semblance of control within an uncontrollable situation. The individual accomplishes this by identifying specific and attainable goals that he or she can reach by gathering information, resolving conflicts, or making plans. These behaviors provide a sense of purpose and a method for overcoming feelings of helplessness (Lazarus & Folkman, 1984). In contrast, *emotion-focused coping* involves a more cognitive response to stress through denial, detachment, the reinterpretation of events, and the application of humor or religious/spiritual faith. In this form of coping, the objective event is not altered, but the individual purposefully changes his or her emotional reaction to the event (Williamson & Dooley, 2001).

Related to emotional regulation is the coping process of *positive reappraisal*. In this type of coping, the individual reframes a stressful situation to see the positive characteristics that are also present. A person might employ positive reappraisal at the inception of a stressor and throughout the stressful experience to assist him or her with managing feelings of despair and to counter increasingly negative emotions (Folkman, 1997). The responses of older adults to the stressors of aging reveal the importance of both cognitive reappraisal and coping. Seniors adjust to role and status loss, limitations of physical health and/or mobility, and relationship changes by identifying new relationships, establishing new patterns of interaction and integration, redefining any restrictions, and identifying the positive aspects of their lives. What is apparent in the research evidence is the significance for older adults of personal perception and the subjective meanings they apply to the changes and losses they encounter (Lazarus & DeLongis, 1983).

Why do some older adults adapt to change with relatively minor difficulty and others cope much less effectively? Baltes and Baltes (1990) have developed a theory of adaptation that emphasizes the interaction between loss and gain in later life and illustrates older adults' potential to experience continued growth. The *principle of selective optimization with compensation* describes a process of adaptation that older adults implement when faced with declines in their functional abilities or threats to their continued social and physical involvement in life's pleasures. This principle is based on three key interacting components: selection, optimization, and compensation. *Selection* refers to individuals' conscious reduction in domains of functioning because of age-related constraints. For example, an older adult diagnosed with a hearing loss may choose to give up certain activities to focus more time on those that cause her little discomfort and still provide her pleasure. *Optimization* occurs when individuals work to improve their performance on the activities they have selected. By focusing their energies on fewer interests, they can experience greater satisfaction and success in those areas. For instance, an older adult who can no longer play the piano because of arthritis may choose to focus his energies on sharing his expertise with promising young piano players. *Compensation* refers to individuals' use of psychological, technological, and environmental aids to assist them in maintaining their social and physical involvement with the world (Baltes & Baltes, 1990). The piano teacher with severe arthritis may use audio and/or video recordings of earlier performances to demonstrate certain techniques to students. The point of this theory is that older adults do not passively accept increasing limitations or functional decline; rather, they combine specific strategies that enable them to maintain enough functional capacity to continue enjoying and participating in life. Finally, successful adjustment to later-life challenges may also be influenced by having meaning or a purpose in later life (Krause, 2007; Reker, 1997; Ryff & Singer, 1998). For example, having a strong sense of identity, setting goals, and reconciling past events can lead to better physical health and improved mental health, and can buffer the negative effects of traumatic or stressful events.

In addition to older adults' individual coping strategies, family members can have considerable influence on an older adult's adaptation to age-related changes as well as their responses to stress. Families' positive influences usually take the form of social support; for example, family members can encourage adaptive behaviors, supply resource information, and provide instrumental assistance to their aging loved ones. Three key types of behaviors constitute social support: aid, affect, and affirmation (Antonucci, 2001). *Aid* consists of tangible types of assistance, such as transportation, help with personal care tasks, and managing the checkbook. *Affect* refers to emotional support, provided through expressions of care and concern for an aging family member. Finally, *affirmation* involves the sharing of values and the acknowledgment of the aging family member's importance.

Most scholars in the area of social support view social relationships as critical to how older adults cope with the challenges of aging (Antonucci, Jackson, & Biggs, 2007; Silverstein et al., 2006). In fact, substantial research evidence supports the assertion that social support has a positive influence on the health and well-being of adults in later life. First, the presence of social support, and even the anticipation of future support, appears to have a buffering effect on stress, mitigating its negative impacts. In addition, anticipated support, defined as a person's belief that support will be provided in the future if needed, appears to have a more significant impact on health and well-being than support already received or the frequency of contact with others (Antonucci et al., 2007). This finding reveals the considerable importance of an older adult's psychological evaluation of his or her support situation in addition to the actual amount or quality of support available.

Again, from an ecological standpoint (Bronfenbrenner, 1979), it is important to recognize that larger social systems play a role in affecting aging individuals' and families' responses to stress. For example, many government and social policies contribute to the circumstances of individuals' retirements and their experiences in retirement. Policies influence the timing and nature of retirement, such as what retirement benefits and resources are available and when they are available (Calasanti, 2000). At the macro level, for example, in Canada, immigrants are ineligible for one of the government's transfer payments called "Old Age Security" (OAS) if they do not meet residency requirements of having lived in the country for more than 10 years. At the exosystem level, gay men and lesbians may feel safe in deliberately created gay-friendly retirement communities so that they can be open about their lives without fearing homophobia or heterosexism (Brotman, Ryan, & Cormier, 2003; Johnson, Jackson, Arnette, & Koffman, 2005). Similarly, for caregiving, exosystem features such as flextime, family leave time, and shared jobs can assist employed caregivers to remain at work. Additionally, government policies around taxation, pensions, and direct compensation influence how stressful caregiving is for individuals and families.

Overall, researchers have identified social relationships (particularly with family and close friends), social support behaviors (both instrumental and emotional), and social policies as critical to the positive adjustment of older adults. Aging families can significantly influence how older adult members cope with age-associated changes, but it is also important to recognize that older adults are resilient, employing creative approaches to adapt to the social and functional limitations they encounter as they age. Moreover, features of the macro-, exo-, and mesoenvironments play significant roles in mediating potentially stressful experiences later in life.

Conclusion

The demographic changes that have taken place over the past century have significantly affected the structure, nature, and resources of aging families in the United States, Canada, and other countries. The implications of current demographic trends for families include more time spent in family relationships, greater geographic distances between family members, greater risk of chronic illness, larger numbers of seniors (particularly women) living alone, and increased opportunities for intergenerational exchange. Because later life is frequently associated with stressful life events and transitions, it is important for researchers and practitioners to understand the strategies that older adults can use to cope effectively as well as the role of family systems and other systems in the positive adjustment of older adults. Due to the heterogeneity that exists among older adults and their families, perceptions of particular events such as retirement and caregiving as stressful, as well as how individuals and families cope with these changes, will continue to vary. Researchers and practitioners attempting to document the adaptive strategies that aging families apply may benefit by exploring more fully the resilience of older adults and the inherent ability of seniors to grow and develop despite advancing age.

Suggested Internet and Reading Resources

General Information for Seniors

Eldercare Locator: by phone toll-free (800) 677–1116 or www.eldercare.gov

Retirement

Social Security Administration: http://www.socialsecurity.gov

Center for Retirement Research at Boston College: http://crr.bc.edu

Family Caregiving

National Alliance for Caregiving: http://www.caregiving.org

Canadian Health Care System: http://www.hc-sc.gc.ca/hcs-sss/index_e.html

Moos, R. H., Brennan, P. L., Schutte, K. K., & Moos, B. S. (2006). Older adults coping with negative life events: Common processes of managing health, interpersonal, and financial/work stressors. *International Journal of Aging and Human Development, 62*(1), 39–59.

Stawski, R. S., Sliwinski, M. J., Almeida, D. M., & Smyth, J. M. (2008). Reported exposure and emotional reactivity to daily stressors: The roles of adult age and global perceived stress. *Psychology and Aging, 23*(1), 52–61.

Note

1. The 1990 estimate by the U.S. Census Bureau has been described as inflated due to overreporting (Krach & Velkoff, 1999). The Social Security Administration estimated 28,000 centenarians in 1990 (Himes, 2002).

References

Aldwin, C. M. (1990). The elders life stress inventory: Egocentric and nonegocentric stress. In M. A. P. Stephens, J. H. Crowther, S. E. Hobfoll, & D. L. Tennenbaum (Eds.), *Stress and coping in later-life families* (pp. 49–69). New York: Hemisphere.

Aldwin, C. M., Sutton, K. J., Chiara, G., & Spiro, A., III. (1996). Age differences in stress, coping, and appraisal: Findings from the normative aging study. *Journal of Gerontology: Psychological Sciences, 51*(4), 179–188.

Aldwin, C. M., Yancura, L. A., & Boeninger, D. K. (2007). Coping, health, and aging. In C. M. Aldwin, C. L. Park, & A. Spiro (Eds.), *Handbook of health psychology and aging* (pp. 210–226). New York: Guilford.

Antonucci, T. C. (2001). Social relations: An examination of social networks, social support, and sense of control. In J. E. Birren & K. W. Schaie (Eds.), *Handbook of the psychology of aging* (pp. 427–453). San Diego, CA: Academic.

Antonucci, T. C., Jackson, J. S., & Biggs, S. (2007). Intergenerational relations: Theory, research, and policy. *Journal of Social Issues, 63*(4), 679–693.

Baltes, P. B., & Baltes, M. M. (1990). Psychological perspectives on successful aging: The model of selective optimization with compensation. In P. B. Baltes & M. M. Baltes (Eds.), *Successful aging: Perspectives from the behavioral sciences* (pp. 1–34). Cambridge, UK: Cambridge University Press.

Blieszner, R., & Bedford, V. H. (1995). The family context of aging: Trends and challenges. In R. Blieszner & V. H. Bedford (Eds.), *Handbook of aging and the family* (pp. 3–12). Westport, CT: Greenwood.

Boss, P. G. (1987). Family stress. In M. B. Sussman & S. K. Steinmetz (Eds.), *Handbook of marriage and the family* (pp. 695–723). New York: Plenum.

Boss, P. G. (1999). *Ambiguous loss: Learning to live with unresolved grief.* Cambridge, MA: Harvard University Press.

Bossé, R., Aldwin, C. M., Levenson, M. R., & Workman-Daniels, K. (1991). How stressful is retirement? Findings from the normative aging study. *Journal of Gerontology: Psychological Sciences, 46*(1), 9–14.

Bossé, R., Levenson, M. R., Spiro, A., III, Aldwin, C. M., & Mroczek, D. K. (1992). For whom is retirement stressful? Findings from the normative aging study. In B. Vellas & J. L. Albarède (Eds.), *Facts and research in gerontology: 1992* (pp. 223–237). New York: Springer.

Bossé, R., Spiro, A., III, & Kressin, N. R. (1996). The psychology of retirement. In R. T. Woods (Ed.), *Handbook of the clinical psychology of ageing* (pp. 141–157). Oxford, UK: John Wiley.

Bronfenbrenner, U. (1979). *The ecology of human development.* Cambridge, MA: Harvard University Press.

Brotman, S., Ryan, B., & Cormier, R. (2003). The health and social service needs of gay and lesbian elders and their families in Canada. *The Gerontologist, 43,* 192–202.

Brown, E. (2007). Care recipients' psychological well-being: The role of sense of control and caregiver type. *Aging and Mental Health, 11*(4), 405–414.

Brubaker, T. H. (1990). A contextual approach to the development of stress associated with caregiving in later-life families. In M. A. P. Stephens, J. H. Crowther, S. E. Hobfoll, & D. L. Tennenbaum (Eds.), *Stress and coping in later-life families* (pp. 29–47). New York: Hemisphere.

Calasanti, T. M. (2000). Incorporating diversity. In E. W. Markson & L. A. Hollis-Sawyer (Eds.), *Intersections of aging* (pp. 188–202). Los Angeles: Roxbury.

Chao, E. L., & Rones, P. L. (2007). *Women in the labor force: A databook. (Report 1002).* Washington, DC: U.S. Government Printing Office. Retrieved June 25, 2008, from http://www.bls.gov/cps/wlf-databook-2007.pdf

Charles, S. T., & Almeida, D. M. (2007). Genetic and environmental effects on daily life stressors: More evidence for greater variation in later life. *Psychology and Aging, 22*(2), 331–340.

Davey, A., & Szinovacz, M. (2004). Dimensions of marital quality and retirement. *Journal of Family Issues, 25,* 431–464.

Folkman, S. (1997). Positive psychological states and coping with severe stress. *Social Science & Medicine, 45,* 1207–1221.

Folkman, S. (2001). Revised coping theory and the process of bereavement. In M. S. Stroebe, R. O. Hansson, W. Stroebe, & H. Schut (Eds.), *Handbook of bereavement research: Consequences, coping, and care* (pp. 563–584). Washington, DC: American Psychological Association.

Gierveld, J. D. J. (2002). The dilemma of repartnering: Considerations of older men and women entering new intimate relationships in later life. *Ageing International, 27*(4), 61–78.

He, W., Sengupta, M., Velkoff, V. A., & DeBarros, K. A. (2005). 65+ in the United States: 2005. *Current Population Reports.* Washington, DC: U.S. Bureau of the Census. Retrieved June 5, 2008, from http://www.census.gov/prod/2006pubs/p23–209.pdf

Hetzel, L., & Smith, A. (2001). *The 65 years and over population: 2000* (Census 2000 brief C2KBR/01–10). Washington, DC: U.S. Bureau of the Census. Retrieved June 5, 2008, from http://www.census.gov/prod/2001pubs/c2kbr01–10.pdf

Himes, C. L. (2002). Elderly Americans. *Population Bulletin 56*(4). Washington, DC: Population Reference Bureau. Retrieved June 5, 2008, from http://www.prb.org/Source/ACFD30.pdf

Hooyman, N. R., & Kiyak, H. A. (2007). *Social gerontology: A multidisciplinary perspective* (8th ed.). Boston: Allyn & Bacon.

Johnson, M. J., Jackson, N. C., Arnette, J. K., & Koffman, S. D. (2005). Gay and lesbian perceptions of discrimination in retirement care facilities. *Journal of Homosexuality, 49*(2), 83–102.

Johnson, R. W. (2008). Choosing between paid elder care and unpaid help from adult children: The role of relative prices in the care decision. In M. E. Szinovacz & A. Davey (Eds.), *Caregiving contexts: Cultural, familial, and societal implications* (pp. 35–69). New York: Springer.

Krach, C. A., & Velkoff, V. A. (1999). *Centenarians in the United States, U.S. Census Bureau Current Population Report.* Washington, DC: U.S. Census Bureau.

Krause, N. (2007). Evaluating the stress-buffering function of meaning in life among older people. *Journal of Aging and Health, 19*(5), 792–812.

Lawrence, A. R., & Schigelone, A. R. S. (2002). Reciprocity beyond dyadic relationships. *Research on Aging, 24*(6), 684–704.

Lazarus, R. S., & DeLongis, A. (1983). Psychological stress and coping in aging. *American Psychologist, 38,* 245–254.

Lazarus, R. S., & Folkman, S. (1984). *Stress, appraisal, and coping.* New York: Springer.

Marshall, V., Clarke, P., & Ballantyne, P. (2001). Instability in the retirement transition: Effects on health and well-being in a Canadian study. *Research on Aging, 23,* 379–409.

Moos, R. H., Brennan, P. L., Schutte, K. K., & Moos, B. S. (2006). Older adults' coping with negative life events: Common processes of managing health, interpersonal, and financial/work stressors. *International Journal of Aging and Human Development, 62*(1), 39–59.

Munnell, A. H., Aubry, J., & Muldoon, D. (2008). *The financial crisis and private defined benefit plans* (No. 8–18). Chestnut Hill, MA: Center for Retirement Research at Boston College.

Munnell, A. H., & Muldoon, D. (2008). *Are retirement savings too exposed to market risk?* (No. 8–16). Chestnut Hill, MA: Center for Retirement Research at Boston College.

National Alliance for Caregiving & AARP. (2005). *Caregiving in the U.S.* Washington, DC: Author. Retrieved June 24, 2008, from http://www.caregiving.org/data/04execsumm.pdf

Nuttman-Shwartz, O. (2004). Like a high wave: Adjustment to retirement. *The Gerontologist, 44*(2), 229–236.

Pearlin, L. I., Aneshensel, C. S., Mullan, J. T., & Whitlatch, C. J. (1996). Caregiving and its social support. In R. H. Binstock & L. K. George (Eds.), *Handbook of aging and the social sciences* (4th ed., pp. 283–302). San Diego, CA: Academic.

Pillemer, K., Suitor, J. J., Mock, S. E., Sabir, M., Pardo, T., & Sechrist, J. (2007). Capturing the complexity of intergenerational relations: Exploring ambivalence within later-life families. *Journal of Social Issues, 63*(4), 775–791.

Pinquart, M., & Sörensen, S. (2003). Differences between caregivers and noncaregivers in psychological health and physical health: A meta-analysis. *Psychology and Aging, 18*, 250–267.

Price, C. A. (2002). Professional women's retirement: The impact of employment. *Journal of Women & Aging, 14*, 41–57.

Price, C. A., & Joo, E. (2005). Exploring the relationship between marital status and women's retirement satisfaction. *International Journal of Aging and Human Development, 61*, 37–56.

Reiss, D. (1981). *The family's construction of reality*. Cambridge, MA: Harvard University Press.

Reker, G. T. (1997). Personal meaning, optimism, and choice: Existential predictors of depression in community and institutional elderly. *The Gerontologist, 37*, 709–716.

Roberts, R. E., Richards, L. N., & Bengtson, V. L. (1991). Intergenerational solidarity in families: Untangling the ties that bind. *Marriage and Family Review, 16*, 11–46.

Rosenthal, C. J., Martin-Matthews, A., & Keefe, J. M. (2007). Care management and care provision for older relatives amongst employed informal care-givers. *Ageing and Society, 27*, 755–778.

Ryff, C. D., & Singer, B. (1998). The role of purpose in life and personal growth in positive human health. In P. T. Wong & P. S. Frye (Eds.), *The human quest for meaning* (pp. 213–235). Mahwah, NJ: Lawrence Erlbaum.

Silverstein, M., Gans, D., & Yang, F. M. (2006). Intergenerational support to aging parents: The role of norms and needs. *Journal of Family Issues, 27*(8), 1068–1084.

Solinge, H. V., & Henkens, K. (2005). Couples' adjustment to retirement: A multiactor panel study. *Journals of Gerontology: Social Sciences, 60B*, S11–S20.

Stawski, R. S., Sliwinski, M. J., Almeida, D. M., & Smyth, J. M. (2008). Reported exposure and emotional reactivity to daily stressors: The roles of adult age and global perceived stress. *Psychology and Aging, 23*(1), 52–61.

Stephens, M. A. P. (1990). Social relationships as coping resources in later-life families. In M. A. P. Stephens, J. H. Crowther, S. E. Hobfoll, & D. L. Tennenbaum (Eds.), *Stress and coping in later-life families* (pp. 1–20). New York: Hemisphere.

Szinovacz, M. (2003). Contexts and pathways: Retirement as institution, process, and experience. In G. A. Adams & T. A. Beehr (Eds.), *Retirement: Reasons, processes, and results* (pp. 6–52). New York: Springer.

Szinovacz, M., & Davey, A. (2005). Retirement and marital decision making: Effects on retirement satisfaction. *Journal of Marriage and Family, 67*, 387–398.

Uhlenberg, P., & Cheuk, M. (2008). Demographic change and the future of informal caregiving. In M. E. Szinovacz & A. Davey (Eds.), *Caregiving contexts: Cultural, familial, and societal implications* (pp. 9–33). New York: Springer.

U.S. Census Bureau. (2008). *Facts for features: Older Americans month,* Series CB08-FF.06. Washington, DC: Government Printing Office. Retrieved June 5, 2008, from http://www.census.gov/Press-Release/www/releases/archives/cb08ff-06.pdf

Watzlawick, P., Weakland, J. H., & Fisch, R. (1974). *Change: Principles of problem formation and problem resolution.* New York: W. W. Norton.

Williamson, G. M., & Dooley, W. K. (2001). Aging and coping: The activity solution. In C. R. Snyder (Ed.), *Coping with stress: Effective people and processes* (pp. 240–258). Oxford, UK: Oxford University Press.

Zimmerman, L., Mitchell, B., Wister, A., & Gutman, G. (2000). Unanticipated consequences: A comparison of expected and actual retirement timing among older women. *Journal of Women & Aging, 12,* 109–128.

4 Death, Dying, and Grief in Families

Colleen I. Murray, Katalin Toth,
Barbara L. Larsen, and Shane Moulton

Tears came to Mary's eyes when she watched television coverage of the Gulf Coast's devastation from Hurricane Katrina. Although the 90-year-old didn't know anyone living in the area, she mourned. A photo of her father, who died in an accident 82 years ago, sat nearby on the table carefully placed amidst other precious images from her lifetime. In the months that followed, she felt sorrow when hurricane survivors lamented that their neighborhood was destroyed and that a way of life had disappeared; having outlived all of her friends and family, she too was grieving as the last survivor for a lost world—one that was alive in her memory, but one that soon nobody would know. Mary's neighbor, Catherine, watched the same television coverage while caring for her two young children. She too mourned the losses experienced by those she did not know, but she put signs on her lawn in support of the victims and sent some of her children's stuffed animals to the relief agencies in hopes of comforting other children. At the same time, Gulf Coast refugees publicized their grief on Internet cemeteries and memorials.

The public images of death and grief that we see today are often those of terrorism, war, natural disaster, or celebrity death. Many hold ambivalent views regarding displays of mourning for people one never knew in life, or for publicizing one's grief, expressions Tony Walter (2008) calls the *new public mourning*. Although mourning may be a major source of social integration, most grieving is private and involves pain from personal relationships, even in cases where expression is vicariously triggered by a public tragedy. Most adults in industrialized countries today die from degenerative illnesses, and most young people die from sudden or violent causes. Overall, we live in an environment where death is invisible and denied, yet we have become desensitized to its vast media presence. Inconsistencies appear related to the extent families are personally affected by death—whether they define loss as happening to "one of us" or "one of them." Our chapter addresses enduring processes and areas of change related to death in families.

Annually, there are more than 2.4 million deaths in the United States, affecting 8 to 10 million surviving immediate family members, including 2 million children and adolescents (Kung, Hoyert, Xu, & Murphy, 2008). Death is a crisis that all families encounter and is recognized as the most stressful life event families face, although most do not need counseling to cope, and the study of loss as a family system phenomenon only recently received visibility (Nadeau, 2008; Shapiro, 2001; Walsh & McGoldrick, 1991).

Etiology of "Invisible Death" and Its Consequences

From at least the Middle Ages through the 17th century, death was viewed as natural and inevitable (Aries, 1974). A movement to deny the realities of death began during the 18th century, and by the 20th century, a lack of firsthand familiarity with death fostered an era in which death became sequestered, privatized, and invisible. Factors contributing to this lack of familiarity with death include increased life expectancy, changes in leading causes of death from communicable diseases to chronic and degenerative diseases (although there is renewed concern about increases in communicable diseases), redistribution of death from the young to old, decreased mortality rates, and increased duration of chronic illnesses (Kung et al., 2008). Geographic mobility and family social reorganization also resulted in reduced intergenerational contact and fewer opportunities to participate in death-related experiences (Rando, 1993). As a result of the development of life-extending technologies, (a) most deaths occur in health care settings rather than at home, (b) care has become dominated by efforts to delay death by all means available, (c) we question our assumptions of what constitutes life and death, and (d) families are confronted with decisions of prolonging dying or terminating life of loved ones (Doka, 2005).

Although families have limited direct contact with death, they are bombarded with its presentation via news media (Murray & Gilbert, 1997). These frequent, violent portrayals of death as unnatural contribute to desensitization, as well as personal traumatization of the bereaved. Media-orchestrated emotional invigilation in reporting of celebrity death and mass tragedies leaves viewers with illusions of intimacy and grieving, or concern that their behavior differs from what everyone else is doing (Walter, 2008). Individuals who did not personally know the deceased can go through rituals of mourning and "virtually" attend the funeral through television or the Internet, without feeling the depth of pain and depression of actual grief. Viewers may confuse their emotional response with the real grief experienced by loved ones of the deceased, and since their "recovery" is quick, they may be insensitive to the amount of time required to "return to normal" when they experience real grief.

These changes have increased the stress that families experience when coping with death. Those in industrialized countries do not view dying and bereavement as normal lifespan experiences; rather, they compartmentalize death, frequently excluding children from family experiences. Adaption to loss has been hampered by lack of cultural supports that could assist families to integrate death into their ongoing life and the lack of instrumental social supports to help manage daily life disruptions in child care, housework, and finances (Walsh & McGoldrick, 1991). Often a minimum of rituals exists surrounding death, roles of the chronically ill or bereaved are not clearly defined, and geographic distance hinders completion of "unfinished business" and dealing with the loss (Shapiro, 2001).

Although death and grieving are normal, the bereaved can experience physical, psychological, and social consequences as a part of the coping process, or as related stressors. Even though few studies utilize physiological measures, research suggests that bereavement can result in negative consequences for physical health, including illness, aggravation of existing medical conditions, increased use of medical facilities, and presence of new symptoms and complaints (Stroebe, Schut, & Stroebe, 2007). During anticipatory bereavement and the months following a loss, physiological changes are indicative of acute heightened arousal (i.e., increased levels of cortisol and cathecholamines, change in immune system competence, and sleep complaints). However, there are changes in neuroendocrine function, immune system competence, and sleep patterns that endure for years (Hall & Irwin, 2001). Intrusive thoughts and avoidance behaviors are correlated with sleep disturbances, which appear to intensify effects of grief, resulting in a decreased number and function of natural killer cells (Ironson et al., 1997). Although bereavement may be related to long-lasting changes, Rosenblatt (2000) found that the narratives of bereaved parents contained sparse reference to any personal health problems.

Epidemiologic studies cannot assess direct causal relationships between bereavement and illness, but researchers have suggested that bereavement is an antecedent of disease (Christakis & Allison, 2006; Hall & Irwin, 2001). Risk factors for increased morbidity and mortality include self-damaging or neglectful behaviors during bereavement, additional stress symptoms, elevated physiological arousal, and depression, as well as being male or Caucasian (Elwert & Christakis, 2006). Physiological resiliency appears to be related to coping strategies, social support networks, and healthy sleep.

Consequences of bereavement for mental health also are difficult to measure. Characteristics typically associated with grief are ones that would evoke concern in other circumstances. High rates of depression, insomnia, suicides, and anorexia may exist in conjunction with consumption of drugs, alcohol, and tobacco (Stroebe et al., 2007). Lack of differentiation between grief and depression has been problematic as they represent distinct, although related reactions to bereavement. Spurred by the recommendation that the forthcoming edition of the *Diagnostic and Statistical Manual of Mental*

Disorders (DSM-V) includes a new disorder labeled *complicated grief* or *prolonged grief disorder* (i.e., the first disorder to be identified as the result of the normal experience of grief), clinicians and scholars are engaged in the difficult task of distinguishing normal from complicated grief in a manner that does not mislabel nonpathological grief, stigmatize bereavement as a pathological condition, deprive those in need of professional assistance, or result in the loss of natural support systems (c.f., Parkes, 2005; Rubin, Malkinson, & Witztum, 2008).

Research has suggested that individuals identify bereavement as a social stressor, reporting lack of role clarity and support (Rando, 1993; Rosenblatt, 2000; Weiss, 2008). Changes in social status, conflicts in identity, disputes over family inheritance, and loss of roles, income, or retirement funds that may result from the death of a family member can contribute to social isolation. Changes in family communication patterns and relationships with people outside the family are common.

Paradoxically, growth may also be an outcome of loss. *Posttraumatic growth* is both a process and outcome in which, following trauma, growth occurs *beyond* an individual's previous level of functioning (Tedeschi & Calhoun, 2008). Growth outcomes occur in *perception of self* (e.g., as survivor rather than victim, and self-reliant yet with heightened vulnerability), *interpersonal relationships* (e.g., increased ability to be compassionate or intimate, to self-disclose important information, and to express emotions), and *philosophy of life* (e.g., reorganization of priorities, greater appreciation of life, grappling with meaning and purpose of life, spiritual change, and sense of wisdom). In contrast, terror management theory (Pyszcznski, Solomon, & Greenberg, 2003) suggests that what appears to be growth is actually cognitive coping, which protects or distances us from traumatic events and buffers fear of death.

Theories of Grieving

Theories are necessary for understanding complex response to loss and the sometimes counterintuitive phenomena that occur during bereavement (e.g., posttraumatic growth). They range from individualistic intrapersonal approaches to an interpersonal study of group influence. Scholars have proposed individual-based theories focusing on developmental stages or trajectories for the dying (e.g., Kübler-Ross, 1969) or survivors (e.g., Rando, 1993), derived from works of Freud (1917/1957) or Bowlby (1980). Such theories differ in number of stages identified, but they all assume that grief follows three basic phases, including periods of shock, denial, and disorganization; extremes including intense separation pain, volatile emotions, and active grief work; and resolution, acceptance, and withdrawal of energy from the deceased and reinvestment. Critics of these theories question the definition of "normal" grief and assumptions about how people "should" respond, including beliefs that (a) intense emotional distress or depression is inevitable, (b) failure to experience distress is indicative of pathology, (c) working through loss is important—intense distress will end with recovery, and (d) by working through loss, individuals can achieve resolution and intellectual acceptance (Silver & Wortman, 2007).

Others purport that stage theories have not been supported in research and view these theories as problematic because they are population-specific and misrepresent progress toward adjustment as linear (Weiss, 2008). Critics contend that progress is not always forward and that grief processes may have no definite ending (Rosenblatt, 2000). They argue that emphasis should not be on recovery or closure, but on continuing bonds, relearning relationships, and renegotiating meaning of loss over time (Klass, 2001; Weiss, 2008). Rather than dichotomizing relinquishing and retaining bonds, Boerner and Heckhausen (2003) suggest that transformation involves both disengagement from the deceased's physical absence and connection through mental representations. A recent longitudinal test of stage theory suggests that yearning is the dominant negative indicator during the first 2 years postloss and that acceptance increases across time (Maciejewski, Zhang, Block, & Prigerson, 2007). However, it has received criticism that its data do not represent normal patterns of grieving (c.f., Letters, 2007).

Concern regarding developmental theories also deals with viewing grief as passive, with few choices for grievers. Critics contend that grieving is active, presenting the bereaved with challenges, choices, and opportunities; and that the bereaved are active participants relearning the world in terms of physical surroundings, relationships, and who they are (Weiss, 2008). They question the necessity of "grief work"—traditionally viewed as an essential cognitive process of confronting loss. Margaret Stroebe and her colleagues suggest that grief work is not a universal concept, its definitions and operationalizations are problematic, few studies have yielded substantial conclusions, and findings were intended for understanding of processes, rather than prescriptions for recovery (Stroebe et al., 2000). Archer (2008) suggests that it may be cognitive restructuring rather than grief work that is related to adjustment following loss.

Among individually centered process-based models is Rando's (1993) "Six R's" model, which assumes the need to accommodate loss. Processes include recognition of loss, reacting to separation, recollection and reexperiencing the deceased and the relationship, relinquishing old attachments and assumptive world, readjusting to move into a new world without forgetting the old, and reinvesting (p. 45). In contrast, the dual process model of coping (M. Stroebe & Schut, 2001) suggests that active confrontation of loss is not necessary for a positive outcome, and there may be circumstances when denial, avoidance of reminders, and repressive strategies are essential. The model concurs with social-functional research that minimizing expression of negative emotions and using laughter as dissociation from distress may improve functioning (Bonanno, 2001). The dual process assumes that most individuals experience ongoing oscillation between *loss orientation* (coping with loss through grief work, dealing with denial, and avoiding changes) and *restoration orientation* (adjusting to various life changes triggered by death, changing routines, transitioning to a new equilibrium, avoiding or taking time off from grief). There is movement between coping with loss and moving forward with differences for individuals, type of loss, culture, and gender.

Although scholars have focused on dying or bereaved individuals, death does not occur in isolation. Individual process models have not been broadened to aid in understanding families, except for some psychoanalytic attempts. Archer (2008) suggests that rather than using Bowlby's work to look at the breaking of attachment bonds, it can instead be used to address the relationship between styles of attachment and grieving, thus going beyond the individual. Mikulincer and Shaver (2008) argue that Bowlby's work on the attachment behavioral system and pair bonds as related to bereavement has been misunderstood, and there is recent evidence from experiments and clinical observations in support of these psychodynamic processes. The bereaved form new attachment bonds while maintaining a symbolic attachment to the deceased, and they integrate that relationship into their new reality (i.e., a focus on both the loss and restoration). Those with insecure attachments have difficulty in this oscillating between this hyperactivation and deactivation of the attachment system, overemphasizing one or the other.

Theories need to integrate three approaches to explaining grief, including (1) continuing bonds and mental representations of the relationship, (2) meaning of the bereavement and maintenance of a meaningful world, and (3) loss of relationship supports from the deceased and the social network (Weiss, 2008). Work on grief from a family perspective has typically utilized elements of systems theories, particularly through integrative approaches to complex issues. Refined systemic models recognize that multiple griefs exist simultaneously for individuals, families, and communities, and although some thoughts and feelings are shared, others are not (Gilbert, 1996).

Family systems theory focuses on dynamics and provides concepts for describing relationships, offering a nonpathologizing conceptualization of grief as a natural process (Nadeau, 2008). The following premises of systems theory can be useful in examining families' adaptation to dying and death:

1. A family reacts to loss as a system. Although we grieve as individuals, the family system has qualities beyond those of individual members (Jackson, 1965), and all members participate in mutually reinforcing interactions (Walsh & McGoldrick, 1991).

2. Actions and reactions of a family member affect others and their functioning. Interdependence exists because causality is circular rather than linear (Shapiro, 2001).

3. Death disrupts a system's equilibrium, modifies the structure, and requires reorganization in feedback processes, role distribution, and functions (Bowen, 1976).

4. Death may produce an emotional shock wave of serious life events that can occur anywhere in the extended family in the years following loss (Bowen, 1976). Waves exist in an environment of denied emotional dependence and may seem unrelated to the death. They may trigger additional stressor events or increase rigid strategies to maintain stability (Shapiro, 2001).

5. There is no single outcome from death of a member that characterizes all family systems. Various family characteristics, such as feedback processes (Jackson, 1965), patterns of relationship (Shapiro, 2001), and family schema and family paradigm (Boss, 2006), influence the outcome.

Scholars have infrequently applied systems theory in examining death-related reorganization. Loss has traditionally been identified as a historical, individual, or content issue and inappropriate for traditional family systems work (which focused on process, homeostasis, differentiation of self from family, current interaction, and the present) (Nadeau, 2008; Walsh & McGoldrick, 1991). Recent versions of systems theory have focused on balance of change and continuity, as well as the negotiated inclusion of differences to balance self-assertion and cohesion. The family systems–based study of grief exists within a framework that includes intergenerational and family life cycle perspectives (Walsh & McGoldrick, 1991), focusing on change in structural factors such as boundaries, and family dynamics such as roles and rules, as well as meaning making and communication (Nadeau, 2008). An examination of the relationship between individual grief and family system characteristics found that grief symptomatology at 4 to 5 weeks postloss did not predict any family system characteristics or grief symptomatology 6 months later (Traylor, Hayslip, Kaminski, & York, 2003). However, perception of family cohesion, expression of affect, and communication were predictors of later grief.

Particularly useful models are those that simultaneously consider individual, family, and cultural dimensions. Rather than relying on traditional family systems, these models integrate family systems' concepts with other perspectives. Rolland's (1994) family systems–illness model examines the interface of individual, family, illness, and health care team. Rather than identifying the ill individual as the central unit of care, it focuses on the family or caregiving system as a resource that is both affected by and influences the course of illness. This model can be useful for understanding experiences of the individual and family members during the terminal phase of chronic illness, in multiple contexts and across time. Shapiro applied a systemic developmental approach to examine grief as a family process (2001). This clinical model views grief as a developmental crisis influenced by family history, sociocultural context, and family and individual life cycle stages. Grief is a crisis of identity and attachment that disrupts family equilibrium but provides an opportunity for developing growth and stability.

Popular interactionist approaches account for context by incorporating life course, social constructionism, and systems concepts. These models recognize the unique interpretation of internal and external worlds of individuals and families dealing with loss (Harvey, Carlson, Huff, & Green, 2001; Rosenblatt, 2000). They utilize narrative methods, focus on meaning making or account making, and recognize intimate losses as part of a changing identity. These models assume that the accuracy of meaning given to any particular events is of limited importance because it is *meaning itself* that influences family interactions. Interactionist counseling would not help families to just understand and manage grief symptomatology but would also help to reconstruct a meaningful narrative of self, family, and world.

Factors Related to Family Adaptation to Death

Characteristics of the Loss

Some characteristics of the death itself and societal interpretations of a loss can influence family adaptation. For example, when the duration of time before death is far longer or shorter than expected, or the sequence of death in a family differs from expected order, problems may occur. Elderly members are assumed to experience "timely" deaths. Early parental loss, death of a young spouse, and death of a child or grandchild of any age are considered tragic and evoke searches for explanations.

In addition, initial grief reaction to sudden or unexpected death may be more intense than death related to illness (Bowlby, 1980), with survivors experiencing a shattered normal world, a series of concurrent stressors and secondary losses (Murray, 2001), with unfinished business more likely to remain (Lindemann, 1944). Factors existing along a continuum that can affect coping include (a) perceptions of whether the loss was natural or human made, (b) degree of intentionality/premeditation, (c) degree of preventability, (d) amount of suffering, anxiety, or physical pain experienced while dying, (e) number of people killed or affected, (f) degree of expectedness (Doka, 1996, pp. 12–13), (g) senselessness, and (h) whether the survivor witnessed the death or its aftermath or found out about the loss through the media. Differences related to suddenness of death appear short term once internal control beliefs and self-esteem are considered (W. Stroebe & Schut, 2001) and are lessened when families are present during emergency medical procedures, such as during efforts to resuscitate (Kamienski, 2004).

According to the National Center for Health Statistics (Kung et al., 2008), 80% of deaths of teens and young adults are sudden violent accidents, homicide, or suicide. A longitudinal study of parents surviving the sudden death of a child reported that marital satisfaction decreased during the first 5 years after the death; nearly 70% said it took 3 to 4 years to put their child's death in perspective; and at 5 years postdeath, 43% said they still had not found meaning in their child's death (Murphy, 2008). Adults who experience the sudden death of a partner also experience great strain and a need to restructure their lives (Rodger, Sherwood, O'Connor, & Leslie, 2006).

Although popular works often discuss the suicide of an attachment figure as the most difficult loss, there is little empirical evidence to support this contention (W. Stroebe & Schut, 2001). Homicide appears to be most directly related to posttraumatic stress disorder and grief marked by despair. In a mass trauma (a potentially life-threatening event experienced by a large number of people), adaptation appears to be influenced by whether it is a single event or recurring/ongoing, by emotional or geographic distance (with vicarious traumatization possible through media coverage, particularly for those who have experienced other unrelated losses), by attribution of causality, and by the interaction of personal, community, and symbolic losses (Webb, 2004).

Deaths following protracted illness can also be stressful. In such cases, family members have experienced a series of stressors before the death, including increased time commitments for caring, financial strain as a result of cost of care and lost employment, emotional exhaustion, interruption of career and family routines, sense of social isolation, and lack of time for self or other family members (Rabow, Hauser, & Adams, 2004). Although research findings on the existence, role, and multidimensionality of anticipatory grief are inconsistent, protracted illness appears to be associated with trauma and secondary morbidity—that is, difficulties in physical, emotional, cognitive, and social functioning of those closely involved with terminally ill persons (Rando, 1993). Deaths following chronic illness may still be perceived as sudden or unexpected by surviving adults who are not yet "ready," by children whose developmental stage inhibits their understanding that death is inevitable, and following multiple cycles of relapse and improvement. Deaths from trauma and illness have much in common. Similar to families who have witnessed or experienced death through violence, families experiencing prolonged or complicated grief, multiple deaths simultaneously, or a series of deaths in close proximity may display signs of posttraumatic stress disorder, with caregivers experiencing secondary traumatic stress (Anderson, Arnold, Angus, & Bryce, 2008).

Scholars have devoted increased attention to losses unacknowledged by society and *disenfranchised grief*—that is, grief that exists although society does not recognize one's right, need, or capacity to grieve (Doka, 2008). Examples include grief over the loss of unacknowledged personal relationships or those not recognized as significant, such as the death of a former spouse, lover, or extramarital lover; a foster child or foster parent; a stepparent or stepchild; a coworker; or a companion animal. In addition, deaths related to pregnancy (i.e., miscarriage, elective abortion, stillbirth, or neonatal death) may also be disenfranchised. Professional caretakers and first responders, especially those labeled as "heroes" or competently focused on tasks of rescue and recovery, also may suffer unacknowledged grief when they lose those for whom they provide care. Bereaved grandparents, men in general (Gilbert, 1996), and families of deceased addicts or death row inmates may also be disenfranchised. Many people see others, such as young children, older adults, and mentally disabled persons, as incapable of grief or without a need to grieve (Doka, 2008). Disenfranchisement occurs when others assume that the circumstances of a death do not warrant grief, or when bereaved persons are told they are experiencing or expressing grief in inappropriate ways. Societal expectations of who is entitled to grieve change over time; losses that are gaining in recognition involve cohabitors and partners in a gay or lesbian relationship.

People who are grieving various types of death report that they believe their grief has been stigmatized. They feel the discomfort of others who distance themselves, and they experience direct or indirect social pressure to become "invisible mourners" (Rosaldo, 1989). Disenfranchised grief often results from stigmatized losses, particularly when there is the assumption that the death was caused by an individual's disturbed or immoral behavior, or a fear of contagion, such as with AIDS or cancer-related deaths (Doka, 2008). AIDS-related deaths have been stigmatized because of their concentration in the homosexual community, and more recently, in poor inner-city Latino or African American neighborhoods. Survivors may be experiencing multiple losses among family and friends, lack of legal standing, denial of death benefits, and isolation. In inner-city neighborhoods, many of those infected with HIV are women, some with infected children, and many who have already lost companions, siblings, children, and friends. Although HIV disclosure may sometimes bring relationship partners closer together, mothers coping with HIV infection also deal with finding caregivers for children and coordinating safer-sex practices with partners reluctant to use condoms. Stigma also occurs in families that have lost a member to suicide or homicide, resulting in altered identities, provoking feelings of anger and guilt, and experiencing isolation, blame, and injustice—characteristics of revictimization (Bucholz, 2002). Resulting secrecy and blame can distort family communication, isolate members, and diminish social support (Walsh & McGoldrick, 1991).

Factors Affecting Family Vulnerability

Death-related loss involves many secondary losses including personal, interpersonal, material, and symbolic losses. Families have more difficulty adapting to death if other stressors are present, as dealing with a loss does not abrogate other family needs (Murray, 2001). When normative events associated with family life cycle (e.g., new marriage, birth of child, or adolescent's move to increase independence) are concurrent with illness or death, they may pose incompatible tasks (Shapiro, 2001). In addition, the centrality of the deceased's role and the degree of the family's emotional dependence on that individual (i.e., function and position) influence adaptation. Shock waves rarely follow the deaths of well-liked people who played peripheral roles or of dysfunctional members unless dysfunction played a central role in maintaining family equilibrium (Bowen, 1976).

Complications in family adaptation can occur when there is intense and continuous ambivalence, estrangement, or conflict. Chronic mourning and depression have been reported by those with anxious-ambivalent attachments; somatization and cognitive suppression are more common among those with avoidant attachment styles (Mikulincer & Shaver, 2008). Grief after the death of an abuser can result in ambivalence, rage, secrecy, sadness, and shame (Monahan, 2003). During illness, there may be time to repair relationships, but family members may hesitate, fearing that confrontations increase risk of death. Surrogate end-of-life decision makers report a greater ability to resolve family disagreements when they perceive the family as psychologically close or open to communication (Mick, Medvene, & Strunk, 2003).

Resources also influence the bereaved family's vulnerability and assist in meeting demands. They may be tangible (e.g., money or health) or intangible (e.g., friendship, self-esteem, role accumulation, or a sense of mastery). African American evacuees from the aftermath of Hurricane Katrina exhibited greater psychological distress (and a lower sense of recovery) if they were uninsured or experienced home destruction or a human loss (Lee, Shen, & Tran, 2009). The disruption that a bereaved family experiences is mediated by intensity and chronicity of family stress. Adaptation is facilitated by members' emotional regulation capacity, nonreactivity to emotional intensity in the system, cohesion and adaptability, and marital intimacy (Nadeau, 2008; Shapiro, 2001). Research findings on benefits of open communication about loss are mixed. Pennebaker, Zech, and Rime (2001) suggest that confiding in others is related to health after a loss. Others assert that the best predictor of emotional well-being is emotional regulation, not emotion focused coping (Bonanno, 2004; Znoj & Keller, 2002).

Social support networks appear to simultaneously complicate and facilitate grieving. Supporters may listen, but hold unrealistic expectations. Availability of formal or informal networks does not guarantee support, especially in a society that does not sanction the expression of emotions surrounding loss. Some bereaved family members turn to face-to-face or online self-help groups composed of persons who have experienced a similar type of loss—a practice that may be predictive of finding meaning in death during the years that follow. However, rules of some family systems discourage members from sharing intimate information and feelings with persons outside the family. Religious belief also may simultaneously complicate and facilitate grieving. Belief in "God's plan" can help create meaning from loss, but it can create anger toward God for unfairly allowing the death and isolate the individual from familiar spiritual roots.

Family Belief System, Definition, and Appraisal

To understand how a family perceives a death or uses coping strategies, one must understand its assumptions about the world. A common paradigm is the "belief in a just world," which posits that the self is worthy and the world is benevolent, just, and meaningful (Janoff-Bulman, 1992; Lerner, 1980). This paradigm values control and mastery; it assumes fit between efforts and outcomes: One gets what one deserves. Such a view is functional only when something can be done to change a situation. Challenges to the just-world assumption make the world seem less predictable and can lead to cognitive efforts to manage fear of death. Such efforts can lead to blaming chronically ill persons for their conditions and lack of recovery, or to linking adolescent deaths to drug use or reckless behavior as a way of affirming, "It can't happen to my child." In contrast, for those dealing with loss, understanding the complexities, multiple levels of context, and short- or long-term effects of the event will facilitate grief (Murray, 2001).

Family members share some beliefs that are unintentionally but collectively constructed. Family history and experiences with death provide a *legacy* (a way of looking at loss that has been received from ancestors) that is related to how the family will adapt to subsequent loss (Walsh & McGoldrick, 1991). Particularly in relation to several traumatic untimely deaths, a family may have a legacy of empowerment (i.e., family members see themselves as survivors who can be hurt but not defeated) or a legacy of trauma (i.e., family members feel "cursed" and unable to rise above their losses)—either of which can inhibit openness of the system. Families may not recognize transgenerational anniversary patterns or concurrence of a death with other life events, and members may lack emotional memory or have discrepant memories regarding a death (Shapiro, 2001). Members may make unconscious efforts to block, promote, or shift beliefs to maintain consistency with the legacy.

Grief can also be viewed as a process of *meaning construction* that evolves throughout the life of the bereaved. Several factors appear to influence families' construction of the meaning of their losses, including family schema, contact, cutoffs, interdependence, rituals, secrets, coherence, paradigms, divergent beliefs, tolerance for differences, rules about sharing, and situational and stressor appraisals (Nadeau, 2008; Rosenblatt, 2000). Researchers are increasingly noting the importance of making sense of the event, finding benefits from the experience and shaping one's new identity to include the loss (Gibson, 2007). Irrational, violent death may result in meaning making expressed through activism or intense pursuit of numerous small actions.

Families may find additional challenges when experiencing a situation of family boundary ambiguity (i.e., confusion a family experiences when it is not clear who is in and who is out of the system) (Boss, 2006; Carroll, Olson, & Buckmiller, 2007). Ambiguity rises when (a) the facts surrounding a death are unclear, (b) a person is missing but it is unclear if death has occurred, or (c) the family denies the loss. Degree of boundary ambiguity may be more important for explaining adaptation and coping than the presence of coping skills or resources. Both denial and boundary ambiguity initially may be functional because they give a shocked family time to deny the loss and then cognitively reorganize itself before it accepts the fact that the death is real. If a high degree of ambiguity exists over time, the family is at risk for maladaptation. However, evidence that bonds continue to exist after death and that conversations with the dead may be replacing rituals as the normative way bonds are maintained (Klass, 2001) may challenge the notion of boundary ambiguity, suggesting one can recognize loss while holding psychological, emotional, and spiritual connections to deceased loved ones.

Factors of Diversity

Despite Western cultural expectations, most couples experience incongruent grieving, often with one adult whose grief could be called *cognitive and solitary* and the other whose grief is more *social and emotional* (Gilbert, 1996). Perhaps this incongruence can be understood as a family system–level manifestation of M. Stroebe and Schut's (2001) dual process model. A functional system would require a *loss orientation* and *restoration orientation*. Studies of incongruent grieving have suggested that women often display an intuitive grieving style, with more sorrow, guilt, and depression than men (Doka & Martin, 2001). Men are socialized to manage instrumental tasks, such as those related to the funeral, burial, finances, and property. Women are more likely to take on caregiving roles, which require them to engage in both dual processes. However, men are more able to immerse themselves in work and block other intuitive tasks. Reasons for gender-related differences are not well understood but seem influenced by expectations and socialization. Research in this area has been hampered by reliance on studies completed during acute stages of grief and lack of nonbereaved control groups. Longitudinal studies of bereaved persons who have suffered violent or traumatic losses found few gender differences (Boelen & van den Bout, 2002/2003).

With gender controls, despite differences in social support, widowers experience greater depression and health consequences than widows (W. Stroebe & Schut, 2001). It has been thought that men have unrecognized problems because their socialization interferes with active grief processes (Doka & Martin, 2001). Men's response to grief typically includes coping styles that mask fear and insecurity, including remaining silent; taking physical or legal action in order to express anger and exert control; immersion in work, domestic, recreational, or sexual activity; engaging in solitary or secret mourning; and exhibiting addictive behavior, such as alcoholism. Cook (1988) identified a double bind that bereaved fathers experience: Societal expectations are that they will contain their emotions in order to protect and comfort their wives, but that they cannot heal their own grief without the sharing of feelings. Similarly, Doka and Martin (2001) identified a third pattern of grief involving dissonance between the way one experiences grief and the manner it is expressed. For example, some males may experience internal grief feelings but are constrained from expressing them. Much of the problem may not be in men's grieving but rather in our understanding of the mourning process (Cook, 1988), which largely has been formulated through the study of women. As such, concepts of meaning making (Gilbert, 1996) and the dual process model (M. Stroebe & Schut, 2001) may be more relevant for men than concepts of grief work.

Grief is a socially constructed malleable phenomenon, and given current levels of immigration and contact among diverse groups, mourning patterns in the United States can be expected to change. In addition to commonalities, group differences in values and practices continue and present a wide range of normal responses to death. General areas in which differences exist include the following:

- Extent of ritual attached to death (e.g., importance of attending funerals, types of acceptable emotional displays, and degree to which these affairs should be costly)
- Need to see a dying relative
- Openness and type of display of emotion
- Emphasis on verbal expression of feelings, and public versus private (namely, solitary or family) expression of grief
- Appropriate length of mourning
- Importance of anniversary events
- Roles of men and women
- Role of extended family
- Beliefs about what happens after death, particularly related to ideas of suffering, fate, and destiny
- Value of autonomy/dependence in relation to bonds after death
- Coping strategies
- Social support for hospice patients
- Whether certain deaths are stigmatized
- Definition of when death actually occurs
- Barriers to trusting professionals
- Interweaving of religious and political narratives
- Appropriateness of the concept of recovery (Laurie & Neimeyer, 2008; McGoldrick et al., 1991; Rosenblatt, 2008)

Specific Losses

The death of one's child is viewed as the most difficult loss, for it is contrary to expected developmental progression and thrusts one into a marginal social role that has unclear role expectations (Arnold & Gemma, 2008; Murphy, 2008). Deaths ranging from fetal loss to that of an adult child (who may also be a grandparent or a caregiver to older parents) can cause reactions similar to posttraumatic stress (Znoj & Keller, 2002). From an Eriksonian perspective, young-adult parents grapple with death-related issues of identity as a parent and spousal intimacy, middle-aged parents deal with loss of generativity, and elderly parents deal with loss in terms of ego integrity versus despair. Classic attachment and psychoanalytic models appear to be inadequate to address experiences of a parent whose child died. Newer models focus on integrating the deceased child into the parents' psychic and social worlds (Klass, 2001).

Society expects spouses to provide support and comfort during times of stress; however, this may not be possible for bereaved parents who are both experiencing intense grief as individuals, with unique timetables, and may not be "in sync" with each other (Rando, 1993). Sexual expression between bereaved parents can serve as a reminder of the child and elicit additional distress (Rosenblatt, 2000). Parents with an insecure partner attachment experience more symptoms of grief and depression, especially when low marital satisfaction is present (Meij et al., 2007). However, previously reported high divorce rates of bereaved parents appear to be erroneous; research on which they were based is neither longitudinal nor representative and confuses marital distress and divorce.

Most research on sibling death is recent, focused on children and adolescents. Prior work on sibling loss generally was confined to clinical studies; recent work differentiates normal and complicated sibling grief patterns (Silverman, Baker, Cait, & Boerner, 2003). Even in the same family, sibling grief reactions are not uniform or the same as parents, but they can be understood best in relation to individual characteristics (e.g., sex, developmental stage, relationship to the sibling). Scholars have not reported consistent behavioral or at-risk differences in school-age children who experienced parental death or sibling death, but they have found gender differences, with boys more affected by the loss of a parent and girls impacted more by the death of a sibling, especially a sister (Worden, Davies, & McCown, 1999).

Initial negative outcomes and grief reactions of siblings include a drop in school performance, anger, a sense that parents are unreachable, survivor guilt, and guilt from sibling rivalry (even when siblings recognize the irrationality of their beliefs) (Rando, 1993; Schaefer & Moos, 2001). Parents report more frequent and negative symptoms in adolescents than in younger children, with mothers and fathers reporting different problem behaviors (Lohan & Murphy, 2002). Adolescents who use religious coping ascribe more negative meaning to the death, especially when they try to reconcile belief in a loving God with a negative event such as sibling death (Hays & Hendrix, 2008). Although siblings report more family conflict than do parents, siblings rarely direct their anger toward parents, who they perceive to be vulnerable and hence in need of protection from additional pain.

Long-term changes appear to be positive, especially in terms of maturity, which adolescents relate to appreciation for life, coping successfully, and negotiating role changes. Adults who lost siblings in childhood have reported that these losses fostered greater insights into life and death (Schaefer & Moos, 2001).

Siblings have unique bonds that continue following the death of a brother or sister (Packman, Horsley, & Davies, 2006). Deceased siblings also play an identity function for survivors who may feel a need to fulfill roles the deceased children played for parents or to act in an opposite manner in an attempt to show that they are different. In later adulthood, sibling death is the most frequent death of close family members, yet researchers have largely overlooked this loss. Surviving siblings appear to experience functioning and cognitive states similar to those of surviving spouses (Moss, Moss, & Hansson, 2001). Unfortunately, research on sibling grief to date has consisted primarily of cross-sectional investigations that rely on retrospective data, data no more than 2 years beyond the loss, and longitudinal data treated as cross-sectional due to small sample sizes. Research is needed to determine how grief may change over time, particularly in the context of stigmatized losses such as death from AIDS-related illnesses.

The death of a parent can occur during childhood or adulthood. Children's reactions to parental death vary and are influenced by emotional and cognitive development, closeness to the deceased parent, responses of/ interactions with the surviving parent, and perceptions of social support. Researchers have reported evidence of complicated grief, traumatic grief, and posttraumatic growth in parentally bereaved children and adolescents (Melhem, Moritz, Walker, Shear, & Brent, 2007; Wolchik, Coxe, Tein, Sandler, & Ayers, 2008). Adolescents grieving the death of a parent appear to have heightened interpersonal sensitivity, characterized by uneasiness and negative expectations regarding personal exchanges (Servaty-Sieb & Hayslip, 2003). They tend to flee a grieving peer; thus family support may be especially important and instrumental in preventing maladaptive behavior (Silverman et al., 2003). Although many adolescents live in single-parent, divorced, or blended families, researchers have largely ignored the topic of parental death in those contexts or have focused on surviving parents' grief and adjustment.

The death of a parent is the most common form of family loss in middle age. Adult response to this loss is influenced by the meaning of the relationship, roles the parent played at the time of death, anticipation, disenfranchisement, circumstances of the death, impact on the surviving adult child, and maintenance of the parent–child bond while letting go (Moss et al., 2001). Adults whose parents experienced protracted illness or lived in nursing homes prior to death exhibit multidimensional responses to their parents' deaths, including sadness, grief, relief, persistence of memories about the parent, and a sense that the protection against death provided by the parents has vanished. Adults who become "orphaned" may find their identities and remaining relationships impacted.

Adults with mental disabilities who experience parental death have some aspects of grief in common with others but also have unique concerns. When individuals with psychiatric disabilities are faced in midlife with the death of a parent, they often have no preparation for this event. They may suddenly find themselves faced with making funeral arrangements, dealing with financial repercussions of the death, as well as possible residential relocation (Jones et al., 2003).

Among the family losses during adulthood, the death of a spouse has been the most intensively studied; however, less attention has been given to spousal death in early or middle adulthood, widowed parents with dependent children, or death of other life partners such as committed homosexual couples. Loneliness and emotional adjustment are major concerns of spouses who lose a companion and source of emotional support, particularly in a long interdependent relationship in which there was a shared identity based on systems of roles and traditions (Moss et al., 2001). Conjugal bereavement can be especially difficult for individuals whose relationships assumed a sharp division of traditional sex roles, leaving them unprepared to assume the range of tasks required to maintain a household. The death of one's spouse brings up issues of self-definition and prompts the need to develop a new identity. Despite these problems, many bereaved spouses adjust very well, and the death of a partner does not always result in grief for the other (Watford, 2008). Some derive pleasure and independence from the new lifestyle, feeling more competent than when they were married.

An additional loss involves death and the multidimensional families of those in the military. Sacrificing one's life in military operations has historically been extolled as honorable. Generally, family members of a fallen soldier are embraced by their surrounding community, as well as the military organization, with intense support shortly after the loss, and a sense of meaning is constructed to account for, and help justify, the loss. The military's standard operating procedures help create a supportive environment for the surviving family (Bowen, Mancini, Ware, & Nelson, 2003). However, the prevalence and social legitimacy of military deaths have led to a general desensitization of communities to the length of time needed for grieving and impatience waiting for the family to move ahead. Rapid desertion from various support networks can result in family members feeling disenfranchised, as invisible mourners grieving in silence.

In addition, among service members, the lasting impact of combat losses on grieving is often overlooked or assumed to be posttraumatic stress disorder (Papa, Neria, & Litz, 2008). Yet war veterans often experience complicated grief as a result of the deaths of close friends, unit members, or leaders; witnessing the death of other security forces and civilians; or their own killing of enemy insurgents. Studies of veterans of the Vietnam and Israeli Yom Kippur wars suggest that exposure to combat trauma, survivor guilt, and poor postcombat adjustment are related to increased risk of suicide. The close relationships that form within military units reflect attachment, and their losses are subject to grief as with loss of other attachment and family figures. Adjustment difficulties and suicide rates, especially of those with lengthy deployments, are indications that early evidence-based interventions are needed (Figley, 2007).

Conclusion and Summary

Dealing with death involves a process, not an event. It is an experience that all families *will* encounter and is inherent in the nature of close relationships. Despite its importance in the experiences of individuals and families, death still appears to be a taboo subject, and no comprehensive theory exists to account for the complexity and contexts in which grief occurs. Families' adaptation to death varies; factors that influence the process include characteristics of the death, family vulnerability, history of past losses, incompatible life cycle demands, resources, belief systems, and the sociocultural context in which a family lives.

Although loss is a normal experience, it has been treated by theorists and researchers as a problem. At this point, more work needs to focus on processes and strengths, such as the process of coping (rather than problems), and on factors that facilitate growth from loss (rather than those that inhibit growth). Examination of posttraumatic growth is a first step, but it warrants application beyond the individual to assess its applicability to families. Promising areas of study include the interface of grief with technology, such as the effectiveness of Internet support groups, Internet suicide counseling, and grief therapy using virtual reality environments; or the integration of functional magnetic resonance imaging (fMRI) technology to better understand normal versus complicated grief and adaptation processes.

Internet Resources

Association for Death Education and Counseling. 342 N. Main St., West Hartford, CT 06117. www.adec.org

Center for Loss and Life Transition. 3725 Broken Bow Road, Fort Collins, CO 80526. http://www.centerforloss.com

The Compassionate Friends (nondenominational support group for bereaved parents and siblings). P.O. Box 3696, Oak Brook, IL 60522. http://www.compassionatefriends.org

The Dougy Center: The National Center for Grieving Children and Families. P.O. Box 86852, Portland, OR 97286. http://www.dougy.org

Gilbert, K. R. Grief in a family context. [Online course]. Available at http://www.indiana.edu/~famlygrf

GriefNet. [Online grief support]. http://www.griefnet.com

Tragedy Assistance Program for Survivors (TAPS). (Support for all members of the armed services who have been impacted by death). 2001 S Street SW, Suite 300, Washington, DC 20009. www.taps.org

Widowed Persons Service (WPS), American Association of Retired Persons (AARP). 601 E Street NW, Washington, DC 20049. www.aarp.org

References

Anderson, W. G., Arnold, R. M., Angus, D. C., & Bryce, C. L. (2008). Posttraumatic stress and complicated grief in family members of patients in the intensive care unit. *Journal of General Internal Medicine, 23,* 1871–1876.

Archer, J. (2008). Theories of grief: Past, present, and future perspectives. In M. S. Stroebe, R. O. Hansson, H. Schut, & W. Stroebe (Eds.), *Handbook of bereavement research and practice* (pp. 45–65). Washington, DC: American Psychological Association.

Aries, P. (1974). *Western attitudes toward death: From the Middle Ages to the present.* Baltimore: Johns Hopkins University Press.

Arnold, J., & Gemma, P. B. (2008). The continuing process of parental grief. *Death Studies, 32,* 658–673.

Boelen, P. A., & van den Bout, J. (2002/2003). Gender differences in traumatic grief symptom severity after the loss of a spouse. *Omega, 46,* 183–198.

Boerner, K., & Heckhausen, J. (2003). To have and have not: Adaptive bereavement by transforming mental ties to the deceased. *Death Studies, 27,* 199–226.

Bonanno, G. A. (2001). Grief and emotion: A social-functional perspective. In M. S. Stroebe, R. O. Hansson, W. Stroebe, & H. Schut (Eds.), *Handbook of bereavement research: Consequences, coping, and care* (pp. 493–515). Washington, DC: American Psychological Association.

Bonanno, G. A. (2004). Loss, trauma, and human resilience: Have we underestimated the human capacity to thrive after extremely aversive events? *American Psychologist, 59,* 20–28.

Boss, P. (2006). *Loss, trauma, and resilience: Therapeutic work with ambiguous loss.* New York: W. W. Norton.

Bowen, G., Mancini, J. A., Ware, W. B., & Nelson, J. P. (2003). Promoting the adaptation of military families: An empirical test of a community practice model. *Family Relations, 52,* 33–44.

Bowen, M. (1976). Family reaction to death. In P. J. Guerin (Ed.), *Family therapy: Theory and practice.* New York: Gardner.

Bowlby, J. (1980). *Attachment and loss* (vol. 3), *Loss: Sadness and depression.* New York: Basic.

Bucholz, J. A. (2002). *Homicide survivors: Misunderstood grievers.* Amityville, NY: Baywood.

Carroll, J. S., Olson, C. D., & Buckmiller, N. (2007). Family boundary ambiguity: A 30-year review of theory, research, and measurement. *Family Relations, 56,* 210–230.

Christakis, N., & Allison, P. (2006). Mortality after the hospitalization of a spouse. *New England Journal of Medicine, 354,* 719–730.

Cook, J. A. (1988). Dad's double binds: Rethinking fathers' bereavement from a men's studies perspective. *Journal of Contemporary Ethnography, 17,* 285–308.

Doka, K. J. (Ed.). (1996). Commentary. *In Living with grief after sudden loss: Suicide, homicide, accident, heart attack, stroke* (pp. 11–15). Bristol, PA: Taylor & Francis.

Doka, K. J. (2005). Ethics, end-of-life decisions and grief. *Mortality, 10*(1), 83–90.

Doka, K. J. (2008). Disenfranchised grief in historical and cultural perspective. In M. S. Stroebe, R. O. Hansson, H. Schut, & W. Stroebe (Eds.), *Handbook of bereavement research and practice* (pp. 223–240). Washington, DC: American Psychological Association.

Doka, K. J., & Martin, T. (2001). Take it like a man: Masculine response to loss. In D. A. Lund (Ed.), *Men coping with grief* (pp. 37–47). Amityville, NY: Baywood.

Elwert, F., & Christakis, N. (2006). Widowhood and race. *American Sociological Review, 71*, 16–41.

Figley, C. R. (2007). An introduction to the special issue on the MHAT-IV. *Traumatology, 13*, 4–5.

Freud, S. (1917/1957). Mourning and melancholies. In J. Strachey (Ed. and Trans.), *The standard edition of the complete psychological works of Sigmund Freud* (Vol. 14, pp. 243–258). London: Hogarth Press.

Gibson, D. M. (2007). The relationship of infertility and death: Using the relational/cultural model of counseling in making meaning. *The Humanistic Psychologist, 35*, 275–289.

Gilbert, K. R. (1996). "We've had the same loss, why don't we have the same grief?" Loss and differential grief in families. *Death Studies, 20*, 269–283.

Hall, M., & Irwin, M. (2001). Physiological indices of functioning in bereavement. In M. S. Stroebe, R. O. Hansson, W. Stroebe, & H. Schut (Eds.), *Handbook of bereavement research: Consequences, coping, and care* (pp. 473–492). Washington, DC: American Psychological Association.

Harvey, J. H., Carlson, H. R., Huff, T. M., & Green, M. A. (2001). Embracing their memory: The construction of accounts of loss and hope. In R. A. Neimeyer (Ed.), *Meaning reconstruction and the experience of loss* (pp. 231–243). Washington, DC: American Psychological Association.

Hays, J. C., & Hendrix, C. C. (2008). The role of religion in bereavement. In M. S. Stroebe, R. O. Hansson, H. Schut, & W. Stroebe (Eds.), *Handbook of bereavement research and practice* (pp. 327–348). Washington, DC: American Psychological Association.

Ironson, G., Wynings, C., Schneiderman, N., Baum, A., Rodriguez, M., Greenwood, D., Benight, C., Antoni, M., LaPerriere, A., Huang, H. S., Klimas, N., & Fletcher, M. A. (1997). Posttraumatic stress symptoms, intrusive thoughts, loss, and immune function after Hurricane Andrew. *Psychosomatic Medicine, 59*, 128–141.

Jackson, D. (1965). The study of the family. *Family Process, 4*, 1–20.

Janoff-Bulman, R. (1992). *Shattered assumptions: Towards a new psychology of trauma.* New York: Free Press.

Jones, D., Harvey, J., Giza, D., Rodican, C., Barreira, P. J., & Macias, C. (2003). Parental death in the lives of people with serious mental illness. *Journal of Loss and Trauma, 8*, 307–322.

Kamienski, M. C. (2004). Family-centered care in ED. *American Journal of Nursing, 104*, 59–62.

Klass, D. (2001). The inner representation of the dead child in the psychic and social narratives of bereaved parents. In R. A. Neimeyer (Ed.), *Meaning reconstruction and the experience of loss* (pp. 77–94). Washington, DC: American Psychological Association.

Kübler-Ross, E. (1969). *On death and dying.* New York: Macmillan.

Kung, H.-C., Hoyert, D. L., Xu, J., & Murphy, S. L. (2008). Deaths: Final data for 2005. *National Vital Statistics Reports, 56*(10). Hyattsville. MD: National Center for Health Statistics.

Laurie, A., & Neimeyer, R. A. (2008). African Americans in bereavement: Grief as a function of ethnicity. *Omega, 57,* 173–193.

Lee, E.-K. O., Shen, C., & Tran, T. V. (2009). Coping with Hurricane Katrina: Psychological distress and resilience among African American evacuees. *Journal of Black Psychology, 35,* 5–23.

Lerner, M. (1980). When, why, and where people die. In E. S. Schneidman (Ed.), *Death: Current perspectives* (pp. 87–106). Palo Alto, CA: Mayfield.

Lindemann, E. (1944). Symptomology and management of acute grief. *American Journal of Psychiatry, 101,* 141–148.

Lohan, J. A., & Murphy, S. A. (2002). Parents' perceptions of adolescent sibling grief responses after an adolescent or young adult child's sudden, violent death. *Omega, 44,* 77–95.

Maciejewski, P. K., Zhang, B., Block, S. D., & Prigerson, H. G. (2007). An empirical examination of the stage theory of grief. *Journal of the American Medical Association, 297*(7), 716–723.

McGoldrick, M., Almeida, R., Hines, P. M., Garcia-Preto, N., Rosen, E., & Lee, E. (1991). Mourning in different cultures. In F. Walsh & M. McGoldrick (Eds.), *Living beyond loss* (pp. 176–206). New York: Norton.

Meij, L. W., Stroebe, M., Schut, H., Stroebe, W., van den Bout, J., van der Heijden, P. G. M., & Dijkstra, I. (2007). Patterns of attachment and parents' adjustment to the death of their child. *Personality and Social Psychology Bulletin, 33,* 537–548.

Melhem, N. M., Moritz, G., Walker, M., Shear, M. K., & Brent, D. (2007). Phenomenology and correlates of complicated grief in children and adolescents. *Journal of the American Academy of Child and Adolescent Psychiatry, 46,* 493–499.

Mick, K. A., Medvene, L. J., & Strunk, J. H. (2003). Surrogate decision making at end of life: Sources of burden and relief. *Journal of Loss and Trauma, 8,* 149–167.

Mikulincer, M., & Shaver, P. R. (2008). An attachment perspective on bereavement. In M. S. Stroebe, R. O. Hansson, H. Schut, & W. Stroebe (Eds.), *Handbook of bereavement research and practice* (pp. 87–112). Washington, DC: American Psychological Association.

Monahan, K. (2003). Death of an abuser: Does the memory linger on? *Death Studies, 27,* 641–651.

Moss, M. S., Moss, S. Z., & Hansson, R. O. (2001). Bereavement and old age. In M. S. Stroebe, R. O. Hansson, W. Stroebe, & H. Schut (Eds.), *Handbook of bereavement research: Consequences, coping, and care* (pp. 241–260). Washington, DC: American Psychological Association.

Murphy, S. A. (2008). The loss of a child: Sudden death and extended illness perspectives. In M. S. Stroebe, R. O. Hansson, H. Schut, & W. Stroebe (Eds.), *Handbook of bereavement research and practice* (pp. 375–395). Washington, DC: American Psychological Association.

Murray, C. I., & Gilbert, K. R. (1997, June). *British and U.S. reporting of the Dunblane school massacre.* Paper presented at the meeting of the 5th

International Conference on Grief and Bereavement in Contemporary Society/Association for Death Education and Counseling. Washington, DC.

Murray, J. A. (2001). Loss as a universal concept: A review of the literature to identify common aspects of loss in diverse situations. *Journal of Loss and Trauma, 6*, 219–241.

Nadeau, J. W. (2008). Meaning-making in bereaved families: Assessment, intervention, and future research. In M. S. Stroebe, R. O. Hansson, H. Schut, & W. Stroebe (Eds.), *Handbook of bereavement research and practice* (pp. 511–530). Washington, DC: American Psychological Association.

Packman, W., Horsley, H., & Davies, B. (2006). Sibling bereavement and continuing bonds. *Death Studies, 30,* 817–841.

Papa, A., Neria, Y., & Litz, B. (2008). Traumatic bereavement in war veterans. *Psychiatric Annals, 38,* 686–691.

Parkes, C. M. (2005). Special Issue: Complicated grief. *Omega, 52*(1).

Pennebaker, J. W., Zech, E., & Rime, B. (2001). Disclosing and sharing emotion: Psychological, social, and health consequences. In M. S. Stroebe, R. O. Hansson, W. Stroebe, & H. Schut (Eds.), *Handbook of bereavement research: Consequences, coping, and care* (pp. 517–543). Washington, DC: American Psychological Association.

Pyszcznski, T., Solomon, S., & Greenberg, J. (2003). *In the wake of September 11: The psychology of terror.* Washington, DC: American Psychological Association.

Rabow, M. W., Hauser, J. M., & Adams, J. (2004). Supporting family caregivers at the end of life: "They don't know what they don't know." *Journal of the American Medical Association, 291*(4), 483–491.

Rando, T. A. (1993). *Treatment of complicated mourning.* Champaign, IL: Research Press.

Rodger, M. L., Sherwood, P., O'Connor, M., & Leslie, G. (2006). Living beyond the unanticipated sudden death of a partner: A phenomenological study. *Omega, 54,* 107–133.

Rolland, J. S. (1994). *Families, illness, & disability: An integrative treatment model.* New York: Basic Books.

Rosaldo, R. (1989). *Culture and truth: The remaking of social analysis.* Boston: Beacon.

Rosenblatt, P. C. (2000). *Parent grief: Narratives of loss and relationship.* Philadelphia: Brunner/Mazel.

Rosenblatt, P. C. (2008). Recovery following bereavement: Metaphor, phenomenology, and culture. *Death Studies, 32,* 6–16.

Rubin, S. S., Malkinson, R., & Witztum, E. (2008). Clinical aspects of a DSM complicated grief diagnosis: Challenges, dilemmas, and opportunities. In M. S. Stroebe, R. O. Hansson, H. Schut, & W. Stroebe (Eds.), *Handbook of bereavement research and practice* (pp. 187–206). Washington, DC: American Psychological Association.

Schaefer, J. A., & Moos, R. H. (2001). Bereavement experiences and personal growth. In M. S. Stroebe, R. O. Hansson, W. Stroebe, & H. Schut (Eds.), *Handbook of bereavement research: Consequences, coping, and care* (pp. 145–167). Washington, DC: American Psychological Association.

Servaty-Sieb, H. L., & Hayslip, B. (2003). Post-loss adjustment and funeral perceptions of parentally bereaved adolescents and adults. *Omega, 46,* 251–261.

Shapiro, E. R. (2001). Grief in interpersonal perspective: Theories and their implications. In M. S. Stroebe, R. O. Hansson, W. Stroebe, & H. Schut (Eds.),

Handbook of bereavement research: Consequences, coping, and care (pp. 301–327). Washington, DC: American Psychological Association.

Silver, R. C., & Wortman, C. B. (2007). The stage theory of grief. *Journal of the American Medical Association* (Letters Section), *297*, 2692–2694.

Silverman, P. R., Baker, J., Cait, C. A., & Boerner, K. (2003). The effects of negative legacies on the adjustment of parentally bereaved children and adolescents. *Omega, 46*, 335–352.

Stroebe, M., Schut, H., & Stroebe, W. (2007, December). Health outcomes of bereavement. *Lancet, 370*, 1960–1973.

Stroebe, M. S., & Schut, H. (2001). Models of coping with bereavement: A review. In M. S. Stroebe, R. O. Hansson, W. Stroebe, & H. Schut (Eds.), *Handbook of bereavement research: Consequences, coping, and care* (pp. 375–403). Washington, DC: American Psychological Association.

Stroebe, M. S., van Son, M., Stroebe, W., Kleber, R., Schut, H., & van den Bout, J. (2000). On the classification and diagnosis of pathological grief. *Clinical Psychology Review, 20*, 57–75.

Stroebe, W., & Schut, H. (2001). Risk factors in bereavement outcome: A methodoloogical and empirical review. In M. S. Stroebe, R. O. Hansson, W. Stroebe, & H. Schut (Eds.), *Handbook of bereavement research: Consequences, coping, and care* (pp. 349–371). Washington, DC: American Psychological Association.

Tedeschi, R. G., & Calhoun, L. G. (2008). Beyond the concept of recovery: Growth and the experience of loss. *Death Studies, 32*, 27–39.

Traylor, E. S., Hayslip, B., Kaminski, P. L., & York, C. (2003). Relationships between grief and family system characteristics: A cross lagged longitudinal analysis. *Death Studies, 27*, 575–601.

Walsh, F., & McGoldrick, M. (1991). Loss and the family: A systems perspective. In F. Walsh & M. McGoldrick (Eds.), *Living beyond loss* (pp. 1–29). New York: Norton.

Walter, T. (2008). The new public mourning. In M. S. Stroebe, R. O. Hansson, H. Schut, & W. Stroebe (Eds.), *Handbook of bereavement research and practice* (pp. 241–262). Washington, DC: American Psychological Association.

Watford, M. L. (2008). Bereavement of spousal suicide: A reflective self-exploration. *Qualitative Inquiry, 14*, 335–359.

Webb, N. B. (2004). The impact of traumatic stress and loss on children and families. In N. B. Webb (Ed.), *Mass trauma and violence: Helping families and children cope* (pp. 3–22). New York: Guilford.

Weiss, R. S. (2008). The nature and causes of grief. In M. S. Stroebe, R. O. Hansson, H. Schut, & W. Stroebe (Eds.), *Handbook of bereavement research and practice* (pp. 29–44). Washington, DC: American Psychological Association.

Wolchik, S. A., Coxe, S., Tein, J. Y., Sandler, I. N., & Ayers, T. S. (2008). Six-year longitudinal predictors of posttraumatic growth in parentally bereaved adolescents and young adults. *Omega, 58*, 107–128.

Worden, J. W., Davies, B., & McCown, D. (1999). Comparing parent loss with sibling loss. *Death Studies, 23*, 1–15.

Wortman, C. B., & Silver, R. C. (2001). The myths of coping with loss revisited. In M. S. Stroebe, R. O. Hansson, W. Stroebe, & H. Schut (Eds.), *Handbook of bereavement research: Consequences, coping, and care* (pp. 405–429). Washington, DC: American Psychological Association.

Znoj, H. J., & Keller, D. (2002). Mourning parents: Considering safeguards and their relation to health. *Death Studies, 26*, 545–565.

5 Illness and Family Stress

Jeremy B. Yorgason

During recent years, health in the United States has improved in many ways due to increased longevity; a decline in mortality from heart disease, stroke, and cancer; and a continued decline in infant mortality (National Center for Health Statistics, 2007). At the same time, illness is taking a major toll on families and societies. In 2005, for example, $249 billion was paid out of pocket by Americans for medical expenses that included costs for physician visits, hospital bills, and nursing home care (National Center for Health Statistics, 2007). Similar to other stressors addressed in this book, illness typically occurs within the context of family systems, where family members are seen as mutually influential. Therefore, in this chapter, characteristics of illnesses will be addressed, a theoretical model for examining illness stressors and family resilience will be presented, and using this model, research findings relating to three situations, including childhood illness, illness in marriage, and illness of aging parents, will be discussed.

Illness Characteristics

Illness as a stressor is comprised of several characteristics that interact in complex ways. These factors often include (a) type of illness, (b) amount of time since diagnosis or illness phase, (c) life course timing of illness onset, (d) illness intensity, (e) illness severity and threat, (f) illness uncertainty, and (g) projected duration of the illness (see Burman & Margolin, 1992; Rolland, 1994). To consider these characteristics, many studies on illness and families are carried out with small samples that are recruited with particular characteristics in mind, such as having a specific illness (which helps to control for illness intensity, threat, and projected duration to some degree). Other studies recruit through medical arenas, allowing some uniformity in time since diagnosis (e.g., couples seeking treatment as a result of a diagnosis of cancer). Larger-scale studies provide the benefit of tracking changes in health and family relationships across multiple years, with samples that generalize to larger populations. This chapter will include findings from both small- and larger-scale studies, drawing upon the strengths of each approach.

Theoretical Framework

A broad range of theoretical frameworks has been applied to families and health. The majority of these include aspects of family stress theory (e.g., McCubbin & Patterson, 1982) or more recently, a family resilience framework (Walsh, 1998). In this chapter, a combination of McCubbin and Patterson's double ABC-X model (1982), Walsh's family resilience model (1998), and Karney and Bradbury's vulnerability-stress-adaptation model (1995) are presented. A representation integrating these approaches is shown in Figure 5.1.

Health stressors (Figure 5.1) are linked to *individual and family outcomes* through *adaptive processes*. Health stressors are sometimes due to chance (e.g., brain injury resulting from a car accident) and are sometimes caused or influenced by stable characteristics or behaviors called *enduring vulnerabilities* or *enduring characteristics* (e.g., poor eating habits, lack of exercise, and genetic predisposition leading to type 2 diabetes). Health stressors and individual and family outcomes are also moderated by both positive and negative enduring characteristics. For example, when someone with the enduring vulnerability of depression experiences a physical health stressor (such as chronic back pain), the adaptive processes of the family can be different than

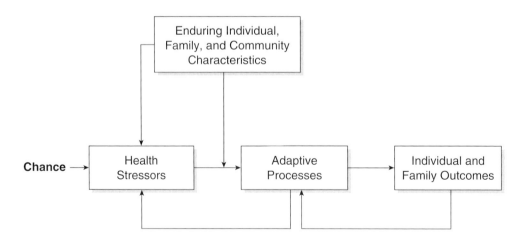

Figure 5.1   Theoretical Model of Illness and Families Integrating Aspects of the Double ABC-X Model, Family Resilience, and the Vulnerability-Stress-Adaptation Model

NOTE: Model adapted from Karney and Bradbury (1995). *Enduring characteristics* are also called *risk factors* and *protective factors* in the resilience literature and *family demands* and *family capabilities* in the family stress literature (see Patterson, 2002).

if the person is not suffering from depression. Adaptive processes include family members' perceptions of the health stressors as well as their use of resources and the implementation of coping activities. The link between health stressors and individual and family outcomes is also mediated by the adaptive processes that families undergo as they respond to stressors; that is, the ways that families adapt to health stressors determine individual and family outcomes to a greater extent than the actual stressors. For example, marital outcomes when a wife has cancer depend on the effectiveness of coping behaviors, perceptions of prognosis, and knowledge about the illness, rather than the sole fact of being diagnosed with cancer. In the model, circular patterns are shown where adaptive processes feed back into stressors, and where individual and family outcomes feed back into adaptive processes. For example, if a wife who is diagnosed with cancer communicates openly with her husband, receives support from him, and works together with him against the illness (positive adaptive processes), additional stressors will likely be managed. In contrast, if couples communicate poorly, are not supportive, and live separate lives (poor adaptive processes), additional stressors are more likely to pile up for the couple.

Resilience can be identified in various parts of the model (Patterson, 2002). First, resilience could be examined by exploring enduring characteristics that lead to more positive family relationships and/or health outcomes. For example, cohesion may help families to adapt more successfully to certain stressors. In this way, enduring characteristics are identified as risk factors and protective factors. Second, resilience could be identified in successful adaptive processes including an individual's or family's optimistic perceptions, helpful coping activities, and new resources that assist with family coping. Resilience could also be assessed by exploring various physical, psychological, and family relationship outcomes. As suggested by Coleman and Ganong (2002), however, resilience may be present in some individuals or in some family relationships but not in others. As a result, resilience does not necessarily include all family members.

When a Child Is Ill

Six months after being diagnosed with cancer, Katie, age 7, is doing fairly well. She has endured weeks and months of medical tests, cancer treatments (including radiation, chemotherapy, and bone marrow transplants), and moving back and forth from the hospital to home. Katie's father is with her and the family as much as possible since the diagnosis, but continues working to keep the bills paid and the insurance coverage in place. Katie's mother is also with her as much as possible, while still caring for their other three children. The best family times are during those weeks that Katie is able to be at home. Despite the challenges the cancer presents, the family is working together and is more united than before. The doctors and nurses are supportive and caring; at times, it seems they are part of the family. Friends, neighbors, people from church, and extended family are also supportive, helping to care for the children, bringing in meals, and sending letters, cards, and gifts. Although the outcome of the cancer is ambiguous, Katie and her family continue fighting, one day at a time.

This vignette provides an example of a life-threatening and possibly disabling childhood illness that requires intense treatment across several months. The 2005 National Health Interview Survey found that approximately 8% of children between the ages of 5 and 17 have some functional limitation resulting from a chronic illness (Federal Interagency Forum on Child and Family Statistics, 2008) with 2% of these children being unable to walk or care for themselves. These percentages may seem small, but with more than 72 million children under the age of 18 in the United States in 2000 (Meyer, 2001), they suggest a substantial number of affected children and families.

Health Stressors

Childhood illness can present various individual and family stressors (for a review, see Cohen, 1999) that are sometimes unique to specific types of illnesses. To date, most studies have focused on specific illnesses, thereby providing details about illness characteristics including onset, duration, and ways that a particular illness can impact families. Illnesses that have been the focus of research include general health problems/chronic illness, asthma, cancer, cerebral palsy, cystic fibrosis, diabetes, Down syndrome, and Rett syndrome. More recent efforts to understand the overall impact of childhood illnesses on families have used a "noncategorical" approach wherein stressors from a variety of illnesses reveal similar strains on families (see Berge & Holm, 2007; Gartstein, Short, Vannatta, & Noll, 1999). This approach acknowledges differences, yet also emphasizes that there may be more similarities than differences involved.

Children with a chronic illness often encounter emotional, behavioral, and school-related problems (Silver, Westbrook, & Stein, 1998). In a study of children with diabetes, for example, Jutras et al. (2003) found that ill children were more likely to report concerns about school performance and the presence of health symptoms than their mothers and siblings. In comparison, siblings of children with a chronic illness may experience unique stressors including feelings of differential treatment resulting from an imbalance in time and attention from parents (Quittner & Opipari, 1994). Sharpe and Rossiter (2002) suggest that illnesses that require daily management regimes put healthy siblings at greater risk than illnesses not requiring daily care. While it might be assumed that such health stressors would drive a wedge between siblings, Sharpe and Rossiter (2002) propose that sibling relationships paradoxically grow closer with illness, resulting in compassion and companionship.

Parents with a child who is chronically ill face stressors that are more intensive and pervasive than typical parental strains (Cohen, 1999). For example, research on families with a medically fragile child in the home indicates that parents experience numerous psychological stressors (Patterson, Leonard, &

Titus, 1992) including dealing with insurance and employer conflicts, being isolated from peer and social networks, grieving losses due to illness, making difficult medical decisions, and communicating with the ill child about the illness (Murray, Kelly-Soderholm, & Murray, 2007). In many cases, the compounded strains are so severe that parents experience symptoms common to post-traumatic stress (e.g., Manne, DuHamel, Gallelli, Sorgen, & Redd, 1998). Mothers and fathers may also experience different stressors depending on the roles they carry out in the family. For instance, mothers are generally more involved in the daily care of the child and in interactions with medical professionals, while fathers focus more on finances and their emotional closeness to the child (Cohen, 1999). Single parents face additional strain as they are often left to attend to each of these roles without the help of another adult.

In summary, families face multiple stressors resulting from childhood illness that have the potential to put all family members at risk, both physically and psychologically. Although illness conditions are important in determining the degree of stress experienced, risk and protective factors, resources, perceptions, and family processes are generally more indicative of individual and family outcomes (Cohen, 1999; McCubbin, Thompson, & McCubbin, 1996).

Enduring Characteristics

Characteristics of families that protect them from the stressors of illness include age, race, gender, socioeconomic status (SES), and structure. Studies indicate that the risk of children having a chronic illness increases with age and is higher for African Americans, boys, and in families with an income below the poverty level (Newacheck & Halfon, 1998). Furthermore, Newacheck and Halfon (1998) suggest that family structure (e.g., single-parent homes) is also predictive of increased risk, although this risk may simply be indicative of lower incomes.

Although age, race, and gender do not always moderate the link between illness and adaptive processes, SES, family structure, and parenting styles may. Lower SES is predictive of higher morbidity, higher percentage of income spent on health care, lower rates of insurance coverage, and higher rates of people not seeking medical care (National Center for Health Statistics, 2007). For example, when a child has asthma, lower family SES has been linked to having problems accessing health care services, lower parental understanding of the illness, less influence over environmental factors that may exacerbate an illness, and greater challenges in meeting family needs (Mansour, Lanphear, & DeWitt, 2000). In addition, having only one parent available to provide physical and emotional care as well as financial support may present increased risks for poorer outcomes. Parenting styles and parent–child interactions may also influence adaptive processes. In a study of children with diabetes, Roper and colleagues (in press) explore how parenting styles are linked with metabolic control (an indicator of healthy diabetes control). Results indicate that mothers' exhibiting an authoritative style of parenting is linked to better disease management practices and metabolic control. In the same study, fathers' and mothers' permissive parenting is correlated with poorer metabolic control.

Adaptive Processes

Adaptive processes among parents and siblings are a major focus of the literature surrounding children's health and can be discussed in terms of coping behaviors, perceptions, and resources. Regarding coping behaviors, family actions can be related to various health, mental health, and relationship outcomes. On the negative side, maternal depression and negative parenting, as well as family conflict, have been linked to dysfunctional child and adult emotional and health outcomes (Cohen, 1999; Lim, Wood, & Miller, 2008; Svavarsdottir & Rayens, 2005). In contrast, a strong indicator of positive outcomes is "balanced coping" (Cohen, 1999; Paterson, 1991). This occurs when illness demands are kept in perspective with other family needs. Balanced coping by parents becomes especially important in attending to the needs of both the ill child and healthy siblings. Other healthy family adaptive processes include (a) reorganizing and accessing resources as a family, (b) engaging in active coping strategies (such as seeking knowledge about the condition), (c) collaborating with medical professionals, (d) maintaining a positive outlook on life and hope for the future, and (e) providing emotional protection to the ill child (Kars, Duijnstee, Pool, van Delden, & Grypdonck, 2008; McCubbin, Balling, Possin, Frierdich, & Bryne, 2002; Mednick et al., 2007). Sometimes adaptive processes that were helpful to families at one time become less helpful over time. In the case of illness in infants or small children, it is best if parents ensure that children receive treatments as scheduled. However, as children move into adolescence, parental control may be less effective.

Illness Perceptions

Perceptions of childhood health stressors account for the link between illness and family resilience. However, perceptions likely differ over time and among family members (Cohen, 1999; Patterson, 1993; Patterson & Garwick, 1994). Families' views of stressors resulting from childhood illnesses likely evolve across diagnosis, treatment, and management phases. Symptoms, diagnoses, and prognoses are often ambiguous, leaving families to deal with the unknown (see Berge & Holm, 2007; O'Brien, 2007; Roper & Jackson, 2007). Garwick and colleagues (1999) indicate that shortly after diagnosis, many families ask the question of "why" the illness occurred. They report that most family members find some explanation for the childhood illness (e.g., biomedical cause, environmental cause, and so forth), but with time many stop asking why the illness happened and focus more on the needs of the child.

After an initial response to childhood illness, family perceptions may begin to diverge and be focused on particular roles. For example, Jutras and colleagues (2003) found that parents were focused on their roles as caregivers and teachers to their children, while ill children were more often concerned about school performance and health symptoms. In comparison, siblings tend to focus on relationships with their parents and the ill child. Although parent, child, and sibling perceptions were focused on different role-related experiences, they were all related to some aspect of wellness (Jutras et al., 2003). Additional research suggests that although mothers and fathers express similar perceptions about caring for their child, their coping responses differ (Copeland & Clements, 1993). Thus, a common family or parental goal of wellness may be more important than shared perceptions and coping strategies.

Resources

A number of family resources have been linked to positive outcomes when childhood illness occurs. Some resources are specific to family functioning, such as maintaining clear boundaries; communicating effectively; being flexible with rules, roles, and expectations; being committed to the family; maintaining a healthy marriage relationship; and maintaining family rituals and routines (Kars et al., 2008; Lee et al., 2004; Patterson, 1991; Retzlaff, 2007). These family resources provide stability for families during times of crisis, ambiguity, and change. Other resources consist of networks outside the family, such as integration in a social system and having social support from family, friends, religious groups, the workplace, and community agencies (Lee et al., 2004; McCubbin et al., 2002; Retzlaff, 2007). These resources translate into help with transportation, child care, tangible resources such as food and financial assistance, emotional support, spiritual support, and workplace flexibility with hours and responsibilities.

Outcomes

Typical outcomes examined in studies of childhood illness include individual (child, parent, sibling) psychological distress, health changes for better or worse in the ill child, and individual child and family functioning (Patterson, 1991). For example, Lim et al. (2008) examined the effect of maternal depression on parenting practices, which predicted higher child internalizing symptoms, followed by increased child asthma disease activity. Other studies have examined outcomes such as increasing chances for survival (Kars et al., 2008), diabetes metabolic control (Stoker et al., under review), and individual functioning (McCubbin et al., 2002). In contrast to individual outcomes, family functioning is more often viewed as part of the adaptive processes that feed into individual outcomes. As seen in Figure 1, outcomes feed back into adaptive processes and, therefore, influence future family functioning. For example, in a study of children with cystic fibrosis, Patterson, Budd, Goetz, and Warwick (1993) found that family processes such as balanced coping, focusing on personal growth, and treatment compliance were predictive of lung health across a 10-year period. These researchers acknowledged that family processes influenced health, and that the health of the child also influenced future family functioning. In other words, these processes operate in a bidirectional nature.

When Spouses Are Ill

After 16 years of marriage, John was diagnosed with multiple sclerosis. Both he and his wife, Janet, are in their 40s and had previously been married and divorced. The diagnosis was a shock to the couple, for they had hoped that his recent health problems were something that could be cured. Shortly after diagnosis, adjusting to symptoms, treatments, and new routines was not too disruptive, as work, family, and other activities continued. However, both John and Janet knew that things would eventually get worse. Janet was committed to their marriage and felt she could deal with doing a little more around the house because she wanted to support John. Perhaps the most difficult thing for Janet was the ambiguity regarding their financial future. She was constantly haunted by her concern regarding the adequacy of her income to pay the bills if or when John had to stop working. Each time John complained about his illness or asked for her help, it would remind her of the challenges they faced. This was not what she had planned for their marriage.

This vignette illustrates the challenges that can result from an off-time illness that is chronic and worsens over time. Studies examining the impact of a general decline in health indicate a minor yet significant decrease in marital quality (Badr & Acitelli, 2005; Booth & Johnson, 1994). In addition, studies investigating the impact of specific health problems report similar findings; however, results present a complex picture of illness and marriage. A variety of specific illnesses have been studied in relation to marital relationships. Some examples include arthritis (e.g., Martire et al., 2006), cancer (e.g., Norton & Manne, 2007), dementia (e.g., Daniels, Lamson, & Hodgson, 2007), diabetes (e.g., Sandberg, Trief, Greenberg, Graff, & Weinstock, 2006), hearing loss (e.g., Yorgason, Piercy, & Piercy, 2007), heart problems (e.g., Coyne et al., 2001), infertility (Peterson et al., 2006), and osteoporosis (Roberto, Gold, & Yorgason, 2004).

Health Stressors

A growing body of literature examines the impact of illness within couple relationships (see reviews by Berg & Upchurch, 2007; Burman & Margolin,

1992) and, in general, finds that the amount of stress varies by type of illness. For example, hearing loss can result in difficulty in communication between spouses (see Yorgason et al., 2007), yet being diagnosed with cancer (see Norton & Manne, 2007) can present a greater life threat along with stress-laden treatments.

Timing of illness onset can influence the amount of stress experienced by a couple. First, if illness onset is somewhat expected, such as in later life or where a clear pattern of family history provided forewarning, couples may adjust better than if it is completely unexpected. Researchers have focused on stress at various points in the illness process (i.e., diagnosis, treatment, management), for example, illness onset prior to the time of diagnosis (see Peyrot, McMurry, & Hedges, 1988) versus directly after diagnosis (see Northouse, Templin, Mood, & Oberst, 1998). Although the stress associated with an illness can be difficult for a couple, illness can also have a positive influence on marital quality. Yorgason, Booth, and Johnson (2008) found that a health decline was related to a *decrease* in marital quality, yet the onset of a disability was related to an *increase* in marital quality. The authors' interpretation of this finding is that a decline in self-rated health likely represents initial changes in health, while the onset of a disability may represent health declines that occur well after health problems have been in process, allowing time for couples to adapt. Similar to this finding, Peyrot and colleagues (1988) indicate that some couples report being emotionally closer due to confronting diabetes together. For these reasons, it is important to consider illness conditions when interpreting findings.

Enduring Characteristics

Age at illness onset is an important moderator of the link between illness stress and adaptive processes. The moderating effect of age is first recognized in studies of couples dealing with illness during mid- and later life (Berg & Upchurch, 2007). In a comparison of 24- through 76-year-olds, Yorgason and colleagues (2008) report that a decline in general health is more strongly related to a decline in marital happiness for young and midlife adults than for older adults. Although some aspects of marital quality were impacted by health in the older group, the effects were weaker and less consistent. This is not surprising given that many health problems are age related and therefore more commonly experienced in later life.

Whether the spouse is ill versus well and female versus male are also important enduring characteristics. Several studies indicate that marital quality is at greater risk for healthy spouses than for ill spouses (Burman & Margolin, 1992). For example, Booth and Johnson (1994) found that spousal declines in health were related to lower marital happiness for the "well" spouse across a 3-year period, and Carter and Carter (1994) reported that "well" spouses perceived that illness had a greater impact on the marital relationship. The effect of being the ill versus well spouse is further compounded by gender, with couples where husbands are ill and the wives are well reporting the greatest amount of distress. For example, in a study of congestive heart failure, Rohrbaugh et al. (2002) found that well female spouses were more distressed than well male spouses. One reason why this trend exists might include financial strain due to the husbands' illness, which could result in a decrease in income. Exceptions to this trend include cases where a serious physical impairment resulted in the well spouse being less concerned about equity in the relationship (see Kuijer et al., 2002) and among couples reporting high marital quality, in which case distress was lower for both males and females (Rohrbaugh et al., 2002). High marital quality prior to the onset of illness may be an enduring characteristic that can buffer the impact of illness-related stress. However, few studies have measured marital quality prior to illness onset; therefore, this characteristic is most often observed within the adaptive process that couples make in response to an illness.

Additional enduring characteristics that can moderate the link between illness and adaptive processes include socioeconomic status (SES), religiosity, and social support. Socioeconomic status, as measured by income, access to health care, and education, often results in resources that lead to more adaptive processes. Alternatively, poverty is a risk factor for many illnesses and often presents barriers to optimal health care, sometimes requiring a greater percentage of one's income to be spent on health care expenses (National Center for Health Statistics, 2007). Religiosity, including beliefs in divine help and social resources linked with religious participation, and social support, in addition to spousal support, have also been established as important stress buffers (Penninx et al., 1997; Schaie, Krause, & Booth, 2004)).

Adaptive Processes and Outcomes

Adaptive processes that mediate the link between illness stressors and outcomes include illness mechanisms, illness-prompted resources, and couple coping and caregiving processes. Illness mechanisms, defined as life changes due to an illness, sometimes account for why illness is disruptive to families. Booth and Johnson (1994) reported that a decrease in finances, division of household labor, and marital problems account for some of the negative effects a health decline can have on marital happiness. Yorgason et al. (2008) also found that psychological distress was a consistent mediator between health decline and marital happiness.

Stress-prompted resources, defined as resources that emerge as a result of an illness, can also influence couple relationships and influence couple interactions. In the case of diabetes, illness-prompted resources might include patient and spousal knowledge about the disease including how to manage it (Trief et al., 2003). On the other hand, meal planning and preparation, grocery shopping, having a shared diet plan, and the monitoring of blood sugar levels all require knowledge of the illness and could bring a couple closer together. In cases of hearing loss, devices such as hearing aids, telephones with volume-adjustment ringers and handsets, and sound receivers at concerts, plays, church, and other venues can lead to better couple communication and the enjoyment of joint pleasures (Yorgason et al., 2007). In cases of life-threatening illnesses such as cancer, medical professionals can provide knowledge that can provide hope for recovery (Hatchett, Friend, Symister, & Wadhwa, 1997), and spirituality can be used as a coping resource that strengthens marriage (Ka'opua, Gotay, & Boehm, 2007).

Regarding couple adaptive processes, communication between spouses is paramount. Poor communication patterns, as illustrated by protective buffering (i.e., hiding negative feelings about the illness to avoid hurting the other spouse), can have negative consequences, such as lower life satisfaction and higher levels of depression and anxiety. In a study of women with breast cancer, Manne and colleagues (2007) reported that husbands who used protective buffering were more distressed over time. Furthermore, the negative effects of protective buffering were stronger when patients (as opposed to "well" spouses) concealed feelings, and when those feelings were concealed among couples in more (as opposed to less) satisfied relationships. Another negative communication pattern that has been linked to negative outcomes can be found in ambivalence over emotional expressiveness (Tucker, Winelman, Katz, & Bermas, 1999). Examples of ambivalence include wanting to express certain emotions but not doing so, not wanting to express certain emotions but doing so, and expressing emotions and then regretting having done so. Although protective buffering is less helpful, couples may find themselves in situations where ambivalence about how to communicate about an illness complicates their situation.

In comparison, good couple communication can facilitate positive outcomes. For example, when one spouse is enduring painful arthritis, better outcomes result when the other spouse is aware of the level of pain being experienced by their partner. Specifically, Martire and colleagues (2006) report that spouses with an accurate perception of their partner's pain respond with less anger and irritation and give more helpful support. Similarly, Schulz, Ready, Beach, Rudy, and Starz (2006) indicate that agreement in reported levels of pain by spouses is related to less pain and better functioning. Good communication may also include talking about the marital relationship in order to facilitate couple adjustment to a chronic illness (Badr & Acitelli, 2005). Thus, open communication about the specifics of an illness and about the marital relationship in general may result in better couple relations.

The caregiving practices couples demonstrate can represent some of the most important adaptive processes to illness. It is common that when an individual is ill, a spouse is called on to provide at least some care. It is important for the caregiver to balance caring behavior while allowing autonomy in the recipient. For example, gaining knowledge about an illness in order to provide support to an ill spouse can be done in a controlling or supportive way (Peyrot et al., 1988). Revenson, Schiaffino, Majerovitz, and Gibofsky (1991) describe this continuum of supportive behavior as the double-edged sword of social support. They report that positive support predicts lower depression, and problematic support predicts higher depression among rheumatoid arthritis patients. Trief and colleagues (2003) suggest that there is a fine line between a helpful reminder of health treatments for diabetes and nagging or pushing a partner to pursue treatment. Also, Kuijer et al. (2000) recommend an appropriate balance where the patient copes well on their own and the spouse provides support of that coping.

In summary, illness can pose significant strains on marriages. Age, gender, SES, marital quality, and social support are moderators of this relationship, while mediators can include illness mechanisms, stress-prompted resources, and couple coping and caregiving processes. In addition, maintaining inter-dependence within the couple relationship appears beneficial as long as the healthy spouse is supportive but not overprotective.

When Aging Parents Are Ill

Diane has been a support to her mother, Thelma, from the time that her father died. In the past few years, however, Thelma has had trouble organizing her bills, remembering if she had taken her medications, and had gotten lost while driving home from the supermarket. Diane's frustrations led her to seek medical advice regarding her mother's situation. Although the doctors weren't 100% sure, they thought Thelma might be developing Alzheimer's disease (which causes deterioration in mental capacity and ultimately results in death). After receiving this probable diagnosis, Diane decided to have her mother live with her and her husband, Greg. This arrangement is providing some relief since they know Thelma is being cared for. However, at the same time, Diane and Greg now have very little time for each other without Thelma being present. To help with the caregiving, Diane takes Thelma to an adult day care three days a week. In addition, Diane now attends a support group for caregivers of persons with Alzheimer's. She finds the respite provided by the adult day care to be a great help, and the support group provides disease information and knowledge of other available community supports. Even though Diane knows Thelma's health will continue to deteriorate, she is beginning to feel equipped to keep Thelma in her home, at least for the present time.

In 2000, it was estimated that 4.5 million people in the United States are living with Alzheimer's disease (Hebert, Scherr, Bienias, Bennett, & Evans, 2003). In addition to Alzheimer's disease, the prevalence of many chronic illnesses increases in later life, such as arthritis, heart disease, stroke, cancer, and diabetes, with approximately 30% of older adults reporting some difficulty performing activities necessary for daily living (Federal Interagency Forum on Aging-Related Statistics, 2008). Although many older adults live with one or more chronic conditions without receiving care from others, research indicates that adult children typically provide care when their parents begin to experience physical immobility, difficulty performing daily activities, and cognitive impairments that affect daily problem solving (Cicirelli, 2000).

Health Stressors

In an aging parent, chronic illness often results in functional impairment, cognitive impairment, and behavior problems (see Bédard, Pedlar, Martin, Malott, & Stones, 2000; Schultz, O'Brien, Bookwala, & Fleissner, 1995) and may be linked to pain, intense medical treatments, and consistent problems over extended periods of time. In the case of Diane's mother, cognitive impairments resulting from Alzheimer's disease eventually resulted in Thelma needing help getting dressed, using the bathroom, preparing meals, and eating. For children who provide care to their aging parents, caregiver strain can be viewed as resulting from the deteriorating health of the parent and the strain of increased care responsibilities. Strain on a caregiver may include overwhelming role demands (e.g., work plus the demands of caregiving), repeatedly dealing with health crises, financial strains, grieving the loss of a parent both physically and socially, and the changing nature of the caregiving role (Cicirelli, 2000; Ott, Sanders, & Kelber, 2007; Pinquart & Sorensen, 2003; Sanders, 2005).

The intensity of caregiver strain is influenced by several factors including a sudden versus expected caregiving role, whether caregiving is full-time or part-time, and length of the illness (Barnes, Given, & Given, 1992; Cicirelli, 2000; Lieberman & Fisher, 1995). Several studies indicate that greater strain is experienced by adult-child caregivers during the initial stages of caring for a parent (Barnes et al., 1992; Townsend, Noelker, Deimling, & Bass, 1989). In contrast, other studies show that the mental and physical health of the caregiver often declines over time due to the burden experienced (Lieberman & Fisher, 1995), suggesting the need to monitor strain throughout the duration of an illness.

Enduring Characteristics

Several factors moderate the link between stress resulting from caring for an ill parent and adaptive processes. Gender, for example, is an important factor because women are more likely to be caregivers. Pinquart and Sorensen (2006) reported that women "provided more caregiving hours, helped with more caregiving tasks, and assisted more with personal care" (p. 33). Furthermore, although male and female caregivers use similar levels of informal and formal support, female caregivers experience higher depression and more health problems because of a discrepancy in caregiving stressors and available supports.

In addition to gender, being married and having siblings influence caregiving of ill parents by adult children. When adult-child caregivers are married, they may receive support from their spouse (Ron 2006), and having a sibling can be either beneficial or detrimental. Having no siblings to help can result in carrying a greater caregiving burden (Barnes et al., 1992). When siblings are present, if they share in caregiving responsibilities, there are fewer negative outcomes (Li, Seltzer, & Greenberg, 1999), but if they do not participate in caring for an ill parent, feelings of resentment and abandonment are more likely (Barnes et al., 1992).

Ethnicity may also influence the likelihood of caregiving, associated stressors, and outcomes. In an analysis of 116 published studies examining ethnic influences in caregiving, Pinquart and Sorensen (2005) report that caregivers from diverse ethnic backgrounds provide more care than their Caucasian counterparts, and are more likely to be single, younger, and with lower SES. African American, but not Hispanic or Asian American, caregivers experience less caregiver burden, while all ethnic minority caregivers report poorer health than Caucasian caregivers. Perhaps due to greater informal support networks, African American caregivers appear more resilient to the negative psychological effects of caring for an ill parent (Haley, West, & Wadley, 1995).

Adaptive Processes

Adaptive processes that mediate the link between caring for an aging parent and the amount of stress experienced include perceptions, resources, and coping activities. From a stress and coping paradigm (Lazarus & Folkman, 1984), the adult-child caregiver's appraisal of the situation will influence outcomes; that is, perceptions of being an effective caregiver are associated with lower levels of depression (Townsend et al., 1989). Resources related to social support are strong indicators of resilience for caregivers and can be helpful by reducing stress, encouraging good health behaviors, and pursuing effective coping activities (Pinquart & Sorensen, 2007). For example, in a study of over 400 Israeli caregivers, extended-family support provided a significant buffer to caregiver burden (Ron, 2006).

In addition to perceptions and resources, family relationships may account for the effects of caregiver strain. For example, in a study of family caregivers for older persons with disabilities, lower-quality care recipient–caregiver relationships were predictive of feelings of role captivity and depression (Lawrence, Tennstedt, & Assman, 1998). In addition, Townsend and Franks (1995) reported that when ill parents had a cognitive impairment, the emotional closeness between the child and parent mediated the relationship between the impairment and feelings of stress as a caregiver. In other words, when the parent–child relationship is positive, caregiver stress is reduced. They also found that conflict between the aging parent and adult child resulted in greater caregiver stress, less effectiveness, and more depression.

Communication between an ill parent and an adult-child caregiver also appears to be an important adaptive process. In a study of satisfying and unsatisfying interactions between parents who had cancer and adult-child caregivers, Harzold and Sparks (2006) reported that communication about the diagnosis and treatment was satisfying to caregivers, whereas parents withholding information about their illness was viewed as unsatisfying. In addition, families sometimes used humor effectively to communicate about sensitive illness issues.

Outcomes

Adult children report both strains and gains as caregivers (Pinquart & Sorensen, 2003). Negative outcomes, including psychological distress, caregiver burden, and physical health, are the most commonly researched. For example, in a longitudinal study of mental health, caregivers experienced substantially higher rates of depression and anxiety than noncaregiving counterparts (Dura, Stukenberg, & Kiecolt-Glaser, 1991). These findings are important because psychological and physical health outcomes among caregivers are often closely intertwined. As indicated by Pinquart and Sorensen (2007), caregivers with higher psychological distress are likely to experience physical repercussions of that strain.

Gains related to being an adult-child caregiver include personal and spiritual growth, feelings of mastery of the caregiving situation, and closeness to the care recipient (e.g., Sanders, 2005). Although gains can represent positive outcomes among caregivers, they are often not observed in studies that use quantitative methods. Rather, qualitative studies that explore both positive and negative outcomes are more likely to tap into both dimensions of the caregiving experience.

In summary, caring for an ill parent involves stressors related to health limitations of the parent, as well as stressors experienced by the adult-child caregiver. Gender is an important contextual factor that influences many aspects of caregiving, including prevalence rates, amount of care, and strain experienced. Enduring protective factors include being married, sharing caregiving responsibilities with siblings, and some ethnic dimensions. More research is needed to explore specific cultural and ethnic mechanisms involved in caregiving. Successful caregiving experiences seem related to social support, relationship quality, and family communication. Prevention and intervention efforts can focus on helping adult-child caregivers balance the gains and strains of caregiving.

Discussion and Conclusion

Commonalities between childhood, spousal, and parental illness provide a sense of what factors are most salient for families dealing with a chronic illness. Despite the stress created by illness, many families facing illness are drawn closer together. Furthermore, research findings suggest that families can experience strains and gains simultaneously.

Enduring characteristics can significantly influence the extent and duration of illness stress and can be used as a target for intervention. Enduring characteristics that cannot be changed, such as gender, age, family structure, and ethnic background, often strongly influence the illness experience of all family members and should be considered when assisting families. For example, illness at any age is a challenge for families, although illness in later life may have less negative impact since it is more expected. Enduring characteristics that can be influenced, such as accessibility to health care, outside social support, and internal family interactions, also can be targeted by professionals as points of intervention. For instance, interacting in positive ways with the medical community and gaining knowledge about an illness can be important buffers to the stress associated with a specific illness. Finally, family patterns that are helpful when facing illness include effective family communication, "balanced" coping, family cohesion, and maintaining clear, yet flexible, boundaries.

Although perceptions of illness change with time, maintaining a positive outlook can be beneficial for individuals and families. This is not always easy, as diagnoses, treatment, and prognoses are often ambiguous. Furthermore, different family members may have differing perceptions of the illness that are related to the roles that each family member carries out (i.e., parent, ill child, sibling). Despite differences, research suggests that balanced coping (i.e., placing the illness in perspective of other aspects of life) is helpful to families. The outcomes of illness, regardless of which family member is ill, are nearly always related to psychological distress, indicating an important target for prevention and intervention.

Although a tremendous amount of research has been conducted in the areas reviewed in this chapter, there is much room for future study. Knowledge of illness and families could be enhanced by addressing methodological concerns, as well as bridging the medical and psychosocial research arenas. From a methodological perspective, the study of illness in families includes a rich blend of qualitative and quantitative studies, and future studies could focus on replicating findings using both approaches. Alternatively, mixed-methods approaches could be used to explore resilience processes in greater depth. Many of the outcomes studied in research to date involve negative measures including psychological and relationship distress; hence, more measures of positive family functioning are needed. Although a growing number of studies are exploring illness longitudinally, the reality is that the windows of data collection often provide only a snapshot of the illness. Future research is needed to understand prediagnosis predictors of resilience, as well as family relationship processes across the different phases of illness. In addition, few studies have examined everyday illnesses in families, such as colds, the flu, a broken limb, mononucleosis, running a temperature, and so forth. More research is also needed to understand similarities in the effects of chronic illnesses in childhood, in adulthood, and in later life. Although a theoretical foundation has been developed, more insight could be gained through basic research in this area. Finally, literature exploring illness and families crosses many disciplines including nursing, medicine, and the social sciences. The influence of medical professionals interacting with families is such an integral aspect of experiencing illness that multidisciplinary research teams would enhance both the medical and the social arenas.

Research exploring childhood illness, illness of a marriage partner, and caring for an ill parent has dramatically increased in recent decades. Findings indicate (a) an increasing knowledge of the stressors that individuals and families face, (b) the enduring characteristics that predispose families to experience illness and act as protective and risk factors once a chronic illness occurs, (c) adaptive processes families often use, (d) and positive and negative outcomes commonly experienced. Research that has been carried out provides a strong base for future work, yet further effort is needed to better understand illness experiences within families.

Additional Resources

Berg, C. A., & Upchurch, R. (2007). A development-contextual model of couples coping with chronic illness across the adult life span. *Psychological Bulletin, 133*, 920–954.

Cohen, M. S. (1999). Families coping with childhood chronic illness: A research review. *Families, Systems & Health, 17*, 149–164.

Morris, V. (2004). *How to care for aging parents.* New York: Workman Publishing.

Pinquart, M., & Sorensen, S. (2003). Associations of stressors and uplifts of caregiving with caregiver burden and depressive mood: A meta-analysis. *The Journals of Gerontology, 58B*, P112–P128.

Alzheimer's Association: www.alz.org

Alzheimers Online: http://alzonline.phhp.ufl.edu

American Cancer Society: www.cancer.org

American Diabetes Association: www.diabetes.org (Diabetes Action: http://www.diabetesaction.org/site/PageNavigator/Tips/tip)

Multiple Sclerosis Association of America: www.msassociation.org

National Center for Health Statistics: http://www.cdc.gov/nchs/

The Wellness Community: Cancer Support, Education, and Hope: http://thewellnesscommunity.org

References

Badr, H. & Acitelli, L. K. (2005). Dyadic adjustment in chronic illness: Does relationship talk matter? *Journal of Family Psychology, 19*, 465–469.

Barnes, C. L., Given, B. A., & Given, C. W. (1992). Caregivers of elderly relatives: Spouses and adult children. *Health & Social Work, 17*, 282–289.

Bédard, M., Pedlar, D., Martin, J. J., Malott, O., & Stones, M. J. (2000). Burden in caregivers of cognitively impaired older adults living in the community: Methodological issues and determinants. *International Psychogeriatrics, 12*, 307–332.

Berg, C. A., & Upchurch, R. (2007). A development-contextual model of couples coping with chronic illness across the adult life span. *Psychological Bulletin, 133,* 920–954.

Berge, J. M., & Holm, K. E. (2007). Boundary ambiguity in parents with chronically ill children: Integrating theory and research. *Family Relations, 56,* 123–134.

Booth, A., & Johnson, D. R. (1994). Declining health and marital quality. *Journal of Marriage and Family, 56,* 218–223.

Burman, B., & Margolin, G. (1992). Analysis of the association between marital relationships and health problems: An interactional perspective. *Psychological Bulletin, 112,* 39–63.

Carter, R. E., & Carter, C. A. (1994). Marital adjustment and effects of illness in married pairs with one or both spouses chronically ill. *The American Journal of Family Therapy, 22,* 315–326.

Cicirelli, V. G. (2000). An examination of the trajectory of the adult child's caregiving for an elderly parent. *Family Relations, 49,* 169–175.

Cohen, M. S. (1999). Families coping with childhood chronic illness: A research review. *Families, Systems & Health, 17,* 149–164.

Coleman, M., & Ganong, L. (2002). Resilience and families. *Family Relations, 51,* 101–102.

Copeland, L. G., & Clements, D. B. (1993). Parental perceptions and support strategies in caring for a child with a chronic condition. *Issues in Comprehensive Pediatric Nursing, 16,* 109–121.

Coyne, J. C., Rohrbaugh, M. J., Shoham, V., Sonnega, J. S., Nicklas, J. M., & Cranford, J. A. (2001). Prognostic importance of marital quality for survival of congestive heart failure. *The American Journal of Cardiology, 88,* 526–529.

Daniels, K. J., Lamson, A. L., & Hodgson, J. (2007). An exploration of the marital relationship and Alzheimer's disease: One couple's story. *Families, Systems, & Health, 25,* 162–177.

Dura, J. R., Stukenberg, K. W., & Kiecolt-Glaser, J. K. (1991). Anxiety and depressive disorders in adult children caring for demented parents. *Psychology and Aging, 6,* 467–473.

Federal Interagency Forum on Aging-Related Statistics. (2008). *Older Americans 2008: Key indicators of well-being.* Federal Interagency Forum on Aging-Related Statistics. Washington, DC: U.S. Government Printing Office.

Gartstein, M. A., Short, A. D., Vannatta, K., & Noll, R. B. (1999). Psycho-social adjustment of children with chronic illness: An evaluation of three models. *Journal of Developmental and Behavioral Pediatrics, 20,* 157–163.

Garwick, A. W., Kohrman, C. H., Titus, J. C., Wolman, C., & Blum, R. W. (1999). Variations in families' explanations of childhood chronic conditions: A cross-cultural perspective. In H. I. McCubbin & A. Thompson (Eds.), *The dynamics of resilient families* (pp. 165–202). Thousand Oaks, CA: Sage.

Haley, W. E., West, C. A., & Wadley, V. G. (1995). Psychological, social, and health impact of caregiving: A comparison of black and white dementia family caregivers and noncaregivers. *Psychology and Aging, 10,* 540–552.

Harzold, E., & Sparks, L. (2006). Adult child perceptions of communication and humor when the parent is diagnosed with cancer: A suggestive perspective from communication theory. *Qualitative Research Reports in Communication, 7,* 67–78.

Hatchett, L., Friend, R., Symister, P., & Wadhwa, N. (1997). Interpersonal expectations, social support, and adjustment to chronic illness. *Journal of Personality and Social Psychology, 73,* 560–573.

Hebert, L. E., Scherr, P. A., Bienias, J. L., Bennett, D. A., & Evans, D. A. (2003). Alzheimer disease in the US population: Prevalence estimates using the 2000 census. *Archives of Neurology, 60,* 1119–1122.

Jutras, S., Morin, P., Proulz, R., Vinay, M. C., Roy, E., & Routhier, L. (2003). Conceptions of wellness in families with a diabetic child. *Journal of Health Psychology, 8,* 573–586.

Ka'opua, L. S., Gotay, C. C., & Boehm, P. S. (2007). Spiritually based resources in adaption to long-term prostate cancer survival: Perspectives of elderly wives. *Health & Social Work, 32*(1), 29–39.

Karney, B. R., & Bradbury, T. N. (1995). The longitudinal course of marital quality and stability: A review of theory, method, and research. *Psychological Bulletin, 118,* 3–34.

Kars, M. C., Duijnstee, M. S. H., Pool, A., van Delden, J. J. M., & Grypdonck, M. H. F. (2008). Being there: Parenting the child with acute lymphoblastic leukemia. *Journal of Clinical Nursing, 17,* 1553–1562.

Kuijer, R. G., Buunk., B. P., Ybema, J. F., & Wobbes, T. (2002). The relation between perceived inequity, marital satisfaction and emotions among couples facing cancer. *British Journal of Social Psychology, 41,* 39–56.

Kuijer, R. G., Ybema, J. F., Buunk, B. P., Majella de Jong, G., Thijs-Boer, F., & Sanderman, R. (2000). Active engagement, protective buffering, and overprotection: Three ways of giving support by intimate partners of patients with cancer. *Journal of Social and Clinical Psychology, 19,* 256–275.

Lawrence, R. H., Tennstedt, S. L., & Assmann, S. F. (1998). Quality of the caregiver-care recipient relationship: Does it offset negative consequences of caregiving for family caregivers? *Psychology and Aging, 13,* 150–158.

Lazarus, R. S., & Folkman, S. (1984). *Stress, appraisal, and coping.* New York: Springer.

Lee, I., Lee, E., Kim, H. S., Park, Y. S., Song, M., & Park, Y. H. (2004). Concept development of family resilience: A study of Korean families with a chronically ill child. *Journal of Clinical Nursing, 13,* 636–645.

Li, L. W., Seltzer, M. M., & Greenberg, J. S. (1999). Change in depressive symptoms among daughter caregivers: An 18-month longitudinal study. *Psychology and Aging, 14,* 206–219.

Lieberman, M. A., & Fisher, L. (1995). The impact of chronic illness on the health and well-being of family members. *The Gerontologist, 35,* 94–102.

Lim, J., Wood, B. L., & Miller, B. D., (2008). Maternal depression and parenting in relation to child internalizing symptoms and asthma disease activity. *Journal of Family Psychology, 22,* 264–273.

Manne, S. L., DuHamel, K., Gallelli, K., Sorgen, K., & Redd, W. H. (1998). Posttraumatic stress disorder among mothers of pediatric cancer survivors: Diagnosis, comorbidity, and utility of the PTSD Checklist as a screening instrument. *Journal of Pediatric Psychology, 23,* 357–366.

Manne, S. L., Norton, T. R., Ostroff, J. S., Winkel, G., Fox, K., & Grana, G. (2007). Protective buffering and psychological distress among couples coping with breast cancer: The moderating role of relationship satisfaction. *Journal of Family Psychology, 21,* 380–388.

Mansour, M. E., Lanphear, B. P., & DeWitt, T. G. (2000). Barriers to asthma care in urban children: Parent perspectives. *Pediatrics, 106,* 512–520.

Martire, L. M., Keefe, F. J., Schulz, R., Ready, R., Beach, S. R., Rudy, T. E., & Starz, T. W. (2006) Older spouses' perceptions of partners' chronic arthritis pain: Implications for spousal responses, support provision, and caregiving experiences. *Psychology and Aging, 21,* 222–230.

McCubbin, H. I., & Patterson, J. M. (1982). Family adaptation to crisis. In H. I. McCubbin, A. E. Cauble, & J. M. Patterson (Eds.), *Family stress, coping, and social support* (pp. 26–47). Springfield, IL: Charles C Thomas.

McCubbin, H. I., Thompson, A. I., & McCubbin, M. A. (1996). *Family assessment: Resiliency, coping and adaptation.* Madison: University of Wisconsin Publishers.

McCubbin, M., Balling, K., Possin, P., Frierdich, S., & Bryne, B. (2002). Family resiliency in childhood cancer. *Family Relations, 51,* 103–111.

Mednick, L., Cogen, F., Henderson, C., Rohrbeck, C. A., Kitessa, D., & Steisand, R. (2007). Hope more, worry less: Hope as a potential resilience factor in mothers of very young children with type 1 diabetes. *Children's Health Care, 36,* 385–396.

Meyer, J. (2001). *Age: 2000: Census 2000 Brief.* U.S. Census Bureau, Washington, DC. Retrieved on June 30, 2008, from: http://www.census.gov/prod/2001pubs/c2kbr01–12.pdf

Murray, C. E., Kelley-Soderholm, E. L., & Murray, T. L., Jr. (2007). Strengths, challenges, and relational processes in families of children with congenital upper limb differences. *Families, Systems, & Health, 25,* 276–292.

National Center for Health Statistics. (2007). *Chartbook on trends in the health of Americans.* Hyattsville, MD: U.S. Government Printing Office.

Newacheck, P. W., & Halfon, N. (1998). Prevalence and impact of disabling chronic conditions in childhood. *American Journal of Public Health, 88,* 610–617.

Northouse, L. L., Templin, T., Mood, D., & Oberst, M. (1998). Couples' adjustment to breast cancer and benign breast disease: A longitudinal analysis. *Psycho-Oncology, 7*(1), 37–48.

Norton, T. R., & Manne, S. L. (2007). Support concordance among couples coping with cancer: Relationship, individual, and situational factors. *Journal of Social & Personal Relationships, 24,* 675–692.

O'Brien, M. (2007). Ambiguous loss in families of children with autism spectrum disorders. *Family Relations, 56,* 135–146.

Ott, C. H., Sanders, S., & Kelber, S. T. (2007). Grief and personal growth experience of spouses and adult-child caregivers of individuals with Alzheimer's disease and related dementias. *The Gerontologist, 47,* 798–809.

Patterson, J. M. (1991). Family resilience to the challenge of a child's disability. *Pediatric Annals, 20,* 491–499.

Patterson, J. M. (1993). The role of family meanings in adaptation to chronic illness and disability. In A. P. Turnbull, J. M. Patterson, S. K. Behr, D. L. Murphy, J. G. Marquis, & J. J. Blue-Banning (Eds.), *Cognitive coping, families, and disability* (pp. 221–238). Baltimore: Brookes Publishing.

Patterson, J. M. (2002). Integrating family resilience and family stress theory. *Journal of Marriage and Family, 64,* 349–360.

Patterson, J. M., Budd, J., Goetz, D., & Warwick, W. J. (1993). Family correlates of a 10-year pulmonary health trend in cystic fibrosis. *Pediatrics, 91,* 383–389.

Patterson, J. M., & Garwick, A. W. (1994). Levels of meaning in family stress theory. *Family Process, 33,* 287–304.

Patterson, J. M., Leonard, B. J., & Titus, C. M. A. (1992). Home care for medically fragile children: Impact on family health and well-being. *Journal of Developmental & Behavioral Pediatrics, 13,* 248–255.

Penninx, B. W. J. H., Van Tilburg, T., Deeg, D. J. H., Kriegsman, D. M. W., Boeke, A. J. P., & Van Eijk, J. T. M. (1997). Direct and buffer effects of social support and personal coping resources in individuals with arthritis. *Social Science and Medicine, 44,* 393–402.

Peterson, B. D., Newton, C. R., Rosen, K. H., & Schulman, R. S. (2006). Coping processes of couples experiencing infertility. *Family Relations, 55,* 227–239.

Peyrot, M., McMurry, J. F., Jr., & Hedges, R. (1988). Marital adjustment to adult diabetes: Interpersonal congruence and spouse satisfaction. *Journal of Marriage and Family, 50,* 363–376.

Pinquart, M., & Sorensen, S. (2003). Associations of stressors and uplifts of caregiving with caregiver burden and depressive mood: A meta-analysis. *The Journals of Gerontology, 58B,* P112–P128.

Pinquart, M., & Sorensen, S. (2005). Ethnic differences in stressors, resources, and psychological outcomes of family caregiving: A meta-analysis. *The Gerontologist, 45,* 90–106.

Pinquart, M., & Sorensen, S. (2006). Gender differences in caregiver stressors, social resources, and health: An updated meta-analysis. *The Journals of Gerontology, 61B,* P33–P45.

Pinquart, M., & Sorensen, S. (2007). Correlates of physical health of informal caregivers: A meta-analysis. *The Journals of Gerontology, 62B,* P126–P137.

Quittner, A. L., & Opipari, L. C. (1994). Differential treatment of siblings: Interview and diary analyses comparing two family contexts. *Child Development, 65,* 800–815.

Retzlaff, R. (2007). Families of children with Rett syndrome: Stories of coherence and resilience. *Families, Systems, & Health, 25,* 246–262.

Revenson, T. A., Schiaffino, K. M., Majerovitz, S. D., & Gibofsky, A. (1991). Social support as a double-edged sword: The relation of positive and problematic support to depression among rheumatoid arthritis patients. *Social Science & Medicine, 33,* 807–813.

Roberto, K., Gold, D., & Yorgason, J. B. (2004). Chronic illness and marital relationships: The influence of osteoporosis on the lives of older couples. *Journal of Applied Gerontology, 23,* 443–456.

Rohrbaugh, M. J., Cranford, J. A., Shoham, V., Micklas, J. M., Sonnega, J. S., & Coyne, J. C. (2002). Couples coping with congestive heart failure: Role and gender differences in psychological distress. *Journal of Family Psychology, 16,* 3–13.

Rolland, J. S. (1994). *Families, illness, and disability.* New York: Basic Books.

Ron, P. (2006). Caregiving offspring to aging parents: How it affects their marital relations, parenthood, and mental health. *Illness, Crisis, & Loss, 14,* 1–21.

Roper, S. O., Call, A., Leishman, J., Ratcliffe, G. C., Mandleco, B. L. Dyches, T. T., & Marshall, E. S. (in press). Type 1 diabetes: Children and adolescents' knowledge and questions. *Journal of Advanced Nursing.*

Roper, S. O., & Jackson, J. B. (2007). The ambiguities of out-of-home care: Children with severe or profound disabilities. *Family Relations, 56,* 147–161.

Sandberg, J., Trief, P. M., Greenberg, R. P., Graff, K., & Weinstock, R. S. (2006). "He said, she said": The impact of gender on spousal support in diabetes management. *Journal of Couple & Relationship Therapy, 5,* 23–42.

Sanders, S. (2005). Is the glass half empty or half full? Reflections on strain and gain in caregivers of individuals with Alzheimer's disease. *Social Work in Health Care, 40,* 57–74.

Schaie, K. W., Krause, N., & Booth, A. (2004). *Religious influences on health and well-being in the elderly.* New York: Springer.

Schulz, R., Ready, R., Beach, S. R., Rudy, T. E., & Starz, T. W. (2006). Older spouses' perceptions of partners' chronic arthritis pain: Implications for spousal responses, support provision, and caregiving experiences. *Psychology and Aging, 21,* 222–230.

Schulz, R., O'Brien, A. T., Bookwala, J., & Fleissner, K. (1995). Psychiatric and physical morbidity effects of dementia caregiving: Prevalence, correlates, and causes. *The Gerontologist, 35,* 771–791.

Sharpe, D., & Rossiter, L. (2002). Siblings of children with a chronic illness: A meta-analysis. *Journal of Pediatric Psychology, 27,* 699–710.

Silver, E. J., Westbrook, L. E., & Stein, R. E. K. (1998). Relationship of parental psychological distress to consequences of chronic health conditions in children. *Journal of Pediatric Psychology, 23,* 5–15.

Stoker, M., Mandleco, B. L., Roper, S. O., Marshall, E. S., & Dyches, T. (under review). *Parenting styles, self-care behaviors, and metabolic control in adolescents with type 1 diabetes: A correlational study.*

Svavarsdottir, E. K., & Rayens, M. K. (2005). Hardiness in families of young children with asthma. *Journal of Advanced Nursing, 50*(4), 381–390.

Townsend, A. L., & Franks, M. M. (1995). Binding ties: Closeness and conflict in adult children's caregiving relationships. *Psychology and Aging, 10,* 343–351.

Townsend, A. L., Noelker, L., Deimling, G., & Bass, D. (1989). Longitudinal impact of interhousehold caregiving on adult children's mental health. *Psychology and Aging, 4,* 393–401.

Trief, P. M., Sandberg, J., Greenberg, R. P., Graff, K., Castronova, N., Yoon, M., & Weinstock, R. S. (2003). Describing support: A qualitative study of couples living with diabetes. *Families, Systems, and Health, 21,* 57–67.

Tucker, J. S., Winelman, D. K., Katz, J. N., & Bermas, B. L. (1999). Ambivalence over emotional expression and psychological well-being among rheumatoid arthritis patients and their spouses. *Journal of Applied Social Psychology, 29,* 271–290.

Walsh, F. (1998). *Strengthening family resilience.* New York: Guilford.

Yorgason, J. B., Booth, A., & Johnson, D. (2008). Health, disability, and marital quality: Is the association different for younger versus older cohorts? *Research on Aging, 6,* 623–648.

Yorgason, J. B., Piercy, F. P., & Piercy, S. K. (2007). Acquired hearing impairment in older couple relationships: An exploration of couple resilience processes. *Journal of Aging Studies, 21,* 215–228.

6 Violence, Abuse, and Neglect in Families and Intimate Relationships

Richard J. Gelles

During the last quarter of the 20th century, violence between intimates and family members was transformed from a private trouble to a social problem that has received increasing professional, public, and policy attention. We now know that violence and abuse between intimates and between parents and children is extensive; occurs across societies, cultures, and historical time; and is not limited to one social, economic, or demographic group. We recognize the social, emotional, economic, and societal costs of violence in families and intimate relationships, and we have come to understand the constraints on the victims that limit their ability to protect themselves and their dependents. Although there are numerous controversies among researchers, practitioners, and policymakers about how to best conceptualize and respond to the problem of violence in families and intimate relationships, one consensus has been reached: There is evidence that virtually every type and form of family and intimate relationship has the potential of being violent. Thus, although the term "family violence" in used throughout the chapter, the scope of this chapter examines violence and abuse in intimate as well as family relationships.

Estimates of Current Prevalence and Incidence

Researchers have used numerous techniques in attempts to produce accurate estimates of the rates of abuse and neglect in families and intimate relationships. However, because scholars have defined abuse and neglect in varying ways and have used differing methodologies to examine the incidence and frequency of these phenomena, no definitive data exist on the extent of abuse and neglect in families or intimate relationships in the United States or other nations. It is clear from the data that are available, however, that family violence is a very serious societal problem.

Child Maltreatment

In 2006, according to the National Child Abuse and Neglect Data System, 1.9 million cases of child maltreatment were reported, from which 3.6 million children were the subjects of investigations by Child Protective Service agencies (U.S. Department of Health and Human Services, 2008). As a result of the investigations, an estimated 905,000 children were considered victims of maltreatment at the hands of parents or caregivers. Of 885,245 victims of maltreatment for whom there are data on type of maltreatment, 142,041 (16%) experienced physical abuse; 567,787 (64.1%) experienced neglect; 78,120 (8.8%) experienced sexual abuse; 58,577 (6.6%) experienced psychological maltreatment; and the remainder experienced medical neglect or other forms of maltreatment (U.S. Department of Health and Human Services, 2008.).

Finkelhor and his colleagues conducted a national survey of child victimization in 2002–2003 (Finkehor, Ormrod, Turner, & Hamby, 2005). The survey collected data on children 2 to 17 years of age. Interviews were conducted with parents and youth. Slightly more than 1 in 7 children (138 per 1,000) experienced child maltreatment. Emotional abuse was the most frequent type of maltreatment. The rate of physical abuse (meaning that children experienced physical harm) was 15 per 1,000, while the rate of neglect was 11 per 1,000. The overall projected extent of maltreatment was 8,755,000 child victims (Finkehor, Ormrod, Turner, & Hamby, 2005).

Dating and Courtship Violence

Overall, studies indicate that the prevalence of nonsexual courtship violence ranges from 9% to 65%, depending on the definitions and research methods used (Silverman, Raj, Mucci, & Hathaway, 2001).

Partner Abuse

Numerous sources of data on violence between spouses and intimate partners are available to researchers. According to the National Crime Victims Survey, 564,392 (2.3 per 1,000) women were victims of intimate-partner violence in the United States in 2005; this represents a decline from 1.1 million (5.8 per 1,000) female victims in 1993. Men were victims of 153,737 (0.9 per 1,000) violent acts at the hands of their intimate partners in 2005, down from 162,870 in 1993 (1.6 per 1,000) (Catalano, 2007). Data from the Bureau of Justice Statistics Supplemental Victimization Survey found that 3.4 million individuals (23.8 per 1,000) age 18 or older were victims of stalking (Baum, Catalano, Rand, & Rose, 2009). Women were at a much greater risk of reporting stalking victimization compared to men (20.0 per 1,000 versus 7.4 per 1,000).

The National Violence Against Women (NVAW) Survey involved telephone interviews with a nationally representative sample of 8,000 women and 8,000 men (Tjaden & Thoennes, 1998). The survey was conducted between November 1995 and May 1996. The NVAW survey assessed lifetime prevalence and annual prevalence (violence experienced in the previous 12 months). Nearly 52% of women surveyed (519 per 1,000, or 52,261,743 women) reported experiencing a physical assault as a child or adult. Nearly 56% of women surveyed (559 per 1,000, or 56,289,623 women) reported experiencing any form of violence, including stalking, rape, or physical assault. The rate of lifetime assault at the hands of an intimate partner was 221 per 1,000 for physical violence and 254 per 1,000 for any form of violence victimization. The rates of forms of violence less likely to cause an injury, such as pushing, grabbing, shoving, or slapping, were the highest (between 160 and 181 per 1,000), while the rates of the most severe forms of violence (used a gun, used a knife, or "beat up") were the lowest (85 per 1,000 for "beat up"; 7 per 1,000 for used a gun). The annual prevalence or incidence of violence was 19 per 1,000 for physical assault (1,913,243 women) and 30 per 1,000 for any form of violence victimization (3,020,910 women). The annual prevalence of women victimized by intimate partners was 13 per 1,000 for physical assault (1,309,061) and 18 per 1,000 (1,812,546 women) for all forms of victimization.

Homicide of Intimates and Children

Approximately 329 husbands and boyfriends were killed by their wives or girlfriends in 2005, whereas 1,182 wives and girlfriends were slain by their husbands or boyfriends. (Catalano, 2007). The number of intimate homicides has declined since 1993. An estimated 1,530 children were killed by parents or caregivers in 2006 (U.S. Department of Health and Human Services, 2008).

Elder Abuse

The National Elder Abuse Incidence Survey found that approximately 450,000 elderly persons living in domestic settings were abused and/or neglected in 1996 (National Center on Elder Abuse, 1998).

Siblings, Parents, Gays, Lesbians, and Transgendered Couples

Physical fights between brothers and sisters are by far the most common form of family violence. Violence between siblings often goes far beyond so-called "normal" violence. A national survey of 2,030 children living in the contiguous states in the United States found that 35% of children experienced a physical assault at the hands of a sibling in the previous year (Finkehor, Ormrod, Turner, & Hamby, 2005). Boys and girls were nearly equally likely to be a victim of sibling violence. The rate of assault was highest for children 6 to 12 years of age (Finkehor, Ormrod, Turner, & Hamby, 2005). According to the U.S. Bureau of Justice Statistics, 119 murders in 2002 involved perpetrators and victims who were siblings (Durose, Harlow, Langan, Motivans, Rantala, & Smith, 2005). Nearly three-quarters (72%) of sibling murders were brother on brother, while 14% were brothers killing sisters.

Parents are also hidden victims of family violence. Each year, according to Straus and Gelles's national surveys, between 750,000 and 1 million parents have violent acts committed against them by their teenage children (Cornell & Gelles, 1982).

Last, intimate-partner violence is not exclusive to heterosexual relationships. Although there are no national statistics or official reports that tabulate the rates of partner violence among gay, lesbian, and transgendered couples, descriptive research consistently uncovers intimate violence among nonheterosexual couples (see, Greenwood, Relf, Huang, Pollack, Canchola, & Catania, 2002; Lockhart, White, Causby, & Isaac, 1994; Tjaden & Thonnes, 2000; Turrell, 2000).

Witnessing Domestic Violence

According to the Bureau of Justice Statistics, there were children in the homes of 38% of female victims of domestic violence and 21% of male victims of domestic violence (Catalano, 2007). Children who witness domestic violence are a unique population warranting research and clinical attention (Rosenberg & Rossman, 1990). Witnessing is at the intersection of child abuse and neglect and domestic violence. Researchers and clinicians report that children who witness acts of domestic violence experience negative behavioral and developmental outcomes, independent of any direct abuse or neglect that they may also experience from their caretakers (Jaffe, Wolfe, & Wilson, 1990; Osofsky, 1995; Rosenberg & Rossman, 1990).

The Costs of Family Violence

It is challenging to estimate the actual costs of domestic violence and child maltreatment. Wang and Holton have estimated that child abuse and neglect have cost those involved approximately $103.8 billion (Wang & Holton, 2007). This estimate is based on the immediate needs of victims and indirect costs (juvenile delinquency, special education, mental health care, adult criminal costs, etc.), as well as long-term costs.

Based on an analysis of the survey data, the U.S. Centers for Disease Control and Prevention (2003) estimate that the cost of intimate-partner assault, rape, and stalking has exceeded $5.8 billion. Of this amount, $4.1 billion was for direct medical and mental health services, $0.9 billion was lost productivity from paid work and household work, and $0.9 billion was in lifetime earnings lost as a result of homicide.

The long-term consequences of child abuse and neglect for individuals differ depending on the age at which abuse or neglect occurs. During childhood, some of the major consequences of maltreatment include problematic school performance and lowered attention to social cues. Researchers have found that children whose parents are "psychologically unavailable" function poorly across a wide range of psychological, cognitive, and developmental areas (Egeland & Sroufe, 1981). Physical aggression, antisocial behavior, and juvenile delinquency are among the most consistently documented consequences in adolescence and adulthood for those abused as children (Aber, Allen, Carlson, & Cicchetti, 1990; Dodge, Bates, & Pettit, 1990; Widom, 1989a, 1989b, 1991). Evidence also suggests that childhood maltreatment increases individuals' later risk of alcohol and drug abuse problems (National Research Council, 1993).

Research on the consequences of childhood sexual abuse indicates that inappropriate sexual behavior, such as frequent and overt sexual stimulation and inappropriate sexual overtures to other children, is often found among victims (Kendall-Tackett, Williams, & Finkelhor, 1993). Widom (1995) found that people who were sexually abused during childhood are at higher risk of arrest for committing crimes as adults, including sex crimes, than are people who did not suffer sexual abuse. However, this risk is no greater than the risk of arrest for victims of other childhood maltreatment, with one exception: Victims of childhood sexual abuse are more likely to be arrested for prostitution than are victims of other forms of maltreatment.

As severe and significant as the consequences of child abuse and neglect are, it is also important to note that the majority of children who are abused and neglected do not show signs of extreme disturbance. Many children have the ability to cope effectively even when they have been physically, psychologically, and/or sexually abused. Researchers have identified a number of factors that appear to influence the effects of child maltreatment, including the child's intelligence level and scholastic attainment, the child's temperament, the child's cognitive appraisal of the events (i.e., how the child views the maltreatment), the child's having a relationship with a significant person, and the types of interventions used to end the maltreatment, including the child's placement outside of the home (National Research Council, 1993).

For female victims of domestic assault, the consequences extend beyond physical injury. Researchers have consistently found a high incidence of depression and anxiety as well as increased risk of suicide attempts among samples of battered women (Christopoulos et al., 1987; Gelles & Harrop, 1989; Hilberman, 1980; National Research Council, 1996; Schechter, 1983; Schumacher, Feldbau-Kohn, Slep, & Heyman, 2001; Walker, 1984).

For society as a whole, the costs of family violence include the time lost from work by victims, the medical care that victims require, and the investment of resources from social and criminal justice agencies.

Factors Associated With Family Violence

The early thinking and writing on family violence was dominated by a mental illness model (Gelles, 1973). There are a number of problems with the psychopathological, or mental illness, model of family violence and abuse. First, most of the conclusions about the causes of family violence are based on studies of a limited number of cases, typically without comparison groups, and that draw conclusions after the data are collected, rather than testing hypotheses developed prior to data collection. Second, such an explanation confuses the cause with consequence: People who abuse their children or partners are mentally ill, we are told; we know they are mentally ill because they have committed an outrageous act of violence or abuse. A third problem is that the psychopathological model ignores the fact that certain societal factors are also related to family violence. The remainder of this section examines those societal factors.

Sex and Gender Differences

Research on child abuse finds that mothers were slightly more likely than fathers to abuse or kill their children (National Research Council, 1998; U.S. Department of Health and Human Services, 2008; Wolfner & Gelles, 1993). Abusive females are typically younger than abusive men. Mothers are the perpetrators of 27.4% of child fatalities, while fathers are perpetrators in 13.1% (U.S. Department of Health and Human Services, 2008). Black, Heyman, and Slep's (2001) review of existing studies that investigated the relationship between parent sex and the likelihood of parent-to-child physical aggression, in nationally representative samples, and not just cases of abuse reported to child protective services, found that parent sex is not associated with parent-to-child physical abuse.

There is considerable debate about the comparative rates of husband-and-wife violence. While some investigators report that the rate of wife-to-husband violence is about the same as the rate of husband-to-wife violence (Moffitt, Caspi, Rutter, & Silva, 2001; Straus, 1999, 2004; Straus & Gelles, 1986), others explain that women are the disproportionate victims of family violence (Dobash & Dobash, 1979; Dobash, Dobash, Wilson, & Daly, 1992; Kurz, 2005; Tjaden & Thoennes, 1998). If one goes by how much harm is done, who initiates the violence, and how easy it is for a victim to escape violence, women clearly are the disproportionate victims of domestic violence.

Boys are the more violent siblings and offspring (Durose, Harlow, Langan, Motivans, Rantala, & Smith, 2005). Mothers and sisters are the more frequent targets of the young or adolescent boys' family violence (Cornell & Gelles, 1982).

Social Characteristics

There are two conflicting positions regarding the relationship between social class and family violence: (1) Violence cuts across all socioeconomic groups and is not a function of social class or income, and (2) violence is caused by low social class and poverty. Although there appears to be an association between lower income and increased risk for family violence (Catalano, 2007; Cunradi, Caetano, & Schafer, 2002; Schumacher, Feldbau-Kohn, Slep, & Heyman, 2001; U.S. Department of Justice, 2004), it is not singularly confined to lower-class families. Victims from lower socioeconomic levels are more likely to go to emergency rooms or clinics, and they are more likely to come to the attention of the authorities if their child is bruised or battered. Similarly, clinics or emergency rooms are the most likely source of medical aid for lower-class battered women. Therefore, family violence is a more observable phenomenon among those with low incomes. Nonetheless, the rates of virtually all forms of family violence are higher among those with low income or who live in disadvantaged neighborhoods (National Research Council, 1998).

Rates of family violence also vary by race. Both official report and self-report survey data suggest that the rates of intimate violence are higher in minority families (Catalano, 2007; National Research Council, 1998). American Indian women report intimate-partner victimization at rates higher than women in other racial or ethnic groups (Catalano, 2007). The rates of violence toward children and between husbands and wives are highest among Hispanics compared to blacks and whites, and higher among blacks compared to whites (Hampton & Gelles, 1991; Hampton, Gelles, & Harrop, 1989; Straus & Smith, 1990). For partner abuse, the higher rates in Hispanic families reflect the economic deprivation, youthfulness, and urban residence of Hispanics, since when these factors are controlled, there is no statistically significant difference between Hispanics and non-Hispanic whites. Kantor, Jasinski, and Aldaronodo (1994) report that Hispanic ethnicity may not be a risk factor itself but may be a marker for other sociodemographic variables that are risk factors for family violence. However, with regard to violence toward children, the differences between Hispanics, blacks, and whites persist even when demographic and socioeconomic factors are controlled.

Stress

Career and life stressors have a medium effect on the likelihood of intimate-partner violence (Stith, Smith, Penn, Ward, & Tritt, 2004). The prevalence of posttraumatic stress in women victims is high, ranging from approximately 33% to 85% (Astin, Lawrence, & Foy, 1993). Kantor and Straus (1987) suggest that men employed in blue-collar occupations reported higher rates of family violence than did men with white-collar employment. Financial difficulties, as well as other factors, such as being a single parent, being a teenage mother, and having sexual problems, are all related to heightened stress that may precipitate violent episodes (Cano & Vivian, 2001; Gelles, 1989; Gelles & Straus, 1988). However, overall life experiences that are perceived as stressful appear to have a more significant connection to physical abuse in families than do daily life stressors (MacEwen & Barling, 1988; McKenry, Julian, & Gavazzi, 1995; Pan, Neidig, & O'Leary, 1994).

Social Isolation

People who are socially isolated from neighbors and relatives are more likely to be violent in the home. One major source of stress reduction, and an insulator to family violence, is being able to call on friends and family for help, aid, and assistance. The more a family is integrated into the community, the more groups and associations they belong to, and the less likely they are to be violent (Milner & Chilamkurti, 1991; Straus et al., 1980). Data from the 1992 National Survey of Families suggest that experiencing satisfaction with social relationships was associated with less intimate-partner violence (Rodriquez, Lasch, Chandra, & Lee, 2001). Social connections, however, do not preclude the possibility of physical violence. In fact, some research suggests that receiving little social support is not associated with an increased risk of partner abuse (Barnett, Martinez, & Keyson, 1996; Zlotnick, Kohn, Peterson, & Pearlstein, 1998).

Intergenerational Transmission

The notion that abused children grow up to be abusive parents and violent adults has been widely expressed in the child abuse and family violence literature, and a history of victimization is a major risk factor for family violence offending (Stith, Smith, Penn, Ward, & Tritt, 2004). Kaufman and Zigler (1987) reviewed the literature that tested the intergenerational transmission of violence hypothesis and concluded that the best estimate of the rate of intergenerational transmission appears to be 30% (plus or minus 5%). Although a rate of 30% intergenerational transmission is substantially less than the majority of abused children, the rate is considerably more than the 2% to 4% rate of abuse found in the general population (Straus & Gelles, 1986). Barnett and Fagan (1993) found that witnessing parental verbal and psychological aggression was also significantly related to later abusive behavior.

Evidence from studies of parental and partner violence indicates that while experiencing violence in one's family of origin is often correlated with later violent behavior, such experience is not the sole determining factor. When the cycle of violence occurs, it is likely the result of a complex set of social, psychological, and interpersonal processes.

Factors Associated With Sexual Abuse of Children

There has been a great deal of research on the characteristics of sexual abusers; however, current research has failed to isolate characteristics, especially demographic, social, or psychological factors, that discriminate between sexual abusers and nonabusers (Black, Heyman, & Slep, 2001; Quinsey, 1984).

One of the key questions raised in discussions about sexual abuse is whether all children are at risk for sexual abuse or whether some children, because of some specific characteristic (e.g., age, sex, or poverty status), are at greater risk than others. Current research is unclear as to definitive factors that can predict future sexual abuse. Finkelhor, Moore, Hamby, and Straus (1997) found that a child's sex does not necessarily predict later victimization. However, Sedlak (1997) asserts that female children are at an increased risk for sexual abuse, and the relationship between a child's sexual victimization and age is also associated with family structure and race.

Theoretical Perspectives

Below, we discuss the major sociological and psychological theories that may help explain the causes and processes of family violence.

Social Learning Theory

Social learning theorists (e.g., Bandura, 1973) posit that most behavior is learned through individuals' experience and observation of their own and others' behaviors. According to this theory, individuals who have experienced or witnessed violence are more likely to use violence than those who have experienced little or no violence. Social learning theory provides support for the belief that family violence is learned. The family is the institution and social group in which people learn the roles of husband, wife, parent, and child. The home is the prime location where people learn how to deal with various stressors, crises, and frustrations. In many instances, the home is also the place where individuals first experience violence. Not only do people learn violent behavior, but they learn how to justify being violent. For example, when a child hears a father say, "This will hurt me more than it will hurt you," or a mother say, "You have been bad, so you deserve to be spanked," this contributes to the child's learning how to justify violent behavior.

Ecological Theory

Garbarino (1977) and Belsky (1980, 1993) have proposed an ecological model to explain the complex nature of child maltreatment. According to this model, parental violence and abuse arise out of a mismatch between parent and child or between the family and its neighborhood or community. For example, a parent who is under a great deal of social stress and has poor coping skills may have a difficult time meeting the needs of a child who is hyperactive. The risk of abuse and violence increases when the functioning of the child and the parent is constrained by developmental problems, such as when the child has learning disabilities and social or emotional handicaps, and when the parent is under considerable stress or has personality problems, such as immaturity or impulsiveness. The risk of abuse is further increased if the family lives in a community where few institutions and agencies offer support to troubled families.

Social Exchange Theory

Many scholars have used social exchange theory to explain the complex dynamics inherent in family violence (Gelles, 1983, 1997). This theory proposes that both partner abuse and child abuse are governed by the principle of costs and benefits. Individuals use abuse when the rewards of doing so are greater than the costs (Gelles, 1983). Exchange theorists assert that inflicting costs on someone who has hurt you is rewarding (e.g., Homans, 1967). The notion of "sweet revenge" is useful for explaining why victims may respond with extreme forms of violence after having been victimized. There is a gain to using violence, and that gain is the achievement of dominance and control over another. The private nature of the family, the reluctance of social institutions and agencies to intervene in family matters— in spite of mandatory child abuse reporting laws and mandatory arrest laws for partner violence—and the low risk of other interventions reduce the costs that abusers face for using violence. In addition, the cultural approval of violence as both expressive and instrumental behavior raises the potential rewards for using violence—the most significant reward being social and interpersonal control and power.

Sociobiological Theory

The sociobiological, or evolutionary, perspective on family violence suggests that violence toward human or nonhuman primate offspring is the result of the reproductive success potential of children and parental investment. This theory's central assumption is that natural selection is the process of differential reproduction and reproductive success (Daly & Wilson, 1980). Males can be expected to invest in offspring when there is some degree of parental certainty (how confident the man is that the child is his own genetic offspring), and females are also inclined to invest under conditions of parental certainty. Parents recognize their own offspring and avoid squandering valuable reproductive effort on the offspring of others. Thus Daly and Wilson (1985) conclude that parental feelings are more readily and more profoundly established with one's own offspring than in cases where the parent–offspring relationship is artificial. Children who are not genetically related to their parental figures (e.g., stepchildren, adopted children, or foster children) and children with low reproductive potential (e.g., handicapped or retarded children) are at highest risk for infanticide and abuse (Burgess & Garbarino, 1983; Daly & Wilson, 1980; Hrdy, 1979). Also, large families can dilute parental energy and lower parents' attachment to children, thus increasing the risk of child abuse and neglect (Burgess, 1979).

Smuts (1992) applies an evolutionary perspective to male aggression against females and argues, as do Daly and Wilson (1988) and Burgess and Draper (1989), that such aggression often reflects male reproductive striving. These scholars postulate that both human and nonhuman male primates use aggression against females both to intimidate the females so that they will not resist future male efforts to mate with them and to reduce the likelihood that the females will mate with other males. Thus males use aggression to control female sexuality to males' reproductive advantage. The frequency of male aggression varies across societies and situations, depending on (a) the strength of female alliances, (b) the amount of support women receive from their families, (c) the strength and importance of male alliances, (d) the degree of equality in male–female relationships, and (e) the degree to which males control the society's economic resources. Male aggression toward females, in the forms of both rape and other physical violence, is high (a) when female alliances are weak, (b) when females lack kin support, (c) when male alliances are strong, (d) when male–female relationships are unbalanced, and (e) when males control societal resources.

General Strain Theory

Sociologist Robert Agnew (1992) asserts that violent behavior may be related to the frustration and anger that result when an individual is treated poorly in social relationships. Agnew outlines three types of strain that increase an individual's feelings of anger and fear. The first is the strain associated with the failure to achieve positively valued goals. This type of strain may result in an individual's using illegitimate means to get what he or she wants. Another type of strain is that caused by the presentation of negative stimuli. Stressful life situations of this type may include such adverse events as criminal victimization, child maltreatment, and interpersonal violence. An individual confronted with such stressors may engage in criminal acts to seek revenge. The third type of strain that Agnew describes is caused by the anticipated or actual loss of positively valued stimuli, such as loss of a loved one or the experience of a major life transition. Difficulties arise when an individual attempts to seek revenge for a loss or tries to prevent major life changes through illegal methods. According to Agnew, the most critical response to strain is anger, which can result in increased aggression and possibly violent criminal behavior.

Pro-Feminist Theory

Pro-feminist theory is the dominant ideological perspective in the field of relational violence. This theory views society through a gendered lens, perceiving women as being controlled by an oppressive patriarchal social system (Gelles, 1993b). Feminist theorists assert that women are the victims of men's culturally sanctioned coercive control (see, e.g., Dobash & Dobash, 1979; Pagelow, 1984; Yllö, 1988, 1993). The central thesis of this perspective is that economic, social, and cultural processes operate directly and indirectly to support a patriarchal (male-dominated) social order and family structure. Patriarchy leads to the subordination of women and causes the historical pattern of systematic violence directed against women.

Attachment Theory

Attachment theory describes the propensity of each individual to form a strong emotional bond with a primary caregiver who functions as a source of security and safety (Bowlby, 1973). The theory proposes that there is a clear association between a person's early attachment experiences and the pattern of affectionate bonds the individual makes throughout his or her lifetime. If an individual forms a strong and secure attachment with an early caregiver, the adult relationships he or she forms later will also have secure attachments. On the other hand, if an individual forms only insecure, anxious, or ambivalent attachments early on, his or her adult attachments will be similarly unsatisfactory. Therefore, according to the theory, attachment difficulties underlie adulthood relational problems. Bowlby (1988) posits that anxiety and anger go hand in hand as responses to risk of loss and that anger is often functional. For certain individuals who have weak and insecure attachments, the functional reaction to anger becomes distorted and is manifested through violent acts against intimates.

Interventions

Protecting Children

Although child protection workers have a wide array of specific service options available, typically they take one of two basic courses to protect victims of child abuse: (1) They remove the children from their homes and place them in foster homes or institutions, or (2) they provide victims' families with social support, such as counseling, food stamps, and day-care services. Neither solution is ideal, and there are there risks in both. For instance, a child may not understand why he or she is being removed from the home. Children who are removed from abusive homes may well be protected from physical damage, but they still suffer the emotional harm that arises from the fact that they still love their parents and do not want to be separated from them. This emotional damage is compounded when the children are unable to understand why they have been removed from their parents and homes. Abused children often feel that they are responsible for their own abuse. In addition, abused children frequently require special medical and/or psychological care, and it is difficult to find suitable residential placements for such children. Children who require special care may become a burden for foster parents or institutions, and this may lead them to be at greater risk of abuse in foster homes or institutions than they were in their homes with their natural parents.

Leaving a child in an abusive or neglecting home and providing social services to the family involve another type of risk. Most child protective service workers are overworked, undertrained, and underpaid. Services that can help to reduce abuse in families, such as crisis day care, financial assistance, assistance in obtaining suitable housing, and transportation, are often limited in availability. This situation can lead to cases in which children who have been reported as abused and investigated by state agencies are killed by their caretakers even though their families are supposedly being monitored by child protection workers. Half of all children who are killed by their caretakers in the United States are killed *after* they have been reported to child welfare agencies (Gelles, 1996).

To date, only a handful of studies have been conducted to evaluate prevention and treatment programs for child maltreatment. In Elmira, New York, Olds, Henderson, Tatelbaum, and Chamberlin (1986) evaluated the effectiveness of a family support program during pregnancy and for the first 2 years after birth for low-income, unmarried, teenage first-time mothers. They found that in a sample of poor, unmarried teenage girls who had received no services during pregnancy, 19% were reported for subsequent child maltreatment. Of the children of the poor, unmarried teenage mothers in the program who were provided with the full complement of nurse home visits during pregnancy and for the first 2 years after birth, 4% had confirmed cases of child abuse and neglect reported to the state child protection agency. Subsequent follow-ups of participants in this home health visiting intervention demonstrated the long-term effectiveness of the program. However, the effectiveness varied depending on the populations receiving the service, the community context, and who made the visits (nurses or others) (Olds et al., 1999).

Protecting Victims of Intimate-Partner Violence

A number of options are available to women who want to escape or be protected from partner violence. One option is to call the police. The most well-known assessment of intervention into domestic violence to date is the Minneapolis Police Experiment, which was designed to examine whether arresting men for violent attacks on their partners would decrease the risk of further violence (Sherman & Berk, 1984). In this study, the police randomly assigned incidents of misdemeanor family assaults to one of three treatments: arrest, separation, or advice/mediation. The households that received the arrest intervention had the lowest rate (10%) of recidivism (relapse into violent behavior), and those in which the abuser and victim were only separated had the highest rate (24%).

Replications of the Minneapolis study, however, found that arrest had no more effect in deterring future arrests or complaints of violence than did separation or counseling (Berk, Campbell, Klap, & Western, 1992; Dunford, Huizinga, & Elliott, 1990; Pate & Hamilton, 1992; Sherman, Smith, Schmidt, & Rogan, 1992). The replications did find that employed men who were arrested were less likely to be violent after the intervention than were men who were not arrested. However, unemployed men who were arrested were actually more likely to be violent after the intervention than were unemployed men who were not arrested.

A second option for a woman who wants to escape an abuser is to go to a shelter or safe house. *If* a shelter is nearby, *if* the woman knows how to get to it, and *if* the shelter has room for her, this is a good option. Shelters provide physical protection, social support, counseling, legal aid, and even occupational counseling. Shelters are the most cost-efficient form of intervention in domestic violence. Researchers have found that the effects of shelters seem to depend on the attributes of the victims. When a victim is actively engaged in taking control of her life, a shelter stay can dramatically reduce the likelihood of new violence. For some victims, a shelter stay may have no impact, whereas for others it may actually lead to an escalation of violence when they return home (Berk, Newton, & Berk, 1986).

Bowker (1983) interviewed women who had been physically abused and who managed to get their partners to stop being violent. These women utilized a number of different interventions, including talking to friends and relatives, threatening their partners, aggressively defending themselves, going to shelters, calling social service agencies, and calling the police. No single action worked best, and Bowker concluded that, ultimately, the crucial factor was a woman's taking a stand and showing her determination that the violence had to stop.

The prevailing legal and criminal response to intimate-partner violence in the United States has produced an escalating number of male batterers who have found their way into the criminal justice system, and then often into court-mandated treatment. The approach most frequently used in programs for batterers is based on the group intervention model (Austin & Dankwort,

1999; Gondolf, 2002). Some of the earliest studies of such programs appeared to demonstrate that group counseling for batterers is effective in reducing subsequent violence (Dutton, 1986; Gondolf, 1987; Pirog-Good & Stets, 1986). However, the quality of these programs is uneven at best, and no particular modality, length, or type of program has been found to be more effective than any other in reducing men's violence (Babcock et al., 2004; Holtzworth-Munroe, 2001; Levesque, 1998). Research suggests that batterer treatment programs may be able to increase their effectiveness by tailoring interventions to specific types of batterers (Cavanaugh & Gelles, 2005; Saunders, 2001).

Many states do not allow court-mandated programs to use alternative interventions for intimate-partner violence, such as couples counseling, individual treatment, family counseling, and group couples counseling, in spite of a lack of empirical support for that stance (Babcock et al., 2004; Holtzworth-Munroe, 2001). In addition, given the high rate of co-occurrence of spouse abuse and physical child abuse (Appel & Holden, 1998), some researchers have suggested that more integrated interventions are needed to address family violence, such as interventions based on a family-level model (Slep & Heyman, 2001).

References

Aber, J. L., Allen, J. P., Carlson, V., & Cicchetti, D. (1990). The effects of maltreatment on development during early childhood: Recent studies and their theoretical, clinical, and policy implications. In D. Cicchetti & V. Carlson (Eds.), *Child maltreatment: Theory and research on causes and consequences* (pp. 579–619). New York: Cambridge University Press.

Agnew, R. (1992). Foundation for a general strain theory of crime and delinquency. *Criminology, 30,* 47–87.

Appel, A. E., & Holden, G. W. (1998). The co-occurrence of spouse and physical child abuse: A review and appraisal. *Journal of Family Psychology, 12,* 578–599.

Arias, I., Samios, M., & O'Leary, K. D. (1987). Prevalence and correlates of physical aggression during courtship. *Journal of Interpersonal Violence, 2,* 82–90.

Astin, M. C., Lawrence, K. J., & Foy, D. W. (1993). Post-traumatic stress disorder among battered women: Risk and resiliency factors. *Violence and Victims, 8,* 17–28.

Austin, J. B., & Dankwort, J. (1999). Standards for batterer programs: A review and analysis. *Journal of Interpersonal Violence, 14,* 152–168.

Babcock, J. C., Green, C. E., & Robie, C. (2004). Does batterers' treatment work? A meta-analytic review of domestic violence treatment. *Clinical Psychology Review, 23,* 1023–1053.

Bandura, A. (1973). *Aggression: A social learning analysis.* Englewood Cliffs, NJ: Prentice Hall.

Barnett, O. W., & Fagan, R. W. (1993). Alcohol use in male spouse abusers and their female partners. *Journal of Family Violence, 8,* 1–25.

Barnett, O. W., Martinez, T. E., & Keyson, M. (1996). The relationship between violence, social support, and self-blame in battered women. *Journal of Interpersonal Violence, 11,* 221–233.

Baum, K, Catalano, S., Rand, M., & Rose, K. (2009) *Stalking victimization in the United States.* Washington, DC: U.S. Department of Justice, Office of Justice Programs.

Belsky, J. (1980). Child maltreatment: An ecological integration. *American Psychologist, 35,* 320–335.

Belsky, J. (1993). Etiology of child maltreatment: A developmental-ecological analysis. *Psychological Bulletin, 114,* 413–434.

Berk, R. A., Campbell, A., Klap, R., & Western, B. (1992). The deterrent effect of arrest incidents of domestic violence: A Bayesian analysis of four field experiments. *American Sociological Review, 57,* 698–708.

Berk, R. A., Newton, P., & Berk, S. F. (1986). What a difference a day makes: An empirical study of the impact of shelters for battered women. *Journal of Marriage and Family, 48,* 481–490.

Black, D. A., Heyman, R. E., & Slep, A. M. S. (2001). Risk factors for child physical abuse. *Aggression and Violent Behavior, 6,* 121–188.

Bowker, L. H. (1983). *Beating wife beating.* Lexington, MA: Lexington Books.

Bowlby, J. (1973). *Attachment and loss: Vol. 2. Separation.* London: Hogarth.

Bowlby, J. (1988). *A secure base.* London: Hogarth.

Burgess, R. L. (1979). *Family violence: Some implications from evolutionary biology.* Paper presented at the annual meeting of the American Society of Criminology, Philadelphia.

Burgess, R. L., & Draper, P. (1989). The explanation of family violence: The role of biological, behavioral, and cultural selection. In L. Ohlin & M. Tonry (Eds.), *Crime and justice: A review of research: Vol. 11. Family violence* (pp. 59–116). Chicago: University of Chicago Press.

Burgess, R. L., & Garbarino, J. (1983). Doing what comes naturally? An evolutionary perspective on child abuse. In D. Finkelhor, R. J. Gelles, G. T. Hotaling, & M. A. Straus (Eds.), *The dark side of the families: Current family violence research* (pp. 88–101). Beverly Hills, CA: Sage.

Cano, A., & Vivian, D. (2001). Life stressors and husband-to-wife violence. *Aggression and Violent Behavior, 6,* 481–497.

Catalano, S. (2007) *Intimate partner violence in the United States.* Washington, DC: U.S. Department of Justice, Bureau of Justice Statistics.

Cavanaugh, M. M., & Gelles, R. J. (2005). The utility of male domestic violence offender typologies: New directions for research, policy, and practice. *Journal of Interpersonal Violence, 20,* 155–166.

Centers for Disease Control and Prevention, National Center for Injury Prevention and Control. (2003). *Costs of intimate partner violence in the United States.* Atlanta, GA: Centers for Disease Control and Prevention.

Christopoulos, C., Cohn, D. A., Shaw, D. S., Joyce, S., Sullivan-Hanson, J., Kraft, S. P., et al. (1987). Children of abused women: Adjustment at time of shelter residence. *Journal of Marriage and Family, 49,* 611–619.

Cornell, C. P., & Gelles, R. J. (1982). Adolescent to parent violence. *Urban Social Change Review, 15,* 8–14.

Cunradi, C. B., Caetano, R., & Schafer, J. (2002). Socioeconomic predictors of intimate partner violence among white, Black, and Hispanic couples in the United States. *Journal of Family Violence, 17,* 377–389.

Daly, M., & Wilson, M. (1980). Discriminative parental solicitude: A biosocial perspective. *Journal of Marriage and Family, 42,* 277–288.

Daly, M., & Wilson, M. (1985). Child abuse and other risks of not living with both parents. *Ethology and Sociobiology, 6,* 197–210.

Daly, M., & Wilson, M. (1988). *Homicide.* New York: Aldine de Gruyter.

Daro, D. (1988). *Confronting child abuse: Research for effective program design.* New York: Free Press.

Dobash, R. E., & Dobash, R. P. (1979). *Violence against wives: A case against the patriarchy.* New York: Free Press.

Dobash, R. P., Dobash, R. E., Wilson, M., & Daly, M. (1992). The myth of sexual symmetry in marital violence. *Social Problems, 39,* 71–91.

Dodge, K. A., Bates, J. E., & Pettit, G. S. (1990). Mechanisms in the cycle of violence. *Science, 250,* 1678–1683.

Dunford, F. W., Huizinga, D., & Elliott, D. S. (1990). The role of arrest in domestic assault: The Omaha Police Experiment. *Criminology, 28,* 183–206.

Durose, M. R., Harlow, C. W., Langan, P. A., Motivans, M., Rantala, R. R., & Smith, E. L. (2005). *Family violence statistics: Including statistics on strangers and acquaintances.* Washington, DC: U.S. Department of Justice, Office of Justice Programs.

Dutton, D. G. (1986). The outcome of court-mandated treatment for wife assault: A quasi-experimental evaluation. *Violence and Victims, 1,* 163–176.

Egeland, B., & Sroufe, L. A. (1981). Attachment and early child maltreatment. *Child Development, 52,* 44–52.

Finkehor, D., Ormrod, R., Turner, H., & Hamby, S. H. (2005). The victimization of children and youth: A comprehensive national survey. *Child Maltreatment, 10,* 5–25.

Finkelhor, D., Moore, D., Hamby, S. L., & Straus, M. A. (1997). Sexually abused children in a national survey of parents: Methodological issues. *Child Abuse & Neglect, 21,* 1–9.

Garbarino, J. (1977). The human ecology of child maltreatment. *Journal of Marriage and Family, 39,* 721–735.

Gelles, R. J. (1973). Child abuse as psychopathology: A sociological critique and reformulation. *American Journal of Orthopsychiatry, 43,* 611–621.

Gelles, R. J. (1983). An exchange/social control theory. In D. Finkelhor, R. J. Gelles, G. T. Hotaling, & M. A. Straus (Eds.), *The dark side of families: Current family violence research* (pp. 151–165). Beverly Hills, CA: Sage.

Gelles, R. J. (1989). Child abuse and violence in single parent families: Parent absence and economic deprivation. *American Journal of Orthopsychiatry, 59,* 492–501.

Gelles, R. J. (1992). Poverty and violence toward children. *American Behavioral Scientist, 35,* 258–274.

Gelles, R. J. (1993a). *Husband to wife violence by income.* Unpublished manuscript.

Gelles, R. J. (1993b). Through a sociological lens: Social structure and family violence. In R. J. Gelles & D. R. Loseke (Eds.), *Current controversies on family violence* (pp. 31–46). Newbury Park, CA: Sage.

Gelles, R. J. (1996). *The book of David: How preserving families can cost children's lives.* New York: Basic Books.

Gelles, R. J. (1997). *Intimate violence in families* (3rd ed.). Thousand Oaks, CA: Sage.

Gelles, R. J., & Harrop, J. W. (1989). Violence, battering, and psychological distress among women. *Journal of Interpersonal Violence, 4,* 400–420.

Gelles, R. J., & Straus, M. A. (1988). *Intimate violence*. New York: Simon & Schuster.

Gondolf, E. W. (1987). Evaluating progress for men who batter: Problems and prospects. *Journal of Family Violence, 2*, 95–108.

Gondolf, E. W. (2002). *Batterer intervention systems: Issues, outcomes, and recommendations*. Thousand Oaks, CA: Sage.

Greenwood, G. L., Relf, M. V., Huang, B., Pollack, L. M., Canchola, J. A., & Catania, J. A. (2002). Battering victimization among a probability-based sample of men who have sex with men. *American Journal of Public Health, 92*, 1964–1969.

Hampton, R. L., & Gelles, R. J. (1991). A profile of violence toward black children. In R. L. Hampton (Ed.), *Black family violence* (pp. 21–34). Lexington, MA: Lexington Books.

Hampton, R. L., Gelles, R. J., & Harrop, J. W. (1989). Is violence in black families increasing? A comparison of 1975 and 1985 national survey rates. *Journal of Marriage and Family, 51*, 969–980.

Hilberman, E. (1980). Overview: "The wife-beater's wife" reconsidered. *American Journal of Psychiatry, 137*, 1336–1346.

Holtzworth-Munroe, A. (2001). Standards for batterer treatment programs: How can research inform our decisions? *Journal of Aggression, Maltreatment, and Trauma, 5*, 165–180.

Homans, G. C. (1967). Fundamental social processes. In N. J. Smelser (Ed.), *Sociology*. New York: John Wiley.

Hrdy, S. B. (1979). Infanticide among animals: A review, classification, and examination of the implications for reproductive strategies of females. *Ethology and Sociobiology, 1*, 13–40.

Jaffe, P. G., Wolfe, D. A., & Wilson, S. K. (1990). *Children of battered women*. Newbury Park, CA: Sage.

Kantor, G. K., Jasinski, J. L., & Aldarondo, E. (1994). Sociocultural status and incidence of marital violence in Hispanic families. *Violence and Victims, 9*, 207–222.

Kantor, G. K., & Straus, M. A. (1987). The "drunken bum" theory of wife beating. *Social Problems, 34*, 212–230.

Kaufman, J., & Zigler, E. (1987). The intergenerational transmission of abuse is overstated. In R. J. Gelles & D. R. Loseke (Eds.), *Current controversies on family violence* (pp. 209–221). Newbury Park, CA: Sage.

Kendall-Tackett, K. A., Williams, L. M., & Finkelhor, D. (1993). The impact of sexual abuse on children: A review and synthesis of recent empirical studies. *Psychological Bulletin, 113*, 164–180.

Kurz, D. (2005). Men's violence toward women is a serious social problem. In D. Loseke, R. J. Gelles, & M. M. Cavanaugh (Eds.), *Current controversies on family violence* (2nd ed., pp. 79–96). Thousand Oaks, CA: Sage.

Levesque, D. (1998). *Violence desistance among battering men: Existing intervention and the application of the transtheoretical model of change*. Unpublished doctoral dissertation, University of Rhode Island, Kingston.

Lockhart, L. L., White, B. W., Causby, V., & Isaac, A. (1994). Letting out the secret: Violence in lesbian relationships. *Journal of Interpersonal Violence, 9*, 469–492.

Loseke, D. R., & Kurz, D. (2004). Men's violence toward women is a serious social problem. In D. R. Loseke, R. J. Gelles, & M. M. Cavanaugh (Eds.), *Current controversies on family violence* (2nd ed., pp. 79–96). Thousand Oaks, CA: Sage.

MacEwen, K. E., & Barling, J. (1988). Multiple stressors, violence in the family of origin, and marital aggression: A longitudinal investigation. *Journal of Family Violence, 3*, 73–87.

McKenry, P. C., Julian, T. W., & Gavazzi, S. M. (1995). Toward a biopsychosocial model of domestic violence. *Journal of Marriage and Family, 57*, 307–320.

Milner, J. S., & Chilamkurti, C. (1991). Physical child abuse perpetrator characteristics: A review of the literature. *Journal of Interpersonal Violence, 6*, 345–366.

Moffitt, T. E., Caspi, A., Rutter, M., & Silva, P. A. (2001). *Sex differences in antisocial behaviour conduct disorder, delinquency and violence in the Dunedin Longitudinal Study.* Cambridge, UK: Cambridge University Press.

National Center on Elder Abuse. (1998). *The National Elder Abuse Incidence Study.* Washington, DC: American Public Human Services Association.

National Research Council. (1993). *Understanding child abuse and neglect.* Washington, DC: National Academy Press.

National Research Council. (1996). *Understanding violence against women.* Washington, DC: National Academy Press.

National Research Council. (1998). *Violence in families: Assessing prevention and treatment programs.* Washington, DC: National Academy Press.

Olds, D. L., Henderson, C. R., Jr., Kitzman, H. J., Eckenrode, J. J., Cole, R. E., & Tatelbaum, R. C. (1999). Prenatal and infancy home visitation by nurses: Recent findings. *Future of Children, 9*(1), 44–65.

Olds, D. L., Henderson, C. R., Jr., Tatelbaum, R. C., & Chamberlin, R. (1986). Preventing child abuse and neglect: A randomized trial of nurse home visitation. *Pediatrics, 78*, 65–78.

Osofsky, J. (1990). The effects of exposure to violence on young children. *American Psychologist, 50*, 782–788.

Pagelow, M. D. (1984). *Family violence.* New York: Praeger.

Pan, H. S., Neidig, P. H., & O'Leary, K. D. (1994). Predicting mild and severe husband-to-wife aggression. *Journal of Consulting and Clinical Psychology, 62*, 975–981.

Pate, A. M., & Hamilton, E. E. (1992). Formal and informal social deterrents to domestic violence: The Dade County Spouse Assault Experiment. *American Sociological Review, 57*, 691–697.

Pirog-Good, M. A., & Stets, J. E. (1986). Programs for abusers: Who drops out and what can be done. *Response, 9*(2), 17–19.

Quinsey, V. L. (1984). Sexual aggression: Studies of offenders against women. In D. N. Weisstub (Ed.), *Law and mental health: International perspectives* (Vol. 1, pp. 84–121). New York: Pergamon.

Rodriguez, E., Lasch, K. E., Chandra, P., & Lee, J. (2001). Family violence, employment status, welfare benefits, and alcohol drinking in the United States: What is the relation? *Journal of Epidemiology and Community Health, 55*, 172–178.

Rosenberg, M., & Rossman, R. (1990). The child witness to marital violence. In R. T. Ammerman & M. Hersen (Eds.), *Treatment of family violence: A sourcebook* (pp. 183–210). New York: John Wiley & Sons.

Saunders, D. (2001). Developing guidelines for domestic violence offenders: What can we learn from related fields and current research? In R. A. Geffner & A. Rosenbaum (Eds.), *Domestic violence offenders: Current interventions, research, and implications for policies and standards* (pp. 235–248). New York: Haworth.

Schechter, S. (1983). *Women and male violence.* Boston: South End.

Schumacher, J. A., Feldbau-Kohn, S., Slep, A. M. S., & Heyman, R. E. (2001). Risk factors for male-to-female partner physical abuse. *Aggression and Violent Behavior, 6,* 281–352.

Sedlak, A. J. (1997). Risk factors for the occurrence of child abuse and neglect. *Journal of Aggression, Maltreatment, and Trauma, 1,* 149–187.

Sherman, L. W., & Berk, R. A. (1984). The specific deterrent effects of arrest for domestic assault. *American Sociological Review, 49,* 261–272.

Sherman, L. W., Smith, D. A., Schmidt, J. D., & Rogan, D. P. (1992). Crime, punishment, and stake in conformity: Legal and informal control of domestic violence. *American Sociological Review, 57,* 680–690.

Silverman, J., Raj, A., Mucci, L., & Hathaway, J. (2001). Dating violence against adolescent girls and associated substance use, unhealthy weight control, sexual risk behavior, pregnancy and suicidality. *Journal of the American Medical Association, 286,* 572–579.

Slep, A. M. S., & Heyman, R. E. (2001). Where do we go from here? Moving toward an integrated approach to family violence. *Aggression and Violent Behavior, 6,* 353–356.

Smuts, B. (1992). Male aggression against women: An evolutionary perspective. *Human Nature, 3,* 1–44.

Stith, S. M., Smith, D. B., Penn, C. E., Ward, D. B., & Tritt, D. (2004). Intimate partner physical abuse perpetration and victimization risk factors: A meta-analytic review. *Aggression and Violent Behavior, 10,* 65–98.

Straus, M. A. (1999). The controversy over domestic violence by women: A methodological, theoretical, and sociology of science analysis. In X. B. Arriaga & S. Oskamp (Eds.), *Violence in intimate relationships* (pp. 17–44). Thousand Oaks, CA: Sage.

Straus, M. A. (2004). Women's violence toward men is a serious social problem. In D. R. Loseke, R. J. Gelles, & M. M. Cavanaugh (Eds.), *Current controversies on family violence* (2nd ed., pp. 55–78). Thousand Oaks, CA: Sage.

Straus, M. A., & Gelles, R. J. (1986). Societal change and change in family violence from 1975 to 1985 as revealed in two national surveys. *Journal of Marriage and Family, 48,* 465–479.

Straus, M. A., Gelles, R. J., & Steinmetz, S. K. (1980). *Behind closed doors: Violence in the American family.* New York: Doubleday/Anchor.

Straus, M. A., & Smith, C. (1990). Violence in Hispanic families in the United States: Incidence rates and structural interpretations. In M. A. Straus & R. J. Gelles (Eds.), *Physical violence in American families: Risk factors and adaptations to violence in 8,145 families* (pp. 341–367). New Brunswick, NJ: Transaction.

Tjaden, P., & Thoennes, N. (1998). *Prevalence, incidence, and consequences of violence against women: Findings from the National Violence Against Women Survey* (NCJ Publication No. 172837). Washington, DC: U.S. Department of Justice.

Tjaden, P., & Thoennes, N. (2000). *Extent, nature, and consequences of intimate partner violence* (NCJ Publication No. 181867). Washington, DC: U.S. Department of Justice.

Turell, S. C. (2000). A descriptive analysis of same-sex relationship violence for a diverse sample. *Journal of Family Violence, 15,* 281–294.

United States Department of Justice. (2004). *When violence hits home: How economics and neighborhood play a role.* Washington, DC: Office of Justice Programs.

U.S. Department of Health and Human Services, Administration on Children, Youth and Families. (2008). *Child maltreatment 2006.* Washington, DC: Government Printing Office.

Walker, L. E. (1984). *The battered woman syndrome.* New York: Springer.

Wang, C. T., & Holton, J. (2007). *Total estimated cost of child abuse and neglect in the United States.* Chicago: Prevent Child Abuse America.

Widom, C. S. (1989a). Child abuse, neglect, and violent criminal behavior. *Criminology, 27,* 251–271.

Widom, C. S. (1989b). The cycle of violence. *Science, 244,* 160–166.

Widom, C. S. (1991). Childhood victimization and adolescent problem behaviors. In M. E. Lamb & R. Ketterlinus (Eds.), *Adolescent problem behaviors* (pp. 127–164). Hillsdale, NJ: Lawrence Erlbaum.

Widom, C. S. (1995). *Victims of childhood sexual abuse: Later criminal consequences* (National Institute of Justice research in brief). Washington, DC: U.S. Department of Justice, Office of Justice Programs.

Wolfner, G. D., & Gelles, R. J. (1993). A profile of violence toward children. *Child Abuse & Neglect, 17,* 197–212.

Yllö, K. A. (1988). Political and methodological debates in wife abuse research. In K. A. Yllö & M. Bograd (Eds.), *Feminist perspectives on wife abuse* (pp. 28–50). Newbury Park, CA: Sage.

Yllö, K. A. (1993). Through a feminist lens: Gender, power, and violence. In R. J. Gelles & D. R. Loseke (Eds.), *Current controversies on family violence* (pp. 47–62). Newbury Park, CA: Sage.

Zlotnick, C. K., Kohn, R., Peterson, J., & Pearlstein, T. (1998). Partner physical victimization in a national sample of American families. *Journal of Interpersonal Violence, 13,* 156–166.

7

Families Coping With Alcohol and Substance Abuse

Judith Fischer,
Kevin P. Lyness, and Rachel Engler

A prominent approach to the study of alcohol and families involves a biopsychosocial focus (Zucker, Boyd, & Howard, 1994). This perspective organizes the prediction of pathological alcohol involvement (and, by extension, more general substance abuse) through consideration of biological contributions, psychological factors, and social influences. Conjoining this model with the family stress and coping model (see McKenry & Price, 2005) acknowledges the contribution of these biopsychosocial factors at each juncture: stressor, resource, perception, coping, and managing. We pay particular attention to the mediating and moderating effects that intervene between two variables, such as those that occur when associations between parent drinking and offspring drinking are worked through (mediated) or altered (moderated) by other variables.

Some definitions are in order. *Substance use,* as we use the term in this chapter, includes both experimental and regular use. *Substance misuse* refers to the excessive consumption of a substance. *Substance abuse* and *substance dependence* are clinical designations involving serious and persistent problems with substances. The major distinction between abuse and dependence is in the level of use; that is, substance dependence includes spending a great deal of time using, unsuccessful attempts to control the substance use, and, for some, the presence of tolerance and withdrawal. If tolerance and withdrawal are present, the diagnosis is substance dependence with physiological dependence (American Psychiatric Association, 2000). Designations used in this chapter reflect those chosen by the authors cited.

In organizing the following literature review, we take a family developmental approach. Timing is an important part of the stress and coping model. Stressors may be time limited, but they may also extend over long periods. Particular situations may not be considered stressors at one developmental period but may be stressors at another. For example, Biederman, Faraone,

Monuteaux, and Feighner (2000) found that *childhood* exposure to parental substance use disorders conferred a twofold risk on offspring, but *adolescent* exposure was associated with a threefold risk for the emergence of substance use disorders. Perceptions, resources, and problem solving may be greater or lesser depending on individual and family development. Coping that is effective in the short term may moderate the long-term impacts of a stressor or lead to a pileup of stressors over time. In any given family, the substance misuser may be the parents, the offspring, or both. Treatments vary depending on whether the child in the family or the adult is the presenting patient. And when intervening with an alcoholic parent, the ages of the children in the family need to be taken into account (Kelley & Fals-Stewart, 2008).

This review covers four topics within the context of families: (1) children and their parents coping with the challenges posed by substances, (2) adolescents who use and abuse substances, (3) bidirectional effects, and (4) intervention strategies. Throughout the chapter we put the emphasis on both the family stresses involved and the search for explanations of resilience in these situations of families coping with substance abuse. The chapter concludes with an illustrative vignette. Given limitations of space, we are unable to extend our discussion in this chapter beyond the contexts of families with children and adolescents. Information on other important topics related to families and substance misuse may be found in Arendt and Farkas (2007) for fetal alcohol spectrum disorder, Leonard and Eiden (2007) for adult couples, and Stelle and Scott (2007) for elders in families.

Children and Substance Abuse Problems

Most research on childhood substance abuse has focused on 8- to 11-year-olds. A number of scholars have documented the fact that children this young are using and even abusing substances (Griffin, Botvin, Epstein, Doyle, & Diaz, 2000; Loveland-Cherry, Leech, Laetz, & Dielman, 1996; McDermott, Clark-Alexander, Westhoff, & Eaton, 1999). According to McDermott et al. (1999), 18% of fifth graders may be described as active drinkers, having consumed alcohol in the previous 30 days. In 2007, almost 40% of eighth graders had consumed more than a few sips of alcohol (Johnston, O'Malley, Bachman, & Schulenberg, 2008).

Child Characteristics

Research on substance abuse prior to adolescence tends to focus on childhood predictors of *later* adolescent and adult use and abuse (cf., Zucker, 2008) rather than correlates of *actual* substance use in childhood. Early alcohol initiation is strongly predicted by the presence of conduct disorders

(Sartor, Lynskey, Heath, Jacob, & True, 2006). A considerable body of literature suggests that behavioral undercontrol or behavioral disinhibition (failure to inhibit behavioral impulses) in childhood, especially among males, is an important precursor of later adolescent problems with substance use and abuse (Dubow, Boxer, & Huesmann, 2008; Zucker, 2008).

Cognitions (expectancies, beliefs, and values) about alcohol use appear in children as young as 3 to 6 years old (Zucker, Fitzgerald, Refior, Pallas, & Ellis, 2000), particularly among children in alcoholic families. Dunn and Goldman (1996) found that children 8 to 11 years old reported alcohol expectancies that were similar to those reported by adults. Children's favorable attitudes toward alcohol and intentions to use alcohol at age 10 are associated with a higher probability of drug abuse and dependency at age 21 (Guo, Hawkins, Hill, & Abbott, 2001). Examining young children's cognitions and behaviors is important to understanding childhood and later substance use and misuse. McDermott et al. (1999) have suggested that emphasizing health concerns as a reason not to use alcohol is likely to be ineffective with children, but it may be useful to correct children's misconceptions about alcohol-related norms and risks before they begin active use. Strong parental antialcohol norms have promoted more negative alcohol-related cognitions among seventh and eighth graders.

The child characteristics that scholars have found to be related to *childhood* substance use include a mix of behavioral and cognitive variables: less competence (Jackson, Henriksen, & Dickinson, 1997), more tolerance to deviance, more deviant self-image, more susceptibility to peer pressure, and greater reported peer use (Loveland-Cherry et al., 1996). In addition, childhood factors related to adolescent or young adult use include IQ and educational attainment (Dubow et al., 2008), children (age 10) living in a neighborhood with more trouble-making youth, antisocial friends, frequent alcohol use by best friends, frequent contact with antisocial friends, and high levels of bonding with antisocial friends (Guo et al., 2001). Childhood antisocial behavior is a recurring and important correlate of later use (Dubow et al., 2008; Fitzgerald, Puttler, Refior, & Zucker, 2007; Leonard & Eiden, 2007).

Parent Factors

Jacob and Johnson (1997) conceptualize parenting influence on children as alcohol-specific effects and non-alcohol-specific effects. *Alcohol-specific effects* involve the behaviors of the parents with respect to alcohol and how these parental behaviors are related to the child's behavior and cognition. Frequently studied are the effects of being a child of an alcoholic (COA). Weinberg, Dielman, Mandell, and Shope (1994) found that fifth and sixth graders had higher odds of current alcohol misuse and heavy alcohol use when there was greater mother or father drinking levels, a substance-specific influence. In general, parents' substance-specific influences on preadolescents have predictive utility for later adolescent and adult use and abuse (Dishion, Capaldi, & Yoerger, 1999). *Non-alcohol-specific effects* reflect the general aspects of the family environment that are related to children's deviant behavior, cognition, and substance use. Parenting practices and behaviors such as supervision, discipline, and nurturance of children; communication with children; and parental divorce and remarriage reflect the operation of non-substance-specific influences as do having clear family rules and monitoring (Guo et al., 2001).

Non-substance-specific factors are studied as operating alone, together with alcohol-specific factors, and as part of feedback loops. The non-substance-specific variables of low income, parental aggression, and low marital satisfaction have been found to be important correlates of child adjustment (Fals-Stewart, Kelley, Cooke, & Golden, 2003). In turn, child-hood maladjustment is an important predictor of greater harmful drinking at age 42 (24% more) (Maggs, Patrick, & Feinstein, 2008). The combination of parental alcoholism (alcohol-specific) with parental antisocial behavior (non-alcohol-specific) has been shown to predict child externalizing behavior, itself a predictor of more harmful drinking as an adult (Fals-Stewart et al., 2003; Fitzgerald et al., 2007; Maggs et al., 2008). A number of studies have provided evidence that parent reactions to children's difficult behaviors are followed by additional child maladaptation (Dishion et al., 1999; Wong, Zucker, Puttler, & Fitzgerald, 1999). As well, parental divorce has been shown to be a lesser risk factor for preadolescents than for adolescents (Needle, Su, & Doherty, 1990).

In sum, children with conduct problems, particularly in stressful homes, are at high risk for later substance use problems. Parenting responses that emphasize increased monitoring may make child externalizing problems worse. Clearly, help for parents in dealing with difficult children is warranted. In addition, the problems seem to extend beyond parenting to parents' own issues with substances, their relationships with each other, and their relationships with society.

Adolescents and Youth and Substance Abuse Problems ____

In the United States, the period of adolescence, roughly ages 13 to 19, is characterized by dramatic increases in substance use. The period of youth or young adulthood, up to age 25, is generally the time during which substance use and abuse peak (National Institute on Alcohol Abuse and Alcoholism, 2000). Monitoring the Future's annual surveys of 50,000 students in the 8th, 10th, and 12th grades document the latest figures. "Nearly three quarters of students (72%) have consumed alcohol (more than just a few sips) by the end of high school. . . . In fact, more than half (55%) of the 12th graders and nearly a fifth (18%) of the 8th graders in 2007 report having been drunk at least once in their life" (Johnston et al., 2008, p. 41).

From the late 1990s to 2007, substance use among adolescents generally declined. Despite this decline, however, data from the Monitoring the Future surveys show large shifts in behavior from those in the eighth grade to those in the twelfth grade. Scholars' attempts to account for these age-related changes, and to explain the use of substances in adolescence, have generated a substantial body of literature in which certain themes stand out. Researchers have looked at (a) adolescent characteristics, such as expectancies, achievements, moods, behaviors, stressors, personality, roles, and clinical diagnoses, as well as demographics of gender, ethnicity, school, and neighborhood; (b) substance-specific family characteristics, such as parent substance use and alcohol-specific parenting practices; and (c) non-substance-specific influences such as parenting styles, family dysfunction, family stressors, family socioeconomic status, and parent–adolescent communication. It should be noted that most of the research documents factors that are involved in greater risk. However, research on moderating variables highlights areas where there may be factors involved in resilience (doing well despite adversity).

Fitting primarily within the resources component of the stress and coping model, four important models link family history of alcoholism to adolescent pathological alcohol involvement: (1) positive affect regulation (produce positive feelings), (2) deviance proneness (demonstrate deficient socialization of which alcohol use is a part), (3) negative affect regulation (relieve negative emotions), and (4) pharmacological vulnerability (have physical sensitivity to the effects of alcohol) (Sher, Grekin, & Williams, 2005). In their research on moderators, scholars have sought to specify for whom and under what conditions associations hold between and among variables (Fischer & Wampler, 1994; Jacob & Johnson, 1997).

Adolescent Characteristics

Just as research has identified *childhood* behavioral disinhibition as an important factor in the prediction of early and later onset of substance use, there is a similar picture of the influence of *adolescent* behavioral disinhibition (Zucker, 2008). The relationship between high sensation seeking/impulsivity and substance use has been found to be moderated by gender, with a stronger association for males than for females (Baker & Yardley, 2002). The authors suggested that societal pressures and expectations placed upon females may help to explain this finding; such expectations may be protective for young women.

Researchers have examined problems related to both delinquency and substance use (deviance proneness) in adolescents over time, with mixed results (Mason & Windle, 2002). Mason and Windle found that early delinquency appeared to have enduring consequences in adolescence for boys, whereas Merline, Jager, and Schulenberg (2008) reported that later alcohol use disorders among women were related to earlier theft and property damage behaviors. Among girls, apparent links between drug use and delinquency were based on the shared influences of third variables such as conduct problems (Mason & Windle, 2002).

Evidence for a negative emotions or internalizing pathway is mixed. For example, in the research of Englund, Egeland, Olivia, & Collins (2008), children with internalizing problems at age 7 reported less alcohol use in adulthood; however, at age 11, children with internalizing problems reported more alcohol use during young and middle adulthood for both genders and, for males, more alcohol use during adolescence. Parenting is related to offspring depression that is, in turn, related to alcohol abuse in college men and women (Patock-Peckham & Morgan-Lopez, 2007).

Adolescent expectancies about the effects of substances are factors in substance use and misuse (Chen, Grube, & Madden, 1994). Research has found early expectancies to be predictive of later heavy drinking in boys but not in girls (Griffin et al., 2000). Neither mediating nor moderating effects of this association are well known. However, Barnow, Schuckit, and Lucht's (2002) research on German adolescents pulled together some of these threads. In their sample, adolescents with *alcohol problems* had more behavioral problems, more perceived parental rejection, less parental warmth, and more association with substance-using peers than did adolescents without alcohol problems. *Alcoholic* adolescents demonstrated all of these characteristics plus aggression/delinquency. Thus, adolescents lacking the self-control resource were more vulnerable to alcoholism. A review of general coping supports these conclusions: (1) Adolescent coping is enhanced by warm, close relationships with parents, and (2) self-regulation plays an important role in adolescent coping (see Aldwin, 2007).

Apart from adolescent delinquency, Windle (2000) found that a number of factors operated directly and indirectly on adolescent substance use over time. Stressful life events were related to drinking to cope and directly to adolescent alcohol problems. High activity levels and sociability of the adolescent were linked to substance use by peers and were thereby indirectly related to adolescent substance use and problems with alcohol. Adolescent self-control forms a link between parental monitoring and adolescent substance use (Chapple, Hope, & Whiteford, 2005). Regretfully, there is a reduced likelihood that stressed parents or those who themselves engage in deviant behavior will encourage or teach their children self-control.

Age of drinking onset in adolescence is a strong predictor of later alcohol abuse and disorder (Tyler, Stone, & Bersani, 2006); adolescents who began drinking at 12 years or younger were at increased risk for developing later abuse and dependence compared with adolescents who held off until age 16 or older. Males reported drinking before age 12 at a rate almost three times that of females. Other factors influencing early alcohol initiation are conduct disorders, externalizing disorders, attention-deficit/hyperactivity disorder (ADHD), parental alcohol dependence, and being male (Sartor et al., 2006). Associations between early drinking status and later problem behaviors remain even after controls are employed for a number of demographic and family variables (Ellickson, Tucker, & Klein, 2003). Findings such as these suggest that early drinking is an important risk in and of itself for later problems with alcohol.

Substance-Specific Parenting Factors

Many researchers have documented associations between parental drinking and adolescent drinking (Sher et al., 2005). Involved in these associations are all the elements of the stress and coping model. Not only is there greater risk for alcohol problems among children of alcoholics (COAs) and earlier initiation of drinking, but such children also show telescoped trajectories; that is, the interval from first using alcohol to the development of alcohol disorders is shorter (Hussong, Bauer, & Chassin, 2008). Peak age for first signs of an alcohol disorder is age 18. Considering the important transitions that accompany this age period (graduating high school, employment, romantic involvements), experiencing an alcohol disorder could disrupt the timing and success of these events and relationships. Fischer and colleagues have documented pathways from alcohol misuse of parents both to young adults' difficulties with particular romantic relationships (e.g., Fischer et al., 2005) and to the initiation and maintenance of dating relationships in general (Fischer, Wiersma, Forthun, Pidcock, & Dowd, 2007).

Researchers have frequently found that a family history of alcoholism is an important element in adolescent development of substance use problems. Children are thought to imitate behaviors modeled by their parents, but such an effect has failed to appear in studies of adopted children (Sher et al., 2005), and in an offspring-of-twin research design, such effects were modest at best (Slutske et al., 2008). Although sibling substance use is also a significant predictor of adolescent substance use (Vakalahi, 2002), in line with the results of parent drinking, it may be that the sibling effect is less about modeling and more about social influence and availability. As Pandina and Johnson (1990) cautioned, a family history of alcoholism does not inevitably produce an offspring with alcohol abuse or other problems, and a family without alcoholism does not necessarily protect offspring from developing substance use problems. Furthermore, siblings from the same family may be concordant or discordant for alcohol use. Fischer and Wiersma (2008) reported that 18% of siblings were different in alcohol use, primarily in adolescence, and that this difference appeared to reflect a niche-seeking strategy when there was more parental drinking.

If parental use of alcohol is associated with adolescent use, then parental recovery from alcoholism or cessation of alcohol-related problems should reflect a reduction in family stress and an alteration in children's expectancies and alcohol-related behaviors. However, researchers have found mixed outcomes in the offspring of recovering alcoholics (e.g., Pidcock & Fischer,

1998). Family recovery is a stressful endeavor, and attention needs to be given to children when other family members go through recovery (Lewis & Allen-Byrd, 2007).

Mediators of associations between parental substance abuse and adolescent behavior identify mechanisms and processes in the transmission of adolescent alcoholism. Parenting styles represent one such mediator. Monitoring and supervision constitute one dimension of parenting style; warmth and support constitute another. When parents abuse substances, their ability to provide appropriate levels of monitoring and support may be compromised, thereby providing a mediating pathway to adolescent substance use and abuse (Barnes, Reifman, Farrell, & Dintcheff, 2000). Furthermore, because parents are regarded as sources of information for children, it is important to consider what parents tell their children about substance use and abuse (i.e., alcohol-specific parenting practices). Surveys indicate that parents do talk to their seventh- through twelfth-grade children about drugs, but their levels of communication vary for different substances: 70% discuss cigarettes, 66% discuss alcohol, and 53% discuss marijuana "a lot," but the proportion of parents who say they discuss Ecstasy "a lot" drops to just 24% ("Survey Finds," 2003). In addition, the effectiveness of parental communication about substance use varies. Although Chassin, Presson, Todd, Rose, and Sherman (1998) found that mothers' smoking-specific conversations with their adolescents were associated with lowered risk of adolescent smoking, Ennett, Bauman, Foshee, Pemberton, and Hicks (2001) indicated that for adolescents who were already using substances, parent–child communication on the topic actually made the situation worse. These researchers recommend that parents begin communicating with their children about substance use before the children initiate use.

Alcohol-specific parenting strategies could be a mechanism through which monitoring and other parenting practices work. Parental provision of alcohol and access to alcohol in the home increases the likelihood that adolescents will express greater intent to use as well as greater actual alcohol use (Komro, Maldonado-Molina, Tobler, Bonds, & Muller, 2007). Nonetheless, the findings have not been consistent from study to study, suggesting the presence of moderating effects.

Gender of the offspring and gender of the drinking parent are important moderators. Consistently, associations of predictors with drinking outcomes are stronger and more stable for males compared to females (Merline et al., 2008; Zucker, 2008). Greater male vulnerability may be genetic (Zucker, 2008). Maternal drinking is an often overlooked factor in offspring drinking but has been documented as playing an important role (Englund et al., 2008; White, Johnson, & Buyske, 2000). Tyler et al. (2006) attribute maternal influences to mothers' stronger role in child rearing.

Other moderating factors that have been found to alter the association between parental drinking and offspring outcomes include expectations, peer orientations, ethnicity, family functioning, family structure, family cohesion, parental support, personality of the offspring, and family roles of the offspring (Fischer & Lyness, 2005). However, buffering effects by one parent of the negative effects of the other parent's drinking has not been one of the moderators (Curran & Chassin, 1996), and parental support loses its effectiveness among adolescents with higher levels of undercontrol (King & Chassin, 2004). With respect to resilience, Fischer and Wampler (1994) investigated the buffering effects of personality and family roles (hero, mascot, scapegoat/lost child) on the associations between offspring alcohol misuse and both family history of addictions and family dysfunction. They found that personality was a moderator of the association of family addictions with offspring drinking for both males and females, but family roles such as hero buffered offspring drinking only with respect to family dysfunction. Other research points to the importance of avoiding the role of parentified child in families with parental alcohol misuse. Such avoidance was related to higher self-concept, an indication of more resilience in these particular 10- to 18-year-old children (Godsall, Jurkovic, Emshoff, Anderson, & Stanwyck, 2004). The kind of coping a child engages in, such as active coping, is important to adjustment (Smith et al., 2006); unfortunately, parental alcoholism is more likely to lead to children using avoidant coping, a tactic associated with poorer adjustment. Andrews, Hops, and Duncan (1997) concluded that although a good parent–child relationship is important to positive child adjustment, it may not always be protective in situations in which parents use substances.

Non-Substance-Specific Parenting Factors

Supervision and support are important parenting variables that operate regardless of parental substance use or abuse to influence adolescent outcomes. For example, based on their research on 9- to 17-year-olds, Coombs and Landsverk (1988) suggest that "for a youngster to remain free from substances, it is advantageous if parents set clear behavioral limits and maintain interpersonally satisfying relationships with their children" (p. 480). Among other benefits, these parenting practices may reduce stress, increase resources, and encourage active coping. Abstaining youth have parents who do not use punishment to maintain control but instead clarify appropriate behavior and reinforce that behavior; such parents also have warm relationships with their children. Increased family involvement, support, and bonding during adolescence are protective factors that predict less problem alcohol use in adulthood (Galaif, Stein, Newcomb, & Bernstein, 2001; Vakalahi, 2002). Maternal hostility toward their 24- to 42-month-old children predicted age 19 alcohol use for females although not for males (Englund et al., 2008). On the other hand, White et al. (2000) failed to find an association of parental warmth/hostility in the adolescent period with later offspring adult drinking. The timing of the parenting behavior could be a factor in these differing findings.

Adolescent demands for autonomy may create parent–child stressors and disrupted parenting. Dishion and McMahon (1998) provide the following definition of parental monitoring: "[It] includes both structuring the child's home, school, and community environments, and tracing the child's behavior in those environments. . . . [It] should be developmentally, contextually, and culturally appropriate" (p. 66). Good intentions are necessary but not sufficient to bring about successful parental monitoring practices. In a sample of high-risk adolescents, parental monitoring was a protective factor against alcohol and other drug use. However, for this protection to emerge, adolescents had to report that their parents *always* monitored them rather than just *sometimes* (Shillington at al., 2005).

Some scholars have theorized that single-parent family structure creates distress in adolescents that may lead to greater affect and mood alteration through substance use. In addition, the lower levels of supervision and availability of parents in single-parent households may also lead to greater substance experimentation and abuse. Reflecting the stress approach, Jeynes's (2001) research of nationally representative U.S. 12th graders found that adolescents who had experienced more recent parental divorce drank more alcohol. But other variables, including parent unavailability, family quality, peer acceptance/self-esteem, and deviant peer involvement, serve as mediators between parental divorce and adolescent alcohol use (Curry, Fischer, Reifman, & Harris, 2004). In addition to the absence of the nonresident father, factors such as weak attachment and limited monitoring are also associated with adolescent alcohol use (Jones & Benda, 2004). The association between single-parent homes and alcohol use may hold only during adolescence (Merline et al., 2008). Divorce is not the only family structure risk factor in that adolescents who transition from a single-parent family to a stepfamily increase their risk of initiating alcohol use (Kirby, 2006). There is some support, however, for the idea that instead of family structure, parent and peer relationships are better at explaining adolescent alcohol consumption (Crawford & Novak, 2008).

Regardless of intactness of family of origin, parental support is an important correlate of adolescent alcohol use, but the association is also mediated by other factors, such as religiosity, peer alcohol use, and school grades (Mason & Windle, 2002). Furthermore, students who received good grades elicited greater parental support. According to Bogenschneider, Wu, and Raffaelli (1998), mothers' responsiveness acted indirectly on adolescent alcohol use by helping to weaken adolescents' orientation to peers. Maternal depression, a condition that could reduce maternal support, contributed to adolescent and young adult problem drinking (Alati et al., 2005).

Wills and Cleary (1996) suggested that parent support buffers adolescent substance use by reducing the effects of risk factors and increasing the effects of protective factors. Family support moderates the effects of peers on adolescent substance use (Frauenglass, Routh, Pantin, & Mason, 1997). In a study of Hispanic eighth graders, Frauenglass et al. (1997) found that parent support was protective against the effects of peer modeling on tobacco and marijuana use. The combination of supervision and acceptance, an *authoritative* parenting style, has been identified as a particularly important factor, both concurrently and longitudinally, in the reduced use of substances (Adalbjarnardottir & Hafsteinsson, 2001). Among older adolescents, more indulgent and less controlling parents have been found to be related to substance abuse more often than have authoritative parents. Tucker, Ellickson, and Klein (2008) indicated that adolescents living in permissive homes were nine times more likely to drink heavily in the 9th grade and three times more likely to drink heavily in the 11th grade compared with children from nonpermissive homes. In general, the more the parent used alcohol, the more permissive were the alcohol rules for the adolescent. The more permissive the alcohol rules, the more the adolescent drank. Despite living in a permissive home environment, there were factors predicting less heavy drinking for these adolescents: social influences, alcohol beliefs, and resistance self-efficacy (Tucker et al., 2008).

In addition to parenting style, the quality of parent–child communication is important. Kafka and London (1991) established the value of an adolescent's having at least one parent with whom the adolescent has "open" communication. They found reduced levels of substance use among high school–age adolescents who had such a parent. However, openness of communication may not be enough; Humes and Humphrey (1994) suggested that parents also need to be sensitive to adolescents' needs.

Trauma is another important pathway to adolescent problem behavior. Effects of trauma can be ameliorated by parenting behaviors of support and monitoring (Luster & Small, 1997). Adolescents in substance abuse treatment programs have reported more physical, sexual, and violent victimization compared with controls (National Institute on Alcohol Abuse and Alcoholism, 1997). The dual risks of COA status and sexual abuse in adolescence have been related to higher levels of adolescent problems, including chemical abuse, than that found in adolescents with only one risk factor (Chandy, Blum, & Resnick, 1996). Moreover, such experiences are related to lengthier periods of treatment and less treatment cooperation (Mulsow, 2007). Adolescents experiencing *current* abuse have been shown to have more problem behaviors, such as binge drinking, than adolescents with histories of *prior* abuse (Luster & Small, 1997). Employing a national data set, Kilpatrick et al. (2003) found connections between substance abuse and dependence during adolescence and (a) family alcohol problems, (b) having been a witness to violence, and (c) having been a victim of physical assault. Posttraumatic stress disorder (PTSD) occurred when sexual assault was added to the mix. Those who develop alcohol misuse subsequent to trauma are more at risk for future assault (Mulsow, 2007). The effects of secondhand abuse (i.e., childhood abuse of parents of substance-abusing adolescents) may also be at work through its association with greater parental alcohol dependence (Peters, Malzman, & Villone, 1994).

In sum, difficulties in making the transition from childhood to adolescence are compounded when alcohol and drugs enter the picture. Parents' use of substances gains added importance, creating stressors, influencing perceptions, detracting from resources, and hindering coping. Parents' flexibility in coping with adolescents' emerging needs for autonomy and independence should be gender sensitive, given that socialization pressures continue to differ for boys and girls. More resilient adolescents in the face of parental alcoholism, poorer parenting, and trauma tend to be female, less disinhibited, and more parentally supported and monitored.

Bidirectional Processes

Throughout this chapter, the studies we cited have primarily focused on a particular direction of effects from parent to child: alcohol abuse in parents *leads to* child and adolescent alcohol use and misuse; parenting practices help or hinder adolescent resistance to alcohol use. Other research suggests that bidirectional effects are at work. The title of one article put the issue as "Can your children drive you to drink?" (Pelham & Lang, 1999). A series of experimental studies documented an affirmative answer. Adoptive parents (Finley & Aguiar, 2002) of children whose biological parents had alcohol, antisocial, depressive, or other psychiatric disorders experienced double the risk of developing their own psychiatric or alcohol-related problems compared to adoptive parents of children without such a predisposition. Rather than parenting practices being a result of parental substance use disorders, parents' discipline was *elicited* by sons' neurobehavioral disinhibition (ND); this ND was in turn related to sons' substance use disorders (Mezzich et al., 2007). Commenting on studies such as these, Leonard and Eiden (2007) stated, "Alcoholic parents are at higher risk for having children with behavior problems, and children's behavior problems may increase parental stress and lead to more drinking" (p. 299). Deater-Deckard (2004) suggested that parents may need family support, training in coping responses, and social policies such as parental leave to alleviate parenting stress.

Issues in Prevention and Treatment

Although we have focused on families coping with substance use and misuse in the discussion above, limiting prevention and treatment efforts to "the person" in the family with the substance use problem is not sufficient to address the multiple levels of factors that are implicated in a person's substance use problem. There is no one place to start. In fact, alcohol misuse in families can extend back generations (Garrett & Landau, 2007). The substance-abusing parent certainly needs help, but so do the children in the family. As the above review illustrates, the stress and coping model highlights the importance of all the components—stressors, perceptions, resources, problem-solving skills, coping skills, and bidirectional effects—found in families dealing with substance abuse. Helping parents to effectively manage a behaviorally disinhibited child may interrupt the negative sequence of events from childhood to young adulthood. But helping children cope with a substance-abusing parent is also critical. Prevention of both early onset of substance use and early conduct disorder problems is a key factor in positive youth development. Fitzgerald et al. (2007) suggested that children from antisocial alcoholic families would benefit from interventions that begin in infancy. Other pathways that children follow are sorted out in middle childhood, suggesting that interventions begin before this critical time. Bolstering the case for early intervention, Aldwin's (2007) developmental approach identifies coping as embedded in the social ecology of the family throughout the lifespan beginning with infant and even prenatal coping behaviors.

Although medicating children who have ADHD has been found to be effective in preventing later substance use, not all behaviorally disinhibited children have ADHD. Nor is medication the sole answer for multifaceted family problems. If children and adults are dually diagnosed (e.g., alcohol abuse/dependence with PTSD), it is important to treat both (Mulsow, 2007). It is also necessary to deal with such family background issues as stresses surrounding grief, loss, and trauma (Garrett & Landau, 2007) for which alcohol abuse is a symptom.

Effective programs aimed at treating or preventing substance abuse involve multiple components and multiple points of entry (Boyd & Faden, 2002). These programs may be expensive; they may require commitments of time, energy, and other resources from schools and communities as well as the dedication of skilled leaders. There is no "magic bullet" for treating or preventing substance abuse. Nor is there one for producing resilient children.

Currently in the United States, too many parents and children are in need of treatment services, but substance abuse treatment is expensive, and effective programs are scarce, particularly for those whose addiction issues have led to impoverishment and lack of insurance. At the societal level, reductions in access to treatment and program resources have contributed to a pileup of unmet needs (Etheridge, Smith, Rounds-Bryant, & Hubbard, 2001). Even when substance-abusing parents or children go into treatment and recovery, the relapse rates are discouraging (Alford, Koehler, & Leonard, 1991). For example, because an important concomitant of recovery is the disruption of family dynamics, programs need to address changes in family dynamics to prevent relapse and to prevent children in the family from experiencing additional difficulties (Lewis & Allen-Byrd, 2007). Fischer, Pidcock, and Fletcher-Stephens (2007) describe three evidence-based programs for alcohol-abusing adolescents that include the family as well as the adolescent. Dealing with family dynamics is only one goal of comprehensive intervention, however. As we noted in the earlier version of this chapter (Fischer & Lyness, 2005), to prevent relapse, programs must also consider settings and situations beyond the family itself, such as (a) effective aftercare services; (b) safe havens for children of addicted parents; (c) school, college, and community policies; (d) cultural and subcultural norms and behaviors; and (e) support for recovery, important for singly diagnosed and dually diagnosed alike.

Drawing on the general literature on coping and the effects of coping on mental health, Aldwin (2007) concludes: "Interventions that serve . . . to enhance individual feelings of control (where appropriate) have been unequivocally demonstrated to have positive effects on both mental and physical health" (p. 208). In addition, Aldwin states that a key aspect of the development of positive coping is the focus on self-regulation that implies choice, consistency, and continuity, particularly in goal-directed coping. One implication of this self-regulation focus in coping in recent interventions has been in the development of *mindful coping* (Aldwin).

Conclusion

An encouraging aspect of recent studies examining how families cope with substance abuse is the inclusion of multiple variables, multiple perspectives, multiple waves of data collection spanning infancy to middle age, and sophisticated data analysis techniques. This very richness presents challenges to the scholars who report such research because the findings are embedded in complex webs of interrelated results. Studies that examine the changing nature of predictors across different developmental ages provide valuable information for prevention and risk reduction (e.g., Guo et al., 2001). With this information, programs can begin to focus on the key developmental periods specific to identified predictors.

With only a few exceptions, the literature we have reviewed in this chapter has largely reported on research with families of European heritage. However, the Monitoring the Future surveys repeatedly find lower rates of substance use among African American youth than among European American adolescents (Johnston, O'Malley, Bachman, & Schulenberg, 2008). Even when similar rates are reported across ethnic groups, as with marijuana use, researchers should not assume that predictors and pathways to substance use are analogous. Furthermore, the consequences of use are greater for African American than European American youth (Jones, Hussong, Manning, & Sterrett, 2008). Future research must reflect the diversity of families coping with substance abuse, not just in terms of ethnicity and culture but also in terms of emerging understandings of the broad spectrum of close relationships covered by the term *families*. We have included in this review research on families with children and adolescents that we believe illuminates family scholars' understandings of families coping with substance abuse.

Illustrative Vignette

Karl is a 13-year-old boy who has been getting into trouble for drinking at school. This is not Karl's first time in trouble—he is often disruptive and aggressive and seems to lack impulse control. When he was younger, his parents (at the urging of the school) had him tested for ADHD, but the results were inconclusive, and the psychiatrist did not recommend medication. Karl's parents are typically punitive and have been known to use physical punishment, and Karl has reported not feeling supported by his parents. Moreover, Karl's parents have been considering getting a divorce. His father is a heavy drinker, although he has never been diagnosed with a substance abuse problem. Karl sees his father come home from work each night and drink five to six beers as he complains about his day. Recently, his father reports that the stress of dealing with Karl has led to increased drinking in order to cope. Karl has learned from this that drinking is a good way to relieve stress, and this reinforces his positive attitudes toward alcohol. Karl's parents do not know most of his friends, but the school reports that Karl hangs out with a slightly older group of kids who are known to drink and party. Karl has never felt that he fits in very well with his peers, but this current group of friends seems more accepting of his impulsive nature. Karl has an older sister who has not gotten into trouble with substances, and who has always been more controlled and inhibited. The school has recommended that the family see a therapist.

The family therapist, knowing some of the literature on stress and coping as well as alcohol and substance abuse, engaged a multifaceted approach. The therapist first addressed parental behaviors and coping, including the quality of the marriage, parenting styles, and Karl's father's drinking, with a focus on increasing self-regulation capacities in both parents and in Karl. Partly as a result of increased self-awareness, Karl's father decided to cut down on his drinking and made a commitment to work on the marriage. Both parents agreed to specific behavioral interventions designed to interrupt Karl's disinhibited behavior patterns. The therapist also helped Karl find other, less maladaptive ways of coping, along with implementing interventions with Karl at the school that helped him develop a different peer group (particularly focusing on Karl's propensity for aggression). Finally, the therapist intervened with Karl directly about his drinking behavior, knowing that Karl's early onset of drinking places him at risk for later serious substance abuse problems. Karl was able to talk about using alcohol as a means of coping with rejection and reported some success with making new friends. The therapist also helped Karl by specifically focusing on self-regulation by developing positive goal structures and increasing his focus on choices he makes in coping. He still struggles with anger, but he is able to talk with his father about his choices at times. For all of the family members, the interventions focused on active coping and building in each a sense of control and mindfulness.

Suggested Internet Resources

National Institute on Alcohol Abuse and Alcoholism (an institute within the National Institutes of Health): http://www.niaaa.nih.gov

National Institute on Drug Abuse: http://www.drugabuse.gov

Monitoring the Future (information on adolescent substance use and abuse): http://www.monitoringthefuture.org

Harvard School of Public Health, College Alcohol Study (information on adolescent and young adult binge drinking in college): http://www.hsph.harvard.edu/cas

UNC Carolina Population Center, information about the National Longitudinal Survey of Adolescent Health): http://www.cpc.unc.edu/projects/addhealth

References

Adalbjarnardottir, S., & Hafsteinsson, L. G. (2001). Adolescents' perceived parenting styles and their substance use: Concurrent and longitudinal analyses. *Journal of Research on Adolescence, 11,* 401–423.

Alati, R., Kinner, S. A., Najman, J. M., Mamum, A. A., Williams, G. M., O'Callaghan, M., & Bor, W. (2005). Early predictors of adult drinking: A birth cohort study. *American Journal of Epidemiology, 162*(11), 1098–1107.

Aldwin, C. M. (2007). *Stress, coping, and development: An integrative perspective* (2nd ed.). New York: Guilford.

Alford, G. S., Koehler, R. A., & Leonard, J. (1991). Alcoholics Anonymous–Narcotics Anonymous model inpatient treatment of chemically dependent adolescents: A 2-year outcome study. *Journal of Studies on Alcohol, 52,* 118–126.

American Psychiatric Association. (2000). *Diagnostic and statistical manual of mental disorders* (4th ed., text rev.). Washington, DC: Author.

Andrews, J. A., Hops, H., & Duncan, S. C. (1997). Adolescent modeling of parent substance use: The moderating effect of the relationship with the parent. *Journal of Family Psychology, 11,* 259–270.

Arendt, R. E., & Farkas, K. J. (2007). Maternal alcohol abuse and fetal alcohol spectrum disorder: A life-span perspective. *Alcoholism Quarterly, 25*(3), 3–20.

Baker, J. R., & Yardley, J. K. (2002). Moderating effect of gender on the relationship between sensation seeking-impulsivity and substance use in adolescents. *Journal of Child and Adolescent Substance Abuse, 12*(1), 27–43.

Barnes, G. M., Reifman, A., Farrell, M. P., & Dintcheff, B. A. (2000). The effects of parenting on the development of adolescent alcohol misuse: A six-wave latent growth model. *Journal of Marriage and the Family, 62,* 175–186.

Barnow, S., Schuckit, M. A., & Lucht, M. (2002). The importance of a positive family history of alcoholism, parental rejection and emotional warmth, behavioral problems and peer substance use for alcohol problems in teenagers: A path analysis. *Journal of Studies on Alcohol, 63,* 305–312.

Biederman, J., Faraone, S. V., Monuteaux, M. C., & Feighner, J. A. (2000). Patterns of alcohol and drug use in adolescents can be predicted by parental substance use disorders. *Pediatrics, 106,* 792–797.

Bogenschneider, K., Wu, M., & Raffaelli, M. (1998). Parent influences on adolescent peer orientation and substance use: The interface of parenting practices and value. *Child Development, 69,* 1672–1688.

Boyd, G. M., & Faden, V. (2002). Overview. *Journal of Studies on Alcohol, 14*(Suppl.), 6–13.

Chandy, J. M., Blum, R. W., & Resnick, M. D. (1996). History of sexual abuse and parental alcohol misuse: Risk, outcomes and protective factors in adolescents. *Child and Adolescent Social Work Journal, 13,* 411–432.

Chapple, C. L., Hope, T. R., & Whiteford, S. W. (2005). The direct and indirect effects of parental bonds, parental drug use, and self-control on adolescent substance use. *Journal of Child & Adolescent Substance Abuse, 14*(3), 17–38.

Chassin, L., Presson, C. C., Todd, M., Rose, J. S., & Sherman, S. J. (1998). Maternal socialization of adolescent smoking: The intergenerational transmission of parenting and smoking. *Developmental Psychology, 34,* 1189–1201.

Chen, M., Grube, J. W., & Madden, P. A. (1994). Alcohol expectancies and adolescent drinking: Differential prediction of frequency, quantity, and intoxication. *Addictive Behaviors, 19,* 521–529.

Coombs, R. H., & Landsverk, J. (1988). Parenting styles and substance use during childhood and adolescence. *Journal of Marriage and Family, 50,* 473–482.

Crawford, L. A., & Novak, K. B. (2008). Parent-child relations and peer associations as mediators of the family structure-substance use relationship. *Journal of Family Issues, 29*(2), 155–184.

Curran, P. J., & Chassin, L. (1996). A longitudinal study of parenting as a protective factor for children of alcoholics. *Journal of Studies on Alcohol, 57*(3), 305–313.

Curry, L., Fischer, J., Reifman, A., & Harris, K. (2004, March). *Family factors, self-esteem, peer involvement, and adolescent alcohol misuse.* Poster presented at the biennial meeting of the Society for Research on Adolescence, Baltimore.

Deater-Deckard, K. (2004). *Parenting stress.* New Haven, CT: Yale University Press.

Dishion, T. J., Capaldi, D. M., & Yoerger, K. (1999). Middle childhood antecedents to progressions in male adolescent substance use: An ecological analysis of risk and protection. *Journal of Adolescent Research, 14,* 175–205.

Dishion, T. J., & McMahon, R. J. (1998). Parental monitoring and the prevention of child and adolescent problem behavior: A conceptual and empirical formulation. *Clinical Child and Family Psychology Review, 1,* 61–75.

Dubow, E. F., Boxer, P., & Huesmann, L. R. (2008). Childhood and adolescent predictors of early and middle adulthood alcohol use and problem drinking: The Columbia County Longitudinal Study. *Addiction, 103*(Suppl. 1), 36–47.

Dunn, M. E., & Goldman, M. S. (1996). Empirical modeling of an alcohol expectancy memory network in elementary school children as a function of grade. *Experimental and Clinical Psychopharmacology, 4,* 209–217.

Ellickson, P. L., Tucker, J. S., & Klein, D. J. (2003). Ten-year prospective study of public health problems associated with early drinking. *Pediatrics, 111,* 949–955.

Englund, M. M., Egeland, B., Olivia, E. M., & Collins, W. A. (2008). Childhood and adolescent predictors of heavy drinking and alcohol use disorders in early adulthood: A longitudinal developmental analysis. *Addiction, 103*(Suppl. 1), 23–35.

Ennett, S. T., Bauman, K. E., Foshee, V. A., Pemberton, M., & Hicks, K. A. (2001). Parent-child communication about adolescent tobacco and alcohol use: What do parents say and does it affect youth behavior? *Journal of Marriage and Family, 63,* 48–63.

Etheridge, R. M., Smith, J. C., Rounds-Bryant, J. L., & Hubbard, R. L. (2001). Drug abuse treatment and comprehensive services for adolescents. *Journal of Research on Adolescents, 16,* 563–589.

Fals-Stewart, W., Kelley, M. L., Cooke, C. G., & Golden, J. C. (2003). Predictors of the psychosocial adjustment of children living in households of parents in which fathers abuse drugs: The effects of postnatal parental exposure. *Addictive Behaviors, 28,* 1013–1031.

Finley, G. E., & Aguiar, L. J. (2002). The effects of children on parents: Adoptee genetic dispositions and adoptive parent psychopathology. *Journal of Genetic Psychology, 163*(4), 503–506.

Fischer, J. L., Fitzpatrick, J. A., Cleveland, B., Lee, J.-M., McKnight, A., & Miller, B., (2005). Binge drinking in the context of romantic relationships. *Addictive Behaviors, 30,* 1496–1516.

Fischer, J. L., & Lyness, K. P. (2005). Families coping with alcohol and substance abuse. In P. S. McKenry & S. J. Price (Eds.), *Families and change: Coping with stressful events and transitions* (3rd ed., pp. 155–178). Thousand Oaks, CA: Sage.

Fischer, J. L., Pidcock, B. W., & Fletcher-Stephens, B. J. (2007). Family response to adolescence, youth and alcohol. In J. L. Fischer, M. Mulsow, & A. W. Korinek (Eds.), *Familial responses to alcohol problems* (pp. 27–41). Binghamton, NY: The Haworth Press.

Fischer, J. L., & Wampler, R. S. (1994). Abusive drinking in young adults: Personality type and family role as moderators of family-of-origin influences. *Journal of Marriage and the Family, 56,* 469–479.

Fischer, J. L., & Wiersma, J. D. (2008, November). *Patterns of sibling drinking in adolescence and young adulthood.* Presented at the National Council on Family Relations Annual Meeting, Little Rock, AR.

Fischer, J. L., Wiersma, J. D., Forthun, L. F., Pidcock, B. W., & Dowd, D. (2007, November). *Parent drinking, college student drinking, difficulties with friendships and difficulties with dating.* Presented at the National Council on Family Relations Annual Meeting, Pittsburg, PA.

Fitzgerald, H. E., Puttler, L. I., Refior, S., & Zucker, R. A. (2007). Family response to children and alcohol. In J. L. Fischer, M. Mulsow, & A. W. Korinek (Eds.), *Familial responses to alcohol problems* (pp. 11–25). Binghamton, NY: The Haworth Press.

Frauenglass, S., Routh, D. K., Pantin, H. M., & Mason, C. A. (1997). Family support decreases influence of deviant peers on Hispanic adolescents' substance use. *Journal of Clinical and Child Psychology, 26,* 15–23.

Galaif, E. R., Stein, J. S., Newcomb, M. D., & Bernstein, D. P. (2001). Gender differences in the prediction of problem alcohol use in adulthood: Exploring the influence of family factors and childhood maltreatment. *Journal of Studies on Alcohol and Drugs, 62,* 486–493.

Garrett, J., & Landau, J. (2007). Family motivation to change: A major factor in engaging alcoholics in treatment. In J. L. Fischer, M. Mulsow, & A. W. Korinek (Eds.), *Familial responses to alcohol problems* (pp. 65–83). Binghamton, NY: The Haworth Press.

Godsall, R. E., Jurkovic, G. J., Emshoff, J., Anderson, L., & Stanwyck, D. (2004). Why some kids do well in bad situations: Relation of parental alcohol misuse and parentification to children's self-concept. *Substance Use & Misuse, 39,* 789–809.

Griffin, K. W., Botvin, G. J., Epstein, J. A., Doyle, M. M., & Diaz, T. (2000). Psychosocial and behavioral factors in early adolescence as predictors of heavy drinking among high school seniors. *Journal of Studies on Alcohol, 61,* 603–606.

Guo, J., Hawkins, J. D., Hill, K. G., & Abbott, R. D. (2001). Childhood and adolescent predictors of alcohol abuse and dependence in young adulthood. *Journal of Studies on Alcohol and Drugs, 62,* 754–762.

Humes, D. L., & Humphrey, L. L. (1994). A multi-method analysis of families with a polydrug-dependent or normal adolescent daughter. *Journal of Abnormal Psychology, 103,* 676–685.

Hussong, A. M., Bauer, D., & Chassin, L. (2008). Telescoped trajectories from alcohol initiation to disorder in children of alcoholic parents. *Journal of Abnormal Psychology, 117,* 63–78.

Jackson, C., Henriksen, L., & Dickinson, D. (1997). The early use of alcohol and tobacco: Its relation to children's competence and parents' behavior. *American Journal of Public Health, 87,* 359–364.

Jacob, T., & Johnson, S. (1997). Parenting influences on the development of alcohol abuse and dependence. *Alcohol Health and Research World, 21,* 204–210.

Jeynes, W. H. (2001). The effects of recent parental divorce on their children's consumption of alcohol. *Journal of Youth and Adolescence, 30,* 305–319.

Johnston, L. D., O'Malley, P. M., Bachman, J. G., & Schulenberg, J. E. (2008). *Monitoring the Future national results on adolescent drug use: Overview of key findings, 2007* (NIH Publication No. 08-6418). Bethesda, MD: National Institute on Drug Abuse. Downloaded Nov. 21, 2008, from http://www.monitoringthefuture.org/pubs/monographs/overview2007.pdf

Jones, D. J., Hussong, A. M., Manning, J., & Sterrett, E. (2008). Adolescent alcohol use in context: The role of parents and peers among African American and European American youth. *Cultural Diversity and Ethnic Minority Psychology, 14*(3), 266–273.

Jones, K. A., & Benda, B. B. (2004). Alcohol use among adolescents with non-residential fathers: A study of assets and deficits. *Alcoholism Treatment Quarterly, 22,* 3–25.

Kafka, R. R., & London, P. (1991). Communication in relationships and adolescent substance use: The influence of parents and friends. *Adolescence, 26,* 587–597.

Kelley, M. L., & Fals-Stewart, W. (2008). Treating parental drug abuse using learning sobriety together: Effects on adolescents versus children. *Drug and Alcohol Dependence, 92*(1–3), 228–238.

Kilpatrick, D. G., Ruggiero, K. J., Acierno, R., Saunders, B. E., Resnick, H. S., & Best, C. L. (2003). Violence and risk of PTSD, major depression, substance abuse/dependence, and comorbidity: Results from the national survey of adolescents. *Journal of Consulting and Clinical Psychology, 71,* 692–700.

King, K. M., & Chassin, L. (2004). Mediating and moderated effects of adolescent behavioral undercontrol and parenting in the prediction of drug use disorders in emerging adulthood. *Psychology of Addictive Behaviors, 18,* 239–249.

Kirby, J. B. (2006). From single-parent families to stepfamilies: Is the transition associated with adolescent alcohol initiation? *Journal of Family Issues, 27*(5), 685–711.

Komro, K. A., Maldonado-Molina, M. M., Tobler, A. L., Bonds, J. R., & Muller, K. E. (2007). Effects of home access and availability of alcohol on young adolescents' alcohol use. *Addiction, 102,* 1597–1608.

Leonard, K. E., & Eiden, R. D. (2007). Marital and family processes in the context of alcohol use and alcohol disorders. *Annual Review of Clinical Psychology, 3,* 285–310.

Lewis, V., & Allen-Byrd, L. (2007). Coping strategies for the stages of family recovery. In J. L. Fischer, M. Mulsow, & A. W. Korinek (Eds.), *Familial responses to alcohol problems* (pp. 105–124). Binghamton, NY: The Haworth Press.

Loveland-Cherry, C. J., Leech, S., Laetz, V. B., & Dielman, T. E. (1996). Correlates of alcohol use and misuse in fourth-grade children: Psychosocial, peer, parental, and family factors. *Health Education Quarterly, 23,* 497–577.

Luster, T., & Small, S. A. (1997). Sexual abuse history and problems in adolescence: Explaining the effects of moderating variables. *Journal of Marriage and the Family, 59,* 131–142.

Maggs, J. L., Patrick, M. E., & Feinstein, L. (2008). Childhood and adolescent predictors of alcohol use and problems in adolescence and adulthood in the National Child Development Study. *Addiction, 103*(Suppl. 1), 7–22.

Mason, W. A., & Windle, M. (2002). Reciprocal relations between adolescent substance use and delinquency: A longitudinal latent variable analysis. *Journal of Abnormal Psychology, 111,* 63–76.

McDermott, R. J., Clark-Alexander, B. J., Westhoff, W. W., & Eaton, D. K. (1999). Alcohol attitudes and beliefs related to actual alcohol experience in a fifth-grade cohort. *Journal of School Health, 69,* 356–361.

McKenry, P. C., & Price, S. J. (2005). Families coping with change. In P. S. McKenry & S. J. Price (Eds.), *Families and change: Coping with stressful events and transitions* (3rd ed., pp. 1–24). Thousand Oaks, CA: Sage.

Merline, A., Jager, J., & Schulenberg, J. E. (2008). Adolescent risk factors for adult alcohol use and abuse: Stability and change of predictive value across early and middle adulthood. *Addiction, 103*(Suppl. 1), 84–99.

Mezzich, A. C., Tarter, R. E., Kirisci, L., Feske, U., Day, B., & Gao, Z. (2007). Reciprocal influence of parent discipline and child's behavior on risk for substance disorder: A nine-year prospective study. *American Journal of Drug and Alcohol Abuse, 33*(6), 851–867.

Mulsow, M. (2007). Treatment of co-morbidity in families. In J. L. Fischer, M. Mulsow, & A.W. Korinek (Eds.), *Familial responses to alcohol problems* (pp. 125–140). Binghamton, NY: The Haworth Press.

National Institute on Alcohol Abuse and Alcoholism. (1997). *Youth drinking: Risk factors and consequences* (Alcohol Alert 37). Retrieved December 20, 2004, from http://www.niaaa.nih.gov/publications/aa37.htm

National Institute on Alcohol Abuse and Alcoholism. (2000). Drinking over the life span: Issues of biology, behavior, and risk. In National Institute on Alcohol Abuse and Alcoholism, *Tenth special report to the U.S. Congress on alcohol and health: Highlights from current research.* Retrieved December 20, 2004, from http://www.niaaa.nih.gov/publications/10report/chap01.pdf

Needle, R. H., Su, S. S., & Doherty, W. J. (1990). Divorce, remarriage, and adolescent substance use: A prospective longitudinal study. *Journal of Marriage and the Family, 52,* 157–169.

Pandina, R. J., & Johnson, V. (1990). Serious alcohol and drug problems among adolescents with a family history of alcoholism. *Journal of Studies on Alcohol, 51,* 278–282.

Patock-Peckham, J. A., & Morgan-Lopez, A. A. (2007). College drinking behaviors: Mediational links between parenting styles, parental bonds, depression, and alcohol problems. *Psychology of Addictive Behaviors, 21*(3), 297–306.

Pelham, W. E., & Lang, A. R. (1999). Can your children drive you to drink Stress and parenting in adults interacting with children with ADHD. *Alcohol Research and Health, 23*(4), 292–298.

Peters, K. R., Malzman, I., & Villone, K. (1994). Childhood abuse of parents of alcohol and other drug misusing adolescents. *International Journal of the Addictions, 29*(10), 1259–1268.

Pidcock, B. W., & Fischer, J. L. (1998). Parental recovery as a moderating variable of adult offspring problematic behaviors. *Alcoholism Treatment Quarterly, 16,* 45–57.

Sartor, C. E., Lynskey, M. T., Heath, A. C., Jacob, T., & True, W. (2006). The role of childhood risk factors in initiation of alcohol use and progression to alcohol dependence. *Addiction, 102,* 216–225.

Sher, K. J., Grekin, E. R., & Williams, N. A. (2005). The development of alcohol use disorders. *Annual Review of Clinical Psychology, 1,* 493–523.

Shillington, A. M., Lehman, S., Clapp, J., Hovell, M. F., Sipan, C., & Blumberg, E. J. (2005). Prenatal monitoring: Can it continue to be protective among high-risk adolescents? *Journal of Child and Adolescent Substance Abuse, 15*(1), 1–15.

Slutske, W. S., D'Onofrio, B. M., Turkheimer, E., Emery, R. E., Harden, K. P., Heath, A. C., & Martin, N. G. (2008). Searching for an environmental effect of parental alcoholism on offspring alcohol use disorder: A genetically informed study of children of alcoholics. *Journal of Abnormal Psychology, 117*(3), 534–551.

Smith, C. L., Eisenberg, N., Spinrad, T. L., Chassin, L., Sheffield Morris, A., Kupfer, A., Liew, J., Cumberland, A., & Valiente, C. (2006). Children's coping strategies and coping efficacy: Relations to parent socialization, child adjustment, and familial alcoholism. *Development and Psychopathology, 18,* 445–469.

Stelle, C. D., & Scott, J. P. (2007). Alcohol abuse by older family members: A family systems approach. In J. L. Fischer, M. Mulsow, & A. W. Korinek (Eds.), *Familial responses to alcohol problems* (pp. 43–63). Binghamton, NY: The Haworth Press.

Survey finds parents unresponsive to Ecstasy threat. (2003, November 3). *Alcoholism and Drug Abuse Weekly.* Retrieved February 28, 2004, from http://www.drugfreeamerica.org

Tucker, J. S., Ellickson, P. L., & Klein, D. J. (2008). Growing up in a permissive household: What deters at-risk adolescents from heavy drinking? *Journal of Studies on Alcohol and Drugs, 69,* 528–534.

Tyler, K. A., Stone, R. T., & Bersani, B. (2006). Examining the changing influence of predictors on adolescent alcohol misuse. *Journal of Child and Adolescent Substance Abuse, 16*(2), 95–114.

Vakalahi, H. F. (2002). Family-based predictors of adolescent substance use. *Journal of Child and Adolescent Substance Abuse, 11*(3), 1–15.

Weinberg, N. Z., Dielman, T. E., Mandell, W., & Shope, J. T. (1994). Parental drinking and gender factors in the prediction of early adolescent alcohol use. *International Journal of the Addictions, 29,* 89–104.

White, H. R., Johnson, V., & Buyske, S. (2000). Parental modeling and parenting behavior effects on offspring alcohol and cigarette use: A growth curve analysis. *Journal of Substance Abuse, 12*(3), 287–310.

Wills, T. A., & Cleary, S. D. (1996). How are social support effects mediated? A test with parental support and adolescent substance use. *Journal of Personality and Social Psychology, 71,* 937–952.

Windle, M. (2000). Parental, sibling, and peer influences on adolescent substance use and alcohol problems. *Applied Developmental Science, 4,* 98–110.

Wong, M. M., Zucker, R. A., Puttler, L. I., & Fitzgerald, H. E. (1999). Heterogeneity of risk aggregation for alcohol problems between early and middle childhood: Nesting structure variations. *Development and Psychopathology, 11,* 727–744.

Zucker, R., Boyd, G., & Howard, J. (Eds.). (1994). *The development of alcohol problems: Exploring the biopsychosocial matrix of risk* (National Institute on Alcohol Abuse and Alcoholism Research Monograph No. 26). Rockville, MD: U.S. Department of Health and Human Services.

Zucker, R. A. (2008). Anticipating problem alcohol use developmentally from childhood into middle adulthood: What have we learned? *Addiction, 103,* 100–108.

Zucker, R. A., Fitzgerald, H. E., Refior, S. K., Pallas, D. M., & Ellis, D. A. (2000). The clinical and social ecology of childhood for children of alcoholics: Description of a study and implications for a differentiated social policy. In H. E. Fitzgerald, B. M. Lester, & B. S. Zuckerman (Eds.), *Children of addiction: Research, health, and policy issues* (pp. 109–141). New York: Routledge/Falmer.

8 Mental Illness and Family Stress

Angie M. Schock-Giordano and Stephen M. Gavazzi

The terms *mental health* and *mental illness* fall on a continuum rather than reflect two distinct categories. On one end of the continuum, mental health is characterized by "successful performance of mental function, resulting in productive activities, fulfilling relationships with other people, and the ability to adapt to change and to cope with adversity," while on the opposite end, mental illness is described as "health conditions that are characterized by alterations in thinking, mood, or behavior associated with distress and/or impaired functioning," (U.S. Department of Health and Human Services, 1999, p. 4). This chapter will emphasize the experiences of individuals and their families as they cope with stressors associated with mental illness. Fortunately, our society is becoming more knowledgeable about identifying symptoms and is more willing to seek help from mental health professionals. Society is also becoming more sensitive to the fact that mental health and mental illness are family issues as well as individual concerns. Mental illness affects individuals of all ages; however, the family experience of coping with mentally unhealthy members can vary greatly based on which member is experiencing the impairment.

Facets of mental illness, such as the display and severity of symptoms, as well as the individual's and family's ability to cope with a disorder, are influenced by social, psychological, and biological factors. Therefore, understanding the impact of daily stressors and the ways in which individuals and family members cope with stress are topics that must be integrated into any discussion of mental illness. In this chapter, we present the most recent research findings related to the causes, courses, and treatment of mental illness as a family event. We discuss topics relevant to families coping with mentally ill members in reference to the ABC-X model of family stress, and we use personal narratives throughout the chapter to illustrate the links between family issues and components of the ABC-X model.

Family Stress Theory and Mental Illness _____

Walter is a 36-year-old married father of two young boys who recently returned from a 1-year tour of duty serving as a military officer in Iraq. Walter has been home for 7 months, but on a daily basis, he still talks to his wife, Rosa, about the overwhelming feelings of worry and guilt he has over the status of the war and the incidents that he saw take place; he has even displayed some uncharacteristic angry outbursts toward his two young sons. Walter sleeps only 2 to 3 hours per night due to reoccurring nightmares and has not been able to return to work at the military base. His recent condition has frightened Rosa, but she has not talked with her husband about this because she was raised in a family culture in which one does not discuss mental illness. Recently, Walter has begun spending his evenings meeting and talking with several officers in his unit who also have returned from Iraq and who have been experiencing similar problems.

Walter's situation appears to reflect symptoms associated with posttraumatic stress disorder (PTSD), a condition that may be an emerging problem in the near future among the many U.S. military men and women who have served recently in wars overseas. Many of the issues that Walter is facing correspond with the elements of the ABC-X model, and many of the topics that we discuss in this chapter can be illustrated through his story. For example, in the model, A refers to the stressor event, which is the family member's mental illness. For Walter, this would include the causes and symptoms of his PTSD. Thus, we discuss below the numbers of individuals in the United States who are affected by mental illness, with particular emphasis on the demographic characteristics (e.g., gender, age, socioeconomic status, and ethnicity) associated with mental illness. In addition, we review research related to the causes of mental illness, including genetic linkages, family environment contributions, and the combination of heredity and family relationships.

In the ABC-X model, B represents available resources that can exist within the individual, within the family system, and within the community. For Walter, his wife Rosa and the men's support group where he discusses his problems would be considered two main resources. In this chapter, we discuss family strengths and the positive outcomes that families can achieve by coping successfully with mental illness. We also discuss the community resources that exist for families coping with mental illness, such as treatment programs (e.g., psychoeducation), community-based organizations (e.g., the National Alliance for the Mentally Ill), Web-based support systems, and social policy efforts.

The C element in the family stress theory model refers to the family's perceptions of the family member's mental illness. In Walter's family, his wife Rosa has not addressed his symptoms, largely because her family of origin did not openly recognize or discuss mental illness. We review the literature pertaining to the concept of "expressed emotion," illustrating how family members' views of mental illness can translate into behaviors and attitudes that have a direct impact on the well-being of mentally ill family members. Another important issue discussed in this chapter is the notion of *subjective burden* (i.e., a family member's appraisal of the illness and/or the caregiving experience). For instance, a significant subjective burden for many families with mentally ill members involves the stigma attached to mental illness, both within the family and in society in general, which can be influenced by cultural and family belief systems.

Epidemiology of Mental Illness

Epidemiologists study disease patterns in given populations to determine how many people in those populations suffer from particular illnesses. Two terms from the field of epidemiology are used to estimate the occurrence of mental illness in a population: *incidence,* which refers to new cases of particular mental illnesses that occur during a set period of time, and *prevalence,* which refers to new and existing mental illnesses that have been observed during a set period or during one point in time (U.S. Department of Health and Human Services, 1999). Sometimes, however, it can be difficult to identify "cases." For example, although an individual may experience particular symptoms, the duration and/or intensity of the symptoms may not reach the threshold necessary for a diagnosis of mental illness (Kupfer, First, & Regier, 2002). In addition, most epidemiological studies survey members in households across the country and neglect to gather information from homeless persons or those living in institutions such as shelters, treatment centers, hospitals, and prisons (U.S. Department of Health and Human Services, 1999). Despite these limitations, current patterns of mental illness in the U.S. population can be described by using available information about the incidence and prevalence of various disorders.

As previously mentioned, the term *mental illness* is not entirely separate from *mental health* in that many people may experience mental health problems at some level of severity throughout life. Serious mental illnesses that can be officially diagnosed by mental health professionals using standard criteria often are classified into two groups of problem behaviors: internalizing disorders and externalizing disorders. Internalizing disorders involve a major disturbance in moods and emotions, and may include symptoms such as anxiety, sadness, worry, and guilt (although the features of these disturbances can vary widely). The two main types of internalizing disorders are mood disorders and anxiety disorders. Externalizing disorders, in contrast, are characterized by aggressive, impulsive, and/or delinquent behaviors, and can include a range of mild to severe acting-out behaviors. The two main types of externalizing disorders are disruptive behavior disorders and attention-deficit/hyperactivity disorders (McMahon & Estes, 1997; Zahn-Waxler, Klimes-Dougan, & Slattery, 2000).

Rates of Mental Illness in the U.S. Population

Several large-scale studies have been conducted in the United States to provide estimations of mental illness rates. For instance, the National Institute of Mental Health's Epidemiological Catchment Area study (Regier, Burke, & Burke, 1990) and the National Comorbidity Survey (NCS) (Kessler et al., 1994) supplied gross estimates of the prevalence of mental disorders in the U.S. population. More recently, the National Comorbidity Survey Replication (NCS-R) (Kessler & Merikangas, 2004) was completed and represents the most up-to-date statistics on mental disorders in the country. These epidemiological studies typically supply statistics on *lifetime prevalence rates* (i.e., the number of persons who will experience the disorder over the course of their lives), and *12-month prevalence rates* (i.e., the number of persons who have experienced the disorder in a given year).

The NCS-R surveyed 9,282 English-speaking adults over the age of 18 in U.S. households between 2001 and 2003. Results indicated that nearly half of all respondents (46.4%) experienced a psychiatric disorder at least once in their lives (Kessler et al., 2005), and 26.2% experienced a mental disorder within the past 12 months (Kessler, Chiu, Demler, & Walters, 2005). Using the 2004 census data, these findings translate into an estimate that nearly 56 million people in the United States will experience a diagnosable mental disorder in a given year (National Institute of Mental Health, 2008).

In addition, using the NCS-R data, lifetime prevalence rates and 12-month prevalence rates were reported for many major mental illnesses. Specifically, the lifetime prevalence rate for anxiety disorders (e.g., panic disorder, generalized anxiety disorder, phobias, posttraumatic stress disorder, obsessive-compulsive disorder) was 28.8% and the 12-month rate was reported to be 18.1%. For mood disorders (e.g., major depressive disorder, dysthymia, bipolar disorder), the lifetime prevalence rate was 20.8% and the 12-month rate was reported to be 9.5%. The lifetime prevalence rate for impulse control–related disorders (e.g., conduct disorder, attention-deficit/hyperactivity disorder) was reported to be 24.8% and the 12-month rate was 8.9%. For substance use disorders, the lifetime rate was 14.6% and the 12-month rate was 3.8%. Finally, for social phobias, the lifetime and 12-month prevalence rates were 12.1% and 7.1%, respectively (Kessler, Chiu, Demler, & Walters, 2005; Kessler, et al., 2005).

Gender Differences

Several gender differences appear to be associated with vulnerability to certain mental health disorders. For example, data from the earlier NCS and the more recent NCS-R are consistent in indicating that adult women have higher prevalence rates for affective disorders and anxiety disorders, whereas men have higher rates for substance abuse disorders, impulse control disorders

(Kessler et al., 1994, 2005), and antisocial personality disorders (Regier et al., 1988). In fact, rates of depressive disorders (i.e., major depressive disorder, dysthymic disorder, and bipolar disorder) are twice as high for women (12%, or 12.4 million women) as they are for men (6.6%, or 6.4 million men) in the United States (Narrow, 1998). However, it may be that men and women experience depression differently and may have unique ways of coping. For instance, men are more likely to report fatigue, sleep problems, irritability, and loss of interest in their employment or leisure activities rather than feelings of sadness, overwhelming guilt, or worthlessness that women report. Furthermore, men are more likely than women to self-medicate with alcohol and illicit drugs as a form of coping with depressed thoughts. In relation to suicide, four times as many men die from suicide as do women (Weissman et al., 1999), yet women attempt suicide two to three times more often than do men (Kochanek, Murphy, Anderson, & Scott, 2004).

With regard to seeking assistance, research suggests women are more likely than men to pursue treatment of any kind for mental health issues (Wang, Lane, & Olfson, 2005). Reasons for this trend may include the reduced stigma of treating mental illness for women as compared to men and women's greater ability to consciously recognize mental health symptoms. In addition, when seeking assistance, women are more likely to utilize primary care providers and outpatient services, whereas men seek treatment through specialists and inpatient care, which can ultimately result in men receiving more adequate care when they do seek help (Wang, Lane, & Olfson, 2005).

Age

Data from the NCS suggest that the highest rates of mental illness are found in persons between 25 and 34 years of age, with prevalence declining at later ages (Kessler et al., 1994). Incidences of some disorders tend to be related to age, however, such as varying forms of dementia. For instance, Alzheimer's disease, which is the most common type of dementia, occurs most frequently among older adults. This incurable disease is estimated to affect 4.5 million Americans, with 10% of adults over 65 years and nearly 50% of those over 85 years diagnosed with the disease (National Institute on Aging, 2005).

Depression is another common mental health problem among older adults. Estimated rates of major depression among seniors who live in the community range from 1%–5%, but rates increase to 11.5% for those who are patients in hospitals and up to 13.5% for elders who need at-home health care assistance (Hybles & Blazer, 2003). It appears that depression risks increase among the older adult population when their capacity to function becomes limited. In addition, depression has been related to high suicide rates among older adults. In particular, people who were over 65 years of age in 2004 accounted for 16% of suicide deaths in the United States, yet this group represents only 12% of the overall population (Centers for Disease Control and Prevention, 2005).

Mental illness among children and adolescents is an emerging area of study as researchers begin to acknowledge and diagnose the psychiatric impairment of youth (Mash & Barkley, 1996). Reports indicate that rates of serious emotional disturbances among children and adolescents are between 9% and 13% (Friedman, 1996), suggesting that nearly 75 million children in the United States have mental disorders. Estimated mental illness prevalence rates among U.S. preschoolers, preadolescents, and adolescents are 12%, 15%, and 18%, respectively (National Institute of Mental Health, 1991; Roberts, Attkisson, & Rosenblatt, 1998). However, more recent data for adolescents are expected to be forthcoming in the NCS-A (NCS of Adolescents) report, a data collection effort conducted by the researchers of the NCS-R study that will yield a more current estimation of childhood and adolescent mental disorder rates.

Gender differences among mental disorders in children and adolescents also exist. Prevalence rates for autism have been estimated to be at 3.4 cases per 1,000 children 3 to 10 years of age (Yeargin-Allsopp et al., 2003), yet rates are four times greater among boys than girls (National Institute of Mental Health, 2008). In contrast, the prevalence rate for major depression among teenagers is almost three times greater among girls than boys (12.7% of girls and 4.6% of boys), with an estimated 8.5% of adolescents between 12 and 17 years having experienced a major depressive episode in the past year (Office of Applied Studies , 2007). Also, these data from 2004 and 2006 show that depression rates increase with age, which is consistent with other research suggesting that rates of mental illness in the young vary among different age cohorts (preschoolers, preadolescents, and adolescents) (Roberts, Attkinsson, & Rosenblatt, 1998). Depression is related to suicide; therefore, statistics show that suicide rates among young adults are disproportionately high (Minino, Arias, Kochanek, Murphy, & Smith, 2002). In fact, suicide is the third leading cause of death among those 10 to 24 years of age, and more than 90% of those who commit suicide have some type of a mental disorder (National Alliance on Mental Illness, 2007).

Race and Ethnicity

Only recently have large-scale studies been completed that include prevalence rates of mental illness among African Americans, Latinos, Asian Americans, and Native Americans. As a result, the limited information available concerning mental illness rates among racial and ethnic minority groups in the United States is based on few national epidemiological studies. For instance, the NCS-R, mentioned previously, collected data from Latinos and African Americans, though the sample was limited to English-speaking Latinos and such important factors as country of origin or immigration status were not considered (Alegria et al., 2008). The National Latino and Asian

American Study (NLAAS), conducted between 2002 and 2003, gathered information pertaining to the prevalence of mental illness disorders and mental health treatment/service usage in the United States. The sample consisted of 2,554 Latinos and 2,095 Asian Americans. Respondents were stratified into ethnic subgroup categories (e.g., Puerto Rican, Cuban, Mexican, Other Latinos, Chinese, Vietnamese, Filipino, and Other Asians) to allow for within-ethnic-group comparisons (Center for Multicultural Mental Health Research, 2008).

Data from these recent studies suggest that most rates of mental disorder are lower for Latinos and African Americans compared to Caucasians (Alegria et al., 2008; Breslau et al., 2006; Kessler et al., 2005). Specifically, lifetime prevalence rates were significantly lower for inter-nalizing disorders (e.g., anxiety disorder, depression, social phobia) and substance use disorders, and lifetime prevalence rates were lower for non-U.S.-born Latinos versus those born in the United States. When within-group comparisons among Latinos were investigated, differences emerged based on country of origin; for example, Mexicans were at higher risk for anxiety and depressive disorder compared to Cubans, Puerto Ricans, and other Latinos (Alegria et al., 2008). Thus, it is imperative to consider important ethnic group variables, such as nativity and generation status, when conducting studies of immigrants who have been born and raised in the United States. Furthermore, research is needed to identify reasons for lower mental illness rates among non-Caucasians in the United States and what role certain protective factors such as ethnic identity, religiosity, lifestyle choices, and cultural values might have in contributing to mental health.

Etiology of Mental Illness

Phillip is a 13-year-old boy who has recently been diagnosed with ADHD and bipolar disorder. His symptoms first surfaced at school when his grades dramatically dropped last year after experiencing severe distress over completing classroom assignments. He is also regularly getting into physical fights with other students on the playground. His mother, Shirley, is a stay-at-home mother, while, Jimmy, the father, is a full-time physician. Shirley and Jimmy have disagreed on the severity of Phillip's condition, and their many years of obvious marital discord now focuses daily on whether Phillip needs professional help. Shirley is especially distraught because she cannot convince her husband to attend family therapy. Also, she not only recognizes Phillip's aggressive behaviors in her husband, but Phillip is also echoing his father's defiance in not wanting to seek help for his symptoms. Just recently, Phillip came home from school complaining about the "mean kids" in his class who have been teasing him, and he told his mom that he "wants to die and never see them again."

Because all family members are a part of the family system, it is difficult to discuss the etiology (i.e., the causes or origins) of mental disorders in family members without adopting a family-oriented perspective. Moreover, it is necessary to understand the role of at least one parent (mother and/or father) in an individual's psychopathology since even molecular, genetic-based research studies have at their core the implication of family heritage.

The family-oriented view is consistent with the biopsychosocial model of disease (Engel, 1977), which contends that the causes, courses, and outcomes of all illnesses are influenced by interactions among biological predis-positions, genetic and psychological vulnerability, and stressful family or life events. Thus, multiple factors play roles in the etiology of mental illness, and the relative importance of the various factors differs among individuals and across the stages of the life span. In Phillip's case, he may have inherited a predisposition for his condition from his father, and/or he may be displaying the effects of growing up surrounded by a family plagued with constant marital discord. In addition, Phillip is currently experiencing daily stress at school caused by his poor performance and fights with his peers. In sum, multiple factors have contributed to Phillip's condition and the feelings of hopelessness that have resulted.

Research on the etiology of mental illness parallels this biopsychosocial framework, such that studies utilizing a family-oriented perspective on mental disorders can be organized into three categories: (1) studies that examine how the presence of a mental disorder in a parent puts his or her offspring at risk and the contribution of shared genes on siblings' mental health outcomes (genetic linkage research), (2) studies that assess the relationship between various family environmental factors and the subsequent mental health status of family members (family environment research), and (3) studies that attempt to examine the simultaneous influence of both genetic linkage and family environment to the development of mental disorders.

Genetic Linkage Research

Genetic linkage research explores the relationship between the presence of a mental disorder in one family member and the concurrent or eventual manifestation of mental illness in other family members. To increase our understanding of how shared genes can cause mental illness among family members and to clarify the unique contributions of genetic influences and family environmental influences, researchers have implemented studies of twins and children who have been adopted. For example, researchers compare disorder rates among monozygotic twins (who share 100% of their genes) and dizygotic twins (who share only 50% of their genes) to evaluate the influence of heritability; if disorder rates are significantly higher among monozygotic twins, then heritability is deemed an important factor. Similarly, studies of adopted children generally compare adjustment/mental health similarities in twins who have been reared in separate environments. The results of twin and adoption studies suggest that genetic links are important elements in the onset of many different mental illnesses, such as personality disorders, mood disorders, autism, and substance abuse (Mash & Dozois, 1996). However, it is likely that the extent of genetic contributions may vary across specific disorders (Eley, 2001). Efforts in molecular genetics indicate that it may be useful to examine particular genes or genetic markers for links to mental illness (Plomin, DeFries, Craig, & McGuffin, 2003). Recent genetic research has focused on the relationships between genetic markers and anxiety (Eley, 2001), antisocial behavior (Eley, Lichtenstein, & Moffitt, 2003), and mood disorders (Morley, Hall, & Carter, 2004; Preisig, 2006).

Family Environment Research

Many family environmental factors have been shown to be related to the development of mental disorders, including family stressors, numerous family relationship variables (e.g., conflict, support, and relationship quality), and expressed emotion. Researchers have found interrelationships among particular family stressors, such as maternal physical and mental health, divorce, parental death, and everyday hassles (Forehand, Biggar, & Kotchick, 1998; Kahng, Oyserman, Bybee, & Mowbray, 2008; Sheeber, Hops, & Davis, 2001). For example, Forehand et al. (1998) found that half of the mothers in their sample of 285 families of adolescents (ages 11–15) reported experiencing two or more family stressors. Additionally, adolescents from those families with multiple stressors showed more depressive symptoms 6 years later compared with adolescents from less stressful family environments. In a more recent study, higher levels of parenting stress and lower levels of nurturing behaviors were positively associated with the level of symptom severity of mothers diagnosed with a serious mental illness (Kahng, Oyserman, Bybee, & Mowbray, 2008).

Family conflict, parenting approaches, and family members' relationship quality also have been associated with youth reports of mental illness. For example, family conflict, parental hostility, and harsh discipline have been related to adolescents' internalizing and externalizing disorders. Specifically, one longitudinal study found parent–adolescent disagreements during early adolescence predicted internalizing symptoms several years later among a sample of late adolescents (Reuter, Scaramella, Wallace, & Conger, 1999). Furthermore, high levels of negative parenting characteristics (e.g., using harsh discipline and feeling frustrated, angry, or impatient with their child) have been associated with antisocial behaviors in children (Larsson, Viding, & Plomin, 2008). Also, in a study of families with two siblings diagnosed with ADHD, results suggested that 40% of the siblings' impairment was accounted for by family conflict (Pressman, Loo, & Carpenter, 2006).

Several studies also suggest that family members' relationship quality and overall family environment are related to the mental health of children and adolescents. For instance, Sheeber, Hops, Alpert, Davis, and Andrews (1997) found that less supportive family environments and less facilitative behavior during problem-solving discussions were associated with adolescent depressive symptomatology, and Rowe and Liddle (2003) showed that low levels of family cohesion and poor attachment relationships were related to adolescent substance abuse. In addition, Puig-Antich et al. (1993) found that depressed adolescents reported poorer-quality relationships with parents and siblings than did nondepressed adolescents. When overall family environment has been assessed, it has been related to (a) boys' major depression, conduct disorder, ADHD, and alcohol use and (b) girls' major depression, conduct disorder, ADHD, operational defiant disorder, and posttraumatic stress disorder (Halloran, Ross, & Carey, 2002).

Research on Expressed Emotion

The research on expressed emotion (EE; see Brown, Birley, & Wing, 1972) has been very influential in the movement toward a family-oriented perspective on mental disorders. In addition, the concept of EE aligns with the C element in the ABC-X model of family stress, such that EE represents an individual's perceptions. Specifically, the concept of EE has traditionally been comprised of two factors: (1) the level of emotional (over)involvement among family members and (2) the degree to which family members display critical attitudes toward and/or make hostile comments about the family member who has a mental disorder (Vaughn & Leff, 1976). More recent studies have further identified behavior patterns within the emotional overinvolvement factor, noting the particular ways in which family members display inappropriate intrusiveness, distress, and self-sacrificing behaviors toward a mentally ill family member (Fredman, Baucom, Miklowitz, & Stanton, 2008).

Extensive research on EE has found that individuals suffering from a multitude of illnesses (e.g., schizophrenia, mood disorders, ADHD, panic disorders, eating disorders, posttraumatic stress disorder, alcohol abuse, Alzheimer's disease, and personality disorders) who live with high-EE (i.e., overinvolved, critical, or hostile) family members are more likely to experience relapse (i.e., another episode of symptoms) than are persons with the same illnesses who live with low-EE family members (Barrowclough & Hooley, 2003; Miklowitz, 2007).

Some researchers have attempted to gain a more complete understanding of exactly why EE is associated with psychiatric relapse. Barrowclough and Hooley (2003) note that growing evidence suggests that "high- and low-EE family members differ in the beliefs they hold about patients and the problem behaviors associated with the patient's illness" (p. 850) such that high-EE relatives tend to blame mentally ill family members for their abnormal behavior, whereas low-EE family members perceive the individual's behavior to be out of his or her control and a product of the illness. One implication of these research findings is the need to educate family members regarding the severity and origins of the patient's symptoms as a way of decreasing family

EE levels. Lopez, Nelson, Snyder, and Minz (1999) contend that the goal of family treatment should be a "flexible attributional stance," in which family members neither attribute all aspects of the patient's behavior to factors beyond the patient's control nor assume that the patient could easily control his or her symptoms. Thus, the recognition that abnormal behaviors are distinct from the individual's personality and largely out of that person's control would increase the possibility that family members would act in a less critical fashion toward the patient (Fristad, Gavazzi, & Soldano, 1999).

Research Examining Both Genetic Linkage and Family Environment

In recent years, there has been a tremendous amount of growth in research combining genetic and environmental factors within the same study (Costello, Foley, & Angold, 2005; Jaffee, 2007). The biopsychosocial model emphasizes the value in combining genetic and environmental variables when studying the etiology of most mental disorders, such that heredity can provide an individual with a predisposition to a mental illness, but the likelihood that the illness will manifest is largely determined by environmental and family influences. Two directions have emerged in gene–environment research: (1) the gene–environment correlation approach focusing on the manner and extent that genetic factors shape family environmental variables (e.g., a parent's mental disorder creates a discordant marital relationship and family environment), and (2) the gene–environment interaction approach examining how the effects of one factor vary across levels of another factor (e.g., the impact of a negative family environment on a child's mental health is evident in only extremely unhealthy family situations) (Lau & Eley, 2008). Combined gene–environment research has been used to assess several different environmental factors in studies with twins and siblings with depressive symptoms (Lau & Eley, 2008) and externalizing behaviors (Button, Lau, Maughan, & Eley, 2001). Also, the gene–environment approach has been used when discussing the causes of anxiety disorder (Gregory & Eley, 2007) and specific antisocial behaviors (Larsson, Viding, & Plomin, 2008).

Assessment of Family Resources

Ron and Barbara are a middle-aged couple who have recently begun to care for Ron's mother, Lucille, who has been diagnosed with Alzheimer's disease. Since Lucille first moved in with Ron and Barbara, her condition has deteriorated rapidly, and she is now approaching the need for

(Continued)

(Continued)

around-the-clock care. Ron and Barbara are struggling to pay for all of the medical treatment that Lucille needs, and the family is experiencing additional financial problems because Barbara had to quit her job to provide full-time care for her mother-in-law. Other adjustments the couple has had to make are also creating stress, and Barbara has limited her contact with friends in the neighborhood due to Lucille's occasional embarrassing behaviors. Although Ron and Barbara have been unsuccessful in locating local programs and resources for families caring for elders with Alzheimer's in their community, they have joined an online support group. Their search for resources on the Internet seems to have brought the couple closer to each other. They have grown to understand that many other couples who have sustained similar hardships involving family caretaking have found their relationships strengthened as a result. In addition, Ron and Barbara have decided to organize a support group at their local hospital for other families in their community who are caring for family members with Alzheimer's.

For Ron and Barbara, the stressors that are currently affecting the family include the financial burdens and daily tasks associated with caregiving; the stigma of the mental disorder, which has led Barbara to reduce contact with neighbors; and the lack of community resources available to help the family cope. However, as a result of their providing care for Ron's mother, the couple has discovered several family strengths, such as the improved quality of their relationship and their ability to organize a local support group.

Nearly three-fourths of patients released from mental hospitals following an illness episode return to live at home with family members (Shankar & Muthuswamy, 2007). As a result, it is imperative to understand the impact of mental disorders on families. Specifically, mental health professionals must have a reliable and valid understanding of what family members have and do not have at their disposal in terms of skills and resources for coping with and adapting to a member who is mentally ill. Because each individual family is different, it is important to recognize that the circumstance of caregiving may vary considerably as a result of a caregiver's "age, their years of caregiving experience, the stage of illness in the family member, the level of support the caregiver experiences, their stage in the family lifecycle, and their relationship to the care recipient" (Shankar & Muthuswamy, 2007, p. 303).

Scholars have argued that although families who provide care to a mentally ill family member do experience stress, many of these families also exhibit positive aspects and strengths as a result of their coping with mental illness (Doornbos, 1996; Hawley & DeHaan, 1996; Kramer, 1997; Morano, 2003; Walsh, 1996). One such strength is often referred to as *resiliency* in the family literature. Other positive concepts are also discussed in the literature on caregiving, such as caregiver esteem (the extent to which participating in caregiving enhances an individual's self-esteem), uplifts of caregiving (caregiving events that evoke joy), caregiver satisfaction (benefits an individual receives as a result of his or her efforts at caregiving), caregiver gain (positive return received as a result of caregiving), and meaning through caregiving (finding higher levels of meaning through the caregiving experience) (Hunt, 2003).

In a nationwide study, Marsh et al. (1996) asked 131 family members of patients with serious mental illness to respond to a set of open-ended questions concerning the development of personal, family, and patient resilience. They found that 99.2% of their respondents reported the presence of some form of personal resilience, 87.8% reported family resilience, and 75.6% reported patient resilience. Examples of the resilience dimensions the respondents mentioned included family support/bonding, insight and caregiving competencies, and gratification through advocacy initiatives for constructive changes in the mental health system.

On the other hand, many scholars have focused on understanding the stressors related to family caregiving and mental illness. These stressors typically are described as the "burdens" associated with having a family member suffering from a mental disorder. These burdens have been characterized as being of two types: objective and subjective (Hunt, 2003). Objective burdens are the observable and tangible stressors or costs related to caregiving and mental illness (Jones, 1996), whereas subjective burdens are those based in individuals' perceptions about or appraisal of the illness and/or the caregiving experience (Nijober, Triemstra, Tempelaar, Sanderman, & Van den Bos, 1999).

Objective burdens usually are measured in terms of economic hardships faced by a family, often calculated as the amount of money the illness has cost the family in outright payment or copayment for medical expenses as well as lost wages. Objective burdens also include many other tangible family costs related to the care and treatment of an ill member, such as the costs of providing transportation, food, clothing, and insurance, and other disruptions to the household.

The amount of subjective burden a caregiver experiences is related to his or her perceptions about the family member and the mental illness. Research has shown that caregivers who experience high levels of subjective burden are at greatest risk for negative health outcomes, such as depression (Nijober et al., 1999). One of the most severe subjective burdens that families with mentally ill members experience is the stigma attached to mental disorders; this psychological burden can lead to lower self-esteem levels, reduced social contacts, job loss, and family relationship difficulties (Mittleman, 1985; Wahl & Harman, 1989). In addition, others have studied the health risks associated with caring for a mentally ill family member, revealing that nearly one-third of the sample of caregivers reported feeling stressed, frustrated, bored, easily upset, and mentally exhausted (Curtin & Lilley, 2001).

Community-Based Resources

Therapy

The family therapy profession has greatly influenced the family-oriented perspective regarding major mental disorders. Some of the earliest writings in the field of family therapy blamed families, directly and indirectly, for "causing" mental disorders in family members (Selvini Palazzoli & Prata, 1989). From this perspective, therapeutic interventions were designed to disrupt unhealthy family interactions in order to eliminate symptoms of the disorder.

Today, family-based treatment is considered to be any modality that involves family members as necessary participants in the course of treatment, and the combined use of family treatment and other forms of treatment (e.g., use of medications, cognitive therapy) is increasingly common. In a 10-year review of recent family-based treatments for a range of mental illnesses, Diamond and Josephson (2005) outline several challenges for the future study of family treatment, including the need (a) for empirically based treatment evaluations, (b) to match treatment approaches to respective mental disorders, (c) to implement multisystem-level approaches, (d) to identify which negative family behaviors are common across disorders, (e) to uncover the most effective basic tenets of treatment, and (f) to disseminate successful treatment models into the community.

Psychoeducational Approach

Most family therapists have moved away from positions of blame. Examples of this trend can be found in the work of those who utilize a psychoeducational approach when addressing mental disorders in a family context (McFarlane, 1991). A psychoeducational approach typically includes three elements: education, training in coping skills, and social support. The relative emphasis placed on each component varies, however (Marsh, 1998). Therapists using this approach encourage family members to learn all they can about the mental disorder, to become fully educated about the facts surrounding assessment and treatment. Nonblaming attributions about mental disorders and knowledge about the disorder's symptoms, course, and treatment are thought to be indicators of the effectiveness of psychoeducational programming (see Fristad, Gavazzi, & Mackinaw-Koons, 2003). In contrast to therapeutic approaches, which are designed to eliminate particular disorders, a psychoeducational approach largely seeks to prevent the *return* of a disorder as well as to alleviate the pain and suffering of family members.

Internet-Based Resources

Internet usage continues to expand as family members browse the Web to locate (a) information about mental illness symptoms and diagnoses, (b) agencies and organizations that provide family services in the community, and (c) online support groups and family networks that may be experiencing similar challenges when coping with mental illness (Weinberg, Schmale, Uken, & Wessell, 1995). In fact, online support groups appear to provide many of the same benefits as in-person resources (Bacon, Condon, & Fernsler, 2000) while offering the additional advantages of convenience and expediency (Salem, Bogar, & Reid, 1997). Given the recent estimate that approximately three-quarters of U.S. citizens with diagnosable mental disorders will never receive direct and necessary treatment (Norcross, 2000), Internet-based services may be the only resources available to many in need. It is still imperative, though, that one should receive an evaluation from a licensed professional when diagnosing mental illness.

Social Policy

In recent years, the most significant changes in Americans' social attitudes toward mental illness and in policymaking decisions surrounding mental disorders have come about as the result of the work of grassroots organizations such as the National Alliance for the Mentally Ill (NAMI) and its related affiliates. NAMI has the dual focus of (a) advocating for patient (and family) rights and (b) providing general public education about mental disorders (Howe & Howe, 1987). NAMI has a state organization in every state, along with more than 1,200 local affiliates. The organization also produces a magazine, the *Advocate,* and their Web site offers e-newsletters and a blog in their aggressive efforts to disseminate mental health information.

Recently, NAMI has published a comprehensive report that is "the first comprehensive survey and grading of state adult public mental healthcare systems conducted in more than 15 years," that " includes tables that indicate each state's overall grade as well as its grade in each of four categories: infrastructure, information access, services, and recovery" (NAMI, 2006). Unfortunately, the report concludes that the overall national grade of a D is of poor quality, and that a higher quality of state mental health systems must include the following 10 characteristics: (1) comprehensive services and support, (2) integrated systems, (3) sufficient funding, (4) consumer- and family-driven systems, (5) safe and respectful treatment environments, (6) accessible information for consumers and family members, (7) access to acute care and long-term care treatment, (8) cultural competence, (9) health promotion and mortality reduction, and (10) an adequate mental health workforce.

Future Directions

In this chapter, we have applied concepts from the ABC-X model of family stress to organize our discussion of issues relevant to families coping with mentally ill family members. In particular, we have reviewed the characteristics of the stressor event (A, mental illness), such as demographic trends and potential causes of mental disorders. We have also outlined community resources (B) as we described current treatment approaches, supportive organizations, and policy initiatives aimed at improving family life. Finally, we have reviewed examples of family perceptions (C) through our discussion of family burdens and family attitudes/behaviors exhibited by family members toward the mentally ill member. Although great strides have been made with regard to these issues since earlier editions of *Families & Change* have been published, scholars today need to put forth a clear and detailed agenda to guide further work in this area.

Based on our analysis of the present situation, we offer the following suggestions concerning future research and intervention efforts. First, scholars need to continue to focus on mental illness prevalence rates in the population—in particular, on how mental illness may have disproportionate impacts on those persons in greatest need of assistance (e.g., children and elders, men in families, socioeconomically disadvantaged families, and ethnic families that still stigmatize the mentally ill). Similarly, it is important for professionals to develop more effective ways to deliver services and assistance to those groups most in need. Second, scholars need to identify strategies that will maximize family participation in community-based programs (Schock & Gavazzi, 2004) as well as techniques that will help researchers and practitioners to evaluate program effectiveness (Diamond & Josephson, 2005). Third, advances in technology will allow researchers to further disentangle the contributions of heredity and family environment to the development and continuance of mental illness. Finally, on a larger scale, we must continue to reduce the stigma attached to mental illness in American society and work to achieve a higher quality of mental health services that are easily available and affordable to all families in need.

Suggested Internet Resources

American Academy of Child and Adolescent Psychiatry: http:// www .aacap.org

American Psychological Association: http://www.apa.org

National Alliance for the Mentally Ill: http://www.nami.org

National Institute of Mental Health: http://www.nimh.nih.gov

Office of the Surgeon General (site for the publication *Mental Health: A Report of the Surgeon General*): http://www.surgeongeneral.gov/library/mentalhealth/home.html

Suggested Readings

Costello, J. E., Foley, D. L., & Angold, A. (2005). 10-year research update review: The epidemiology of child and adolescent psychiatric disorders. *Journal of the American Academy of Child and Adolescent Psychiatry, 45,* 8–25.

Diamond, G., & Josephson, A. (2005). Family-based treatment research: A 10-year update. *Journal of the American Academy of Child & Adolescent Psychiatry, 44,* 872–887.

National Alliance on Mental Illness. (2007). *Mental illness: Facts and numbers.* Arlington, VA: National Alliance on Mental Illness.

National Institute of Mental Health. (2008.). *The numbers count: Mental disorders in America.* Retrieved April 8, 2008, from http://www.nimh.nih.gov/health/publications.

U.S. Department of Health and Human Services. (1999). *Mental health: A report of the surgeon general.* Rockville, MD: Author.

References

Alegria, M., Canino, G., Shrout, P. E., Woo, M., Duan, N., Vila, D., Torres, M., Chen, C., & Meng, X. (2008). Prevalence of mental illness in immigrant and non-immigrant U.S. Latino groups. *American Journal of Psychiatry, 165,* 359–369.

Bacon, E. S., Condon, E. H., & Fernsler, J. I. (2000). Young widows' experience with an Internet self-help group. *Journal of Psychosocial Nursing, 38,* 24–33.

Barrowclough, C., & Hooley, J. M. (2003). Attributions and expressed emotion: A review *Clinical Psychology Review, 23,* 849–880.

Breslau, J., Aguilar-Gaxiola, S., Kendler, K., Su, M., Williams, D., & Kessler, R. C. (2006). Specifying race-ethnic differences in risk for psychiatric disorder in a USA national sample. *Psychological Medicine, 36,* 57–68.

Brown, G. W., Birley, J. L. T., & Wing, J. K. (1972). Influence of family life on the course of schizophrenic disorders: A replication. *British Journal of Psychiatry, 121,* 241–258.

Button, T. M. M., Lau, J. Y. F., Maughan, B., & Eley, T. C. (2007). Parental punitive discipline, negative life events and gene-environment interplay in the development of externalizing behavior. *Psychological Medicine, 38,* 29–39.

Center for Multicultural Mental Health Research (2008). National Latino and Asian American Study: Background and aims of the NLAAS. Retrieved June 18, 2008, from http://www.multiculturalmentalhealth.org/nlaas.asp.

Centers for Disease Control and Prevention, National Center for Injury Prevention and Control. (2005). Web-Based Injury Statistics Query and Reporting System (WISQARS) [online]. Retrieved March 23, 2008, from http://www.cdc.gov/ncipc/wisqars.

Costello, J. E., Foley, D. L., & Angold, A. (2005). 10-year research update review: The epidemiology of child and adolescent psychiatric disorders. *Journal of the American Academy of Child and Adolescent Psychiatry, 45,* 8–25.

Curtin, T., & Lilley, H. (2001). *Caring across community 2000–2001: Carer education project for carers from culturally and linguistically diverse backgrounds.* Canberra, Australia: Carers Association of Australia.

Diamond, G., & Josephson, A. (2005). Family-based treatment research: A 10-year update. *Journal of the American Academy of Child & Adolescent Psychiatry, 44*, 872–887.

Doornbos, M. M. (1996). The strengths of families coping with serious mental illness. *Archives of Psychiatric Nursing, 10*, 214–220.

Eley, T. C. (2001). Contributions of behavioral genetics research: Quantifying genetic, shared environmental and nonshared environmental influences. In M. W. Vasey & M. R. Dadds (Eds.), *The developmental psychopathology of anxiety* (pp. 45–59). New York: Oxford University Press.

Eley, T. C., Lichtenstein, P., & Moffitt, T. E. (2003). A longitudinal behavioral genetic analysis of the etiology of aggressive and nonaggressive antisocial behavior. *Development and Psychopathology, 15*, 383–402.

Engel, G. L. (1977). The need for a new medical model: A challenge for biomedicine. *Science, 196*, 129–136.

Forehand, R., Biggar, H., & Kotchick, B. A. (1998). Cumulative risk across family stressors: Short- and long-term effects for adolescents. *Journal of Abnormal Child Psychology, 26*, 119–128.

Fredman, S. J., Baucom, D. H., Miklowitz, D. J., & Stanton, S. E. (2008). Observed emotional involvement and overinvolvement in families of patients with bipolar disorder. *Journal of Family Psychology, 22*, 71–79.

Friedman, R. M. (1996). *Prevalence of serious emotional disturbance in children and adolescents.* Unpublished manuscript, Center for Mental Health Services, Washington, DC.

Fristad, M. A., Gavazzi, S. M., & Mackinaw-Koons, B. (2003). Family psychoeducation: An adjunctive intervention for children with early onset bipolar disorder. *Biological Psychiatry, 53*, 1000–1008

Fristad, M. A., Gavazzi, S. M., & Soldano, K. W. (1999). Naming the enemy: Learning to differentiate mood disorder "symptoms" from the "self" that experiences them. *Journal of Family Psychotherapy, 10*, 81–88.

Gavazzi, S. M., Fristad, M. A., & Law, J. C. (1997). The Understanding Mood Disorders Questionnaire. *Psychological Reports, 81*, 172–174.

Gregory, A. M., & Eley, T. C. (2007). Genetic influences on anxiety in children: What we've learned and where we're heading. *Clinical Child and Family Psychology, 10*, 199–212.

Halloran, E. C., Ross, G. J., & Carey, M. P. (2002). The relationship of adolescent personality and family environment to psychiatric diagnosis. *Child Psychiatry & Human Development, 32*, 201–216.

Hawley, D. R., & DeHaan, L. (1996). Toward a definition of family resilience: Integrating life-span and family perspectives. *Family Process, 35*, 283–298.

Howe, C. W., & Howe, J. W. (1987). The National Alliance for the Mentally Ill: History and ideology. In A. B. Hatfield (Ed.), *Families of the mentally ill: Meeting the challenges* (pp. 23–42). San Francisco: Jossey-Bass.

Hunt, C. K. (2003). Concepts in caregiver research. *Journal of Nursing Scholarship, 35*, 27–33.

Hybels, C. F., & Blazer, D. G. (2003). Epidemiology of late-life mental disorders. *Clinics in Geriatric Medicine, 19*, 663–696.

Jaffee, S. R. (2007). Gene-environment correlations: A review of the evidence and implications for prevention of mental illness. *Molecular Psychiatry, 12*, 432–442.

Jones, S. (1996). The association between objective and subjective caregiver burden. *Archives of Psychiatric Nursing, 10,* 77–84.

Kahng, S. K., Oyserman, D., Bybee, D., & Mowbray, C. (2008). Mothers with serious mental illness: When symptoms decline does parenting improve? *Journal of Family Psychology, 22,* 162–166.

Kessler, R. C., Chiu, W. T., Demler, O., & Walters, E. E. (2005). Prevalence, severity, and comorbidity of 12-month *DSM-IV* disorders in the national comorbidity survey replication. *Archives of General Psychiatry, 62,* 617–709.

Kessler, R. C., McGonagle, K. A., Zhao, S., Nelson, C. B., Hughes, M., Eshleman, S., et al. (1994). Lifetime and 12-month prevalence of *DSM-III-R* psychiatric disorders in the United States. *Archives of General Psychiatry, 51,* 8–19.

Kessler, R. C., & Merikangas, K. R. (2004). The national comorbidity survey replication (NCS-R): Background and aims. *International Journal of Methods in Psychiatric Research, 13,* 93–121.

Kochanek, K. D., Murphy, S. L., & Anderson, R. N., & Scott, C. (2004). Deaths: Final data for 2002. *National Vital Statistics Report, 12,* 1–115.

Kramer, B. J. (1997). Gain in the caregiver experience: Where are we? What next? *Gerontologist, 37,* 218–232.

Kupfer, D. J., First, M. B., & Regier, D. A. (Eds.). (2002). *A research agenda for DSM-V.* Washington, DC: American Psychiatric Association.

Larsson, H., Viding, E., & Plomin, R. (2008). Callous-unemotional traits and antisocial behavior: Genetic, environmental, and early parenting characteristics. *Criminal Justice and Behavior, 35,* 197–211.

Lau, J. Y. F., & Eley, T. C. (2008). Disentangling gene-environment correlations and interactions on adolescent depressive symptoms. *The Journal of Child Psychology and Psychiatry, 49,* 142–150.

Lopez, S. R., Nelson, K. A., Snyder, K. S., & Minz, J. (1999). Attributions and affective reactions of family members and course of schizophrenia. *Journal of Abnormal Psychology, 108,* 307–314.

Marsh, D. T. (1998). *Serious mental illness and the family: The practitioner's guide.* New York: John Wiley.

Marsh, D. T., Lefley, H. P., Evans-Rhodes, D., Ansell, V. I., Doerzbacher, B. M., LaBarbera, L., et al. (1996). The family experience of mental illness: Evidence for resilience. *Psychiatric Rehabilitation Journal, 20,* 3–12.

Mash, E. J., & Barkley, R. A. (Eds.). (1996). *Child psychopathology.* New York: Guilford.

Mash, E. J., & Dozois, D. J. (1996). Child psychopathology: A developmental systems perspective. In E. J. Mash & R. A. Barkley (Eds.), *Child psychopathology* (pp. 3–63). New York: Guilford.

McFarlane, W. R. (1991). Family psychoeducational treatment. In A. S. Gurman & D. P. Kniskern (Eds.), *Handbook of family therapy* (Vol. 2, pp. 363–395). New York: Brunner/Mazel.

McMahon, R. J., & Estes, A. M. (1997). Conduct problems. In E. J. Mash & L. G. Terdal (Eds.), *Assessment of childhood disorders* (3rd ed., pp. 130–193). New York: Guilford.

Miklowitz, D. J. (2007). The role of the family in the course and treatment of bipolar disorder. *Association for Psychological Science, 16,* 192–196.

Minino, A. M., Arias, E., Kochanek, K. D., Murphy, S. L., & Smith, B. L. (2002). Deaths: Final data for 2000. Hyattsville, MD: National Center for Health Statistics.

Mittleman, G. (1985). First person account: The pain of parenthood of the mentally ill. *Schizophrenia Bulletin, 11*, 300–303.

Morano, C. (2003). Appraisal and coping: Moderators or mediators of stress in Alzheimer's disease caregivers? *Social Work Research, 27*, 116–128.

Morley, K. I., Hall, W. D., & Carter, L. (2004). Genetic screening for susceptibility to depression: Can we and should we? *Australian and New Zealand Journal of Psychiatry, 38*, 73–80.

Narrow, W. E. (1998). *One-year prevalence of depressive disorders among adults 18 and over in the U.S.: NIMH ECA prospective data.* Unpublished table.

National Alliance on Mental Illness. (2006). *Grading the states: A report on America's health care system for serious mental illness.* Arlington, VA: National Alliance on Mental Illness.

National Alliance on Mental Illness. (2007). *Mental illness: Facts and numbers.* Arlington, VA: National Alliance on Mental Illness.

National Institute of Mental Health. (1991). *Implementation of the national plan for research on child and adolescent mental disorders* (Publication No. PA-91–46). Washington, DC: U.S. Department of Health and Human Services.

National Institute of Mental Health. (2008.). *The numbers count: Mental disorders in America.* Retrieved April 8, 2008, from http://www.nimh.nih.gov/health/publications.

National Institute on Aging. (2005). *Progress report on Alzheimer's disease 2004–2005* (NIH Publication No. 05–5724). Bethesda, MD: National Institute on Aging.

Nijober, C., Triemstra, M., Tempelaar, R., Sanderman, R., & Van den Bos, G. (1999). Determinants of caregiving experiences and mental health of partners of cancer patients. *Cancer, 86*, 577–588.

Norcross, J. C. (2000). Here comes the self-help revolution in mental health. *Psychotherapy, 37*, 370–377.

Office of Applied Studies. (2007). *Results from the 2006 National Survey on Drug Use and Health: National findings* (DHHS Publication No. SMA 07–4293, NSDUH Series H-32). Rockville, MD: Substance Abuse and Mental Health Services.

Plomin, R., DeFries, J. C., Craig, I. W., & McGuffin, P. (2003). Behavioral genomics. In R. Plomin & J. C. DeFries (Eds.), *Behavioral genetics in the postgenomic era* (pp. 531–540). Washington, DC: American Psychological Association.

Preisig, M. (2006). Genetics of bipolar disorder: A review. *Schweizer Archiv für Neurologie und Psychiatrie, 157*, 366–377.

Pressman, L. J., Loo, S. K., & Carpenter, E. M. (2006). Relationship of family environment and parental psychiatric diagnosis to impairment in ADHD. *Journal of the American Academy of Child & Adolescent Psychiatry, 45*, 346–354.

Puig-Antich, J., Kaufman, J., Ryan, N. D., Williamson, D. E., Dahl, R. E., Lukens, E., et al. (1993). The psychosocial functioning and family environment of depressed adolescents. *Journal of the American Academy of Child and Adolescent Psychiatry, 32*, 244–253.

Regier, D. A., Boyd, J. H., Burke, J. D., Jr., Rae, D. S., Myers, J. K., Kramer, M., et al. (1988). One month prevalence of mental disorders in the United States. *Archives of General Psychiatry, 45*, 977–986.

Regier, D. A., Burke, J. D., Jr., & Burke, K. C. (1990). Comorbidity of affective and anxiety disorders in the NIMH Epidemiologic Catchment Area Program. In J. D. Maser & C. R. Cloninger (Eds.), *Comorbidity of mood and anxiety disorders* (pp. 113–122). Washington, DC: American Psychiatric Press.

Reuter, M. A., Scaramella, L., Wallace, L. E., & Conger, R. D. (1999). First onset of depressive or anxiety disorders predicted by the longitudinal course of internalizing symptoms and parent-adolescent disagreements. *Archives of General Psychiatry, 56,* 726–732.

Roberts, R. E., Attkisson, C. C., & Rosenblatt, A. (1998). Prevalence of psychopathology among children and adolescents. *American Journal of Psychiatry, 155,* 715–725.

Rowe, C. L., & Liddle, H. A. (2003). Substance abuse. *Journal of Marital & Family Therapy, 29,* 97–120.

Salem, D. A., Bogar, G. A., & Reid, C. (1997). Mutual help goes on-line. *Journal of Community Psychology, 25,* 189–207.

Schock, A. M., & Gavazzi, S. M. (2004). A multimethod study of father participation in family-based programming. In R. D. Day & M. E. Lamb (Eds.), *Conceptualizing and measuring father involvement* (pp. 149–184). Mahwah, NJ: Lawrence Erlbaum.

Selvini Palazzoli, M., & Prata, G. (1989). *Family games: General models of psychotic processes in the family.* New York: W. W. Norton.

Shankar, J., & Muthuswamy, S. S. (2007). Support needs of family caregivers of people who experience mental illness and the role of mental health services. *Families in Society: The Journal of Contemporary Social Services, 88,* 302–310.

Sheeber, L., Hops, H., Alpert, A., Davis, B., & Andrews, J. (1997). Family support and conflict: Prospective relations to adolescent depression. *Journal of Abnormal Child Psychology, 25,* 333–344.

Sheeber, L., Hops, H., & Davis, B. (2001). Family processes in adolescent depression. *Clinical Child and Family Psychology Review, 4,* 19–35.

U.S. Department of Health and Human Services. (1999). *Mental health: A report of the surgeon general.* Rockville, MD: Author.

Vaughn, C. E., & Leff, J. P. (1976). The measurement of expressed emotion in the families of psychiatric patients. *British Journal of Social and Clinical Psychology, 15,* 157–165.

Wahl, O. F., & Harman, C. R. (1989). Family views of stigma. *Schizophrenia Bulletin, 15,* 131–139.

Walsh, F. (1996). The concept of family resilience: Crisis and challenge. *Family Process, 35,* 261–281.

Wang, P. S., Lane, M., & Olfson, M. (2005). Twelve-month use of mental health services in the United States: Results from the national comorbidity survey replication. *Archives of General Psychiatry, 62,* 629–640.

Weinberg, N., Schmale, J. D., Uken, J., & Wessell, K. (1995). Computer-mediated support groups. *Social Work With Groups, 17,* 43–54.

Weissman, M. M., Bland, R. C., Canino, G. J., Greenwald, S., Hwu, H. G., Joyce, P. R., et al. (1999). Prevalence of suicide ideation and suicide attempts in nine countries. *Psychological Medicine, 29,* 9–17.

Yeargin-Allsopp, M., Rice, C., Karapurkar, T., Doemberg, N., Boyle, C., & Murphy, C. (2003). Prevalence of autism in a U.S. metropolitan area. *Journal of the American Medical Association, 289,* 49–55.

Zahn-Waxler, C., Klimes-Dougan, B., & Slattery, M. J. (2000). Internalizing problems of childhood and adolescence: Prospects, pitfalls, and progress in understanding the development of anxiety and depression. *Development and Psychopathology, 12,* 443–466.

9

Economic Stress and Families

Suzanne Bartholomae and Jonathan Fox

For many American families, money can be a major source of stress. Anxiety over money is a familiar phenomenon to most of us, whether it is stress from unemployment, making ends meet, or decisions on how to spend, save, earn, or manage money. Most of us have encountered economic stress and are familiar with what it feels like to be concerned about our finances. As American families face a worsening economy and economic uncertainties, many struggle to cope with the fear, anger, worry, anxiety, and even depression that can accompany an economic downturn and uncertainty.

Economic stress is the by-product of conditions in the national, regional, or local economy; for example, recession, unemployment, and poverty rates identify general economic conditions within which families function. Economic stress can be described as either *normative* (resulting from expected milestones in the family life cycle, such as marriage or birth of a child) or *situational* (stemming from unexpected events, such as divorce, retirement, or illness). In addition, economic stress associated with life events may be *temporary* (e.g., a short-term drop in income due to job loss) or *chronic* (e.g., a long-term income loss because of a permanent work-limiting disability).

In this chapter, we start by reviewing economic conditions and family financial status. Using the Family Economic Stress Model as a framework, we then discuss the outcomes associated with economic stress. Next, we review the research on economic stress and its interaction with resources and problem solving. Finally, using a family economic life cycle, we discuss coping strategies for negative economic events.

Defining and Measuring Economic Stress

Family researchers often use the term *economic or financial stress* interchangeably with such terms as *economic or financial distress, hardship, pressure,* and *strain*. Voydanoff and Donnelly (1988) have decomposed the concept of economic stress into objective and subjective dimensions of employment and income. Objective dimensions of economic stress include *employment instability* and *economic deprivation*. A lack of regular work and income generally defines employment instability. Economic deprivation can be defined by declining real or relative income. To assess these concepts, researchers examine patterns of employment and changes in income over time, for example, by comparing various individual, couple, and family outcomes associated with employed versus unemployed status.

The subjective dimensions of economic stress, which Voydanoff and Donnelly (1988) label *employment uncertainty* and *economic or financial strain*, are based on individuals' perceptions of employment and income. Employment uncertainty refers to the probability of unemployment and can be defined as a person's perception of the security of his or her current employment and prospects for future employment. Economic strain or pressure can be defined as "the perceived adequacy of financial resources, financial concerns and worries, and expectations regarding one's future economic situation" (Voydanoff & Donnelly, 1988, p. 98). Financial strain represents the psychological aspects of economic stress and is thought to be related to, but independent of, income. Families of similar income levels can have considerably different experiences based on their access to economic resources, like home ownership, and characteristics like family size and number of dependents (Kahn & Pearlin, 2006). Researchers have generally assessed levels of financial strain by using Likert scale items. Individuals rate how often they worry about their finances, how satisfied they are with their financial situation, their level of difficulty paying bills, and whether they have enough money for basic necessities and/or have money left over at the end of the month. The components of economic distress are unique to each individual and family system, particularly the perception of the event; however, as a whole, Voydanoff and Donnelly's (1988) typology has been found to be useful as a tool for assessing the economic conditions of individuals and families (Fox & Chancey, 1998).

Economic Conditions of the American Family _____

The following excerpt from Elizabeth Warren's testimony before the Senate Finance Committee describes how America's changing economy has created more challenging circumstances for today's families and how, relative to previous generations, making ends meet is getting harder for middle-class families. No official government definition exists for the term *middle class*; however, using the three middle quintiles of the Census Bureau's income distribution, middle-class household income is shown as ranging from $19,178 to $91,705 (Cashell, 2007).

The rules of the game have changed. For today's middle-class families, hard work and good intentions are no longer enough. Go to school, get a good job, do your work, don't go crazy with spending, and everything will work out. That formula may have worked in their parents' day, but today families face a tough, new world. There are opportunities to be sure, but there are also new costs and hidden dangers.

———

America was once a world of three economic groups that shaded each unto the other—a bottom, a middle, and a top—and economic security was the birthright of all those who could make it to the middle. Today the lines dividing Americans are changing. No longer is the division on economic security between the poor and everyone else. The division is between those who are prospering and those who are struggling, and much of the middle class is now on the struggling side.

———

The economy has changed, and middle-class families are struggling to change with it. Laws like Social Security, Medicare, FHA, consumer product safety, fair credit reporting, and a host of other statutes were designed to help middle-class Americans cope with the risks in the economy of the mid-20th century. With a strong safety net to back them up, Americans innovated at a rate unparalleled in world history. Today's families face new costs and new risks, and they need help so that they too can achieve security and prosperity for themselves and a stronger, healthier economy for everyone.

———

Elizabeth Warren

Testimony before Senate Finance Committee

May 10, 2007

By many measures, poor and middle-income families are experiencing mounting financial pressures due to long-term shifts in the American economy and the employment sector, as well as current deteriorating economic conditions (Weller & Logan, 2008). In a recent poll, more than half (58%) of American adults rated the U.S. economy as poor and 74% believe economic conditions in the country are getting worse. More than half think their personal finances are getting worse (Discover Financial Services, 2008). A feeling of financial insecurity is on the rise among Americans. Another poll found that almost half (47%) of adults surveyed said they were worried about their personal economic security, an increase from 24%—almost double—from 2007 (Weller & Logan, 2008).

Measures of Family Economic Well-Being

Most measures of economic well-being can be explained and vary substantially by demographic characteristics, such as age, gender, education, minority group status, work status (for example, retired or not working), region of the country, marital status, and housing status (for example, homeowners versus renters). This chapter reports on economic status related to families.

Income: Family Livelihood

One of the most important indicators of family economic well-being is income. In 2006, families earned a median income of $59,894 (DeNavas-Walt, Proctor, & Smith, 2007). Personal income levels have not kept pace with the cost of living due to stagnating wages; for example, between 2000 and 2004, real median family income dropped by 3% (Mishel, Bernstein, & Allegretto, 2006). Wages represent the largest share of family income and have also fallen. The Federal Reserve reported a 6.2% decline in the median amount of wages between 2001 and 2004 (Bucks, Kennickell, & Moore, 2006). Family income is strongly associated with education; families headed by college-educated individuals have a substantially higher income compared to those with lower levels of education (Bucks, Kennickell, & Moore, 2006). Since 1963, women's income has increased for all education levels, with college-educated women experiencing the greatest gains. Among men, earnings have actually declined for all but college graduates who saw some increases in income (White & Rogers, 2001). Incomes are not neatly apportioned across families; in fact, family incomes have grown less equal. Aggregating the total income of all households by quintile, the share of aggregate income held by the lowest quintile was 3.4%, whereas the highest quintile was 50.5% (DeNavas-Walt, Proctor, & Smith, 2007). These figures demonstrate the inequality between families at the bottom of the income distribution versus Americans at the top.

If a family's total income is less than the official government-designated poverty threshold, then that family and every individual in it is considered in poverty. Poverty status is determined by total household income and the number of individuals in the household. In 2007, a family of four with a total income below $20,650 was considered in poverty. Equivalent numbers were $17,170, $13,690, and $10,210 for a three-, two-, and one-person family, respectively (Federal Register, 2007). Poverty data from the U.S. Census show that 9.8% of American families were in poverty in 2006, approximately 7.7 million families. Current poverty figures are fueled by the home-mortgage crisis, rising food and energy costs, and the widening disparity in income, wealth, and education (Billitteri, 2007). For the first time in a decade, the poverty rate dropped from 12.6% in 2005 to 12.3% in 2006. Among family households in poverty, female-headed households represent the largest proportion (28.3%), followed by male-headed (13.2%) and married-couple households (4.9%) (DeNavas-Walt, Proctor, & Smith, 2007). The day-to-day reality of families living in poverty goes beyond worry or anxiety about money. Families in poverty live without many of the basics that most of us take for granted, including safe and quality living conditions, a healthy diet, and medical care. For adults, it might be going without a hot cooked meal each day and for children, not having toys. Regardless, the persistent hardship experienced by families living in poverty is damaging to the health and well-being of all family members (Wadsworth & DeCarlo Santiago, 2008).

Families are experiencing increased pressure and/or need to secure two or more sources of income (Warren, 2007). Married-couple households had the highest median income ($69,716), relative to other family household types—$31,818 and $47,078 for female- and male-headed family households, respectively (DeNavas-Walt, Proctor, & Smith, 2007). Married-couple households have experienced a growth in median income over the past several decades; however, the growth comes from adding a working mother's second paycheck (Warren, 2007). Among married-couple families with children under 18, recent estimates from the U.S. Bureau of Labor Statistics (2008b) show that in 62.2% of the families, both parents were employed and 97.3% had one employed parent. In 2007, among all married-couple families, just over half (51.7%) were dual earners, whereas in 19.8% of the families, only the husband worked and in 6.6%, only the wife was the main wage earner. In 2005, wives earned more than husbands in 25% of dual-earner marriages, an increase from 16% in 1981 (U.S. Bureau of the Census, 2005). Dual-earner families are more vulnerable financially because they have no safety net from a backup earner in case of illness or job loss. Two-income families budget both paychecks in order to meet financial obligations; thus, the implications of job loss or illness are potentially more serious than for a single-earner family where the other person can enter the labor market to make up for an income loss (Warren, 2006, 2007).

Net Worth: A Measure of Family Wealth

Net worth is an equally important indicator of family economic well-being. Net worth consists of a family's total assets (money accumulated in savings, checking, and retirement accounts including 401(k) plans and individual retirement accounts; real estate including home equity; stock holdings; and other assets such as cars, furniture, etc.) minus total liabilities (money owed on debts such as mortgages, credit cards, and student loans). In 2002, the median net worth of American households was $58,905. Inequality is evident in the distribution of net worth. Households in the lowest income quintile had a median net worth of $5,466 compared to $188,712 for households in the highest quintile (Gottschalk, 2008). The types of assets held vary by household wealth. Portfolios with stocks, bonds, and other investment generating financial assets tend to be held by wealthier households, whereas lower-income households hold most of their wealth in home equity through home ownership. For example, the highest household income quintile is five times more likely to own stocks, mutual funds, IRAs, and Keough accounts compared to the lowest quintile (Gottschalk, 2008). The difference in asset holdings contributes to wealth disparity. Research has shown that longer marriages accumulate more wealth (Lupton & Smith, 2003) and that there is a link between assets and marital satisfaction (Shaninger & Buss, 1986).

In the United States, members of ethnic minority groups often lack the social, legal, and economic supports afforded members of the majority culture. Whether resulting from structural discrimination or a lack of meaningful and equal employment opportunities, such circumstances greatly influence economic behaviors and outcomes (Burden & Klerman, 1984). Compared with whites, members of ethnic minority groups have lower net worth (Gottschalk, 2008) and greater rates of poverty (DeNavas-Walt, Proctor, & Smith, 2007), generating economic vulnerability and disadvantage. However, ethnic minority groups also have resources, such as particular family structures, family dynamics, value systems, and childrearing practices that traditionally have served as buffers against economic stress (Gomel, Tinsley, Parke, & Clark, 1998; Lincoln, 2007). For example, black families historically have dealt with economic adversity with the help of extended kin networks, reciprocal intergenerational relations, and strong bonds with community, church, and friends (Taylor et al., 1990). Such social networks provide direct and in-kind assistance that can moderate the impacts of economic stressors (Lincoln, 2007).

Home Ownership, Home Equity, and the Housing Crisis

Home equity—the value of a home less the amount owed on the mortgage—constitutes a family's greatest financial asset and share of net worth. In 2002, median home equity was $73,697 and made up 41.7% of total net worth (Gottschalk, 2008). Since the early 1990s, home ownership rates have generally been on an upward trend, narrowly ranging from 64% to 68%. In 2008, the home ownership rate in the United States was 67.8% (U.S. Census Bureau, 2008).

The home mortgage is a family's biggest expense. Record home foreclosures in the United States have contributed to the current housing crisis and signal severe financial distress. Nationwide in 2008, a total of 2,330,483 properties were involved in a foreclosure filing, an increase of 81% from 2007 and 225% from 2006 (Realytrac, 2009). Subprime mortgages, a product developed for poor credit and/or low-income borrowers, precipitated the housing crisis by qualifying high-risk households. In 2002, the subprime mortgage market was 6% of all mortgage originations; this increased to more than 20% in 2006 (Agarwal & Ho, 2007). The foreclosure inventory rate increased to 1.22% for prime loans (loans issued to credit-worthy borrowers) and to 10.74% for subprime loans. The delinquency rate, which includes mortgages with at least one payment past due, was 6.35% for all mortgages, its highest since data collection started in 1979. The delinquency rate for prime loans was 3.71% versus 18.79% for subprime loans (Mortgage Bankers Association, 2008).

For American families, home equity is fundamental to building wealth (Mishel, Bernstein, & Allegretto, 2006). Falling home prices, also associated with the housing crisis, threaten family financial security. Federal Reserve (2008) estimates show that Americans' net worth has fallen by 3%, partly because of falling home values and the slump in the stock market. Home equity as a share of home values has fallen to a record low of 46.2%. In 2007, recent estimates show a 2.5% drop in the total value of all homes, the largest drop since 1974 (Weller, 2008). Home prices declined 3.1% over the past year (as of May 2008), the largest drop in the 17-year history of the national house price index (Office of Federal Housing Enterprise Oversight, 2008). The repercussion of the subprime foreclosures can be felt by other American households as the spillover in the community is projected to impact more than 40.6 million neighboring homes whose values will depreciate an estimated $356 billion over the next few years (Pew Charitable Trusts, 2008). Even more sobering, an estimated 2 million children will suffer as their families' homes are lost to subprime mortgage foreclosures. Home foreclosure and frequent moves produce behavioral problems, learning deficiencies, health problems due to the family's inability to afford health insurance, and emotional distress such as shame and anxiety (Lovell & Isaacs, 2008). The estimate will reach beyond 2 million children once renters who were displaced by foreclosures are included.

Employment Instability and Insecurity

Unemployment resulting from job dismissal, factory closing, forced early retirement, or any other type of job loss introduces a set of constraints, disruptions, and stressors to the family system. The stress an individual or family experiences as a result of job loss is greatly influenced by the amount and types of hardships that accompany unemployment or a loss of income. Unemployment is often an unpredictable occurrence, leaving families and individuals with little or no time to prepare for its consequences.

Poor labor market conditions in the United States indicate a weak economy. In 2008, relative to the same period a year earlier, the number of unemployed Americans rose from 6.9 million to 8.5 million, with the jobless rate increasing from 4.5% to 5.5%, the highest rate since 2004 (U.S. Bureau of Labor Statistics, 2008a). The American economy had a record number of job losses—the loss of jobs posted the first 6 months of 2008 indicate the weakest economic expansion since the Great Depression (Weller, 2008). In 2006, employment in the manufacturing sector was at its lowest level in more than half a century, hurting families with the least education the most.

Numerous studies have established that unemployment is instrumental in causing high levels of psychological, emotional, and physical stress. Symptoms commonly associated with job loss include depression, anxiety, strained family relationships, role anxiety, damaged self-esteem, and depletion of financial resources (McKee-Ryan, Song, Wanberg, & Kinicki, 2005; Voydanoff & Donnelly, 1988). The harmful effects of unemployment in terms of subjective economic stress have also been documented. The threat of being laid off and perceived job instability has been associated with poor physical health and high depressive symptoms (Maurier & Northcott, 2000). Financial strain has been identified as a predictor of psychological distress among samples of unemployed adults (Creed & Klisch, 2005) and unemployed older adolescents (Ullah, 1990) as well as a predictor of greater depression levels among a sample of older adults (Krause, 1987). Aside from the financial implications, other impacts associated with unemployment include loss of time structure, loss of social status associated with the job, disrupted social networks, reduced opportunities for social contact, and reduced goals and task demands (Creed & Klisch, 2005).

Cost of Living: Financial Strain From Uncertainty

Besides languishing wages and unfavorable labor market conditions, American families are facing increasing uncertainty in the cost of living. Nationwide, gas and energy prices have been volatile. For example, the price for regular gasoline increased by 27.9% in 2007; prices for energy rose 188.1% since June 2000 (Logan & Weller, 2008a). As of April 2009, energy prices dropped 25.1% from a year earlier. According to the Consumer Price Index, food costs were up 4% in 2007, and between April 2008 and April 2009, prices were up 3.3%. In April 2009, the price of basic family necessities like dairy products declined by 5.5% since the previous year (U.S. Bureau of Labor Statistics, 2009). A recent national poll found that roughly 66% of American adults said they anticipated higher household expenses, up from 46% 6 months earlier. Over half (56%) said they plan to spend less money on discretionary personal expenses, such as entertainment or eating out, an increase from 49% 6 months earlier (Discover Financial Services, 2008). Due to high gasoline prices in the summer of 2008, about 41% reported that they cut entertainment expenses and 15% reported cuts in travel/vacations or gas and food (Discover Financial Services, 2008). In the summer of 2009, families are facing gas prices that are 39% lower than the previous summer, and AAA estimates a 1.5% increase in automobile travel of 50 miles or more on holiday weekends (Schwartz, 2009). Such unpredictability of markets can be a significant stressor on families as planned activities and family routines are adjusted.

The cost of health insurance is so prohibitive that many Americans are going without coverage. The Census estimated that 47 million Americans were without health insurance in 2006, an increase from 2005 (44.8 million) (DeNavas-Walt, Proctor, & Smith, 2007), with families spending 74% more on health insurance than they did 30 years ago (Warren, 2007). The proportion of Americans who are provided health insurance by their employers declined from 69% in 1979 to 59.7% in 2006 (Mishel, Bernstein, & Allegretto, 2006; Weller, 2008). The inequality of health insurance coverage can be seen between low- and high-wage workers—only 19% of the lowest-wage earners were covered by their employers' health insurance plan, while 72% of the highest-wage workers received coverage (Mishel, Bernstein, & Allegretto, 2006).

Household Debt and Families: Borrowing Against the Future

Faced with budget constraints due to rising prices and unfavorable economic conditions, families increasingly borrow against their future. Not all household debt is bad; debt is a financial instrument that can be used to create opportunities. For example, student loan debt creates human capital that has long-term returns. Of the various types of debt, the most threatening to the long-term financial well-being of families is high-interest consumer credit used to purchase nondurable goods and services (i.e., items and services that typically do not last longer than the payment period and yield no economic return while being held). Paying for dinner in a restaurant with a high-interest credit card is the classic example of this kind of debt.

Relative to other types of consumer loans, credit card loans have grown the fastest. Credit bureaus report that the average American household has 13 debt obligations; 9 are credit cards, including bank, gas, retail, and phone cards, and 4 are installment loans, including mortgage, auto, and student loans (myfico.com, 2008). Among families who use credit cards, 58% carry outstanding balances on their cards, with an average balance of $2,200 (Bucks, Kennickell, & Moore, 2006). In 2005, household debt was more than 130% of disposable personal income, with middle-income families dedicating 20% of their income to debt repayment. Some families owe an excess of 40% of their income to debt repayment, roughly 14% of middle-income families and 25% of low-income families. Research has shown that Americans are working more hours than they would like in order to be able to make payments on their consumer debt (Clarkberg & Moen, 2001). Household debt becomes problematic when large amounts of debt are assumed and/or other financial obligations cannot be met.

The ability to meet debt obligations, credit card use, and frequency of late payments made by credit users are all important factors in assessing subjective economic stress (Avery, Calem, & Canner, 2003). Financial satisfaction appears to be directly related to credit practices and attitudes. Attitudes among married couples about consumer debt may predict frequent marital conflict. Couples may recognize that consumer debt constrains future choices and may resent the time and money required to make debt payments (Dew, 2007). Lown and Ju (1992) found that families with higher debt-to-income ratios were less satisfied with their overall financial situation than were families with lower ratios; they also found that families who used credit cards for convenience rather than installment purchases were more satisfied with their finances. Worries about debt repayment and meeting financial emergencies have been found to be associated with lower levels of perceived financial well-being (Porter & Garman, 1993). Stress associated with credit card debt has also been found to have negative effects on physical subjective self-reported health (Drentea & Lavrakas, 2000).

Research findings suggest that ethnic minority groups vary in their access to, sources of, and utilization of financial resources (Gomel et al., 1998). Prior to the passage of the Equal Credit Opportunity Act in 1975, creditors routinely discriminated against some applicants based on gender, race, and ethnicity. Since that time, however, the availability of credit to previously underserved families has steadily increased, and credit usage levels now appear to be similar across groups.

Bankruptcy: Ultimate Family Financial Distress

Personal bankruptcies and home foreclosures are linked to rising household debt and signal severe economic stress in families (American Bankruptcy Institute, 2008). The rate of personal bankruptcies reached an all-time high in 2005 when a total of 2,078,415 nonbusiness bankruptcies were recorded, implying that roughly 1.8% of the nation's households filed for personal bankruptcy. With Congress's passage of the Bankruptcy Abuse Prevention and Consumer Protection Act of 2005 (BAPCPA), a law designed to make it more difficult for consumers to be protected by bankruptcy, consumer bankruptcy filings dropped by 70% in 2006 to 617,660 (Administrative Office of the U.S. Courts, 2006). Despite this tougher law, consumer bankruptcy filings were up 30% during the first 6 months of 2008, relative to the same time frame a year earlier (American Bankruptcy Institute, 2008). Policy analysts forecast that consumer bankruptcy rates will reach the levels recorded before BAPCPA's passage, particularly given the adversity faced by families in the current economic environment. Proponents of the BAPCPA conjecture that individuals who declared bankruptcy were abusing the system to avoid their debt obligation or were out-of-control spenders. In reality, the majority of bankruptcy filings occur because of reasons beyond the control of the family, such as job loss, divorce, or illness coupled with a lack of health insurance (Logan & Weller, 2008b).

Savings: Family Safety Net

When faced with challenging economic conditions, families who maintain a cash reserve in an emergency savings account can steer clear of financial disaster and continue to meet their financial obligations. However, many American families are more vulnerable during weak economic conditions because they have less to save or are saving less. A recent survey indicated that the proportion of families who could withstand an unspecified emergency equal to 3 months' income decreased to 29.4% in 2007, from 30.5% in 2005 and 39.4% in 2000 (Weller & Logan, 2008). Another recent survey on savings found that half of Americans (52%) said they currently cannot afford to save or are saving inadequately (Consumer Federation of America, 2007). Approximately 37% of American adults reported not having money left over after paying all of their regular bills for the month (Discover Financial Services, 2008). The Consumer Federation of America (2007) report found that respondents were pessimistic about their ability to save, with many blaming credit card debt and impulsive spending as barriers. Between 2001 and 2004, the Survey of Consumer Finance reported a three-percentage-point drop in the proportion of families—roughly 56% of families—who said their spending was less than their income.

The proportion of American families that save has been steadily declining; about 41% of families report that they save regularly (Bucks, Kennickell, & Moore, 2006). Regardless of income and education, married couples save at higher rates than other types of families (Lupton & Smith, 2003). The personal savings rate of Americans averaged around 9% in the 1980s, dropped to 5% in the 1990s, and since the millennium has hovered around 0%, with the current 12-month average personal savings rate at 0.7% through April 2008. Interestingly, the rate jumped to 5.0% in May 2008 due to the Economic Stimulus Act of 2008, which provided rebates to eligible tax payers (Bureau of Economic Analysis, 2008).

Among families who do save, the top three motives for families' saving were retirement (34.7% of families), liquidity or cash reserve (30% of families), and education (11.6% of families). It appears that roughly one-third of families are taking precautionary measures by saving for liquidity-related reasons (Bucks, Kennickell, & Moore, 2006). Financial professionals recommend a 3- to 6-month emergency savings fund to provide for living expenses in the case of income loss, but most Americans aren't meeting the recommended provision. American adults were asked to estimate how many months they would be able to continue living at their current lifestyle if they had a sudden loss of income; 27% could not maintain their lifestyle even 1 month. Approximately 18%, 11%, and 27% responded 1, 2, and 3 months, respectively, and 23% could live 6 months or more. For individuals making less than $40,000 a year, the proportion jumped to 40% versus 14% of individuals who make more than $75,000 a year (Discover Financial Services, 2008). Thus, many American families with no safety net hang on the precipice of financial disaster.

The Family Economic Stress Model

The Family Economic Stress Model attributed to Conger and Elder (1994) links economic hardship to child and family outcomes through changes in personal mental health, marital quality, and parenting. The process begins with external economic pressures such as involuntary job separation or a general countrywide economic downturn leading to financial strains placed on mothers and fathers. These pressures result in declines in parental mental health, which challenges both marital quality and parenting practices. Finally, compromised parenting yields negative family outcomes most often observed in declines in child mental health and behavior. The Family Economic Stress Model has been applied to models of family and child outcomes in diverse economic systems and cultures, performing equally well in Finland's welfare state (Solantaus, Leinonen, & Punamaki, 2004), communist China (Shek, 2005), and capitalist economies such as the United States (Conger & Elder, 1994).

Economic stress in the family manifests itself directly by influencing individual well-being and indirectly by influencing family interaction (Conger et al., 1990; Elder & Caspi, 1988). Economic factors (e.g., unemployment, low income, excessive debt levels) have negative effects on the mental health and well-being of individuals (Kahn & Pearlin, 2006; McKee et al., 2005). Researchers have consistently found a relationship between economic stress and individual distress, which can take the form of increased levels of anger, hostility, depression, anxiety, somatic complaints, and poor physical health (Kahn & Pearlin, 2006; Lincoln, 2007; McKee et al., 2005). Even the association between economic strain and suicide has been linked (Stack & Wasserman, 2007). Economic stress within the family system amplifies the fragility and interdependence of all family members.

The adverse effects of economic stress on family functioning and family relationships have also been well documented. Economic stress has been found to decrease family satisfaction and cohesion (Voydanoff, 1991) and often forces family members to adapt their roles and responsibilities. For example, if a family experiences an income decline because of one member's job loss, other family members may be required to contribute to household resources by finding employment (Elder & Caspi, 1988). With a loss in income, a family may have to reduce discretional spending, perhaps reluctantly substituting the family vacation for a "staycation" (a stay-at-home vacation). Economic stress can also lead to diminished relationship quality in the family through the strain and disruption caused by changes in social activities as well as changes in the support provided by social networks (Voydanoff, 1991).

The marital relationship may be altered by economic stress. When a couple faces economic hardship, the quality of the marital relationship often declines (Conger, Reuter, & Elder, 1999; Cutrona et al., 2003). Several recent studies support the Family Economic Stress Model with respect to marital outcomes (Dew, 2007; Kinnunen & Feldt, 2004). The stress process is modeled as a couple's negative economic circumstances increasing financial strain, which increases individual psychological distress, which in turn negatively impacts marital stability and adjustment (Kinnunen & Feldt, 2004). Economic stress results in increased financial disputes and thus greater marital tension and discord (Dew, 2007; Gudmunson et al., 2007). A recent study showed that financial strain increased the incidence of couple disagreements and fighting and decreased the couple's quality time together; ultimately, these factors mediated the relationship between financial strain and marital instability (Gudmunson et al., 2007). Economic stress has been found to be related to an increase in negative exchanges and a reduction in positive exchanges between spouses (Conger et al., 1990). For example, financial strain affects the marital relationship of an unemployed couple through spousal withdrawal of social support and social undermining (Vinokur, Price, & Caplan, 1996). Economic strain increases husbands' hostility and decreases their supportiveness and warmth (Conger et al., 1990). Another reaction to economic stress in interpersonal relations is competitiveness between spouses.

Parents facing economic stress may find that the quality of their parenting suffers. Parental well-being is affected by economic stress; that is, studies have found elevated psychological distress (Gutman, McLoyd, & Tokoyawa, 2005), general life stress, depressive symptoms, and decreased feelings of efficacy (Mistry, Lowe, Renner, & Chien, 2008). Dimished parental well-being influences parenting behaviors, childrearing practices, and the quality of parent–child interactions (Gutman et al., 2005; Mistry et al., 2008; Solantus et al., 2004). Economic stress has been shown to affect parenting practices by reducing warmth and affective support (Mistry et al., 2008); increasing inconsistent, controlling, and punitive discipline (Grant et al., 2000; Mistry et al., 2008; Solantus et al., 2004); and lowering levels of parent involvement and supportiveness (Lempers & Clark-Lempers, 1997; Waanders, Mendez, & Downer, 2007). Levels of maternal warmth and social support and the provision of child learning experiences in the home are also affected negatively by economic stress (Klebanov, Brooks-Gunn, & Duncan, 1994). In one study, parents under economic pressure reported feeling less effective in their roles as disciplinarians. These same parents were observed to be less affectionate in their interactions with their children than were other parents. The researchers suggest that the diminished feelings these parents had in the parenting role resulted indirectly from the effects of economic pressure on their psychological well-being, which included lowered feelings of efficacy and heightened depressive levels (Mistry, Bandewater, Huston, & McLoyd, 2002). Greater financial strain reduces positive parent–adolescent relations—measured as shared activities and supportiveness—and increases negative parent–adolescent relations—measured as frequency of conflict and aggressive interactions such as shouting or acting angry (Gutman et al., 2005).

Economic stress has been associated with specific child outcomes, both short and long term, through limited resources, limited opportunities, and diminished human capital development. Children who experience economic stress have been found to exhibit greater levels of depression, psychological distress, and anxiety (Grant el al., 2000; Gutman et al., 2005); more aggressive and antisocial behaviors (Solantaus et al., 2004); decreased levels of self-esteem, self-efficacy, mastery, life satisfaction, and resourcefulness (Gutman et al., 2005; Shek, 2003); diminished school performance (Gutman et al., 2005); and increased substance abuse and psychiatric morbidity (Shek, 2003). Family economic stress has also been linked to a greater prevalence of psychosomatic symptoms and chronic illness (Pederson, Madsen, & Kohler, 2005). Fathers' negativity resulting from economic pressure has been found to increase children's risk of depression and aggression (Elder et al., 1992), whereas maternal financial stress has been shown to decrease the quality of the mother–child relationship, resulting in greater levels of depression and loneliness (Lempers & Clark-Lempers, 1997). Maternal financial strain has been found to be associated with lower school performance and greater sexual experience among African American adolescent girls (Coley & Chase-Lansdale, 2000).

Compared with other adolescents, adolescents who worry frequently about their families' finances have reported suffering more from various somatic complaints, including stomachaches, loss of appetite, depression, sleeplessness, and lack of concentration (Reinharcit Pederson et al., 2005; Wadsworth & Santiago, 2008). Additionally, compared with other types of stress (e.g., school, social, health), economic stress is the most strongly related to adolescents' self-perceived health. Adolescents' perceptions of their relationships with their parents are also negatively affected by economic stress (Ho et al., 1995) as parents and children frequently disagree about control over money. When adolescents and their parents are in agreement over family finances, in contrast, the adolescents' satisfaction with family life and their own money management skills are increased (Williams & Prohofsky, 1986).

Coping With Economic Stress

The characteristics of financially challenged families—such as adaptability, cohesion, and authority patterns—that are in place both prior to and during a stressor event, like financial difficulties, are important in that they can alter the relationship between the event (such as unemployment and its associated hardships) and individual and family reactions. Families experiencing economic stress from their financial situation can draw on individual (e.g., education), psychological (e.g., self-efficacy), social (e.g., social support), relational (e.g., marital relationship), and financial (e.g., savings) resources to cope with their situation (Elder & Caspi, 1988).

Individuals with positive self-evaluations, such as high self-esteem or self-worth, and a strong sense of personal control or mastery over their situation are better prepared to manage their financial difficulties. As such, these qualities can weaken the link between financial stress and mental health outcomes (McKee-Ryan et al., 2005). For example, self-efficacy has been found to be an effective moderator in the context of economic stress (McKee-Ryan et al., 2005), determining how an individual reacts to a given stressor event. Studies of unemployment have found that high self-efficacy successfully predicts reemployment (McKee-Ryan et al., 2005). Financial resources, such as savings and unemployment compensation, are also important in mediating the effect economic stress has on psychological and health outcomes. The impact of job loss can be alleviated by income, liquid assets, and public assistance (McKee-Ryan et al., 2005) as well as the continuation of fringe benefits such as health insurance, severance pay, and pensions (Voydanoff, 1983).

As outlined in the Family Economic Stress Model, some social resources such as integration into family and social networks and quality of one's interpersonal relationships are diminished by financial strain. For example, a recent study found that financial strain was associated with lower levels of social support and higher levels of negative interactions (Lincoln, 2007).

According to Elder and Caspi (1988), families respond to economic loss by restructuring resources and relationships. Restructuring may relieve the situation without improving it, or it may be an adaptive coping strategy. For those struggling with chronic economic issues, several coping strategies have been identified as effective in breaking the links established in the Family Economic Stress Model. For example, coping strategies such as problem solving, social support such as talking to others, acceptance of the situation, positive thinking, and distraction have been associated with fewer somatic complaints as well as anxious and depressive symptoms among families suffering from chronic economic stress (Wadsworth & Santiago, 2008).

_____ Family Financial Planning as a Coping Resource

Family financial planning can mitigate the psychological and social damage caused by economic stress, family vulnerability, and exposure to economic stress. The family life cycle model developed by Ando and Modigliani (1963) is a common framework for understanding saving and consumption behavior of families. Families are assumed to maximize lifetime satisfaction by balancing high- and low-income periods with saving, and investing is assumed to increase a family's satisfaction and decrease economic stress. Over the family life cycle, spending is expected to be smooth and stable as the family maintains a standard of living with the use of savings during low-income periods. However, actual consumption patterns are often affected by changing family needs and wants, situational stressors, and significant historical events (Fox, 1995). Part of the gap between the theory of household resource allocation over time and actual resource allocation is explained by the nonnormative factors that are so prevalent among American families, including unanticipated unemployment, divorce, casualty losses, and unanticipated health care expenses (Fan, Chang, & Hanna, 1992).

The family economic life cycle is comprised of three key phases, identified by the relationship between expenditure and earning levels that define the life cycle savings hypothesis. These phases, which we discuss in turn, can serve as guidelines for addressing economic stress. When families employ systematic money management strategies, they can reduce or eliminate conflict during tough financial times. For example, research has shown that couples have fewer finance-related arguments when they use financial management strategies such as record keeping, goal-setting practices, and saving (Godwin, 1994). Couples under economic pressure who use effective problem-solving skills reduce marital conflict and thus marital distress (Conger et al., 1999). A study of married couples found that when a spouse thinks his or her spouse mismanages money, the odds of divorce greatly increase (Amato & Rogers, 1997).

Phase I. Family Formation: Starting a Family and a Credit and Debt Management Program

In the family formation phase, a family is expected to accumulate significant amounts of debt through the use of installment and consumer credit, largely as a result of the purchase of a home and expenses of child rearing. Families in this phase typically make up 30% of the U.S. population, yet they hold nearly 60% of the debt (Kapoor, Dlabay, & Hughes, 1999, p. 156). Planning for payment against this debt and worrying about possible default can easily become a source of stress within a family.

A family can avoid much of the stress that can come with debt by following a plan of debt management. To make such a plan, the family needs to (a) establish credit goals or debt limits; (b) explore, understand, and make good choices among the various sources of credit; and (c) make fair comparisons between the costs of different types of credit (Garman & Forgue, 2007). Once family members have set their goals and tolerable debt levels, they can study their available credit options. Sources of credit range from very informal (relatives and friends) to very formal (banks or banklike institutions). Most salient in the family's credit decision should be the determination of the actual cost of credit. In the simplest form, the cost of credit is represented by the interest rate. Saving current income is a primary mechanism through which families achieve financial goals and prepare for financial emergencies. Saving is also thought to provide a sense of economic control. In the event of economic stress (e.g., income loss or unemployment), an emergency fund in the form of savings serves as a safeguard or a coping resource.

Phase II. Repaying Debt and Saving for Retirement

In the second phase of the family economic life cycle, the time at which most household heads reach their peak earning years, many families plan to accumulate wealth in anticipation of a substantial decrease in earned income in retirement. Reduced or stabilized living expenses that do not exceed income mark this phase. As income increases with workplace experience and household formation nears completion, immediate financial demands are expected to subside, and the family has an opportunity to accumulate savings and pay off debt accumulated in the formation stage. However, during these peak earning years, many families are challenged by the repayment of accumulated debt, college education expenses, and deferral of the proper amount of consumption until retirement when reduced earnings are anticipated.

Families use tax planning, investment, and asset protection strategies to move assets from one point in the life cycle to another. Unfortunately, the complexity of these financial strategies can often become a source of additional economic stress in families (Aldana & Liljenquist, 1998). As a result, many families now seek the help of family financial managers to retire the debt accumulated in the previous phase and invest any surplus in financial assets.

The most important action a family can take in this phase is to determine accurately the extent of the family's debt. Once the amount of debt is clear, the family can allocate savings toward debt repayment, retiring the loans with the highest interest first, thus "investing" in the highest-return assets earlier. This method of thinking of debt repayment in similar terms as saving for future financial goals helps financial managers justify an emphasis on debt repayment early in the financial life cycle, potentially relieving some of the stress involved in delaying savings for retirement and longer-range financial goals.

A number of nonprofit organizations, such as Consumer Credit Counseling Services, have been established to assist families with the debt management process. Typically, such an organization will help a family reestablish payment terms for debt with payments that are more manageable. Often, the counseling service will collect a lump-sum payment from the family and redistribute the money to the family's creditors, thus relieving family members of the stress involved in direct contact with creditors. Research findings suggest that working with credit counselors can have positive impacts on individuals' financial well-being and health (Kim, Garman, & Sorhaindo, 2003). However, using such a debt management system can also have significant drawbacks. The process itself is often reported as a negative event in credit bureau files, and participants must agree to discontinue any use of credit while they are working with the debt management agency.

As families struggle to retire the debt they have accumulated in the formation stage, they may encounter significant additional educational expenses as children approach college age. Educational spending pressures have risen steadily in the United States over the past two decades as tuition increases have consistently outpaced increases in wages. The widespread perception of the hopelessness of this situation is expressed in most families' unwillingness to plan for or begin saving for children's education. A recent survey found that less than one quarter (24%) of Americans are taking advantage of plans, like Coverdell Savings Accounts or 529 plans, to save for their children's education (Country Financial, 2008). Parents of college students face competing pressures, whether to save for their retirement or their children's education goals; about 25% of all families use retirement assets to pay for college expenses (Todd & DeVaney, 1997).

Recent empirical studies of the adequacy of retirement savings consistently have found that American families are underfinancing their retirement. These families will need to either increase their savings or reduce their living standards below expected levels upon retirement. In a recent survey, approximately 66% of workers reported that they (and/or their spouse) had saved money for retirement, and even fewer (60%) reported that they were currently saving. Among those who do save, roughly half have accumulated less than $25,000, excluding their home and defined benefit plan, showing that they are likely not on track for retirement at preretirement consumption levels (Helman, VanDerhei, and Copeland 2007).

Garman and Forgue (2007) outline the formal process of retirement planning; families can use their guidelines to determine the levels of savings they need to meet their retirement spending needs. As with all financial planning prescriptions, the process begins with goal setting. Goals are set based on income needs in retirement. Anticipated retirement resources are then evaluated, these are subtracted from retirement needs, and a savings gap is estimated. Additional annual contributions needed to fill this gap are then calculated, and investment decisions are made to match individual investor risk-tolerance levels and specific financial goals in retirement. In this final part of the retirement planning and saving process, a wide range of tax, investment, and insurance planning tools are available to families. It is at this point that many families rely on financial managers to cope with the complexities of the financial planning process. In fact, the sheer breadth of the field of financial planning appears to be a source of economic stress in families. Aldana and Liljenquist (1998) confirm that lack of financial education and understanding about financial matters is a significant determinant of financial strain. Researchers have also found that families who receive professional advice about finances and retirement are more satisfied with their current financial situation than are families who do not receive such advice (Kim et al., 2003).

Phase III. Living in Retirement and Planning for Intergenerational Transfers

In the third phase of the family economic life cycle, consumption expenditures are again expected to outpace earnings as families tap savings and investment income for expenditures in retirement. At this end of the life cycle, some families face the problem of living on reduced incomes, whereas others need to distribute excess assets among family members and/or favorite charities. These wealth transfers, and planning for them, can easily become an additional source of family stress and conflict through competition for assets.

The quality of the retirement experience relies on financial security. One study found that retirement income in the form of pensions increased positive attitudes toward retirement 6, 12, and 24 months after retirement (van Solinge & Henkens, 2008). Another study found that 41% of the retired individuals in the sample said that adjusting to retirement was a financially difficult process, whereas only 12% of newlyweds and 23% of new parents reported difficulties with financial adjustments (Pollan & Levine, 1995). Similarly, Hira and Mugenda (1998) found that 35% of retirees were dissatisfied with their current level of savings. However, for the majority of retired Americans, financial stress and dissatisfaction levels appear to be minimal in comparison with the levels found among those in other stages of the family financial life cycle. Relative to younger and employed Americans, retirees have been shown to pay closer attention to their long-range financial plans. Davis and Carr (1992) found that retirees, in comparison with persons in other age groups, were least likely to use formal or informal written budgets; however, those retirees who did use budgets were more likely than those in any other age groups to use budgets that covered a period longer than a month.

In the simplest form of the family life cycle savings model, families are assumed to hold no bequest motives, with every dollar spent during the lifetimes of the immediate family members. Clearly, an important extension of this life cycle framework is consideration of the impact and process of passing wealth between generations (Modigliani, 1988). Stress resulting from the estate planning or intergenerational transfer portion of a family financial plan likely comes directly from (a) perceived legal complexities associated with asset transfers before and after death and (b) changing roles of family members in the financial management process (Edwards, 1991). The goal of estate planning is to maximize compliance with the decedent's wants while minimizing the erosion of wealth through taxes and transaction costs.

Summary

Economic stress exacts social and psychological costs on the quality of family life. Families have been shown to vary significantly in their vulnerability to changing economic events. Marital status, children in the household, and ethnicity are among the characteristics that help to explain the differences between families who deal well with changing economic circumstances and those who move into crisis. Differing levels of resources and adoption of coping strategies further explain family resilience under economic stress. In this chapter, we have offered the process of family financial planning over distinct life cycle stages as a general preventive strategy, to help families reduce the social and psychological costs associated with economic stress.

Suggested Internet Resources

Kiplinger offers a wide selection of financial planning tools, ranging from financial statements to decision-making worksheets on home and car buying: http://www.kiplinger.com/tools

Federal Trade Commission, Bureau of Consumer Protection, provides educational resources and links to information covering consumer rights, protection, and fraudulent practices: http://www.ftc.gov/ftc/consumer.htm

American Bankruptcy Institute provides information on getting help with debt consolidation, debt management, and the bankruptcy process: http://www.abiworkd.org

Consumer Credit Counseling Services, a nonprofit organization, offers assistance with debt management: http://www.credit-counselors.cc

American Savings Education Council offers resources for families wanting to get started with savings: http://www.asec.org/tools

Vanguard Retirement Planning Center provides educational materials for those just starting with investments: http://www.vanguard.com

Certified Financial Planner Board of Standards and National Association of Personal Financial Advisors provide assistance in selecting a financial planner: http://www.cfp.net/learn and http://www.napfa.org

Estate Planning Links and Crash Course in Wills and Trusts provide information on estate planning: http://www.estateplanninglinks.com and http://mtpalermo.com

References

Administrative Office of the U.S. Courts. (2006). *2005–2006 calendar year comparison.* Retrieved June 14, 2008, from http://www.uscourts.gov/bnkrpctystats/bankrupt_ftable_dec2006.xls

Agarwal, S., & Ho, C. T. (2007). *Comparing the prime and subprime mortgage markets.* Chicago Fed Letter, Issue 241. Retrieved June 1, 2008, from http://www.chicagofed.org/publications/fedletter/cflaugust2007_241.pdf

Aldana, S. G., & Liljenquist, W. (1998). Validity and reliability of a financial strain survey. *Financial Counseling and Planning, 9*(2), 11–18.

Amato, P. R., & Rogers, S. J. (1997). A longitudinal study of marital problems and subsequent divorce. *Journal of Marriage and Family, 59*(3), 612–624.

American Bankruptcy Institute. (2008). *Consumer bankruptcy filings in first half of 2008 up 30 percent from a year ago.* Retrieved July 4, 2009, from http://www.abiworld.org/AM/Template.cfm?Section=Home&TEMPLATE=/CM/ContentDisplay.cfm&CONTENTID=53632

Ando, A., & Modigliani, F. (1963). The life cycle hypothesis of saving. *American Economic Review, 53*(1), 55–84.

Avery, R. B., Calem, P. S., & Canner, G. B. (2003). An overview of consumer data and credit reporting. *Federal Reserve Bulletin, 89,* 47–73.

Billitteri, T. J. (2007). Domestic poverty: Is a new approach needed to help the poorest Americans? *CQ Researcher, 17,* 721–743.

Bucks, B. K., Kennickell, A. B., & Moore, K. B. (2006). Recent changes in U.S. family finances: Evidence from the 2001 and 2004 Survey of Consumer Finances. *Federal Reserve Bulletin, 92,* A1–A38.

Burden D. S., & Klerman, L. V. (1984). Teenage parenthood: Factors that lessen economic dependence. *Social Work, 29*(1), 11–16.

Bureau of Economic Analysis (2008). Personal income and outlays: May 2008. U.S. Department of Commerce. June 27, 2008, tp://www.bea.gov/newsreleases/national/pi/2008/pdf/pi0508.pdf

Cashell, B.W. (2007). *Who are the middle class?* CRS Report to Congress. [Electronic Version]. Washington, DC: The Library of Congress.

Clarkberg, M., & Moen, P. (2001). The time-squeeze: Is the increase in working time due to employer demands or employee preferences? *American Behavioral Scientist, 44*(7), 1115–11137.

Coley, R. L., & Chase-Lansdale, P. L. (2000). Welfare receipt, financial strain, and African-American adolescent functioning. *Social Service Review, 74*(3), 380–404.

Conger, R. D., & Elder, G. H. (1994). *Linking economic hardship to marital quality and instability. Families in troubled times: Adapting to change in rural America.* New York: Aldine De Gruyter.

Conger, R. D., Elder, G. H., Jr., Lorenz, F. O., Conger, K. J., Simons, R. L., Whitbeck, L. B., et al. (1990). Linking economic hardship to marital quality and instability. *Journal of Marriage and Family, 52*(2), 643–656.

Conger, R. D., Reuter, M. A., & Elder, G. H., Jr. (1999). Couple resilience to economic pressure. *Journal of Personality and Social Psychology, 76*(1), 54–71.

Consumer Federation of America. (2007). *More than half of Americans say they are not saving adequately.* Retrieved June 30, 2008, from http://www. consumerfed .org/ pdfs/CFA_Wachovia_Savings_Press_Release_ 12_10_07.pdf

Country Financial. (2008). *Americans' college choices limited despite early saving.* Retrieved July 14, 2008, from http://www.countryfinancialsecurityindex.com/ trendrelease.php?tid=8&menu=N

Creed, P. A., & Klisch, J. (2005). Future outlook and financial strain: Testing the personal agency and latent deprivation models of unemployment and well-being. *Journal of Occupational Healthy Psychology, 10*(3), 251–260.

Cutrona, C. E., Russell, D. W., Abraham, W. T., Gardner, K. A., Melby, J. M., Bryant, C., et al. (2003). Neighborhood context and financial strain as predictors of marital interaction and marital quality in African American couples. *Personal Relationships, 10*(3), 389–409.

Davis, E. P., & Carr, R. A. (1992). Budgeting practices over the life cycle. *Financial Counseling and Planning, 3*(1), 3–16.

DeNavas-Walt, C., Proctor, B. D., & Smith, J. (2006). *Income, poverty, and health insurance coverage in the United States: 2006.* U.S. Census Bureau, Current Population Reports P60–233. Washington, DC: U.S. Government Printing Office.

Discover Financial Services. (2008). *Discover U.S. spending monitor.* Retrieved July 13, 2008, from http://www.discoverfinancial.com/surveys/spending_files/ DSMSummaryJun08.pdf

Drentea, P., & Lavrakas, P. J. (2000). Over the limit: The association among health, race and debt. *Social Science & Medicine, 50*(4), 517–529.

Dew, J. (2007).Two sides of the same coin? The differing roles of assets and consumer debt in marriage. *Journal of Family and Economic Issues, 28*(1), 89–104.

Edwards, K. P. (1991). Planning for family asset transfers. *Financial Counseling and Planning, 2*(1), 55–78.

Elder, G. H., Jr., & Caspi, A. (1988). Economic stress in lives: Developmental perspectives. *Journal of Social Issues, 44*(2), 25–45.

Elder, G. H., Conger, R. D., Foster, E. M., & Ardelt, M. (1992). Families under economic pressure. *Journal of Family Issues, 13*(1), 5–37.

Fan, X. J., Chang, Y. R., & Hanna, S. (1992). Optimal credit use with uncertain income. *Financial Counseling and Planning, 3*(3), 125–132.

Federal Reserve. (2008). *Flow of funds accounts of the United States.* Retrieved July 1, 2008, from http://www.federalreserve.gov/releases/z1/Current/z1r-1.pdf

Fox, G. L., & Chancey, D. (1998). Sources of economic distress: Individual and family outcomes. *Journal of Family Issues, 19*(6), 725–749.

Fox, J. J. (1995). Household demand system analysis: Implications of unit root econometrics for modeling, testing and policy analysis. *Consumer Interests Annual, 41,* 195–201.

Garman, E. T., & Forgue, R. E. (2007). *Personal finance* (9th ed.). Boston: Houghton Mifflin.

Godwin, D. D. (1994). Antecedents and consequences of newlyweds' cash flow management. *Financial Counseling and Planning, 5*(4), 161–190.

Gomel, J. N., Tinsley, B. J., Parke, R. D., & Clark, K. M. (1998). The effects of economic hardship on family relationships among African American, Latino, and Euro-American families. *Journal of Family Issues, 19*(4), 436–467.

Gottschalk, A. O. (2008). *Net worth and the assets of households: 2002.* Current Population Reports P70–115 issued April 2008. Washington, DC: U.S. Census Bureau.

Grant, K., Poindexter, L., Davis, T., Mi Hyon, C., McCormick, A., & Smith, K. (2000). Economic stress and psychological distress among urban African American adolescents: The mediating role of parents. *Journal of Prevention & Intervention in the Community, 20*(1/2), 25–37.

Gudmunson, C. G., Beutler, I. F., Israelsen, C. L., McCoy, J. K., & Hill, E. J. (2007). Linking financial strain to marital instability: Examining the roles of emotional distress and marital interaction. *Journal of Family and Economic Issues, 28*(3), 357–376.

Gutman, L. M., McLoyd, V. C., & Tokoyawa, T. (2005). Financial strain, neighborhood stress, parenting behaviors, and adolescent adjustment in urban African American families. *Journal of Research on Adolescence, 15*(4), 425–449.

Helman, R., VanDerhei, J., & Copeland, C. (2007). *The retirement system in transition: The 2007 Retirement Confidence Survey.* EBRI Issue Brief No. 304 (April). Washington, DC: Employee Benefit Research Institute.

Hira, T. K., & Mugenda, O. (1998). Predictors of financial satisfaction: Differences between retirees and non-retirees. *Financial Counseling and Planning, 9*(2), 75–83.

Ho, C. S., Lempers, J. D., & Clark-Lempers, D. S. (1995). Effects of economic hardship on adolescent self-esteem: A family mediation model. *Adolescence, 30*(117), 117–131.

Holden, K. C., & Smock, P. J. (1991). The economic costs of marital dissolution: Why do women bear a disproportionate cost? *Annual Review of Sociology, 17,* 51–78.

Kahn, J. R., & Pearlin, L. I. (2006). Financial strain over the life course and health among older adults. *Journal of Health & Social Behavior, 47*(1), 17–31.

Kapoor, J. R., Dlabay, L. R., & Hughes, R. J. (1999). *Personal finance* (5th ed.). Boston: Irwin/McGraw-Hill.

Kim, J., Garman, E. T., & Sorhaindo, S. (2003). Relationships among credit counseling clients' financial well-being, financial behaviors, financial stressor events, and health. *Financial Counseling and Planning, 14*(2), 75–87.

Kinnunen, U., & *Feldt,* T. (2004). Economic stress and marital adjustment among couples: Analyses at the dyadic level. *European Journal of Social Psychology, 34*(5), 519–532.

Klebanov, P. K., Brooks-Gunn, J., & Duncan, G. J. (1994). Does neighborhood and family poverty affect mothers' parenting, mental health, and social support? *Journal of Marriage and Family, 56*(2), 441–455.

Krause, N. (1987). Chronic strain, locus of control, and distress in older adults. *Psychology and Aging, 2*(4), 375–382.

Krause, N. (1997). Anticipated support, received support, and economic stress among older adults. *Journal of Gerontology: Psychological Sciences, 52,* 284–293.

Lempers, J. D., & Clark-Lempers, D. S. (1990). Economic hardship, parenting, and distress in adolescence. *Child Development, 60*(1), 25–39.

Lempers, J. D., & Clark-Lempers, D. S. (1997). Economic hardship, family relationships, and adolescent distress: An evaluation of a stress-distress mediation model in mother-daughter and mother-son dyads. *Adolescence, 32*(126), 339–356.

Lincoln, K. D. (2007). Financial strain, negative interactions, and mastery: Pathways to mental health among older African Americans. *Journal of Black Psychology, 33*(4), 439–462.

Logan, A., & Weller, C. E. (2008a). *Rising gas prices add to the strain on families' already squeezed budgets.* Retrieved July 15, 2008, from www.americanprogress .org/issues/2008/06/pdf/food_gas.pdf

Logan, A., & Weller, C. E. (2008b). *Bankruptcies back on the wrong track: Bankruptcy rates on the rise again despite the Bankruptcy Abuse Prevention and Consumer Protection Act of 2005.* Retrieved July 15, 2008, from www.american progress.org/issues/2008/06/pdf/food_gas.pdf

Lovell, P., & Isaacs, J. (2008). *The impact of the mortgage crisis on children.* First Focus. Retrieved July 11, 2008, from http://www.firstfocus.net/Download/ HousingandChildrenFINAL.pdf

Lown, J. M., & Ju, I. (1992). A model of credit use and financial satisfaction. *Financial Counseling and Planning, 3*(3), 105–124.

Lupton, J. P., & Smith, J. P. (2003). Marriage, assets, and savings. In S. A. Grossbard-Shechtman (Eds.), *Marriage and the economy* (pp. 129–151). Cambridge, UK: Cambridge University Press.

Maurier, W. L., & Northcott, H. C. (2000). Job uncertainty and health status for nurses during restructuring of health care in Alberta. *Western Journal of Nursing Research, 22*(5), 623–641.

Mckee-Ryan, F. M., Song, Z., Wanberg, C. R., & Kinicki, A. J. (2005). Psychological and physical well-being during unemployment: A meta-analytic study. *Journal of Applied Psychology, 90*(1), 53–76.

Mishel, L., Bernstein, J., & Allegretto, S. (2006). The state of working America 2006/2007. Ithaca, NY: ILR Press.

Mistry, R. S., Bandewater, E. A., Huston, A. C., & McLoyd, V. C. (2002). Economic well-being and children's social adjustment: The role of family process in an ethnically diverse low-income sample. *Child Development, 73*(3), 935–951.

Mistry, R. S., Lowe, E. D., Renner, A. D., & Chien, N. (2008). Expanding the Family Economic Stress Model: Insights from a mixed-methods approach. *Journal of Marriage and Family, 70*(1), 196–209.

Modigliani, F. (1988). The role of intergenerational transfers and life cycle saving in the accumulation of wealth. *Journal of Economic Perspectives, 2*(2), 15–40.

Mortgage Bankers Association. (2008). *Delinquencies and foreclosures increase in latest MBA National Delinquency Survey.* Retrieved July 13, 2008, from http://www.mortgagebankers.org/NewsandMedia/PressCenter/62936.htm

myfico.com. (2008). *Average credit statistics.* Retrieved July 13, 2008, from http:// www.myfico.com/CreditEducation/AverageStats.aspx

Office of Federal Housing Enterprise Oversight. (2008). *Decline in house prices accelerates in first quarter.* Retrieved July 13, 2008, from www.ofheo.gov/media/pdf/ 1q08hpi.pdf

Pederson, R. C., Madsen, M., & Kohler, L. (2005). Does financial strain explain the association between children's morbidity and parental non-employment? *Journal of Epidemiology and Community Health, 59*(4), 316–321.

Pew Charitable Trusts. (2008). *Defaulting on the dream: States respond to America's foreclosure crisis.* Retrieved July 13, 2008, from http://www.pewtrusts.org/ uploadedFiles/wwwpewtrustsorg/Reports/Subprime_mortgages/defaulting_ on_the_dream.pdf

Pollan, S. M., & Levine, M. (1995, January). The rise and fall of retirement. *Worth, 5,* 64–76.

Porter, N. M., & Garman, E. T. (1993). Testing a conceptual model of financial well-being. *Financial Counseling and Planning, 4*(3), 135–164.

Realytrac. (2009). *Foreclosure activity increases 81 percent in 2008.* Retrieved May 20, 2009, from http://www.realytrac.com/ContentManagement/pressrelease.aspx?channelid=9&ItemID=5681

Reinharcit Pedersen, C., Madsen, M., & Köhler, L. (2005). Does financial strain explain the association between children's morbidity and parental non-employment? *Journal of Epidemiology & Community Health, 59*(4), 316–321.

Schaninger, C. M., & Buss, W. C. (1986). A longitudinal comparison of consumption and finance handling between happily married and divorced couples. *Journal of Marriage and the Family, 48*(1), 129–136.

Schwartz, A. A. (2009). *Memorial Day weekend will lure more travelers with gas at $2.33.* Retrieved May 21, 2009, from http://www.bloomberg.com/apps/news?pid=20603037&sid=aPhoK4X.ueLE&refer=home.

Shek, D. T. L. (2003). Economic stress, psychological well-being and problem behavior in Chinese adolescents with economic disadvantage. *Journal of Youth and Adolescence, 32*(4), 259–266.

Solantaus, T., Leinonen, J., & Punamaki, R.-L. (2004). Children's mental health in times of economic recession: Replication and extension of the Family Economic Stress Model in Finland. *Developmental Psychology, 40*(3), 412–429.

Stack, S., & Wasserman, I. (2007). Economic strain and suicide risk: A qualitative analysis. *Suicide & Life-Threatening Behavior, 37*(1), 103–112.

Taylor, R. J., Chatters, L. M., Tucker, M. B., & Lewis, E. (1990). Developments in research on Black families: A decade review. *Journal of Marriage and the Family, 52*(4), 275–295.

Todd, K. J., & DeVaney, S. A. (1997). Financial planning for retirement by parents of college students. *Financial Counseling and Planning, 8*(1), 25–32.

Ullah, P. (1990). The association between income, financial strain and psychological well-being among unemployed youths. *Journal of Occupational Psychology, 63*(4), 317–330.

U.S. Bureau of the Census. (2005). Table F-22. *Married-couple families with wives' earnings greater than husbands' earnings: 1981 to 2005 (selected years).* Historical Income Tables—Families. Retrieved July 1, 2008, from http://www.census.gov/hhes/www/income/histinc/f22.html

U.S. Bureau of the Census (2008). Table 14. Homeownership rates by area: 1960 to 2008. Retrieved July 13, 2008, from http://www.census.gov/hhes/www/housing/hvs/annual08/ann08t14.xls

U.S. Bureau of Labor Statistics. (2008a). *Why has unemployment risen? Insights from labor force flows. Summary 08–05/June 2008.* Retrieved July 18, 2008, from http://www.bls.gov/opub/ils/pdf/opbils66.pdf

U.S. Bureau of Labor Statistics. (2008b). *Employment characteristics of families in 2007.* Retrieved July 18, 2008, from http://www.bls.gov/news.release/pdf/famee.pdf

U.S. Bureau of Labor Statistics. (2009). Consumer Price Index: April 2009. Retrieved May 1, 2009, from http://www.bls.gov/news.release/archives/cpi_05152009.pdf

van Solinge, H., & Henkens, K. (2008). Adjustment to and satisfaction with retirement: Two of a kind? *Psychology & Aging, 23*(2), 422–434.

Vinokur, A. D., Price, R. H., & Caplan, R. D. (1996). Hard times and hurtful partners: How financial strain affects depression and relationship satisfaction of unemployed persons and their spouses. *Journal of Personality and Social Psychology, 71*(1), 166–179.

Voydanoff, P. (1983). Unemployment: Family strategies for adaptation. In C. R. Figley & H. I. McCubbin (Eds.), *Stress in the family: Vol. 2. Coping with catastrophe* (pp. 90–102). New York: Brunner/Mazel.

Voydanoff, P. (1991). Economic distress and family relations: A review of the eighties. *Journal of Marriage and Family, 52*(4), 1099–1115.

Voydanoff, P., & Donnelly, B. W. (1988). Economic distress, family coping, and quality of family life. In P. Voydanoff & L. C. Majka (Eds.), *Families and economic distress: Coping strategies and social policies* (pp. 95–115). Newbury Park, CA: Sage.

Waanders, C., Mendez, J. L., & Downer, J. T. (2007). Parent characteristics, economic stress and neighborhood context as predictors of parent involvement in preschool children's education. *Journal of School Psychology, 45*(6), 619–636.

Wadsworth, M. E., & Santiago, C. D. (2008). Risk and resiliency processes in ethnically diverse families in poverty. *Journal of Family Psychology, 22*(3), 399–410.

Warren, E. (2006). The middle class on the precipice. Retrieved July 10, 2008, from http://harvardmagazine.com/2006/01/the-middle-class-on-the.html

Warren, E. (2007). *The new economics of the middle class: Why making ends meet has gotten harder.* Retrieved July 13, 2008, from http://finance.senate.gov/hearings/testimony/2007test/051007testew.pdf

Weller, C. E. (2008). *Economic snapshot.* Retrieved July 13, 2008, from http://www.americanprogress.org/issues/2008/07/pdf/ju108_econ_snapshot.pdf

Weller, C. E., & Logan, A. (2008). *America's middle class still losing ground.* Retrieved August 2, 2008, from www.americanprogress.org/issues/2008/07/middle_class_squeeze.html

White, L., & Rogers, S. J. (2001). Economic circumstances and family outcomes: A review of the 1990s. In R. M. Milardo (Ed.), *Understanding families into the new millennium: A decade in review* (pp. 254–270). Minneapolis, MN: National Council on Family Relations.

Williams, F. L., & Prohofsky, S. S. (1986). Teenagers' perception of agreement over family expenditures, employment, and family life. *Journal of Youth and Adolescence, 15,* 243–257.

10

Divorce

A Risk and Resilience Perspective

Mark A. Fine,
Lawrence H. Ganong, and David H. Demo

The word *divorce* conjures up images of divided families, vulnerable children, failed marriages, forgotten commitments, long and expensive legal battles, resentment, hostility, bitterness, and economic hardship. It is understandable that people do not think positively about divorce. Few, if any, adults marry with the expectation, and certainly not the hope, that their marriages will one day be dissolved, nor do most children hope that their parents will divorce and live apart.

Nevertheless, large proportions of American families have experienced or are experiencing parental divorce, a phenomenon that cuts across racial and ethnic groups, albeit to varying degrees. Although a smaller proportion of African Americans marry than do European Americans, a much higher percentage of African American marriages end in divorce than is the case for European Americans (Orbuch & Brown, 2006). In the 1990s, approximately 47% of African American marriages resulted in separation within 10 to 15 years, compared with 28% of European American marriages (Cherlin, 1998). The divorce rate for Latinos is lower than that for both European Americans and African Americans (Umana-Taylor & Alfaro, 2006). Partly because of these ethnic differences in divorce rates, from 1970 to 1994, the percentage of white children living with two parents (including stepparents) fell from 90% to 80%; for African American children, the percentage declined from 60% to 33%; and for Hispanic children, the percentage decreased from 80% to 65% (Teachman, 2000). These figures have stabilized into this century. In 2004, 78% of white children, 87% of Asian American children, 68% of Hispanic children, and 38% of African American children lived with two parents. A higher percentage of African American children lived with a single parent in 2004 than did white non-Hispanic or Hispanic children (54% compared with 20% and 28%, respectively).

In this chapter, we provide an overview of what we know about divorce, the consequences it has on family members, and interventions designed to help those who are experiencing this family stressor. To accomplish these goals, we first provide a brief review of family systems theory and how it helps to illuminate processes and outcomes relevant to divorce, with an emphasis on how a risk and resiliency perspective adds to the utility of family systems theory. Second, we describe historical trends and patterns. Third, we present information on factors that predict and may cause divorce. Fourth, we review the literature on the consequences of divorce for parents and children, emphasizing risk and resiliency factors that help predict how family members will adjust to this stressor. Finally, we describe and evaluate interventions that may facilitate divorce adjustment, focusing on parenting education for divorcing parents and divorce mediation and one of its variants—collaborative divorce.

Family Systems Theory With a Risk and Resiliency Extension

Family systems theory views the family as a system of interconnected individuals, with changes in one or more members or relationships having reverberating effects throughout the entire family (Klein & White, 2007). In addition, families, as systems, influence their environments and, in turn, are influenced by the circumstances and contexts around them.

With reference to divorce, family systems theory suggests that the family needs to be viewed in its entirety because it may be misleading to focus on only particular individuals or dyads within the family. For example, family systems theorists contend that one cannot understand how children are affected by divorce without understanding how children are affected by their parents and by extrafamilial institutions (e.g., the school), and how parents are affected by divorce (i.e., because children are ultimately influenced by the effects that divorce has on their parents). Therefore, in this chapter, we are sensitive to the systems view that the effects of divorce on children and parents need to be considered holistically and not in isolation from other processes and effects occurring within the family.

As useful as family systems theory has proven to be, it needs to be supplemented by other theories to delineate more precisely *how* divorce affects family members and the family system. A risk and resiliency perspective is helpful for achieving this purpose. Risk factors increase the likelihood of negative outcomes, whereas resilience refers to processes by which an individual (or group) overcomes difficult circumstances, "bounces back" from adversity, and becomes stronger in the face of a crisis (Walsh, 2002). The risk–resilience perspective addresses why some parents and children in divorced families cope relatively well with this transition, whereas others do not adapt as successfully. A risk–resilience approach places the research focus on understanding *variation* in responses to the challenges posed by divorce and life in a single-parent household (Demo, Aquilino, & Fine, 2005). For example, research has suggested that living in a single-parent family increases the risk of children experiencing behavioral problems at school from 10% (in first-marriage families) to 20% (Amato, 2000b). Although this suggests a heightened risk from living in a single-parent family, this finding also indicates that *most* children in single-parent families do *not* develop behavioral problems at school. The risk–resilience perspective attempts to identify factors that account for these differential outcomes to the same stressor.

In the risk–resilience framework, outcomes depend on the interplay among risk and protective factors and mechanisms (Margolin, Oliver, & Medina, 2001). Risk factors increase the likelihood of undesirable outcomes, whereas risk mechanisms are the processes by which a particular stressor (e.g., parental divorce) leads to adjustment difficulties. Protective factors are characteristics that promote adaptation to difficult circumstances, as well as family and contextual factors that buffer the effects of severe risk. Protective mechanisms are the ways in which protective factors have their positive effects. One type of protective factor—coping resources—refers to the social, economic, psychological, emotional, and physical assets on which family members can draw (Ahrons, 1994). Adaptation is facilitated to the extent that there are protective factors that are strong enough to help individuals and families cope with the risks that accompany stressors such as divorce.

History and Context

Although it is commonly believed that the divorce rate was low through the 1950s and then soared in recent decades, the divorce rate actually increased steadily from the mid-19th century through the 1970s (Teachman, Tedrow, & Hall, 2006). The divorce rate then stabilized at a high level in the early 1980s and declined modestly since then (Amato & Irving, 2006; Hurley, 2005; Teachman et al., 2006). Martin (cited in Hurley, 2005) has suggested that this drop was due to a decline in divorce rates among individuals with college degrees.

There are several reasons why the divorce rate rose dramatically after World War II. One important consideration is that the nuclear family of the late 1940s and 1950s—the family form that is often used as a standard by which contemporary families are judged—was an aberration (Cherlin, 1992). Following the instability and hard times of the Great Depression and World War II, high value was placed on family life, contributing to a short-term drop in the divorce rate. The postwar economic boom stimulated growth in the middle class, the standard of living improved, marriage and birth rates rose, and divorce rates dropped.

Although the male-breadwinner, female-homemaker marriages of the late 1940s and 1950s were much *more* susceptible to divorce than marriages begun earlier, mid-20th-century marriages are viewed with nostalgia (Coontz, 1992), partly because they were significantly *less* likely than contemporary marriages to end in divorce. Often overlooked in such simple historical comparisons, however, is that "traditional" marriages are characterized by inequities and burdens for women, who often perform disproportionate shares of unpaid domestic work, child care, caregiving for aging parents, and other aspects of family labor in addition to paid labor outside the home (Bianchi, Robinson, & Milkie, 2006; Erickson, 2005). Thus, although "traditional" marriages during this period were less likely than contemporary marriages to end in divorce, there were costs to this stability.

The cultural climate in the United States during the 1960s and 1970s featured an increasing emphasis on individualism. From the late 1950s to the late 1980s, singlehood, cohabitation, childlessness, and nonmarital sexual relations became more acceptable, whereas opposition to abortion and divorce weakened (Amato, 2004; Demo & Fine, 2010). For many, concerns with self-fulfillment and career development diminished their commitment to family, rendering marriage and other intimate relationships vulnerable (Coontz, 1992).

Economic factors also contributed to rising divorce rates. Changing work patterns, diminished occupational opportunities, men's declining labor force involvement, stagnant wages for white men and declining wages for African American men, and massive underemployment for millions of lower-income wage earners created domestic turmoil for many families (Coleman, Ganong, & Warzinik, 2007; Teachman, 2000). Although women earn less than men for the same work, their reduced economic dependence on men made divorce a more acceptable alternative for women in unhappy marriages. Heckert, Nowak, and Snyder (1998) observed that compared to "traditional" marriages in which the husband earned the majority of family income, the greatest likelihood of marital disruption occurred for marriages in which wives earned 50% to 75% of family income. It is important to note, however, that in many families, particularly those with lower incomes, wives' earnings relieve economic pressure, stabilize marriage, and prevent marital dissolution (Heckert et al., 1998).

Many observers have argued that higher divorce rates are a result of declining levels of marital satisfaction in recent decades (Amato, Johnson, Booth, & Rogers, 2003; Bradbury, Fincham, & Beach, 2000). However, although overall levels of marital satisfaction have declined, there is little evidence that this decline led to an increase in the divorce rate (Amato et al., 2003). Perhaps a more plausible explanation of the increase in the divorce rate in the late 1960s and 1970s is that many individuals, especially women, recognized that marriage was not meeting their personal needs (Amato, 2004; Cherlin, 2004). In this context, it is not surprising that two-thirds of divorces are initiated by women (Amato & Irving, 2006; Sweeney, 2002).

However, it should be noted that the relationship between marital quality and attitudes toward divorce is bidirectional. In one direction, low levels of marital quality, because they may bring the possibility of divorce to the forefront of one's thinking, may lead to an increasingly more favorable attitude toward divorce. In the other direction, having favorable attitudes toward divorce, because individuals know that they have an acceptable option should their relationship deteriorate, may erode marital quality over time by decreasing the quantity and quality of marital interaction and increasing marital conflict (Amato & Rogers, 1999).

Other factors serve to undermine marital stability. Individuals often have unrealistic, idealistic, and romanticized notions about marriage. Married couples today are spending significantly less time with each other than they did 20 years ago (Amato et al., 2003). These conditions—personal fulfillment being strongly valued, lofty expectations not being satisfied, declines in marital interaction, and the perception that acceptable alternatives are available—increase the probability of divorce. Because it is unlikely that there will be substantial changes in these conditions in the near future (see Teachman et al., 2006, for projections about divorce rates), the divorce rate in the United States is likely to remain at or near current levels.

Factors That Predict and Cause Divorce

The risk and resilience perspective encourages us to explore the complicated issues of which factors are predictive of some couples staying together while others dissolve their relationship and the causal mechanisms underlying *why* these factors are predictive of marital (in)stability. There is consistent evidence that several demographic, individual difference, and relationship variables contribute to a higher probability of divorce (i.e., they constitute risk factors) (Rodrigues, Hall, & Fincham, 2006). Unfortunately, we know much less about how relationship processes relate to the likelihood of divorce than we do about the influence of demographic and individual difference factors (Amato, 2004; Rodrigues et al., 2006).

Demographic risks include (a) being African American, (b) living in the western and southern parts of the United States, (c) living in an urban area, (d) cohabitating premaritally, (e) having a premarital birth, (f) being young at the time of marriage, (g) having less education, (h) being married for a shorter amount of time, (i) being remarried, (j) having divorced parents, and (k) being nonreligious. In terms of individual difference variables, divorce risk is positively related to neuroticism (i.e., a generalized tendency to experience negative emotions, such as sadness, anger, guilt, fear, and embarrassment), psychopathology, thinking of divorce, and higher levels of self-monitoring (i.e., the ability and motivation to control one's presentation to others). Finally, with respect to relationship variables, divorce risk is related to dissatisfaction with marriage, lower levels of commitment to the relationship, marital aggression, and more negativity than positivity in marital interactions (Rodrigues et al., 2006).

Identifying risk factors is considerably easier to do than identifying the *causes* of divorce. Determining the causes of relationship dissolution is extremely difficult because there are important distinctions between what people report to be the cause of their breakup and what may have actually caused the breakup (Powell & Fine, 2009). Research has suggested that people who are going through a divorce typically construct a public account of what happened in their relationship that led to its termination. These narrative accounts often present the individual in a positive light, minimizing his or her role and attributing the dissolution to either one's ex-spouse/partner or to circumstances beyond one's control. Thus, these stories may be both incomplete and inaccurate with respect to how the events surrounding the divorce actually unfolded. In addition, individuals may come to actually believe their stories, even if they were distortions of the "truth."

By contrast, researchers attempt to identify the causes of divorce when they look for regularities in factors that lead to divorce across a population. Whereas the divorced individual's perspective identifies his or her subjective view of what caused the dissolution of the relationship, the researcher's perspective uses empirical investigations to identify factors that seem to account for divorce in the general population. Thus, the divorced individual's account and the researcher's perspective have different goals and may reach apparently divergent conclusions. For example, many individuals blame the termination of their relationship on infidelity. However, because many relationships survive instances of infidelity, the researcher perspective suggests that infidelity is seldom the primary cause of dissolution. Each perspective taps a different, but important, aspect of the complex picture of why dissolution occurs.

What do ex-spouses typically report when asked "what went wrong" in their marriages? Wives report more dissatisfaction with marriage than do husbands (Amato et al., 2003). Common complaints by wives include husbands' authoritarianism, mental cruelty, verbal and physical abuse, excessive drinking, lack of love, neglect of children, emotional and personality problems, and extramarital sex. Men describe their former wives as nagging, whining, faultfinding, and immature (Hetherington & Kelly, 2002). It is common for women and men to share the views that communication problems, unhappiness, and incompatibility led to the divorce. Former spouses' descriptions of their marriages underscore that traditional gender scripts and power imbalances in marriage, work, and parenthood often have undesirable, even harsh, consequences for family members. However, as previously noted, partners' accounts of the end of their romantic relationships are socially constructed to create a story that is acceptable to themselves as well as to their families and social networks. Thus, such accounts should be interpreted cautiously, as they may not accurately portray the events as they actually occurred.

Divorce and Its Aftermath

Researchers have reached quite different conclusions regarding the effects of divorce on family members (Fine & Demo, 2000). For example, some have argued that children and adults experience severe, long-term postdivorce adjustment problems, some of which become more severe over time (e.g., Wallerstein & Blakeslee, 1990). Others, however, using larger and more representative samples, have found moderate and short-term effects for adults (Braver, Shapiro, & Goodman, 2006) and children (Barber & Demo, 2006). We have been persuaded by Emery's (1999) attempt to reconcile these differing scholarly conclusions as they pertain to children. Emery concluded that (a) divorce is a stressful experience for children; (b) divorce leads to higher levels of clinically significant adjustment and mental health problems among children; (c) most children are resilient and adjust well to divorce over time; (d) children whose parents divorce report considerable pain, unhappy memories, and continued distress; and (e) postdivorce family interaction patterns greatly influence adjustment following divorce. According to Emery, different researchers have reached varying conclusions regarding the consequences of divorce because they have tended to focus their efforts on one or two of these areas of inquiry at a time to the exclusion of the others. For example, Wallerstein's emphasis on pain and stress may accurately characterize one aspect of the experience of the children and families she studied, but she did not explore more objective long-term indices of adjustment. Others who found few long-term effects may not have placed the same level of emphasis as did Wallerstein on the pain and stress of the experience.

A second reason why investigators have reached differing conclusions is that there is considerable variability in the nature of adjustment to divorce (Demo & Fine, 2010; Fine & Demo, 2000). Individuals differ, sometimes considerably, in how they respond to divorce and in their *perceptions* of their adjustment to divorce. As feminist researchers emphasize, family life is perceived, defined, and experienced differently by each family member (e.g., McGraw & Walker, 2004). Rather than a unitary or "core" family reality, there are multiple and sometimes conflicting realities. Understanding divorce requires us to understand the perspectives of all family members regarding their pre- and postdivorce family histories, relationships, and experiences.

A third reason why researchers have drawn different conclusions about divorce effects is that many of these effects are modest. Because effect sizes in divorce studies are often small, they are difficult to measure consistently across investigations and may be more reactive than larger, more robust effects would be to the measures used, the size and representativeness of the samples, and other aspects of study design.

It is important to note that adjustment to divorce occurs within a society that typically has held negative views of divorce (Ganong & Coleman, 2004). Although public disapproval of divorce has softened (Cherlin, 2004; Usdansky, 2009), divorced individuals still confront stigma. In response, divorced individuals develop elaborate accounts to explain the divorce to themselves and to others (Hopper, 1993, 2001).

Gerstel (1990) found that the circumstances associated with social disapproval are different for women than for men. Compared to childless women, divorced mothers experienced harsher disapproval, particularly if they had young children, whereas divorced men did not perceive any differences in social reactions based on whether or not they were parents. Men who had been sexually involved outside the marriage prior to separation reported experiencing greater disapproval than did other men. Gerstel concluded that the processes associated with social rejection and stigma reflect "a gender-based ideology of divorce—and marriage" (1990, p. 464). With this in mind, we now consider the specific consequences of divorce in several important life domains.

Economic Consequences

Women are more likely to be economically disadvantaged after divorce than are men. Of course, some women and men fare better financially than others; having a high predivorce standard of living is a protective factor that lessens the negative economic impact of divorce. Nevertheless, despite this individual variation, a clear pattern is that the economic well-being of divorced women and their children plunges in comparison to predivorce levels, while divorced men often enjoy a *better* financial situation postdivorce (Sayer, 2006).

The economic costs of divorce are greater for women because most divorces involve children, and mothers continue to devote substantially more time and money than fathers to caring for children (Walzer, 2004). The time women invest in child care and other unpaid family labor restricts not only their income but also their educational and occupational opportunities. Women are less likely to work if they have young children, and family demands prompt many employed women to reduce time spent in paid work (Garey, 1999). Another major reason why women fare more poorly financially after divorce than men is that fathers tend not to comply fully with child support awards. Many mothers receive irregular or incomplete child support payments, and a substantial minority receives nothing (Manning & Smock, 2000; Pirog & Ziol-Guest, 2006). Even when fathers comply fully, child support awards are typically too low to meet the costs of raising children, and they are typically not indexed for inflation (Pirog-Good & Brown, 1996).

Institutionalized sexism and gender discrimination in the wage workplace also contribute to women's sustained postdivorce economic decline. Most employment opportunities for women are in low-paying or temporary work, which offers little opportunity for advancement. Women's lower earnings relative to men's, when combined with the inadequacies of child support payments and the lack of affordable child care, doom many women and their families to long periods of economic hardship following divorce.

Psychological Adjustment

In some cases, it is fairly straightforward to think of changes associated with divorce as *consequences* of divorce, such as changes in the size or composition of friendship networks or income. But some changes may predate the divorce, and the timing of these changes is more difficult to assess. For example, how do we determine whether an adult's postdivorce adjustment problems are attributable to chronic strains associated with single-parenting, long-term mental or physical health problems, family conflict or abuse that occurred prior to the divorce, or some combination of these (and perhaps other) factors? It is extremely difficult to tease apart these varying possibilities.

Although several studies have examined the course of adult psychological adjustment following divorce, most have involved cross-sectional designs, relied on clinical or convenience samples, or failed to include comparison groups. Still, there are some consistent findings. In a rare longitudinal study, Coysh, Johnston, Tschann, Wallerstein, and Kline (1989) examined a predominantly white, middle- and high-income clinical sample of divorced adults. They found that an important predictor of both women's and men's postdivorce psychological adjustment was their *pre*divorce adjustment. For both sexes, better coping and emotional functioning prior to divorce were associated with more effective coping and less anger and emotional distress after divorce. Preseparation communication and shared decision making regarding childrearing also were associated with more cooperative involvement between parents after divorce.

There are interesting similarities and differences in the ways that women and men respond to family experiences preceding and following divorce. Both divorced women and divorced men who are involved in relationships with new partners adjust better psychologically and emotionally than others without such relationships (i.e., having a new romantic relationship serves as a protective factor) (Hetherington & Kelly, 2002; Wang & Amato, 2000). Yet women appear to be bothered more by pre- and postdivorce family issues, tensions, and conflicts. For men, "new relationships were able to undo, with surprising rapidity, the narcissistic injury engendered by the divorce" (Coysh et al., 1989, p. 68). In contrast, "women appear to be more affected by the residual hostility from the past marriage and problematic relations between partners and children in their new marriages or relationships" (p. 68).

There are a number of possible explanations for sex differences in postdivorce adjustment. Women, in general, are more deeply committed to marriage, parenthood, and family life than men; women devote substantially more time and energy to these activities than men; and women are better attuned than men to family members' needs, the emotional climate of the marriage, and marital problems (Hetherington, 2003; Hochschild, 2003). Having invested more in the relationship, it is reasonable that the dissolution of the relationship inflicts greater emotional pain on women than on men. Other factors certainly contribute to women's postdivorce distress, including their worsened economic position and the chronic stresses associated with coordinating employment and single-parenting (Braver et al., 2006; Sayer, 2006).

As bleak a picture as this paints for many divorced women, there is considerable evidence to suggest that divorce is a short-term crisis, with stress increasing as the divorce approaches, then subsiding postdivorce as life is reorganized and individuals adjust to new routines and lifestyles (Demo & Fine, 2010). Many divorced women may feel that even with the demands placed on them following divorce, they prefer their current situation to the lives they had when they were married.

The evidence on race differences in adjustment to divorce is limited, but it appears that compared to their white counterparts, African American women receive more social support postdivorce (Orbuch & Brown, 2006). Kitson (1992) suggested that although African Americans view divorce as regrettable, the higher divorce rate among African Americans prompts greater acceptance and less stigma. Social, emotional, and financial adjustment to divorce appears to be very similar among whites and African Americans (Amato, 2000b).

Children's Adjustment

Perhaps no issue surrounding divorce generates more concern or stirs more controversy than children's adjustment to divorce, and the research literature on the subject is voluminous (e.g., see Amato, 2000b; Barber & Demo, 2006). Here, we briefly summarize what we know about how children are influenced by processes associated with divorce, highlight the variability found in children's ability to adapt to divorce, and offer some explanations for these patterns.

As is the case for most adults, the evidence suggests that most children and adolescents experience adjustment difficulties (but not necessarily at *clinical* levels) for 1 to 2 years during the period leading up to and immediately following parental separation and divorce (Hetherington & Kelly, 2002). This is usually the period when marital and family conflicts intensify, when legal battles are fought, and when relationships with residential and nonresidential parents are restructured and renegotiated. On average, however, the adjustment of children and adolescents following divorce is only moderately, although significantly, lower than that of their counterparts in continuously intact first-marriage families (Barber & Demo, 2006; Demo & Fine, 2010). Differences in children's psychological well-being *within* family types tend to be far larger in magnitude than differences *between* family types.

Factors that are protective of children's postdivorce adjustment are the provision of economic resources; having positive, nurturing relationships with both parents; low levels of interparental and family conflict (Barber & Demo, 2006; Demo & Fine, 2010); and higher levels of predivorce adjustment

(Strohschein, 2005). It is widely speculated that reduced involvement with nonresidential parents is damaging to children's well-being. Heightening this concern are studies showing that in many cases, paternal involvement following divorce is infrequent and that fathers' contact typically diminishes over time (King, Harris, & Heard, 2004). But the broader picture is both more complex and more encouraging. Children live in a wide variety of family situations following parents' divorce, including arrangements in which nonresidential fathers (especially African American fathers) maintain regular contact with their children (King & Heard, 1999). Many children change residences (some several times) to live with a different parent (Amato, 2000a), children living with their fathers typically have relatively frequent contact with nonresidential mothers (Maccoby & Mnookin, 1992), and most children and adolescents adapt well to diverse forms of postdivorce family life (Demo & Fine, 2010; King & Heard, 1999). These patterns demonstrate that traditional definitions of family structure (e.g., father present or father absent) and broad generalizations of postdivorce parenting (e.g., "deadbeat dads") obscure substantial temporal and cultural variation in residential and visitation processes (King & Heard, 1999).

There is evidence, however, that the frequency of contact with the nonresidential parent has little effect on children's well-being (Amato & Gilbreth, 1999; King et al., 2004). One plausible explanation for this is that the frequency of parental contact may be unrelated to the history and/or quality of the relationship, which may be strongly related to children's outcomes. For example, although low levels of paternal involvement appear to be the norm for children in mother-only families, for some children this means seeing less of a nurturing and supportive father, whereas for others it means seeing less of a detached or abusive father. On the other hand, the *quality* of children's relationships with both parents affects children's adjustment to divorce (Marsiglio, Amato, Day, & Lamb, 2000). There is also consistent evidence that children's adjustment is enhanced if they have a good relationship with at least one (but not necessarily both) of their parents (Hetherington, Bridges, & Insabella, 1998).

A serious problem confronting many children following divorce is prolonged economic hardship. Although children's postdivorce residential arrangements are variable and change over time, roughly two-thirds of children live with their mother, 10% live with their father, and the remainder have dual residences or live in other arrangements (Amato, 2000a; King et al., 2004). As we have seen, postdivorce, most women and children experience a sharp, long-term decline in their standard of living. Economic hardship is associated with lowered parental well-being, less effective and less supportive parenting, inconsistent and harsh discipline, and distressed and impaired socioemotional functioning in children (Demo & Cox, 2000; Pong & Ju, 2000; Sun & Li, 2002, 2007). It should be clear, however, that these adverse effects are products of chronic financial stress and can be experienced by children in divorced and nondivorced families alike.

Multiple Family Transitions and Children's and Parents' Adjustment

Although research indicates that most children and adolescents who experience their parents' divorce score in the normal (or nonclinical) range on measures of adjustment, a small but growing minority may be at prolonged risk because of multiple transitions in family living arrangements. Transitions in family living arrangements refer to changes in family structure, marital status, or household living arrangements that mark the beginning or the end of cohabiting, marital, or remarried relationships. As children age, the likelihood increases that they will experience family structure change, as does the probability that they will experience more than one family transition. According to Cavanagh and Huston (2008), more than one in four children in the NICHD Study of Early Child Care and Youth Development experienced two or more family transitions by the end of fourth grade.

What effects do multiple family transitions have on children? Each family structure transition can be emotionally stressful, so there is the potential that the cumulative effect of multiple transitions across childhood and adolescence may be quite harmful. When parents and their romantic partners move into and out of the household, there are disruptions in adult sources of support, nurturance, supervision, and discipline. Changes in parenting behaviors, family routines, and emotional attachments are often accompanied by changes in residences, schools, neighborhoods, and peer groups. Analyses of data from three waves of the Fragile Families Study found that the frequency of mothers' partnership transitions was associated with increases in children's aggressive and anxious/depressive behavior at age 3 (Osborne & McLanahan, 2007). Although a single partnership change was associated with only a modest detrimental effect, the effects were additive, resulting in large effects for children who experienced multiple transitions. Furthermore, the pattern of accumulating effects of multiple transitions was obtained across white, black, and Hispanic children.

For adults, given the relatively high divorce rates for first and subsequent marriages, multiple divorces are quite common; approximately 17% of adults experience two or more divorces (Amato, 2004). Furthermore, there is some evidence that the frequency of family transitions (i.e., marriage, divorce, cohabitation, singlehood) is related to higher levels of depression for women (Cavanagh & Huston, 2006).

In sum, multiple family structure transitions have modest detrimental effects for women, and perhaps men, but these negative consequences for adults are smaller in magnitude than are the comparable effects for children. Perhaps the effects on adults are smaller because adults (to varying degrees) choose to make these transitions whereas children's transitions are often decided for them, because many adults have more sophisticated and effective coping skills than children, and/or because some adults may become more accustomed to divorce stressors (and presumably less affected by them) with each subsequent divorce.

Interventions

The past 35 years have seen the rise of what has been called the "divorce industry," consisting of professionals from a variety of fields who make their living from divorce (Bohannon, 1984). The divorce industry has led to the development of new professions such as family mediation and expanded opportunities for attorneys, therapists, school counselors, family life educators, parent educators, and social workers, among others.

In this section, we consider two types of interventions that attempt to improve the lives of those who have experienced divorce: parenting education for divorcing parents and family mediation. These two were selected because they are becoming increasingly popular, have already affected large numbers of divorced families and involve some degree of collaboration between legal and nonlegal professionals.

Parenting Education for Divorcing Parents

In no arena is the "divorce industry" more apparent than in the area of parenting education for divorcing parents. Partly because of an increased awareness of the stresses that divorce places on children, attention has been focused on helping children adjust more effectively to divorce. In recent years, the most frequent way this has been addressed is through educational programs that prepare parents to help their children cope with divorce. Parent education for separated and divorced parents is available in all but four states (Pollett & Lombreglia, 2008), and most of these programs are court mandated (Blaisure & Geasler, 2006; Fine et al., 1999). These programs are offered in schools, universities, community agencies, and family courts (Cookston, Sandler, Braver, & Genalo, 2007), and they range widely in length and number of sessions, instructional methods, and educational goals. In general, these programs address child-focused, parent-focused, and/or court-focused content, including (a) post-divorce reactions of children and parents, (b) children's needs and reactions to divorce at different ages, (c) the benefits of cooperative postdivorce parenting, and (d) the emotional costs of placing children in the middle of parental disputes (Blaisure & Geasler, 2006).

The quality of the evaluations of these programs has lagged far behind programmatic development (Blaisure & Geasler, 2006; Fine et al., 1999; Pollett & Lombreglia, 2008). Evaluations of these programs, when conducted, have primarily consisted of "consumer satisfaction" questionnaires that ask participants how satisfied they were with various aspects of the program (Blaisure & Geasler, 2006). Results from these questionnaires typically show that consumers are very satisfied with the programs (Fine et al., 1999; Pollett & Lombreglia, 2008), which is not surprising given that clients usually report having positive experiences with a wide range of interventions.

However, client satisfaction does not necessarily mean that the programs are successful in achieving their primary goal—fostering behavioral change. Unfortunately, we know relatively little about the short- and long-term effectiveness of these parenting education programs in effecting behavior change. The few studies examining such change have yielded mixed results. Some have reported that compared to parents who do not attend such programs, parents in divorce education programs were more willing to seek outside help (DeLuse, Braver, & Sandler, 1995), litigated less often (Arbuthnot, Kramer, & Gordon, 1997), and engaged in less conflict (Arbuthnot & Gordon, 1996; Bacon & McKenzie, 2004; Shifflet & Cummings, 1999). Not all evaluation studies report success, however; several researchers have reported no differences between program participants and controls (Douglas, 2004; Kramer & Washo, 1993; McKenry, Clark, & Stone, 1999), and often findings are mixed, with program parents benefiting on some outcomes but not others (Bacon & McKenzie, 2004; Cookston et al., 2007; Shifflet & Cummings, 1999; Thoennes & Pearson, 1999).

These educational programs have political and intuitive appeal, so the absence of supportive evidence of effectiveness has not deterred (and probably will not deter) their widespread use and dissemination. However, without sound evaluation findings, courts and legislatures will find it increasingly difficult to justify mandating such programs. Thus, evaluations of these programs that extend beyond consumer satisfaction are very much needed.

Given that the primary targets of parent education for divorcing parents are *children*, one might wonder why children themselves are not the direct recipients of intervention. There are a number of reasons why parents are the direct recipients of these educational sessions, including that (a) they are more amenable to such interventions, (b) they perhaps have the insight and motivation to benefit from the material presented, and (c) it is logistically easier to require adults than children to attend such a session. Nevertheless, there are a number of programs developed for children whose parents are divorced/divorcing (Pedro-Carroll, 1997). Many of these are school-based programs that focus on helping children adapt socially and emotionally; becoming aware of their feelings about themselves, their parents, and the divorce; expressing feelings in appropriate ways; learning to cope with frustration; learning to get along with others; and enhancing self-esteem. There is some evidence that these group interventions are effective (Barber & Demo, 2006), but few programs have been adequately evaluated in controlled studies, and findings from the evaluation studies that have been conducted are not consistent or clear-cut.

Divorce Mediation

Mediation is one of a class of alternative dispute resolution approaches—they are considered "alternative" because they are less adversarial than traditional legal procedures and seek to reach agreements in a more cooperative manner. Divorce mediation consists of an impartial third party helping a divorcing or divorced couple identify, discuss, and, hopefully, resolve disagreements related to the divorce (Sbarra & Emery, 2006). Mediation has grown rapidly and is mandated in several states (Sbarra & Emery, 2006). Mediation usually addresses some or all of five areas of potential conflict: (1) property division, (2) spousal support, (3) child support, (4) custody, and (5) visitation (Beck & Sales, 2001; Sbarra & Emery, 2006). Successful mediation allows the divorcing couple to maintain control of decisions in these domains and results in each party feeling some ownership over the divorce agreement (Sbarra & Emery, 2006).

Mediation is based on the principle of cooperative negotiation, which is unlike the typically adversarial nature of the U.S. legal system, which views the parties as disputants who compete with each other for limited resources. In contrast to psychotherapy, mediation targets more specific, pragmatic, concrete, and immediate issues. Emery (1999) has described the core of mediation as "renegotiating family relationships" (p. 379). The negotiation of relationships is not achieved by exploring psychological issues, but rather by helping the (ex)partners agree on issues regarding child rearing.

Although early evidence was promising, recent reviews of the body of research have suggested that there are no short-term differences between mediation and more traditional adversarial approaches in enhancing psychological well-being and/or the quality of coparenting (Beck & Sales, 2001; Sbarra & Emery, 2006). The lack of positive mediation short-term effects may be due to overly high expectations about what a brief intervention such as mediation can reasonably accomplish and/or a lack of measures that are sensitive to the nuanced ways that mediation may be helpful.

Nevertheless, mediation has been shown to be effective on some dimensions. In the Charlottesville Mediation Study (Sbarra & Emery, 2006), parents consistently preferred mediation over litigation in terms of both the process (e.g., feeling understood) and perceived outcomes (e.g., one's rights being protected) of the intervention. Furthermore, in a long-term (12-year) follow-up, nonresidential parents who went through mediation had considerably more contact (both face-to-face and by telephone) with their children than did those who had litigated settlements. However, a potential drawback of this additional contact is that ex-partners reported being more attached to each other than partners who went through litigation.

Mediation has its critics. First, some have expressed concern that men's greater power places women at a disadvantage in negotiating and that mediators do not take these power differentials into account (Menzel, 1991). On the other hand, noting that women are more satisfied than are men with both litigated and mediated settlements, Emery (1995) has suggested that it is not that women are disadvantaged in mediation, but rather that men are disadvantaged in litigation. Thus, according to this view, men have more to gain in mediation than they often do in litigation, which leads them to be more satisfied with mediated agreements.

Second, mediation is not an appropriate strategy for some couples. Spouses who cannot communicate and problem solve with each other, whether because one or both spouses have personality characteristics that prohibit cooperative problem solving or because the couple has dysfunctional interactional patterns, are inappropriate candidates for mediation.

Third, there has been controversy regarding who can be effective mediators. Mediators generally fall into one of two groups: lawyers and mental health professionals. Some have argued that lawyers are best suited to be mediators because of their knowledge of the law, whereas others have suggested that mental health professionals have greater knowledge of the psychological and emotional aspects of how children, parents, and families cope with divorce. Consistent with Emery's (1995) prediction, mediation has not and probably will not become a separate profession, but it has developed within both the mental health and legal professions.

Finally, there is some controversy pertaining to whether mediation should be mandated, used only in select cases, or voluntary. As Emery (1995) notes, there are some cases when mediation may be inappropriate, such as when a child and/or a spouse has been abused. Nevertheless, because mandating mediation typically requires that a couple attend and participate in a session but does not mean that the parties must reach a settlement, there are strong reasons to require mediation except in selected cases.

Collaborative Divorce

Collaborative divorce, a variant of mediation, is based on the idea that better and longer-lasting solutions will be achieved if the spouses work together rather than compete with one another to maximize their own personal gain (see collaborativedivorce.net, nd). In collaborative divorce, both parties commit to not pursuing litigation as long as the negotiations continue. To make sure that the collaborative divorce lawyers have no incentive to fail, all involved parties agree that the lawyers will withdraw from the case if the collaborative divorce process ends without an agreement reached and if litigation begins. We consider collaborative divorce to be a variant of divorce mediation because the two are very similar with one major exception—in mediation, an objective third party, the mediator, helps the parties reach a mutually acceptable agreement, whereas in collaborative divorce, each spouse retains his or her own personal attorney.

Collaborative divorce is relatively new (the term and perhaps the idea were developed by a Minnesota lawyer—Stu Webb—in 1990) and there are no known empirical studies that have evaluated its effectiveness. However, information on the Web site (collaborativedivorce.net) states that many lawyers and clients report that it can be quicker, less expensive, and less distressing than the typical adversarial process. As is the case with mediation, its key limitation is that it is not appropriate when spouses and/or couples do not have the necessary conflict resolution skills, personality characteristics, or relational patterns. For these couples, the traditional adversarial process may be the only viable option.

Conclusion

Divorce has become almost a normative experience in the 21st century. Although there is considerable variation in children's and adults' emotional adjustment to divorce (see Demo & Fine, 2010), most children and adults adapt well to a variety of postdivorce family forms and function in the normal ranges of adjustment. Among the small percentage who experience lingering difficulties, the problems can often be traced to poor adjustment preceding the divorce; predivorce family tension, stress, conflict, and hostility; postdivorce economic decline; postdivorce conflict between the exspouses; and multiple transitions in family living arrangements.

Divorce is more widely accepted and less stigmatized today than in the past, but it still tends to be viewed negatively and is often blamed for many individual and societal problems. Opposition to divorce also has legal and political implications as, from time to time, there have been efforts to make it more difficult for married couples to obtain divorces, such as longer waiting periods and requiring participation in counseling before the divorce is granted. The evidence reviewed in this chapter suggests that divorce is a prevalent (and sometimes even necessary) aspect of family life, and we believe that little is likely to be gained by restricting divorce and further stigmatizing divorce. Our position is that it makes more sense for family researchers, practitioners, and policymakers to focus attention and resources on identifying risk and protective factors and processes that are related to how effectively people adjust to divorce. For example, what can be done to help parents keep their children out of the middle of their conflicts? What are the best ways for parents to communicate their impending divorce to their children? How do support networks facilitate the adjustment of divorcing parents? Exploring these and other issues from research, practice, and policy perspectives will, in our opinion, be more helpful than devoting resources to trying to prevent divorce.

With specific reference to interventions, attention also needs to be devoted to designing programs that better prepare and educate divorcing adults—parents and nonparents alike—for the financial, coparenting, and personal stresses, transitions, and challenges they will face in a variety of postdivorce family forms. Client satisfaction with educational programs for divorcing parents is impressive, but little research has evaluated the short- and long-term impact of these programs on parenting effectiveness, parent–child relationships, or child well-being. Programs designed specifically for children are also needed. Finally, while there is a growing body of evidence suggesting that divorce mediation and collaborative divorce have numerous advantages over conventional adversarial divorces, more research is needed that evaluates when mediation is most effective and for which groups it is particularly well suited. The challenge will be to explore these and other interventions as ways of normalizing divorce and facilitating healthy adjustment to this stressor.

Suggested Internet Resources

American Bar Association Family Law Section: (http://www.abanet.org/family/welcome/html)

Books on divorce and several related issues: (http://www.amazon.com) 1–800–201–7575

Children's and parenting books: (http://www.any-book-in-print.com) 1–800–227–2591

Divorceinfo: (http://www.divorceinfo.com/)

Divorce Net: (http://www.divorcenet.com/)

Divorce Online: A resource for those facing divorce: (http://www.divorce-online.com)

Share Kids: (http://www.sharekids.com/)

Shared Parenting: (http://www.vix.com/crc/sp/)

Single Parents Association: (http://www.singleparents.org)

The Divorce Support Page: (http://www.divorcesupport.com)

References

Ahrons, C. (1994). *The good divorce: Keeping your family together when your marriage comes apart.* New York: HarperCollins.

Amato, P. R. (2000a). Diversity within single-parent families. In D. H. Demo, K. R. Allen, & M. A. Fine (Eds.), *The handbook of family diversity* (pp. 149–172). New York: Oxford University Press.

Amato, P. R. (2000b). The consequences of divorce for adults and children. *Journal of Marriage and the Family, 62,* 1269–1287.

Amato, P. R. (2004). Divorce in social and historical context: Changing scientific perspectives on children and marital dissolution. In M. Coleman and L. Ganong (Eds.), *Handbook of contemporary families: Considering the past, contemplating the future* (pp. 265–281). Thousand Oaks, CA: Sage.

Amato, P. R., & Gilbreth, J. G. (1999). Nonresident fathers and children's well-being: A meta-analysis. *Journal of Marriage and the Family, 61,* 557–573.

Amato, P. R., & Irving, S. (2006). Historical trends in divorce and dissolution in the United States. In M. A. Fine & J. H. Harvey (Eds.), *Handbook of divorce and relationship dissolution* (pp. 41–57). Mahwah, NJ: Lawrence Erlbaum.

Amato, P. R., Johnson, D., Booth, A., & Rogers, S. (2003). Continuity and change in marital quality between 1980 and 2000. *Journal of Marriage and Family, 65,* 1–22.

Amato, P. R., & Rogers, S. J. (1999). Do attitudes toward divorce affect marital quality? *Journal of Family Issues, 20,* 69–86.

Arburthnot, J., & Gordon, D. A. (1996). Does mandatory divorce education for parents work? *Family and Conciliation Courts Review, 34,* 60–81.

Arbuthnot, J., Kramer, K. M., & Gordon, D. A. (1997). Patterns of relitigation following divorce education. *Family and Conciliation Courts Review, 35,* 267–279.

Bacon, B. L., & McKenzie, B. (2004). Parent education after separation/divorce: Impact of the level of parental conflict on outcomes. *Family Court Review, 42,* 85–98.

Barber, B. L., & Demo, D. H. (2006). The kids are alright (at least, most of them): Links between divorce and dissolution and child well-being. In M. A. Fine & J. H. Harvey (Eds.), *Handbook of divorce and relationship dissolution* (pp. 289–311). Mahwah, NJ: Lawrence Erlbaum.

Beck, C. J. A., & Sales, B. D. (2001). *Family mediation: Facts, myths, and future prospects.* Washington, DC: American Psychological Association.

Bianchi, S. M., Robinson, J. P., & Milkie, M. A. (2006). *Changing rhythms of American family life.* New York: Russell Sage Foundation.

Blaisure, K. R., & Geasler, M. J. (2006). Educational interventions for separating and divorcing parents. In M. A. Fine & J. H. Harvey (Eds.), *Handbook of divorce and relationship dissolution* (pp. 575–602). Mahwah, NJ: Lawrence Erlbaum.

Bohannon, P. (1984). *All the happy families.* New York: McGraw-Hill.

Bradbury, T. N., Fincham, F. D., & Beach, S. R. H. (2000). Research on the nature and determinants of marital satisfaction: A decade in review. *Journal of Marriage and the Family, 62,* 964–980.

Braver, S. L., Shapiro, J. R., & Goodman, M. R. (2006). Consequences of divorce for parents. In M. A. Fine & J. H. Harvey (Eds.), *Handbook of divorce and relationship dissolution* (pp. 313–337). Mahwah, NJ: Lawrence Erlbaum.

Cavanagh, S. E., & Huston, A. C. (2006). Family instability and children's early problem behavior. *Social Forces, 85,* 551–581.

Cavanagh, S. E., & Huston, A. C. (2008). The timing of family instability and children's social development. *Journal of Marriage and Family, 70,* 1258–1269.

Cherlin, A. J. (1992). *Marriage, divorce, and remarriage* (2nd ed.). Cambridge, MA: Harvard University Press.

Cherlin, A. J. (1998). Marriage and marital dissolution among black Americans. *Journal of Comparative Family Studies, 29,* 147–158.

Cherlin, A. J. (2004). The deinstitutionalization of American marriage. *Journal of Marriage and Family, 66,* 848–861.

Coleman, M., Ganong, L., & Warzinik, K. (2007). *Family life in 20th century America.* Westport, CT: Greenwood.

Collaborativedivorce.net (nd). Accessed on September 2, 2008.

Cookston, J. T., Braver, S. L., Griffin, W., DeLuse, S. R., & Miles, J. C. (2007). Effects of the Dads for Life intervention on interparental conflict and co-parenting in the two years after divorce. *Family Processes, 46,* 123–137.

Cookston, J. T., Sandler, I. N., Braver, S. L., & Genalo, T. (2007). Predicting readiness to adopt evidence-based programs for divorcing families: Champions, attitudes, and access to funding. *American Journal of Orthopsychiatry, 77,* 573–581.

Coontz, S. (1992). *The way we never were: American families and the nostalgia trap.* New York: Basic Books.

Coysh, W. S., Johnston, J. R., Tschann, J. M., Wallerstein, J. S., & Kline, M. (1989). Parental postdivorce adjustment in joint and sole physical custody families. *Journal of Family Issues, 10,* 52–71.

DeLuse, S. R., Braver, L. S., & Sandler, I. N. (1995). *Who volunteers for programs to help their children: A test of a recruitment method and a theoretical extension.* Paper presented at the Society for Community Research and Action Biennial Conference, Chicago, IL.

Demo, D. H., Aquilino, W. S., & Fine, M. A. (2005). Family composition and family transitions. In V. Bengtson, A. Acock, K. Allen, P. Dilworth-Anderson, & D. Klein (Eds.), *Sourcebook of family theory and research* (pp. 119–134). Thousand Oaks, CA: Sage.

Demo, D. H., & Cox, M. J. (2000). Families with young children: A review of research in the 1990s. *Journal of Marriage and the Family, 62,* 876–895.

Demo, D. H., & Fine, M. A. (2010). *Beyond the average divorce.* Thousand Oaks, CA: Sage.

Douglas, E. M. (2004). The effectiveness of a divorce education program on father involvement. *Journal of Divorce & Remarriage, 40,* 91–101.

Emery, R. E. (1995). Divorce mediation: Negotiating agreements and renegotiating relationships. *Family Relations, 44,* 377–383.

Emery, R. E. (1999). *Marriage, divorce, and children's adjustment* (2nd ed.). Thousand Oaks, CA: Sage.

Erickson, R. J. (2005). Why emotion work matters: Sex, gender, and the division of household labor. *Journal of Marriage and Family, 67,* 337–351.

Fine, M. A., Coleman, M., Gable, S., Ganong, L. H., Ispa, J., Morrison, J., & Thornburg, K. R. (1999). Research-based parenting education for divorcing parents: A university-community collaboration. In T. R. Chibocos & R. M. Lerner (Eds.), *Serving children and families through community-university partnerships: Success stories* (pp. 251–258). Norwell, MA: Kluwer.

Fine, M. A., & Demo, D. H. (2000). Divorce: Societal ill or normative transition? In R. M. Milardo & S. W. Duck (Eds.), *Families as relationships* (pp. 135–156). Chichester, UK: Wiley.

Ganong, L., & Coleman, M. (2004). *Stepfamily relationships: Development, dynamics, and interventions.* New York: Kluwer/Plenum.

Garey, A. I. (1999). *Weaving motherhood and work.* Philadelphia: Temple University Press.

Gerstel, N. (1990). Divorce and stigma. In C. Carlson (Ed.), *Perspectives on the family: History, class, and feminism* (pp. 460–478). Belmont, CA: Wadsworth.

Heckert, D. A., Nowak, T. C., & Snyder, K. A. (1998). The impact of husbands' and wives' relative earnings on marital disruption. *Journal of Marriage and the Family, 60,* 690–703.

Hetherington, E. M. (2003). Intimate pathways: Changing patterns in close personal relationships across time. *Family Relations, 52,* 318–331.

Hetherington, E. M., Bridges, M., & Insabella, G. M. (1998). What matters? What does not? Five perspectives on the association between marital transitions and children's adjustment. *American Psychologist, 53,* 167–184.

Hetherington, E. M., & Kelly, J. (2002). *For better or for worse.* New York: Norton.

Hochschild, A. (with Machung, A.) (2003). *The second shift: Working parents and the revolution at home* (rev. ed.). New York: Viking/Penguin.

Hopper, J. (1993). The rhetoric of motives in divorce. *Journal of Marriage and the Family, 55,* 801–813.

Hopper, J. (2001). The symbolic origins of conflict in divorce. *Journal of Marriage and Family, 63,* 430–445.

Hurley, D. (2005, April 19). Divorce rate: It's not as high as you think. *New York Times.*

King, V., Harris, K. M., & Heard, H. E. (2004). Racial and ethnic diversity in non-resident father involvement. *Journal of Marriage and Family, 66,* 1–21.

King, V., & Heard, H. E. (1999). Nonresident father visitation, parental conflict, and mothers' satisfaction: What's best for child well-being? *Journal of Marriage and the Family, 61,* 385–396.

Kitson, G. C. (1992). *Portrait of divorce: Adjustment to marital breakdown.* New York: Guilford.

Klein, D. M., & White, J. M. (2007). *Family theories* (2nd ed.). Thousand Oaks, CA: Sage.

Kramer, L., & Washo, C. A. (1993). Evaluation of a court-mandated prevention program for divorcing parents. *Family Relations, 42,* 179–186.

Maccoby, E. E., & Mnookin, R. H. (1992). *Dividing the child: Social and legal dilemmas of custody.* Cambridge, MA: Harvard University Press.

Manning, W. D., & Smock, P. J. (2000). Swapping families: Serial parenting and economic support for children. *Journal of Marriage and the Family, 62,* 111–122.

Margolin, G., Oliver, P. H., & Medina, A. M. (2001). Conceptual issues in understanding the relation between interparental conflict and child adjustment. In J. H. Grych & F. D. Fincham (Eds.), *Interparental conflict and child development* (pp. 9–38). Cambridge, UK: Cambridge University Press.

Marsiglio, W., Amato, P. R., Day, R. D., & Lamb, M. E. (2000). Scholarship on fatherhood in the 1990s and beyond. *Journal of Marriage and the Family, 62,* 1173–1191.

McGraw, L., & Walker, A. (2004). Gendered family relations: The more things change, the more they stay the same. In M. Coleman & L. Ganong (Eds.), *Handbook of contemporary families: Considering the past, contemplating the future* (pp. 174–191). Thousand Oaks, CA: Sage.

McKenry, P. C., Clark, K. A., & Stone, G. (1999). Evaluation of a parent education program for divorcing parents. *Family Relations, 48,* 129–137.

Menzel, K. E. (1991). Judging the fairness of mediation: A critical framework. *Mediation Quarterly, 9,* 3–20.

Orbuch, T. L., & Brown, E. (2006). Divorce in the context of being African American. In M. A. Fine & J. H. Harvey (Eds.), *Handbook of divorce and relationship dissolution* (pp. 481–498). Mahwah, NJ: Lawrence Erlbaum.

Osborne, C., & McLanahan, S. (2007). Partnership instability and child well-being. *Journal of Marriage and Family, 69,* 1065–1083.

Pedro-Carroll, J. (1997). The Children of Divorce Intervention Program: Fostering resilient outcomes for school-aged children. In G. W. Albee & T. P. Gullotta (Eds.), *Primary prevention works* (pp. 213–238). Thousand Oaks, CA: Sage.

Pirog, M. A., & Ziol-Guest, M (2006). Child support enforcement: Programs and policies, impacts and questions. *Journal of Policy Analysis and Management, 25,* 943–990.

Pirog-Good, M. A., & Brown, P. R. (1996). Accuracy and ambiguity in the application of state child support guidelines. *Family Relations, 45,* 3–10.

Pollet, S. L., & Lombreglia, M. (2008). A nationwide survey of mandatory parent education. *Family Court Review, 46,* 375–394.

Pong, S., & Ju, D. (2000). The effects of change in family structure and income on dropping out of middle and high school. *Journal of Family Issues, 21,* 147–169.

Powell, D., & Fine, M. A. (2009). Relationship dissolution, causes. In H. T. Reis & S. Sprecher (Eds.), *Encyclopedia of human relationships.* (Vol. 1; pp. 436–440). Thousand Oaks, CA: Sage.

Rodrigues, A. E., Hall, J. H., & Fincham, F. D. (2006). What predicts divorce and relationship dissolution. In M. A. Fine & J. H. Harvey (Eds.), *Handbook of divorce and relationship dissolution* (pp. 85–112). Mahwah, NJ: Lawrence Erlbaum.

Rollie, S., & Duck, S. (2006). Divorce and dissolution of romantic relationships: Stage models and their limitations. In M. A. Fine & J. H. Harvey (Eds.), *Handbook of divorce and relationship dissolution* (pp. 223–240). Mahwah, NJ: Lawrence Erlbaum.

Sayer, L. C. (2006). Economic aspects of divorce and relationship dissolution. In M. A. Fine & J. H. Harvey (Eds.), *Handbook of divorce and relationship dissolution* (pp. 385–406). Mahwah, NJ: Lawrence Erlbaum.

Sbarra, D. A., & Emery, R. E. (2006). In the presence of grief: The role of cognitive emotional adaptation in contemporary divorce mediation. In M. A. Fine & J. H. Harvey (Eds.), *Handbook of divorce and relationship dissolution* (pp. 553–573). Mahwah, NJ: Lawrence Erlbaum.

Shifflet, K., & Cummings, E. M. (1999). A program for educating parents about the effects of divorce and conflict on children: An initial evaluation. *Family Relations, 48,* 79–89.

Strohschein, L. (2005). Parental divorce and child mental health trajectories. *Journal of Marriage and Family, 67,* 1286–1300.

Sun, Y., & Li, Y. (2002). Children's well-being during parents' marital disruption process: A pooled time-series analysis. *Journal of Marriage and Family, 64,* 472–488.

Sun, Y., & Li, Y. (2007). Racial and ethnic differences in experiencing parents' marital disruption during late adolescence. *Journal of Marriage and Family, 69,* 742–762.

Sweeney, M. (2002). Remarriage and the nature of divorce. *Journal of Family Issues, 23,* 410–440.

Teachman, J., Tedrow, L., & Hall, M. (2006). The demographic future of divorce and dissolution. In M. A. Fine & J. H. Harvey (Eds.), *Handbook of divorce and relationship dissolution* (pp. 59–82). Mahwah, NJ: Lawrence Erlbaum.

Teachman, J. D. (2000). Diversity of family structure: Economic and social influences. In D. H. Demo, K. R. Allen, & M. A. Fine (Eds.), *The handbook of family diversity* (pp. 32–58). New York: Oxford University Press.

Thoennes, N., & Pearson, J. (1999). Parent education in the domestic relations court: A multisite assessment. *Family & Conciliation Courts Review, 37,* 195–218.

Umaña-Taylor, A. J., & Alfaro, E. C. (2006). Divorce and relationship dissolution among Latino populations in the United States. In M. A. Fine & J. H. Harvey (Eds.), *Handbook of divorce and relationship dissolution* (pp. 515–530). Mahwah, NJ: Lawrence Erlbaum.

Usdansky, M. L. (2009). A weak embrace: Popular and scholarly depictions of single-parent families, 1900–1998. *Journal of Marriage and Family, 71,* 209–225.

Wallerstein, J. S., & Blakeslee, S. (1990). *Second chances.* New York: Ticknor & Fields.

Walsh, F. (2002). A family resilience framework: Innovative practice applications. *Family Relations, 51,* 130–137.

Walzer, S. (2004). Encountering oppositions: A review of scholarship about motherhood. In M. Coleman & L. H. Ganong (Eds.), *Handbook of contemporary families: Considering the past, contemplating the future* (pp. 209–223). Thousand Oaks, CA: Sage.

Wang, H., & Amato, P. R. (2000). Predictors of divorce adjustment: Stressors, resources, and definitions. *Journal of Marriage and the Family, 62,* 655–668.

11 Stress and Coping Within the Context of Stepfamily Life

Kay Pasley and Michelle Lee

Evidence suggests that most Americans marry or form marriagelike relationships sometime during their adulthood (see Seltzer, 2000; Teachman & Tedrow, 2008). However, approximately 40% to 50% of those who do so ultimately see their relationship end, primarily through divorce or dissolution (Bramlett & Mosher, 2002; Teachman & Tedrow, 2008), although with increasing age, death of a spouse becomes more common. Whether persons marry or cohabit, when these relationships end, many of the participants go on to form new relationships or remarry—often in a relatively short period. Using the most recent data available from 2004, approximately 68.8% of men and 74.2% of women had married. Of those, 14.9% of men and 16.3% of women had married at least twice (U.S Census Bureau, n.d.; see Table 3).

Furthermore, many of these new unions include children from past unions and, thus, form stepfamilies. As a result, the effects of these relationship changes are experienced by both adults and children and can have far-reaching effects (see Coleman, Ganong, & Fine, 2000; Hetherington, 2003). With the addition of new spouses and/or partners, an intricate network of relationships is established among biological parents, stepparents, and social parents whose shared interests include both biological children and stepchildren. Because these families do not operate in isolation, they are also influenced by elements in the broader social context, such as extended-family members, educational arenas, and other elements in neighborhoods and communities.

Researchers suggest that there are many difficulties inherent in stepfamily life that can result in relationship dissolution and children and stepchildren being at greater risk for negative outcomes (e.g., Coleman et al., 2000; Falci, 2006; Friesther, Jay, & Svare, 2004; Harper & McLanahan, 2004; Tillman, 2008). Although there is a slightly higher divorce rate for second marriage, recent evidence shows that it takes about the same time for first and later marriages to dissolve (Kreider, 2005).

In this chapter, we discuss the issues that complicate families with children who form stepfamilies, whether these relationships follow remarriages or repartnerships for the parents. In doing so, we focus primarily on the sources of stress that affect adjustment to these new relationships and the influence of the broader social context on this process. We end with recommendations of strategies to effectively manage the stress and ultimately strengthen stepfamily life.

What Is a Stepfamily?

The literature is replete with various terms that have been used as a substitute for *stepfamily*. These include, but are not limited to, *blended, merged, reconstituted, combined,* and *remarried*. Although these alternative terms are most commonly used in the popular press, scholars have also adopted them (e.g., Ge, Natsuaki, Neiderhiser, & Reiss, 2007; Halpern-Meekin & Tach, 2008). Among the popular press, the implicit assumption is that such terms lack the negative connotation associated with *step,* and this may be the case among some scholars who fail to define what is meant by terms such as *blended* (e.g., Ge et al., 2008; Portie & Hill, 2005). Other scholars differentiate between blended and stepfamilies by suggesting that the former is "formed when parents in a stepfamily give birth to a shared child, so they contain both stepchildren and shared children" (Halpern-Meekin & Tach, 2008, p. 437). Still other scholars use the terms interchangeably (e.g., Rigg & Pryor, 2007) or use *blended* in place of *stepfamily,* although the definition is "biological mother and stepfather" (see Laursen, 2005, p. 51). Furthermore, research scholars (e.g., Coleman & Ganong, 2004) argue that the use of such terms fosters a different kind of bias. For example, referring to stepfamilies as blended families implies that members in stepfamilies should give up their unique and separate identities to adopt a single-family identity. Doing so implicitly excludes nonresident parents and their families and can result in defensive reactions from children (Visher & Visher, 1996). The spread of alternative terms to describe stepfamilies led to a discussion and recommendation by the leadership of the Stepfamily Association of America in 2000 to reaffirm the use of *stepfamily,* because the meaning of the term was commonly understood (personal communication, Dr. Marjorie Engel, January 7, 2008).

Teachman and Tedrow (2008) argue that the definition of stepfamily has changed somewhat, because many stepfamilies today are formed as a result of repartnering, in the case of cohabitation, rather than from divorce or, as was typical in the distant past, the death of a spouse. They also argue that the inclusion of unmarried couples mirrors the current debates regarding what constitutes a family (Harris, 2008; Weigel, 2008). As part of this debate and specific to stepfamilies, Teachman and Tedrow asked whether stepfamilies include cohabitors and gay and lesbian couples, as well as whether stepfamilies must result only from marriage. Results reported by Weigel (2008) show that the general public is more inclusive in defining families than in the past, such that the boundaries between married and nonmarried stepfamilies have blurred.

Here, we use a broad and inclusive definition of stepfamily. We include both families formed through marriage and those formed through cohabitation. In addition, where data are available, we examine the similarities and differences between these groups of stepfamilies.

How Prevalent Are Stepfamilies?

Clear definitions are essential when we attempt to determine the prevalence of stepfamilies. Different data sources use slightly different definitions, and as a result, there are differences in the numbers and estimates offered. Importantly, it has been suggested that the number of stepfamilies and stepchildren are underestimated (Adamsons & Pasley, 2006; Teachman & Tedrow, 2008). Specifically, one common data source is the U.S. Census. According to these data, stepfamilies are defined as those including two adults who reside together and where one parent is not biological. Children or stepchildren are designated as those 18 years and younger, residing with a parent or stepparent. In contrast, and indicative of the problems in this area, if a child resides with her nonrepartnered biological mother but regularly visits her biological father and his new wife (the child's new stepmother), the stepfamily situation would not be counted as such. Instead, the child would be designated as living with a single parent. If the child is older than 18 and resides with a biological parent and stepparent, according to the U.S. Census, this family is also not counted as a stepfamily.

Estimating the number of stepfamilies is further complicated by the increase in nonmarital childbearing followed by a first marriage where only one adult is the biological parent. Thus, the other adult is a stepparent to that child, and their relationship is that of a stepparent–stepchild relationship. Still other couples had children as part of a cohabiting relationship, ended that relationship, and are now repartnered with others, but no marriage occurred. By our definition in this chapter, these families would be included as stepfamilies; however, they would not be counted as such in the U.S. Census. Attempts have been made to estimate the prevalence of stepfamilies that include cohabitors. The results of one study (Bumpass, Raley, & Sweet, 1995) suggest that about 25% of mothers and 33% of children enter stepfamilies from a never-married status. Other estimates suggest that these figures may be higher, such that about two-thirds of mothers and children enter stepfamilies through cohabitation rather than through marriage (Bumpass & Lu, 2000). Still other data using an urban cohort found that almost 60% of unmarried couples had at least one child from a prior relationship and, thus, were stepfamilies (Carlson & Furstenberg, 2006).

Our point here is that even our best estimates fail to give us a complete picture of the prevalence of these families. That is, about 9% of married couples and 12% of cohabiting couples have a stepchild residing in the household (Teachman & Tedrow, 2008). However, recall that these estimates do not recognize children (a) who reside with a resident single parent but whose nonresident parent is remarried or repartnered, (b) who are older than 18 years, or (c) who reside in a family unit composed of a same-sex couple where one adult is the biological parent and the other adult partner functions as a stepparent. In spite of these limitations and the issue of underestimation, scholars agree that the increase in their prevalence is due to cohabitation rather than marriage or remarriage (Teachman & Tedrow, 2008).

The Stepfamily as a Complex System

Commonly, scholars offer insight into the complex issues facing stepfamilies and the nature of interaction among members by adopting a family systems perspective (Pasley & Moorefield, 2004). This perspective encourages us to see all parts of the family as interconnected; for example, Pasley and Ihinger-Tallman (1997) used the concept of interconnection to reflect "how the behavior and expression of one component (individual or dyad) of a family influences and is influenced by all others" (p. 73). Furthermore, this perspective suggests that a family is both nested within a larger social context and influenced by and influences persons and institutions outside the family (Cox & Paley, 1997). The family systems perspective also suggests that any family is best understood by examining the whole rather than parts of the whole. Thus, looking at only the couple and ignoring the influence of the stepparent–stepchild relationships on the couple would result in less understanding of the couple's experience in a stepfamily. Systems (e.g., a stepfamily) and subsystems (e.g., couple dyad, parent–child dyad, stepparent–stepchild dyad, sibling dyads) are also influenced by their boundaries, which serve as a border between the system and the outside. Boundaries affect the flow of information, people, other objects, and energy (White & Klein, 2008). Unlike first-marriage families where all children are biologically related to the couple, stepfamilies must have more permeable boundaries to allow a nonresident parent to maintain his or her relationship with his or her biological child. Also, there is often a wider and more complex extended-family network with which a stepfamily must interact. Commonly, there are former in-laws who want to maintain contact with the grandchild coupled with new stepgrandparents who may also desire contact.

We apply a family systems perspective to our discussion of stepfamily life. Our goal is to identify the nature of interaction within and between two primary subsystems relevant to a stepfamily: couple subsystem and the parent–child or stepparent–stepchild subsystem. We also address the influences of systems outside the stepfamily to more fully understand the complex nature of family relationships and processes.

The Couple Subsystem

The original-couple subsystem experiences dramatic changes as a result of the dissolution of the relationship. This subsystem must leave behind an often extensive and intimate pattern of living together over time where there were habits, rituals, rules, and routines that created a shared and often long history. When the relationship dissolves, the adults terminate the couple subsystem while working to maintain a coparental relationship as former spouses/partners. As part of this transition, it is not uncommon that former spouses continue some of their routines and rituals after divorce (Hetherington, 1993).

Upon remarriage or repartnering, the new couple is the most recent and vulnerable subsystem, because they lack a shared history. Building habits, rituals, rules, and routines through experiences together becomes a necessary part of adjustment. Furthermore, many of the routines, rituals, and other forms of intimate behaviors (e.g., assistance with household maintenance, sharing holidays, communication of anecdotes about the children) that were part of the original-couple subsystem and continued after the divorce now must either end or change. Such change can leave former spouses feeling threatened by a new stepparent, who often has more ongoing interaction with the child (e.g., Adamsons & Pasley, 2006). Even communication between formers spouses can become more complicated, because there can be a lack of clarity or explicit communication about expectations for the new step-parent in handling matters, especially those having to do with child rearing (Hetherington & Kelly, 2002). However, there is a need for the boundaries between the two households to be adequately permeable to allow for interaction on behalf of the children. There is some evidence, however, that permeable boundaries can result in ambiguity, and such ambiguity is associated with marital stress particularly (e.g., Stewart, 2005).

The Parent–Child Subsystem

Like the original-couple subsystem, the parent–child subsystem also has a shared history that is disrupted by divorce. In fact, this life event commonly results in multiple changes that affect parents and children alike. For example, when parents divorce, relocation is common, so not only do children move from being in a two-parent family to living with one parent and visiting the other, but the typical routines of daily life also change. Children spend less time with the nonresident parent, often attend a new school, develop new friendships, and become familiar with a new neighborhood (Amato, 2000). Furthermore, the resident parent must develop new routines with the child and assumes sole care when the child resides with her or him in a single-parent family. Parent–child relations also change as children take on added responsibilities that require greater maturity (Hetherington, 1993).

Because the nonresident parent must develop new routines when the child is in his care, and this may be restricted by custody and access agreements, daily contact, for example, is often not possible, so other forms of contact must be established. Thus, the nonresident parent is forced to redefine his or her identity and parental behaviors in light of new limitations and determine how to best parent the child. Children can be confused with these changes, and the subsequent renegotiation of rules may prove to be difficult for both parent and child (e.g., Adamsons & Pasley, 2006; Pasley & Braver, 2003).

Although we use the language of divorce and remarriage, we recognize that many children are born outside of marriage and begin their lives with two parents (Bumpass & Lin, 2000; Bumpass & Lu; Manning, Smock, & Majumdar, 2004). When these relationships end, we anticipate that similar kinds of issues arise for these families and result in changes to the nature of the parent–child relationship. There is some research to support this (e.g., Cooper, Osborne, Beck, & McLanahan, 2008; Manning & Smock, 2000).

If either parent remarries or repartners, then another round of changes must occur to accommodate the new family member(s). This results in parents and children struggling to renegotiate roles and rules in order to develop comfortable habits and routines in this new context that continues to include the two households of the resident and nonresident parents. Some of the changes may include bringing additional children into the family, so competition for attention and other resources increases, and children are highly sensitive to perceived unfair treatment. Changes may also result from another relocation, which has a domino effect noted earlier. Furthermore, it requires that the interactions between parents and between parents and children must be renegotiated in order to bring the new outsiders into what were possibly once two single-parent family units.

Systems on the Outside

Becoming a stepfamily does not occur in isolation. In fact, there are intimate outsiders who have a vested interest in what happens inside the family. These include former and current in-laws, grandparents, aunts and uncles, and other family members. In addition, there are influential others from other systems outside the family, such as teachers from the educational system. These individuals also have a stake in what happens in children's lives. Depending on the family unit, outsiders can affect life on the inside and insiders can affect life on the outside. For example, there is a growing body of literature on grandparenting after divorce and remarriage that suggests a desire on the part of grandparents to remain connected (e.g., Christensen & Smith, 2002). This literature also identifies the complexity of maintaining such relationships, especially among paternal grandparents (Lussier, Deater-Deckard, Dunn, & Davies, 2002). There is other literature that provides insight into the complexity of stepgrandparenting from both the view of the stepgrandparent and the view of the stepgrandchild (Ganong, 2008). Specific to cohabiting couples, there is research demonstrating the potential negative influence of grandparents on repartnerships among low-income, minority couples due to these relationships being embedded in a much larger extended family (Carlson & Furstenberg, 2005; Jarrett, Roy, & Burton, 2002).

Other external systems such as those associated with educational and medical treatment can affect stepfamily life. Contacting teachers and other school-based professionals is often the first step taken by members of stepfamilies when seeking help (Pasley & Ihinger-Tallman, 1997). The assumptions that educational personnel make about these complex families and the policies and procedures within educational systems can ease or cause stress for these families. For example, teachers may assume that the man who brings a child to school regularly is the father of that child; the mother and stepfather may also present themselves as the parents of the child. They then expect him to attend the parent–teacher conference, and they fail to extend an invitation to the nonresident father, which results in conflict between the parents that spills over into the mother–stepfather relationship. Similarly, it is not uncommon that physicians fail to discriminate between parent and stepparent in gaining permission for the treatment of children. The assumption is often that the adult accompanying the child is the child's parent.

_____ Sources of Stress in Stepfamilies: An Overall Picture

Several scholars have discussed sources of stress common to stepfamilies (e.g., Ganong, Coleman, & Hans, 2006; Pasley & Ihinger-Tallman, 1982). Pasley and Ihinger-Tallman (1982) were the first to do so, and they identified three key sources of stress. These include "(a) merging of different family 'cultures,' (b) differing rules of resource distribution (e.g., time, energy, material goods, and affection), and (c) feelings of loyalty or disloyalty about prior and present family members" (p. 183). They argued that these sources of stress are influenced by the structural complexity found in various types of remarried families, including those that form stepfamilies (e.g., his children only, her children only, his and hers together). They suggested that stress also depends on whether children are present, the age of the children (e.g., independent adult children versus dependent children), and with whom the children reside.

Issues of Shared Culture

Becoming a stepfamily through marriage (or cohabitation) is similar to moving to a foreign country. In this new family environment, members do not share the same history or experiences; this is evident in that the meaning of language is different, the food is different, the customs around money may be different, and the behavioral expectations are often different. It is realistic to expect that adjusting to life in a foreign country requires time to acquire the language and to learn the customs of the new culture. Similarly, adjusting to a new family environment takes time; yet, unrealistic expectations for "instant adjustment" are common (Papernow, 1993; Visher & Visher, 1988). Furthermore, individual variation (e.g., temperament, cognitive abilities) will result in varied adjustment patterns with some members making a successful adjustment with relative ease, whereas others require more time or never successfully adjust (Amato, 2003; Hetherington, 2003; Hetherington & Kelly, 2002).

Different Rules of Resource Distribution

Another source of stress results from bringing together two units (commonly a biological mother and her child or children from a previous marriage and a stepfather) where different rules apply to daily living. When new members are added, the existing resources of time, energy, affection, and money are redistributed among all members, often resulting in a perceived sense of loss. This is especially true of children who are accustomed to receiving all of the attention from their single parents, but who now must accept the loss of attention that is directed to a new spouse or partner and perhaps his or her children (e.g., Cartwright & Seymour, 2002). Understandably, when there are more members in a family, there are competing demands on time and resources within the household and across households, so fewer resources are available to individual members (Manlove, Logan, Ikramullah, & Holcombe, 2008). Interestingly, evidence suggests that both children and stepchildren receive equal amounts of attention, although the level of attention overall diminished (Hofferth & Anderson, 2003). In some instances, younger children may actually get more attention from a new stepparent or an older stepsibling, but the loss of attention from the parent is still felt. Also, there is some evidence that in cohabitating couples where men have children from multiple women, the competing demands may result in redirecting resources from their prior children to their newest children (e.g., Manning & Smock, 2000).

Beyond resources, many of the rules by which families live are implicit, such that members often learn family rules by breaking them, observing others break them, or being taught directly about rules. Some rules are never discussed but are still understood. For example, one parent might assign household tasks to children based on gender, whereas a stepparent might assign the same tasks based on age. When these families join, conflict can erupt from such differences about how to distribute household responsibilities. Both families know the rules that were part of their earlier family and implicitly assume that there is no need to discuss this rule in the newly formed family.

Within stepfamilies, however, there is a need to make rules explicit, so those who were not part of the original rule-making process can understand the expectations for behavior. In spite of this need, evidence suggests there is little discussion of rules prior to the merging of families (Ganong et al., 2006). As a result, the newest family members may break the rules or makes other unintentional mistakes. It is in this context of having done something objectionable where the discussion about rules, if it is to occur, takes place, and stress is a common part of this process.

Feelings About Loyalty

Loyalty conflicts arise when individuals feel torn or caught between people they love and care about. In a stepfamily, this conflict can occur between the parents' love and concern for their child and their love and concern for a new spouse or partner. For example, clinical evidence (Browning, 1994; Papernow, 1993, 2008) shows that it is common for one's children to act in such a way that demands the parent to side with them against the new stepparent. In doing so, the resulting conflict leaves the parent feeling as if he or she must choose between his/her child and the new partner, and this can be stressful for all involved.

Loyalty conflicts are also experienced by children. Recent research on the communication patterns in stepfamilies (Afifi, 2003; Golish, 2003) shows that "feeling caught" is a common experience reported by children when they are triangulated on issues arising between parents and stepparents. Dunn, O'Connor, and Cheng (2005) found that children are more likely to side with a parent than a stepparent during arguments between these adults. Feeling caught in between parents and stepparents or taking sides in adult arguments are forms of triangulation, and such triangulation is stressful for children. Furthermore, children who were triangulated were reported by their parents to score higher on internalizing and externalizing problem behaviors (Dunn et al., 2005).

Loyalty conflicts that arise place family members in a difficult situation. Believing that one must choose between significant people can undermine any attempts to develop cohesion in the new stepfamily whether it is formed through marriage or by cohabitation. In fact, some recent evidence suggests that among nonmarried couples characterized by multiple-partner fertility, there is fertile ground for loyalty conflicts to develop among multiple grandparents, parents, and new partners (Carlson & Furstenberg, 2006), and this complexity serves as a source of stress.

Some loyalty conflicts can also stem from the competing developmental needs that accompany stepfamily formation. For example, the importance of spending time alone to solidify the new-couple relationship can conflict with the parenting demands associated with having children. These conflicting demands might emerge when remarrying partners with children try to decide whether to take a family honeymoon or one restricted to the couple. Another example of competing developmental needs as a source of stress occurs when a man with young adult children partners with a woman who has young preschool-aged children. In this case, one partner's life cycle stage entails greater independence from daily childrearing demands, whereas the other partner is experiencing a stage of greater childrearing demands and need for cohesion. Both developmental stages are appropriate; yet, when combined, they can result in greater stress and conflict.

A Comment About Structural Complexity in Stepfamilies

From a family systems perspective, the more members in the system, the more complicated the interaction and family processes become. Thus, there are more opportunities for stress to be experienced. In fact, evidence shows that having a larger family more negatively affects child outcomes for those in stepfamilies and single-parent families than for those in first-marriage families (Kerr & Beaujot, 2002). Unlike first-marriage families, stepfamilies typically have at least one nonresident parent, usually the father. From the child's perspective, his or her "family" also includes this nonresident parent and associated extended-family members (e.g., uncles, cousins, grandparents) who maintain interest in the child's life. Within the more intimate circle, the new stepfamily might include children from more than one prior union, as well as any children the couple decides to conceive. (About half of all remarriages produce a "common" child within the first couple of years; Bramlett & Mosher, 2002.)

Evidence shows that several factors inherent in the structural complexity influence the amount and nature of stress experienced in a repartnered or stepfamily. We have already mentioned that the presence or absence of children with prior family experience can be stressful. Custody and/or visitation arrangements with children from previous relationships can also prove to be stressful, as can the number of persons directly (immediate-family members) and indirectly (in-laws, former in-laws, former spouses/partners, and so on) involved in the new family. Last, the lack of clarity regarding appropriate behavior within the newly formed family and between current and prior families affects level of stress (e.g., Pasley & Ihinger-Tallman, 1982; Visher & Visher, 1988).

Often distinctions are made regarding structural complexity by referring to stepfamilies as "simple" or "complex." The most common simple stepfamily is one in which the mother has children from a prior marriage or relationship but the husband and new stepfather does not. A complex stepfamily includes children from the earlier unions of both adults. In this latter situation, both parents become stepparents, regardless of where children reside. Neither of these labels account for multiple repartnerings or the inclusion of common children born to the new union. In repartnerings, the current stepfamily might be the second such family structure for a child (about 3% of remarriages are a third or higher-order marriage; see U.S. Census Bureau, n.d., Table 3). Divorce and remarriage or repartnering is common for the grandparent generation, making multiple sets of grandparents available to the child and his or her family structure even more complicated. In any of these situations, the nature of family interaction becomes increasingly complex because of the family structure.

_____ Other Sources of Stress Affecting Stepfamilies

Ganong and associates (2006) identified two fundamental differences in first-marriage families and remarried families that can and do serve as additional sources of stress. One difference is that women come to remarriage or repartnering seeking more power than was common in their past relationships. This is most clear regarding financial matters (vanEeden-Moorefield, Pasley, Dolan, & Engel, 2007). However, women's seeking more power in stepfamilies is evident in their reported desire for any interaction to be more egalitarian than it was in earlier relationships (see Burgoyne & Morrison, 1997). Specifically, these women seek more input into the decision-making process (Pyke, 1994), especially in matters dealing with finances and children (Ganong et al., 2006). Thus, it is not simply about wanting more power; it is about desiring a more egalitarian relationship with the new partner.

Another difference that serves as a source of stress is that new stepfamilies operate under the watchful eyes of intimate "interested third parties" (e.g., children, stepchildren, former spouses). Ganong et al. (2006) suggest that these third parties have "vested interests in the quality and perhaps the stability of the remarriage" (p. 416). Nothing that is done or said remains private, and children are known to carry information from one household to the other (e.g., Ahrons, 1979; MacDonald & DeMaris, 2002). Because children may have limited motivation to see the remarriage succeed, and they may view the stepparent as a disruptive intruder, they behave in ways to effectively demonstrate his or her incompetence (Visher & Visher, 1996). Such behavior on the part of children often creates conflict in the couple relationship (Papernow, 1993).

In addition, former spouses or partners and their families can be intrusive. Especially in the early stages of the remarriage, determining and maintaining clear boundaries around the new-couple dyad, as well as the new stepfamily, pose challenges. The more people who desire access to the children (e.g., former partners, grandparents, etc.), the more challenging it becomes to handle boundary issues, as many of the parental responsibilities must be shared across households (e.g., Adamsons & Pasley, 2006; Adler-Baeder & Higginbotham, 2004; Ahrons, 1979). Working out how to effectively coparent and handle the multiple demands can complicate family interaction.

When asked directly about sources of stress and conflict in relationships, remarried people report that child rearing and finances are the most common (Adler-Baeder & Higginbotham, 2004). Interestingly, Stanley, Markman, and Whitton (2002) noted that first-married couples also identified money and children as the first and second sources of conflict in their relationships. They also noted that the order of these issues were reversed for remarriages; that is, conflict stemming from issues around children and child rearing dominated disagreements between remarried spouses, followed by money issues. There is no research on how nonmarried pairs rank these issues, but we expect that similar patterns occur. Some of the stress regarding these issues may result from the common practice of couples avoiding and ignoring addressing these subjects in anticipation of their marriage (e.g., Coleman, Fine, Ganong, Downs, & Pauk, 2001; Coleman & Ganong, 1989). Other topics that can also be ignored include decision making and division of household labor (Ganong et al., 2006). In the following pages, we explore more closely the extant literature related to issues around child rearing and finances.

Childrearing Issues and Complexities _____

Much has been written about the effects of stepfamily life on child outcomes (Coleman et al., 2000; Pasley & Moorefield, 2004), while less research has focused on the ways in which child rearing in stepfamilies is stressful for parents, stepparents, and nonresident parents. Therefore, our focus is to examine how child rearing in stepfamilies can be stress inducing.

Stepparent Role as a Source of Stress

Some scholarship exists on the stepparent role and how individuals manage it effectively. Pasley and Moorefield (2004) summarized the research published between 1980 and 2000 and concluded that the stepparent role was more ambiguous and difficult than that of a biological parent. Because of the variation in role expectations and behaviors, determining the "best" behaviors for stepparents is challenging, especially among new stepparents (e.g., Ganong & Coleman, 2004; Hetherington & Kelly, 2002; Weaver & Coleman, 2005).

There is some evidence that stepparents are granted greater latitude in parenting and that this latitude can cause confusion and ambiguity. For example, stepfathers are expected to assume less parenting responsibility in both the daily care and control or monitoring of children than are resident parents (e.g., Hetherington & Kelly, 2002). However, when the stepparent is a stepmother, especially to young children, there is also an implicit assumption that she takes on the primary childrearing role (Nielsen, 1999;

Svare, Jay, & Mason, 2004). Some argue that beyond the unspoken expectations for women to assume certain roles in any family, stepmother families frequently have more complex structures, including his, hers, and our children (e.g., Dunn, Davies, O'Connor, & Sturgess, 2000). Also, research shows that stepmothers assume a greater portion of family work—which they believe they should do—and when this occurs, the stepmother's relationships with their stepchildren do not fare as well (Ceglian & Garner, 2000). A common conclusion is that the stepmother role is more difficult and stressful than that of the stepfather, and there are research findings to support this idea (see Coleman & Ganong, 2004; Pasley & Moorefield, 2004, for reviews).

Young adult stepchildren have been reported to describe the roles assumed by stepparents as legitimate and not legitimate (e.g., Baxter, Braithwaite, Bryan, & Wagner, 2004)—an indication of confusion on the part of even adult stepchildren. Other evidence shows that stepfathers are perceived more negatively compared with fathers (e.g., Claxton-Olfield, Garber, & Gilcrist, 2006) and more positively compared with stepmothers (e.g., Schrodt, 2006). The overall conclusion from this body of research is that the lack of clarity regarding what stepparents should and should not do results in feeling unsure and insecure regarding one's place in the family and what is expected.

The Process of Stepparenting

Being treated as an intimate outsider in a newly formed stepfamily complicates any attempts by a stepparent to engage in parenting behaviors. It is not uncommon that stepfathers especially try to assume a more active part in parenting than the mother or her children thinks is appropriate (e.g., Bray & Kelly, 1998; Hetherington & Kelly, 2002). This is often compounded by the lack of discussion about how and when to discipline whose children and, thus, is a reason why child rearing is a primary issue in stepfamilies. A typical response by the biological parent is to take the side of his or her child, and this effectively undermines any attempts by the stepparent to exert control (e.g., Bray & Kelly, 1998; Pasley & Moorefield, 2004).

Specific to stepfathers, there is some research showing that they exert less monitoring behaviors than do biological fathers (Fisher, Leve, O'Leary, & Leve, 2003) and control their own negative feelings better (Bray & Kelly, 1998; Hetherington, 1993). However, the reaction from stepchildren to attempts by stepfathers to limit, control, or monitor behavior is often negative (e.g., Pasley & Moorefield, 2004). This is true even when he exerts authoritative control strategies (e.g., warmth coupled with control). In this context, stepfathers commonly adopt a more disengaged stepparenting style, and over time, this style is associated with improved quality in the stepfather–stepchild relationship (Hetherington & Kelly, 2002). Yet, there is some evidence that his disengagement is associated with more tension in the mother–child relationship (DeLongis & Preece, 2002).

New findings (Flouri, 2004) suggest that when stepfathers see their stepchildren as well adjusted, they are more likely to be involved rather than disengaged (Bray & Kelly, 1998; Hetherington & Kelly, 2002) and such involvement is perceived positively by the stepchild (e.g., MacDonald & DeMaris, 2002). Other findings (Golish & Caughlin, 2002) show that the communication from stepchildren to stepparents is infrequent and such infrequency is believed to contribute to the often less positive stepparent–stepchild relationship Taken together, Pasley and Moorefield (2004) suggested that

> poor communication, lack of warmth, fewer positive expressions, and less support and monitoring may combine to foster children's feeling more disconnected and more resistant to change (parental remarriage) and agents of change (stepparents). (p. 321)

Thus, the nature of interaction between them can and often does set the tone for the way in which life is experienced by other members in stepfamilies. In addition, there is some evidence that confirms that stepparenting a stepdaughter is fraught with more conflict than stepparenting a stepson (e.g., Hetherington & Kelly, 2002).

Evidence also suggests that stepfathers develop more positive relationships with stepchildren in general than do stepmothers (Bray & Kelly, 1998; Coleman & Ganong, 2004). These findings are drawn from multiple studies using reports from stepparents (e.g., Marsiglio, 2004; Svare et al., 2004) and those using reports from young adult stepchildren (e.g., Moore & Cartwright, 2005). For example, results from a 20-year study (Ahrons & Tanner, 2003) of children of divorce whose parents remarried and formed stepfamilies indicate that of those who experienced the remarriage of both parents, their father's remarriage was more difficult for them because of changes in the quality of the father–child relationship, which became stressful.

When the resident stepparent is a stepmother, negativity and conflict are stronger and more frequent than with a resident stepfather (e.g., MacDonald & DeMaris, 1996). This may be due to the more engaged behavior on the part of the stepmother, as women often report that they take on more parenting behaviors because their husbands do not assume such responsibility (e.g., Nielsen, 1999).

Many scholars have identified factors that affect stepparenting beyond sex of the stepparent and sex of the stepchild. Among them, two factors stand out: age of the stepchild and structural complexity of the stepfamily. Regarding age of the stepchild, stepparent–stepchild relationships are more conflicted when the stepchild is an adolescent (e.g., Feinberg, Kan, & Hetherington, 2007; Golish & Caughlin, 2002; Hetherington & Kelly, 2002).

Furthermore, recent research indicates that there is more conflict between adults in stepfamilies of greater complexity. Specifically, findings show that children are exposed to more conflict when they reside within complex stepfamilies where both adults are stepparents to their partner's children compared to simple stepfamilies where only one adult is a stepparent (e.g., Jenkins, Simpson, Dunn, Rasbash, & O'Connor, 2005). It is likely that communication becomes increasingly complicated as membership in the family expands, and there are multiple people representing vested interests in one set of issues over another.

Within-Family Interaction

Much has been written about the nature of the stepparent–stepchild relationship, especially in terms of its effects on children. However, the vast majority of this literature addresses the relationship between resident step-parents and stepchildren. A conclusion that can be made from this literature is that parenting someone else's children is not the same as parenting one's own children. As noted earlier, because the stepparent is an outsider to an already established unit, the principle of homeostasis from family systems theory suggests that this established unit will operate in such a way to further exclude the outsider (Pasley & Ihinger-Tallman, 1997). Thus, greater understanding about stepfamily life comes from examining the linkages among relationships within the family beyond that of just the stepparent and stepchild.

MacDonald and DeMaris (2002) reported several findings of interest regarding these linkages. They found that when the quality of the mother–child relationship was good, the stepfather–stepchild relationship was better than when the mother–child relationship was characterized by conflict and negativity. DeLongis and Preece (2002) found that when stepfathers withdrew from conflict with their wives, their wives reported more conflict with their own children. Findings from a study of families in the United Kingdom (Shelton, Walters, & Harold, 2008) showed that the mechanism through which interparental conflict affects child adjustment differs for children in first-marriage and remarriage families. In first-marriage families, children's outcomes are mostly affected through their appraisals of threat and their own experience of self-blame. However, for children in stepfather families, neither appraisal nor self-blame helped to explain their outcomes. Instead, it was the way in which interparental conflict (between the mother and stepfather) resulted in more hostile and rejecting parenting that, in turn, affected children's outcomes.

Although limited in volume, studies of nonmarried stepfamilies also shows that the quality of the mother's relationship with her children is associated with the quality of her relationship with her partner. That is, when their romantic relationship ended, the quality of parenting between the mother and child was diminished (e.g., Thomson, Mosely, Hanson, & McLanahan, 2001).

Coparental Relationships Across Households

One relationship that has received little attention is that which occurs between the resident and nonresident parents and/or the resident and nonresident stepparents (Ganong et al., 2006). We label these as coparenting relationships, because they are linked by their interactions around shared children. Adamsons and Pasley (2006) discussed a number of factors that influence coparenting after divorce, including the quality of the parents' predivorce relationship, the nature of the divorce process, custody and visitation arrangements, postdivorce relationships with former spouses, and time since divorce. They also identified remarriage and new-family formation as influencing coparenting. Importantly, from the divorce literature, findings show that when children become involved in interparental conflict, their involvement is associated with higher levels of externalizing and internalizing behavior problems after divorce than those children residing in intact, first-marriage families (e.g., Dunn et al., 2005; Shelton et al., 2008).

When parents remarry or repartner, new coparenting relationships are introduced. Although limited, some evidence suggests that many of the contentious issues that were part of the earlier divorce resurface with the remarriage of one or both parents. Such resurfacing can result in increased antagonism and conflict between former partners, and this negativity is often coupled with reduced cooperation between former partners (Buehler & Ryan, 1994; Hetherington, 2003). Encouragingly, there is evidence that over time such conflict is reduced (see Braithwaite, McBride, & Schrodt, 2003).

Conflict among coparents is shown to affect other relationships as well. For example, when coparenting conflict increases, fathers in stepfamilies become more negative toward adolescent stepchildren, whereas those in intact families becomes less negative (Feinberg, Kan, & Hetherington, 2007). MacDonald and DeMaris (2002) found that when conflict between bioparents was high, the stepfather–stepchild relationship suffered; when this conflict was also coupled with frequent father–child contact, the stepfather–stepchild relationship suffered even more. Still other research shows that when a positive stepfather–stepchild relationship exists, the frequency and regularity of contact with the nonresident father is reduced (Dunn, Cheng, O'Connor, & Bridges, 2004). Also, when nonresident fathers remarry, some see their children as a source of stress because of his added responsibilities to his new family. Such added responsibility is associated with his disengagement from his first family (e.g., Ganong & Coleman, 2004). This later finding also is true for nonmarried partners (e.g., Carlson & Furstenberg, 2005; Manning & Smock, 2000).

Marsiglio and Hinojosa (2007) explored ways in which stepfathers reported developing coparental relationships with fathers. They examined how these two men became allies, suggesting that from the stepfather's perception, doing so is associated with his romantic relationship security, his perceiving the father as worthy, and his being a parent.

Extended Kin

Extended kin is a topic that has received limited attention by scholars. As mentioned earlier, a number of studies, however, have examined the relationship between stepgrandparents and stepgrandchildren (e.g., White, 1994). For example, Ganong (2008) concluded that stepgrandparents are a heterogeneous group whose functions and expectations are "unexplored and unknown" (p. 397). He was the first to describe the experiences of stepgrand-parents by differentiating three types: a stepparent who raised stepchildren and becomes a stepgrandparent when a stepchild has his or her own child; a parent whose adult child marries a person with a child from a prior relationship; and a later-life remarriage to a person with adult children and grandchildren. However, he also noted that the extant literature treated stepgrandparents as if they were homogeneous.

Most of the research indicates that physical proximity enhanced the relationship among extended kin (e.g., Clawson & Ganong, 2002; Ganong & Coleman, 2006a). Maintaining relationships across generations shows that women tend to mediate these relationships (e.g., Schmeeckle, 2007), and that parents of resident stepparents have more contact than do those of nonresident stepparents (Lussier et al., 2002). In addition, there are a number of studies addressing the perceived responsibility and obligations across generations (e.g., Coleman, Ganong, Hans, Rothrauff, & Sharp, 2005; Ganong & Coleman, 2006). These findings suggest that more obligations are associated with biological relationships compared with steprelationships, although more frequent contact between stepparents and stepchildren is associated with a heightened sense of obligation between these two.

Finances as a Source of Stress

Our discussion demonstrates the importance of child rearing as a source of stress in stepfamilies. This emphasis is warranted given that child-related issues are identified as the primary source of difficulty by those in remarriages (Stanley et al., 2002). Although much less studied, finances and money management are also identified as major sources of difficulty. Scholar agree (e.g., Ganong et al., 2006; Pasley & Ihinger-Tallman, 1982; vanEeden-Moorefield et al., 2007) that the difficulty is less about available resources than about the decisions regarding how to distribute resources and the meaning attached to such distribution. In fact, Amato (2000) and Vogler (2005) show that remarriage is associated with increased economic status and reduced economic stress among women.

Evidence also shows that women in remarriages report more say in financial matters than women in first marriages, and this greater say is associated with greater diversity in the use of resources in stepfamilies (e.g., Burgoyne &

Morrison, 1997). There is some speculation that the desire for more input into financial management is a carryover from the economic independence of women during and after divorce (Vogler, 2005).

It is not uncommon that some separation of finances continues after remarriage; a common reason for this is the complexity of supporting children from past and/or current relationships, as well as individuals (especially women) wanting to retain some financial independence. In fact, studies document the use of several financial management styles: one-pot, two-pot, combined one- and two-pot styles (e.g., Coleman & Ganong, 1989; Pasley, Sandras, & Edmundson, 1994; vanEeden-Moorefield et al., 2007). Findings related to management styles show that women who report more financial changes (e.g., sold their home, quit a job) as a result of a remarriage also more frequently reported adopting a one-pot or combination style of money management in remarriage (vanEeden-Moorfield et al., 2007). Unexpectedly, research has failed to show a link between financial management styles and martial quality (Pasley et al., 1994); however, Lown and Dolan (1994) showed a positive link between the use of a one-pot style and reports of higher marital cohesion, with those using a two-pot style reporting the least marital cohesion. Furthermore, there is a link between financial management and relationship stability, such that more frequent dissolution is reported among couples who maintain two pots and make autonomous decisions (Vogler, Lyonette, & Wiggins, 2008).

Ganong and associates (2006) speculated that with greater structural complexity in the stepfamily, there is greater opportunity for conflict around finances and resource issues. However, the findings from a recent study (vanEeden-Moorefield et al., 2007) did not support this speculation.

Lastly, there is much less information on financial resources and management styles among nonmarried stepfamilies. A notable exception is the work of Vogler (2005). She reported that financial security can be enhanced through remarriage, and there is evidence to support this finding (Vogler, Brockmann, & Wiggins, 2006, 2008). Furthermore, Vogler and associates found that cohabiting partners and cohabiting parents are less likely to comingle resources than are married couples and parents.

Implications for Working With Stepfamilies

Scholars have written extensively about the implications of this body of research for working with stepfamilies, including issues related to public policy (e.g., Malia, 2008; Papernow, 2008; Pasley, Dollahite, & Ihinger-Tallman, 1993; Pasley, Rhoden, Visher, & Visher, 1996). These include recommendations that to provide appropriate and helpful services to stepfamilies, practitioners must first understand the complexity and diversity of these families and be able to address their own biases with regard to what constitutes a legitimate family form (e.g., Adler-Baeder & Higginbotham, 2004). This is especially important in working with cohabiting couples, including gay and lesbian couples raising children together (e.g., Berger, 1998, 2000; Lynch, 2000). Beyond merely recognizing their own limitations, professionals must also be able to suspend and/or transcend stereotypical beliefs in favor of a more positive or at least neutral stance.

In addition to exploring personal beliefs, practitioners must also appreciate differences in stepfamilies related to structural complexity, developmental stages of the individuals and the family system itself, as well as the influences of all relevant outside systems. Recognizing that stepfamily life is not static and will change over time is essential (Papernow, 1993, 2008). Part of this realization stems from extensive knowledge of the extant empirical literature and writings by clinicians known for their expertise in working with stepfamilies who advocate for practitioners gaining such knowledge (e.g., Pasley et al., 1996; personal communication, S. Browning, September 10, 2008; Visher, Visher, & Pasley, 2003).

Taking a psychoeducational approach is a useful first step in working with stepfamilies and an approach that has been recommended (e.g., Adler-Baeder & Higginbotham, 2004; Pasley & Ihinger-Tallman, 1997). To do so effectively, we reiterate the strong belief that practitioners must be well versed in the relevant research literature and be able to provide appropriate resources related to empirical findings. They must also be able to articulate their under-standing of the research as informative and useful to the families with whom they work. Because members of stepfamilies can become quickly disillusioned in the early stages of their family development, advising them about the process of stepfamily development as multistage and requiring an appreciable amount of time is warranted (Papernow, 2008). Such information serves the primary purpose of normalizing experiences, as stepfamilies commonly see their lives as unique, which can result in feelings of isolation (Visher & Visher, 1988; Visher et al., 2003). Also, providing information about the process of stepfamily development can give them a road map of somewhat predictable experiences and measurable tasks to be met.

Narrative approaches that are typically used in clinical work with step-families have also been recommended (Christian, 2005). Such approaches encourage individuals to talk about their perceptions of their experiences and are one way to develop a positive family story (narrative) that all members can share (White & Epston, 1990). Professionals who are successful in working with stepfamilies ask questions that allow members to tell their story by reporting their experiences while simultaneously challenging any dominant social narratives about stepfamily life (e.g., "wicked" stepmother). In fact, it is conceivable that the stories stepfamilies tell are already influenced by the broader cultural bias of being deficient compared with a traditional two-parent family or representing an "incomplete institution" (Cherlin, 1978). Such stories inherently contain elements of failure that can reify problems. When used effectively, narrative approaches provide opportunities to move beyond societal expectations to explore what is more relevant to the specific family. Thus, both the therapist and the family can gain insight into their problems and successes, and it is this latter insight that is most powerful (Papernow, 2008).

We recognize that many stepfamilies have difficulty with many of the issues noted here, including the merging of cultures, distribution of resources, loyalty conflicts, boundaries, and negotiating roles and rules (especially where discipline and affection are concerned). Inherent in all of these difficulties are often unexpressed and unmet expectations. Interventions with stepfamilies that allow for the exploration of expectations are essential, especially as they relate to making unspoken expectations explicit and bringing those expectations into one's consciousness (e.g., Adler-Baeder & Higginbotham, 2004; Papernow, 2008; Whitton, Nicholson, & Markman, 2008). Once expectations are identified, family members can begin the process of negotiating which expectations are important and realistic.

Communication skills and problem-solving training is an important recommendation for stepfamilies (see Beaudry, Boisverty, Simard, Parent, & Blais, 2004; Markman & Halford, 2005; Whitton et al., 2008). Such training is important to families in general, but because of the added complexity of stepfamily life, these skills are essential. The research on communication strengths within stepfamilies identifies areas that promote success, such as "everyday talk," more openness, spending regular time together as a family, and promoting positive relationships between family subsystems (e.g., Golish, 2003; Schrodt, Soliz, & Braithwaite, 2008). Thus, professionals can promote a focus on "solution talk" versus "problem talk" in their work with stepfamilies (Weiner-Davis, 2002).

Others have recommended that combining communication skills training with components that address parenting skills might reduce some of the added risk of stress in stepfamily living (e.g., Forgatch, DeGarmo, & Beldavs, 2005). These recommendations provide a comprehensive and focused approach to the development of skills and are key to fostering adjustment over time.

Finally, abundant research has produced much knowledge about the problems that accompany life in stepfamilies. However, there remains little written on the strengths and successes of stepfamilies. Both research and practice should continue to emphasize a shift from deficit models toward models of resiliency (Walsh, 2006). Evidence-based assessments and interventions are crucial to program and policy development; yet, these must include identifiable strengths as a valuable contribution.

Reading Resources

Cavanagh, S. E. (2008). Family structure history and adolescent adjustment. *Journal of Family Issues, 29,* 944–980.

Ganong, L. H., & Coleman, M. (2004). *Stepfamily relationships: Development, dynamics, and intervention.* New York: Plenum.

National Stepfamily Resource Center: http://www.stepfamilies.info/

Pryor, J. (Ed.). *The international handbook of stepfamilies: Policy and practice in legal, research, and clinical environments.* Hoboken, NJ: John Wiley & Sons.

Teachman, J. (2008). Complex life course patterns and the risk of divorce in second marriage. *Journal of Marriage and Family, 70,* 294–305.

References

Adamsons, K., & Pasley, K. (2006). Coparenting following divorce and relationship dissolution. In M. A. Fine & J. H. Harvey (Eds.), *Handbook of divorce and relationship dissolution* (pp. 241–262). Mahwah, NJ: Lawrence Erlbaum.

Adler-Baeder, F., & Higginbotham, B. (2004). Implications of remarriage and stepfamily formation for marriage education. *Family Relations, 53,* 448–458.

Afifi, T. (2003). "Feeling caught" in stepfamilies: Managing boundary turbulence through appropriate communication privacy rules. *Journal of Social and Personal Relationships, 20,* 729–755.

Ahrons, C. R. (1979). The binuclear family: Two households, one family. *Alternative Lifestyles, 2,* 499–515.

Ahrons, C. R., & Tanner, J. (2003). Adult children and their fathers: Relationship changes 20 years after parental divorce. *Family Relations, 52,* 340–351.

Amato, P. R. (2000). Consequences of divorce for adults and children. *Journal of Marriage and the Family, 62,* 1269–1287.

Amato, P. R. (2003). Reconciling divergent perspectives: Judith Wallerstein, quantitative family research, and children of divorce. *Family Relations, 52,* 332–339.

Baxter, L. A., Braithwaite, D. O., Bryant, L, & Wagner, A. (2004). Stepchildren's perceptions of the contradictions in communication with stepparents. *Journal of Social and Personal Relationships, 21,* 447–467.

Beaudry, M., Boisverty, J. M., Simard, M., Parent, C., & Blais, M. C. (2004). Communication: A key component to meeting the challenges of stepfamilies. *Journal of Divorce & Remarriage, 42,* 85–104.

Berger, R. (1998). The experiences and issues of gay stepfamilies. *Journal of Divorce & Remarriage, 29*(3/4), 93–102.

Berger, R. (2000). Gay stepfamilies: A triple-stigmatized group. *Families and Society, 81,* 501–516.

Braithwaite, D., McBride, C., & Schrodt, P. (2003). "Parent-teams" and the everyday interactions of co-parenting in stepfamilies. *Communication Reports, 16,* 93–111.

Bramlett, M., & Mosher, W. (2002). *Cohabiation, marriage, divorce, and remarriage in the United States. Vital Health Statistics,* Series 23, No. 22. Hyattsville, MD: National Center for Health Statistics.

Bray, J., & Kelly, J. (1998). *Stepfamilies.* New York: Broadway Books.

Browning, S. W. (1994). Treating stepfamilies: Alternative to traditional family therapy. In K. Pasley & M. Ihinger-Tallman (Eds.), *Stepparenting: Issues in theory, research, and practice* (pp. 175–198). Westport, CT: Greenwood.

Buehler, C., & Ryan, C. (1994). Former spouse relationships and noncustodial father involvement during marital and family transitions: A closer look at remarriage following divorce. In K. Pasley & M. Ihinger-Tallman (Eds.), *Stepparenting: Issues in theory, research, and practice* (pp. 127–150). Westport, CT: Greenwood.

Bumpass, L. L., & Lu, H. (2000). Trends in cohabitation and implication for children's family contexts in the United States. *Population Studies, 54,* 29–41.

Bumpass, L. L., Raley, R. K., & Sweet, J. (1995). The changing character of stepfamilies: Implications of cohabitation and nonmarital childbearing. *Demography, 32,* 425–436.

Burgoyne, C. B., & Morrison, V. (1997). Money in remarriage: Keeping things simple and separate. *The Sociological Review, 45,* 363–395.

Carlson, M. J., & Furstenberg, F. F., Jr. (2006). The prevalence and correlates of multipartnered fertility among urban U.S. parents. *Journal of Marriage and Family, 68,* 718–732.

Cartwright, C., & Seymour, F. (2002). Young adults' perceptions of parents' responses in stepfamilies: What hurts? What helps? *Journal of Divorce & Remarriage, 37*(3/4), 123–141.

Ceglian, C. P., & Garner, S. (2000). Attachment style and the "wicked stepmother" spiral. *Journal of Divorce & Remarriage, 34*(1/2), 111–129.

Cherlin, A. J. (1978). Remarriage as an incomplete institution. *American Journal of Sociology, 84,* 634–650.

Christensen, F., & Smith, T. (2002). What is happening to satisfaction and quality of relationships between step/grandparents and step/grandchildren? *Journal of Divorce & Remarriage, 37*(1/2), 117–133.

Christian, A. (2005). Contesting the myth of the "wicked stepmother": Narrative analysis of an online stepfamily support group. *Western Journal of Communication, 69,* 27–47.

Clawson, J., & Ganong, L. (2002). Adult stepchildren's obligations to older stepparents. *Journal of Family Nursing, 8,* 50–72.

Claxton-Oldfield, S., Garber, T., & Gilcrist, K. (2006). Young adults' perceptions of their relationships with their stepfathers and biological fathers. *Journal of Divorce & Remarriage, 45*(1/2), 165–177.

Coleman, M., Fine, M. A., Ganong, L. H., Downs, K. J. M., & Pauk, N. (2001). When you're not the Brady bunch: Identifying perceived conflicts and resolution strategies in stepfamilies. *Personal Relationships, 8,* 55–73.

Coleman, M., & Ganong, L. (1989). Financial management in stepfamilies. *Lifestyles: Family and Economic Issues, 10,* 217–232.

Coleman, M., & Ganong, L. (2004). *Stepfamily relationships: Development, dynamics, and interventions.* New York: Kluwer.

Coleman, M., Ganong, L., & Fine, M. (2000). Reinvestigating remarriage: Another decade of progress. *Journal of Marriage and the Family, 62,* 1288–1307.

Coleman, M., Ganong, L. H., Hans, J. C., Rothrauff, T. C., & Sharp, E. A. (2005). Filial obligations in post-divorce stepfamilies. *Journal of Divorce & Remarriage, 43*(3/4), 1–27.

Cooper, C., Osborne, C., Beck, A., & McLanahan, S. (2008, May). *Partnership stability and child well-being during the transition to elementary school.* Fragile Families Working Paper Series, WP08–07-FF.

Cox, M. J., & Paley, B. (1997). Families as systems. *Annual Review of Psychology, 48,* 243–267.

DeLongis, A., & Preece, M. (2002). Emotional and relational consequences of coping in stepfamilies. *Marriage and Family Review, 34*(1/2), 115–138.

Dunn, J., Cheng, H., O'Connor, T. G., & Bridges, L. (2004). Children's perspectives on their relationships with their nonresident fathers: Influences, outcomes and implications. *Journal of Child Psychology and Psychiatry, 45,* 553–566.

Dunn, J., Davis, L., O'Connor, T. G., & Sturgess, W. (2000). Parents' and partners' life course and family experiences: Links with parent-child relationships in different family settings. *Journal of Child Psychology and Psychiatry, 41,* 955–968.

Dunn, J., O'Connor, T. G., & Cheng, H. (2005). Children's responses to conflict between their different parents: Mothers, stepfathers, nonresident fathers, and nonresident stepmothers. *Journal of Clinical Child and Adolescent Psychology, 34,* 223–234.

Falci, C. (2006). Family structure, closeness to residential and nonresidential parents, and psychological distress in early and middle adolescence. *The Sociological Quarterly, 47,* 123–146.

Feinberg, M. E., Kan, M. L., & Hetherington, E. M. (2007). The longitudinal influence of coparenting conflict on parental negativity and adolescent maladjustment. *Journal of Marriage and Family, 69,* 687–702.

Fisher, P., Leve, L., O'Leary, C., & Leve, C. (2003). Parental monitoring of children's behavior: Variations across stepmother, stepfather, and two-parent biological families. *Family Relations, 52,* 45–52.

Flouri, E. (2004). Correlates of parents' involvement with their adolescent children in restructured and biological two-parent families: The role of child characteristics. *International Journal of Behavioral Development, 28,* 148–156.

Forgatch, M. S., DeGarmo, D. S., & Beldavs, Z. G. (2005). An efficacious theory-based intervention for stepfamilies. *Behavior Therapy, 36,* 1–13.

Freisthler, B., Jay, S., & Svare, G. M. (2004). Drinking in young adulthood: Is the stepparent a risk factor. *Journal of Divorce & Remarriage, 41(3/4),* 99–114.

Ganong, L. H. (2008). Intergenerational relationships in stepfamilies. In J. Pryor (Ed.), *The international handbook of stepfamilies: Policy and practice in legal, research, and clinical environments* (pp. 394–420). Hoboken, NJ: John Wiley & Sons.

Ganong, L. H., & Coleman, M. (2004). *Stepfamily relationships: Development, dynamics, and interventions.* Columbia: University of Missouri Press.

Ganong, L. H., & Coleman, M. (2006a). Patterns of exchange and intergenerational responsibilities after divorce and remarriage. *Journal of Aging Studies, 20,* 265–278.

Ganong, L. H., & Coleman, M. (2006b). Responsibilities to stepparents acquired in later life: Relationship quality and acuity of needs. *Journal of Gerontology: Social Sciences, 61B,* S80–S88.

Ganong, L. H., Coleman, M., & Hans, J. A. (2006). Divorce as a prelude to stepfamily living and the consequences of redivorce. In M. A. Fine & J. H. Harvey (Eds.), *Handbook of divorce and relationship dissolution* (pp. 409–434). Mahwah, NJ: Lawrence Erlbaum.

Ge, X, Natsuaki, M. N., Neiderhiser, J. M., & Reiss, D. (2007). Genetic and environmental influences on pubertal timing: Results from two national sibling studies. *Journal of Research on Adolescence, 17,* 767–788.

Golish, T. (2003). Stepfamily communication strengths: Understanding the ties that bind. *Human Communication Research, 29,* 41–80.

Golish, T., & Caughlin, J. (2002). "I'd rather not talk about it": Adolescents' and young adults' use of topic avoidance in stepfamilies. *Journal of Applied Communication Research, 30,* 78–106.

Halpern-Meekin, S., & Tach, L. (2008). Heterogeneity in two-parent families and adolescent well-being. *Journal of Marriage and Family, 70,* 435–451.

Harper, C. C., & McLanahan, S. S. (2004). Father absence and youth incarceration. *Journal of Research on Adolescence, 14,* 369–397.

Harris, S. R. (2008). What is family diversity? Objective and interpretive approaches. *Journal of Family Issues, 29,* 1407–1425.

Hetherington, E. M. (1993). An overview of the Virginia Longitudinal Study of Divorce and Remarriage with a focus on early adolescence. *Journal of Family Psychology, 7,* 39–96.

Hetherington, E. M. (2003). Intimate pathways: Changing patterns in close personal relationships across time. *Family Relations, 52,* 318–331.

Herthington, E. M., & Kelly, J. (2002). *For better or worse.* New York: Norton.

Hofferth, S. L., & Anderson, K. G. (2003). Are all dads equal? Biology versus marriage as a basis for paternal investment. *Journal of Marriage and Family, 65,* 213–232.

Jarrett, R., Roy, K., & Burton, L. (2002). Fathers in the 'hood: Qualitative research on African American men. In C. Tamis-LeMonda & N. Cabrera (Eds.), *Handbook of father involvement: Multidisciplinary perspectives* (pp. 211–248). Hillsdale, NJ: Lawrence Erlbaum.

Jenkins, J., Simpson, A., Dunn, J., Rasbash, J., & O'Connor, T. G. (2005). Mutual influence of marital conflict and children's behavior problems: Shared and non-shared family risks. *Child Development, 76,* 24–39.

Kerr, D., & Beaujot, R. (2002). Family relations, low income, and child outcomes: A comparison of Canadian children in intact-, step-, and lone-parent families. *International Journal of Comparative Sociology, 43,* 134–152.

Kreider, R. M. (2005). *Number, timing, and duration of marriages and divorces: 2001.* Current Population Reports, P70–97. Washington, DC: U.S. Census Bureau.

Laursen, B. (2005). Conflict between mothers and adolescents in single-mother, blended, and two-biological-parent families. *Parenting: Science and Practice, 5*(4), 47–70.

Lown, J. M., & Dolan, E. M. (1994). Remarried families' economic behavior: Fishman's model revisited. *Journal of Divorce & Remarriage, 22*(1/2), 103–119.

Lussier, G., Deater-Decker, K., Dunn, J., & Davies, L. (2002). Support across two generations: Children's closeness to grandparents following parental divorce and remarriage. *Journal of Family Psychology, 16,* 363–376.

Lynch, J. (2000). Considerations of family structure and gender composition: The lesbian and gay stepfamily. *Journal of Homosexuality, 40*(2), 81–95.

MacDonald, W. L., & DeMaris, A. (1996). The effects of stepparents' gender and new biological children. *Journal of Family Issues, 17,* 2–25.

MacDonald, W. L., & DeMaris, A. (2002). Stepfather-stepchild relationship quality: The stepfather's demand for conformity and the biological father's involvement. *Journal of Family Issues, 23,* 121–137.

Malia, S. E. C. (2008). How relevant are U.S. family and probate laws to stepfamilies? In J. Pryor (Ed.), *The international handbook of stepfamilies: Policy and practice in legal, research, and clinical environments* (pp. 545–572) Hoboken, NJ: John Wiley & Sons.

Manlove, J., Logan, C., Ikramullah, E., & Holcombe, E. (2008). Factors associated with multiple-partner fertility among fathers. *Journal of Marriage and Family, 70,* 536–548.

Manning, W. D., & Smock, P. J. (2000). "Swapping" families: Serial parenting and economic support for children. *Journal of Marriage and the Family, 62,* 111–122.

Manning, W. D., Smock, P. J., & Majumdar, D. (2004). The relative stability of marital and cohabiting relationships for children. *Population Research and Policy Review, 23,* 135–159.

Markman, H. J., & Halford, W. K. (2005) International perspectives on couple relationship education. *Family Process, 44,* 139–146.

Marsiglio, W. (2004). When stepfathers claim stepchildren: A conceptual analysis. *Journal of Marriage and Family, 66,* 22–39.

Marsiglio, W., & Hinojosa, R. (2007). Managing the multifather family: Stepfathers as father allies. *Journal of Marriage and Family, 69,* 845–862.

Moore, S., & Cartwright, C. (2005). Adolescents' and young adults' expectations of parental responsibilities in stepfamilies. *Journal of Divorce & Remarriage, 43,* 109–127.

Nicolson, J., Phillips, M., Peterson, C., & Battistutta, D. (2002). Relationship between the parenting styles of biological parents and stepparents and the adjustment of young adult stepchildren. *Journal of Divorce & Remarriage, 26,* 57–76.

Nielsen, L. (1999). Stepmothers: Why so much stress? A review of the research. *Journal of Divorce & Remarriage, 20,* 115–148.

Papernow, P. L. (1993). *Become a stepfamily: Patterns of development in remarried families.* San Francisco: Jossey-Bass.

Papernow, P. L. (2008). A clinician's view of "stepfamily architecture." In J. Pryor (Ed.), *The international handbook of stepfamilies: Policy and practice in legal, research, and clinical environments* (pp. 423–454). Hoboken, NJ: John Wiley & Sons.

Pasley, K., & Braver, S. (2003). Reconceptualizing and measuring father involvement in divorced, nonresident fathers. In R. D. Day & M. E. Lamb (Eds.), *Measuring father involvement* (pp. 217–240). Mahwah, NJ: Lawrence Erlbaum.

Pasley, K., Dollahite, D. C., & Ihinger-Tallman, M. (1993). Bridging the gap: Clinical applications of research findings on the spouse and stepparent roles in remarriage. *Family Relations, 42,* 315–322.

Pasley, K., & Ihinger-Tallman, M. (1982). Stress in remarried families. *Family Perspective, 16,* 181–190.

Pasley, K., & Ihinger-Tallman, M. (1997). Stepfamilies: Continuing challenges for the schools. In T. N. Fairchild (Ed.), *Crisis intervention strategies for school-based helpers* (pp. 60–100). Springfield, IL: Charles C Thomas.

Pasley, K., & Moorefield, B. (2004). Stepfamilies: Changes and challenges. In M. Coleman & L. Ganong (Eds.), *Handbook of contemporary families: Considering the past, contemplating the future* (pp. 317–330). Thousand Oaks, CA: Sage.

Pasley, K., Rhoden, L., Visher, E. B., & Visher, J. S. (1996). Successful stepfamily therapy: Client's perspective. *Journal of Marital and Family Therapy, 22,* 343–357.

Pasley, K., Sandras, E., & Edmundson, M. E. (1994). The effects of financial management strategies on quality of family life in remarriage. *Journal of Family and Economic Issues, 15,* 52–70.

Portie, T., & Hill, N. R. (2005). Blended families: A critical review of the current research. *The Family Journal: Counseling and Therapy for Couples and Families, 13,* 445–451.

Pyke, K. D. (1994). Women's employment as a gift or a burden? Marital power across marriage, divorce, and remarriage. *Gender and Society, 8,* 73–91.

Rigg, A., & Pryor, J. (2007). Children's perceptions of families: What do they really think? *Children & Society, 21,* 17–30.

Schmeeckle, M. (2007). Gender dynamics in stepfamilies: Adult stepchildren's views. *Journal of Marriage and Family, 69,* 174–189.

Schrodt, P. (2006). Typological examination of communication competence and mental health in stepchildren. *Communication Monographs, 73,* 309–333.

Schrodt, P., Soliz, J., & Braithwaite, D. O. (2008). A social relations model of everyday talk and relational satisfaction in stepfamilies. *Communication Monographs, 75,* 190–217.

Seltzer, J. A. (2000). Families formed outside of marriage. *Journal of Marriage and the Family, 62,* 1247–1268.

Shelton, K. H., Walters, S. L., & Harold, G. T. (2008). Children's appraisals of relationships in stepfamilies and first families. In J. Pryor (Ed.), *The international handbook of stepfamilies: Policy and practice in legal, research, and clinical environments* (pp. 250–276). Hoboken, NJ: John Wiley & Sons.

Stanley, S. M., Markman, H. J., & Whitton, S. (2002). Communication, conflict, and commitment: Insights on the foundations for relationship success from a national survey. *Family Process, 41,* 659–675.

Stewart, S. D. (2005). Boundary ambiguity in stepfamilies. *Journal of Family Issues, 26,* 1002–1029.

Svare, G. M., Jay, S., & Mason, M. A. (2004). Stepparents on stepparenting: An exploratory study of stepparenting approaches. *Journal of Divorce & Remarriage, 41*(3/4), 81–97.

Teachman, J., & Tedrow, L. (2008). The demography of stepfamilies in the United States. In J. Pryor (Ed.), *The international handbook of stepfamilies: Policy and practice in legal, research, and clinical environments* (pp. 3–29). Hoboken, NJ: John Wiley & Sons.

Thomson, E., Mosely, J., Hanson, T. L., & McLanahan, S. (2001). Remarriage, cohabitation, and changes in mothering behavior. *Journal of Marriage and Family, 63,* 136–154.

Tillman, K. H. (2008). "Non-traditional" siblings and the academic outcomes of adolescents. *Social Science Research, 37,* 88–108.

U.S. Census Bureau. (n.d.). *Survey of Income and Program Participation (SIPP) Report, Table 3: Marital History for People 15 Years and Over, by Age and Sex: 2004.* Retrieved November 18, 2008, from http://www.census.gov/population/www/socdemo/ marrdiv.html.

vanEeden-Moorefield, B., Pasley, K., Dolan, E., & Engel, M. (2007). From divorce to remarriage: Financial management and security among remarried women. *Journal of Divorce & Remarriage, 47*(3/4), 21–42.

Visher, E. B., & Visher, J. S. (1988). *Old loyalties, new ties.* New York: Brunner/Mazel.

Visher, E. B., & Visher, J. S. (1996). *Therapy with stepfamilies.* New York: Brunner/Mazel.

Visher, E. B., Visher, J. S., & Pasley, K. (2003). Remarriage families and stepparenting. In F. Walsh (Ed.), *Normal family processes: Growing diversity and complexity* (3rd ed., pp. 153–175). New York: Guilford.

Vogler, C. (2005). Cohabiting couples: Rethinking money in the household at the begging of the twenty first century. *The Sociological Review, 53,* 1–29.

Vogler, C., Brockmann, M., & Wiggins, R. D. (2006). Intimate relationships and changing patterns of money management at the beginning of the twenty-first century. *The British Journal of Sociology, 57,* 455–482.

Vogler, C., Brockmann, M., & Wiggins, R. D. (2008). Managing money in new heterosexual forms of intimate relationships. *The Journal of Socio-Economics, 37,* 552–576.

Vogler, C., Lyonette, C., & Wiggins, R. D. (2008). Money, power, and spending decisions in intimate relationships. *The Sociological Review, 56,* 117–143.

Walsh, F. (2006). *Strengthening family resiliency* (2nd ed.). New York: Guilford.

Weaver, S. E., & Coleman, M. (2005). A mothering but not a mother role: A grounded theory study of nonresidential stepmother role. *Journal of Social and Personal Relationships, 22,* 477–497.

Weigel, D. J. (2008). The concept of family: An analysis of laypeople's views of family. *Journal of Family Issues, 29,* 1426–1447.

Weiner-Davis, M. (2002). *The divorce remedy: The proven 7-step program for saving your marriage.* New York: Simon & Schuster.

White, J. M., & Klein, D. M. (2008). *Family theories* (3rd ed.). Thousand Oaks, CA: Sage.

White, L. (1994). Growing up with single parents and stepparents: Long-term effects on family solidarity. *Journal of Marriage and the Family, 56,* 935–948.

White, M., & Epston, D. (1990). *Narrative means to therapeutic ends.* New York: Norton.

Whitton, S. W., Nicholson, J. M., & Markman, H. J. (2008). Research on interventions for stepfamily couples: The state of the field. In J. Pryor (Ed.), *The international handbook of stepfamilies: Policy and practice in legal, research, and clinical environments* (pp. 455–484). Hoboken, NJ: John Wiley.

12 Lesbian- and Gay-Parent Families

Development and Functioning

Abbie E. Goldberg

An ecological or systems approach to human development recognizes that individuals exist within, are influenced by, and interact with multiple intersecting contexts, including their families, friends, neighborhoods, communities, and workplaces, as well as broader societal institutions and ideologies (Bronfenbrenner, 1977; Whitechurch & Constantine, 1993). Such interactions shift throughout the life cycle, as people develop, establish relationships, and create families and communities. This approach is particularly useful in the study of lesbian, gay, and bisexual (LGB) individuals, whose lives, relationships, and families are increasingly visible in society (Savin-Williams, 2008). LGB individuals are increasingly recognized as members of numerous systems, including the health care system, the legal system, organizations and workplaces, schools, families, communities, and neighborhoods. By extension, LGB individuals necessarily impact and are impacted by these systems (e.g., they may experience stigmatization and stress as a function of their devalued status; Meyer, 2003). Thus, attention to LGB people's experiences and interactions within these varied contexts is warranted.

This chapter will discuss research on various aspects of lesbian, gay, and bisexual (LGB) people's experiences. Special attention will be paid to the situational and contextual forces that impact LGB persons' experiences as they move through the life course, particularly those that may pose challenges for sexual minorities and their families. Topically, this chapter will begin with a discussion of LGB people's "coming out" experiences, as well as their experiences forming and maintaining intimate relationships, with attention to the barriers they face in doing so (e.g., lack of recognition and stigma). Next, the multiple barriers that LGB people face in becoming parents will be discussed (e.g., challenges in accessing fertility treatments; discrimination in the adoption process) with attention to the resourcefulness that they display in the face of such barriers. Research on LGB parents and their children will be also be highlighted, with a focus on the stressors that LGB-parent families experience in relation to three major overlapping contexts: their families of origin, schools, and the legal system. Finally, a discussion of the implications of this research, along with suggestions for teachers, therapists, social workers, health care providers, and other professionals with regard to supporting LGB-parent families, will conclude the chapter.

Coming Out and Being Out

The process of "coming out" is one that is unique to the life experience and life cycle of sexual minorities. According to Cass's (1979) stage model (perhaps the most widely known framework for understanding the coming out process), individuals move from a state of questioning and confusion ("Could I be gay?") to acceptance and tolerance of one's nonheterosexual identity ("I am gay, and I will be okay") to pride and synthesis of their LGB identity ("This is a part of who I am and I need to let people know who I am"). Thus, the coming out process is conceptualized as one that is relatively linear and proceeds according to a series of predefined and continuous stages. Contemporary scholars, however, have suggested that coming out is an ongoing process that is not necessarily linear, but is often marked by contradiction and change and both pride and shame (e.g., Dindia, 1998). Furthermore, scholars have increasingly argued for a conceptual distinction between individual sexual identity and group membership identity (McCarn & Fassinger, 1996); that is, a woman may come to terms with her same-sex erotic feelings and intimacy (and may ultimately identify as a lesbian) without identifying with or becoming active within the lesbian community. Consequently, the failure to disclose one's sexual orientation in diverse contexts should not necessarily be interpreted as implying an incomplete sexual identity (Tomlinson & Fassinger, 2003).

Scholars have also increasingly emphasized the importance of considering the varied situational and contextual forces that impact individual decisions to come out. In deciding whether to disclose their sexual orientation, LGB people must consider their immediate social contexts and potential threats associated with disclosure (e.g., verbal or physical harassment, social humiliation and rejection, loss of housing or employment), how well they know the individual at hand, and the ease of concealment. Broader contextual factors, such as characteristics of one's family, friendship network, workplace environment, and community, will also influence the coming out process. Individuals from highly religious and/or politically conservative families, for example, may be particularly fearful of rejection and social alienation (Boon & Miller, 1999) and may resist or delay coming out to family members. Social class and occupation may also impact the degree to which individuals are "out" in various aspects of their lives. For example, working-class sexual minorities, who are often employed in male-dominated, blue-collar workplaces, may experience less freedom to be "out" at work than their middle-class counterparts (McDermott, 2006).

Race and ethnicity may also impact coming out. Racial and ethnic minority sexual minorities may face multiple forms of marginalization, because they are vulnerable to racism in the gay/lesbian community and to homophobia within their own families and communities (Green, 2007). For example, racial minority sexual minorities may be stared at or whispered about (indirect racism) or refused entry (direct racism) in gay bars that serve predominantly white clienteles (Green, 2007; Greene & Boyd-Franklin, 1996). Likewise, racial/ethnic minority gay men and lesbians are often aware of hostile attitudes regarding homosexuality within their immediate and extended families of origin, and thus may hesitate to come out because they do not wish to lose the emotional and material support that family members provide (Green, 2007) and/or because they do not wish to show disrespect for their cultural upbringing. For example, Merighi and Grimes (2000) found that African American, Mexican American, and Vietnamese American gay men struggled with wanting to establish their own gay identity while also respecting certain cultural norms and ideals. They were aware that their families would respond to their coming out as the "end to the family lineage" and as a source of shame and embarrassment; therefore, they were cautious about making their sexual identity widely known.

And yet, coming out may be important for multiple reasons. First, failure to come out may restrict individuals' ability to meet potential partners as well as their ability to maintain healthy relationships. Second, closeting (i.e., hiding one's sexual orientation) necessarily limits the amount of support that sexual minorities have available to them (Caron & Ulin, 1997), which may create feelings of isolation and intrapersonal conflict, and, in turn, lead to mental health problems (Garnets & Kimmel, 2003). At the same time, closeting oneself is a protective and adaptive strategy in certain contexts, and men and women who are not "out" in all areas of their lives are not necessarily less psychologically healthy than those who are (Beals & Peplau, 2001). Furthermore, sexual minorities who closet themselves in certain situations do not necessarily experience ambivalence or inner conflict, but instead recognize that such closeting is often necessary to survival (Anderson & Holliday, 2004).

Same-Sex Relationships

Coming out may precede or occur alongside the formation of same-sex relationships. Same-sex unions share many characteristics with heterosexual unions, but they are also defined by certain unique characteristics, including the partners' shared gender, the stigmatized nature of homosexuality, and the absence of legal, structural, and social supports to protect and maintain these relationships. Despite the stigmatized nature of these relationships and in contradiction to stereotypes of lesbians and gay men as incapable of forming lasting relationships (Baker, 2005), many lesbians and gay men are members of committed same-sex relationships. According to the 2000 U.S. Census, at least 1.2 million people reported being in same-sex intimate-partner relationships and sharing a household (Simmons & O'Neil, 2001); these estimates are probably conservative, because many same-sex couples likely concealed their relationships on the census. In addition, studies have begun to compare the quality of same-sex relationships and heterosexual relationships (e.g., in terms of perceived relationship quality and satisfaction) and have found few differences between the two groups (Kurdek, 1998; Mackey, Diemer, & O'Brien, 2004). Several studies have found that lesbian couples report higher relationship quality than heterosexual couples (Balsam, Beauchaine, Rothblum, & Solomon, 2008; Kurdek, 2001), a finding that may in part reflect the absence of structural barriers that govern heterosexual relationships; that is, in the absence of fundamental relationship "constraints" such as legal support, family support, and children, relationships that are not highly rewarding are perhaps more easily terminated. Indeed, Kurdek (2006) found that gay and lesbian couples were more likely to separate than were heterosexual married couples with children (i.e., couples with multiple institutionalized barriers to leaving). On the other hand, gay and lesbian *parents* may be no more likely to separate than their heterosexual counterparts. A study of 73 lesbian couples with children found that 30 couples had split up by the time their children were 10 years old (Gartrell et al., 2005, 2006), which is comparable to rates among heterosexual couples (national survey statistics indicate that at least one-third of heterosexual couples terminate their first marriages within 10 years; Bramlett & Mosher, 2001). More research is needed to examine how access to marriage and civil unions, and the presence of children, individually and collectively contribute to relationship stability among lesbian and gay couples.

Characteristics of Healthy Relationships: Same-Sex Couples

The characteristics of healthy or stable relationships among same-sex couples may lend insight into the nature and dynamics of these relationships. That is, what factors appear to promote relationship quality? By extension, what variables appear to contribute to instability in same-sex relationships?

Equality

Some scholars suggest that perceptions of egalitarianism in the relationship, that is, the extent to which partners perceive themselves as sharing decision-making power, household management, and so forth, may be particularly important in same-sex couples, in that both partners may be particularly sensitive to power imbalances due to their stigmatized status in society (Blumstein & Schwartz, 1983). Lesbian partners, in particular, may be especially likely to value equality in their intimate relationships, given their common socialization as women and, therefore, their exposure to inequity in a variety of interpersonal and institutional contexts (Blumstein & Schwartz, 1983). Research does suggest that lesbians tend to place a greater valuing of equality in their appraisals of "ideal" relationships (Kurdek, 1995) and are also more likely to perceive equal power in their relationships, compared to heterosexual and gay couples (Kurdek, 1998). Additionally, lesbians and gay men tend to share housework more equitably with their partners compared to heterosexual couples (Solomon, Rothblum, & Balsam, 2005). This sharing appears to be facilitated by financial, educational, occupational, and social resources. Carrington (2002) studied the division of labor among gay and lesbian couples and found that equal sharing of domestic labor was most common among financially comfortable couples who relied on paid help, and also among couples in which both partners had flexible schedules.

Perceptions of equality have in turn been linked to relationship outcomes in same-sex couples. For example, Kurdek (1998) found that higher perceived equality was associated with higher relationship satisfaction among same-sex couples. Furthermore, Kurdek (2007) found that lesbian and gay partners' satisfaction with the division of labor affected relationship satisfaction and stability over time, via the mediating influence of perceived equality in the relationship. Increasing discrepancies between ideal and actual levels of equality over time have also been linked to declines in relationship quality for both lesbian and gay partners (Kurdek, 1995).

Conflict and Difference

Few couples can avoid any conflict or disagreement in their relationships. Indeed, lesbian, gay, and heterosexual couples tend to report a similar frequency of arguments in their relationships (Peplau & Fingerhut, 2007) and to disagree about similar topics, such as finances, sex, and household tasks (Kurdek, 2006). Likewise, research suggests that higher levels of conflict are associated with lower levels of relationship quality in both heterosexual and same-sex relationships (Balsam et al., 2008).

Some sources of conflict may be specific to same-sex couples. Given the unique relational context of same-sex relationships (e.g., partners' shared gender and shared status as stigmatized minorities), same-sex couples may encounter certain unique interpersonal patterns and challenges with regard to conflict management. Mackey, O'Brien, and Mackey (1997) found that gay men in long-term committed relationships tended to avoid discussing their thoughts, feelings, and frustrations until difficulties threatened their relationships. Perhaps such dynamics arise from the "double dose" of male socialization that characterizes gay men's relationships (i.e., men are socialized to mask or avoid emotional distress and vulnerability). Lesbian couples struggled in other areas (Mackey et al., 1997). For example, in the early stages of their relationships, women often avoided confronting interpersonal differences in an effort to maintain relational harmony. As their relationships progressed, however, they became less avoidant of these differences and were increasingly likely to address them. The authors suggest that this change might have been facilitated by women's declining fears of being abandoned by their partners and greater perceived security in their current relationships.

Lesbian and gay partners may also differ from one another in important ways that may cause conflict. For example, racial/ethnic differences between partners may create the potential for stress and misunderstanding. Specifically, racial/ethnic minority lesbians and gay men with white partners may experience alienation within their relationships if they feel that their partners cannot empathize with the intersecting forces of sexism, heterosexism, and racism that they face (Pearlman, 1996). Likewise, white partners may feel guilty about internalized and/or institutional racism and attempt to compensate for their privilege, a strategy that may leave both partners feeling frustrated and angry. Furthermore, interracial same-sex couples may be more identifiable than two women or men of the same ethnic group, thereby eliciting strong homophobic and racist reactions from outsiders (Greene & Boyd-Franklin, 1996) and possibly placing them at risk for victimization. This perceived risk may lead couples to avoid racially homogeneous settings and to prefer diverse racial atmospheres (Steinbugler, 2005). Despite the challenges that interracial same-sex couples face, however, they often maintain healthy committed relationships. For example, Peplau, Cochran, and Mays (1997) found that, on average, interracial couples did not differ from same-race couples in terms of relationship satisfaction. Thus, many interracial same-sex couples are able to successfully navigate their differences, and the stigma their relationships endure, to create satisfying and lasting relationships.

Social Support and Recognition

The relationships of lesbians and gay men are necessarily impacted by their social networks. Specifically, the support (or lack of support) they receive from their families of origin, their friends, their communities, their workplaces, and from their state and national governments has profound implications for their individual and relational health. Research indicates that lesbian and gay partners perceive less social support from family members compared to heterosexual couples (Kurdek, 2001), which may have implications for the quality of their intimate relationships (Caron & Ulin, 1997) and mental health (Goldberg & Smith, 2008). Certain sexual minorities are particularly at risk for diminished familial support; for example, racial/ethnic minority sexual minorities and gay men and lesbians in interracial relationships are vulnerable to nonsupport (Greene, 2000). Additionally, gay couples in which one or both partners are diagnosed with HIV/AIDS frequently experience rejection by and alienation from their families of origin (Paul, Hays, & Coates, 1995).

Lesbians and gay men also face legal nonsupport and lack of recognition. Their relationships are denied many of the legal protections and securities that are routinely afforded to heterosexual couples (Herek, 2006). Denial of marriage rights disallows them of numerous benefits, including automatic financial decision-making authority on behalf of a spouse, the ability to make medical decisions for an incapacitated partner, and the ability to file joint income tax returns (Pawelski et al., 2006). On a symbolic level, the failure to grant legal recognition to committed same-sex couples undermines the commitment that partners have made to each other and may threaten the stability of their unions. Likewise, legal and social recognition of same-sex couples has the capacity to strengthen gay/lesbian relationships and, in turn, individual well-being (Herek, 2006). Solomon and colleagues (2005) studied couples that had obtained civil unions in Vermont and found that 54% of same-sex couples reported positive changes in their love and commitment for each other as a result of having a civil union. Thus, the execution of legal documents may have a protective and stabilizing function with regard to relationships (Herek, 2006). Couples that are unable to acquire civil unions or civil marriages can, of course, pursue certain legal safeguards to alleviate their vulnerability (e.g., wills, powers of attorney for health care and finances, the naming of a health care surrogate, and advanced medical directives); however, the cost of obtaining a lawyer to obtain such safeguards is prohibitive for many LGB persons and couples. Hence, financially disadvantaged LGB persons and couples are rendered particularly vulnerable in the absence of civil marriage.

Becoming Parents, Forming Families

Many lesbians and gay men become parents in the context of heterosexual relationships; that is, they become parents before coming out as gay/lesbian. Other lesbians and gay men become parents in the context of same-sex committed relationships,[1] a phenomenon that has become increasingly common due in part to advancements in reproductive technology and increasingly tolerant attitudes regarding gay/lesbian parenting and adoption (Savin-Williams, 2008). The U.S. Census estimates that approximately 1 in 20 male same-sex couples and 1 in 5 female same-sex couples were raising children in 1990; in 2000, these figures had risen to 1 in 5 for male couples and 1 in 3 for female couples (Gates & Ost, 2004). Furthermore, of note is that gay/lesbian parents currently represent a sizeable minority of *adoptive* parents. Specifically, of the quarter million children that are living in households headed by same-sex couples in the United States, 4.2% are either adopted or foster children, almost double the figure for heterosexual couples (Gates & Ost, 2004). Again, these estimates are likely conservative, due to the fact that some individuals chose to conceal the same-sex nature of their relationship on the census.

Alternative Insemination

Lesbian and gay couples who wish to become parents may consider several potential routes to parenthood: alternative insemination (among lesbian couples), adoption, foster care, surrogacy, or more complex parenting arrangements (e.g., a lesbian couple and a gay couple may choose to coparent). The most common routes to parenthood in intentional lesbian- and gay-parent families are alternative insemination and adoption. Each of these presents unique challenges. Lesbian couples that choose insemination must decide who will carry the child, a decision that may have profound legal implications, in that the biological mother is automatically the legal parent, and only about half of U.S. states allow the nonbiological mother to become a legal parent to her child via a second-parent adoption[2] (Pawelski et al., 2006). Lesbian couples also confront legal anxieties in the context of deciding whether to use sperm from a known or unknown donor. Indeed, women who choose unknown donors often do so out of a desire to avoid potential custody challenges (Goldberg, 2006). Women who pursue insemination via known donors may also experience legal worries but at the same time feel strongly that their child deserves access to their biological heritage (Touroni & Coyle, 2002). They may also choose known donors because they wish to avoid interfacing with official, potentially heterosexist institutions such as sperm banks and fertility clinics (Touroni & Coyle, 2002).

Social change, combined with the increasing visibility of lesbian mothers, has gradually facilitated greater awareness of (and more sensitive treatment of) lesbians who seek out donor insemination; however, reports of insensitive and inappropriate treatment by health care providers continue to appear in the literature (Goldberg, 2006; Wilton & Kaufman, 2000). For example, doctors may refuse to inseminate based on moral or ethical grounds (Goldberg, 2006). Additionally, some insurance carriers justify their decision to cover only married women on the basis that they treat infertility, and when a woman in a married couple seeks to inseminate, it is because of a medical problem "within the couple" (e.g., genetic risk) or because of infertility "within the couple" (e.g., the husband is infertile) (Agigian, 2004). Sexual minority women also routinely encounter clinic forms that are inappropriate for lesbian and bisexual patients (e.g., they assume a heterosexual two-parent family), as well as health care providers who fail to acknowledge the nonbirthing partner at office visits and prenatal classes (Goldberg, 2006; Wilton & Kaufman, 2000).

Adoption

Some lesbian and gay couples pursue adoption as a means of becoming parents. Specifically, couples may pursue international adoption, public domestic adoption (through the child welfare system), and private domestic adoption (e.g., through a lawyer or agency). Private domestic adoptions may in turn be "open" or "closed." Open adoption (which is increasingly common in U.S. private domestic adoptions) refers to a continuum of openness that allows birth parents and adoptive parents to have information about and to communicate with each other before and/or after placement of the child. Closed adoptions refer to arrangements in which the birth parents and adoptive parents do not exchange identifying information and there is no contact whatsoever between the birth parents and the adoptive parents.

Lesbian and gay couples may choose private domestic open adoption because they are attracted to the possibility of maintaining contact with birth parents and/or being able to provide their child with (possibly ongoing) information about their birth parent(s) (Goldberg, Downing, & Sauck, 2007). They may also be drawn to open adoption because of the greater likelihood of adopting an infant compared to international or public adoption (Goldberg et al., 2007). On the other hand, prospective adoptive parents may select international adoption to avoid the long wait associated with domestic private adoptions of healthy infants (Hollingsworth & Ruffin, 2002). Gay and lesbian prospective parents may be particularly drawn to international adoption for this reason; that is, many sexual minorities suspect that birth mothers (who often choose the adoptive parents in open adoption arrangements) are unlikely to choose them because they are gay, and they therefore worry they will end up waiting "forever" (Goldberg et al., 2007). Such concerns are not unrealistic: Some birth parents specifically protest the placement of their child with gay/lesbian parents (Brodzinsky, 2003). However, gay and lesbian couples who pursue international adoption must weigh such considerations against the reality that if they choose to adopt internationally, they must closet their relationship; no country allows same-sex couples to adopt, and therefore same-sex couples who choose this route must choose one partner to pose as a single parent. This situation can create intra- and interpersonal tension and stress, in that one partner is virtually invisible in the adoption process (Goldberg et al., 2007). The nonlegal partner may in turn experience feelings of inadequacy, invisibility, anxiety, or jealousy, whereas the legal partner may feel burdened with feelings of guilt and/or overresponsibility. Finally, gay/lesbian couples who seek to adopt through the public welfare system are typically motivated in part by finances and/or altruistic reasons (e.g., the wish to give a child a permanent family) (Downing, Richardson, Kinkler, & Goldberg, 2009). Additionally, gay men and lesbians may believe that they have the best chance of adopting via the public welfare system, in that the number of children in foster care far exceeds the number of heterosexual prospective adoptive parents. And yet, while it is true that gay men and lesbians may be welcomed by some child welfare workers and social service agencies, reports of insensitive practices by child welfare workers do appear in the literature (e.g., Goldberg et al., 2007).

Upon settling on an adoption route, prospective adoptive parents must then choose an agency and/or lawyer, a process that can be particularly challenging and time-consuming for gay/lesbian couples. Given their vulnerability in the adoption process, it is not surprising that many lesbians and gay men expend significant time and effort researching potential adoption agencies for evidence that they are open to working with sexual minorities (Goldberg et al., 2007). Indeed, one survey found that 35% of adoption agencies did not even accept applications from gay men and lesbians (Brodzinsky, 2003). Furthermore, even if gay men and lesbians select agencies that they believe to be accepting and affirming, they may still encounter heterosexism further into the adoption process. Sexual minorities often encounter forms, materials, and support groups that seem to focus on heterosexual couples only (e.g., they presume a history of infertility) (Goldberg et al., 2007). They may also confront adoption professionals who hold discriminatory stereotypes and attitudes toward gay men and lesbians and who sabotage potential adoptive placements. And because of their vulnerability in the adoption process, gay and lesbian prospective parents may be silent about such incidents, so as not to "make waves" and further jeopardize their chances of adopting.

Other Challenges

All gay men and lesbians, regardless of what route to parenthood they choose, are vulnerable to additional challenges as they make their way toward parenthood. For example, lesbians and gay men may not benefit from the societal support that heterosexual couples receive when they become parents: They may face nonsupport from other (heterosexual) parents, as well as resistance from their families of origin. Lesbian couples who become parents via insemination also encounter the unique challenge of negotiating various asymmetries in their relationship, that is, during pregnancy, with regard to breastfeeding, and in the partners' genetic relatedness to the child (Goldberg & Perry-Jenkins, 2007). Such asymmetries may create feelings of jealousy on the part of the nonbirth mother and/or conflicts over who the child "belongs" to. Inseminating lesbian couples may also negotiate legal asymmetries, in that the birth mother may be the only partner legally related to the child. Adoptive lesbian and gay couples start out on more equal footing, although legal inequities (e.g., in couples who live in states in which same-sex couples cannot coadopt and must therefore choose one partner to adopt as a single parent) can cause tensions and conflicts. Such issues are initially negotiated during the transitional stage of becoming parents, but likely continue to be relevant as lesbians and gay men shape their lives as parents and families.

There is evidence that many lesbians and gay men adopt transracially and/or transculturally (Gates, Badgett, Macomber, & Chambers, 2007). Specifically, national data sets suggest that 47% of adopted children of same-sex couples are nonwhite, compared to 37% of adopted children of married heterosexual couples (Gates et al., 2007). Lesbian/gay transracial adoptive households may face additional challenges related to their multiply stigmatized and highly visible family structure, in that these families are vulnerable to the stresses associated with both heterosexism *and* racism. For example, both parents and children may experience discrimination and rejection on the basis of their family's racial/ethnic makeup as well as on the basis of parents' sexual orientation. Because of their visibility, they may also be faced with intrusive questions about the whys and hows of their family's creation.

Gay- and Lesbian-Parent Families: Experiences and Challenges

A growing body of research has focused on parent and child functioning within LGB-parent households. This research has served to dispel concerns about the potentially negative impact of growing up with LGB parents and has also provided insight into the dynamics and functioning of LGB household members. Despite concerns that the sexual orientation of gay parents will negatively affect children in both indirect and direct ways, research is consistent in indicating that sexuality is not relevant to men's and women's parenting capacities and parent–child relationships. Specifically, studies that have compared lesbian, gay, and heterosexual parents in terms of parenting stress, parenting skills, and parental warmth and involvement have found few differences based on family structure (Bos, van Balen, & van den Boom, 2007; Golombok et al., 2003; Leung, Erich, & Kanenberg, 2005). Some studies have found that sexual minorities may have less conventional parenting values than heterosexual women and men. Specifically, lesbian mothers appear to be less interested in fostering conformity in their children (Bos et al., 2007) and tend to have more gender-neutral preferences for their children's play, compared to heterosexual mothers (Hoeffer, 1981), and may also be more accepting of a range of sexualities in their children (Tasker & Golombok, 1997).

Similarly, studies suggest that children who grow up with LGB parents do not appear to differ remarkably from children of heterosexual parents in terms of their emotional and behavioral adjustment. Studies have found few differences between the two groups in terms of self-esteem, depression, behavioral problems, or social functioning (Golombok et al., 2003; Tasker & Golombok, 1997; Wainright, Russell, & Patterson, 2004). Furthermore, although Tasker and Golombok (1997) found that young adults with lesbian mothers were more likely to express openness to and acceptance of same-sex relationships, they were no more likely to *identify* as gay as compared to young adults with heterosexual mothers. Other research has also found that children of lesbian and gay parents are no more likely to assume a homosexual identification compared to children of heterosexual parents (e.g., Bailey, Bobrow, Wolfe, & Mikach, 1995).

The fact that LGB parents and their children demonstrate such positive outcomes suggests remarkable resilience, given that they develop in a heterosexist society and are exposed to stigma and nonsupport in multiple intersecting, overlapping contexts. Specifically, gay/lesbian parents and their children are vulnerable to nonsupport and alienation from their families of origin. They are also vulnerable to misunderstanding and mistreatment in the school context, and also confront lack of recognition and support in the legal sphere.

The Family Context

Lesbian and gay parents may perceive less support from members of their family of origin than do heterosexual parents (Goldberg & Smith, 2008), but tend to report greater support from family members than lesbian/gay nonparents (DeMino, Appleby, & Fisk, 2007). It seems that family members may become more supportive once a child enters the picture. For example, Goldberg (2006) found that lesbians' perceptions of support from their own and their partners' families increased across the transition to parenthood. Thus, some family members may push their feelings about homosexuality aside and seek to repair problematic or damaged relationships in the interest of developing a relationship with a new grandchild or niece or nephew. Of course, not all family members become more supportive and involved across the transition to parenthood. Some LGB parents confront reduced support from their families upon announcing their intention to parent. For example, their families may express opposition to their decision to parent on moral and/or religious grounds, or because they believe that life as a gay-parent family will be too difficult.

The level of support that LGB-parent families receive may depend on whether the child is biologically related to the family of origin. Some research suggests that biological mothers' families may be more involved in children's lives than nonbiological mothers' families (Patterson, Hurt, & Mason, 1998). Importantly, the establishment of *legal* ties may foster greater investment and involvement by extended-family members: Hequembourg and Farrell (1999) observed that when nonbiological lesbian mothers secured second-parent adoption rights (thereby legally validating their relationship with their children), their own parents often became more willing to acknowledge them as parents and to emotionally invest in their grandchildren.

Families' level of support can also vary depending on the racial/ethnic match between parent and child, such that gay and lesbian parents who adopt across racial lines may encounter particular resistance and nonsupport from family members (Johnson & O'Connor, 2002). Family members may be uncomfortable acknowledging their new grandchild or niece or nephew based on their own racist beliefs. They may also find it difficult to embrace a child that looks different from them. Additionally, family members may experience (and express) concerns about the many challenges and vulnerabilities that the children might be exposed to because of their multiple marginalized statuses (Johnson & O'Connor, 2002).

The School Context

Both LGB parents and their children are also vulnerable to alienation and stigma within the school setting. A recent study conducted by the Gay, Lesbian, and Straight Education Network (GLSEN) that focused on lesbian, gay, bisexual, and transgendered (LGBT) families' experiences in education found that more than half (53%) of over 500 LGBT parents described various forms of exclusion from their children's school communities (i.e., being excluded or prevented from fully participating in school activities and events, being excluded by school policies and procedures, and being ignored) (Kosciw & Diaz, 2008). For example, parents were told that they could not be aides in their children's classrooms, that only one parent was allowed to attend a school event, and that their offers to assist with creating a more inclusive classroom (e.g., reading *Heather Has Two Mommies* to the class) were not welcome. Furthermore, 26% of LGBT parents reported being mistreated by other parents (e.g., being stared at or ignored). Importantly, parents whose children's schools had comprehensive safe school policies (i.e., policies that protect both students and their parents from harassment or exclusion based on actual or perceived sexual orientation or gender) tended to report lower levels of mistreatment than parents whose children's schools did not have such policies (Kosciw & Diaz, 2008).

GLSEN's survey also found that 40% of the 154 students surveyed reported being verbally harassed in school because of their family (e.g., being called names such as "fag," "lesbo," and "devil's daughter"). Furthermore, although the vast majority of students in the study identified as heterosexual, 38% reported being verbally harassed at school because of their real or perceived sexual orientation (i.e., they were assumed to be gay because their parents were gay) (Kosciw & Diaz, 2008). Such data would appear to suggest that peer teasing and bullying are quite common; however, it is important to recognize that such experiences tend to be relatively prominent at certain developmental periods and relatively minimal at others. Gartrell et al. (2000) found that 18% of mothers reported that their 5-year-old children had experienced some type of homophobia from peers or teachers. However, by the age of 10, almost half of children had reportedly experienced some form of homophobia (e.g., teasing) (Gartrell et al., 2005). Similarly, a study of gay and lesbian parents and their children in Australia found that no children in kindergarten through Grade 2 had experienced bullying; 44% of children in Grades 3 to 6 had experienced bullying related to their parents' sexual orientation; 45% of children in Grades 7 to 10 had experienced bullying or harassment; and 14% of children in Grades 11 to 12 had experienced bullying (Ray & Gregory, 2001). Those who did not encounter bullying attributed it to the geographical area that they lived in or the type of school that they attended (e.g., progressive private schools). Thus, middle- and upper-middle-class LGB parents may be at an advantage with regard to protecting their children from bullying: Their social and financial resources allow them some choice in where they live, and they may therefore favor areas and schools that are known to be more inclusive and progressive.

The Legal Context

The legal sphere also presents challenges for LGB parents and their families. First, gay and lesbian parents lack legal recognition of their relationships in the vast majority of states. Second, they may also lack legal recognition of their parental status. Specifically, many states do not allow openly gay/lesbian couples to coadopt (i.e., to adopt their child jointly). Gay and lesbian couples living in these states must select one partner to perform the official adoption (as a single parent), resulting in a situation in which the child has only one legal parent. Fortunately, in approximately half of U.S. states, the as-of-yet nonlegal partner may complete a second-parent adoption, thereby enabling their child to have two legal parents (Pawelski et al., 2006). Similarly, lesbian couples that create their families via insemination may seek a second-parent adoption for the nonbiological, nonlegal partner. However, many same-sex couples live in states where they are unable to pursue second-parent adoptions; thus, many LGB-parent families consist of one legal parent and one parent whose relationship to their child is not legally recognized or protected. Such lack of recognition is problematic in that the nonlegal parent's parental status is constantly being questioned and/or denied (e.g., by their child's school, their pediatrician, family members, etc.), which can create feelings of insecurity and vulnerability in the nonlegal parent, the child, and the family system in general.

Furthermore, the inequality in parents' legal relationships to their children can have devastating consequences if couples dissolve their relationships. In such situations, the parental status of the legal parent (who is often also the biological parent) is virtually always affirmed. In one study of 77 lesbian couples that consisted of a birth mother and a nonbirth mother, 30 couples had separated by the time that their children were 10. Of these 30 couples, custody was shared after 13 of them separated, and the birth mother retained sole or primary custody in 15 cases (Gartrell et al., 2006). Couples in which the comother had obtained a second-parent adoption were more likely to share custody, thereby highlighting the importance of legal supports for family stability (and, in turn, child well-being).

_____ Conclusions and Suggestions for Practitioners

Same-sex couples and their children are vulnerable to social and legal challenges at multiple stages of the life course and in multiple settings. Such challenges undermine the integrity of sexual minorities' family relationships and threaten their emotional and physical well-being. And yet, LGB parents and their children demonstrate remarkable resilience in the face of such challenges. This resilience is likely facilitated by the formation of strong and stable relationships that are characterized by equality, mutuality, and compassion (Connolly, 2005; Kurdek, 1998); access to and engagement with an active and/or visible LGBT community (Russell & Richards, 2003); and perceptions of support and affirmation from one's family and/or friendship network (Russell & Richards, 2003). Indeed, LGB individuals and parents appear to demonstrate many of the characteristics that are associated with resiliency, including the ability to create reciprocal and meaningful support systems, a driving will to overcome and triumph over adversity, persistent hope, and a sense of purpose (Golding, 2006). For example, there is evidence that lesbians and gay men seek to establish strong social networks, particularly in the absence of unqualified support from their family of origin (Golding, 2006). Additionally, lesbians and gay men are increasingly likely to pursue and successfully achieve parenthood, despite the numerous obstacles and challenges that they encounter along the way (thereby demonstrating their driving will to triumph over adversity) (Goldberg, 2006). Many lesbians and gay men are also characterized by a strong commitment to parenthood, viewing parenthood as their main purpose in life (Lassiter, Dew, Newton, Hays, & Yarbrough, 2006).

Of course, the fact that LGB parents and their children demonstrate remarkable resilience by no means legitimates the heterosexism that they face in their everyday lives. Scholars, practitioners, educators, and policymakers are urged to work on behalf of LGB persons and families to identify and ameliorate the conditions that underlie and perpetuate the social stress and oppression that sexual minorities must endure. By destabilizing systems of oppression and inequality, we can begin to improve the social conditions in which sexual minorities live.

Therapists and practitioners who work with same-sex couples should be attentive to the unique dimensions of their relationships as compared to heterosexual relationships, but at the same time should remain cognizant of the ways in which same-sex couples' relational difficulties may reflect "universal" relationship conflicts. Furthermore, therapists should be sensitive to the many variables that impact the formation, nature, and stability of same-sex relationships, such as similarities/differences between partners in terms of outness, race, and so on. Finally, and perhaps most importantly, therapists should maintain a heightened awareness of the ways in which both subtle and overt forms of societal stigma and exclusion may contribute to existing individual and relational problems. For example, in treating a socially isolated lesbian couple, a therapist should recognize the potential systemic causes of their isolation and should resist blaming the couple for their lack of social connectedness.

Practitioners and institutions (e.g., gynecologists, social workers, adoption agencies) that work with lesbian and gay couples during the transitional stage of becoming parents should strive to communicate a philosophy of inclusion and acceptance. Pink triangles or rainbow decals can be posted inconspicuously in hospitals, offices, and waiting rooms. Facilitators of prenatal education classes and adoption support groups can strive to utilize inclusive language (e.g., terms such as *partner*) (Goldberg, 2006). Additionally, practitioners (e.g., lawyers, social workers) who work with prospective lesbian and gay parents should aim to educate couples in advance about the legal barriers that they may face (e.g., in obtaining coparent or second-parent adoptions). Specifically, they should assist them in understanding the consequences of such barriers (e.g., the fact that their child will have one legal parent) as well as considering other legal safeguards (e.g., living wills, medical powers of attorney, financial powers of attorney, hospital visitation authorizations) to offset the challenges posed by these barriers.

School educators and personnel are encouraged to take steps to reduce stigmatization of LGBT-parent families by actively creating a climate of acceptance and inclusion of these families within schools and classrooms. School educators and administrators, for example, may choose to seek out ongoing training and education about diverse families (e.g., via organizations such as the Gay, Lesbian, and Straight Education Network: www.glsen.org). Such training will support them in advocating for diverse families and actively fighting discrimination and prejudice against children resulting from their parents' sexual orientations. Educators can create "safe spaces" at their schools by visibly marking places and people that are "safe" for children with LGBT parents (as well as LGBT students themselves). This is usually accomplished via a pink triangle sticker or some other easily identifiable LGBT symbol. When students, staff members, and teachers place these stickers on their bags, offices, or lockers, this serves as a symbol of affirmation and indicates that they are "safe" to approach for support or guidance. Educators and school personnel can also train student allies who wish to be involved in building safe spaces and creating a more affirmative school climate. School personnel may also wish to educate the larger school community about the importance of maintaining safe spaces for all students affected by anti-LGBT bias.

Finally, at the policy and legal levels, greater protections are clearly needed for LGB-parent families. State laws that discriminate against gay- and lesbian-parent families (e.g., by preventing gay and lesbian parents from adopting their own children) render families vulnerable to stigma and serve to legitimize the treatment of LGB-parent family members as second-class citizens. Widespread legal recognition of LGB-parent families will help to foster acceptance of these families, ensure the protection of these families via the provision of standard rights and benefits, and promote the stability and security of LGB-parent families and their children, thereby contributing to their health and well-being.

Notes

1. These families are often referred to as "planned" or "intentional" lesbian- and gay-parent families

2. Second-parent adoptions allow nonlegal parents to adopt their partners' children without requiring the biological parents to give up their parental rights. These adoptions have historically been used by heterosexual stepparents to adopt their wives' or husbands' children. Some courts have interpreted the second-parent adoption to apply in same-sex couples, whereas others have not.

Suggested Resources

For LGB Couples and Parents

Clifford, D., Hertz, F., & Doskow, E. (2007). *A legal guide for lesbian and gay couples* (10th ed.). Berkeley, CA: Nolo. A resource for couples containing legal information relevant to children, domestic partnership benefits, marriage, powers of attorney, wills and estate planning, contracts, and property.

Lev, A. I. (2004). *The complete lesbian and gay parenting guide.* New York: Penguin Press. Provides in-depth information for lesbian and gay parents and prospective parents on issues as diverse as alternative insemination, adoption, surrogacy, solo parenting, and adjusting to the realities of parenting.

For Researchers and Practitioners

Johnson, S. M., & O'Connor, E. (2002). *The gay baby boom: The psychology of gay parenthood.* New York: New York University Press.

Kosciw, J. G., & Diaz, E. M. (2008). *Involved, invisible, ignored: The experiences of lesbian, gay, bisexual, and transgender parents and their children in our nation's K–12 schools.* New York: Gay, Lesbian, and Straight Education Network.

Relevant Informational Web Sites

The Human Rights Campaign (HRC) is the largest national LGBT civil rights organization. The HRC Web site contains research, resources, and information about a wide range of topics, including coming out, being gay in the military, gay parenting, and adoption laws and gay-friendly adoption agencies: www.hrc.org

The Family Equality Council (formerly Family Pride) is the national advocacy organization committed to securing family equality for LGBT parents, guardians, and allies. The Web site contains links to blogs and parenting support groups: www.familyequality.org

The Gay, Lesbian, and Straight Education Network (GLSEN) is an organization dedicated to research, education, and advocacy pertaining to the safety of LGBT students and children of LGBT parents. They have published several reports that are intended to inform educators, policymakers, and the public about the school-related experiences of LGBT parents and their children, as part of GLSEN's continued efforts to ensure safe and harassment-free school environments for all children. These reports can be accessed via their Web site: www.glsen.org

Children of Lesbians and Gays Everywhere (COLAGE) is a national organization that serves youth with LGBT parents. The Web site provides advice and resources to youth with LGBT parents; it also serves as a clearinghouse for information and research related to children of LGBT parents: www.colage.org

References

Agigian, A. (2004). *Baby steps: How lesbian alternative insemination is changing the world.* Middletown, CT: Wesleyan University Press.

Anderson, S. C., & Holliday, M. (2004). Normative passing in the lesbian community: An exploratory study. *Journal of Gay & Lesbian Social Services, 17,* 25–38.

Bailey, J. M., Bobrow, D., Wolfe, M., & Mikach, S. (1995). Sexual orientation of adult sons of gay fathers. *Developmental Psychology, 31,* 124–129.

Baker, P. (2005). *Public discourses of gay men.* London: Routledge.

Balsam, K. F., Beauchaine, T. P., Rothblum, E. D., & Solomon, S. (2008). Three-year follow-up of same-sex couples who had civil unions in Vermont, same-sex couples not in civil unions, and heterosexual married couples. *Developmental Psychology, 44,* 102–116.

Beals, K. P., & Peplau, L. A. (2001). Social involvement disclosure of sexual orientation, and the quality of lesbian relationships. *Psychology of Women Quarterly, 25,* 10–19.

Blumstein, P., & Schwartz, P. (1983). *American couples: Money, work, sex.* New York: William Morrow.

Boon, S., & Miller, R. J. (1999). Exploring the links between interpersonal trust and the reasons underlying gay and bisexual males' disclosure of their sexual orientation to their mothers. *Journal of Homosexuality, 37,* 45–68.

Bos, H. M. W., van Balen, F., & van den Boom, D. C. (2007). Child adjustment and parenting in planned lesbian-parent families. *American Journal of Orthopsychiatry, 77,* 38–48.

Bramlett, M. D., & Mosher, W. D. (2001). *First marriage, dissolution, divorce and remarriage: United States: Advance data from vital and health statistics, No. 323.* Hyattsville, MD: National Center for Health Statistics.

Brodzinsky, D. M. (2003). *Adoption by lesbians and gay men: A national survey of adoption agency policies, practices and attitudes.* Retrieved on March 27, 2008, from http://www.adoptioninstitute.org/whowe/Gay%20and%20Lesbian%20Adoption1.html

Bronfenbrenner, U. (1977). Toward an experimental ecology of human development. *American Psychologist, 32,* 513–531.

Caron, S. L., & Ulin, M. (1997). Closeting and the quality of lesbian relationships. *Families in Society, 78,* 413–419.

Carrington, C. (2002). *No place like home: Relationships and family life among lesbians and gay men.* Chicago: University of Chicago Press.

Cass, V. C. (1979). Homosexual identity formation: Testing a theoretical model. *Journal of Homosexuality, 4,* 219–235.

Connolly, C. M. (2005). A qualitative exploration of resilience in long-term lesbian couples. *The Family Journal, 13,* 266–280.

DeMino, K. A., Appleby, G., & Fisk, D. (2007). Lesbian mothers with planned families: A comparative study of internalized homophobia and social support. *American Journal of Orthopsychiatry, 77,* 165–173.

Dindia, K. (1998). "Going into and coming out of the closet": The dialectics of stigma disclosure. In B. M. Montgomery & L. A. Baxter (Eds.), *Dialectical approaches to studying personal relationships* (pp. 83–108). Mahwah, NJ: Lawrence Erlbaum.

Gagnon, A. C., Riley, A., Toole, M., & Goldberg, A. E. (2007). *Motivations to parent in lesbian adoptive couples.* Poster presented at the American Psychological Association annual conference, San Francisco, CA, August 2007.

Gates, G., Badgett, M. V. L., Macomber, J. E., & Chambers, K. (2007). *Adoption and foster care by gay and lesbian parents in the United States.* Washington, DC: The Urban Institute.

Gates, G., & Ost, J. (2004). *The gay and lesbian atlas.* Washington, DC: The Urban Institute.

Garnets, L., & Kimmel, D. (2003). *Psychological perspectives on lesbian and gay male experience.* New York: Columbia University Press.

Gartrell, N., Banks, A., Reed, N., Hamiliton, J., Rodas, C., & Deck, A. (2000). The National Lesbian Family Study: 3. Interviews with mothers of five-year-olds. *American Journal of Orthopsychiatry, 70,* 542–548.

Gartrell, N., Deck, A., Rodas, C., Peyser, H., & Banks, A. (2005). The National Lesbian Family Study: 4. Interviews with 10-year-old children. *American Journal of Orthopsychiatry, 75,* 518–524.

Gartrell, N., Rodas, C., Deck, A., Peyser, H., & Banks, A. (2006). The USA National Lesbian Family Study: Interviews with mothers of 10-year-olds. *Feminism & Psychology, 16,* 175–192.

Goldberg, A. E. (2006). The transition to parenthood for lesbian couples. *Journal of GLBT Family Studies, 2,* 13–42.

Goldberg, A. E., Downing, J. B., & Sauck, C. C. (2007). Choices, challenges, and tensions: Perspectives of lesbian prospective adoptive parents. *Adoption Quarterly, 10,* 33–64.

Goldberg, A. E., & Perry-Jenkins, M. (2007). The division of labor and perceptions of parental roles: Lesbian couples across the transition to parenthood. *Journal of Social & Personal Relationships, 24,* 297–318.

Goldberg, A. E., & Smith, J. Z. (2008). Social support and well-being in lesbian and heterosexual preadoptive parents. *Family Relations, 58,* 281–294.

Golding, A. C. (2006). Redefining the nuclear family: An exploration of resiliency in lesbian parents. *Journal of Feminist Family Therapy, 18,* 35–65.

Golombok, S., Perry, B., Burston, A., Murray, C., Mooney-Somers, J., Stevens, M., & Golding, J. (2003). Children with lesbian parents: A community study. *Developmental Psychology, 39,* 20–33.

Green, A. I. (2007). On the horns of a dilemma: Institutional dimensions of the sexual career in a sample of middle-class, urban, Black, gay men. *Journal of Black Studies, 37,* 753–774.

Greene, B. (2000). African American lesbian and bisexual women. *Journal of Social Issues, 56,* 239–249.

Greene, B., & Boyd-Franklin, N. (1996). African American lesbians: Issues in couples therapy. In J. Laird and R. Green (Eds.), *Lesbians and gays in couples and families: A handbook for therapists* (pp. 251–271). San Francisco: Jossey-Bass.

Hequembourg, A., & Farrell, M. (1999). Lesbian motherhood: Negotiating marginal-mainstream identities. *Gender & Society, 13,* 540–555.

Herek, G. M. (2006). Legal recognition of same-sex relationships in the United States: A social science perspective. *American Psychologist, 61,* 607–621.

Hoeffer, B. (1981). Children's acquisition of sex-role behavior in lesbian-mother families. *American Journal of Orthopsychiatry, 51,* 536–544.

Hollingsworth, L., & Ruffin, V. M. (2002). Why are so many U.S. families adopting internationally? A social exchange perspective. *Journal of Human Behavior in the Social Environment, 6,* 81–97.

Johnson, S. M., & O'Connor, E. (2002). *The gay baby boom: The psychology of gay parenthood.* New York: New York University Press.

Kosciw, J. G., & Diaz, E. M. (2008). *Involved, invisible, ignored: The experiences of lesbian, gay, bisexual, and transgender parents and their children in our nation's K-12 schools.* New York: Gay, Lesbian, and Straight Education Network.

Kurdek, L. A. (1995). Developmental changes in relationship quality in gay and lesbian cohabiting couples. *Developmental Psychology, 31,* 86–94.

Kurdek, L. A. (1998). Relationship outcomes and their predictors: Longitudinal evidence from heterosexual married, gay cohabiting, and lesbian cohabiting couples. *Journal of Marriage and the Family, 60,* 553–568.

Kurdek, L. (2001). Differences between heterosexual non-parent couples and gay, lesbian, and heterosexual parent couples. *Journal of Family Issues, 22,* 727–754.

Kurdek, L. A. (2006). Differences between partners from heterosexual, gay, and lesbian cohabiting couples. *Journal of Marriage and Family, 68,* 509–528.

Kurdek, L. A. (2007). The allocation of household labor by partners in gay and lesbian couples. *Journal of Family Issues, 28,* 132–148.

Lassiter, P. S., Dew, J., Newton, K., Hays, D. G., & Yarbrough, B. (2006). Self-defined empowerment for gay and lesbian parents: A qualitative examination. *The Family Journal, 14,* 245–252.

Leung, P., Erich, S., & Kanenberg, H. (2005). A comparison of family functioning in gay/lesbian, heterosexual and special needs adoptions. *Children & Youth Services Review, 27,* 1031–1044.

Mackey, R. A., Diemer, M. A., & O'Brien, B. A. (2004). Relational factors in understanding satisfaction in the lasting relationships of same-sex and heterosexual couples. *Journal of Homosexuality, 47,* 111–136.

Mackey, R. A., O'Brien, B. A., & Mackey, E. F. (1997). *Gay male and lesbian couples: Voices from lasting relationships.* Westport, CT: Praeger.

McCarn, S. R., & Fassinger, R. E. (1996). Revisioning sexual minority identity formation: A new model of lesbian identity and its implications for counseling and research. *The Counseling Psychologist, 24,* 508–534.

McDermott, E. (2006). Surviving in dangerous places: Lesbian identity performances in the workplace, social class, and psychological health. *Feminism & Psychology, 16,* 193–211.

Merighi, J. R., & Grimes, M. D. (2000). Coming out to families in a multicultural context. *Families in Society, 81,* 32–41.

Meyer, I. (2003). Prejudice, social stress, and mental health in lesbian, gay, and bisexual populations: Conceptual issues and research evidence. *Psychological Bulletin, 129,* 674–697.

Patterson, C. J., Hurt, S., & Mason, C. D. (1998). Families of the lesbian baby boom: Children's contact with grandparents and other adults. *American Journal of Orthopsychiatry, 68,* 390–399.

Paul, J., Hays, R., & Coates, T. (1995). The impact of the HIV epidemic on U.S. gay male communities. In R. Savin-Williams & C. Patterson (Eds.), *Lesbian, gay and bisexual identities over the lifespan: Children to adults* (pp. 436–561). New York: Harcourt Brace.

Pawelski, J. G., Perrin, E. C., Foy, J. M., Allen, C. F., Crawford, M. D. M., Kaufman, M., et al. (2006). The effects of marriage, civil union, and domestic partnership laws on the health and well-being of children. *Pediatrics, 118,* 349–364.

Pearlman, S. F. (1996). Loving across race and class divides: Relational challenges and the interracial lesbian couple. *Women & Therapy, 19,* 25–35.

Peplau, L. A., Cochran, S. D., & Mays, V. M. (1997). A national survey of the intimate relationships of African American lesbians and gay men: A look at commitment, satisfaction, sexual behavior, and HIV disease. In B. Greene (Ed.), *Ethnic and cultural diversity among lesbians and gay men* (pp. 11–38). Thousand Oaks, CA: Sage.

Peplau, L. A., & Fingerhut, A. W. (2007). The close relationships of lesbians and gay men. *Annual Review of Psychology, 58,* 373–408.

Ray, V., & Gregory, R. (2001). School experiences of the children of lesbian and gay parents. *Family Matters, 59,* 28–34.

Russell, G. M., & Richards, J. A. (2003). Stressor and resilience factors for lesbians, gay men, and bisexuals confronting antigay politics. *American Journal of Community Psychology, 31,* 313–328.

Savin-Williams, R. C. (2008). Then and now: Recruitment, definition, diversity, and positive attributes of same-sex populations. *Developmental Psychology, 44,* 135–138.

Simmons, T., & O'Neil, G. (2001, September). *Households and families: 2000* (U.S. Census Bureau Publication No. C2KBR/01–8). Washington, DC: U.S. Census Bureau.

Solomon, S. E., Rothblum, E. D., & Balsam, K. F. (2005). Money, housework, sex, and conflict: Same-sex couples in civil unions, those not in civil unions, and heterosexual married siblings. *Sex Roles, 52,* 561–575.

Steinbugler, A. C. (2005). Visibility as privilege and danger: Heterosexual and same-sex interracial intimacy in the 21st century. *Sexualities, 8,* 425–443.

Tasker, F. L., & Golombok, S. (1997). *Growing up in a lesbian family: Effects on child development.* London: Guilford.

Tomlinson, M. J., & Fassinger, R. E. (2003). Career development, lesbian identity development, and campus climate among lesbian college students. *Journal of College Student Development, 44,* 845–860.

Touroni, E., & Coyle, A. (2002). Decision-making in planned lesbian parenting: An interpretative phenomenological analysis. *Journal of Community & Applied Social Psychology, 12,* 194–209.

Wainright, J., Russell, S., & Patterson, C. (2004). Psychosocial adjustment, school outcomes, and romantic relationships of adolescents with same-sex parents. *Child Development, 75,* 1886–1898.

Whitechurch, G. G., & Constantine, L. L. (1993). Systems theory. In P. G. Boss, W. J. Doherty, R. LaRossa, W. R. Schumm, & S. K. Steinmetz (Eds.), *Sourcebook of family theories and methods: A contextual approach* (pp. 325–352). New York: Plenum.

Wilton, T., & Kaufman, T. (2000). Lesbian mothers' experiences of maternity care in the UK. *Midwifery, 17,* 203–211.

13 Adaptation Among Immigrant Families

Resources and Barriers

Kevin Ray Bush,
Stephanie A. Bohon, and Hyoun K. Kim

_____Immigrant Families in the United States

According to recent Census Bureau (2006) estimates, approximately 37.5 million immigrants are living in the United States, accounting for approximately 12.5% of the total population. The majority of foreign-born individuals living in the United States were born in Latin America (53.5%), Asia (26.8%), and Europe (13.3%); the remaining foreign-born individuals are from African countries, Canada, Australia, and elsewhere. These estimates do not include the estimated 12 million immigrants who are assumed to be living in the United States without proper documentation (Passel, 2006).

Immigrants to the United States include foreign-born individuals who plan to settle permanently as well as those who plan long-term but temporary stays, including students in U.S. universities. Immigrants can be categorized as economic migrants (i.e., those who come to the United States seeking better jobs and pay), family migrants (i.e., those who come to join family members already living here), or involuntary migrants (i.e., refugees who are fleeing political violence or extreme environmental devastation in their home countries). The term *first-generation immigrant* is typically used to refer to a foreign-born individual who has immigrated to the United States. The children of first-generation immigrants who are born in the United States (and, therefore, are U.S. citizens) are thus referred to as *second-generation immigrants*, and their children (the grandchildren of first-generation immigrants) as *third-generation immigrants*. In this chapter, we discuss families living in the United States in which at least some members are foreign-born.

For most immigrants, the decision to move to the United States is heavily influenced by family events and processes (Landale, 1997; Rumbaut, 1997; Suarez-Orozco, Suarez-Orozco, & Todorova, 2008). This is true even when individuals—rather than families—immigrate. In places such as Mexico, families often select one or two members to immigrate, in order to maximize their household resources (Massey, Durand, & Malone 2002). The following three hypothetical visa applicants help to illustrate this point:

Marianne is a German national applying for permanent U.S. residency. She is engaged to an American soldier whom she met when he was stationed in her hometown. She wants to marry her fiancé and live with him in the United States.

Maria is applying for a family reunification visa so that she can join her husband, Hector, who immigrated to the United States from Mexico 5 years ago. Maria's sister and brother-in-law also live in the United States.

Purvish is a native of India who is seeking a work permit so that he can move to California and work at his uncle's software company. Purvish is single, and if his visa is approved, he plans to live with his extended family in the United States.

These cases demonstrate how families influence individuals' decisions to immigrate. U.S. officials decide whether or not to approve visa applications on a case-by-case basis, but most migration decisions are made within the contexts of families or at least take family considerations into account. Therefore, the phenomenon of migration, whether of individuals or of families, needs to be understood at the family level (Landale, 1997). Unfortunately, most of the research on immigrants to date has tended to focus on individuals. As a result, traditional examinations of this process provide only a partial analysis.

Because of the wide diversity among immigrant families, in general, it is impossible to describe one profile or set of experiences that is common to every immigrant family (Rumbaut, 1997). At the macro level, immigration policies and the broader social, historical, political, and economic contexts of the United States and immigrants' home countries influence the migration process and experience (Rumbaut, 1997). For example, over the years, U.S. immigration policies have changed, affecting the eligibility and capability of individuals and families who wish to immigrate. The 1965 amendments to the Immigration and Nationality Act of 1952 created a "family reunification" category of immigrants whereby applicants for visas who had family members already living in the United States were given preferential application status. The 1986 Refugee Act made it easier for families facing dire circumstances because of political violence or extreme environmental conditions in their home countries to immigrate as refugees.

Beginning in 1990, however, policies shifted that made family migration more difficult. The Immigration Act of 1990 shifted the balance of visa applicants away from family reunification in favor of work-related criteria (Sorenson, Bean, Ku, & Zimmerman, 1992). More specifically, the 1990 act gave preference to individuals who have education and credentials in particular fields (e.g., the biological and physical sciences) and those willing to invest large sums of money in the U.S. economy. Two additional laws passed in 1996, the Illegal Immigration Reform and Immigrant Responsibility Act and the Personal Responsibility and Work Opportunity Reconciliation Act, also limited legal family reunification migration and led to an increase in unauthorized immigration (Massey et al., 2002).

Immigrant families in the United States tend to be more diverse than ever before in terms of country of origin, language, socioeconomic status, and other social and demographic characteristics. Because of this diversity, we cannot discuss each distinct immigrant group here, but rather we focus on the general barriers, stressors, resources, and patterns of adaptation common among most immigrant families, with emphasis on the two largest immigrant groups in the United States, Asians and Latinos. Given this focus, we want to be careful to underscore the fact that great variation exists within each of these broad categories (i.e., Asians and Latinos) and within specific cultural/ethnic groups of immigrants (e.g., Koreans and Mexicans).

Acculturation and Adaptation

The United States is a nation of immigrants, and the patterns of immigration as well as the reasons people immigrate vary substantially. A common characteristic among the majority of immigrant families, however, is stress associated with immigration. Many of the values, beliefs, and strategies that immigrant families and individuals have followed in order to function successfully in their home cultures differ from U.S. norms. An immigrant family's system will experience stress to the extent that members find that strategies (i.e., rules and roles relating to established patterns of interaction) they have used in the past to accomplish family tasks (e.g., providing for family, establishing and maintaining rules, facilitating identity development and socialization) are not as effective in the social, economic, and political contexts of the United States (e.g., McCubbin, Thompson, Thompson, & Fromer, 1998). Therefore, in addition to the typical normative (e.g., family transitions) and nonnormative (e.g., natural disasters) stressors that families encounter, immigrant families experience unique stress and change related to migration and acculturation.

Acculturation—that is, the process of adjusting to a new culture or society—involves potential changes in identity, values, behaviors, attitudes, interactions, and relationships (Berry, 2001). All family systems have their own unique rules that define appropriate behaviors and interactions that are influenced by cultural and ethnic values as well as socioeconomic status and other sociodemographic factors (Boss, 2002; McCubbin et al., 1998). As family members encounter stress or pressure to change, the family system also experiences pressure to change. Family systems theory highlights the importance of interactions among individuals and family subsystems (e.g., parental, marital, and child) and the resultant meanings and structures that emerge out of these interactions (Whitechurch & Constantine, 1993). Thus, changes within a family are viewed as being processed by the entire family system, rather than by a single member. Moreover, stress is viewed as an agent of change rather than as inherently negative.

As a family system changes, individual family members change their ways of interacting in accordance with the new rules for interaction. For example, it is fairly common for Mexican immigrants to the United States to experience "family stage migration" (Hondagneu-Sotelo, 1994) in which one or two family members immigrate at a time. That is, the father might immigrate first, leaving his wife and children behind, thus creating the need for changes in family strategies. As a man on his own, the father must now accomplish many tasks—such as laundry, cooking, and other chores—typically performed by his wife. In turn, the wife, who is now the de facto head of the family's household in Mexico, must take on many of the roles she previously shared with her husband (e.g., socialization and discipline of children) as well as family tasks that had been her husband's sole responsibility (e.g., managing the family's finances). When she and the children eventually migrate to the United States, the husband's and wife's roles must be renegotiated, often resulting in something entirely new (Hondagneu-Sotelo, 1994).

The effects of acculturation are complicated by other factors as well, including family members being at different stages in the acculturation process. Some members (particularly children) may assimilate rapidly, adopting values and beliefs of the mainstream U.S. culture (Berry, 2001). Some members may experience separation; that is, they may retain the values and beliefs of their cultures of origin and reject those of the mainstream U.S. culture. The most common form of adaptation among immigrants is integration, or the blending of aspects of both the home culture and the new culture (Berry, 2001), as most immigrants find it impractical to ignore the practices of their host country and also find it comforting to retain some of the traditions of their homelands.

Common Barriers and Stressors Experienced by Immigrant Families

Scholars have identified a wide variety of stressors that immigrant families may experience. The salience and impact of particular stressors, however, vary depending on the families' ethnicities, cultures, reasons for immigrating, and other social and contextual factors. Stressors exist at the community or society level (e.g., immigration policies and discrimination), the family level (e.g., change and conflict within intergenerational and marital relationships), and the individual level (e.g., depression, isolation, identity development). Immigrant families face various barriers (i.e., hindering structural factors and individual characteristics) in the adaptation process, including (a) lack of English-language fluency, (b) diminished social support networks, (c) conflict in family relationships, (d) lowered socioeconomic status, (e) poor housing conditions, (f) lack of familiarity with U.S. norms, (g) family separation/ reunification, (h) fear of deportation, and (i) discrimination. Such barriers can be sources of stress for families and their individual members, therefore creating change within family systems.

Language Barriers

The ability to speak English is closely related to daily functioning in U.S. society; it is likely to determine employment opportunities as well as an individual's level of social participation in the mainstream culture (Bhattacharya & Schoppelrey, 2004). The inability to read signs, posted warnings, food labels, job applications, and materials related to children's schooling is a frustrating experience for many immigrants and can lead to increased pressure to learn English. However, adult family members are often unable to attend classes to learn English because they need to work to provide for the family, they have to stay home to care for children (Atiles & Bohon, 2002; Bhattacharya & Schoppelrey, 2004), or they lack access to transportation (Bohon, Stamps, & Atiles, 2008). Lack of fluency in English can lead to experiences of discrimination and can make it difficult for immigrants to establish social support networks in the United States.

Diminished Social Support Networks

When families move to the United States and leave behind most of their extended-family members and friends, they are faced with the task of navigating a new culture without familiar social supports. Because the lack of social support can serve as a barrier to family functioning, immigrant families need to establish new support networks in the United States; they may also need to redefine family and family relationships, such as changes in roles, boundaries, and patterns of interaction (Falicov, 2003).

Immigrant women from cultures that adhere to traditional gender roles (e.g., where women's roles are restricted primarily to the socialization and nurturance of children and to family relationships) may find themselves at a distinct disadvantage in the United States. In traditional Asian cultures, for example, extrafamilial relationships are not considered necessary for women, as women have multiple supports available to them within the extended-family structure (Serafica, Weng, & Kim, 2000). Furthermore, in cases where women do have extrafamilial relationships, these relationships are mediated through family/kin system interactions rather than through the women's individual efforts. When women from such Asian cultures immigrate to the United States, they are not prepared for establishing and maintaining interpersonal relationships outside their families (Serafica et al., 2000).

Conflict in Intergenerational Relationships

Maintaining harmony in intergenerational relationships can be a major challenge for immigrant families. As family members adjust to their new country, their levels of acculturation may vary across age and gender, which can serve as barriers to family functioning and lead to changes within intergenerational relationships (Kwak, 2003). Children usually acculturate more quickly than their parents, which can lead to conflict as parents focus on values and practices from their culture of origin, while children integrate more values and practices from the mainstream host culture (Suarez-Orozco et al., 2008). Typically, children learn cultural norms and practices from their parents, but the messages that immigrant children receive from their parents may conflict with those they receive from their U.S.-born peers and teachers. For example, second- and third-generation immigrants are more likely to engage in premarital sex, cohabit, and marry at later ages compared to first-generation immigrants (Chen, Harris, & Guo, 2005).

As immigrant children become more acculturated than their parents, the likelihood of intergenerational conflict and communication problems increases. Such conflict may result in children rejecting some or all of the values of the family's culture of origin (Kwak, 2003), leading to higher levels of stress for the family. Immigrant children often find themselves serving as translators for other, less acculturated family members; many take on the role of family liaison or "cultural broker" between their families and the new society. In such situations, children are likely to feel the stress of adult responsibilities, whereas their parents may feel the stress of role reversal that comes from relying on children for their survival and well-being (Bhattacharya & Schoppelrey, 2004; Kwak, 2003). See Box 13.1 for examples of cultural brokers.

Box 13.1   Immigrant Children as Cultural Brokers: Advantage or Disadvantage to Development?

The terms *cultural broker* and *language broker* refer to one who serves as a guide or broker between two cultures or language groups. Since immigrant children are typically exposed to English sooner and more intensively than their parents, children often are placed in situations where they serve as the cultural broker for their parents and/or other family members. Child cultural brokers can be called upon to translate notes from school, bills, or bank statements, as well as to translate and interact as their parents' agent in conversations with banks, businesses, schools, hospitals, and other institutions where limited English proficiency restricts parents' direct involvement.

There is a debate among researchers regarding whether children who serve in such roles (or their families) suffer negative consequences (Trickett & Jones, 2007). Some assert that cultural brokering is a form of "adultification," "parentification," or "role reversal," which can impede normal development for the child if she or he spends too much time in an adult role without being allowed to mature normally, gradually developing autonomy with supportive relationships with parents. Scholars taking this view also suggest that having children serve as cultural brokers undermines the traditional power relationship between parents and children, perhaps even increasing parents' dependence on their child's serving as a cultural broker.

There are many situations in which cultural brokering has a negative consequence. Imagine, for example, that a child who is being reprimanded by a teacher must relate this reprimand to his or her parent. The child is forced into a situation where translating accurately will likely result in negative consequences, but telling a lie requires betraying the trust of parents who rely on the child as their broker. In other situations, children often do not understand the nuances of language that can result in faulty translations and the subsequent consequences. Some words that have several meanings in one language may have only one meaning in English, or vice versa. A child may inadvertently tell a doctor that his 2-year-old sister fell off a ladder (a case of poor supervision), when, in fact, she fell down the stairs (an accident). When children misinterpret language, and there are negative consequences for the family, the child is then burdened with the guilt of causing trouble for his or her family.

Scholars on the other side of the debate assert that children serving as cultural brokers are more bicultural, have higher academic achievement, and have more self-confidence (Buriel, Perez, De Ment, Chavez, & Moran, 1998). These positive outcomes are assumed to be the result of placing children in adult contexts and exposing them to more sophisticated language (such as that used at banks) that they must learn in order to be effective. Female children from patriarchal cultures may particularly benefit from their elevated role.

The following stories of Won Jee and Jose illustrate examples of children serving as cultural brokers and the advantages and disadvantages to these roles:

- Won Jee is 15 and emigrated to the United States with her parents from China when she was 2 years old. Because her parents work in Chinatown, it was not necessary for them to speak English until they needed to enroll Won Jee in elementary school. One of the teachers from Won Jee's early childhood program went with her parents to register her for school. As time went on and Won Jee became more fluent in English, her parents became more and more reliant on her to translate just about everything for the family, from doing their taxes, helping them purchase a car, attending parent–teacher conferences for her younger siblings, and paying the household bills. In her first year of high school, Won Jee barely passed, but she was afraid to tell her parents, since she felt that her duties as the family translator were more important than her schoolwork. Eventually, Won Jee dropped out of high school and obtained a job at the same restaurant where her parents work in Chinatown.

(Continued)

(Continued)

- Jose immigrated to the United States with his family from Mexico when he was 2. In elementary school, Jose was placed in a dual-immersion program where instruction took place in both Spanish and English. This type of environment allowed interaction with U.S.-born children learning Spanish as well as other immigrant children learning English. Neither of his parents completed high school in Mexico and both work in a Mexican restaurant in the United States where English is not necessary, thus they rely heavily on Jose to help them navigate the culture outside of their Spanish-speaking workplace and community. Jose's translating chores required him to learn more about the English language and U.S. culture than he would have learned otherwise. For example, when his parents had problems obtaining medical care, Jose went to the library and learned all he could about resources for immigrant families and the health care system. Eventually, Jose applied for and received several scholarships for college. After graduating from law school several years later, Jose returned to his childhood community in now works as an immigration lawyer helping immigrant families.

Discussion Questions

1. Discuss the positive and negative consequences of serving as a child cultural broker for each of these youth.

2. Identify and discuss factors that mediated or influenced whether the experience produced positive or negative results for each child.

Conflict and Change in Marital Relationships

Previous studies have found acculturation to be related to marital conflict (e.g., Flores, Tschann, Marin, & Pantoja, 2004). Married immigrant couples may find it difficult to carry out the family and spousal roles they learned in their cultures of origin and are likely to experience pressure to change their family relationships and roles. For example, immigrant wives often need to work outside the home in order to help support their families, and as a result, they gain independence and status, whereas their husbands may experience a loss of status and/or power or lowered self-esteem (Chun & Akutsu, 2003). As the women in these couples gain economic power, the potential increases for conflicts and changes in their family systems (Chung, Tucker, & Takeuchi, 2008).

Cultural values impact couple and family interaction, roles, and how conflict is perceived and expressed. For example, more acculturated Mexican immigrants have been found to use more direct communication and conflict negotiation, whereas those less acculturated use conflict avoidance strategies, perhaps more in line with traditional cultural expectations of smooth and respectful familial relationships and less acceptance of open expressions of conflict (Flores et al., 2004).

Different levels of acculturation within couples can also increase the difficulty of renegotiating family and marital roles. Researchers suggest that

Asian immigrant men are more traditional and tend to assimilate into U.S. culture less readily than do Asian immigrant women, who tend to show more egalitarian attitudes (e.g., Chia, Moore, Lam, Chuang, & Cheng, 1994); such differences can create significant tension between spouses. Chung et al. (2008) found higher rates of male-to-female partner violence among Asian American families; Asian wives are at greater risk for partner violence when they earn as much or more than their husbands and play a greater role in decision-making processes. Conversely, when the husbands had greater authority over decisions, the risk of husbands' violence toward their wives decreased significantly. This suggests that traditional gender roles and women's newly gained economic power can be a significant source for marital violence among immigrant families.

Poor Housing Conditions

For the first few years they are in the United States, many immigrants live in housing that is, by most U.S. standards, inferior (Bhattacharya & Schoppelrey, 2004), although it may be superior to what was available to the immigrants in their home countries. A major family stressor related to immigrants' living conditions is overcrowding (Bhattacharya & Schoppelrey, 2004). In fact, immigrant children are approximately four times as likely to be living in crowded housing conditions compared to native-born children (Capps, 2001).

Families in the United States also tend to spend more time inside their houses than do families in developing countries, which intensifies the feeling of overcrowding when occupancy levels are high. In addition, immigrant families often discover that it is not always safe to let children play outdoors because of limited common green space and dangerous motor vehicle traffic. When children must spend most of their time crowded indoors, particularly in housing of inferior construction quality, they can develop illnesses such as asthma. Moreover, residential overcrowding has been linked with negative parenting behaviors (less responsiveness and lower levels of monitoring), increased chances of child maltreatment, and poorer child outcomes including psychological distress and lower social and cognitive competence (Evans, 2006).

Lack of Familiarity With U.S. Norms

Immigrant families often experience stress as they adjust to life in the United States because they do not fully understand American social norms, including those related to child care and child rearing. Violating these norms results in a variety of sanctions, ranging from ridicule to having their children removed from their homes. For example, immigrant parents may not be aware of laws requiring that small children be restrained in special seats when riding in a car (Atiles & Bohon, 2002). Moreover, parents following traditional cultural practices of child rearing (e.g., cosleeping) or folk medicine ("cupping" or "coining") might be perceived as meeting criteria for neglect or abuse by uninformed child protection authorities in the United States (c.f. Coleman, 2007).

The problem of family violence that exists in some immigrant families is exacerbated by immigrants' lack of understanding concerning U.S. cultural and legal norms. Because of language barriers, many immigrants do not fully understand the laws regarding family violence. Additionally, cultural barriers (e.g., cultural values from their countries of origin regarding gender hierarchies and family strategies related to keeping family problems within the family) may prevent families from seeking needed help. In a study with parole officers, Atiles and Bohon (2003) found that one common pattern among new Latin American immigrants is for a woman who has been abused by her husband to report the abuse to police, only to discover that the husband's arrest results in severe repercussions for the family. If the man is a first-time offender, his punishment often consists of a large fine and probation. The offender is also forced to pay monthly probation costs and the cost of mandated counseling. The economic impact of an arrest for domestic violence can be severe for an immigrant family, usually exacerbating stressors that may have contributed to the violence in the first place (Atiles & Bohon, 2002).

A related barrier to immigrant adjustment is lack of familiarity with the U.S. educational system (Bhattacharya & Schoppelrey, 2004). New immigrants from developing countries may not understand that children are required to attend school or that children enrolled in school must attend every weekday unless they are excused (Bohon, Macpherson, & Atiles, 2005). Moreover, immigrant parents may not understand the expectation of parental involvement in children's education.

Separation and Reunification

In the majority of immigrant families, members do not migrate at the same time, thus it is very common for children and parents, as well as spouses, to endure long periods of separation. Reunification of the entire family can sometimes span many years (e.g., Arnold, 1991), and many families run into unexpected delays including those related to finances, immigration laws/ processes, housing issues, divorces, and remarriages (Suarez-Orozco et al., 2008).

During the separation, stress experienced by the loss of a family member leads to the changes in the family system as family roles must be renegotiated. Often separation is experienced as ambiguous loss, thus adjustment can take more time and is difficult to accomplish (Boss, 2002). Since the parent, child, or other family member is not gone permanently, the family members' loss may go unacknowledged or unsupported (Boss, 2002). Moreover, family members who are not willing or able to renegotiate roles are thus less likely to accomplish necessary tasks, at least with the same level of competence as prior to the separation.

Reunification can also be stressful for family members. Successful reunification between children and parents depends on many factors including coparenting between the caregiver in the country of origin and the immigrant parent(s). That is, the quality of the relationships among the caregiver in the country of origin, the child, and the immigrant parent contribute to the quality of parent–child relationships and well-being upon reunification (e.g., Arnold, 1991). The quality of communication (e.g., letters, phone calls, remittances) between separated family members is also highly predictive of adjustment at reunification (Suarez-Orozco et al., 2008).

Fear of Deportation

Families often consist of mixed immigration statuses, such as being citizens (e.g., children who were born in the United States), legal immigrants with work permits, or undocumented immigrants. The legal or citizenship status of immigrants in the United States varies considerably. Although a majority of immigrants in the United States are legal through various types of immigration statuses (e.g., work permits, citizenship, etc.), it is estimated that approximately 12 million immigrants in the United States are undocumented (Passel, 2006). Besides serving as a constant stressor, the fear of deportation can also hinder integration with the host culture, such as discouraging interaction with nonimmigrants as well as social institutions. For example, parents may not communicate with schools or attend parent–teacher conferences for fear of deportation.

Discrimination

Immigrant families often experience barriers to adjustment as the result of discrimination based on factors such as, race, ethnicity, and religion. In more than two centuries of U.S. history, discrimination against immigrants has persisted unceasingly, with little change except the group being defamed. Over time, Irish, Chinese, Italian, Japanese, Eastern European, and Latino immigrants have all been subjected to public resentment and official sanctions (Espenshade, 1995). One of the very first U.S. immigration laws—the Chinese Exclusion Act of 1882—barred Chinese immigrants from becoming U.S. citizens and effectively halted Chinese immigration for more than 60 years, breaking apart many Chinese families (Gyory, 1998). In the 1940s, 110,000 Japanese-origin men, women, and children—the majority of whom were U.S. citizens—were forcibly evacuated from their homes and relocated to concentration camps. As a result, many lost their family farms and other important family resources (Hakim, 1995). After the attacks on the Pentagon and World Trade Center on September 11, 2001, hate crimes against persons of Middle Eastern descent increased precipitously, and the U.S. government instituted "antiterror" policies that made Middle Eastern and South Asian immigrants even greater targets for discrimination and prejudice (Bozorgmehr & Bakalian, 2004). Discrimination-related stressors often combine with other stressors to place immigrant families at increased risk for poor adaptation.

The issues of illegal immigration in the United States and concern regarding the negative impact of this immigration on U.S. society has sparked debates, protests, and hurried inadequate legislation without much concern for immigrants who are already in the United States (Suarez-Orozco et al., 2008). Issues such as whether and how to deport illegal immigrants and their families, some of whom might be U.S. citizens, inadvertently place them in a tenuous position. As a result, many immigrants face daily discrimination ranging from verbal abuse to physical abuse, as well as barriers related to employment, education, and other opportunities that most people in the United States take for granted.

Inadequate Public Policies and Programs

One of the most problematic barriers that immigrant families face is the failure of U.S. social policies to address the needs of immigrants (Fix & Zimmerman, 1997; Suarez-Orozco et al., 2008). The only forms of government assistance that are available to immigrants (with the exception of refugees) are mainstream public assistance programs such as Temporary Assistance to Needy Families (TANF) (Capps, Kenney, & Fix, 2003; Fix & Zimmerman, 1997). The 1996 Personal Responsibility and Work Opportunity Reconciliation Act (commonly known as "welfare reform") recently increased restrictions on immigrants' ability to receive public assistance, extending the amount of time in the United States necessary for eligibility for most programs for the poor from 3 to 5 years. The law also bars immigrants from receiving food stamps or Supplemental Security Income (SSI) (Massey et al., 2002). The federal government closely monitors immigrants' enrollment in public assistance programs, and any attempt to enroll before the end of the 5-year waiting period is grounds for deportation. This level of punishment may discourage many immigrants from ever applying for assistance; immigrant enrollment in public assistance programs is far lower than enrollment among the U.S.-born (Tumlin & Zimmerman, 2003). The 1996 changes to the laws governing public assistance also definitively barred unauthorized immigrants from nearly all income-based assistance programs (Massey et al., 2002).

Refugee families have considerably more financial and other resources available to them than do other immigrant families in the United States. Unfortunately, only immigrants who have been officially recognized by the U.S. government as refugees are eligible to receive such assistance. Too often, for political reasons, the federal government grants only *economic immigrant* status to immigrant families who flee their homelands to escape violence, thereby cutting them off from refugee assistance programs (Zucker & Zucker, 1992).

Lack of Economic Resources

Socioeconomic status is both a predictor and an indicator of acculturation and adaptation. Although immigrant families exist across the socioeconomic continuum, many exist at the lower levels, with children in immigrant families experiencing twice the poverty rate of native-born families in the United States (Van Hook, 2003). Often the work experience and training that immigrants have had in their countries of origin are not recognized in the United States, and so many educated professional immigrants are forced to take jobs for which they are overqualified (Austria, 2003; Bhattacharya & Schoppelrey, 2004). Whether such employment is temporary or long term, it is typically less financially and psychologically rewarding than the work for which these immigrants were trained. Many immigrants who were professionals (e.g., lawyers, architects, accountants) in their home countries are unable to find employment in their fields and become owners of small businesses (Austria, 2003) or taxi drivers (Bhattacharya & Schoppelrey, 2004).

Immigrant families with greater economic resources have more options regarding the neighborhoods and communities in which they choose to live; this, in turn, is related to the educational and occupational opportunities of family members (Suarez-Orozco et al., 2008). Poor immigrant families, of course, have fewer choices, and this can increase the amount of stress these families face and affect their family systems' ability to make the adjustments necessary for them to achieve a good quality of life in the United States. The story in Box 13.2 illustrates barriers and stressors that impoverished immigrant families are likely to encounter.

Box 13.2   Barriers and Stressors of an Impoverished Immigrant Family

Maria migrated from Juarez, Mexico, to Atlanta with her three children to join her husband, Jaime, who has been living in the United States since 1998. Although Jaime has a work permit ("green card"), Maria and the children are undocumented. They live in a poor neighborhood and share a small trailer with Jaime's brother, Jose, his wife, and their two children. Because they cannot afford a car, Jose and Jaime share a ride to work with other men who work for the same construction company. Jose's wife works as a maid in a hotel. Each morning she catches a bus at 6:00 a.m., leaving her two toddlers in Maria's care until she returns in the evening.

Maria spends most of her day caring for her own toddler and her niece and nephew while her two older children go to school. Maria has never seen the buildings where her children attend the sixth and tenth grades, but she worries because she hears rumors that there are gangs at the high school. In Mexico, Maria had a small garden and her children would play nearby while she tended it. She would walk with the children to the village to buy things the family needed. In Atlanta, however, she is afraid to walk to the store. There are no sidewalks, and she worries that the toddlers will run into the street. Sometimes Jaime goes with his coworkers to the store after work. Maria is embarrassed that her husband has to shop "like a wife."

(Continued)

(Continued)

Maria and Jaime are saving money to buy a home, but it is hard to save much on Jaime's income. Maria wants to get a job, but there are not many jobs available for women without green cards that she could reach by bus. Maria would also like to learn English, but she has few opportunities, as there are no English-speaking people in her neighborhood. She has heard that some churches offer free English classes, but it is too expensive for her to take three children along on the bus. She knows that her children will have a better life in the United States than they would have had in Mexico, but she worries that she is a burden to her husband because she has little to contribute to the household.

Discussion Questions:

1. What are some of the social-level barriers that Maria and her family may be facing? List the potential barriers and examples of how they impact Maria's family.

2. If you found yourself in Maria's situation, what would you do to improve it? Discuss resources that would help Maria or someone in her situation.

3. Discuss how family stress theory and/or other theories would explain Maria's family.

Common Resources and Adaptation Among Immigrant Families

Family adaptation is defined as the extent to which the internal functions of a family system (e.g., roles and perceptions) and/or external reality (e.g., social and economic contexts) are altered to achieve a system–environment fit (e.g., Boss, 2002; McCubbin et al., 1998). Adaptation involves long-term change, whereas adjustment is short-term change the family system makes in order to function successfully in different contexts (Boss, 2002). Although few scholars have examined migration and acculturation processes at the family level, a discussion of the various resources and patterns of adaptation seen among immigrant families will help to illustrate the process of change.

Resources that can aid immigrant families' adaptation exist at the society, community, family, and individual levels. Society- and community-level resources include immigration policies and programs and social support networks and services, such as those provided by religious institutions and ethnic enclaves and communities. Family-level resources include shared family values and traditions, such as religion and familism, which can assist in maintaining effective family cohesion and communication and in establishing new social support networks. Individual-level resources include the ability to speak English, education, monetary resources, and familiarity with U.S. norms. Immigrant families' use of any of these resources depends on their perceptions of stressors as well as on their definitions of and goals for adaptation.

Perceptions of Barriers and Stressors

Immigration leads to changes in the events that individuals and families perceive as stressful, as well as changes in methods of coping with stressors (Boss, 2002). Obviously, when families encounter barriers, they experience these barriers as stressors. However, what any given family considers a barrier (and, therefore, a stressor) depends not only on the perception and meaning the family attaches to particular events but also on how the family defines adaptation. For example, some immigrant families may perceive their children's increasing fluency in the English language as an asset to the family, whereas others might perceive it as a threat to the stability of the family. Culture, religion, education, resources, and prior experience are all important influences on families' perceptions of stressors and their subsequent responses.

Cultural Values

Value systems and associated behaviors serve as important influences within families (McCubbin et al., 1998). Shared values such as family cohesion, respect for elders, filial piety, and emphasizing family goals over individual goals can greatly increase the ability of a family system to maintain coherence during change by facilitating clear communication and similar definitions of stressors and adaptation goals among family members. That is, shared cultural values serve to maintain a cohesive and familiar family environment, thus facilitating support and effective coping.

Shared family values such as self-sufficiency, perseverance, and familism bolster family adaptation by guiding the reframing of stressors into more manageable challenges. For example, an immigrant family that followed patri- archal norms in their home country may find that the wife has better employment opportunities than the husband. Viewing this stressor as a great opportunity for the wife to enter the workforce and for the husband to spend more time with the children would be consistent with values that emphasize the importance of the family unit over the individual. By reframing the stressor in this way, the family facilitates change in the family system that allows the family to meet its needs through the reversal of some spousal roles. The likelihood of such a change is dependent on the acculturation level of both spouses and the relative importance and flexibility of roles and values (e.g., patriarchy) within the family system.

Immigration Policies and Programs

Qualified legal immigrants to the United States are entitled to participate in mainstream public assistance programs such as TANF (Capps et al., 2003). Additionally, immigrants officially recognized as political asylum refugees by the U.S. government are very likely to take advantage of special government assistance programs for refugees (Bohon, 2001). These include family resettlement programs, special language classes, and work training. Cities such as Atlanta, Georgia, and Portland, Oregon, are attractive destinations for refugee families, as many nongovernment refugee assistance agencies have been established in these locations to help families adjust to life in the United States. Refugees are also eligible for college financial aid, TANF, food stamps, and other assistance without going through the waiting periods required of other immigrants.

There are also government programs that help immigrants, regardless of their income. For example, the Civil Rights Act of 1964 and subsequent legislation requires that all public schools teach English to children who are not native English speakers. Therefore, all immigrant families with school-age children should have at least one English speaker or an English learner in their home, provided that the children are in school. Local places, like Portland, Oregon, have also established day labor centers to ensure that workers, usually immigrants, have a safe place to wait for temporary work and are fairly paid for their labor (Ten Eyck, 2008).

Religion and Spirituality

Religious and spiritual beliefs and activities can serve as important resources for immigrants by fostering social support, adaptive coping strategies, self-efficacy, family cohesion, and community closeness. Among African immigrants, for example, spiritual well-being has been found to be related to lower levels of stress, higher levels of family hardiness (ability to resist stress and cope effectively), and higher levels of coping resources (Kamya, 1997). Similarly, seeking religious support has been found to serve as a protective factor for health outcomes among Mexican immigrants, with those experiencing higher levels of discrimination benefiting the most from religious support seeking (Finch & Vega, 2003).

For immigrant families, churches and other types of religious and spiritual organizations can also facilitate the formation of friendships and support networks with individuals and families from their native cultures (Min, 2005). For example, the church is an important aspect of life for most Korean immigrants, fostering social support, a sense of belonging, and preservation of Korean cultural traditions (Min, 2005).

Ethnic Communities and Enclaves

Ethnic communities—that is, neighborhoods populated primarily by individuals and families from the same culture—can play very significant roles in the lives of immigrants. They provide the opportunity to adjust to life in a new country while living in somewhat familiar surroundings (e.g., language, food, and other customs). Ethnic communities can also provide new immigrant families with social support in that they make it relatively easy for family members to form new friendships with individuals who have similar backgrounds but more experience and knowledge of their new country (Sanders & Nee, 1987).

Ethnic enclaves are extreme forms of ethnic communities in that they are larger and many of their economic activities are separated from those of the larger surrounding city (Bohon, 2001). The most famous ethnic enclaves are Little Havana in Miami, Little Tokyo in Honolulu, and the Chinatowns of San Francisco, Los Angeles, and New York. Immigrants who live in ethnic enclaves rarely have to venture outside the enclave boundaries to provide for their daily needs (Portes & Manning, 1986), unlike those who live in ethnic neighborhoods, most of whom work outside their neighborhoods in the larger community.

Living and working in ethnic enclaves is one method by which immigrant families cope with the problems of prejudice and discrimination (e.g., Fernandez-Kelly & Schauffler, 1994). Immigrants are not minorities within the enclave, and they are likely to have skills and work habits that are valued in the production of goods within ethnic enclaves. Many of the employers in ethnic enclaves also allow women to bring their children with them to work, so these women can simultaneously fulfill the role of both homemaker and wage earner (Fernandez-Kelly & Schauffler, 1994).

Latino Immigrant Families

Latinos constitute the largest minority group in the United States, and Latino immigrants account for more than half of the total foreign-born population (U.S. Bureau of the Census, 2006). However, the size of this population and the somatic similarity of its members often mask the considerable diversity that exists among Latino immigrants in the United States. Although less diverse than Asian immigrants in terms of languages, religions, dietary customs, and even appearance, Latino immigrants also come from numerous countries under a variety of situations. Some, like many Cubans, are refugees who have been granted political asylum. Others, like many Mexicans, are economic migrants seeking better jobs for themselves and better schools for their children. Since 1990, an increasing number of Latino immigrants are undocumented and thus do not have the same access to jobs and education as others (Massey et al., 2002). Some small groups are completely different from those typically envisioned as Latino immigrants. For example, some Guatemalan immigrants are indigenous Mayans who speak little Spanish and have few cultural practices that are similar to the majority of the people who live in their home country.

Most of the Latin American immigrants in the United States have their origins in Mexico or Cuba (U.S. Bureau of the Census, 2006), and these two groups, in many ways, represent the extreme ends of the spectrum of Latino immigrants. Cuban Americans, for example, are more likely than other Latino groups to have features commonly considered to be "Anglo," including blond or red hair and blue eyes. Mexican Americans are much more likely to have features that accord with common stereotypes of Latinos (i.e., dark hair and eyes and darkish skin), although there is considerable phenotypical variation among individuals in this group (Murguia & Telles, 1996). Furthermore, indicators of the socioeconomic status of Latino immigrants (e.g., income, housing values, and educational attainment) show trends that are typically below those of nonimmigrant whites and above those of nonimmigrant blacks, but Cubans and Mexicans are at the extremes of that spectrum as well (del Pinal & Singer, 1997). That is, Cubans are the most well-off of all Latino immigrants, reporting average incomes higher than those of non-Latino whites, whereas Mexicans are the most impoverished of the Latin American immigrants (U.S. Bureau of the Census, 2006). Despite these differences, Latino immigrants do not show the extremely wide variations in socioeconomic status seen among Asian groups.

For decades, the United States has depended on Latin American laborers to fill vacant positions in agriculture, construction, and other areas (Massey et al., 2002); thus there is a long history of legal Latin American migration from Mexico. The fact that the United States shares a large border with Mexico also makes it somewhat easier for Latin American immigrants (especially Mexicans) to enter the United States illegally. It is interesting to note that among the immigrants who clandestinely enter the United States from Mexico, those least likely to be apprehended are those who have family members already residing in this country, suggesting that family members share important information on border crossing (Singer & Massey, 1998).

Latino immigrant families do not experience some stressors to the degree that other immigrant families might. Strength in numbers allows Latino immigrants to overcome many of the barriers that Asian immigrants face, particularly language barriers. Prior to 1990, the majority of Latino immigrants lived in a handful of states in fewer than a dozen metropolitan areas (del Pinal & Singer, 1997), making it relatively easy for local governments and industries to offer goods and services for this population. In Miami, Houston, and Los Angeles, for example, the notes that schoolteachers send home for their students' parents are printed in English on one side and Spanish on the other (Bohon et al., 2005). Street signs in these cities are often in both languages. Government service providers such as school counselors, family social workers, and police officers are often bilingual in English and Spanish. Businesses find it profitable to offer goods that Latino immigrants want to buy and to hire bilingual workers (Portes & Stepick, 1993). However, an increasing number of Latino families are forgoing these advantages by migrating to nontraditional places in the U.S. South, West, and Midwest, where the Latino populations are much smaller (Atiles & Bohon, 2002).

Another advantage that Latino immigrant families have, primarily because of the large numbers of such families in the United States, is their large extended-family support networks (Landale & Oropesa 2007). These networks serve as practical resources to families (e.g., by allowing for more communal child-care arrangements and more car-sharing options), and they also allow families to share stressful events and the burdens of adapting to life in a new country with many supportive others. However, the large number of Latino immigrants in the United States also sometimes works to this group's disadvantage. As Taylor (2000) notes, the size of an out-group is usually the biggest predictor of prejudicial attitudes among members of the in-group. Where minority groups are small, prejudice against members of those groups is less prevalent. When minority groups are large, the reverse is true. This helps to account for the long history of discrimination against members of the two largest minority groups in the United States, African Americans and Latinos (Spain, 1999).

Asian Immigrant Families

Asians (including Pacific Islanders) are the fastest-growing minority group in the United States and account for approximately 25% of the total foreign-born population and 48% of the foreign-born population who are naturalized U.S. citizens (U.S. Census Bureau, 2004). Although Asians are often considered a monolithic group, great diversity exists within this population. Individuals with origins in at least 60 different Asian groups currently live in the United States; most of these groups have their own languages, religious traditions, and political, cultural, and migration histories (Austria, 2003; Lin & Cheung, 1999). The largest subgroup within the Asian population living in the United States is Chinese (2.7 million), followed by Filipino (2.4 million) and Asian Indian (1.9 million) (U.S. Census Bureau, 2004). The numbers of Southeast Asian (i.e., Vietnamese, Cambodian, Laotian, and Hmong) immigrants have also increased in recent years (Austria, 2003). Chinese, Korean, and Indo-Chinese immigrants are more likely to settle in their own ethnic enclaves, whereas Filipinos and Asian Indian immigrants tend to reside in suburbs.

One of the inherent problems in understanding the experiences of Asian immigrants in the United States is that researchers have often paid little attention to sociocultural differences within distinct Asian groups, thus failing to recognize the potential influences of such differences on acculturation processes (Chun & Akutsu, 2003). For example, unlike Chinese, Japanese, and Korean immigrants, most of whom left their home countries voluntarily to seek better economic and educational opportunities, a majority of Southeast Asians arrived in the United States after being "forced" to leave their countries. Consequently, compared with other Asian immigrants, Southeast Asians are often less prepared for the new environment (e.g., poor English ability) and had limited exposure to Western culture at the time of their immigration (Ying & Akutsu, 1997). Given the wide diversity among

Asian immigrants, each subgroup may face unique barriers and stressors in the process of adaptation.

One unique barrier that Asian immigrants face is the myth of Asian Americans as the "model minority" (Austria, 2003; Min, 2005). That is, Asians are often perceived as the most highly educated and economically successful ethnic minority group in the United States. Various statistics do indicate that Asian Americans represent the minority group with the highest household income and college and advanced degree (professional or PhD) attainment rate. For instance, their 2005 median family income was $61,094, which is 120% of the median for non-Hispanic white households (U.S. Census Bureau, 2006). Asian Americans are considered successful when examining other domains of social life such as low rates of divorce, crime, and violence (Sue, 2002). However, Asian immigrants tend to have more family members working in the labor force, they make less money for additional years of education attained, and recent or first-generation Asian immigrants earn less money than non-Hispanic whites (Fong, 2007). In addition, and to illustrate within-group diversity, among Southeast Asian immigrants, 30% to 60% of Laotians, Cambodians, and Hmong are living in poverty, whereas only 10% of all Asians in the United States live below the poverty line (U.S. Bureau of the Census, 2000). Scholars have argued that the model minority perception leads to overgeneralizations and exclusion from many policies and programs (e.g., Austria, 2003).

The model minority image further exacerbates several problems that Asian immigrants may face, such as physical and psychological adjustment problems, because it leads social service providers to virtually ignore the needs of Asians (Alvarez, Juang, & Liang, 2006; Austria, 2003). For example, because Asian American children, on average, tend to have higher levels of educational achievement than European American children, many policymakers assume that all Asian youth are academically successful and psychologically healthy (Austria, 2003). However, Asian immigrants are also found to experience greater family dysfunction than other ethnic minority groups (Tsai-Chae & Nagata, 2008); levels of family conflict are significantly higher among Asian American college students (Lau, Jernewall, Zane, & Myers, 2002), which is, in turn, linked to psychological problems including anxiety and depression (Farver, Narang, & Bhadha, 2002). Furthermore, the 2000 National Youth Tobacco Survey of the American Legacy Foundation reported that Asian American high school students had the highest smoking initiation rate (42.5%) among all racial/ethnic groups, and approximately 18% of Asian American youths start smoking during grade school (Appleyard, Messeri, & Haviland, 2001). Asian immigrants also tend to be victims of racially motivated harassment and vandalism and physical assaults, with 29% of the hate crimes directed at Asian Americans (National Asian American Pacific Legal Consortium, 2002). Taken together, these findings suggest that Asian immigrant youth might be at increased risk for developmental, social, and emotional difficulties related to cultural adjustment (Yeh et al., 2003).

A major issue in the adaptation process for Asian immigrants is their tendency to underutilize mainstream health services (Sue, 2002). Epidemiological surveys show that the rates of mental disorders among Asian Americans are comparable to other ethnic groups (Sue, 2002). In fact, research findings also suggest that Asian immigrants experience major adjustment problems, especially Southeast Asian refugees, who tend to have high levels of depression and related issues (e.g., Sue et al., 1994). Costs, location, availability, limited knowledge of resources/services, and lack of English-language proficiency have been proposed to explain "underutilization" of services (Sue, 2002). However, the most influential factor would be traditions and belief systems such as Buddhism and Confucianism, which have profound influence on the recognition of mental health symptoms, help-seeking processes, and responses to various treatment modalities (Lin & Cheung, 1999). Asians emphasize coping mechanisms that rely on interdependent relationships and familial commitment (Yeh et al., 2003) and tend to delay seeking professional help until they exhaust all other personal resources (Lin & Cheung, 1999). Given the fast-growing Asian population in the United States, prevalence rates of mental health issues are likely to increase, and untreated cases incur significant cost to individuals, families, and society.

Conclusion

As an immigrant family faces social contexts in the United States that differ from those of their home country, the family system experiences stress, which can lead to changes in family strategies. In turn, changes in the family system can establish more adaptive rules, roles, and corresponding patterns of interaction within the family. That is, despite the long list of barriers and potential stressors that an immigrant family may face, stress is not necessarily negative. Stress on the family system can lead to change that is positive and increases adaptation. Religion, spirituality, ethnic communities and enclaves, shared cultural values, and informal and formal social support can serve as resources that aid immigrant families in adaptation.

Intervention efforts aimed at assisting immigrant families must consider the perspectives and social contexts of the target families (Santisteban & Mitrani, 2003). Interventions that violate the families' belief systems or that are not applicable to the families' particular social contexts will likely fail. Prior to beginning treatment with an immigrant family, it is important to assess characteristics and strategies of the family system, such as boundary hierarchies and methods of communication and conflict negotiation (Santisteban & Mitrani, 2003). For example, in a family that views children's open disagreement with parents as disrespectful, the parents are not likely to respond well to an intervention approach that instructs the children to tell the parents about their perceptions of parental and/or family rules. In such a case, the parents are likely to view the intervention as increasing the problem.

Interventions that are less direct and that build on the strengths of the family's hierarchical values are likely to be more successful for such a family.

In addition, it is equally important to assess acculturation levels of each member as these influence values and interactions with the family system. For example, among immigrants from Mexico, interventions with more acculturated individuals and families require a different focus than less acculturated individuals and families because of the different perceptions and expression of conflict (Flores et al., 2004). That is, interventions with more acculturated individuals and families must be sensitive to more direct power struggles as the individual or family attempts to integrate cultural expectations from both their home and host cultures. In contrast, interventions with less acculturated individuals and families must be sensitive to the values, roles, and expectations from the home-country culture that influence the family system (e.g., less acceptance of open conflict). Needless to say, when there are individuals at different levels of acculturation within the family, interventions need to be more complex and tailored to fit the needs of the family and its members.

Currently, some human service programs exist to aid immigrant families, but many more are needed, especially for nonrefugee immigrant families (Fix & Zimmerman, 1997). Decreasing the 5-year waiting period for eligibility in mainstream public assistance programs may be a good starting point. Bilingual programs are also needed to assist immigrant families in navigating their new country; such programs could raise immigrants' awareness and knowledge of the services and resources available to them and also help them to gain familiarity with U.S. cultural and legal norms (e.g., those concerning the educational system, child care, and domestic violence).

Suggested Internet and Reading Resources _____

Note: Some of the resources listed below do not have information available in languages other than English.

The U.S. Department of Health and Human Services provides links to other federal departments and agencies within the DHHS that address issues relevant to immigrant families: http://www.hhs.gov

The Office for Civil Rights provides general information regarding discrimination, rights to receive services and benefits from DHHS-funded programs, guidance for filing complaints concerning discrimination, immigrants' access to DHHS-funded services, and more; information is available in several languages other than English, including Spanish, Chinese, Korean, Polish, Russian, Tagalog, and Vietnamese: http://www.hhs.gov/ocr

The Office of Refugee Resettlement in the Administration for Children and Families within the DHHS provides links to eligibility requirements and information regarding services across the United States: http://www.acf.hhs.gov/programs/orr

Catholic Charities Diocese of San Diego and Jewish Family and Children's Services of Pittsburgh are examples of private organizations that provide direct services to immigrants (e.g., counseling, education, and assistance in applying for residence, citizenship, and social service programs) as well as referrals: http://www.ccdsd.org and http://www.jfcspgh.org/refugee.asp

Lansford, J. E., Deater-Decker, K., & Bornstein, M. H. (2007). *Immigrant families in contemporary society.* New York: Guilford.

Massey, D. S., Durand, J., & Malone, N. J. (2002). *Beyond smoke and mirrors: Mexican immigration in an era of economic integration.* New York: Russell Sage.

Suarez-Orozco, C., Suarez-Orozco, M. M., & Todorova, I. (2008). *Learning a new land: Immigrant students in American society.* Cambridge, MA: Belknap Press.

References

Alvarez, A. N., Juang, L., & Liang, C. T. H. (2006). Asian Americans and racism: When bad things happened to "model minorities." *Cultural Diversity and Ethnic Minority Psychology, 12,* 477–492.

Appleyard, J., Messeri, P., & Haviland, M. L. (2001). Smoking among Asian American and Hawaiian/Pacific Islander youth: Data from the 2000 National Youth Tobacco Survey. *Asian American Pacific Islander Journal of Health, 9,* 5–14.

Arnold, E. (1991). Issues of reunification of migrant West Indian children in the United Kingdom. In J. L. Roopnarine & J. Brown (Eds.), *Caribbean families: Diversity among ethnic groups* (pp. 243–258). Greenwich, CT: Ablex.

Atiles, J. H., & Bohon, S. A. (2002). The needs of Georgia's new Latinos: A policy agenda for the decade ahead. *Public Policy Research, 3,* 1–51.

Atiles, J. H., & Bohon, S. A. (2003). Camas calientes: Housing adjustments and barriers to social and economic adaptation among Georgia's rural Latinos. *Southern Rural Sociology, 19*(1), 97–122.

Austria, A. M. (2003). People of Asian descent: Beyond myths and stereotypes. In J. D. Robinson & L. C. James (Eds.), *Diversity in human interactions: The tapestry of America* (pp. 63–75). New York: Oxford University Press.

Berry, J. W. (2001). A psychology of immigration. *Journal of Social Issues, 57,* 615–631.

Bhattacharya, G., & Schoppelrey, S. L. (2004). Preimmigration beliefs of life success, postimmigration experiences, and acculturative stress: South Asian immigrants in the United States. *Journal of Immigrant Health, 6,* 83–92.

Bohon, S. A. (2001). *Latinos in ethnic enclaves: Immigrant workers and the competition for jobs.* New York: Routledge.

Bohon, S. A., Macpherson, H., & Atiles, J. H. (2005). Educational barriers for new Latinos in Georgia. *Journal of Latinos and Education, 4,* 43–58.

Bohon, S., Stamps, K., & Atiles, J. (2008). Transportation and migrant adjustment in Georgia. *Population Research & Policy Review, 27*(3), 273–291.

Boss, P. G. (2002). *Family stress management: A contextual approach* (2nd ed.). Thousand Oaks, CA: Sage.

Bozorgmehr, M., & Bakalian, A. (2004, August). *Post-9/11 anti immigrant government initiatives: The response of Middle Eastern and South Asian American organizations.* Paper presented at the annual meetings of the American Sociological Association, San Francisco, CA.

Buriel, R., Perez, W., De Ment, T., Chavez, D., & Moran, V. (1998). The relationship of language brokering to academic performance, biculturalism, and self-efficacy among Latino adolescences. *Hispanic Journal of Behavioral Sciences, 20*(3), 283–297.

Capps, R. (2001). *Hardship among children of immigrants: Findings for the 1999 National Survey of America's Families.* Washington, DC: Urban Institute.

Capps, R., Kenney, G. M., & Fix, M. E. (2003). *Health insurance coverage of mixed status immigrant families.* Washington, DC: Urban Institute.

Chen, P., Harris, K. M., & Guo, G. (2005, August). *Cohabit or marry: Union formation patterns among young adults of different immigrant generations.* Paper presented at the annual meetings of the American Sociological Association, Philadelphia, PA.

Chia, R. C., Moore, J. L., Lam, K., Chuang, C. J., & Cheng, B. S. (1994). Cultural differences in gender role attitudes between Chinese and American students. *Sex Roles, 31,* 3–30.

Chun, K. M., & Akutsu, P. D. (2003). Acculturation among ethnic minority families. In K. M. Chun, P. B. Organista, & G. Marín (Eds.), *Acculturation: Advances in theory, measurement, and applied research* (pp. 95–119). Washington, DC: APA.

Chung, G. H., Tucker, M. B., & Takeuchi, D. (2008). Wives' relative income production and household male dominance: Examining violence among Asian American enduring couples. *Family Relations, 57,* 227–238.

Colman, D. L. (2007). The role of the law in relationships within immigrant families. In J. E. Lansford, K. Deater-Decker, & M. H. Bornstein (Eds.), *Immigrant families in contemporary society* (pp. 287–303). New York: Guilford.

del Pinal, J., & Singer, A. (1997). Generations of diversity: Latinos in the United States. *Population Bulletin, 52*(3), 122–139.

Espenshade, T. J. (1995). Unauthorized immigration to the United States. *Annual Review of Sociology 21,* 195–216.

Evans, G. W. (2006). Child development and the physical environment. *Annual Review of Psychology, 57,* 423–451.

Falicov, C. J. (2003). Immigrant family processes. In F. Walsh (Ed.), *Normal family processes: Growing diversity and complexity* (pp. 280–300). New York: Guilford.

Farver, J. A. M., Narang, S. K., & Bhadha, B. R. (2002). East meets West: Ethnic identity, acculturation, and conflict in Asian Indian families. *Journal of Family Psychology, 16*(3), 338–350.

Fernandez-Kelly, P. M., & Schauffler, R. (1994). Divided fates: Immigrant children in a restructured U.S. economy. *International Migration Review, 28,* 662–690.

Finch, B. K., & Vega, W. A. (2003). Acculturation stress, social support, and self-rated health among Latinos in California. *Journal of Immigrant Health, 5,* 109–117.

Fix, M. E., & Zimmerman, W. (1997). *Welfare reform: A new immigration policy for the United States.* Washington, DC: Urban Institute.

Flores, E., Tschann, J. M., Marin, B. V., & Pantoja, P. (2004). Marital conflict and acculturation among Mexican American husbands and wives. *Cultural Diversity and Ethnic Minority Psychology, 10*(1), 39–52.

Fong, R. (2007). Immigrant and refugee youth: Migration journeys and cultural values. *Prevention Researcher, 14*(4), 3–5.

Gyory, A. (1998). *Closing the gate: Race, politics, and the Chinese Exclusion Act.* Chapel Hill: University of North Carolina Press.

Hakim, J. (1995). *A history of us: War, peace and all that jazz.* New York: Oxford University Press.

Hondagneu-Sotelo, P. (1994). *Gendered transitions: Mexican experiences of migration.* Berkeley: University of California Press.

Kamya, H. A. (1997). African immigrants in the United States: The challenge for research and practice. *Social Work, 42,* 154–165.

Kim, H. K., & McKenry, P. C. (1998). Social networks and support: A comparison of African Americans, Asian Americans, Caucasians, and Hispanics. *Journal of Comparative Family Studies, 29,* 313–334.

Kwak, K. (2003). Adolescents and their parents: A review of intergenerational family relations for immigrant and non-immigrant families. *Human Development, 46,* 115–136.

Landale, N. S. (1997). Immigration and the family: An overview. In A. Booth, A. C. Crouter, & N. S. Landale (Eds.), *Immigration and the family: Research and policy on U.S. immigrants* (pp. 281–291). Mahwah, NJ: Lawrence Erlbaum.

Landale, N., & Oropesa, R. (2007). Hispanic families: Stability and change. *Annual Review of Sociology, 33*(1), 381–405.

Lau, A. S., Jernewall, N. M., Zane, N., & Myers, H. F. (2002, August). Correlates of suicidal behaviors among Asian American outpatient youths. *Cultural Diversity and Ethnic Minority Psychology, 8*(3), 199–213.

Lin, K.-M., & Cheung, F. (1999). Mental health issues for Asian Americans. *Psychiatric Services, 50,* 774–780.

Massey, D. S., Durand, J., & Malone, N. J. (2002). *Beyond smoke and mirrors: Mexican immigration in an era of economic integration.* New York: Russell Sage.

McCubbin, H. I., Thompson, E. A., Thompson, A. I., & Fromer, J. E. (Eds.). (1998). *Resiliency in Native American and immigrant families.* Thousand Oaks, CA: Sage.

Min, P. G. (2005). *Asian Americans: Contemporary trends and issues.* Thousand Oaks, CA: Pine Forge Press.

Murguia, E., & Telles, E. E. (1996). Phenotype and schooling among Mexican Americans. *Sociology of Education, 69,* 276–289.

National Asian American Pacific Legal Consortium. (2002). *Audit of violence against Asian Pacific Americans. Remembering: A ten-year retrospective.* Retrieved May 15, 2009, from http://www.advancingequality.org/files/2002_Audit.pdf

Passel, J. S. (2006). *Size and characteristics of the unauthorized migrant population in the U.S.* Washington, DC: Pew Hispanic Center.

Portes, A., & Manning, R. (1986). The immigrant enclave: Theory and empirical examples. In S. Olzak & J. Nagel (Eds.), *Competitive ethnic relations* (pp. 47–68). Orlando, FL: Academic Press.

Portes, A., & Stepick, A. (1993). *City on the edge: The transformation of Miami.* Berkeley: University of California Press.

Rumbaut, R. G. (1997). Ties that bind: Immigration and immigrant families in the United States. In A. Booth, A. C. Crouter, & N. S. Landale (Eds.), *Immigration and the family: Research and policy on U.S. immigrants* (pp. 3–46). Mahwah, NJ: Lawrence Erlbaum.

Sanders, J., & Nee, V. (1987). Limits of ethnic solidarity in the enclave economy. *American Sociological Review, 52,* 745–773.

Santisteban, D. A., & Mitrani, V. B. (2003). The influences of acculturation processes on the family. In K. M. Chun, P. B. Organista, & G. Marín (Eds.), *Acculturation: Advances in theory, measurement, and applied research* (pp. 121–135). Washington, DC: APA.

Serafica, F. C., Weng, A., & Kim, H. K. (2000). Asian American women's friendships and social networks. In J. L. Chin (Ed.), *Relationships among Asian American women* (pp. 151–175). Washington, DC: APA.

Singer, A., & Massey, D. A. (1998). The social process of undocumented border crossing among Mexican migrants. *International Migration Review, 32,* 561–592.

Sorenson, E., Bean, F. D., Ku, L., & Zimmerman, W. (1992). *Immigrant categories and the U.S. job market: Do they make a difference?* (Urban Institute Report No. 92–1). Washington, DC: Urban Institute Press.

Spain, D. (1999, May). America's diversity: On the edge of two centuries. *Population Reference Bureau Reports on America, 1*(2), 1–12.

Suarez-Orozco, C., Suarez-Orozco, M. M., & Todorova, I. (2008). *Learning a new land: Immigrant students in American society.* Cambridge, MA: Belknap Press.

Sue, S. (2002). Asian American mental health: What we know and what we don't know. In W. J. Lonner, D. L. Dinnel, S. A. Hayes, & D. N. Sattler (Eds.), *Online readings in psychology and culture* (Unit 3, Chapter 4) (http://www.wwu.eud/~culture). Center for Cross-Cultural Research, Western Washington University, Bellingham, WA.

Sue, S., Nakamura, C. Y., Chung, R. C.-Y., & Yee-Bradbury, C. (1994). Mental health research on Asian Americans. *Journal of Community Psychology, 23,* 61–67.

Taylor, M. C. (2000). The significance of racial context. In D. O. Sears, J. Sidanius, & L. Bobo (Eds.), *Racialized politics: The debate about racism in America* (pp. 118–136). Chicago: University of Chicago Press.

Ten Eyck, Tiffany. (2008). "Uneasy reception for Portland day labor center." *Labor Notes.* Retrieved August 5, 2008, from labornotes.org

Trickett, E., & Jones, C. (2007). Adolescent culture brokering and family functioning: A study of families from Vietnam. *Cultural Diversity & Ethnic Minority Psychology, 13*(2), 143–150.

Tsai-Chae, A., & Nagata, D. (2008). Asian values and perceptions of intergenerational family conflict among Asian American students. *Cultural Diversity & Ethnic Minority Psychology, 14*(3), 205–214.

Tumlin, K. C., & Zimmerman, W. (2003). *Immigrants and TANF: A look at immigrant welfare recipients in three cities.* Washington, DC: Urban Institute.

U.S. Bureau of the Census. (2000). *Statistical abstract of the United States.* Washington, DC: Government Printing Office.

U.S. Bureau of the Census. (2004). *Cumulative births, deaths, and migration, 2000–2003.* Retrieved April 26, 2004, from http://eire.census.gov/popest/estimates.php

U.S. Bureau of the Census. (2006). [Data retrieved using American FactFinder utility]. Retrieved August 1, 2008, from http://factfinder.census.gov

Van Hook, J. (2003). *Poverty grows among children of immigrants in the U.S.* Retrieved July 17, 2008, from http://www.migrationinformation.org/USfocus/display.cfm?ID=188

Whitechurch, G. G., & Constantine, L. L. (1993). Systems theory. In P. G. Boss, W. J. Doherty, R. LaRossa, W. R. Schumm, & S. K. Steinmetz (Eds.), *Sourcebook of family theories and methods: A contextual approach* (pp. 325–352). New York: Plenum.

Yeh, C. J., Arora, A. K., Inose, M., Okubo, Y., Li, R. H., & Greene, P. (2003). The cultural adjustment and mental health of Japanese immigrant youth. *Adolescence, 38,* 481–496.

Ying, Y., & Akutsu, P. D. (1997). Psychological adjustment of Southeast Asian refugees: The contribution of sense of coherence. *Journal of Community Psychology, 25,* 125–139.

Zucker, N. L., & Zucker, N. F. (1992). From immigration to refugee redefinition: A history of refugee and asylum policy in the United States. *Journal of Policy History, 4,* 54–70.

14 Stress and Coping in African American Families

Pearl E. Stewart

African American families are systems in the midst of change. In some respects, such as decreasing rates of marriage and increasing age of first marriages, these changes mirror changes in society at large, in pattern if not always in degree. Other changes, such as place of residence and child-rearing practices, are influenced and guided by socioeconomic status and the implications of race, racism, and culture.

African Americans currently represent 13.4% of the U.S. population (Lamanna & Reidman, 2009). In addition to showing numerical growth, African Americans are also growing with respect to intragroup diversity. There are now more African Americans among the middle class than at any other time in the history of the United States, yet a substantial proportion of African Americans continue to live in poverty. This diversity can create significant social and economic tensions within the African American community and within extended-family groups that have historically provided resources for coping with stressors experienced by African Americans. In addition, the continuing existence of racism and the prejudice and discrimination that are practiced as a result of that racism lead to significant stressors in the lives of African Americans.

A discussion of all the stressors that affect the immediate and long-term functioning of African American families is beyond the scope of a single chapter. As a result, this chapter will focus on several broad topics that illustrate common issues and stressors encountered by African American families. The impact of changing socioeconomic status on the African American family structure and family relationships, workplace issues for emerging middle-class African Americans, and African American fathering will be addressed. This chapter will also explore methods including utilization of extended-family networks, racial socialization, and spirituality used by African Americans to cope with daily and long-term stressors.

Theoretical Perspectives

Family Ecological Systems Perspective

The family ecological perspective is an appropriate lens through which African American families and their experiences can be viewed because it provides an opportunity to consider the various contexts in which families and individuals interact with each other. In addition to family contexts, ecological theory examines the interconnectedness and interdependence of the family unit as well as the social, physical, and historical contexts in which the family unit exists (Littlejohn, Blake, & Darling, 1993; Scannapieco & Jackson, 1996; Sudarkasa, 1997). These interconnections, which are well documented in the literature on African American families, may be seen in the form of extended-family structures and kinship patterns such as multigenerational households that share financial and/or caregiving responsibilities, families who live in close proximity to one another, and fictive kin relationships that may not be recognized by the larger society (Chatters, Taylor, & Jayakody, 1994). Bronfenbrenner (1979, 1986) proposes a model that looks at the development of families and individuals within the context of five embedded environmental levels. These contexts promote, support, or inhibit individual and/or family change and development.

The outermost context or level is represented by the *chronosystem*, which speaks to the passage of time and its influence on the individual and/or family (Bronfenbrenner, 1986). Placement in historical time influences behaviors by determining what resources or barriers exist for individuals or families in a historical context. Today, many of the formal and legal barriers to employment, housing, and education have been removed for African American families, yet other issues have arisen. For example, the need to be computer literate and to have Internet access is a product of historical time. As the need to utilize computer technology—to fully participate in economic and educational opportunities—has increased, so has the acknowledgement that African Americans are overrepresented among those lacking access to that technology (Horton, 2004). This lack of access creates stressors related to educational and employment opportunities.

The next system level, the *macrosystem,* represents the cultural and institutional patterns that impact and control society as a whole, for example, the values and norms of larger society that impact social expectations and legal rules, the policies that support the rules, and the ways in which those rules are enforced. These patterns might be described as cultural ideology (Bronfenbrenner, 1986). The history and legacy of slavery, segregation, and racism impact who makes and enforces the rules and roles in the African American community and thus represent macrosystem effects.

The *exosystem* represents the social structures "... both formal and informal that do not themselves contain the developing person but impinge upon or encompass the immediate settings in which that person is found, and thereby influence, delimit or even determine what goes on there" (Bronfenbrenner, 1979, p. 515). Access to employment, the availability of quality education, and access to housing are indicative of exosystem effects.

The *mesosystem* is composed of the interactions and interrelationships between the primary settings or environments that impact the life of the individual. Those interactions may be between parents, peers, schools, churches, or other organizations. Given the history of racism, prejudice, and discrimination toward African Americans in the United States, interactions with institutions such as schools, law enforcement, and, where applicable, public and child welfare may result in negative biases and negative expectations on both sides of an interaction.

The *microsystem* involves the individual and the settings in which the individual is actively involved (Bronfenbrenner, 1979). Those environments or settings include the family, home, classroom, or work environments, as well as churches or peer groups. It is within the context of these environments and the interactions between them that much of an individual's development is facilitated. As Bronfenbrenner and Morris (1997) state:

> Especially in its early phases, but also throughout the life course, human development takes place through processes of progressively more complex reciprocal interactions between an active, evolving biopsychological organism and the persons, objects and symbols in its immediate external environment. (p. 996)

The family system is arguably the most important aspect of an African American's microsystem and can define, in tone and content, the interactions between the family and other ecological system levels. For example, if school personnel accept only nuclear models of families as legitimate and strong, they may reject the efforts of an extended-family system to meet a student's needs (holding meetings when biological parents are unavailable). For some families, this may be an acceptable way to meet the need for family/school contact. In contrast, the school may view it as an indication of a disorganized or chaotic family system. A negative confrontation over this issue can set the tone for all future interactions and may result in a failure to meet the needs of students.

Stressors for African American Families

Changes in Socioeconomic Status

Changing socioeconomic status, whether related to the increase in economic resources and associated responsibilities or the challenges of living in poverty, has a dramatic impact on all aspects of family life. The impact of changing socioeconomic status is particularly salient for African American families for several reasons. First, there has been a documented rise in the number of middle-class African Americans (Attewell, Lavin, Domina, & Levey, 2004; Pattillo, 2003). This increase has been accompanied by greater exposure to other cultures and belief systems, lifestyle changes, and the need to reconcile that exposure and change with traditional African American values and family expectations. There is potential for both positive and negative outcomes of socioeconomic gains; however, few have acknowledged the stressors that may accompany higher levels of socioeconomic standing. Second, a disproportionate percentage of African Americans continue to live in poverty. Long-term exposure to poverty creates and exacerbates stressors that can lead to negative outcomes for individuals and families. For example, lack of access to health care, caused by the lack of health insurance or by a lack of health care providers, can lead to premature death, chronic disability, or the inability to maintain employment. Other stressors caused by poverty include living in substandard housing, poor nutrition and limited access to educational and employment opportunities.

Emerging Middle Class

The media, and to some extent research, often give the impression that all African Americans are, and have always been, impoverished. In reality, a small number of African American "small businessmen, ministers, teachers and undertakers with a few lawyers, doctors and pharmacists" (Harris, 1999, p. 40) have always served the African American community. Legislation (e.g., Civil Rights Act & Affirmative Action hiring practices) and changes in attitude opened educational and employment opportunities for people of color. Although disparities continue to exist among U.S. racial/ethnic groups with respect to social experience, finances, and the accumulation of wealth, a substantial proportion of African Americans now work in occupations that define them as middle class (Pattillo, 2003).

Definitions of what constitutes the middle class vary, however; in 2001, between 25% and 50% of all African American families were middle class as defined by income and job title (Attewell et al., 2004; McHinnon & Humes, 2000), and 30% of African American households earned $50,000 or more annually (Lamanna & Reidman, 2009). Measuring income represents one way of assigning social class; however, job type is another method of determining middle-class status with those having white-collar jobs being classified as middle class (Pattillo-McCoy, 2000). Persons holding white-collar jobs with incomes at the lower end of the middle-class spectrum are disproportionately African American (Pattillo-McCoy, 2000; Shapiro, 2004). Even with problematic definitions, it is clear that the African American middle class has grown from being few in number to a significant proportion of the African American population.

This unprecedented growth has brought with it both costs and benefits for African American families. Positive changes in income, while relieving the financial strains of poverty, may come at the cost of having to distance oneself from those who provided the financial, social, and instrumental support that allowed the transition from poverty (Rapp, 1992). In breaking or loosening ties with the extended family, African Americans may be sacrificing not only an important support system but also an important part of their culture (Boyd-Franklin, 2003; MacAdoo, 1997). In this way, a positive outcome (increased resources) actually results in an additional stressor (distancing from a primary source of support).

The impact of exposure to differing values and behaviors is seen more clearly as the African American middle class grows. The emphasis on individualism and independence, characteristic of larger U.S. society, rather than on communalism and interdependence, characteristic of the African American community, is one example. Under the doctrine of independence, individual maintenance of resources is accepted, expected, and necessary in order to maintain middle-class status. Furthermore, making those resources available to family members outside the nuclear unit is viewed as unnecessary and an intrusion on the hard work or good fortune of the high achiever. Reconciling these competing value systems can be especially stressful for those newly arrived in the middle class. As Martin and Martin (1978) indicate:

> It is not always easy for a well off member to maintain kinship ties. There are two important reasons: first, American middle class values are not always compatible with extended family values: and, second, a middle class way of life may provide a "better off" family member with a social and cultural orientation different from that of his relatives. Middle class family values are not oriented toward the welfare of aunts, uncles, cousins, unwed mothers or even aging parents to the extent that extended family values are. Middle class values, in short, are more compatible with the nuclear than the extended family. For African Americans, these two behaviors violate basic cultural tenets on which family relationships (blood, marriage or fictive) are built. (p. 76)

In addition to the loss of social support and the reconciliation of competing values, newcomers to the middle class do not have the resources (e.g., savings and other forms of wealth) as others do who were born to the middle class. In fact, many African Americans hold jobs that represent the lowest income groups in the middle class (Lamanna & Riedman, 2009; Shapiro, 2004), resulting in a very real danger of losing middle-class status as one strives to meet extended-family obligations (Billingsley, 1992; Shapiro, 2004).

Another potential stressor for some middle-class African Americans or for those striving to transition from poverty is the reality that contact and interaction with extended-family members may be constrained by the semilegal or illegal lifestyles that less financially secure relatives adopt in order to survive (Stewart, 2003). This necessary distancing may be viewed as a personal choice rather than as a mechanism to protect middle-class status and has implications for even the most basic and appropriate family contacts (e.g., failure to attend family events such as funerals, weddings, and other rites of passage or to visit).

Changing Socioeconomic Status and Family Relationships

As some family members learn new roles and negotiate the expectations of changed socioeconomic circumstances, it is necessary to negotiate family relationships that are affected by socioeconomic variation. Because African American extended families can be large and common definitions of family use a nuclear-family perspective, issues related to intrafamilial variation in social class are less well documented. In the nuclear-family model, socioeconomic status is often based on the income and social position of parents; therefore, all nuclear-family members tend to occupy the same socioeconomic status (Ross, 1995). In African American extended families, which are by definition more inclusive, there is a greater chance that members will occupy varying levels of social status. Variation in social status is even more stress inducing if some members "change" status during their lifetime rather than maintain the status inherited or occupied by parents and/or other family members. Ross (1995) emphasizes change that can cause intrafamilial tension:

> when one family member achieves significantly more (or less) than others, and then does not fit with the family group because of attempts to differentiate, manifested by changes of interests, points of view, and, often, decreasing contact with the family of origin. (p. 340)

Changes in socioeconomic status may lead to changes in residence and the acquisition of new friends (Martin & Martin, 1978). This expansion of boundaries and acquaintances may be normal (Ross, 1995), especially among those experiencing middle-class membership for the first time. These new relationships may also be necessary if the new middle-class member is to maintain middle-class status. The middle-class member may be expanding his or her circle of acquaintances without intending to distance himself or herself from family members, but misunderstandings about motives in these situations may cause family strain. Extended-family members may see this social expansion as an attempt to create distance by associating with new people. This misunderstanding, combined with a lack of communication, may cause hostility and impact relationships in the extended-family group. Despite these issues and tensions, research with African Americans has indicated a desire and effort to maintain family ties regardless of differences in socioeconomic class (Boyd-Franklin, 2003; Heflin & Pattillo, 2006).

The following example taken from a study of intrafamilial changes in socioeconomic status illustrates stressors that may come with greater socioeconomic status (Stewart, 2003).

> Eva is a middle-class member of a large extended family; the rest of her family lives largely in poverty. She and her husband are employed in the legal system. When asked about the frequency and type of contact with extended-family members, she reports far less contact than do other family members. "I don't know. It seems like since I'm not living like that no more, everything is different between us all. Don't get me wrong. I'm happy not to be poor. It's good to be comfortable—not to struggle—and be able to help other people do better. But I lost some stuff too. People don't always want to hear about that part. Used to be we saw each other all the time, every day. Not now. I think some of it is just growing up, but then I remember that all of them still see each other. Some of it is not having time. I got my job and the kid's activities. But really, most of it is I can't be around my family and some of the stuff they do and neither can my kids. I work with the law and some of that stuff isn't really legal. A lot of people do it, but still I can't take the risk for myself or my husband. My family don't tell me about it but I still know. I grew up around it. Survival, you know. I can't blame them for surviving. Some of them got no choice."

This case study illustrates several points raised and provides clear connections to the chosen theoretical contexts. For this woman, gains in socioeconomic status came at the cost of loosening primary microsystem contacts. She has been able to restructure those contacts because her hold on middle-class status is firm. At the same time, even though she and her husband have well-paying jobs, savings, and own their home, it is not possible for her to openly defy social class lines.

Challenges to Professionals

As African Americans move into professional fields, they have encountered stressors, which are not family generated, but impact family life. Though possessing credentials that equal or exceed those of white colleagues, African Americans in professional fields may be viewed as "Affirmative Action hires" who are viewed as less qualified than their white colleagues (Brayboy, 2003; Jackson & Stewart, 2003). In the following example, an African American social services professional was held to a different standard and treated with suspicion because of her family connections. The speaker had limited her interaction with her impoverished family members to protect her middle-class status and tailored her decision making to demonstrate her worth in the workplace even if those decisions did not always meet the standards of best practice. (She is the sister to the speaker in the previous example.)

Eva and her husband can do more financially when the need comes up 'cause they got more. I do what I can, but if I gave them (her extended family) all they need, I would be right back there with them. This sounds bad but I can't go back to that. Most of them understand that but some of them don't. And the people at the job who know where I come from, they are always watching me, waiting for me to step wrong, questioning my decisions where other people don't get questioned. If I advocate for a family—or try to explain how a poor family might view an intervention or even suggest a way to do things so that the clients are served and the job gets what it wants—people wonder if I might be oversympathetic. So I have to be more objective than everybody else so that my integrity and professionalism aren't questioned. It makes me mad and sometimes it just makes me tired.

This speaker is less able to support family members financially than her more financially secure sister. Though her job would seem to lend itself to greater contact with her family or other impoverished families, the work environment is an additional stressor. She feels constantly under surveillance by those who have power and make policy and dictate how policy should be implemented. This speaker was clear that many decisions were made based on biased ideas about the way that those living in poverty think and on the misinterpretation of actions by both clients and service providers. She is aware of being one of the few African American employees in the agency, and is equally aware that there are no African Americans in positions of power and no mechanisms through which to voice her concerns without fear of retribution. Energy invested daily in ensuring that she is seen as an objective and competent professional reduces productivity, causes resentment, and creates issues in other aspects of life.

African Americans Living in Poverty

Although discussions of middle-class African Americans are important and timely, issues related to African Americans who live in poverty must not be neglected. Impoverished African Americans continue to struggle with a variety of intersecting stressors such as a lack of affordable and quality housing, lack of access to health care, inadequate employment, and lack of educational opportunities. Changes to the welfare system initiated by the Personal Responsibility and Work Opportunity Reconciliation Act of 1996 were aimed at promoting self-sufficiency. These changes included (a) limiting welfare payments to 5 years, (b) creating "block" grants that gave states discretionary power to determine benefit eligibility, (c) federal mandates to increase workforce participation and (d) an emphasis on marriage. These strategies have not always been successful and have, in fact, increased the level of stress in the lives of impoverished African Americans (Seccombe, 2007). For example, many individuals who found jobs and left welfare rolls remain in poverty but are counted among the successes of welfare reform (Blank, 2002). Today, 27.7% of African American families and 33% of African American children live below the federal poverty line (Seccombe, 2007).

These disproportionately high numbers do not include African American families who are among the working poor—those who work regularly but lack income stability. This population, though sometimes difficult to define, often consists of individuals who work for minimum or near minimum wages yet do not have access to benefits such as vacation and sick leave and are not eligible for employer-sponsored health insurance (Lamanna & Reidman, 2009; Seccombe, 2007). In 2003, 20% of the nation's poor were individuals who worked for at least 27 weeks of the year and three in every five worked full-time (U.S. Department of Labor, 2005). In addition, the working poor may work at two or three jobs in order to support themselves and their families (Gringeri, 2001). This situation adds stressors because the worker is denied time with family members and the ability to supervise his or her children while not being able to provide for more than the family's basic needs.

Members of the working poor span all races and ethnicities; however, those of African descent are more than twice as likely as whites to be among this population (U.S. Department of Labor, 2005). Race and social policy are often confounding factors for the working poor searching for employment or for ways to improve their social position. The debate continues as to whether current welfare policy has truly moved former Temporary Assistance to Needy Families (TANF) recipients toward self-sufficiency or merely removed them from the public assistance rolls (Edin & Lein, 1997; Seccombe, 2006). However, there is little question that the combination of restructuring the welfare system and the loss of high-paying manufacturing jobs has forced former and current welfare recipients, who have limited education and training, into the low-wage job market (Whitener, Gibbs, & Kusmin, 2003). Such jobs provide little opportunity for advancement; thus, the "work your way up" assumptions that guide "work first" programs are based on false premises (Gringeri, 2001).

Fathering

Issues related to parenting are stressors for African Americans because there are tasks required in addition to those required of other parents. Parenting is viewed as one of the primary tasks of family life, and African American parents have goals and aspirations for their children that are similar to those of other racial and ethnic groups. Among those goals is the desire to have children who are self-sufficient and competent (Peters, 2007). However, factors such as racism, socioeconomic status, single-parenting, and societal attitudes about the efficacy of African American parents may negatively impact the parenting experience for African American families.

For the most part, research on African American parenting has focused on mothering and single parents who are impoverished. If any attention is given to African American fathers, they are, more often than not, depicted as being unimportant or absent from the lives of their children (Cochran, 1997; Coles, 2001; Thomas, Krampe, & Newton, 2008). African American fathers are generally portrayed as nonresponsible individuals with no desire to be involved with their children, and although a majority of African American children do not live with their fathers, it does not mean that men play no role in the lives of their children (Thomas et al., 2008).

Recent research provides a view of African American fathers that is more complex than has been the case in the past and reveals that many are making significant efforts to be present in the lives of their children. For example, nonresidential African American fathers tend to live in close proximity to their children (Bryant & Zimmerman, 2003), visit their children more frequently than other racial and ethnic groups (Coles, 2001; Thomas et al., 2008), and are more likely than fathers of other racial and ethnic groups to provide primary care for their children (Coles, 2003; Hamer & Marchioro, 2002). This has been linked to increased cognitive development and a decrease in negative behaviors in the children (Dubowitz, Lane, Greif, Jensen, & Lamb, 2006).

Low-income fathers, who cannot always provide economic support to their children, recognize the need to contribute and find alternative ways to participate in their lives (Hamer, 2007). For example, low-income fathers report spending time with their children, providing emotional support, and serving as a positive role model—all vital parental functions. A study by Roy (1999) indicated that African American men provided care for their children as well as financial support. The inability of low-income fathers to provide financial support has been a primary factor in negative attitudes toward African American fathers. Lack of access to well-paying jobs, and, thus, the inability to provide money, creates feelings of stress for fathers because they are unable to meet societal and legal expectations (Dubowitz et al., 2006). In such situations, fathers may involve themselves in underground economies in order to meet those needs (Roy, 1999; Woldoff & Cina, 2007). Many low-income fathers do this knowing that it sets a negative example for their children and that it may place themselves and others in danger, but they feel there are no other options if they are to meet financial expectations (Woldoff & Cina, 2007).

Single Fathers

As the number of single-father families has grown in the population at large, so has the number of African American single fathers. African American fathers are more likely to be single parents than men from other racial and ethnic groups, though the exact percentage is unclear (Coles, 2003).

Socioeconomic status plays a role in the strategies used in parenting by single African American fathers. Coles (2001) reports that white-collar fathers are more likely to take on the role of single fathers than are less affluent men, yet Eggebeen, Snyder, and Manning (1996) determined that low-income men are increasingly likely to be single parents. For example, more affluent men have the ability to pay for child care, have jobs that allow for more flexibility in meeting parenting tasks, and are more likely to have health insurance than are men of lower economic status (Hamer & Marchioro, 2002). Another important trend is the likelihood that an African American father will gain custody of a child from a woman to whom he has never been married, often by mutual consent. This eliminates the need for legal battles that could drain financial resources and prove emotionally damaging to the child.

The stressors associated with parenting for African American women are also relevant to single, African American fathers. These men are also coping with a number of exosystem and macrosystem issues over which they have little or no control, but which influence their ability to parent or their willingness to parent. For example, the need to rear children in neighborhoods where poverty, crime, and violence are endemic creates unique stressors and tasks. Letiecq (2007) identified five such tasks: (1) close and constant monitoring of children, (2) teaching neighborhood safety strategies such as safe paths to and from specific areas, (3) self-defense, (4) reducing exposure to media, and (5) avoiding other types of violence and community activism. Other significant stressors include the availability of employment that pays a living wage and access to reliable, affordable child care. Alleviation of either of these stressors can have a major impact on parenting patterns and life chances for all family members. For example, higher wages could allow the family to move to a safer area and provide a wider range of child-care options.

For those of higher socioeconomic status, issues of economics may cause less stress, but workplace issues, such as the constant need to prove oneself, could result in African American fathers having little energy to address parenting concerns. Accessing support from within the family system has long been a tradition for African American single parents. One participant in Roy's (1999) study stated that if he could not provide what was needed and the mother could not provide it, then there was a host of other family members who could combine resources to provide what was needed.

Resources for Coping

Extended-Family Supports

African Americans have long relied on their extended family as a resource for coping with ordinary (caregiving, transportation, advice) and extraordinary (long-term poverty, long-term care of children or elders, racism) stressors. For African Americans, the drive to maintain strong family relationships and to utilize those relationships before considering outside sources is supported by cultural mandates as well as instrumental, social, and emotional needs. These relationships are often connected to an extended rather than a nuclear idea of family and are part of a culture and tradition that reaches back to West African roots and holds implicit meanings for African Americans (Littlejohn-Blake & Darling, 1993; Scannapieco & Jackson, 1996; Sudarkasa, 1997). African American families, for example, may include fictive kin, that is, those who are not related by blood, marriage, or adoption but who have the status, rights, and obligations of family members (Littlejohn-Blake & Darling, 1993).

Extended-family connections and obligations may not be apparent or seem relevant to those accustomed to nuclear-family ideals. They may be, however, as important and binding as nuclear-family obligations for African Americans. Single-parent families, for example, may have extensive family support or ongoing social and/or financial obligations to their extended-family systems that remain hidden to outsiders (Stewart, 2007). Fictive kin may be called upon to meet family needs if blood kin or marital kin are unavailable, unable, or unwilling to do so. These hidden connections can result in actions being viewed by those with limited experience with extended-family systems as inappropriate.

The following is an example of a fictive kin relationship that proved vital to the well-being of siblings in the child welfare system.

Two African American males, ages 6 and 8, are placed in foster care due to their mother's addiction issues. They were removed from the home of an older woman (Grandma Jean) where they frequently stayed when their mother was "off." The boys have been in the foster care system for a number of months and have had a number of individual placements before a sibling placement is found for them in a foster care setting. As part of the therapeutic process, the boys are asked to complete a "family ecomap" identifying people who take care of them. Each boy identifies their "Grandma Jean" as a primary caregiver. Within weeks of their placement, a telephone call is received from Grandma Jean, who wants to know if the boys are safe and if she can see them. Because she is not a "real" relative, CPS (Child Protective Services) did not consider her contacts with the boys to be important or appropriate, and the provider agency is told to ignore the calls. Later, the provider agency, with the support of the boys' therapist, identifies Jean, the "fictive" grandmother, to be a more stable influence in the boys' lives than their mother or any of their blood kin. CPS reluctantly agrees to allow contact. Jean has valuable information about the boys' needs and information about the whereabouts of their mother, which results in communication between the mother and the agency. As a result, contact with Grandma Jean provides the boys with a sense of continuity.

In the situation described, CPS was initially unable to move beyond their definitions of family to meet the needs of these children. This was true even though the regulations were written in a manner that allowed Jean to be included in the lives of these boys at the discretion of the CPS staff person.

While those working with African American families cannot and should not assume the presence of a large extended-kin network, it is important to assess both the level of informal support available and the ability of that system to meet the needs of its members. Recognition and respect for the desire, willingness, and competence of the family system to care for their members validates such care as culturally appropriate. This, of course, implies an acceptance on the part of agencies, organizations, and individuals that such care is appropriate and valuable.

Racial Socialization

Although we currently live in a society where there is greater interaction among varying races and ethnicities than ever before, the need for African American parents to attend to the racial socialization of their children has not been eliminated. Racial socialization is "the process by which African American parents raise children to have positive self concepts in an environment that is racist and sometimes hostile" (Thomas & King, 2007, p. 137). It could be argued that African American parents must aim toward raising children who are grounded in their culture, have an understanding of Eurocentric values and attitudes, and recognize the influence of oppression and racism on their daily lives and life opportunities. It could be further argued that African American children must be able to blend the three aspects if they are to be healthy and productive individuals (Thomas & King, 2007). African American parents are stressed by the need to accomplish this socialization without promoting feelings of hostility or pervasive distrust toward society at large.

Racial socialization is marked by several tasks. Among those tasks is the provision of skills (cognitive, expressive, and instrumental) to cope with the impact of racism (Brown & Krishnakumar, 2007). The ways in which parents teach children to cope can be dependent on the way in which that parent was socialized, the parents' experience of discrimination, and by the parents' expectations that the child will encounter hostility or discrimination (Hughes, Rodriguez, Smith, Johnson, Stevenson, & Spicer, 2006). Second, a person's place of residence impacts racial socialization, with integrated neighborhoods receiving higher levels of socialization than segregated neighborhoods (Caughy, O'Campo, Nettles, & Lohrfink, 2006). The depth of a discussion and the topics discussed will also vary with respect to a child's age and cognitive ability (Hughes et al., 2006). In some situations, for example, children are taught to confront issues directly, while in others, avoidance or disengagement might be a safer and/or more beneficial strategy in the long term. Finally, gender has been found to affect racial socialization messages. Females are often given messages related to racial pride (Hughes et al., 2006), the timing of relationships and mate selection, as well as the importance of education and financial independence, perhaps reflecting the intersection of racism and sexism (Thomas & King, 2007). In comparison, males are more likely to receive messages about negative racial stereotypes, racial barriers, and ways to overcome those barriers (Hughes et al., 2006; Thomas, 1999; Thomas & King, 2007).

The skills and coping strategies taught as a result of racial socialization can be linked to all levels of the family ecological paradigm. For example, children raised in the current historical time frame (chronosphere) have some protection from blatant acts of racism, yet more subtle forms of racist attacks still exist. Institutional forms of discrimination, for example, can still shape futures based on the policies developed and the attitudes of those who enforce policy (exosphere). Discrimination experienced during interactions with peers of the same and different races and ethnicities as well as with school systems, recreational contexts, and work environments represents challenges within the mesosystem that children may encounter. With these environmental challenges comes the need for parents to teach children to attend to outward signs of inequity and prejudicial messages but to also negotiate subtle and often well-hidden barriers. These skills may be particularly important to the growing number of middle-class African Americans with children who are exposed to the hidden barriers but may think that middle-class status protects them.

The experiences of Kevin, who grew up in poverty but who is now firmly entrenched in the middle class, provide some context for some issues related to both residency and racial socialization. His initial belief that the combination of changed societal attitudes and his relative wealth would protect his children from racism proved faulty.

Though Kevin does not recognize the lessons he was taught by his parents as racial socialization, he can articulate the message about survival and how the world is structured for him as an African American male. As a young man, he was aware that white people would consider him a threat, especially if he was in the vicinity of any "trouble" or if he spent time with trouble makers (negative stereotypes). In school, he experienced blatant racism and barriers to success as well as gestures of support. For example, he had coaches who discouraged him from pursuing academics in favor of sports even though his chances of being a professional athlete were slim. There were teachers with a clear bias against African American students in the college preparatory curriculum. However, he also had teachers who supported him and who served as mentors.

——— •·• ———

After completing college, marrying, and having children, Kevin and his wife purchased a home in a moderately integrated and seemingly welcome neighborhood where their children would receive a quality education and be safe. Kevin admits to not thinking about racial socialization at that point because he believed that his middle-class status would protect his children from the bulk of those issues. He felt that raising his children with messages of racial pride, knowledge of extended family, a sense of independence, a value for education, and high self-esteem would be sufficient. He was shocked and disappointed when his oldest daughter encountered her first racial slur in their safe and friendly neighborhood. He and his wife realized that additional racial socialization messages and skills needed to be incorporated into their parenting. These words sum up his thoughts: "I need my kids to be ready for anything. I learned that education and money don't make racism go away and it can only protect you from so much. So from now on, I will make sure my kids are proud and ready."

His response was not unlike that of parents in the research who teach their children the skills needed to survive in their environmental context. Kevin recognized, after trial and error, that overt and covert racism are still present as potential stressors for his children. He and his wife made a decision to combine positive messages with skills that would help them to cope. Those skills included how to recognize the barriers and ways to react when insulted or threatened, skills that had been taught to them as children and believed to be unnecessary for their children.

Religion and Spirituality

Religion and spirituality have been identified as significant sources of coping for African Americans. The role of religion and spirituality in the lives of African Americans is demonstrated in the work of Chatters, Taylor, and Lincoln (1999), who found that 80% of African Americans considered religion to be very important in their lives. African Americans seek comfort through prayer more often compared to those in other racial and ethnic groups (Letiecq, 2007; Watt, 2003), and spirituality has been called a "fundamental attribute or cornerstone of African American family life" (Letiecq, 2007, p. 113) that provides a sense of interconnectedness among the individual, family and community (Moore-Thomas & Day-Vines, 2008). Though the actual mechanism for this connectedness is unclear, most agree that it begins with the feeling of love and connection between the individual and a higher power and then flows to the family and the community (Letiecq, 2007; Mattis & Jagers, 2001; Watt, 2003).

This sense of connectedness allows for the development of a "church family," who provides support and may influence the lives and decisions of African American families (Billingsley, 1992; Carter-Black, 2001; Jackson & Stewart, 2003). When blood or marital kin are unavailable, the church family provides companionship as well as instrumental support such as child care, money, transportation, food, and other goods. These services can be essential in helping African Americans cope when personal resources are inadequate. Historically, this support has been essential to African American survival because African Americans have not always been able or willing to access government-sponsored resources (Gammon, 2000).

The connection to a higher power helps African Americans cope because it provides a source of hope as well as structure. Recent research has indicated that spirituality has coping implications for parenting and adolescent development. Parents who have a strong religious affiliation are guided in their parenting by their religious values (Letiecq, 2007). In addition to helping parents cope by providing a structure and value system in which to rear children, connection to a religious community provides activities in which children can be involved. These activities reinforce the values held by parents and therefore provide an ally for parents against negative behaviors that may be exhibited elsewhere (Mattis & Jagers, 2001). African American religious communities have a long history of community outreach that encompasses families as well as those with addictions and other social problems. In a discussion of the importance of religion in the lives of adolescents, Moore-Thomas and Day-Vines (2008) report that religion is viewed as important for 60% of adolescents and that 72% prayed regularly. For adolescents, spirituality mitigates behaviors such as delinquency, substance abuse, and early sexual activity while promoting positive community involvement, prosocial behavior, resiliency, and coping skills (Mattis & Jagers, 2001; Moore-Thomas & Day-Vines, 2008). The importance of religion as a coping strategy for African Americans is well documented and touches all aspects of family life.

Conclusion and Recommendations

As the African American population continues to grow and diversify, the opportunities for stress increase. Some of these stressors are inherent in the lives of all families, and others are the result of the dynamic interaction among the ecological levels that are unique to African Americans' lives and behaviors. For example, in many cases, African Americans will be able to rely on traditional coping methods such as family support and spirituality. In other situations, the outside interventions must be accessed. These sources might include child welfare, income and/or housing support, mental health services, or services to assist elders. However, in some cases, these interventions add stress to the lives of both clients and staff. In order to address such situations, the following thoughts might be useful.

For those who work with African American individuals and families, staff training or retraining is required. This cross-cultural training should focus not only on the differences between racial and ethnic groups but on ways to negotiate differences. Attention should be given to negotiating peer–workplace relationships as well as client–staff relationships. Jackson and Stewart (2003) found that many white-collar African Americans have a significant degree of workplace stress due to the lack of attention to this issue. Furthermore, ignoring the normal conflicts that arise in a multicultural environment adds to workplace stress for African Americans. This is particularly relevant for middle-class African Americans since the presumption of many is that education has produced a level of cultural understanding that makes racist attitudes rare and laws have made racism and discrimination all but irrelevant. In spite of some areas of progress, however, African Americans in white-collar jobs, despite higher levels of education, may still be subject to the glass ceiling.

A Final Note

Barack Obama's election to the presidency of the United States heralds a time of optimism and a unique opportunity for change in both fact and attitude. Since his election also occurs at a time of economic crisis, it is uncertain what additional stressors may be faced by African American families or how the resilience of those families will work to support their members. President Obama's plans seem to offer both short- and long-term support for the middle class, as well as those living in poverty. His commitment to education at all levels offers particular promise for those seeking to utilize education as a way to relieve financial stress in the future. His stated intent to create jobs, in addition to providing immediate relief to those in financial crisis, combined with educational initiatives, has the potential to ameliorate the lives of families and individuals. Finally, his visibility as a person of African descent, in a position of great power and prestige, may assist in instilling hope and self-esteem in generations of African American young people who previously had no aspirations to such positions. However, these plans and policies must still be tested in an ecological system that may be less open to change than necessary for success. For example, while our current placement in time (chronosystem) with its economic and demographic shifts seems conducive to change, the cultural and institutional patterns that control societal norms and values (macrosystem) may be less than supportive of these changes. At the present time, there is no way to know if the election of Barack Obama will represent positive changes for the diverse body of African American families or if those families will be caught in a backlash as macrosystem forces attempt to maintain the institutional patterns that supported and promoted the racism and discrimination that has shaped the lives and life chances of African American families.

Suggested Internet Resources

The mission of the National Association for the Advancement of Colored People is to ensure the political, educational, social, and economic equality of rights of all persons and to eliminate racial hatred and racial discrimination:

http://www.naacp.org/home/index.htm

Child Welfare Information Gateway provides reading on issues relevant to working with African American families:

http://www.childwelfare.gov/systemwide/cultural/families/african.cfm

ACORN, the Association of Community Organizations for Reform Now, is the nation's largest community organization of low- and moderate-income families, working together for social justice and stronger communities:

http://www.acorn.org/

The Circle Brotherhood Association is a group of African American men practicing, and dedicated to, the quality of life, successful manhood and parenting, economic growth and development, and the pursuit of excellence and spiritual development:

http://www.math.buffalo.edu/~sww/circle/circle.html

Suggested Readings

Attewell, P., Lavin, D., Domina, T., & Levey, T. (2004). The black middle class: Progress, prospects, and puzzles. *Journal of African American Studies, 8*, 6–19.

Letiecq, B. L. (2007). African American fathering in violent neighborhoods: What role does spirituality play? *Fathering: A Journal of Theory, Research, & Practice about Men as Fathers, 5*, 111–128.

Stewart, P. (2007). Who is kin: Family definition in African American families. *Human Behavior in the Social Environment, 15*, 163–182.

Sudarkasa, N. (1997). African American families and family values. In H. P. MacAdoo (Ed.), *Black families* (pp. 9–40). Thousand Oaks, CA: Sage.

References

Attewell, P., Lavin, D., Domina, T., & Levey, T. (2004). The Black middle class: Progress, prospects, and puzzles. *Journal of African American Studies, 8*, 6–19.

Billingsley, A. (1992). *Climbing Jacob's ladder.* New York: Simon & Schuster.

Blank, R. M. (2002). Evaluating welfare reform in the United States. *Journal of Economic Literature, 40*, 1105–1166.

Boyd-Franklin, N. (2003). *Black families in therapy.* New York: Guilford.

Brayboy, B. M. J. (2003). The implementation of diversity in predominantly white colleges and universities. *Journal of Black Studies, 34*, 72–86.

Bronfenbrenner, U. (1979). *Toward an experimental ecology of human development. American Psychologist, 32*(7), 513–531.

Bronfenbrenner, U. (1986). Ecological systems theory. *Annuals of Child Development, 6*, 187–249.

Bronfenbrenner, U., & Morris, P. A. (1997). The ecology of developmental processes. In W. Damon (Editor-in-Chief) & R. M. Lerner (Vol. Ed.), *Handbook of child psychology: Volume 1. Theoretical models of human development* (5th ed., pp. 993–1024). New York: Wiley Press.

Brown, T., & Krishnakumar, A. (2007). Development and validation of the adolescent racial and ethnic socialization scale (ARESS) in African American families. *Journal of Youth & Adolescence, 36*, 1072–1085.

Bryant, A. L., & Zimmerman, M. A. (2003). Role models and psychosocial outcomes among African American adolescents. *Journal of Adolescent Research, 18*, 36–67.

Carter-Black, J. (2001). The myth of the tangle of pathology: Resilience strategies employed by middle class African American families. *Journal of Family Social Work, 6*, 75–100.

Caughy, M., O'Campo, P., Nettles, S., & Lohrfink, K. (2006). Neighborhood matters: Racial socialization of African American children. *Child Development, 77*(5), 1220–1236.

Chatters, L. M., Taylor, R. J., & Jayakody, R. (1994). Fictive kinship relations in black extended families. *Journal of Comparative Family Studies, 25*, 297–312.

Chatters, L. M., Taylor, R. J., & Lincoln, K. D. (1999). African American religious participation: A multi-sample comparison. *Journal for the Scientific Study of Religion, 38*, 132–145.

Cochran, D. (1997). African American fathers: A decade review of the literature. *Families in Society, 78*, 340–351.

Coles, R. (2001). The parenting roles and goals of single Black full-time fathers. *Western Journal of Black Studies, 25*, 101–116.

Coles, R. (2003). Black single custodial fathers: Factors influencing the decision to parent. *Families in Society, 84*, 247–258.

Dubowitz, H., Lane, W., Greif, G., Jensen, T., & Lamb, M. (2006). Low-income African American fathers' involvement in children's lives: Implications for practitioners. *Journal of Family Social Work, 10*, 25–41.

Edin, K., & Lein, L. (1997). *Making ends meet: How single mothers survive welfare and low wage work*. New York: Russell Sage Foundation.

Eggebeen, D. J., Snyder, A. R., & Manning, W. D. (1996). Children in single father families in demographic perspective. *Journal of Family Issues, 17*, 441–465.

Gammon, E. A. (2000). Examining the needs of culturally diverse, rural caregivers who have adults with severe developmental delays living with them. *Families in Society: The Journal of Contemporary Human Services, 81*, 174–184.

Gringeri, C. (2001). The poverty of hard work: Multiple jobs and low wages in family economies of rural Utah households. *Journal of Sociology & Social Welfare, 28*, 3–22.

Hamer, J. (2007). What it means to be daddy: Fatherhood for Black men living away from their children. In S. J. Ferguson (Ed.), *Shifting the center: Understanding contemporary families* (2nd ed., pp. 431–446). Mountain View, CA: Mayfield.

Hamer, J., & Marchioro, K. (2002). Becoming custodial dads: Exploring parenting among low-income and working-class African American fathers. *Journal of Marriage and Family, 64*, 116–129.

Harris, R. L. (1999). The rise of the Black middle class. *World and I, 14*(2), 40–42.

Heflin, C., & Pattillo, M. (2006). Poverty in the family: Race, siblings, and socioeconomic heterogeneity. *Social Science Research, 35*(4), 804–822.

Horton, J. (2004). Is the serpent eating its tail? The digital divide and African Americans. *Journal of Technology Studies, 30*, 17–25.

Hughes, D., Rodriguez, J., Smith, E., Johnson, D., Stevenson, H., & Spicer, P. (2006). Parents' ethnic-racial socialization practices: A review of research and directions for future study. *Developmental Psychology, 42*, 747–770.

Jackson, P., & Stewart, Q. (2003). A research agenda for the Black middle class: Work stress, survival strategies, and mental health. *Journal of Health & Social Behavior, 44*(3), 442–455.

Lamanna, M. A. & Reidman, A. (2009). *Marriages and families: Making changes in a diverse society* (10th ed.). Belmont, CA: Thompson Wadsworth.

Letiecq, B. L. (2007). African American fathering in violent neighborhoods: What role does spirituality play? *Fathering: A Journal of Theory, Research, & Practice about Men as Fathers, 5,* 111–128.

Littlejohn-Blake, S., & Darling, C. (1993). Understanding the strengths of African American families. *Journal of Black Studies, 23,* 460–471.

MacAdoo, H. P. (1997). Upward mobility across generations in the African American family. In H. P. MacAdoo (Ed.), *Black families* (pp. 139–162). Thousand Oaks, CA: Sage.

MacAdoo, H. P. (2007). Religion in African American families. In H. P. MacAdoo (Ed.), *Black families* (pp. 97–100). Thousand Oaks, CA: Sage.

Martin, E. P., & Martin, J. M. (1978). *The Black extended family.* Chicago: University of Chicago Press.

Mattis, J. S., & Jagers, R. J. (2001) A relational framework for the study of religiosity and spirituality in the lives of African Americans. *Journal of Community Psychology, 29,* 519–539.

McHinnon, J., & Humes, K. (2000). The Black population in the United States: March 1999. *United States Census Bureau. Current Population Reports, Series P20–530.* Washington, DC: U.S. Printing Office.

Moore-Thomas, C., & Day-Vines, N. (2008). Culturally competent counseling for religious and spiritual African American adolescents. *Professional School Counseling, 11,* 159–165.

Pattillo, M. (2003). Negotiating Blackness, for richer or for poorer. *Ethnography, 4,* 61–93.

Pattillo-McCoy, M. (2000). The limits of out-migration for the Black middle class. *Journal of Urban Affairs, 22,* 225–241.

Peters, M. F. (2007). Parenting of young children in Black families: A historical note. In H. P. MacAdoo (Ed.), *Black families* (pp. 203–218). Thousand Oaks, CA: Sage.

Rapp, R. (1992). Family and class in contemporary America: Notes toward an understanding of ideology. In B. Thorne with M. Yalom (Eds.), *Rethinking the family: Some feminist questions* (pp. 49–70). Boston: Northeastern University Press.

Ross, J. L. (1995). Social class tension within families. *The American Journal of Family Therapy, 23,* 338–350.

Roy, K. (1999). Low-income single fathers in an African American community and the requirements of welfare reform. *Journal of Family Issues, 20*(4), 432–457.

Scannapieco, M., & Jackson, S. (1996). Kinship care: The African American response to family preservation. *Social Work, 41,* 190–196.

Seccombe, K. (2006). *So you think I drive a Cadillac? Welfare recipient's perspectives on the system and its reform.* Boston: Allyn & Bacon.

Seccombe, K. (2007). *Families in poverty.* Boston: Allyn & Bacon.

Shapiro, T. M. (2004). *The hidden cost of being African American.* New York: Oxford University Press.

Stewart, P. (2003). Change and continuity in a rural, African American extended family: A case study. *Dissertation Abstracts Online* (AAT No. 3085483).

Stewart, P. (2007). Who is kin: Family definition in African American families. *Human Behavior in the Social Environment, 15,* 163–182.

Sudarkasa, N. (1997). African American families and family values. In H. P. MacAdoo (Ed.), *Black families* (pp. 9–40). Thousand Oaks, CA: Sage.

Thomas, A. (1999). Racism, racial identity, and racial socialization: A personal reflection. *Journal of Counseling & Development, 77*(1), 35–36.

Thomas, A., & King, C. (2007). Gendered racial socialization of African American mothers and daughters. *Family Journal, 15*(2), 137–142.

Thomas, P., Krampe, E., & Newton, R. (2008). Father presence, family structure, and feelings of closeness to the father among adult African American children. *Journal of Black Studies, 38*(4), 529–546.

U.S. Department of Labor, Bureau of Labor Statistics. (2005). Report 983. *A profile of the working poor 2003.* Washington, DC: Bureau of Labor Statistics.

Watt, S. K. (2003). Come to the river: Using spirituality to cope, resist and develop identity. *New Directions for Student Services, 104,* 29–40.

Whitener, L. A., Gibbs, R., & Kusmin, L. (2003). Rural welfare reform: Lessons learned. *Amber Waves, 1*(3), 38–44.

Woldoff, R., & Cina, M. (2007). Regular work, underground jobs, and hustling: An examination of paternal work and father involvement. *Fathering: A Journal of Theory, Research, & Practice about Men as Fathers, 5,* 153–173.

15

Homeless Families

An Extreme Stressor

Elizabeth W. Lindsey and Christina A. Sanchez

The 1980s and 1990s saw the emergence of a new and growing social problem for American society—homeless families. Historically, homeless persons were primarily men who were invisible to most Americans because they generally lived in "Skid Row" areas. However, by the early 1980s, the homeless population in the United States increasingly included single women and families with children, and during the 1990s, families headed by single women were the fastest-growing segment of the homeless population (Letiecq, Anderson, & Koblinsky, 1998).

The vast majority of homeless families are headed by women. Thus, this chapter will focus on mother-headed homeless families, rather than try to include the small percentage of father-headed or two-parent homeless families, about which much less is known. Information about homelessness, in general, will also be included to provide a context for understanding the extent and nature of family homelessness.

Many of the studies referred to in this chapter are from the 1980s and 1990s. The increasing prevalence of family homelessness during those decades led researchers to study what was then a new phenomenon. While family homelessness has not declined in recent years, the pace of research has slowed. Thus, to provide a comprehensive picture of family homelessness, findings from some older, groundbreaking studies will be included.

What Is Homelessness?

In 1987, the Stewart B. McKinney Homeless Assistance Act (P.L. 100–77) provided an official definition of homelessness:

an individual who lacks a fixed, regular, and adequate nighttime residence; . . . who has a primary nighttime residence that is either a supervised public or private shelter designed to provide temporary living accommodations; an institution that provides a temporary residence for individuals intended to be institutionalized; or a public or private place not designed for, or ordinarily used as, a regular sleeping accommodation for human beings. (cited in Buckner, 1991, p. 19)

This definition leaves room for varying judgments regarding the meaning of a regular and adequate residence. For instance, Ellie and her four children live in a mobile home with her father, his second wife, and their three children (see Box 15.1).

Box 15.1   The Porter Family

Ellie is a 38-year-old African American woman with five children: Solana, 20; Jerome, 15; Kathy, 14; Tamika, 11; and Larry, 9. Ellie has never been married to any of her children's fathers. Ellie and her children have been homeless three times.

After her mother died, Ellie began using alcohol and drugs to cope with the pain of her loss and with problems she was having with her children. She was living with Johnny, who was an addict. She spent most of her money on drugs and was not able to pay her bills. When Johnny went to jail for stealing a television, Ellie decided to try to give up drugs. When her roommate turned out to be using drugs, Ellie and the children went into a family shelter, and Ellie made a commitment to stay drug free. She and the children remained in the shelter for 30 days until she received a housing subsidy and found an apartment. Within a couple of weeks, Ellie realized she had moved into a part of town where drugs were being sold and gangs were active. While living there, Solana became pregnant, the other children "got wild," and Ellie began using drugs again, describing herself as "suicidal." Johnny was released from jail during this time, and they decided to move to Atlanta.

In Atlanta, they found a church-sponsored program that provided an apartment to them for 30 days while they tried to find a place of their own. Because of difficulties getting paperwork from the previous school system, she was unable to enroll the children in school in Atlanta. So she took the children back to their hometown, Acton, to stay with her father for about a month. Ellie and Johnny both got jobs, and after 30 days they were referred to a transitional housing program run by another ministry program. They brought the children back to Atlanta and lived in a furnished five-bedroom house for 3 months while they saved up enough money for their own place. They located a new apartment, and Ellie gave the money to Johnny to take to the landlord. Johnny absconded with the cash, and Ellie and four of her children ended up in a women's shelter in Atlanta.

Jerome returned to stay with Ellie's sister because he was too old to stay in the shelter. Kathy, who was 12 at the time, was diagnosed with renal cell carcinoma and was hospitalized for 10 days. Ellie spent most of her time at the hospital, and shelter staff and residents cared for the other children. Ellie and the children moved into one of the Atlanta housing projects, which Ellie described as a "rough" environment. She lived there for a year before she decided to return to Acton. In an attempt to save money for the move, she gave her minister her AFDC check to keep for her, but he stole the money. Ellie moved in with her sister back in Acton, but the two did not get along, and Ellie began using drugs again.

Ellie entered a treatment program and has been clean ever since. She moved in with her father, his second wife, and their three children in a mobile home because she believes his strictness supports her efforts to stay drug free. Ellie receives public assistance and food stamps. She contributes money to her father for expenses and buys food for herself and her children. Ellie is now attempting to cope with the possibility that Kathy is having a recurrence of carcinoma.

Discussion Questions

1. Ellie and her family experienced multiple episodes of homelessness, serious health issues, and were victimized by people they trusted. What strengths do you observe in Ellie that you think may have helped her cope with all of these challenges?

2. How does Ellie's life illustrate the idea that during a shortage of affordable housing, the most vulnerable families will be at most risk for becoming homeless?

3. How likely do you think it is that this family will become homeless again?

4. What do you think the impact of this family's experiences may have been on the children?

Is living in this type of "doubled-up" situation being homeless?

Beth lived with her two daughters in a small garage that had been "renovated into a dinky little rat hole" and then on a friend's screened-in porch (see Box 15.2).

Box 15.2   The Johnson Family

Beth Johnson is a 35-year-old white woman with two daughters, Marie, 15, and Daisy, 13. Beth lived with her grandmother for most of the first 6 years of her life, as her parents had divorced before she was born. At age 6, Beth went to live with her mother and her stepfather, who sexually abused her. At age 13, Beth went into foster care until she was 18, when she returned to live with her mother and stepfather. She married Tim in 1978 when she was 8 months pregnant with Marie.

After several years, Beth left Tim and moved in with her mother and stepfather until her stepfather, who she describes as "crazy," became angry with her and threw them out. She and the girls lived in a borrowed car that she parked in front of the local welfare agency for about 3 weeks while she waited for her public assistance and food stamp applications to be

(Continued)

(Continued)

approved. When her assistance began, Beth found a small garage that had been "renovated into a dinky little rat hole," where they lived for a year. They then moved into an apartment with an air conditioner that ran up enormous electric bills that Beth was unable to pay. She and the girls were evicted, and they moved into a friend's screened-in porch for 2 or 3 weeks. Next she moved into a friend's garage, where they lived for about 2 months. They ran a power cord for electricity and had a sofa, a bed, a hot plate, and an ice chest.

Beth eventually went to school to become an LPN and secured a job in a nursing home. While moving a patient, she herniated a disk. Because she was not aware of a problem until a few days later, the nursing home insisted the incident had not occurred on the job. She continued to work and received pain-control treatment, but about a month after the accident, she had to have surgery and was hospitalized for 3 weeks. Three weeks after leaving the hospital, she lost the lease on her trailer, and many of her belongings were repossessed.

Beth and the girls entered a family shelter where they remained for 3 or 4 months. Beth hired an attorney to try to secure compensation for her injury, and her case was finally settled out of court. With a lump-sum payment of $9,000, Beth was able to pay off all her bills, regain possession of the belongings that had been repossessed, and find a new place to live.

Discussion Questions

1. How many times do you think Beth and her children were homeless? Were they homeless when they were living in the garage? What about the time they stayed on the screened-in porch?

2. In what ways does Beth's life illustrate how attachment theory can predict who may be vulnerable to becoming homeless?

3. How do you think this family's experiences with homelessness might have effected Marie's and Daisy's education?

Was this family homeless? People might disagree about whether these two families had "fixed, regular, and adequate living arrangements." They had roofs over their heads, unlike families that live in their cars or camp out in parks or wooded areas, but both of these families' situations were precarious, and most would probably agree that a screened-in porch is "not designed for, or ordinarily used as, a regular sleeping accommodation for human beings." The lack of specificity in the definition of homelessness is one reason why it is so difficult to get an accurate picture of homelessness in the United States.

How Many Homeless People Are There? _____

The extent and scope of homelessness in the United States has been very difficult to establish. Studies of homelessness are not only complicated by inconsistent definitions of homelessness, they are also usually limited to counting those on the streets or in shelters, and thus miss the more transient homeless population. In addition, each of the various methods of counting has its flaws. Point-in-time estimates may focus on counting all homeless people who can be located at a specific point in time (for example, one 24-hour period, one week, or one month) or using more sophisticated probability sampling methods. However, most cases of homelessness are temporary situations, and a more accurate measure of homelessness is the number of individuals and families who experience homelessness over time as well as the proportion of the U.S. population that has ever experienced homelessness.

The most recent comprehensive study of homelessness, the National Survey of Homeless Assistance Providers and Clients (NSHAPC), was conducted in 1995–1996 (Burt, Aron, Douglas, Valente, Lee, & Iwen, 1999). That study indicated that on any given day, at least 800,000 people were homeless in the United States, including about 200,000 children in homeless families. The authors estimated that during a typical year, between 900,000 and 1.4 million children were homeless with their families. Thirty-four percent of all homeless service users were members of homeless families. Of these, 23% were minor children (under 18), and 11% were their parents. Approximately 84% of homeless families were headed by women.

Later studies have not been as comprehensive and are probably underestimates of family homelessness but do provide more recent information. In 2007, the U.S. Department of Housing and Urban Development (USDHUD, 2007a) estimated that of the 1.6 million people who used an emergency shelter or transitional housing facility between October 2006 and September 2007, 500,000 were persons in families. There were approximately 131,000 sheltered family households during that period.

That same year, the U.S. Conference of Mayors (2007) reported that 23% of homeless persons using emergency or transitional shelter services in urban areas were members of households with children. Ten of the cities studied reported an increase in the number of homeless family households as compared with 2006.

Homelessness is not a purely urban phenomenon, but there is much less information available about the extent of rural homelessness. Accurately counting the rural homeless population is even more challenging than getting an accurate count of urban homelessness because people in rural communities are more likely to be invisible as they sleep in cars or campers, in national parks or campgrounds, and in overcrowded situations with friends or relatives. Estimates of the percentage of homeless families in rural areas have ranged from 7% to 14% of the total homeless population (Burt et al., 1999; Rollison & Pardeck, 2006).

Pathways to Homelessness

There are many precipitants of homelessness: economic events such as (a) eviction, inability to pay rent, or job loss; (b) relationship events including women leaving abusive situations and disagreements with friends or relatives with whom they were living; and (c) unsafe living conditions such as a house fire, drug use or sales, condemned structures, or lack of heat or electricity. Burt et al. (2001) reported that the main reasons women who were homeless with children gave for leaving their last place of residence were (a) couldn't pay rent (20%), (b) abuse or violence in the household (16%), (c) landlord made client leave (8%), and (d) problem with residence or area where residence is located (8%). Of the housing officials that responded to the 2007 U.S. Conference of Mayors survey, 57% indicated that poverty was the most common individual or social cause for family homelessness, followed by domestic violence (39%), unemployment (26%), and family disputes (17%). Lack of affordable housing (87%) and low-paying jobs (30%) were the most common structural causes.

Weitzman, Knickman, and Shinn (1990) discovered that the pathways by which families become homeless differ according to their living situation prior to seeking shelter. Families who had had their own home experienced a rapid descent into homelessness after losing their own residence because of an eviction, rent-related problems, or building problems. These mothers tended to be older and to have fewer problems. The second group experienced a "slow slide from primary tenancy to homelessness" (p. 133) as their housing grew more marginal over time. They had left their own place of residence at least a year earlier and had lived with others for most of that time. These women were more likely to have had substance abuse and mental problems and to have active involvement with a child protective services agency. The third group of families had never had a stable residence of their own, and doubling up in crowded apartments with relatives or friends was a permanent way of life. Of these, 68% cited problems with the primary tenant as the main reason they became homeless. Also, 60% of these women had parents who had received public assistance; this group had the least education and work experience of the three groups.

Families become homeless for a variety of reasons. An overriding theme is poverty and women's inability to access adequate housing when current living situations are threatened, whether by personal, interpersonal, or economic crises.

Who Are Homeless Families?

A typical sheltered homeless family is comprised of a mother and two or three children (USDHUD, 2007a). African American families tend to be overrepresented in the homeless population. More than half of sheltered homeless family members (55%) were African American, while only 26% of persons in all poor families in the United States were African American.

White non-Hispanics and Hispanics tend to be underrepresented in the population of homeless families.

Characteristics of Homeless Mothers

In the NSHAPC study (Burt et al., 2001), 65% of mothers who were homeless with their minor children were between 22 and 34 years of age, and 12% were 21 years and under. Forty-five percent of these women were black non-Hispanic, 34% were white non-Hispanic, and 16% were Hispanic. A majority of mothers were never married (46%), 39% were divorced or separated, and 15% were married. Homeless mothers tend to have limited education: 53% reported not graduating from high school, 20% had a high school diploma or GED, and 27% had education beyond high school. In 2007, the USDHUD (2007a) found that more than half of homeless families (54%) had been staying with family or friends or had been living in a housing unit they owned or rented before they entered a shelter. The median length of stay in homeless facilities was longer for families (30 nights) than for individuals (14 nights).

Earlier studies have shown that many homeless mothers have highly inconsistent work histories (Bassuk, Rubin, & Lauriat, 1986; Burt & Cohen, 1989; Goodman, 1991a), which is reflected in their low income levels. In 1996, homeless families, overall, had an income of only 43% of the 1996 federal poverty level, and 58% of homeless women with children received Aid to Families with Dependent Children (Burt et al., 2001). Although these families had some income, it was still not adequate to pay for housing without additional assistance.

Although mental illness and substance abuse do not appear to be present among homeless mothers to the same extent as among single homeless men and women, they are at greater risk for these problems than the general population. In the NSHAPC study, 40% of homeless mothers reported they had experienced alcohol problems in their lifetimes, 46% had experienced drug problems, and 54% had mental health problems (Burt et al., 2001). While many homeless mothers suffer from some form of mental illness (usually depression), mental health concerns do not appear to be a major factor in causing family homelessness (Bassuk & Rosenberg, 1988). There is evidence that both homeless and housed poor mothers experience comparable rates of depression that are extremely high as compared with the general population (Bogard, McConnell, Gerstel, & Schwartz, 1999; Goodman, 1991a). Bogard et al. (1999) asserted that depression among both low-income housed and homeless mothers may be a result of their experiences of long-term poverty, and "that both poverty and homelessness are key factors in *causing* depressive symptoms" (p. 54) rather than depression causing homelessness.

Many homeless women have experienced extremely traumatic childhood events, including sexual and physical abuse and being in foster care (Shinn,

Knickman, & Weitzman, 1991; Weinreb, Buckner, Williams, & Nicholson, 2006). Homeless mothers frequently also experience abusive adult relationships and may be fleeing domestic violence. In one study of homeless and housed poor women, only 11% of the entire sample had *not* been physically or sexually abused at some point in their lives, leading the author to conclude that "women who are poor are unlikely to escape some form of physical violation" (Goodman, 1991a, p. 497). The effects of victimization can also negatively impact substance use, coping mechanisms, health and mental health, and positive relationship formation both with family members and service providers (Weinreb et al., 2006).

Despite the challenges homeless mothers face, they also exhibit areas of strength. For example, Dail (1990) reported "surprisingly good overall psychosocial status" (p. 298) among a sample of homeless mothers. Coping strategies that homeless mothers reported using included (a) doing something to confront their problems directly, (b) getting social support, (c) having patience and enduring hardships, (d) thinking positively, (e) having religious beliefs, (f) exhibiting a willingness to ask for and accept help, and (g) finding purpose in helping others (Banyard, 1995; Lindsey, 1996). While mothers who are homeless with their children may have difficulty fulfilling some aspects of their roles as parents, many are able to keep their families intact and find ways to cope with the stress of homelessness and conditions that precipitate homelessness.

Homeless Children and the Impact of Homelessness

Children who are homeless with one or more parents are distinguished from homeless youth who are considered unaccompanied minors. Fifty-three percent of children under age 18 living with homeless parents are male, and 75% are under age 12 (Burt et al., 2001). One reason for the young age of homeless children may be that many family shelters, including those for survivors of domestic violence, do not allow male teenagers to stay in the shelters. In such cases, male children may have to stay on their own in adult shelters, stay with family or friends, or become wards of the state. Also, mothers may be less willing to leave their younger children with family and friends, and family and friends may be more willing to temporarily house older children.

There has been much research on the impact of homelessness on children because of concern for how homelessness disrupts their lives and, potentially, their healthy development. Despite this volume of research, however, it remains unclear how the conditions of homelessness and poverty differentially affect children.

Buckner (2008) differentiates between earlier and later studies of the impact of homelessness on children. "First-generation" studies, using data collected primarily during the 1980s, focused on identifying characteristics and needs of homeless children. "Second-generation" studies, conducted during the 1990s and later, tended to use more sophisticated research designs to study more conceptually complex questions.

Early research on homeless children, reviewed by Rafferty and Shinn (1991) and Molnar, Rath, and Klein (1990), found (a) poorer living conditions (e.g., poor sanitation; exposure to cold, damp, and mold; and communal sleeping and bathing arrangements), (b) poorer health (including chronic health conditions, malnutrition, elevated lead levels, and iron deficiencies), (c) more mental health problems (including high rates of anxiety, low self-esteem, stress, depression, trauma, and behavioral problems), (d) more developmental problems (including delays in social and personal development, language, and gross and fine motor skills), and (e) more problems in educational achievement among homeless children as compared with housed poor children and the general population of children. Later studies have shown inconsistent differences between homeless and housed poor children, with both groups doing more poorly than middle-class children (Buckner, 2008).

Bucker (2008) notes that most adverse effects seem to be more related to poverty than to being homeless. That is, homeless and poor housed children are more at risk for having mental health/behavioral, health, and education problems than are children in the general population. Differences between the groups of homeless and housed poor children are inconsistent, although being exposed to homelessness does appear to increase children's risk of adverse outcomes. Buckner (2008) discusses a "continuum of risk," with some children experiencing very little risk and others experiencing much more. He describes three types of risk factors:

> risks that are specifically related to being homeless (e.g., stressful conditions within a shelter); risks that are shared by children from low-income families more broadly (e.g., exposure to community violence); and risks that all children, regardless of family income, have in common (e.g., biological and certain family-related factors). (pp. 722–723)

Children who experience homelessness are exposed to all three sets of risk factors, while low-income children are exposed to only two sets. Children who are neither homeless nor poor are exposed to only one set.

The experience of homelessness is stressful for both children and their parents. Buckner and Bassuk (1997) found that children's emotional and behavioral difficulties were more often associated with their mother's emotional distress than with their homeless condition. Family violence and economic distress can contribute to problematic aggressive behavior among homeless children, which, in turn, "appeared to lead to social isolation and avoidance" (Anooshian, 2005, p. 373). Box 15.3 describes the experience of a mother and her son fleeing domestic violence.

Box 15.3   The Aycock Family

Susan, a 43-year-old white woman, became homeless after leaving her abusive husband, Earl. Earl was verbally and physically abusive to Susan and verbally abusive to Terry, their 9-year-old son. During the last year they lived together, he began using drugs, and she began to fear for her life. Police were called to their house on three separate occasions, and finally Susan decided to leave for good. The police took her and Terry to a domestic violence shelter. Earl found out where they were staying and began to harass shelter staff. Susan and Terry moved to a shelter in a different town.

When Susan first arrived at the shelter, she was "in a daze" and "really a mess." She was afraid Earl would find out where they were, and she was panicking over how she would support herself and Terry. She applied for public assistance and food stamps and moved into a transitional family shelter. There were no housing subsidies available at the time, and Susan could not afford housing on her own without help. Susan filed for divorce, and for the first time in years, she felt unafraid. She finally received housing assistance so she and Terry could move into an apartment of their own. She found a job as a secretary and is no longer eligible for any type of public assistance. However, so far, she cannot afford medical coverage for herself or Terry.

Discussion Questions

1. How do you think Terry might have been affected by what happened in his family?

2. What are some challenges Susan might have faced in trying to help Terry adjust to the change in their lives?

3. How likely do you think it is that Susan and Terry might find themselves homeless again at some point in the future?

Page and Nooe (2002) found significant associations between children's distress and mother's childhood risks, chronicity of homelessness, residential instability, and concern over sufficiency of food. Homeless children have also reported that they were grieving for lost friends and possessions, friends, and family, and many felt shame and anger at their parents because of the family's situation (Walsh, 1992).

"Second-generation" studies of education and academic achievement support earlier findings that homeless children tend to do poorly in terms of academic performance, although not always more poorly than housed low-income children (Buckner, 2008). School-age homeless children experience termination or consistent interruption of their education and rarely receive the same services as their peers (Hicks-Coolick, Burnside-Eaton, & Peters, 2003). Numerous barriers to homeless children's educational success have been identified including residency and guardianship requirements, problems in obtaining school records, and lack of transportation, clothes, supplies, and health services (Hicks-Coolick et al., 2003; Newman, 1999; Rafferty & Shinn, 1991). The McKinney Homeless Assistance Act required states to provide homeless children with equal access to public education. However, school personnel responsible for providing services to homeless children often lack knowledge of the act or understanding of its requirements (Hernandez Jozefowicz-Simbeni & Israel, 2006).

There is evidence that children who experience homelessness are more likely than other children to come to the attention of child welfare authorities. In an analysis of 8,251 children of homeless families in New York City, Park, Metraux, Brodbar, and Culhane (2004) found that 18% received child welfare services during the 5-year period following their first admission to a shelter. Another 6% had received such services prior to their first shelter admission.

Huntington, Buckner, and Bassuk (2008) found that homeless children are not a homogeneous group with respect to their mental health, adaptive functioning, and academic achievement. Using data from a 1992–1995 study of homeless and housed low-income mothers and their children, the researchers identified higher- and lower-functioning groups of children. The higher-functioning group had lower levels of behavioral problems and higher adaptive and academic achievement scores, while the lower-functioning group had the opposite pattern. Among preschool children, 18% were doing well across all three domains, and the same percentage was doing poorly across all three domains. Among school-age children, 23% were doing well across all three domains, and 12% were doing poorly across all three domains. There were two areas of difference on demographic variables between the higher- and lower-functioning groups: Children in the lower-functioning group had higher rates of physical and sexual abuse, and mothers of children in the lower-functioning group reported higher levels of mental distress. Huntington et al. (2008) noted that this study was similar to others that have documented subgroups of children "doing relatively well in the face of hardship" (p. 749) such as childhood cancer, parental illness or depression, and divorce. They emphasize the importance of not assuming that all homeless children are "uniform in terms of their characteristics and needs" (p. 749).

Theories About Causes of Homelessness

The primary reasons for the increase in homelessness during the last two decades of the 20th century were an increase in overall poverty and a decline in affordable rental housing. These structural changes in American society put increasing numbers of poor individuals and families at risk of not being able to meet basic living expenses, including housing. The question then becomes, why do some poor people become homeless and others do not? The most comprehensive theories and explanations for why individuals and families become homeless involve structural, individual, and social factors.

Structural and Socioeconomic Factors

Many researchers and policy experts view the increase in homelessness as primarily a structural problem related to poverty and lack of low-cost housing (e.g., Buckner, 1991; Edelman & Mihaly, 1989; McChesney, 1990; Rossi & Wright, 1987). From 1977 to 1987, there was a "virtual decimation of the low-income housing supply in most large American cities" accompanied by a substantial increase in the urban poverty population, resulting in increased homelessness (Wright & Lam, 1987, p. 48). In addition, the number of new housing units decreased during the recessions of 1980–1982, and federal appropriations for subsidized housing declined 80% in constant dollars during the 1980s (Edelman & Mihaly, 1989; McChesney, 1990; Rossi & Wright, 1987).

Lack of sufficient affordable housing has continued to be a problem. In 1995, there were nearly two low-income renters for every low-cost housing unit, and three out of every five renters paid more than half of their incomes for rent and utilities (Center on Budget and Policy Priorities, 1998). The USDHUD (2007b) reported that the number of households with "worse case housing needs in 2005 was 5.99 million, a statistically significant increase of 817,000 households (16%) from the 5.18 million in 2003" (p. 1).

McChesney (1990) asserted that homelessness is primarily due to an imbalance in the ratio between the number of low-cost housing units available and the number of poor families who need such housing. She wrote,

> Homelessness is like a game of musical chairs. The more people playing the game, and the fewer the chairs, the more people left standing when the music stops . . . if homelessness is the net result of the aggregate low-income housing ratio, then . . . homelessness is not caused by individual characteristics or behaviors . . . At most, personal characteristics operate as selection mechanisms. (p. 195)

At the core of the problem of homelessness is extreme poverty. Poverty rates increased during the 1970s and 1980s, and then decreased somewhat in the 1990s. In 1993, the poverty rate was 15.1%, but between 1993 and 2000, it fell each year, reaching 11.2% in 2000 (National Poverty Center, 2006). However, by 2004, poverty was on the rise again with 12.7% of all persons living in poverty; in 2007, the rate was 12.5%.

Historically, poverty rates are highest for families headed by single women. The number of female-headed families rose more than 84% from 1970 to 1984, primarily because of the increased divorce rate, no-fault divorces laws, low rates of child support, and an increase in never-married women having children (Sullivan & Damrosch, 1987). In 2004, 28.4% of households headed by single women were poor, and both African American and Hispanic female-headed households had poverty rates of just under 40% (National Poverty Center, 2006).

Individual Factors

Individual-level factors that predispose people to becoming homeless include youth, low income, ethnicity, physical disabilities (Shinn & Weitzman, 1990) and abuse, separation from one's family of origin, and exposure to domestic violence as adults (Bassuk et al., 1986; Goodman, 1991a). Also included in this category would be individual factors that imply housing loss (such as eviction), factors that result in an increased demand for housing (such as pregnancy), or factors that result in a decrease in material resources (such as job loss or loss of welfare benefits). As discussed earlier, while poor mothers are at greater risk for mental health and substance abuse problems than the general population, there is no evidence that these individual factors are a major causal factor in family homelessness.

Social Factors

Social support is generally thought to serve as a safety net, act as a buffer for dealing with stressful events, and enhance positive coping (Letiecq et al., 1998). Disaffiliation theory and attachment theory have been used to explain why certain people have such limited support networks that they become homeless. According to Crystal (1984), "disaffiliation was seen as extending to most aspects of social living, including family ties, conventional living arrangements, employment, and internalization of socially accepted norms and values" (p. 2). Using attachment theory, Passero, Zax, and Zozus (1991) explained how family history can lead to extreme disaffiliation and inability to use social networks. They suggested that "children who experience high degrees of abuse and family discord, low degrees of parental involvement, and poor family organization and social integration are likely to experience later difficulty in seeking out caregivers" (p. 70). Studies documenting high rates of early-childhood disruptive experiences among homeless women indicate that they may be at particular risk for poor attachment and consequent social disaffiliation.

Social network theory has also been used to explain homelessness, although the idea that poor social networks are a causal factor in homelessness is not entirely supported by research. While several studies have found that homeless families and individuals have small or less supportive social networks (Bassuk, 1990; Bassuk et al., 1986; Dail, 1990; Letiecq et al., 1998; Passero et al., 1991), others have documented no differences between poor housed and homeless families on measures of social support or network size (Goodman, 1991b; Molnar, Rath, Klein, Lowe, & Hartmann, 1991; Toohey, Shinn, & Weitzman, 2004). In fact, Shinn, Knickman, Ward, Petrovic, and Muth (1990) found that homeless families actually have stronger support networks than other poor families and concluded that homeless mothers turned to friends and relatives until "their safety nets had worn too thin to support them any longer" (p. 1186).

Hudson (1998) studied variation in county homelessness rates by looking at the relationship between homelessness and a number of demographic characteristics, indicators of personal disability, economic conditions, family support variables, income and social services support, housing conditions, and extreme poverty. He found that while disability indicators did not play a major role in explaining homelessness, other conditions, such as urbanization, racial minority status, family supports, and economic opportunity, were important. Hudson asserts that a "family breakup, when combined with marginal educational and career preparation, especially among minorities in major urban areas with an unstable and competitive services economy, may be one of the events precipitating eventual homelessness" (p. 308).

In summary, socioeconomic variables best explain the prevalence of homelessness. In the context of a low-income housing shortage, individual and social levels of analysis can be useful in predicting which families and individuals are most vulnerable to becoming homeless. However, many factors that are seen as precursors of homelessness may, in fact, be consequences of homelessness, because the condition of homelessness itself can lead to disruptions in social ties, depression, substance abuse, job loss, and reduction in coping abilities.

Impact of Homelessness on Family Relationships _____

According to Ziefert and Brown (1991), "the parenting role disintegrates quickly when a family becomes homeless. . . . Family boundaries are often fragmented and parent roles abdicated . . . [or] parent roles are rigidly conceived and performed" (p. 217). While entry into a shelter ensures that certain basic needs are met, shelter life may actually be antithetical to parent–child relationships. Boxil and Beaty (1990) noted "the difficulty mothers and their children as family units face in establishing and maintaining *ordered mother/child relationships*" (pp. 53–54). Hausman and Hammen (1993) described homelessness as a "double crisis: the disruptive and traumatizing experience of losing a home as well as impediments to a parent's ability to function as a consistent and supportive caregiver" (p. 358). Homeless mothers (Lindsey, 1997) and service providers (Hausman & Hammen, 1993) have identified three factors that can disrupt parent–child relationships: shelter conditions or environment, the mothers' own emotional state, and the children's emotional state, temperament, and behavior.

The shelter environment, with its rules and characteristics of group living, often results in mothers no longer having control over daily family routines such as when and what their children eat, when children go to bed, how they discipline their children, or when children bathe (Boxil & Beaty, 1990; Cosgrove & Flynn, 2005; Hausman & Hammen, 1993; Lindsey, 1997). Most shelters have very strict rules against corporal punishment, which often leaves mothers without access to their primary form of discipline at the same time they are expected to control their children in a group living situation. The public nature of mothering that occurs in shelters means that family interactions are often observed by other residents and staff. Thus, parents find their decisions and actions judged by others and often feel as though they have lost their roles as "provider, family leader, organizer and standard setter" (Boxil & Beatty, 1990, p. 60) while living in a shelter.

Parents' emotional state influences the extent to which they are able to effectively manage the challenges and constraints of shelter life and their children's reactions to being homeless. Torquati (2002) found that parental self-esteem and physical health both mediated the significant relationship between stress and negative parenting; in one- and two-parent homeless families, however, negative parental affect did not predict negative parenting. This last finding is at odds with other research that has shown that homelessness may to lead to parental distress, a splintering of the family unit, discouragement of positive views of parents and parental roles, and a decrease in the responsiveness to a child's needs (Hernandez Jozefowicz-Simbeni & Israel, 2006). In one study, 52% of homeless mothers reported that "child problems" were a frequent source of stress for them (second only to housing problems) (Banyard, 1995).

How Do Families Emerge From Homelessness?

Service providers and formerly homeless parents cite several factors that seem to help families emerge from homelessness: (a) increase in income, (b) support from friends and family, (c) access to affordable housing, (d) knowing how to use the social service system, (e) internal strengths, and (f) motivation (Dornbusch, 1994). Schwartz (2004) found that the most important factor in determining a successful housing search among homeless families is the size of the family's social network.

Lindsey (1997) used the term "restabilization" to refer to the process by which mother-headed families emerge from homelessness. In-depth interviews with formerly homeless mothers identified three stages in this process: (1) meeting immediate family needs, (2) creating a new home, and (3) maintaining stability once they had moved into permanent housing. These same mothers identified three major factors that they believed affected the process by which they were able to successfully rehouse their families: (1) their children, (2) personal and external resources, and (3) the socioeconomic context within which they were living (Lindsey, 1996).

Services for Homeless Families

Many families come to shelters as the first step toward searching for housing. Schwartz (2004) reported that 44% of participants in his study had other housing alternatives available to them (such as doubling up with family), but they came to the shelter in the hopes that they would have a better chance of securing housing. Bucker (2008) noted that when "being homeless reduces a family's wait for a Section 8 housing certificate/voucher or other form of housing assistance, then some families may decide it is worth it in the long run to seek admittance to a family shelter" (p. 730).

The McKinney Homeless Assistance Act was the first federal legislation that included funding for homeless programs, including housing and food assistance, substance abuse treatment, education, and job training. In 1994, the USDHUD began to require coordinated community-wide applications for homeless program funding under the reauthorized McKinney-Vento Act. Local jurisdictions began to develop planning bodies to coordinate housing and services for homeless families and individuals. The most comprehensive of these plans include a full continuum of care: (a) prevention, (b) outreach and assessment, (c) emergency shelter, (d) transitional housing, (e) permanent supportive housing, (f) permanent affordable housing, and (g) supportive services.

Emergency Shelters

Emergency shelters provide an initial safety net for those who have lost housing. They generally provide a stay ranging from one night to several months, but this length of stay is usually inadequate for families to secure the necessary resources to move into permanent housing. In most emergency shelters, families are provided with few services and little support. During the day, families are left to their own devices to secure housing, visit public assistance offices, pursue education, and, in general, to take care of their own and their children's needs. Shelters designed specifically for women fleeing domestic violence are usually considered emergency shelters. Several studies have documented mothers' suggestions for improving shelter life for families, including access to day care, more physical space to cater to their children's needs, and more professional training for staff in shelters on children's rights and needs, early intervention, and cultural sensitivity (Cosgrove & Flynn, 2005; Hicks-Coolick et al., 2003). The U.S. Conference of Mayors annual surveys have documented insufficient emergency shelter resources for families for an extended period of time, and in 2007 all cities surveyed predicted that there would be increases in requests from households with children in 2008, citing the foreclosure crisis and the increase in poverty.

Transitional Services

Transitional housing programs provide families with a place to live, along with supportive services they may need to move toward stability. Transitional shelter services tend to provide families with apartments for up to 2 years and offer a variety of services such as life skills training, education on budgeting, job training, educational programs for adults and children, employment assistance, support in finding permanent housing, and substance abuse programs.

Many transitional programs offer or even require that residents participate in mental health services. Bogard et al. (1999) asserted that homelessness programs that assume a causal link between mental health problems and homelessness and "indiscriminately deliver mental health services to homeless mothers" (p. 46) may be misguided. These researchers found that mental health services had little impact on depression levels among homeless mothers, but that isolation from their social networks led to increased depression. They concluded that more emphasis should be put on rapid reintegration into the community through providing housing rather than on providing mental health services.

Long-Term Supportive Housing

There is evidence that when permanent housing is linked with the services that vulnerable families need, most families will be able to live independently and succeed in their own stable housing (Burt, 2001; Rog, Holupka, & Mccombs-Thornton, 1995). Long-term (also called service-enhanced) housing is permanent housing with supportive services such as case management, child care, social support, health and mental health care, substance abuse treatment, job services, and transportation assistance as well as programs aimed at the needs of children. Long-term settings, unlike transitional settings, are often scattered site housing with services brought to the family, and often these services are provided by existing community agencies. There is evidence that children in long-term supportive housing tend to have good access to health care, but that such programs often do not adequately provide mental health services for children (Gewirtz, Hart-Shegos, & Medhanie, 2008).

While a comprehensive service system can be successful in helping homeless families become restabilized, the prevalence of homelessness will not actually decrease while there is a scarcity of low-cost housing. Burt (2001) noted that without housing, virtually nothing else works. Increasingly, communities are taking action to encourage the development and maintenance of affordable housing as well as developing other programs (such as housing trust funds, rental assistance programs, and negotiations with landlords) to prevent homelessness.

Interventions With Homeless Families

Little has been written about direct interventions with homeless families outside the context of emergency, transition, and long-term support services.

However, several researchers have suggested promising ways to address some of the issues homeless families face, including recommendations for service models and interventions.

Health and Mental Health Services

Weinreb, Nicholson, Williams, and Anthes (2007) described the Homeless Families Program that integrates behavioral services for homeless mothers and children with primary health care provided at a community health center. The "primary health care visits provide the opportunity for basic health screening and preventative services for the homeless, as well as a context for screening, assessment, treatment and referral to mental health and substance abuse services" (p. 142). The program was based on evidence that women with mental health problems are more likely to seek treatment from a medical professional than a mental health professional. Also, women who have experienced victimization, as many homeless women have, are likely to have comorbid health conditions that may result in more frequent utilization of health care services, therefore increasing interaction with primary health care professionals. Finally, although mothers suffering from a mental illness have stated that they feel they are being judged as parents because they meet criteria for a mental disorder, when homeless mothers bring their children in for a health care visit, they are praised for their efforts to take care of their children. Thus, homeless mothers are more likely to seek and be open to treatment of mental health issues if that treatment is in a primary health care context.

The program is comprehensive, including health, mental health, and substance abuse services. Because there are so many barriers to service access for homeless families, the program is highly flexible. Services may be offered at a shelter or home, at schools, in court, or at the health center. Families can make appointments or drop in at the health center. The intensity of services is based on family needs and goals, and transportation is provided as needed. The program is family centered and uses a strengths-based perspective. To address the fact that so many homeless women have experienced trauma, violence, and victimization, the services provided are "trauma informed" to "recognize the impact of trauma on the functioning of women and children" (Weinreb et al., 2007, p. 146).

The authors provide process outcome results such as types of services families have used, focus of client–staff interactions, length of service, and roles of various health and mental health professionals. While the service model has not been evaluated for outcomes or compared with other service models for effectiveness, initial results seem to support the premise that the primary care setting may offer the most opportune environment for both physical and mental health diagnosis, treatment, assessment, and early intervention for homeless children and their mothers.

Interventions Aimed at Children

Because homeless children frequently exhibit behavior and self-esteem problems, often in school, behavior management techniques and mental health promotion activities may be useful in empowering homeless youth to create success in their educational setting. One such program has been evaluated by Nabors, Sumajin, Zins, Rofey, and Berberich (2003). This 2-month, all-day program, provided over the course of a summer, included classroom and small-group mental health promotion activities, counseling, and parent training classes. The behavior management system involved positive reinforcement through giving bracelets, which could be traded for toys or games weekly. Positive behaviors that merited a bracelet included completing work, following instructions, and prosocial behaviors. Mental health promotion activities were conducted weekly with the whole classroom and in small groups daily. Activities focused on topics such as anger management, self-esteem, positive classroom behavior, relaxation, problem solving, and social skills.

Findings from this study pointed to a moderate improvement in the behavior of those children who attended the entire 7 weeks. Both mothers and teachers reported that the children were exhibiting normal levels of behavioral and emotional functioning. On average, boys received fewer rewards than girls, and younger children earned more rewards than older youth. The authors indicated that there was a need for additional research to investigate whether the behavioral changes were sustained throughout the school year and to determine if these interventions would be best utilized at a younger age.

Multiple-Family Group Intervention

The multiple-family group (MFG) intervention has been successfully used with families experiencing a variety of problems. Parents and children from multiple families meet together with group facilitators to learn from one another, share concerns, and create a supportive network. MFG is a type of mutual aid that empowers families while providing encouragement and support.

Davey (2004) evaluated the use of MFG with a group of homeless families. Initially, the groups were to follow an 8-week format. However, due to families' transitions in and out of shelters and challenges in maintaining attendance over such a long time span, the format was changed into a weekend retreat from 5 p.m. to 8 p.m. on Fridays and 9 a.m. to 4 p.m. on Saturdays, and transportation was provided. The retreat focused on strengthening families and providing an environment in which families could have fun together. Within this focus there were four main components: building trust, communication skills, managing stress, and decision-making responsibilities. Upon completion of the retreat, the majority of parents reported satisfaction with the retreat and stated that it was helpful in helping families to feel positively about themselves. Parents also reported that they were better able to recognize and deal with stress. The author concluded that MFG seems to offer the conditions necessary to build a social support network and increase coping abilities (Davey, 2004).

All three of these suggested interventions will require additional research to examine their effectiveness with homeless mothers and children. Regardless of the type of intervention or service offered, all services offered to homeless families should be provided in a way that is respectful of clients. Homeless mothers have described feeling the stigma of homelessness when accessing services and report feeling dehumanized, humiliated, and disrespected (Cosgrove & Flynn, 2005).

Future Directions

In the nearly 30 years since family homelessness became recognized as a social problem in the United States, we are still grappling with how, as a society, to respond. The conditions that originally created the phenomenon of family homelessness, extreme poverty and a shortage of affordable housing, continue and may even become worse in the next few years as more families are affected by the current financial crisis. Many families are only "one paycheck away" from losing their housing, and middle-class families who lose their homes to foreclosure or bankruptcy will put increasing pressure on the low-income housing market. Such conditions will leave highly vulnerable families, those with serious individual and social risk factors, even less likely to be able to secure housing.

While homeless shelters and services are important in helping families meet emergency and transitional needs, what is most needed is more attention to preventing families from becoming homeless in the first place. Structural societal changes such as increasing the stock of affordable housing and policies aimed at reducing poverty (e.g., creation of jobs that pay a living wage, a minimum wage and public assistance benefits that are indexed to inflation) will be necessary to reduce the prevalence of family homelessness. With 30 years of research, we know what risk factors predispose families to becoming homeless. Social policy and programs should focus on assessing and helping families manage the individual and social factors that place them at high risk, providing financial assistance and support services to families before they become homeless. For families that do become homeless and that remain highly vulnerable even after securing new housing, ongoing supportive services and housing assistance may be needed to help them avoid becoming homeless again. Future research should focus on what services and interventions are most effective in helping to prevent homelessness and in helping families emerge from homelessness into stable living situations.

We should never lose sight of the humanity of poor housed and homeless persons, adults and children. Many of these parents demonstrate great strength and persistence as they continue to hold their families together through the stress and distress of poverty and homelessness. Homeless mothers and children hold up a mirror to our society, reflecting how much we truly value the dignity and worth of all persons and how much we are willing to take responsibility, as a society, for the consequences of economic and social policy that inevitably leaves the most vulnerable among us at great risk.

Additional Internet Resources

National Alliance to End Homelessness: www.endhomelessness.org/

National Coalition for the Homeless: www.nationalhomeless.org

The Urban Institute: http://www.urban.org/

U.S. Conference of Mayors: http://www.usmayors.org/

U.S. Department of Housing and Urban Development: http://www.hud .gov/

References

Anooshian, L. J. (2005). Violence and aggression in the lives of homeless children. *Journal of Family Violence, 20*(6), 373–387.

Banyard, V. L. (1995). Daily survival narratives from mothers who are homeless. *American Journal of Community Psychology, 23*(6), 871–889.

Bassuk, E. L. (1990). Who are the homeless families? Characteristics of mothers and children. *Community Mental Health Journal, 26*(5), 425–433.

Bassuk, E. L., & Rosenberg, L. (1988). Why does family homelessness occur? A case-control study. *American Journal of Public Health, 78*(7), 783–788.

Bassuk, E. L., Rubin, L., & Lauriat, A. S. (1986). Characteristics of sheltered homeless families. *American Journal of Public Health, 76*(9), 1097–1101.

Bogard, C. J., McConnell, J. J., Gerstel, N., & Schwartz, M. (1999) Homeless mothers and misdirected policy. *Journal of Health and Social Behavior, 40,* 46–62.

Boxill, N. A., & Beaty, A. L. (1990). Mother/child interaction among homeless women and their children in a public night shelter in Atlanta, Georgia. *Child and Youth Services, 14*(1), 49–64.

Buckner, J. C. (1991). Pathways into homelessness: An epidemiological analysis. In D. J. Rog (Ed.), *Evaluating programs for the homeless* (Special issue]. *New Directions for Program Evaluation, 52,* 17–30.

Buckner, J. C. (2008). Understanding the impact of homelessness on children: Challenges and future research directions. *American Behavioral Scientist, 51*(6), 721–736.

Buckner, J. C., & Bassuk, E. L. (1997). Mental disorders and service utilization among youths from homeless and low-income housed families. *Journal of the American Academy of Child and Adolescent Psychiatry, 36,* 508–524.

Burt, M. R. (2001). *What will it take to end homelessness?* Retrieved September 1, 2008, from http://www.urban.org/publications/310305.html

Burt, M. R., Aron, L. Y., Douglas, T., Valente, J., Lee, E., & Iwen, B. (1999). *Homelessness: Programs and the people they serve.* Washington, DC: Urban Institute.

Burt, M. R., Aron, L. Y., Lee, E., & Valente, J. (2001). Helping America's homeless: Emergency shelter or affordable housing? Washington, DC: Urban Institute.

Burt, M. R., & Cohen, B. E. (1989). Differences among homeless single women, women with children, and single men. *Social Problems, 36*(5), 508–524.

Center on Budget and Policy Priorities. (1998). *In search of shelter: The growing shortage of affordable rental housing.* Retrieved September 21, 2008, from http://www.cbpp.org/615hous.htm

Cosgrove, L., & Flynn, S. (2005). Marginalized mothers: Parenting without a home. *Analysis of Social Issues and Public Policy, 5*(1), 127–143.

Crystal, S. (1984). Homeless men and homeless women: The gender gap. *Urban and Social Change Review, 17*(2), 2–6.

Dail, P. W. (1990). The psychosocial context of homeless mothers with young children: Program and policy implications. *Child Welfare, 9*(4), 291–308.

Davey, T. L. (2004). A multiple-family group intervention for homeless families: The weekend retreat. *Health & Social Work, 29*(4), 326–328.

Dornbusch, S. M. (1994). Additional perspectives on homeless families. *American Behavioral Scientist, 37*(3), 404–411.

Edelman, M. W., & Mihaly, L. (1989). Homeless families and the housing crisis in the United States. *Children and Youth Services Review, 11,* 91–108.

Gewirtz, A., Hart-Shegos, E., & Medhanie, A., (2008). Psychosocial status of homeless children and youth in family supportive housing. *American Behavioral Scientist, 51*(6), 810–823.

Goodman, L. (1991a). The prevalence of abuse among homeless and housed poor mothers: A comparison study. *American Journal Orthopsychiatry, 61*(4), 489–500.

Goodman, L. (1991b). The relationship between social support and family homelessness: A comparison study of homeless and housed mothers. *Journal of Community Psychology, 19,* 321–332.

Hausman, B., & Hammen, C. (1993). Parenting homeless families: The double crisis. *American Journal of Orthopsychiatry, 63*(3), 358–369.

Hernandez Jozefowicz-Simbeni, D. M., & Israel, N. (2006). Services to homeless students and families: The McKinney-Vento Act and its implications for social work practice. *Children & Schools, 28*(1), 37–44.

Hicks-Coolick, A., Burnside-Eaton, P., & Peters, A. (2003). Homeless children: Needs and services. *Child & Youth Care Forum, 32*(4), 197–209.

Hudson, C. G. (1998). *An interdisciplinary model of homelessness: The dynamics of social disintegration.* New York: Mellen.

Huntington, N., Buckner, J. C., & Bassuk, E. L. (2008). Adaptation in homeless children: An empirical examination using cluster analysis. *American Behavioral Scientist, 51*(6), 737–755.

Letiecq, B. L., Anderson, E. A., & Koblinsky, S. A. (1998). Social support of home-less and housed mothers: A comparison of temporary and permanent housing arrangements. *Family Relations, 47,* 415–421.

Lindsey, E. W. (1996). Mothers' perceptions of factors influencing the process of restabilization among homeless families. *Families in Society, 77*(4), 203–215.

Lindsey, E. W. (1997). The process of restabilization for mother-headed homeless families: How social workers can help. *Journal of Family Social Work, 2*(3), 49–72.

McChesney, K. Y. (1990). Family homelessness: A systemic problem. *Journal of Social Issues, 46*(4), 191–205.

Molnar, J. M., Rath, W. R., & Klein, T. P. (1990). Constantly compromised: The impact of homelessness on children. *Journal of Social Issues, 46*(4), 109–124.

Molnar, J. M., Rath, W. R., Klein, T. Y., Lowe, C., & Hartmann, A. (1991). *Ill fares the land: The consequences of homelessness and chronic poverty for children and families in New York City.* New York: Bank Street College of Education.

Nabors, L., Sumajin, I., Zins, J., Rofey, D., & Berberich, D. (2003). Evaluation of an intervention for children experiencing homelessness. *Child & Youth Care Forum, 32*(4), 211–225.

National Poverty Center. (2006). *Poverty in the United States: Frequently asked questions.* Retrieved September 21, 2008, from http://www.npc.umich.edu/poverty/

Newman, R. (1999). *Educating homeless children: Witness to a cataclysm.* New York: Garland.

Page, T., & Nooe, R. M. (2002). Life experiences and vulnerabilities of homeless women: A comparison of women unaccompanied versus accompanied by minor children, and correlates with children's emotional distress. *Journal of Social Distress & the Homeless, 11*(3), 215–232.

Park, J. M., Metraux, S., Brodbar, G., & Culhane, D. P. (2004). Child welfare involvement among children in homeless families. *Child Welfare, 83*(5), 423–436.

Passero, J. M., Zax, M., & Zozus, R. T., Jr. (1991). Social network utilization as related to family history among the homeless. *Journal of Community Psychology, 19*(1), 70–78.

Rafferty, Y., & Shinn, M. (1991). The impact of homelessness on children. *American Psychologist, 46*(11), 1170–1179.

Rog, D. J., Holupka, C. S., & McCombs-Thornton, K. L. (1995). Implementation of the homeless families program: 1. Service models and preliminary outcomes. *The American Journal of Orthopsychiatry, 65*(4), 502–513.

Rollinson, P. A., & Pardeck, J. T. (2006). *Homelessness in rural America: Policy and practice.* New York: Haworth.

Rossi, P. H., & Wright, J. D. (1987). The determinants of homelessness. *Health Affairs, 6*(1), 19–32.

Schwartz, M. (2004). *Gimme shelter: Helping networks and housing searches among homeless families.* Paper presented at the American Sociological Association Annual Meeting, San Francisco, CA.

Shinn, M., Knickman, J. K., Ward, D., Petrovic, N. L., & Muth, B. J. (1990). Alternative models for sheltering homeless families. *Journal of Social Issues, 46*(4), 175–190.

Shinn, M., Knickman, J. R., & Weitzman, B. C. (1991). Social relationships and vulnerability to becoming homeless among poor families. *American Psychologist, 46*(11), 1180–1187.

Shinn, M., & Weitzman, B. C. (1990). Research on homelessness: An introduction. *Journal of Social Issues, 46*(4), 1–11.

Sullivan, P. A., & Damrosch, S. P. (1987). *Homeless women and children.* In R. D. Bingham, R. E. Green, & S. B. White (Eds.), *The homeless in contemporary society* (pp. 82–98). Newbury Park, CA: Sage.

Toohey, S. M., Shinn, M., & Weitzman, B. C. (2004). Social networks and homelessness among women heads of household. *American Journal of Community Psychology, 33*(1/2), 7–19.

Torquati, J. C. (2002). Personal and social resources as predictors of parenting in homeless families. *Journal of Family Stress, 23*(4), 463–485.

U.S. Conference of Mayors. (2007). *A status report on hunger and homelessness in America's cities: A 23-city survey.* Washington, DC: Author.

U.S. Department of Housing and Urban Development. (2007a). *Annual homeless assessment report to Congress.* Washington, DC: Author.

U.S. Department of Housing and Urban Development. (2007b). *Affordable housing needs 2005: Report to Congress.* Washington, DC: Author.

Walsh, M. E. (1992). *Moving to nowhere: Children's stories of homelessness.* Westport, CT: Auburn House.

Weinreb, L. F., Buckner, J. C., Williams, V., & Nicholson, J. (2006). A comparison of the health and mental health status of homeless mothers in Worcester, Mass.: 1993 and 2003. *American Journal of Public Health, 96*(8), 1444–1448.

Weinreb, L., Nicholson, J., Williams, V. & Anthes, F. (2007). Integrating behavioral health services for homeless mothers and children in primary care. *American Journal of Orthopsychiatry, 77*(1), 142–152.

Weitzman, B. C., Knickman, J. R., & Shinn, M. (1990). Pathways to homelessness among New York City families. *Journal of Social Issues, 46*(4), 125–140.

Wright, J. D., & Lam, J. A. (1987). Homelessness and the low-income housing supply. *Social Policy, 17,* 48–53.

Ziefert, M., & Brown, K. S. (1991). Skill building for effective intervention with homeless families. *Families in Society, 72*(4), 212–219.

16 Everyday Hassles and Family Stress

Heather M. Helms,
Jill K. Walls, and David H. Demo

For many American families, daily life involves negotiating a maze of activities that includes cooking, cleaning, running errands, paying bills, dropping off and picking up children, commuting to and from work, tending to pets, scheduling appointments, attending events (community, religious, and school related), returning phone calls, caring for aging family members, and remembering birthdays—often while parents also fulfill the duties of full- or part-time jobs. These routinized experiences define the rhythm of family life, and family members can experience them at times as rewarding and at other times as hassles. Whether family members perceive a particular event to be a hassle, a pleasure, or both can depend on any number of factors. For example, women and men define and react to hassles differently, socioeconomic resources and work schedules make it easier for some families and harder for others to deal with daily hassles, and differences in personality characteristics and coping resources influence how individual family members experience and respond to everyday hassles.

In this chapter, we discuss the everyday hassles that researchers have examined in studies of daily stress and family life. We first define the kinds of events that constitute such hassles and then describe the methods researchers use to study them, including the means by which researchers explore *invisible* dimensions of family work. We then examine how everyday hassles are associated with family functioning, paying particular attention to the variability in family members' experiences. We present Karney and Bradbury's (1995) vulnerability-stress-adaptation (VSA) model as a helpful way to frame the research on daily hassles and family stress, focusing on the diversity that exists both across and within families in each of the three domains proposed in the model. Because elements of context such as socioeconomic factors, workplace policies, and macrosocietal patterns introduce opportunities and constraints for family members that are likely to affect the links between each element of the model, we adapt Karney and Bradbury's model by nesting it within the ecological niches that families inhabit. In so doing, we underscore how contextual factors moderate the associations between vulnerability, stress, and adaptation. Furthermore, given the gendered meanings attached to many routinized family activities and the often divergent experiences of women and men in families, our approach is necessarily feminist. We close with a discussion of how existing social policies in the United States fail to mesh with the daily reality of most American families, and we offer some suggestions for policy interventions.

What Are Everyday Hassles?

Everyday or daily hassles are the proximal stressors, strains, and transactions of day-to-day life that can be viewed as common annoyances. These events are relatively minor and arise out of routinized daily activities, such as the tasks involved in maintaining a home, caring for family members, working at a paid job, and participating in community activities (DeLongis, Coyne, Dakof, Folkman, & Lazarus, 1982; Serido, Almeida, & Wethington, 2004). Both anticipated and unanticipated events constitute daily hassles (Wheaton, 1999). For example, commuting to work in morning traffic, chauffeuring children to and from school and activities, and working longer hours at particular times of the year (e.g., holiday season for retailers, tax season for accountants) are all daily hassles that families routinize and anticipate. Unanticipated daily hassles, in contrast, are distinct in their episodic nature. Examples of such hassles include an argument with a spouse, a reprimand from a boss, a midday phone call concerning a sick child who needs to be picked up from a child-care center, or a flat tire on the way to work. Although many unexpected daily hassles are relatively minor, they often disrupt the flow of everyday life and thus add to family stress.

Whether anticipated or unanticipated, everyday hassles are distinct from the major life events or transitions discussed in other chapters of this book (e.g., death of a loved one, divorce, job loss). Daily hassles are different from major life events in two important ways. First, everyday hassles represent a more frequent and continuous form of stress than the relatively rare events that constitute major life changes. Because of their frequency, everyday hassles may be more important determinants of family stress than major, but less frequent, life events (Repetti & Wood, 1997b; Serido et al., 2004). Accordingly, the aggregate effects of everyday hassles have the potential to compromise family and individual well-being and even increase vulnerability to major life events. Second, hassles are characterized by relatively minor ongoing stressors that occupy daily living. Although they may contribute to a major life stressor or event, they typically occur in the absence of major life events (Serido et al., 2004). Families experiencing major life changes, however, may also confront daily hassles and continuous stressors. For example, a family member who is adjusting to a major life event such as divorce or job loss may feel heightened stress if he or she misses an appointment or gets a speeding ticket.

Methods for Studying
Everyday Hassles and Family Stress

Researchers who study the links between everyday hassles and family stress have utilized a variety of methods to assess family members' experiences of daily stress. In early studies, researchers defined hassles as "those irritating, frustrating, distressing demands and troubled relationships that grind on us day in and day out" (Miller & Wilcox, 1986, p. 39). Participants in these studies were presented with lists of various kinds of hassles and were asked to rate the frequency and severity with which they had experienced each hassle in the past month (Kanner, Coyne, Schaefer, & Lazarus, 1981). One criticism of this method is that it does not take into account the complexity of individuals' experiences of daily hassles. For example, Lazarus (1999) argued that the likelihood that an individual perceives or experiences a particular event as a hassle depends on the person's appraisal of the event as well as his or her coping resources. To account more fully for individual differences in appraisals of daily hassles, DeLongis, Folkman, and Lazarus (1988) revised Kanner et al.'s (1981) measure of daily hassles to enable respondents to rate how much of a hassle or an uplift they found each category (e.g., work, health, family, friends) to be on a particular day. DeLongis et al.'s revised checklist demonstrates an important shift in scholars' thinking about daily hassles, from viewing hassles as inherently stressful events to viewing them as experiences that individuals might appraise as hassles, uplifts, or both.

Feminist scholars who have used qualitative methods to study everyday, routinized experiences within families have also emphasized the multidimensional nature of daily hassles. Focusing on the routine, gendered experiences of everyday family life, feminist researchers have conducted indepth, face-to-face interviews to uncover valuable insights regarding daily hassles. These studies provide rich sources of information about the nuances of daily family life that include participants' own, often quite complex, appraisals of their experiences. Through the use of these methods, feminist scholars have learned that although women may label many of the routinized tasks of daily life as essential and often unpleasant hassles, they also view these tasks as expressions of care for the people they love. For example, caring for an elderly partner or parent may include providing transportation to activities and doctor's appointments, grocery and clothes shopping, cleaning, and help with personal care. Women are more often responsible for carrying out these types of tasks than are men and, on average, experience them as more stressful than do men, yet regardless of the stress that comes with the added responsibilities of caregiving, many women derive meaning and satisfaction from attending to the needs of their loved ones (Walker, Pratt, & Eddy, 1995).

In addition to underscoring the complex and sometimes contradictory nature of family members' experiences of daily hassles, research using qualitative methods has uncovered routinized aspects of daily family life previously overlooked by researchers. This body of work directs our attention beyond the activities typically identified in survey studies to include emotion work (Dressel & Clark, 1990), kin work (DiLeonardo, 1987), marriage work (Oliker, 1989), the scheduling of family time (Daly, 1996), the feeding of the family (DeVault, 1991), household labor (Coltrane, 2000), child care and care for aging or sick family members (Abel & Nelson, 1990), and volunteer or service work (Hunter, Pearson, Ialongo, & Kellam, 1998).

Over the past decade, researchers have begun to examine whether and how fluctuations in daily stress and hassles affect interactions in families (Larson & Almeida, 1999). These labor-intensive studies generally feature precise temporal sequencing of daily stressors and subsequent interactions with family members. The development of innovative research tools such as time diaries and experience sampling has permitted researchers to obtain detailed accounts of occurrences of daily hassles and resolved problems associated with retrospective recall. In addition, these methods capture dynamic daily experiences that are otherwise static in survey or cross-sectional designs (Almeida, Wethington, & Chandler, 1999). Perhaps the greatest benefit of this body of research is that the methods allow for a within-person examination of the day-to-day fluctuations in everyday hassles and their links with family stress (Almeida, 2005).

Influenced by family systems theory and ecological perspectives, researchers have conducted daily experience studies focusing on how one family member's daily stress is linked to another family member's affect or behavior, as well as the reactivity of men versus women to daily stressors. For example, Larson and Gillman (1999) collected data on single mothers and their adolescent offspring using the experience sampling method (ESM), an approach in which family members carried preprogrammed alarm watches throughout the day for 7 consecutive days and were signaled at random moments. When signaled, they completed brief questionnaires about their activities, companions, and emotional states at those moments. Recently, researchers have coupled multiple methods (i.e., observations of marital and parent–child interactions, daily diary self-report data of mood and workload) with self-collected saliva samples gathered by each family member at four time points on each day of the study (Saxbe, Repetti, & Nishina, 2008). In combination, these time-intensive methods have allowed researchers to examine the complex associations between everyday hassles experienced in the workplace, subsequent marital and family functioning at home, and physiological arousal.

The studies described above have been criticized for their reliance on relatively small, nonrepresentative samples, their use of self-administered checklists to assess daily hassles and stressors, and the time-intensive demands placed on respondents, which often lead to attrition or missing data (Almeida, Wethington, & Kessler, 2002). To address these concerns, Almeida (2005) developed the Daily Inventory of Stressful Events (DISE), a semistructured telephone interview, which he used with a nationally representative sample of 1,483 adults (i.e., the National Study of Daily Experiences). The DISE methodology involves eight consecutive daily telephone interviews in which participants respond to a series of semistructured, open-ended questions about the occurrence of daily stressors across several domains, including arguments or disagreements, work or school, home life, discrimination, and issues involving close friends or relatives. Participants are asked to provide narrative descriptions of all the daily stressors they mention as well as the perceived severity of the stressors. All interviews are tape-recorded, transcribed, and coded. Almeida's methodology is unique in that rather than relying on participants' self-report appraisals of stressors, it uses investigator ratings of objective threat and severity to determine the type of threat each stressor poses (i.e., loss, danger, disappointment, frustration, and opportunity) as well as its severity. Participants' highly specific, brief narratives provide detailed explanations about the types of events that men and women typically experience as daily hassles, and the investigator ratings reduce some of the bias associated with self-report appraisals of stressors. In addition, interviewing participants over 8 consecutive days enables researchers to examine both within-person fluctuations in daily hassles and well-being over time as well as the cumulative effects of everyday hassles across several days rather than relying on single reports about particular days or subjective estimates of daily hassles over several days.

Understanding the Links Between Everyday Hassles and Family Stress

In this section, we examine how family members manage daily hassles and discuss the links between everyday hassles and individual and family functioning. We begin with a discussion of Karney and Bradbury's (1995) VSA model, and then use this model to frame a review of the literature on the effects of everyday hassles for families and their members.

The Vulnerability-Stress-Adaptation Model

The application of theory to the study of everyday hassles and family stress is as varied as the methodologies used. Studies range from the atheoretical to research grounded in life course theory (e.g., Almeida & Horn, 2004; Moen, 2003), the ecological perspective (e.g., Repetti & Wood, 1997a, 1997b), feminist perspectives (e.g., Daly, 2001; DeVault, 1991), emotional transmission paradigms (e.g., Larson & Almeida, 1999), and, most recently, biopsychosocial approaches (e.g., Charles & Almeida, 2007; Saxbe et al., 2008). Originally designed to provide an integrative framework for understanding the empirical research on marital quality and stability, Karney and Bradbury's (1995) VSA model is helpful in that it parsimoniously integrates and expands principles from various social and behavioral theoretical perspectives to explain the ways in which family members' experiences of potentially stressful events may be linked to relational outcomes. In our application of Karney and Bradbury's model, we treat everyday hassles as stressful events and explore how they interact with enduring vulnerabilities and adaptive processes to predict family stress. In addition, we view the opportunities and constraints afforded by the ecological niches that family members inhabit to be central to each element of the model, and we illustrate the adapted model in Figure 16.1.

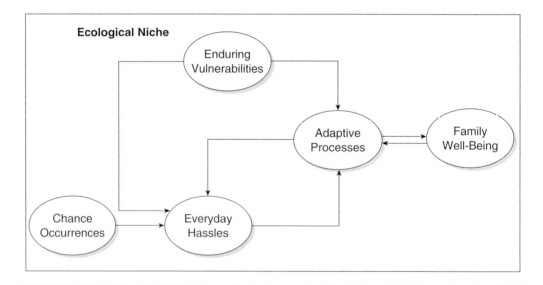

Figure 16.1   Adapted Vulnerability-Stress-Adaptation Model

At the most basic level of their model, Karney and Bradbury (1995) identified three elements that can contribute to our understanding of the links between everyday hassles and family stress. *Adaptive processes*, which play a central role in the model, are the ways in which individuals and families cope with everyday hassles. They are critical to our application of the model because they moderate the associations between daily hassles and family stress. Family stress changes as a function of the way family members behave in response to everyday hassles, and, in turn, family stress can affect how family members appraise daily hassles. For example, some studies suggest that employed spouses and parents withdraw from family interaction following workdays characterized by interpersonal difficulties and high work demands (Repetti & Wood, 1997a; Schulz, Cowan, Cowan, & Brennan, 2004). Additional findings suggest that this type of social withdrawal has short-term benefits, in that solitary time can rejuvenate spouses and parents and buffer children and partners from the transmission of negative emotions (Larson & Gillman, 1999). Rejuvenated parents and protected children are then better able to deal with additional hassles as they unfold. However, the short-term benefits of emotional withdrawal for the individual and the family may be offset over time as repeated instances of withdrawal may erode feelings of closeness in the family, leading to negative interactions, resentment, and more hassles—culminating in higher levels of family stress (Story & Repetti, 2006).

The model also proposes a reciprocal relationship between adaptive processes and *daily hassles*. The level of stress is partially determined by the number, severity, and centrality of daily hassles that the family and its members encounter (Almeida et al., 2002). Interpersonal tensions or arguments have been shown to be linked with both physical symptoms and psychological distress, whereas everyday hassles that disrupt daily routines, threaten physical health, or generate feelings of self-doubt are rated as highly psychologically distressing by adults (Almeida, 2005). Furthermore, the manner in which family members deal with hassles can exacerbate or alleviate family stress. To put it simply, certain days, weeks, and months are better than others; some hassles are easier to manage than others; and some people cope with everyday hassles better than others (Almeida, 2005). In a study of divorced single mothers, Hodgson, Dienhart, and Daly (2001) found that careful planning, scheduling, and multitasking were important coping strategies for mothers of young children. To the extent that the mothers in their study were able to navigate daily hassles, they maintained a sense of control over their family routines. For example:

> I have a certain amount of minutes allotted to get in and out of the day-care center . . . then I have half an hour to get to work so I have it timed to about, I have like six minutes to get them in and out . . . . I can't always, things don't always go that way, smoothly, you know those six minutes to get him dropped off in the morning, I can't guarantee that that happens five days a week, 52 weeks of the year. . . . if I didn't leave the daycare right at the right minute then there's a school bus that I follow all the way down [Highway] 21 . . . there was construction last fall on 21, you know, and there have been situations where I've forgotten things or (child) hasn't settled into daycare. . . . He needed a few extra minutes of comforting. . . . I drop him off the minute it opens and the minute it closes is the minute I'm there to pick him up. (pp. 14–15)

This mother's words illustrate that, as the model suggests, even with the most careful planning around rigid work and child-care schedules, chance events (e.g., bad weather, road construction, forgetfulness, an upset child) can lead to unanticipated hassles, disrupting plans and requiring additional adaptation. For single mothers with young children, backup plans and the anticipation of the unexpected are essential coping strategies for dealing with daily hassles.

A family's ability to adapt to daily hassles is also influenced by the *enduring vulnerabilities* that the family and its members possess. Karney and Bradbury (1995) define enduring vulnerabilities as family members' relatively stable intrapersonal characteristics (e.g., personality, child temperament) and family background variables (e.g., structural and behavioral patterns in family of origin). For example, the extent to which parents are able to refrain from engaging in negative interaction with their children following high-stress days may depend, in part, on the parents' own general level of psychological functioning. Using mood data collected at the end of study participants' workdays as well as self-report and observational data collected in the first few minutes of mother–child interaction at a work-site child-care center, Repetti and Wood (1997a) found that mothers with higher levels of type A behaviors, depression, and anxiety were more likely than other mothers to engage in aversive interactions with their preschoolers on days during which they had experienced either overloads or negative interpersonal interactions at work. Such enduring vulnerabilities can both contribute to family members' appraisals of daily hassles and affect how they adapt to those hassles.

In the VSA model, adaptive processes are hypothesized to be inversely related to family stress; that is, families and their members experience less stress to the extent that they deal with daily hassles in constructive ways. In addition, the model proposes positive associations among family stress, enduring vulnerabilities, and daily hassles. High levels of enduring vulnerabilities and daily hassles are linked with high levels of family stress. However, adaptive processes are expected to moderate this link in such a way that families with average levels of enduring vulnerabilities and daily hassles have higher levels of family stress when adaptive processes are poor and lower levels of family stress when adaptive processes are average or good.

A strength of the VSA model is that it provides an integrative framework that scholars can apply to gain a better understanding of everyday hassles and family stress. The components of the applied model—daily hassles, enduring vulnerabilities, and adaptive processes—and the general paths in the model can help us understand the complex and reciprocal processes operating among the model's components. The model is limited by its inattention to the ecological niches that families and their members inhabit, which leads it to ignore the potential variability that may exist in model paths based on between- and within-family differences. For example, Presser (2004) observes that the United States is moving to a 24-hour, 7-day-a-week economy in which many parents work evenings, nights, rotating hours, or weekends. Although nonstandard work schedules occur for employees of all incomes, low-income families are overrepresented. As demonstrated in the California Childhoods Project conducted by Thorne (2004), the constraints created by a work schedule that is "out of sync" with family life and limited financial resources pose unique challenges for managing everyday hassles.

> . . . We interviewed Betty Jones, a low-income solo African American mother who worked the late afternoon and evening shift as a custodian in an Oakland hospital. Her car had broken down months before and she couldn't afford repairs, so her 11-year-old son Tyrone (all names have been changed) took responsibility for bringing himself and his 6-year-old sister to school on a city bus. After school, Tyrone picked up his younger sister and they walked to a bus stop to begin an hour-long daily ride, including a transfer, from Oakland to San Leandro where their grandmother lived. The grandmother took them with her to her evening job as a custodian in an office building. After she got off work at 10 or 11pm, she drove the kids back to their apartment in a low-income area of Oakland. This scheduling exhausted all of them, and Betty, the children's mother, was concerned about her own mother's willingness to continue watching after grandchildren while cleaning offices at night. Like others we interviewed with very tight budgets, Betty wanted to send her kids to the after-school program located at the public school but she found the fees exorbitant; her income was more than used up by basics like food, rent, and utilities. Betty's swing shift job as a hospital custodian precluded the presence of her children. (pp. 168–169)

It is beyond the scope of this chapter to develop a comprehensive model that can better account for variability in the ecological niches that families inhabit, but we suggest that the current model should be expanded to consider contextual factors and thus better reflect the growing body of research on everyday hassles and family stress.

Daily Hassles

A growing number of researchers using widely varying methodologies have explored the everyday hassles that family members typically experience as well as the different meanings that men and women ascribe to these hassles. With a sample of 1,031 adults, each of whom completed an average of seven daily phone interviews, Almeida and Horn (2004) found that women reported experiencing everyday hassles more frequently than did men. However, they found no differences in the numbers of days that men and women reported experiencing multiple hassles. In addition, these researchers discovered a negative relationship between age and reports of everyday hassles, with a decrease in reports of hassles occurring in old age (i.e., ages 60–74). Compared with older adults, young and midlife adults reported experiencing a hassle or multiple hassles on more days, and they perceived their hassles to be more severe.

The content of the everyday hassles that individuals reported included arguments or tensions, overloads (i.e., having too little time or resources), and hassles regarding respondents' social networks, health care, home management, and work or school. The most frequent type of hassle reported by both men and women, arguments or tensions, is illustrated below.

> I had a problem with an employee. And also today she called and had cancelled something I had ordered three months ago and now I have to start running and searching and waiting for something. It was a big disappointment. It wasn't an argument, it was her fear that she had ordered the wrong thing and she didn't want to go through the stress and stuff. Nor did I obviously. Since she had doubts that she had done the right thing, she cancelled an order. So, it was very stressful for me. (words of a midlife father, Almeida & Horn, 2004, p. 436)

Arguments or tensions accounted for half of all daily stressors reported by men and women, and most of these tensions involved spouses or partners. Overload and network hassles were much less common, occurring on 6% and 8% of the study days, respectively. Women were more likely than men to report hassles involving their social networks (i.e., relatives or close friends), whereas men reported more overloads related to work or school than did women (Almeida, 2005). Examples of overloads and network hassles are illustrated by two middle-aged women.

> I was helping to open and close the store so I had to get up this morning, get my son ready, drag him to work, pick up somebody who didn't have a car, pick them up, take them to work, open the store, make sure they were okay, take him back to kindergarten, drop him off at the bus, go back to work, pick him up from the bus, run to swimming lessons for 45 minutes and then go back to work to close the store. (Almeida & Horn, 2004, p. 436)

> I have a close friend who has emotional problems. My friend also suffers from migraine headaches. I spent quite a bit of time with her today. I tried to comfort her. Yah, it interrupted my routine because I could not be at home to do things. (Almeida & Horn, 2004, p. 436)

Compared with older adults, the younger and midlife adults in Almeida and Horn's study experienced a greater proportion of overloads and reported that hassles caused greater disruption in their everyday routines.

Feminist scholars have focused on gender differences in family members' experiences and the subjective meanings that family members ascribe to routinized hassles. For example, feminist researchers have demonstrated that women perform the bulk of family labor (e.g., cooking, housecleaning, doing laundry), parenting, and caregiving, and this work has multiple and sometimes contradictory meanings for the individuals who perform it. Recent studies involving national surveys and time diaries confirm a "gender gap" in household labor but suggest that it may be narrowing somewhat (Sayer, 2005). These results show that men are spending more time on routine household chores and child care than in the past. Women, however, continue to perform about twice the amount of housework as their husbands (Coltrane, 2000; Sayer, 2005), and mothers spend substantially more solo time caring for children than do fathers (Bianchi & Raley, 2005). Furthermore, even though men's and women's time allocation has become more similar, the types of activities performed remain strongly gendered. Women spend a greater percentage of total time in unpaid labor on routine, time-consuming, and less optional housework (e.g., doing laundry, cooking), whereas men spend a greater percentage of time on occasional household tasks that require less time and regularity (e.g., mowing the lawn, car maintenance). In addition, gender disparities in free time have increased, with women reporting almost 4 hours less free time each week than men (Sayer, 2005). When paid and unpaid work hours are combined, married mothers work more total hours per week than married fathers (Bianchi & Raley, 2005; Sayer, 2005). As evidenced in the words of Meredith, a married mother of a young child, even in situations where couples define their division of family work as equal, inequalities abound when examining the management of everyday hassles.

> In terms of mentally worrying: making sure we have pediatric aspirin, talking to his teachers . . . I would say it's 75-25 . . . I will actually come to work and think we're out of Tylenol, I'd better go out and get some . . . It wouldn't worry Arthur during his workday that there are no clean pajamas. It will actually worry me. I will make a note that if I don't do the wash he has no clean pajamas. That would never worry Arthur. . . . Never! So I carry more mental [stress]. (Deutsch, 1999, p. 159)

Meredith's experiences of tending to the everyday needs of her child underscore feminist characterizations of the often "invisible" nature of the work required to care for children and maintain a home and suggest that if this type of family work were measured directly in large-scale survey studies, gender differences may be even more pronounced.

To understand daily hassles and family stress, one must recognize that family labor is multidimensional and time-intensive, involves both routine and occasional tasks, and is highly variable across and within households. Furthermore, because much of the work is mundane, tedious, boring, and generally performed without pay, most women and men report that they do not like doing it (DeVault, 1991; Robinson & Milkie, 1998). The sheer volume of family labor and caregiving, as well as the ongoing and relentless nature of many of these responsibilities, requires planning, preparation, scheduling, and multitasking—tasks that often fall disproportionately on the shoulders of women. Thus, although caring for family members includes enjoyable aspects, the work itself often creates hassles and family stress. Peg, a school psychologist working 45 hours per week and a married mother of three young children, explains the division of family labor in her home and her frustrations with the arrangement.

> He's not a morning person. He has coffee and sits. That's one of the biggest gripes. When I've had a tough morning, I'll say, "Am I the only one who hears people say, 'more orange juice?' . . . Things build to a head and then I have what you call a meltdown. "I can't do this any-more. This isn't fair. This isn't right. I'm not the only adult in the house!" Then for a few days he'll try to make lunch. It's generally when I'm feeling pressured from everywhere and the stress level just gets to me and then I let it all out. It changes for a short period of time but then reverts right back to the same. (Deutsch, 1999, pp. 50, 53)

Ethan, Peg's husband who works 60 hours per week in the biotechnology business, acknowledges the inequality but explains it in different terms: "[Peg] just naturally jumps in where I kind of wait for her to take the initiative. . . . Maybe I'm not helping as much as I could because I feel like that" (Deutsch, 1999, p. 51). Ethan's response implies that "helping" with the children in the morning is an option for him—something he can opt out of if he doesn't feel like participating.

One explanation for the differences between women and men in the ways they experience everyday hassles focuses on the extent to which individuals interpret their involvement in family labor to be freely chosen or voluntary. Exploring the contextual conditions surrounding family members' experience of emotions, Larson, Richards, and Perry-Jenkins (1994) collected data from married couples using an experience sampling method. Their rich data on the contrasting moods of husbands and wives at work and at home high-light how differently men and women experience these contexts and the everyday hassles they encounter in each domain. For example, employed wives recorded their most positive moods while at work; wives' emotions were generally more positive than were husbands' when they were on the job. However, wives experienced an emotional decline at home during the evening hours, which were filled with housework and child care. In contrast, husbands recorded their most negative emotions in the workplace; at home their moods lightened, in part, because nonwork time included leisure activities. However, even when men performed housework or child care, their moods while they did these tasks were more positive than were those of their wives when they performed the same activities. Further analyses revealed that performing housework and child-care tasks elicited more positive reactions from husbands than from wives because the husbands perceived that they had more choice regarding their involvement in these domains than did the wives.

The reverse is true for paid work. Husbands in Larson et al.'s (1994) study reported low levels of choice while at work, which may be related, in part, to constraints associated with gendered expectations for men to be providers. Employed wives reported more positive moods at work than did employed husbands. For many (but not all) women, an unhurried work pace and a friendly work environment contributed to their positive moods while on the job, demonstrating the importance of social support in the workplace for women's mental health. Collectively, these findings suggest that the transfer of women's and men's routinized experiences in the workplace or at home to emotional distress is a gendered process. The translation of work and family experiences into emotional health or distress may depend, in part, on the degree to which the individual perceives the activity to be freely chosen and whether it provides opportunities for positive social interaction, rather than the characteristics of the activity per se.

In sum, the studies reviewed above suggest that scholars may achieve a better understanding of everyday hassles by considering the ecological contexts in which the hassles occur. A family's construction of gendered expectations is one such context (Allen & Walker, 2000) and contributes to differences in women's and men's perceptions of and reactions to daily hassles. In addition, research has shown that other factors, such as the family's socioeconomic status (Grzywacz, Almeida, Neupert, & Ettner, 2004), exposure to chronic stressors at work or at home (Serido et al., 2004), and nonstandard work schedules (Almeida, 2004), influence the number of everyday hassles that family members experience as well as family members' perceptions of the severity of the hassles.

Adaptive Processes

According to the VSA, the processes that family members use to cope with everyday hassles have important implications for how those hassles affect family interactions. In general, two different patterns of responses have been identified following workdays characterized by heavy workloads or negative interactions with coworkers: (1) increases in marital or parent–child conflict and (2) social withdrawal. These patterns, however, vary across studies, within couples, and by reporter.

In a daily diary study of 166 married couples with children, Bolger, DeLongis, Kessler, and Wethington (1989) found that on days when husbands experienced an argument at work with a coworker or supervisor, they were more likely to return home from work and argue with their wives, but not with their children. For wives, however, the researchers found no significant associations between arguments at work and subsequent arguments with spouses or children. In contrast, a diary study of 43 married couples with children found that wives, but not husbands, reported more marital anger toward their spouse and were more withdrawn from family interaction following workdays characterized by heavy workloads and unpleasant social interactions (Story & Repetti, 2006). In an interesting twist, husbands' reports of their wives' behavior suggested that husbands did not notice their wives' displays of anger or withdrawal on these same days. This may be partially explained by the mediating effect of wives' negative mood following stressful workdays. That is, everyday hassles at work were found to contribute to wives' negative moods, which in turn colored wives' perceptions of their interactions at home. Although husbands did not perceive their wives to be more angry or withdrawn following difficult days at work, wives perceived that they were more irritable and less emotionally available, in part, due to their negative moods. For some families, daily stressors experienced at work may also spill over into interactions with children. For example, Repetti (1994) found that fathers engaged in more expressions of anger toward children and more harsh discipline (i.e., yelling, punishing) following days characterized by negative social interactions at work. In addition, both mothers and fathers have been shown to be less behaviorally and emotionally engaged with their children following busy workdays (Repetti, 1994; Repetti & Wood, 1997a).

How might family members buffer others from the effects of the everyday hassles they encounter? Repetti and Wood's (1997a) research suggests that parents' behavioral and emotional withdrawal may actually protect children from the transmission of their parents' negative work experiences. For example, Bolger et al. (1989) found that when husbands experienced greater-than-usual demands at the workplace, they performed less household labor and child care when they returned home, and their wives compensated for their withdrawal by performing more of the work at home. The parallel pattern did not occur when wives experienced overloads at work. When wives experienced overloads at work, they too performed less work at home (i.e., behavioral withdrawal), but their husbands did not reciprocate by performing more. Bolger et al. (1989) label this an "asymmetry in the buffering effect" (p. 182) and suggest that, in the short term, wives' stepping in for husbands may alleviate husbands' stress and avoid the transmission of stress from husbands' daily hassles to children. However, this short-term adaptive process may prove harmful over time for families—most particularly for wives. Coping in this manner in repeated instances over time may be one factor in explaining the consistent finding that marriage benefits the emotional health of men more than that of women (Amato, Johnson, Booth, & Rogers, 2003). To the extent that women's emotional health plays a key role in child well-being (Demo & Acock, 1996), a pattern of asymmetrical buffering may be detrimental for children in families as well.

More recently, several researchers have inquired as to how patterns of emotional transmission from daily hassles in the workplace to home vary based on the quality of the marital relationship (Schulz et al., 2004; Story & Repetti, 2006). Story and Repetti (2006) found that both husbands and wives in marriages characterized by higher levels of conflict were more likely than their peers in less conflicted marriages to express anger toward their spouse and withdraw from family interaction on evenings following stressful days at work. Similarly, Schulz et al. (2004) found that husbands in more satisfying marriages were less likely than maritally dissatisfied husbands to express anger or criticism toward their wives following emotionally upsetting days at work. Taken together, this research suggests that husbands and wives are more likely to express negative feelings toward their spouses following high-stress days in families where conflicted interactions are common. Spouses in these families also frequently withdraw from family interaction following difficult workdays, perhaps in an attempt to disengage from further negative interactions.

One unexpected finding indicated that some wives in more satisfying marriages actually withdraw more and express more anger following demanding days at work than do wives in less satisfying marriages (Schulz et al., 2004). The authors suggest that a more satisfying marital relationship may create a context in which husbands encourage wives to express their frustrations as a way of coping. It may be that more maritally satisfied husbands facilitate wives' temporary withdrawal from family interactions by increasing their own involvement with child care and housework so that their wives can recuperate (e.g., "Mommy needs some time to relax and unwind because she had a hard day at work."). In turn, wives in more satisfying marital relationships may feel freer than their maritally dissatisfied counterparts to express anger and withdraw from family interaction after difficult workdays because their husbands are willing to hear their complaints and increase their supportive behavior. This research suggests that the nature of the marital relationship may affect the extent to which everyday hassles at work spill over into family interactions and that these patterns may vary by gender. Similarly, the results of other studies suggest that additional family vulnerabilities or strengths (e.g., child conduct problems, overly controlling parenting) may influence the extent to which daily hassles transfer to family stress (Larson & Gillman, 1999; Margolin, Christensen, & John, 1996).

Research from a 10-year, multisite qualitative study suggests that buffering children from the effects of parents' everyday hassles may be a luxury afforded to only middle-class and better-off families (Dodson & Dickert, 2004). In their study of low-income families, Dodson and Dickert (2004) found that these families engaged children, most typically eldest daughters, in child care and housework tasks as a strategy to compensate for the inflexible work hours, low wages, and nonstandard shifts of working-poor parents. Whereas studies of both working- and middle-class families have found that girls, more than boys, assume household labor responsibilities when mothers' work demands are high (e.g., Crouter, Head, Bumpus, & McHale, 2001), low-income families differ in that girls' contributions to family labor are essential for family survival because the demands of parents' work render mothers and fathers unavailable to attend to even the most basic everyday hassles of family life. In this way, parents' workplace demands have direct impacts on eldest daughters' daily experiences in that these girls must contend with the everyday hassles and responsibilities customarily assigned to parents. As a teacher of the low-income adolescent girls participating in Dodson and Dickert's (2004) study observed, "They have to take their little brother to the bus stop in the morning and sometimes that means getting to school late or they are babysitting . . . they are like little mothers" (p. 326). One 15-year-old daughter's own words illustrate that the girls themselves are keenly aware of their responsibilities as child-care providers and assistant housekeepers: "I have to take care of the house and take care of the kids and I don't go outside. I have to stay home. They have to go to work so I take over" (p. 324).

The results of Dodson and Dickert's (2004) study suggest that although this adaptive strategy has both short-term benefits (e.g., children are cared for and household tasks are completed) and long-term benefits (e.g., family cohesion or loyalty, higher levels of social responsibility for adolescents), families use it at considerable cost to eldest daughters. When eldest daughters assume responsibility for the everyday hassles associated with family care-giving, their own education and goals are viewed as secondary to the needs of the family. In Dodson and Dickert's study, teachers, parents, and the girls themselves described lost opportunities for education and extracurricular involvement and, perhaps most disconcerting, lost hope for the eldest daughters' futures.

Enduring Vulnerabilities

Individual differences or enduring vulnerabilities in personality and emotional functioning can both contribute to everyday hassles and affect how family members adapt to them. For example, enduring vulnerabilities play an important role in determining how family members process, interpret, and react to the everyday hassles they encounter. In addition, the extent to which individuals possess relatively stable traits can render them resilient or vulnerable to the transfer of stress from everyday hassles. For example, studies have found exaggerated stress responses to daily hassles among individuals with higher levels of negative affectivity, neuroticism, type A personality traits, depression, and introversion (Almeida, McGonagle, Cate, Kessler, & Wethington, 2002; Repetti & Wood, 1997a) and lower levels of mastery and self-esteem (Almeida, McGonagle et al., 2002; Pearlin, 1999).

Recent research suggests that the extent to which enduring vulnerabilities moderate the links between daily hassles and family stress may differ for men and women. Almeida, McGonagle et al. (2002) asked 166 married couples to complete daily diaries for 42 consecutive days. In each diary entry, participants responded to a short questionnaire about a variety of daily stressors, including arguments with their spouse, as well as a questionnaire designed to assess psychological distress. The analyses addressed the moderating effects of psychological characteristics (i.e., neuroticism, mastery, self-esteem, and extraversion) on the link between marital arguments and psychological distress.

They found that the extent to which wives felt distressed following marital arguments was exacerbated by high levels of neuroticism and attenuated by high levels of mastery, self-esteem, and extraversion. In contrast, self-esteem alone moderated the link between marital arguments and psychological distress for husbands. Almeida, McGonagle et al. (2002) suggested that because personality has been shown to be particularly salient for coping with stressors that are highly threatening or uncontrollable, the different patterns that emerged for husbands and wives in their sample imply that wives may perceive marital arguments as more threatening than do husbands.

Intervention: Toward a New Family-Responsive Policy Agenda

Feminists argue for gender equity in daily tasks as a solution to the disproportionate burdens that mothers, wives, and daughters carry in families (Deutsch, 1999), but they also warn that even with gender equity, many contemporary families would still have too many hassles to manage on their own (Coontz, 2000). In contrast, those ascribing to structural-functionalist views suggest that families function best when women focus on children and home management and men focus on breadwinning (Popenoe, 1996). Rare among scholars but quite prevalent in popular culture are self-help perspectives that frame the link between everyday hassles and family stress as a private matter that individuals can solve by using time more efficiently. Still others emphasize government- or employer-subsidized child- and elder-care services as a mechanism for outsourcing many of the everyday hassles associated with caregiving (Bogenschneider, 2000). We argue that contemporary American families need better opportunities both at home and in the workplace to meet family members' diverse needs, and we support Moen's (2003) conclusion that we must "re-imagine and reconfigure work hours, workweeks, and occupational career paths in ways that address the widening gaps between the time needs and goals of workers and their families at all stages of the life course on the one hand and the time available to them on the other" (p. 7). For example, some families may want to devote more time to paid work outside the home and therefore need ways to simplify aspects of their daily home lives and outsource everyday tasks to readily available, high-quality substitutes. As Valcour and Batt (2003) note, for parents who want to focus more of their time on family obligations, flexibility in the workplace is of paramount importance. They quoted a mother of three children (including 4-year-old twins) who has been married to a business administrator for 15 years:

> I was lucky to work out a job sharing arrangement because there was another woman in my department who did the same thing as me and was also struggling after she had her second baby. So we went to the human resource person and she was supportive but said the company

doesn't have this in place. So we did the research and went to the president of the division and we went through a couple of struggles, but eventually they accepted it. I'm so glad it worked out, because is has been great for me and my family. (p. 320)

As this woman's experience illustrates, workplace policies that enable family members to care for the everyday needs of their members without jeopardizing their financial security or careers are likely to be particularly beneficial for families caring for young children or sick or aging family members.

Although the needs and desires of family members in diverse family forms are likely to change over the life course, they exist in a sociohistorical context that has seen little development in family-responsive workplace policies. For example, the everyday hassles that today's families encounter are situated in a society that is still predicated on a breadwinner-husband, homemaker-wife script in which the breadwinner is assured an adequate wage for family provision and a full-time, linear rise up the occupational ladder and the homemaker manages the everyday nonwork aspects of her husband's life as well as the daily hassles of managing a home and family (Coontz, 2000; Moen, 2003). This outdated script contrasts starkly with the contemporary reality that the majority of American families (e.g., single-parent and dual-earner families) experience as they work in an economy where family-wage jobs are reserved for the highly educated, secure manufacturing jobs are few, job growth is limited to low-wage 24/7 service-sector positions with little security or hope for advancement, and income gains are disproportionately situated within the top 20% of the U.S. income distribution (Jacobs & Gerson, 2005). In addition, existing government and workplace policies have been slow to recognize that working family members have legitimate family demands on their time that may require greater flexibility in the workplace. As long as the culture of the workplace equates work commitment with overwork and fails to recognize the legitimacy of family caregiving as an employee right, those seeking a reasonable balance between work and family life are likely to be penalized (Jacobs & Gerson, 2005). This point is documented by a father of two children (ages 8 and 14) who is employed as a manufacturing production supervisor and married to a part-time educational coordinator:

I wish there were more flexibility, especially in our production environment. I've worked all my life around a rotating-work schedule, but this year alone I lost three excellent employees. They had each become single parents for one reason or another, and there's no way you can get child care in off hours and weekends. It just breaks my heart. Traditionally production has been a male-oriented thing, where one partner stays home with the children and the other one works crazy schedules. . . . the world is changing and the schedule is not. (quoted in Valcour & Batt, 2003, p. 310)

The mismatch between the work environments that family members inhabit and the needs of contemporary families creates a context in which everyday hassles emerge and multiply.

Valcour and Batt (2003) suggest that employers first adopt and promote a family-responsive attitude toward employees and then demonstrate support for this attitude through company policy. A primary objective of this approach is to reduce the often unspoken costs to employees who choose nonstandard work arrangements or take advantage of family-friendly policies (Jacobs & Gerson, 2005). Such an attitude recognizes that all employees, regardless of whether they have spouses, partners, or children at home, are members of families and experience everyday hassles and demands from personal involvements outside the workplace. Valcour and Batt (2003) note that family-responsive employers must offer employees the following:

1. A broad range of work-life programs that provide employees with control over their working time and support in meeting their family and personal needs

2. Adequate pay, benefits, and employment security

3. Work designed to provide employees with discretion and control in meeting work and life demands

4. A workplace culture, transmitted formally by organizational policies and informally by supervisors and coworkers, that values and supports the work-life integration of all employees (pp. 312–313)

Jacobs and Gerson (2005) further emphasize that family responsive reforms must uphold two essential principles: (1) gender equality in opportunity structures and (2) support for employees regardless of socioeconomic location.

Moen (2003) argues that it is not enough for corporations to list such policies on the books. Employers must make continuous efforts to enforce these policies to cultivate a corporate climate that is truly responsive to the needs of families. Moen also suggests that employers and government officials need to keep better records of the variations (and the reasons for them) in employees' work-hour and career-path arrangements in order to track the implications of these variations for employees and corporations. The information gained through such tracking may help to convince employers and politicians of the heterogeneity in employees' experiences both at work and at home and thus persuade them to change outdated workplace policies based on the breadwinner-homemaker template. Finally, and perhaps most important for families' experiences of everyday hassles and stress, employers and policymakers must view employees' vulnerabilities and family circumstances as key human resource, workforce, and labor issues. For family members struggling in uncertain economic times and working in low-wage jobs with inflexible work schedules, everyday hassles such as minor car accidents, sick children, and parent–teacher conferences scheduled during work hours can add strains that they may find hard to manage. Policies that focus on the risks, vulnerabilities, and family lives of workers are likely to attenuate the transfer of stress from everyday hassles to family life.

Suggested Internet and Reading Resources

Families and Work Institute: http://www.familiesandwork.org

Sloan Work and Family Research Network: http://wfnetwork.bc.edu/

Urban Institute: http://www.urbaninstitute.org/

Bianchi, S. M., Casper, L. M., & King, R. B. (2005). *Work, family, health, and well-being*. Mahwah, NJ: Lawrence Erlbaum.

Crouter, A. C., &. Booth, A. (2004). *Work-family challenges for low-income parents and their children*. Hillsdale, NJ: Lawrence Erlbaum.

Hattery, A. (2001). *Women, work, and family: Balancing and weaving*. Thousand Oaks, CA: Sage.

References

Abel, E. K., & Nelson, M. K. (Eds.). (1990). *Circles of care: Work and identity in women's lives*. Albany: State University of New York Press.

Allen, K. R., & Walker, A. J. (2000). Constructing gender in families. In R. M. Milardo & S. Duck (Eds.), *Families as relationships* (pp. 1–17). Chichester, England: John Wiley.

Almeida, D. M. (2004). Using daily diaries to assess temporal friction between work and family. In A. C. Crouter & A. Booth (Eds.), *Work-family challenges for low-income parents and their children* (pp. 127–136). Mahwah, NJ: Lawrence Erlbaum.

Almeida, D. M. (2005). Resilience and vulnerability to daily stressors assessed via diary methods. *Current Directions in Psychological Science, 14*, 64–68.

Almeida, D. M., & Horn, M. C. (2004). Is daily life more stressful during middle adulthood? In C. D. Ryff & R. C. Kessler (Eds.), *A portrait of midlife in the United States* (pp. 425–451). Chicago: University of Chicago Press.

Almeida, D. M., McGonagle, K. A., Cate, R. C., Kessler, R. C., & Wethington, E. (2002). Psychological moderators of emotional reactivity to marital arguments: Results from a daily diary study. *Marriage and Family Review, 34*, 89–113.

Almeida, D. M., Wethington, E., & Chandler, A. L. (1999). Daily transmission of tensions between marital and parent-child dyads. *Journal of Marriage and the Family, 61*, 49–61.

Almeida, D. M., Wethington, E., & Kessler, R. C. (2002). The daily inventory of stressful events: An interview-based approach for measuring daily stressors. *Assessment, 9*, 41–55.

Amato, P. R., Johnson, D. R., Booth, A., & Rogers, S. J. (2003). Continuity and change in marital quality between 1980 and 2000. *Journal of Marriage and Family, 65*, 1–22.

Bianchi, S. M., & Raley, S. B. (2005). Time allocation in families. In S. M. Bianchi, L. M. Casper, & R. B. King (Eds.), *Work, family, health, and well-being* (pp. 21–42). Mahwah, NJ: Lawrence Erlbaum.

Bogenschneider, K. (2000). Has family policy come of age? A decade review of the state of U.S. family policy in the 1990s. *Journal of Marriage and the Family, 62,* 1136–1159.

Bolger, N., DeLongis, A., Kessler, R. C., & Wethington, E. (1989). The contagion of stress across multiple roles. *Journal of Marriage and the Family, 51,* 175–183.

Charles, S. T., & Almeida, D. M. (2007). Genetic and environmental effects on daily life stressors: More evidence for greater variation in later life. *Psychology and Aging, 22,* 331–340.

Coltrane, S. (2000). Research on household labor: Modeling and measuring the social embeddedness of routine family work. *Journal of Marriage and the Family, 62,* 1208–1233.

Coontz, S. (2000). Historical perspectives on family studies. *Journal of Marriage and the Family, 62,* 283–297.

Crouter, A. C., Head, M. R., Bumpus, M. F., & McHale, S. M. (2001). Household chores: Under what conditions do mothers lean on daughters? In A. J. Fuligini (Ed.), *Family obligation and assistance during adolescence* (pp. 23–41). New York: John Wiley.

Daly, K. J. (1996). *Families and time: Keeping pace in a hurried culture.* Thousand Oaks, CA: Sage.

Daly, K. J. (2001). Deconstructing family time: From ideology to lived experience. *Journal of Marriage and Family, 63,* 283–294.

DeLongis, A., Coyne, J. C., Dakof, G., Folkman, S., & Lazarus, R. S. (1982). Relationship of daily hassles, uplifts, and major life events to health status. *Health Psychology, 1,* 119–136.

DeLongis, A., Folkman, S., & Lazarus, R. S. (1988). The impact of daily stress and health on mood: Psychological and social resources as mediators. *Journal of Personality and Social Psychology, 54,* 486–495.

Demo, D. H., & Acock, A. C. (1996). Family structure, family process, and adolescent well-being. *Journal of Research on Adolescence, 6,* 457–488.

Deutsch, F. M. (1999). *Halving it all: How equally shared parenting works.* Cambridge, MA: Harvard University Press.

DeVault, M. L. (1991). *Feeding the family: The social organization of caring as gendered work.* Chicago: University of Chicago Press.

DiLeonardo, M. (1987). The female world of cards and holidays: Women, families, and the work of kinship. *Signs, 12,* 440–453.

Dodson, L., & Dickert, J. (2004). Girls' family labor in low-income households: A decade of qualitative research. *Journal of Marriage and Family, 66,* 318–332.

Dressel, P., & Clark, A. (1990). A critical look at family care. *Journal of Marriage and the Family, 52,* 769–782.

Grzywacz, J. G., Almeida, D. M., Neupert, S. D., & Ettner, S. L. (2004). Socioeconomic status and health: A micro-level analysis of exposure and vulnerability to daily stressors. *Journal of Health and Social Behavior, 45,* 1–16.

Hodgson, J., Dienhart, A., & Daly, K. J. (2001). Time juggling: Single mothers' experience of time-press following divorce. *Journal of Divorce and Remarriage, 35,* 1–28.

Hunter, A. G., Pearson, J. L., Ialongo, N. S., & Kellam, S. G. (1998). Parenting alone to multiple caregivers: Child care and parenting arrangements in black and white urban families. *Family Relations, 47,* 343–353.

Jacobs, J. A., & Gerson, K. (2005). *The time divide*. Cambridge, MA: Harvard University Press.

Kanner, A. D., Coyne, J. C., Schaefer, C., & Lazarus, R. S. (1981). Comparisons of two modes of stress measurement: Daily hassles and uplifts versus major life events. *Journal of Behavioral Medicine, 4,* 1–39.

Karney, B. R., & Bradbury, T. N. (1995). The longitudinal course of marital quality and stability: A review of theory, method, and research. *Psychological Bulletin, 118,* 3–34.

Larson, R. W., & Almeida, D. M. (1999). Emotional transmission in the daily lives of families: A new paradigm for studying family process. *Journal of Marriage and the Family, 61,* 5–20.

Larson, R. W., & Gillman, S. (1999). Transmission of emotions in the daily interactions of single-mother families. *Journal of Marriage and the Family, 61,* 21–37.

Larson, R. W., & Richards, M. H. (1994). *Divergent realities: The emotional lives of mothers, fathers, and adolescents*. New York: Basic Books.

Larson, R. W., Richards, M. H., & Perry-Jenkins, M. (1994). Divergent worlds: The daily emotional experiences of mothers and fathers in the domestic and public spheres. *Journal of Personality and Social Psychology, 67,* 1034–1046.

Lazarus, R. S. (1999). *Stress and emotion: A new synthesis*. New York: Springer.

Margolin, G., Christensen, A., & John, R. S. (1996). The continuance and spillover of everyday tensions in distressed and nondistressed families. *Journal of Family Psychology, 10,* 304–321.

Miller, M. J., & Wilcox, C. T. (1986). Measuring perceived hassles and uplifts among the elderly. *Journal of Human Behavior and Learning, 3,* 38–45.

Moen, P. (Ed.). (2003). *It's about time: Couples and careers*. Ithaca, NY: Cornell University Press.

Oliker, S. J. (1989). *Best friends and marriage*. Berkeley: University of California Press.

Pearlin, L. I. (1999). Stress and mental health: A conceptual overview. In A. V. Horwitz & T. L. Scheid (Eds.), *A handbook for the study of mental health: Social contexts, theories, and systems* (pp. 161–175). New York: Cambridge University Press.

Popenoe, D. (1996). *Life without father*. New York: Free Press.

Presser, H. B. (2004). Employment in a 24/7 economy: Challenges for the family. In A. C. Crouter & A. Booth (Eds.), *Work-family challenges for low-income parents and their children* (pp. 83-105). Mahwah, NJ: Lawrence Erlbaum.

Repetti, R. L. (1994). Short-term and long-term processes linking job stressors to father-child interaction. *Social Development, 3,* 1–5.

Repetti, R. L., & Wood, J. (1997a). The effects of daily stress at work on mothers' interactions with preschoolers. *Journal of Family Psychology, 11,* 90–108.

Repetti, R. L., & Wood, J. (1997b). Families accommodating to chronic stress. In B. H. Gottlieb (Ed.), *Coping with chronic stress* (pp. 191–220). New York: Plenum.

Robinson, J. P., & Milkie, M. A. (1998). Back to the basics: Trends in and role determinants of women's attitudes toward housework. *Journal of Marriage and the Family, 60,* 205–218.

Saxbe, D. E., Repetti, R. L., & Nishina, A. (2008). Marital satisfaction, recovery from work, and diurnal cortisol among men and women. *Health Psychology, 27,* 15–25.

Sayer, L. C. (2005). Gender, time and inequality: Trends in women's and men's paid work, unpaid work and free time. *Social Forces, 84,* 285–303.

Schulz, M. S., Cowan, P. A., Cowan, C. P., & Brennan, R. T. (2004). Coming home upset: Gender, marital satisfaction, and the daily spillover of workday experience into couple interactions. *Journal of Family Psychology, 18*, 250–263.

Serido, J., Almeida, D. M., & Wethington, E. (2004). Chronic stressors and daily hassles: Unique and interactive relationships with psychological distress. *Journal of Health and Social Behavior, 45*, 17–33.

Story, L. B., & Repetti, R. (2006). Daily occupational stressors and marital behavior. *Journal of Family Psychology, 20*, 690–700.

Thorne, B. (2004). The crisis of care. In A. C. Crouter & A. Booth (Eds.), *Work-family challenges for low-income parents and their children* (pp. 165–178). Mahwah, NJ: Lawrence Erlbaum.

Valcour, P. M., & Batt, R. (2003). Work-life integration: Challenges and organizational responses. In P. Moen (Ed.), *It's about time: Couples and careers* (pp. 310–331). Ithaca, NY: Cornell University Press.

Walker, A. J., Pratt, C. C., & Eddy, L. (1995). Informal caregiving to aging family members: A critical review. *Family Relations, 44*, 402–411.

Wheaton, B. (1999). Social stress. In C. S. Aneshensel & J. C. Phelan (Eds.), *Handbook of the sociology of mental health* (pp. 277–300). New York: Kluwer Academic/Plenum.

17

The Impact of Military Duty and Military Life on Individuals and Families

Resources and Intervention

James A. Martin and Michelle D. Sherman

Many aspects of military life have changed as a result of the events that followed the 9/11 attacks on the United States. In particular, the Iraq and Afghanistan wars have profoundly impacted members of the military, their families, and others whose lives are connected to those in uniform. Between October 2001 and January 2009, more than 1.8 million service members deployed at least once during these two conflicts, with many having multiple tours of combat duty. As a result, there is a new generation of veterans who have returned with the physical and emotional scars of war.

Other populations to consider are the veterans of World War II, the Korean War, the Vietnam War, and those who served in the armed forces during the Cold War, the Gulf War, and multiple military actions in places like Somalia and Kosovo. There are millions of family members and loved ones whose lives have also been impacted by the experiences of their service member or veteran. These include the spouses, children, parents, siblings, friends, and the broader communities where these military personnel reside. The goals of this chapter, therefore, are to promote awareness of military duty and military life, increase knowledge about the unique characteristics of members of the military and their families, and to enhance the skills of those involved in providing services to military members, veterans, and their families.

Definitions of the Various Populations Associated With the Military

There are multiple definitions to describe the military populations (e.g., military members, veterans, and family members) addressed in this chapter. The term *military member* refers to individuals currently serving in the armed forces—in either the active-duty or reserve components of the U.S. Army, U.S. Navy, U.S. Marine Corps, and U.S. Air Force (the Army National Guard and Air National Guard are part of the reserves). It also includes members of the Coast Guard in times of war and the noncombatant uniformed services (National Oceanic and Atmospheric Administration Commissioned Corps and the United States Public Health Service Commissioned Corps) whose service involves deployments in support of humanitarian issues and other military missions. The term *veteran* refers to any individual who has served in the active military, naval, or air service and who was discharged or released under conditions other than dishonorable. A veteran also may have served in the National Guard and/or any of the reserves meeting the qualifying Veterans Administration categories for veteran status.

Family members include loved ones who have supported their service member and/or veteran. A family member may be a husband or wife (or intimate partner), parent, stepparent, son, daughter, foster parent, or someone who shares a family or significant relationship with an active military member or a veteran. For example, the Marine Corps permits Marines to designate anyone in this "family member" category to receive official communications from the Marine Corps. A broad definition for family members has also been adopted by the National Guard Bureau and the other reserve components.

Demographic Data

Demographic information about military members, veterans, and their families provides an important context to understand military duties and military life experiences. The specific numbers and percentages cited here will change with time and world events, but characteristics of these populations are not likely to significantly vary even into the next decade. (Updated demographic information is available on the Internet from a variety of government and public sources provided at the end of the chapter.)

The Active-Duty and Reserve Components of Our Armed Forces and Their Families

Military members serve in one of two broad categories, as a member of one of the active-duty components or a member of one of the reserve components. The reserves represent the tradition of the "citizen soldier" that dates back to the Revolutionary War. Unlike the active-duty components, who draw their members from all over the country, most reserve and National Guard units are regionally based and their members are recruited from local areas. National Guard units are actually state militias, and under the U.S. Constitution, they are commanded by their state governor (except when they are called to federal service).

With the advent of the global war on terror, the roles and responsibilities of the reserves (especially the National Guard) have changed dramatically. National Guard members are this nation's domestic "911" force, responding immediately to a wide array of local, state, and even national emergencies (e.g., Hurricane Katrina). Today, the National Guard (and other reserves) no longer serves as only an emergency response force. Rather, they have an important national role responding immediately and mobilizing regularly as a critical component of the armed forces and the U.S. national defense strategy.

Currently, more than 1.4 million men and women serve in the active-duty component of the U.S. Armed Forces with an additional 850,000 individuals serving in the National Guard and other reserves. Between 80% and 85% of active-duty and reserve service members are in the enlisted ranks, and between 15% and 17% of military members are women (Office of the Under Secretary of Defense, Personnel, and Readiness, 2008). Women have taken on an expanding array of military roles and are increasingly being promoted to senior military leadership positions. More than a third of active-duty and reserve members identify themselves as an ethnic minority. Almost all officers have a bachelor's degree (or higher), and almost all enlisted members have a high school diploma (or equivalent). Many senior enlisted members also have bachelor's degrees or advanced technical qualifications.

Both the active-duty and reserve components are composed primarily of young adults. Three fourths of active-duty officers are 40 years or younger, and more than half (53%) of active-duty enlisted members are 25 years or younger. Just over half of active-duty members are married with a majority (70%) of officers and over half (52%) of enlisted members being married (Office of the Under Secretary of Defense, Personnel, and Readiness, 2008). Approximately 7% of active-duty members are in dual-military marriages. Although the reserve members are somewhat older in age than the active-duty members, their marital rates are similar.

More than one-third of active-duty members have children with 5% being single parents. Children of active-duty members are primarily between birth and 5 years old (474,000). In comparison, 34% of reserve members have children and 8% are single parents. Children of reserve members are slightly older than children of active-duty members with most being between the ages of 6 and 14 years (332,000) (Office of the Under Secretary of Defense, Personnel, and Readiness, 2008).

All together, the number of spouses and children of active-duty and reserve military members is approximately 1.8 million and 1.1 million, respectively. A majority (70%) of active-duty military members and their families reside in local civilian communities near military installations with fewer (30%) living in government (or government-leased) housing (Office of the Under Secretary of Defense, Personnel, and Readiness, 2008). During deployment, families of senior and older military members typically stay in their current residence, whereas younger spouses married to junior ranking service members are more likely to return to their home communities seeking the support of immediate families and friends.

Most active-duty service members are stationed at military installations in the continental United States; however, more than 60,000 are stationed in Hawaii, Alaska, or one of the U.S. territories (Office of the Under Secretary of Defense, Personnel, and Readiness, 2008). Comparatively, reserve families, especially those in the National Guard, are scattered across all 50 states and territories. These "citizen soldier" members live in every community including urban, suburban, and especially rural communities where "service" in the National Guard has a strong tradition and often provides an economic supplement to low wages and/or marginal employment.

The U.S. military is a global force currently operating 820 military installations in 39 countries. More than 80,000 service members are stationed in Europe; 70,000 are stationed in East Asia and the Pacific; there are almost 8,000 in North Africa, the Near East, and South Asia; and there are another 3,000 in sub-Saharan Africa. On a typical day, approximately 90,000 service members are somewhere outside the United States—at sea and away from their home and family (Office of the Under Secretary of Defense, Personnel, and Readiness, 2008).

Veterans and Their Families

Today, there are more than 24 million veterans, including more than 2.9 million veterans of World War II, of which 900 are dying daily (National Center for Veterans Analysis and Statistics, 2008). Included in the total number of veterans are 1.8 million females (8% of all veterans). Of these veterans, 7,500 women served mostly as nurses in Vietnam and another 41,000 women were deployed during the Gulf War. The number of female veterans is expected to increase. To date, more than 182,000 women have served in Iraq and/or Afghanistan (about 11% of all deployed personnel). There is no exact number of spouses and children of veterans; however, estimates indicate that 20% of the U.S. population (37 million) are spouses and dependent children of veterans (National Center for Veterans Analysis and Statistics, 2008).

Most living veterans served during a time of war, the largest cohort during the Vietnam era (approximately 8 million). In 2007, the median age of veterans was 60 (61 for men and 47 for women), and almost 40% are 65 or older (National Center for Veterans Analysis and Statistics, 2008). (Veterans from past and present wars live in communities across America, and many still experience the consequences of their military service including the physical, psychological, social, and spiritual residue of combat and other stress exposures associated with military duties and the military lifestyle.)

Veterans' Utilization of Services

Overall, approximately 5.5 million veterans received health care from the Veterans Health Administration (VHA), including more than 255,000 women (Department of Veteran Affairs, 2008). While the reasons are varied, women who served in Iraq and Afghanistan are seeking VHA care at a considerably higher rate than their male counterparts or women from previous wars. Furthermore, the number of women seeking care in the VHA system is expected to double within 5 years.

Veterans have a range of health care options in the VHA system, including medical centers, community-based outpatient clinics, nursing homes, and readjustment counseling centers. Similar to the Department of Defense (DOD), the VHA system has created numerous new positions specifically focused on traumatic brain injury, neuropsychology, suicide prevention, recovery, and trauma or Posttraumatic Stress Disorder (PTSD).

More than 868,000 veterans from service in Afghanistan and/or Iraq have left active duty and are eligible for VHA health care. This includes an approximately equal number of active-duty and National Guard/reserve members. To date, despite extensive VHA outreach, only 40% have accessed VHA health care, and 76,000 of these (22%) have received a PTSD diagnosis (Department of Veteran Affairs, 2008).

Many Iraqi/Afghanistan veterans have experienced considerable trauma during combat deployment(s), and consequently, the reintegration process can be challenging (Bowling & Sherman, 2008). The VHA system, a pioneer in the treatment of combat veterans, has developed considerable expertise in meeting this challenge. According to the National Center for PTSD, 30% of Vietnam War veterans, 10% of Gulf War veterans, 6% to 11% of veterans from Afghanistan, and 12% to 20% of veterans from Iraq have PTSD. Many women, and some men, have also experienced sexual trauma and sexual harassment while in the military, and the VHA system has created specific programs and support for these veterans.

Challenges for Military
Members, Veterans, and Their Families

Since 2003, America has simultaneously conducted two major combat operations, in Afghanistan, which began in 2001, and in Iraq. As of 2008, a total of 1.6 million service members, with the majority being members of the U.S. Army and the Marine Corps, have served one or more tours of combat duty in Iraq or Afghanistan. The term *deployment* refers to any principal activity associated with military service including combat, peacemaking, peacekeeping, humanitarian activities, and a wide range of unit training missions. It is a generic term associated with a military unit's mission-oriented movement from its home installation to some other location in the world.

The average length of deployment for most U.S. Army personnel is 12 to 15 months with Marines often deployed 7 to 9 months depending on their mission requirements. The longest deployments are typically experienced by National Guard and other reserve units who spend significant time away from home for predeployment training. For all, repeated deployments (referred to by the military as "redeployments") have been the norm.

The Consequences of Combat Deployments

The human cost associated with combat operations is often high and always tragic. Previous conflicts for the United States have produced thousands of casualties ranging from 300,000 American deaths in World War II to nearly 50,000 deaths in the Vietnam War. The bloodiest of our wars was the American Civil War where more than 200,000 Union and Confederate soldiers lost their lives. To date, more than 4,200 service members have been killed in Iraq and another 600+ have been killed in and around Afghanistan. Approximately 42,650 service members have been injured in these two conflicts with 18,278 able to return to duty (U.S. Department of Veterans Affairs, 2008).

With the availability of enhanced protective equipment, better combat lifesaver training, and improved battlefield treatments, including rapid evacuation from the battlefield to skilled trauma care, many service members are surviving horrific combat injuries. As a result, however, many service members, and the lives of their loved ones, have been permanently changed. These injuries and the associated physical, emotional, and cognitive difficulties represent the human residue of war.

At the end of 2008, more than 150,000 service members were in Iraq. Although these numbers are expected to decrease over the next 12 to 18 months, the number of service members deployed in Afghanistan (currently more than 30,000) will grow substantially. As our involvement in Iraq diminishes and our engagement in Afghanistan expands, the number of service members killed and wounded, including the behavioral health injuries, referred to as the "invisible wounds of war" (Tanielian & Jaycox, 2008), will continue to mount.

Behavioral Health Consequences for Service Members and Veterans

The behavioral health and relationship consequences of combat deployments are profound. According to a large-scale study done by the RAND Corporation, a nonprofit research organization (Tanielian & Jaycox, 2008), and research by Hoge and colleagues (2004, 2006), many service members serving in Iraq and Afghanistan have encountered significant trauma and are now experiencing prolonged periods of combat-related stress. Specifically, 20% of service members returning from Iraq and 11% returning from Afghanistan report symptoms of PTSD or major depression. In addition, 19% of returning service members report a possible traumatic brain injury and 7% report both a brain injury and PTSD or major depression.

Substance abuse, addiction, and a wide array of other high-risk behaviors also pose serious problems for returning service members (Tanielian & Jaycox, 2008). In particular, alcohol use and alcohol-related problems before and after military combat deployment in Iraq and Afghanistan are a serious concern (Jacobson et al., 2008). Research indicates that active-duty members practice heavy weekly drinking, and younger service members are the most likely to show continued or new problems with alcohol after deployment.

Coinciding with substance abuse issues are widespread reports of increased suicidal ideation among service members and returning veterans with an alarming increase in completion rates. For example, in 2008, the army reported for the fourth straight year an increase in soldier suicide surpassing the suicide rate among civilians. Contributing factors to these recent suicides include relationship trouble, work problems, and legal/financial difficulties. Young, white, unmarried junior enlisted troops were most at risk for attempting suicide, with firearms being the most common method. In an effort to address this problem, the army and the National Institute for Mental Health (NIMH) are collaborating on a 5-year research project exploring the mental and behavioral health of soldiers and the development of intervention strategies.

Relationship Issues Associated With Military and Veteran PTSD

The criteria associated with PTSD typically focus on intrapersonal symptoms (e.g., intrusive thoughts, hypervigilance, flashbacks), yet the interpersonal toll can be significant. Living and/or interacting daily with someone who is chronically angry, emotionally unavailable, preoccupied with the past, socially anxious, and often withdrawn is very difficult. Veterans with PTSD and their spouses report lower marital satisfaction (Jordan et al., 1992), are more likely to get divorced than noncombat veterans (Jordan et al., 1992; Kessler, 2000), and often describe their marital problems as more severe than veterans not experiencing PTSD (Riggs, Byrne, Weathers, & Litz, 1998). Furthermore, partners of veterans with PTSD experience extensive caregiver burden, have poorer psychological adjustment (Calhoun, Beckham, & Bosworth, 2002), and often feel burdened (Beckham, Lytle, & Feldman, 1996) and distressed themselves (Manguno-Mire et al., 2007). When feeling overwhelmed, family members may distance themselves from the veteran, which can increase the intensity of PTSD (Solomon, Mikulincer, & Avitzuer, 1988).

In a study of veterans of the wars in Iraq and Afghanistan (about 15% of whom screened positive for PTSD), concern about relationship problems increased fourfold between homecoming and 6 months later (Milliken, Auchterlonie, & Hoge, 2007). Because these relationship problems (poor communication, difficulties with intimacy, etc.) among veterans experiencing PTSD and their spouses appear to be chronic (Cook, Riggs, Thompson, Coyne, & Sheikh, 2004), it is necessary to monitor these challenges over time.

Due to the impact that PTSD has on both partners, intervening at the relational level can be very beneficial. Assisting both partners in effectively managing stress can lead to the experience of greater intimacy and relationship satisfaction. Interventions that target the relationship can also address trauma symptoms within the context of strengthening the family unit (Johnson, 2002) and facilitate the resolution of family problems that arise as a result of PTSD.

Family Well-Being Including Domestic Violence and Child Maltreatment

There is increasing concern about the well-being of spouses and children/adolescents of military personnel due to the inherent challenges of military family life (Barnes et al., 2007; Chandra et al., 2008; Huebner & Mancini, 2008). The stress associated with extensive duty hours, frequent separations, and periodic relocations (typically far from the support of family and friends) can strain even the strongest of military families. This strain is exacerbated when the returning veteran is carrying the physical and/or behavioral health residue of combat (Bowling & Sherman, 2008).

As a result of these challenges, combat veterans are at increased risk for perpetrating domestic violence, especially those with PTSD (Clark & Messer, 2006; Rentz et al., 2006; Sherman, Sautter, Jackson, Lyons, & Han, 2006). The toll of deployment can be great for the at-home parent(s) as well. Gibbs, Martin, Kupper, and Johnson (2007) report that the rate of child maltreatment in families of enlisted soldiers is 42% higher when military members are deployed in a combat zone than when they are at home. Furthermore, female civilian parents are twice as likely to abuse a child physically and almost four times more likely to neglect a child when their husbands are deployed than at other times. Finally, researchers assessing children of military members serving in Iraq and Afghanistan have identified heightened anxiety, attention difficulties, as well as emotional and behavioral problems among these youth (Chandra et al., 2008). These findings highlight the importance of assessing each family member's functioning throughout the deployment cycle and providing appropriate support to everyone in the family system.

It is essential that individuals working with military and veteran families be cognizant of the risks for violence and routinely screen for domestic abuse and child maltreatment. Clinicians must have knowledge of the state laws and procedures in reporting suspected child abuse and know where to refer clients for issues associated with interpersonal and family violence. Understanding the roles and responsibilities of the service member's commander in these situations is also helpful. Each military service has a comprehensive family violence program interested in and capable of partnering with civilian authorities. These issues are also relevant to veterans in the VHA system where the majority of mental health clinicians are not trained to assess or treat children. Whether providing services to a military member, a veteran, or their family members, having a strong base of community resources is essential for providing competent and comprehensive care.

The Impact of Trauma on Parenting and Veterans' Children

Being a good parent is challenging, but it can be especially difficult for veterans who have experienced trauma. Two critical tasks of effective parenting include (1) developing a healthy attachment/positive emotional connection with the child and (2) helping the child manage strong emotions and learn appropriate behaviors. Trauma survivors often struggle with both of these tasks. First, emotional availability and vulnerability can be difficult for the veteran parent. He or she may want to be attentive and engaged with their child or children, but at the same time, they may be preoccupied with horrific memories. A veteran may feel uncomfortable with a child's playful squeals and active behavior and as a result withdraw from close, warm interactions with them. Many trauma survivors become emotionally numb in order to avoid the pain associated with trauma symptoms. This coping strategy can result in an inability to access the positive feelings that are essential for bonding with children. Consequently, children of veteran parents with PTSD may view their parent as unavailable, distant, or aloof. Older youth may personalize this withdrawal, while younger children may question if their behavior caused this distance.

In addition to the difficulty of accessing emotions, trauma survivors often experience powerful emotions that are hard to control. Veterans may model unhealthy ways of dealing with anger, for example, explosive moods, frequent irritability, and child abuse. Children may model these behaviors at the same time they view their parent as unpredictable, hostile, and frightening. The damage to the child and to the family unit as a result of these angry outbursts is significant.

Professionals who work with children of military families need to assess the children's safety, well-being, and understanding of the family situation. There are several resources that may be useful when working with these children, such as free summer camps for military youth (Operation Purple Camps provided through the National Military Family Association: www.nmfa.org) and trainings for school personnel that focus on the impact of military family life on students (through the Military Child Education Coalition: www.militarychild.org). Age-appropriate DVDs for children about deployment have been distributed nationally at no cost (e.g., *Sesame Street*'s "Talk, Listen, and Connect" and "When Parents Are Deployed") from www.sesameworkshop.org or Military One Source (www.militaryonesource .com). Finally, a resource created for teens whose parent has experienced trauma, *Finding My Way: A Teen's Guide to Living with a Parent Who Has Experienced Trauma* (Sherman & Sherman, 2005), can help teens understand common trauma reactions, realize they are not to blame, identify sources of social support, learn how they can be supportive to others, and provide methods for maintaining hope.

Relationships With Parents and Other Loved Ones

In addition to immediate family members, there are challenges faced by the parents and other loved ones of active military members and veterans. Almost all military members have parents and loved ones who are important in their lives. Service members who are not married (including the majority of young soldiers and Marines) are also at risk for behavioral health problems, risk taking, and relationship problems. Their parents and loved ones are likely to have a primary role in providing care and support to these individuals, yet supportive resources are often limited. Furthermore, many parents lack any knowledge of or a direct connection to their military member's unit or other DOD or VHA network of support.

Clinical Assessment and Intervention Skills _____

Understanding the demographic and intervention information related to military members, veterans, and their families is essential in providing culturally competent care with these populations. This includes an appreciation of the similarities and differences between civilians and these military groups, as well as the diversity within each group as a function of their unique military exposures and/or their military or veteran life stage. Because those not familiar with the armed forces or America's veteran population frequently subscribe to inaccurate stereotypes, it is important that clinicians have a current and accurate picture of today's military members, veterans, and their respective families. By familiarizing themselves with the unique circumstances and challenges of these populations, practitioners can then address their personal and professional biases and/or ignorance in order to result in more effective practices.

Issues of Assessment

Practitioners performing assessments need to consider common, population-specific, behavioral health and relationship risk factors. They also need to acquire information about a person's military history and combat experiences. Among the fundamental questions that a clinician or human services provider would ask are those that pertain to the branch of military the client served with, whether it was with an active-duty or reserve component, whether they served in a combat tour and/or experienced redeployment, and whether they were injured and in what capacity. Gaining background information about why an individual joined the military, what their training involved, what relationships they established during their service, what they liked and disliked about their military experience, how they coped with their time away from family, and their experiences upon returning to civilian life may provide insight into their current state of mind.

In the case of risk assessment of service members and veterans, there are specific areas to explore to assess one's personal and interpersonal resources. Risk factors include the presence of sleep problems, the absence of social support, the presence of physical and/or psychological problems, financial problems, unresolved grief or feelings of loss, and the absence of hope, which can lead to an elevated risk of suicide (L. Sutton, personal communication, August 11, 2008).

Questions that might be useful in working with a spouse, child, parent, or other loved one of a military member might include questions about their details of service (e.g., branch of military, combat tours, injuries, and reintegration into civilian life) and the emotional challenges of being in a relationship with a military member (e.g., coping skills, support networks, relationships challenges).

In any assessment context, strength-based assessments are critical to all interventions. For example, although the service member, veteran, or their family may face enormous stressors, their biopsychosocial strengths, experienced on an individual, family, and community level, must be explored, understood, and celebrated.

In any of these discussions with military members, veterans, and their family members, it is important to understand that military culture is replete with abbreviations and acronyms. For example, a "MOS" is the "Military Occupation Specialty," or the service member's job/duties. It is important to ask questions about military life and service when you do not understand rather than pretend comprehension. Providing a client with the opportunity to explain himself or herself can actually enhance rapport.

Providing Support for Military Members, Veterans, and Their Families

It is important to recognize the formal and informal support services available for service members, veterans, and their families. Many programs and organizations at the federal, state, and community levels (i.e., self-help and grassroots groups) strive to support military families by promoting easy access to services. Given the challenges associated with seeking help for mental health issues (e.g., stigma, fear of loss of status/respect, fear of loss of rank, negative impact on career, distance from provider) (Hoge et al., 2004), outreach becomes critical to facilitating entry into treatment for behavioral health concerns. In order to understand the formal supports available to service members, veterans, and their families, one must understand the services provided by the DOD and/or the VHA, as well as services available from the various military service components and the array of private, nonprofit associations serving these populations. Some services may vary by facility or organization, so site-specific exploration is necessary.

Additional civilian agencies are targeting National Guard and other reserve component members as well as recent Iraq and Afghanistan war veterans for behavioral health and related human services. These include community mental health clinics, substance abuse centers, domestic violence shelters, child protection agencies, probation services, and homeless shelters. In order to properly assess and understand service members, veterans, and their family members, assessment protocols at these civilian community agencies need to be adjusted to ensure that specific military and veteran content areas are adequately explored. Furthermore, these agencies need to be sure that the information they collect will lead to an accurate and informed understanding of treatment needs.

Compared to previous years, a broader knowledge base about interventions that support military personnel and their families is available today. For example, the diagnosis of PTSD was not established until 1980 (*Diagnostic and Statistical Manual of the American Psychological Association*, 3rd Edition, APA, 1980), and subsequent research has led to evidence-based treatments such as prolonged exposure therapy (Foa, Rothbaum, & Hembree, 2007) and cognitive processing therapy (Resick & Schnicke, 1992). Although progress has been made in some areas, other domains (e.g., impact of parental trauma on youth) are still in their infancy.

Individuals working with children or the school system should request that school personnel assess which students are from military families and follow the deployment cycle for each student and/or family. Educators need to be sensitive to the stress during different phases of the deployment cycle and be available to provide extra support to the family during these times. School personnel may wish to seek specialized training on providing support to military youth such as the "Living in the New Normal" professional workshop offered through the Military Child Education Coalition (www.militarychild.org). Family practitioners need to understand the impact of separation and reunification on the family. Within the military culture, the unit is a "surrogate family"; therefore, the relationships within the unit should be considered when providing services. These contextual family systems should be explored more extensively than one might explore a civilian's work environment and relationships.

It is important that individuals who are working with military populations on a regular basis contact DOD or VHA agencies in their region to become informed of military- veteran-specific evidence-based assessment and intervention protocols being used in these settings. The adoption or adaptation of these assessments and/or protocols could greatly enhance clinician effectiveness. Currently, the DOD and VHA are partnering with numerous agencies (e.g., civilian universities, hospitals, private and not-for-profit treatment centers, professional associations, the Substance Abuse and Mental Health Services Administration [SAMHSA], Mental Health America) in promoting empirically supported treatments and best-practice intervention models for common military and veteran behavioral health conditions. In particular, the VHA's National Center for PTSD (NCPTSD) represents the single best source of information. The center's goals are to advance the clinical care and social welfare of veterans through research, education, and training on PTSD and stress-related disorders (www.ncptsd.va.gov). Less well known are the resources available to address the unique needs of military and veteran spouses, of their children, and even of parents and other extended-family members whose lives and personal well-being are often directly linked to these service members and veterans.

Promoting Engagement in Working With Military Families

Engagement is needed at the local, regional, and national levels in support of direct services, clinical and educational programs, and public policies. Programs in the health and human services professions can take a leadership role in collaborating with their professional organizations in an effort to better serve military populations. Graduate schools can encourage their students to assist with the work of governors, mayors, and many other local government initiatives focused on the needs of members of the National Guard and other reserve components. Support for the many not-for-profit initiatives that have emerged in response to the wars in Iraq and Afghanistan to support military members, veterans, and their families is needed. Faith-based initiatives and other volunteer associations have made tremendous contributions and would benefit from the contributions of well-informed, knowledgeable, skilled, compassionate and civically engaged practitioners and professional educators. Many professionals who work with families as individual providers and/or through their agencies have multiple opportunities to become engaged with military members, veterans, and their family members.

Providing pro bono services is another way in which family practitioners and other human service professionals can contribute and have a meaningful experience while assisting military families. For example, there are many behavioral health clinicians supporting programs like Give an Hour (www.giveanhour.org), whose mission is "to develop national networks of volunteers capable of responding to both acute and chronic conditions that arise within our society." Currently, Give an Hour is focusing its efforts on service members and families affected by the wars in Afghanistan and Iraq by asking behavioral health professionals to "give an hour" each week to provide free mental health services to military personnel and their families.

Resiliency Demonstrated by Military Members, Veterans, and Their Families

Military members, veterans, and their families are all challenged by the stress and adversity inherent in military duties and the military lifestyle. Even though these families benefit from adequate life skills preparation and effective support systems to meet these demands, it is important to recognize that they also have multiple strengths that help to buffer the military life stress and that they work to promote access to and utilization of available resources. Many military families are extremely resilient, and these strengths can prove beneficial in coping with subsequent life challenges.

Summary

This chapter provided a road map framed around four interrelated tasks:

1. *Promoting awareness* of our military and veteran populations and their families to support clinical practice

2. *Increasing knowledge* about these groups

3. *Enhancing practice skills* needed to effectively serve military members, veterans, and their families

4. *Increasing engagement* in providing services to these populations

The authors have provided fundamental information in preparation for providing services to military members, veterans, and their families. We encourage readers to treat this information as a foundation and a source of motivation for engaging with military personnel, veterans, and their families. These populations have evolved from a historic commitment of past and present generations who have served in uniform or unselfishly sustained family life at home while their loved ones were defending our nation. Today's military members, veterans, and their families are facing many new and different challenges; however, they continue the tradition of "service before self."

Additional Readings and Internet Resources

BattleMind: A strengths-based approach to deployment mental health: https://www .battlemind.army.mil/

Department of Veterans Affairs: Health Care for Veterans: Provides information on health care benefits and finding local VA facilities: www1.va.gov/ health/index.asp

Deployment Health and Family Readiness Library: Provides deployment health and family readiness information. Includes fact sheets, guides, and other products on a wide variety of topics: http://deploymenthealthlibrary.fhp.osd.mil/home.jsp

MilitaryHOMEFRONT: The official Department of Defense Web site containing reliable information for military members and their families, leaders, and service providers: http://www.militaryhomefront.dod.mil/

Military OneSource: (1-800-342-9647). A "24/7" resource for military personnel and their families: www.militaryonesource.com

National Center for PTSD: Performs research, education, and training on PTSD and stress-related disorders. Has many excellent "fact sheets" on trauma diagnosis, assessment, and treatment: www.ncptsd.va.gov

Operation Enduring Families: A five-session family education program created for veterans/families of the global war on terror: http://www.ouhsc.edu/oef/

SAFE (Support and Family Education) Program: An 18-session family education program used widely in the VA system to support those who care about a veteran living with trauma, PTSD, or mental illness: http://www.ouhsc.edu/safeprogram/

Sherman, M. D., Zanotti, D. K., & Jones, D. E. (2005). Key elements in couples therapy with veterans with combat-related PTSD. *Professional Psychology: Research and Practice, 36*(6), 626–633.

The Defense Centers of Excellence for Psychological Health & Traumatic Brain Injury: A collaborative effort of the VA system and the DOD that establishes quality standards for clinical care; education and training; prevention; patient, family, and community outreach; and program excellence: http://www.health.mil/dcoe.aspx

The National Center for Veterans Analysis and Statistics: For information about veterans, including socioeconomic data, demographic characteristics, the geographical distribution of the veteran population, and other statistical information by the veterans program: http://www.va.gov/vetdata/

References

American Psychiatric Association. (1980). *Diagnostic and statistical manual of mental disorders* (3rd ed.). American Psychiatric Association: Arlington, VA.

Barnes, V. A., Davis, H., & Treiber, F. A. (2007). Perceived stress, heart rate, and blood pressure among adolescents with family members deployed in Operation Iraqi Freedom. *Military Medicine, 172*(1), 4.

Beckham, J. C., Lytle, B. L., & Feldman, M. E. (1996). Caregiver burden in partners of Vietnam War veterans with posttraumatic stress. *Journal of Consulting and Clinical Psychology, 64*, 1068–1072.

Bowling, U. B., & Sherman, M. D. (2008). Welcoming them home: Supporting soldiers and their families in navigating the tasks of reintegration. *Professional Psychology: Research and Practice, 39*(4), 451–458.

Calhoun, P. S., Beckham, J. C., & Bosworth, H. B. (2002). Caregiver burden and psychological distress in partners of veterans with chronic posttraumatic stress disorder. *Journal of Traumatic Stress, 15*(3), 205–212

Chandra, A., Burns, R. M., Tanielian, T., Jaycox, L. H., & Scott, M. M. (2008). *Understanding the impact of deployment on children and families: Findings from a pilot study of Operation Purple Camp participants*. Center for Military Health Policy Research, RAND Corporation. Retrieved January 26, 2009, from http://www.rand.org/pubs/working_papers/2008/RAND_WR566.pdf

Clark, J. C., & Messer, S. C. (2006). Intimate partner violence in the U.S. military: Rates, risks and responses. In C. A. Castro, A. B. Adler, & C. A. Britt (Eds.), *Military life: The psychology of serving in peace and combat. Vol. 3* (pp. 193–219). Bridgeport, CT: Praeger Security International.

Cook, J. M., Riggs, D. S., Thompson, R., Coyne, J. C., & Sheikh, J. I. (2004). Posttraumatic stress disorder and current relationship functioning among World War II ex-prisoners of war. *Journal of Family Psychology, 18*(1), 36–45.

Dean, R. G. (2001). The myth of cross-cultural competence. *Families in Society, 82*(6), 623–630.

Department of Veteran Affairs. (2008, February). *Veterans Affairs Information Pamphlet*. Retrieved February 29, 2009, from http://www1.va.gov/vetdata/docs/Pamphlet_2-1-08.pdf

Foa, E. B., Rothbaum, B. O., & Hembree, E. A. (2007). *Prolonged exposure therapy for PTSD: Emotional processing of traumatic experiences: Therapist guide*. New York: Oxford University Press.

Gibbs, D. A., Martin, S. L., Kupper, L. I., & Johnson, R. E. (2007). Child maltreatment in enlisted soldiers' families during combat-related deployments. *Journal of the American Medical Association, 298*(5), 528–535.

Hoge, C. W., Achterlonie, J. L., & Milliken, C. S. (2006). Mental health problems, use of mental health services and attrition from military service after returning from deployment to Iraq or Afghanistan. *Journal of the American Medical Association, 295*(9), 1023–1032.

Hoge, C. W., Castro, C. A., Messer, S. C., McGurk, D., Cotting, D. I., & Koffman, R. L. (2004). Combat duty in Iraq and Afghanistan, mental health problems, and barriers to care. *New England Journal of Medicine, 351*(17), 1798–1800.

Huebner, A. J., & Mancini, J. A. (2008). Supporting youth during parental deployment: Strategies for professionals and families. *The Prevention Researcher, 15*(5), 10–13.

Jacobson, I. G., Ryan, M. A. K., Hooper, T. I., Smith, T. C., Amoroso, P. J., Boyko, E. J., Gackstetter, G. D., Wells, T. S., & Bell, N. S.(2008). Alcohol use and alcohol-related problems before and after military combat deployment. *Journal of the American Medical Association, 300*(6), 663–675.

Johnson, S. M. (2002). *Emotionally focused couple therapy with trauma survivors: Strengthening attachment bonds*. New York: Guilford.

Jordan, B. K., Marmar, C. R., Fairbank, J. A., Schlenger, W. E., Kulka, R. A., Hough, R. L., & Weiss, D. S. (1992). Problems in families of male Vietnam veterans with posttraumatic stress disorders. *Journal of Consulting and Clinical Psychology, 60*, 916–926.

Kessler, R. C. (2000). Posttraumatic stress disorder: The burden to the individual and to society. *Journal of Clinical Psychiatry, 61*(5), 4–12.

Manguno-Mire, G., Sautter, F., Lyons, J., Myers, L., Perry, D., Sherman, M., Glynn, S., & Sullivan, G. (2007). Psychological distress and caregiver burden in partners of veterans with combat-related PTSD. *Journal of Nervous and Mental Disease, 195*(2), 144–151.

Milliken, C. S., Auchterlonie, J. L., & Hoge, C. W. (2007). Longitudinal assessment of mental health problems among active and reserve component soldiers returning from the Iraq War. *Journal of the American Medical Association, 298*(18), 2141–2148.

National Center for Posttraumatic Stress Disorder. (n.d.). *How common is PTSD?* Retrieved February 19, 2009, from http://www.ncptsd.va.gov/ncmain/ncdocs/fact_shts/fs_how_common_is_ptsd.html?opm=1&rr=rr1363&srt=d&echorr=true

National Center for Veterans Analysis and Statistics. (2008, October). *VA benefits and healthcare utilization.* Retrieved February 19, 2009, from http://www1.va.gov/vetdata/docs/4X6_fall08_sharepoint.pdf

Office of the Under Secretary of Defense, Personnel, and Readiness. (2008, January). *Population representation in the military services.* Retrieved December 26, 2008, from http://www.defenselink.mil/prhome/PopRep_FY06/summary.html

Rentz, E. D., Martin, S. A., Gibbs, D. A., Clinton-Sherrod, M., Hardison, J., & Marshall, S. W. (2006). Family violence in the military. *Trauma, Violence, and Abuse, 7*(2), 93–108.

Resick, P. A., & Schnicke, M. K. (1992). Cognitive processing therapy for sexual assault survivors. *Journal of Consulting and Clinical Psychology, 60,* 748–756.

Riggs, D., Byrne, C. A., Weathers, F. W., & Litz, B. T. (1998). The quality of intimate relationships in male Vietnam veterans: The impact of posttraumatic stress disorder. *Journal of Traumatic Stress 11,* 87–102.

Sherman, M. D., Sautter, F., Jackson, H., Lyons, J., & Han, X. (2006). Domestic violence in veterans with posttraumatic stress disorder who seek couples therapy. *Journal of Marital and Family Therapy, 32*(4), 479–490.

Sherman, M. D., & Sherman, D. M. (2005). *Finding my way: A teen's guide to living with a parent who has experienced trauma.* Edina, MN: Beavers Pond Press.

Solomon, Z., Mikulincer, M., & Avitzuer, E. (1988). Coping, locus of control, social support, and combat-related posttraumatic stress disorder: A prospective study. *Journal of Personality and Social Psychology, 55,* 270–285.

Tanielian, T., & Jaycox, L. H. (Eds.). (2008). *Invisible wounds of war: Psychological and cognitive injuries, their consequences, and services to assist recovery.* Santa Monica, CA: RAND Corporation.

United States Department of Veterans Affairs. (2008, November). *America's wars.* Retrieved February 19, 2009, from http://www1.va.gov/opa/fact/amwars.asp

18

Families, Stress, and Intervention

Melissa J. Herzog

As described in the preceding chapters, families face a multitude of stressors throughout the life course. How well a family manages and adapts to any given stressor event depends on the characteristics of the stressor, the contextual circumstances under which the stressor occurs, and the family's capacity for effective response (Boss, 2002; Burr, Klein, & Associates, 1994; Patterson, 2002). Family stress theory contends that although stress in families is inevitable, it is not inherently negative or positive. It is only when a family's response to a stressor is not effective, and discontent and/or symptoms result, that stress is identified as problematic. Often, it is the combination of increasing discontent and the presence of emotional, physical, behavioral, or relational symptoms that leads a family to seek therapeutic intervention.

This chapter offers a general overview of family stress intervention using a developmental–systemic framework. Additionally, the ABC-X model (Hill, 1958) and the existing body of literature on family stress serve as a foundation from which to (a) address the importance of assessing and classifying the type of stressor event prior to treatment or intervention, (b) review the family processes and family characteristics most often identified as protective factors or beneficial resources in managing stress, and (c) discuss the implications of these processes and characteristics for clinical assessment and intervention with families experiencing stress, providing illustrations of applicable therapeutic strategies. The following case analysis is intended to illustrate the information and ideas put forth throughout the chapter.

Courtney, 42, and David, 44, have been married for 16 years. Together they have two children: Stephen, 13, and Jake, 11. Courtney and David dated for 3 years before they got married, and they describe the early years of their marriage as "happy." When Stephen was born, they describe him as a happy baby and report that the transition to parenthood was relatively smooth.

(Continued)

(Continued)

Two years later, Jake was born and Courtney reports that she saw many differences in early developmental milestones between Jake and Stephen. Jake required far more attention as an infant, but did not seem to offer the same degree of playful interaction. Jake was harder to get along with than Stephen, and although he excelled at learning his ABCs, his overall demeanor was moodier. He was easily frustrated and prone to angry outbursts. Courtney's concern led to frequent visits to the pediatrician, where she was told that second-born children often present additional challenges for parents and there was little cause for concern since Jake's developmental progress appeared to be within the typical range.

———•·•———

Courtney became quite focused on keeping Jake calm despite David's complaints that she was always "giving in." David took a more punitive approach by reacting emotionally and frequently enforcing punishments. Courtney and David often argued about their discrepant approaches to Jake's behavior, resulting in heated verbal attacks on each other's character, followed by withdrawal.

———•·•———

Jake typically initiated social exchanges only with his mother—David's and Stephen's attempts to engage him usually resulted in arguments. Both Stephen and his father complained that trying to talk to Jake was extremely difficult; he was very rigid about rules, did not share or take turns well, and often "droned on" about his favorite topics. Courtney usually intervened during these exchanges, insisting that David and Stephen must be more patient with Jake.

———•·•———

In school, Jake had problems interacting with peers and usually spent time playing alone engaged in his few intense interests. Courtney and David were frequently called to the school for conferences on Jake's grades and seeming distractibility. On a routine doctor visit, Jake's pediatrician offered a diagnosis of ADHD and started a course of medication; Courtney and David disagreed strongly about this decision. They continued to have arguments that began about Jake but quickly escalated in both scope and intensity. David didn't agree with Jake's diagnosis or medication, and he reports that Courtney "doted" on Jake even more than before. Courtney, in turn, reports that David seemed "disinterested" in Jake, and in her, and spent most of his time away from the house with Stephen. This division was often noted in dinnertime conversations—Stephen's attempts to tell his parents about the day's activities were usually derailed when Courtney would bring Jake into the conversation. Jake would "take over" about his usual topics, and when Stephen or David would try to interject, Courtney scolded them for the interruptions.

———•·•———

When Jake began middle school, staff reported that Jake exhibited socially inappropriate behaviors and conversations and was often socially isolated and rejected by his peers. At the recommendation of Jake's school counselor, Courtney took Jake to a child psychologist. After a series of evaluations, the psychologist informed Courtney and David that Jake had Asperger's syndrome (AS).[1] Although his parents felt relieved to have a name for the behavior they had seen in Jake most of his life, they each reported feelings of uncertainty about the diagnosis and what it meant for Jake's future. Since the diagnosis, Courtney's sleep has become erratic as she spends an inordinate amount of time searching the Internet for information about Jake's diagnosis and treatments. David's level of interaction with Jake has not changed much since the diagnosis. He feels that having a label does not change the reality they have been living with since Jake was little.

———◆·◆———

The family lives in a rural community where few local professionals have ever worked with a child with Asperger's. Although well-researched behavioral interventions are available at the university about 90 miles away, the programs are very expensive and are not covered by insurance. Courtney and David currently are not able to enroll Jake in a program, so they have decided to pursue counseling to "fill in the gap" in Jake's treatment.

A Developmental–Systemic Framework

Thinking Developmentally

In the ABC-X model of family stress and crisis, "A" represents an event or occurrence that requires a nonroutine change in a family's functioning. Often such events or occurrences are developmental in nature. As families navigate through life, many of the developmental transitions they experience require them to restructure and redefine family roles and relationships in order to accommodate the changing circumstances (Boss, 2002; Minuchin, 1974). Whereas some transitions are expected and considered normative (the transition to parenthood, a child entering adolescence, retirement), others are unanticipated, or nonnormative (the chronic illness of a family member, the death of a child). For the most part, regardless of normative status, changes and transitions are accompanied by stress (Boss, 1987, 2002; Burr et al., 1994; McCubbin & McCubbin, 1989). As we previously noted, however, stress is not intrinsically negative. For a family with the resources and capacity to manage the stressor and adapt to the transitional state, the outcome may be an improvement in functioning. When a family does not have the ability to adjust and adapt to the changing circumstances, however, the likelihood that family members will experience dissatisfaction, negative symptoms, and crisis increases (McCubbin & McCubbin, 1989; McCubbin & Patterson, 1982; Patterson, 2002).

Families are most likely to seek treatment during transitional developmental periods, when the associated risks of negative stress-related outcomes are greater. As such, practitioners who work with families must have a comprehensive understanding of the family developmental life cycle and the structural accommodations required at each transitional stage (for discussion of the family developmental life cycle, see Carter & McGoldrick, 1988). In the case described above, both sons are in the transition to early adolescence. For Jake in particular, this normative transition is compounded by symptoms associated with his Asperger's diagnosis (Marcus, Kunce, & Schopler, 2005). AS is a developmental disorder characterized by deficits in requisite social skills.

In other words, Jake is socially incompetent compared to his same-age peers. His rigidity against change and his difficulties with social interactions became even more apparent as he began middle school and was forced to interact with a new set of peers. A consideration of Jake's normative developmental transition (i.e., exploration of his personal and social identities) and diagnostic symptoms (i.e., difficulty with understanding the subtleties of social communication) would likely lead his parents to modify their interactions with Jake to provide models for appropriate social interaction, rather than punish or excuse his challenging or socially inappropriate behavior.

Applying the ABC-X model to an assessment of this situation provides additional clarity. The stressor event (A) is the diagnosis of Jake's Asperger's syndrome and its symptomatic behavioral and social patterns. These issues have become especially pronounced as Jake begins his transition to adolescence, which is typically marked by shifting social identities and the salience of peer interaction. His parents have divergent interpretations (B; perceptions) about Jake's behavior—Courtney views them as symptoms of a disorder, whereas David interprets the behavior as manipulative and intentional. These divergent opinions are resulting in drastically different responses (C; resources) from his parents. Courtney responds by attempting to accommodate the behavior, regardless of effects on other family members, and by simultaneously searching for external interventions. David responds with a pattern of withdrawal from Jake and Courtney. Unfortunately, neither approach is remediating the problem; in fact, marital, parent–child, and sibling conflict are all on the rise. A therapist knowledgeable about developmental transitions, and who has a basic understanding of the social and behavioral implications of AS, can assist Courtney and David to better understand their son's current capacities (i.e., shift the perceptions from either "helpless" or "manipulative" to "is able to work through his challenges given some support"). Such a shift in meaning would allow these parents to access a new set of resources to assist Jake's development and would bring the couple back to a state of unification.

Thinking Systemically

The ABC-X model of family stress also highlights that the adaptive management of stressor events is partly influenced by the characteristics and attributes of the family system. Family systems theory (Steinglass, 1987) and the tenets of structural family therapy (Minuchin, 1974) provide a theoretical basis from which to consider the relationship between family dynamics and family stress management. To clearly understand the origins of stress within families, we must understand the properties of the family system. As articulated by family systems theory, the core constructs of organization, morphostasis, and morphogenesis (Steinglass, 1987) provide a framework to explain the development of family processes.

Systems are best defined by their *organization*. A family's structural organization is manifested in the consistent, repetitive, and predictable patterns of interaction produced by the rules and relationships within the family. Three underlying concepts are central to understanding this organizational constancy. First, the principle of *wholeness* suggests that each family is unique because of the specific combination of its elements, implying that the members of a family are intrinsically interrelated—the behavior of one cannot and should not be viewed in isolation from the behavior of the others (Steinglass, 1987). In summarizing the commonalities of stress, Olson (1997) notes that all stressors either begin or end in the family. Thus, whether a stressor is internal (e.g., marital disagreement) or affects one family member through an external source (e.g., a disagreement with a peer at school), the effects of the stressor will have an impact on the entire family system because of the interdependence of the individual members. As seen in our case example, although AS is a diagnosis applicable only to Jake, the social and behavioral challenges of this disorder have impacted the family, as well as their interactions with one another. These interactions, in turn, have influence on the expression of Jake's AS symptoms. Such interdependence is observed not only among individual family members but also among the various *subsystems* within the family. Subsystems are formed when individuals come together to perform specific tasks or functions (e.g., parenting and caring for a child; Minuchin, 1974). For systemic family therapists, the linkages among the parental, marital, and parent–child subsystems should be of interest because of the complexity of their interrelationships (Cowan, Cowan, & Schulz, 1996; Madden-Derdich, 2002). For example, when one parent's relationship with the child is strained and the other parent's is not, a divide in the typical parenting alliance may form, and this divide may spill over into marital interactions. Such a pattern is evident in the current case example. David has always experienced a more contentious relationship with Jake than has Courtney. A therapist would note that over the years, each parent has become entrenched in their particular form of parent–child interaction, with the disagreements about their respective parenting styles precipitating additional conflict about marital issues.

The second organizational principle, *boundaries,* is a metaphorical concept describing the regulation of the type and amount of contact that occurs between individuals and subsystems within the family and between the family unit and their external contexts such as the workplace or school (Steinglass, 1987). Boundaries establish the rules of interaction and define who is part of the system as well as the nature of each member's participation (Boss 1999, 2002; Minuchin, 1974). When boundaries are clear, individuals and subsystems can adequately perform their designated roles and functions. For example, clearly established parental boundaries allow parents to function in a unified way to parent their children in times of stability or stress. When boundary clarity is not present, the result is a state of boundary ambiguity (Boss, 1999, 2002). In this state, neither the membership nor the function of a particular individual or subsystem in the family is readily apparent. This ambiguity interferes with the family's ability to respond successfully when faced with stressors that require adaptive change because the interactional rules and family role definitions are not clearly established and understood. What we see in the current case example are very rigid boundaries between two parent–child dyads: Courtney and Jake are separated from David and Stephen. Such rigid boundaries have created alliances such that the parental subsystem is no longer functioning in a unified way. The rigid separation of these two dyads is also resulting in strain in David's and Jake's parent–child relationship, and in the relationship between Jake and his brother.

Finally, subsystems within families are arranged *hierarchically* (Minuchin, 1974; Steinglass, 1987), with some family members having more power and control than others. In turn, this hierarchical arrangement determines how the subsystems function and who holds decision-making authority in the family. Typically, parents occupy an executive or authoritative function in the family relative to the children. If the hierarchical structure of the family breaks down when a stressor is encountered, symptoms may result. In the current case, we see that there is an implicit breakdown in the parenting hierarchy such that Jake's behaviors, and his mother's complicity with these behaviors, are exerting power over the nature and course of the family's daily tasks and interactions. Although the family is presenting Jake (along with his recent diagnostic label) as the identified client, a common occurrence when dealing with behavioral issues, the overall organization of the family is contributing to the maintenance of the stressful situations. This example highlights the essential need for clinicians to view assessment and treatment planning through developmental and systemic lenses. Intervening solely at the level of the child is unlikely to result in the broader structural and perceptual changes that will be required for the family members to adjust and adapt to the accumulation of stressors.

Although the patterned and predictable behavior within the family is related to organizational structure of the family, family systems theory also suggests that such patterned behavior is the product of *morphostasis,* or the maintenance of and resistance to changes in family interaction (Steinglass, 1987). Families maintain consistency by monitoring the internal environment for signs of change and modifying behavior as needed so that the family can maintain its current structure, interaction patterns, and roles. However, certain circumstances or events can be managed only through the realignment and restructuring of boundaries, rules of interaction, and family role definitions. When a family resists structural reorganization in the face of a stressor event that demands change, stress levels increase and the risk of symptomatic behavior or crisis is amplified. In our case example, although Jake's social and behavioral difficulties have existed since early childhood, the diagnosis is very recent. In the past, Courtney and David were unclear about the nature of Jake's developmental challenges and their roles in helping to remediate some of his social and behavioral problems. Although Courtney is seeking information about AS to learn about effective interventions for adolescents with AS, David appears resistant to change his style of interaction with Jake. Moreover, rather than unifying to confront the diagnosis together, Courtney and David are becoming increasingly entrenched in their roles as "the worrier" and "the denier," roles which have been held for many years.

Finally, inherently linked to morphostasis is the process of *morphogenesis* (Steinglass, 1987). In contrast to morphostasis, this concept relates to the ways in which families grow and change. Morphogenetic reactions to stress and change lead to organizational alterations in the family. Morphogenesis occurs in two distinct ways (Watzlawick, Weakland, & Fisch, 1974). *First-order change* is a temporary reaction to stress in which the interactional patterns within the family are altered in an effort to handle the stress (e.g., Courtney is spending a dramatic amount of time researching AS-specific therapies, which decreases her interactions with the family, and her husband in particular). *Second-order change* is a more dramatic response to stress that involves reorganization of the family's existing structure. Such reorganization may include reconstituting subsystems, strengthening or weakening specific boundaries, and redefining family rules and roles. Through family-based therapy, Jake's parents should be able to shift their perception of Jake's behavior and his abilities and thus approach his communication and behavioral challenges in a more adaptive way that will promote his integration in, rather than domination of, family interaction over time.

Family systems theory and the related tenets of structural family therapy suggest numerous points of entry for clinical interventions in cases of family stress or crisis. Clinicians may intervene at the structural level, focusing on the rules of interaction that guide family roles, or at the level of the behavioral patterns that emerge from this structure. Moreover, certain characteristics of family organization (e.g., flexibility and coherence, described later in this chapter) have been found to be strongly and consistently associated with a family's ability to demonstrate resilience and manage a stressor event. Prior to commencing intervention with a family, however, the clinician must first acquire a thorough understanding of the stressor itself.

_____ Understanding and Assessing the Stressor Event

We have addressed the developmental and systemic context of stressor events and their "normative" or "nonnormative" status. In a clinical setting, however, truly understanding the potential impacts of stressors requires more detailed specification. Stressors can vary widely on a number of dimensions. In her contextual approach to family stress management, Boss (2002) suggests that comprehensive consideration of the qualities of the stressor must precede therapeutic assessment or intervention. The nature of the stressor has the potential to influence a family's perception of the problem, the level of stress they are experiencing, and the stress management strategies they are using. Boss classifies stressors by their *source, type, duration*, and *density*. In a therapeutic application, this system provides the clinician with an objective framework for clearly defining the parameters of a situation, better enabling them to assess a family's resources and to develop management strategies.

Source refers to the origin of the stressor. Is the stressor event internal (the birth of a child, an adolescent's truancy) or external (a school bully, a poor economy) to the family system? Typically, a family has more control over stressors that originate within the family than those originating from external sources. Consequently, interventions for external stressors may be more successful when they are focused on cognitive and perceptual management of the associated stress, whereas internal stressors may offer more extensive points of intervention, including structural, behavioral, cognitive, and perceptual areas. The stressor event in the current case is an internal stressor in the sense that the social challenges and recent diagnosis of Jake's AS are occurring within the family context. Moreover, the interaction patterns within the family have contributed to the maintenance of Jake's behaviors in a very coercive fashion.

In addition to determining whether a stressor is normative or nonnormative, classifying a stressor by *type* encompasses two separate questions. The first is determining whether it is ambiguous or clear; that is, are the particulars surrounding the situation clearly identifiable? It stands to reason that the more information the family and therapist have about the situation, the greater their potential to identify resources and management strategies. As Courtney and David described, they are feeling very uncertain of the meaning of Jake's diagnosis and how such a diagnosis impacts their family. Moreover, there is likely some concern about how Jake may accomplish the developmental tasks of adulthood (i.e., romantic relationships, productive employment) that require the ability to manage a variety of social situations and interactions. The second question is one of whether the stressor is volitional or non-volitional. In other words, did the family seek the situation or was it imposed on them? As a biologically based disorder, Jake's AS diagnosis is certainly not one the family had anticipated or desired. When families enter into stressful circumstances willingly, they have greater ability to identify resources proactively and are more likely to meet the associated challenges with a positive cognitive frame.

The final classification categories, *duration* and *density*, are indicators of intensity. How long has the family been dealing with each stressor, and how many stressors is the family handling simultaneously and/or consecutively? Although Jake's diagnosis is very recent, he and his family have been forced to cope with his behavior and the family's coercive marital and parent–child interaction patterns for years. The family is also recently experiencing the stress associated with both sons entering the transition to adolescence and Jake's increasing social difficulties at school. Experiencing multiple stressors simultaneously or in succession has been termed "stress pileup" (McCubbin & Patterson, 1982). In general, families who are forced to deal with new stressors before they have been able to negotiate previously existing stressors are more vulnerable and more likely to experience negative symptoms (Burr et al., 1994).

As noted above, it is crucial for a clinician working with a stressed family to define the family's stressors and the contextual circumstances surrounding them prior to initiating treatment. A clinician can gain valuable information about the characteristics of a family's stressor events by applying the classification system described above. As noted in the case example, the family is seeking therapy in an effort to remediate *Jake*'s behavioral and social difficulties. By performing a thorough assessment of this stressor, as well as its historical, developmental, and systemic contexts, however, the therapist will be able to determine more clearly the level and types of stress this family has experienced. This information is essential to the therapist's ability to ascertain the resources, management strategies, and interventions that are most likely to facilitate a reduction in stress for the family system and its members. In other words, an adept therapist will recognize that intervening with only Jake likely will not bring about lasting change.

Assessing Resources and Perceptions

Just as the causes and types of stressors vary greatly, so do the ways in which families attempt to cope with or manage stressful circumstances (Burr et al., 1994). Most conceptual models of family stress—including the ABC-X model (Hill, 1958), the double ABC-X model (McCubbin & Patterson, 1983a, 1983b), and the family adjustment and adaptation response model (Patterson, 1988, 2002)—identify both cognitive/perceptual components and resource/capability components when addressing variables that influence the outcomes of individual and family stressors. Accordingly, the next steps in the therapeutic process involve the assessment and identification of family perceptions and resources.

Identifying Meanings and Perceptions

As early as Hill's (1958) first model of family crisis, scholars have theorized that the meanings that families ascribe to stressor events play a central role in determining the degree of stress experienced and the ultimate outcome of that stress. In other words, a family's perceptions of a stressor event may represent a tipping point for whether the family is able to activate the necessary resources and adapt or is pushed into a state of crisis. When stressors occur, family members, both individually and collectively, assign meanings to the situation. This perceptual process encompasses two levels: a cognitive interpretation of the event and the corresponding affective response (Patterson & Garwick, 1994). The family's appraisal of the event determines the behavioral responses of individual family members and the family unit. Thus, coping should be conceptualized as an interrelated set of cognitive, affective, and behavioral processes. From a clinical perspective, the strength of the ascribed meaning that a family gives to a stressor appears to stem from its potential to act as either an added risk or a buffer (Boss, 2002; Patterson, 2002). Families who define stressful conditions optimistically and proactively are more likely to manage those stressors well than are families who ascribe inaccurate or negative interpretations, because they are more likely to make choices that will facilitate adaptation and prevent crisis.

Identifying Resources

Over the past decade, scholars have introduced the concept of resilience to the family stress field (Boss, 2002; Cowan et al., 1996; Patterson, 2002; Walsh, 1998). McCubbin and McCubbin (1988) define family resilience as the "characteristics, dimensions, and properties of families which help families to be resistant to disruption in the face of change and adaptive in the face of crisis" (p. 247). At the clinical level, this concept directs our attention to the capacity of families to cope with the demands they face by applying their arsenals of capabilities and resources to maintain a comfortable level of adjustment and adaptation (Patterson, 1988, 2002).

The next logical therapeutic step is to acquire a thorough understanding of the resources available to the family. A family's *coping resources* are the individual and collective strengths of family members that facilitate their ability to make the necessary systemic adjustments demanded by the circumstances (Boss, 2002; Burr et al., 1994; McCubbin & McCubbin, 1989). Note, however, that coping resources are distinct from coping behaviors or stress management strategies. Resources are the assets of the family that facilitate the members' abilities to implement coping behaviors or management strategies successfully. Unfortunately, individuals and families may not choose to utilize the resources available to them. For example, some families use avoidance strategies by denying that stressors exist or ignoring them in the hopes that problems will resolve themselves (McCubbin & Patterson, 1983a), instead of employing available resources that can help them resolve their problems. It is particularly important for the clinician to identify the availability and utilization of a family's resources, as well as any resource deficits, because this information offers essential direction for treatment planning.

Although resources can exist at individual, family, and community levels, our focus in this chapter is on family-level resources—that is, the internal attributes of the family system that facilitate adjustment and adaptation in times of stress. A review of the literature on family stress reveals that three particular family attributes are consistently beneficial for families faced with stressor events (Hobfoll & Spielberger, 1992). Although terminology varies, the structural characteristics most often identified as integral to successful stress management and coping in families are boundary clarity, cohesion, and flexibility/adaptability.

As mentioned before, boundaries establish family system membership, individuals' roles, and the rules for interaction (Boss 1999, 2002; Minuchin, 1974). When *boundary clarity* exists, family members have established roles, understand the rules of interaction within the family, and experience a healthy balance of autonomy and connection within the family system. Under these circumstances, families are better able to manage both normative and nonnormative changes, thus easing the stress associated with these transitions. In contrast, when boundaries are ill-defined, individual family members' role expectations, as well as functional interaction patterns, are often uncertain. Under these conditions, families are more likely to experience tension and strain when faced with stressors that require adaptive change (Boss, 1980). In the case example, when Jake's social challenges began to escalate during his transition to adolescence, neither parent modified their previously defined roles in an effort to manage and modify Jake's behavior in a consistent fashion. Moreover, Jake was not able to begin experiencing the autonomy that typically increases during adolescence due to the growing alliance he shared with his mother. Developmentally, it should be expected that youth become more capable of managing their own social interactions and behaviors, but Jake was not provided with the time or resources to develop this capability, as his mother would frequently interject on his behalf.

Family *cohesion*, or the level of emotional closeness, unity, and support in a family system, encompasses traits such as loyalty, pride, trust, respect, caring, and shared values (McCubbin & McCubbin, 1989). Compared with noncohesive families, cohesive families tend to be less reactive to stress. The members of cohesive families manage stress by working together. In contrast, families that lack cohesion are apt to become upset when faced with stress; family members tend to show one another minimal understanding, act in a disrespectful manner toward one another, and blame one another. The family described in the case example is lacking in cohesion—the parents have not worked in a unified fashion with respect to Jake's behavior for many years and consequently are experiencing deterioration in their marital relationship. Clearly, these processes are mutually influential: Frequent and hostile conflict further diminishes closeness and intimacy, which, in turn, contributes to the frequency and style of conflict.

Finally, family *flexibility* or *adaptability* refers to a family's ability to balance stability and change (Olson, Russell, & Sprenkle, 1979, 1983). Families have a tendency to resist change and maintain consistent patterns of relational interaction (morphostasis). Although consistency and stability are positive features that facilitate overall functioning, change is inevitable, and families need to be flexible when adaptation is required. Families with rigid structural organization are often incapable of incorporating the systemic changes that accompany normative and nonnormative transitions, and are thus at greater risk of experiencing elevated stress levels, crisis, and associated symptoms and dysfunction. Thus, the ability to balance stability and change serves as a protective factor for families faced with stressor events.

_____ Points of Intervention and Applicable Approaches

Some families choose to participate proactively in intervention programs focused on preventing the negative outcomes of specified stressors or transitions (e.g., premarital counseling or parenting intervention). In therapeutic settings, however, most families seek assistance when their stress has reached intolerable levels or they find themselves in crisis. Therefore, the focus here is on therapeutic interventions with families who enter therapy in a distressed or crisis state and on strategies that therapists can use to help families change the meanings they attribute to stressors and increase family resources in an effort to restore balance.

In considering therapeutic interventions, our goal is to provide examples of clinical approaches that professionals can use to induce change in these specific areas. Although each area (i.e., changing meanings and increasing resources) and its associated treatment strategies are addressed separately below, it must be noted that these two areas are inherently interconnected. Meanings influence resources and behaviors, and, in turn, resources and behaviors influence meanings. Moreover, there is no single best approach to treatment, and therapists may implement these intervention strategies in various orders, simultaneously or sequentially, depending on the circumstances and needs of particular families. In other words, this is not a "cookbook" approach to family stress intervention, but rather a broader conceptual framework that can offer guidance and treatment options to clinicians working with families facing diverse stressor events. Finally, although stress management in families is a combination of familial and individual processes (Boss, 2002; Burr et al., 1994; Nichols, 1987), the focus here is primarily on cognitive, emotional, and behavioral dynamics at the family system level rather than on the inner experiences of individuals that may motivate them to interact in specific ways.

Changing Meanings

When a family experiences a stressor, the family unit and its individual members make a series of attributions about the stress-evoking event (Berg-Cross, 2000; Kelley, 1967). Although attributing meaning to a stressor event is a cognitive process, this perceptual interpretation can influence both the affective and behavioral responses of the family. Practitioners consistently have used cognitively focused intervention strategies across diverse family therapy approaches to clarify potential cognitive distortions and to help families alter their perceptions of the problems. Underlying these strategies is the assumption that once family members alter their perceptions of a particular problem or situation, behavioral and emotional change will follow, allowing new and different resolutions to the problem (Epstein & Baucom, 2002).

The therapeutic reframe is an excellent example of such a strategy. This is a widely utilized technique among therapists applying the structural and strategic models of marriage and family therapy (Minuchin, 1974; Selvini Palazzoli, Boscolo, Cecchin, & Prata, 1978; Watzlawick et al., 1974). The goal of reframing in all of these approaches is the same—to get the individual, couple, or family to view the problem differently in an effort to elicit new behavioral responses. Using our case example, Courtney and David will enter therapy having made attributions about the social and behavioral difficulties they have experienced with Jake. As a clinician, it is critical to understand that their respective beliefs about Jake's ability to "control" his behavior will provide a context for understanding the strategies that have been employed by the family to date (Madsen, 1999). For example, David perceives Jake's socially inappropriate behaviors as rude and willful, whereas Courtney perceives these same behaviors as symptoms of the disorder that cannot be modified without expert help. Unfortunately, both of these interpretations are limited as a problem internal to Jake alone, rather than as a combination of extant challenges and a sequence of behavioral patterns maintained over time by all members of the family.

By encouraging an alternative conceptualization of the problem, reframing offers a viable method to alter the family's meaning of this stressor event. In this example, the therapist may offer a statement to the effect of: "Jake's behavior and communication certainly have been a challenge in your family for quite some time. I wonder how frustrating it must be for Jake to show his ability to behave positively if no one expects that he can." This statement does two things: (1) It removes the attribution of malicious intent Jake's father has ascribed to his behavior by acknowledging that a genuine deficit does exist, and (2) it simultaneously removes the attribution by his mother of Jake as a helpless victim by highlighting his own agency and the importance of clear and consistent models of acceptable behavior. Certainly, acknowledging the role of the challenging behaviors manifest in AS is warranted; however, these behaviors are changeable given contextual modifications. If the parents accept this reframe, they must expand their behavioral responses to the problem to include changes at multiple levels of the family system, including the marital and parental subsystems.

Cognitive and cognitive-behavioral approaches to family stress intervention also take family members' subjective experiences in relationships into account (Epstein & Baucom, 2002). These approaches focus on clarifying potential cognitive distortions and reinterpreting inaccurate perceptions of stressor events. As with reframing, cognitive approaches assume that once family members think differently about a problem or the motivational attributions given to individual family members' actions, behavioral and emotional change will follow (Epstein & Baucom, 2002). Therapists can intervene at the cognitive level by employing a variety of strategies that question the nature of family members' cognitions and the patterns surrounding them. Additionally, cognitive-behavioral therapy (CBT) has demonstrated effectiveness for youth with Asperger's/high-functioning autism in group-based delivery (e.g., Bauminger, 2002). Like the family approach, CBT forces youth who struggle with taking the perspective of others to stop and analyze situations with respect to emotions, intent, and the possible consequences to both actions and reactions. Although the family in our case example does not currently have access to group-based interventions, the family therapist could work with the parents to create strategies for using the CBT structure during "teachable moments" at home. For example, Jake may be allowed the opportunity to plot out a variety of possible responses to given problem situations, consider the repercussions of these responses, and make choices about which option he believes is the most effective. This type of approach provides special attention to the parents and the child as agents of change, and begins to support a unified approach between the parents as coteachers in this model. Moreover, this approach allows for the ineffective reactionary strategies employed by the parents (i.e., David as punitive, Courtney as defending) to be replaced by strategies that are reflective, and proactive for future situations.

A cognitive therapist also may choose to take a more didactic approach. Although probing questions may elicit alternative attributions from some clients, other clients may rely on the therapist's "expertise." In these situations, a psychoeducational approach may be most beneficial (Epstein & Baucom, 2002; Stoddart, 1999). In our case example, the therapist could take such an approach by sharing information about normative adolescent development (e.g., hormonal changes, identity formation, autonomy seeking) that would be applicable for both their sons. In a related way, the therapist could discuss specific characteristics associated with Asperger's syndrome such as deficits in the ability to take the perspective of others and to recognize nonverbal social cues and common figures of speech and to behave accordingly. If David in particular is able to understand these challenges and decrease his perception of Jake as "self-centered," he may be able to alter his own interactional style with Jake by increasing the concreteness of his language (i.e., avoid sarcasm, which may be misunderstood) and by incorporating "teachable moments" about the connection between feelings and behaviors.

In sum, interventions that focus on changing the meanings that families assign to stressors offer avenues for therapeutic change by (a) opening the opportunity for effective and productive behavioral and affective responses that were not possible within the prior perceptual frame and (b) empowering families by helping them gain a more hopeful and optimistic outlook. To maximize the effectiveness of such interventions, however, practitioners need to combine them with therapeutic strategies and approaches that concentrate on improving the structural and interactional attributes of families that function as resources or protective factors.

Enhancing Family Resources

Family-level resources are the attributes of the family system that facilitate adaptation when the family is faced with stressor events. Such resources boost the family's ability to make the systemic adjustments required by changing circumstances. In particular, scholars have identified boundary clarity, flexibility, and cohesion as organizational features of high-functioning family systems. Structural approaches to family intervention, with their emphasis on the linkages among stressors, family organization, and family functioning (Haley, 1987; Minuchin, 1974), offer useful theoretical and applied guidance for clinicians working with families experiencing stress or crisis.

Consistent with the tenets of family stress theory, structural family therapy asserts that family dysfunction (e.g., dissatisfaction or symptomatology) is the result of a family system's failure to modify its organizational patterns when faced with maturational or situational challenges. The approach's attention to identifying the underlying organization of families in terms that provide clear guidelines for diagnosis and treatment is particularly useful for clinicians. Specifically, based on the systemic principles of organization outlined at the beginning of this chapter, structural models focus on establishing an appropriate hierarchical structure with properly functioning subsystems (e.g., parental, marital, sibling) and clear relational boundaries that allow for a balance of individuality and connectedness among family members. Hence structural theory recognizes the dynamic nature of family systems, focusing on the importance of a system having the flexibility to modify its structural features to accommodate changing circumstances when necessary. In the case example, very early in Jake's development, neither of his parents did a particularly good job of modifying their parenting styles to accommodate the social and communicative differences they noticed between Jake and his older brother (e.g., using more concrete language, more specific instructions, etc.). By not making this adjustment early, the trajectory of parent–child interactions became increasingly more coercive and the stress level within the family rose dramatically. Moreover, once the diagnosis was obtained, Courtney and David still did not modify their own behaviors in an effort to decrease the difficult behaviors Jake was exhibiting. In fact, their approaches to parenting became even more divergent and rigid, leading to a breakdown in the parental hierarchy.

Consistent with the family stress literature, the goal of therapy is to increase flexibility, cohesion, and boundary clarity in an effort to enhance the family's ability to manage and cope with stressful events. Within a structural therapy framework, achieving this goal will involve reorganizing the family structure in a manner that incorporates a properly aligned hierarchy, clear boundaries, and well-defined roles. This process will require short-term symptom resolution along the way. It is important to note that a multitude of intervention strategies are possible for accomplishing these changes; we offer here only a sampling of the possibilities.

Theorists and clinicians have frequently asserted that children's problems in a family are often closely interrelated with problems in the marital and/or parental subsystem (Haley, 1987; Minuchin, 1974). Thus, it is critical to consider Jake's behavioral problems within the context of the broader family system. In particular, a systemically trained therapist will be interested in assessing the functionality of the parental subsystem. In other words, are the parents working cooperatively together? Are they parenting consistently? Are they using developmentally appropriate parenting strategies? As has been detailed throughout this chapter, Courtney and David take vastly different approaches to handling Jake's behavior, and this divergence is often expressed in open conflict between the couple. Moreover, neither of their approaches are particularly appropriate for Jake's age nor are they well-suited to some of the challenges associated with AS (i.e., punitive approaches tend to exacerbate undesirable behavior, overly involved approaches tend to decrease the child's motivation to change the behavior).

Parent behavioral training (PBT) is one treatment modality that might assist Courtney and David in managing the stress they are experiencing in parenting. PBT is based on social learning principles and focuses on reducing non-compliant behavior by altering reinforcement processes and modeling appropriate adult behavior in the children's environment (Wierson & Forehand, 1994). This intervention approach assumes that children's problems are the result of inconsistent or inappropriate discipline—in the current case, these issues certainly exacerbate Jake's problematic behavior (Forgatch & Patterson, 1998). PBT, which can be used either proactively or in response to problematic behavior, focuses on teaching parents new parenting skills based on operant techniques.[2] In particular, parents are taught to use contingency management strategies, including consistent rule enforcement, the use of developmentally appropriate expectations and responses, and positive reinforcement (Graziano & Diament, 1992; Wierson & Forehand, 1994).

Two specific examples of such strategies that David and Courtney may be able to implement with Jake are contingency contracting and a token economy. Contingency contracting involves the negotiation of desirable behavior change and is a developmentally appropriate choice for adolescents because they are cognitively able to participate actively in the negotiation process. In establishing a contract, parents agree to make certain changes or allowances contingent upon changes made by the child.

A token economy, in which a child earns points for appropriate behavior (e.g., completing homework on time, a day of good behavior at school, or a day of respectful behavior at home), is also appropriate for adolescents. When the child has accumulated enough points, he or she is allowed to purchase a larger reward on which the parents and child have agreed. Each of these strategies involves a positive or desired reinforcer from the parent in response to socially appropriate behavior and communication by the adolescent. If, for example, Jake especially enjoys playing video games, he may be granted access to extra playing time if he demonstrates an ability to work cooperatively (youth with AS often struggle with taking turns or utilizing the input of others) with his brother during some joint chore assigned by their parents. These types of social negotiation also provide clear models and opportunities for Jake to practice perspective-taking (an area in which youth with AS often experience deficits) as adequate negotiation requires some acknowledgement of the other person's feelings and position about a given situation.

In addition to assessing the parental subsystem, the systemic therapist will be interested in assessing the quality of the marital or spousal subsystem. The marital and parental subsystems are interrelated, with the degree of negative affect and conflict present in marital interactions affecting parent–child interactions in notable ways. In particular, a high level of negative affect and conflict in the marital subsystem is hypothesized to increase the likelihood of parent–child coalitions (i.e., the child is asked to align with one parent in opposition to the other parent) (Minuchin, 1974; Minuchin & Fishman, 1981), reduce the consistency and effectiveness of discipline practices (Fauber, Forehand, Thomas, & Wierson, 1990), and diminish the amount of warmth displayed in parent–child interactions (Engfer, 1988; Fauber et al., 1990). Consequently, a priority in our case example is the improved functioning of the marital and parental subsystems and the reestablishment of parental authoritative positions in the hierarchy of the family. In addition to the cognitive techniques outlined earlier, therapy needs to focus on increasing the level of coherence in the family and improving David's and Courtney's functional capabilities in their marital and parental roles.

Conclusion

In sum, because family systems are dynamic and continually confronted with change, stress is inevitable. Our purpose in this chapter has been to offer a general framework for clinicians and related practitioners who work with families experiencing stress or crisis. In particular, drawing on the available theoretical literature on family stress, we have outlined key areas of clinical assessment and intervention, including the classification of stressor type and the identification of family meanings and resources. Finally, we have offered examples of clinical strategies and approaches that professionals can use to help families change the meanings they attribute to stressors and increase family-level resources.

Notes

1. Asperger's syndrome (AS) is a developmental disorder first described in 1944. It is characterized by deficits in communication and reciprocal social interaction, and by the presence of repetitive or restrictive patterns of thought and behavior. Typically, children with AS are of average or above-average intelligence, do not show delays in language acquisition, and are regarded as "socially awkward" throughout childhood and adolescence. There is no single diagnostic screening for AS, and it may be misdiagnosed as another condition such as ADHD or OCD due to difficulties with attention or the need for routinization. Although classified as an autism spectrum disorder, there is controversy as to whether AS is a distinct syndrome or a milder version of classic autism; often the labels of AS and high-functioning autism (HFA) are used interchangeably.

2. Operant techniques are based on the belief that behavior is determined more by its consequences than by its antecedents. Consequences may be reinforcers that increase the preceding behaviors or may be punishers that decrease the preceding behaviors.

Suggested Internet Resources _____

The American Association of Marriage and Family Therapy provides information on locating a therapist as well as educational materials on family problems: http://www.aamft.org

The Michigan State University Extension program, Furthering Families, offers generalized family stress information including dealing with change, communication and coping: http://www.fcs.msue.msu.edu/ff/familystress.html

The autism-help.org Web site provides information on autism spectrum disorders, including Asperger's, as well as suggestions for social, communication, and behavioral intervention: http://www.autism-help.org

The Yale Child Study Center Developmental Disabilities Clinic provides information from leading researchers in the field on characteristics, diagnosis, and treatment of AS (and other developmental disorders): http://childstudycenter.yale.edu/autism/aspergers.html

References _____

Bauminger, N. (2002). The facilitation of social-emotional understanding and social interaction in high-functioning children with autism: Intervention outcomes. *Journal of Autism and Developmental Disorders, 32,* 283–298.

Beck, J. S. (1995). *Cognitive therapy: Basics and beyond.* New York: Guilford.

Berg-Cross, L. (2000). Attribution. In L. Berg-Cross (Ed.), *Basic concepts in family therapy: An introductory text* (2nd ed., pp. 427–449). New York: Haworth.

Boss, P. G. (1980). Normative family stress: Family boundary changes across the life-span. *Family Relations, 29,* 445–450.

Boss, P. G. (1987). Family stress: Perception and context. In M. B. Sussman & S. K. Steinmetz (Eds.), *Handbook of marriage and the family* (pp. 695–723). New York: Plenum.

Boss, P. G. (1999). *Ambiguous loss: Learning to live with unresolved grief.* Cambridge, MA: Harvard University Press.

Boss, P. G. (2002). *Family stress management: A contextual approach* (2nd ed.). Thousand Oaks, CA: Sage.

Burr, W. R., Klein, S. R., & Associates. (1994). *Reexamining family stress: New theory and research.* Thousand Oaks, CA: Sage.

Carter, E., & McGoldrick, M. (Eds.). (1988). *The changing family life cycle: A framework for family therapy* (2nd ed.). New York: Gardner.

Cowan, P. A., Cowan, C. P., & Schulz, M. S. (1996). Thinking about risk and resilience in families. In E. M. Hetherington & E. A. Blechman (Eds.), *Stress, coping, and resiliency in children and families* (pp. 1–38). Mahwah, NJ: Lawrence Erlbaum.

Engfer, A. (1988). The interrelatedness of marriage and the mother-child relationship. In R. A. Hinde & J. Stevenson-Hinde (Eds.), *Relationships within families: Mutual influences* (pp. 104–118). Oxford, England: Clarendon.

Epstein, N. B., & Baucom, D. H. (2002). *Enhanced cognitive-behavioral therapy for couples: A contextual approach* (pp. 333–373). Washington, DC: American Psychological Association.

Fauber, R., Forehand, R., Thomas, A. M., & Wierson, M. (1990). A mediational model of the impact of marital conflict on adolescent adjustment in intact and divorced families: The role of disrupted parenting. *Child Development, 61,* 1112–1123.

Forgatch, M. S., & Patterson, G. R. (1998). Behavioral family therapy. In F. M. Dattilio (Ed.), *Case studies in couple and family therapy: Systemic and cognitive perspectives* (pp. 85–107). New York: Guilford.

Graziano, A. M., & Diament, D. M. (1992). Parent behavioral training: An examination of the paradigm. *Behavior Modification, 16,* 3–38.

Haley, J. (1987). *Problem-solving therapy* (2nd ed.). San Francisco: Jossey-Bass.

Hill, R. (1958). Social stresses on the family: Generic features of families under stress. *Social Casework, 39,* 139–150.

Hobfoll, S. E., & Spielberger, C. D. (1992). Family stress: Integrating theory and measurement. *Journal of Family Psychology, 6,* 99–112.

Kelley, H. H. (1967). Attribution theory in social psychology. In D. Levine (Ed.), *Nebraska symposium on motivation: Vol. 15* (pp. 192–238). Lincoln: University of Nebraska Press.

Madden-Derdich, D. A. (2002). The role of emotion in marriage and family therapy: Past, present, and future. *Marriage and Family Review, 34,* 165–179.

Madsen, W. C. (1999). *Collaborative therapy with multi-stressed families.* New York: Guilford.

Marcus, L. M., Kunce, L. J., & Schopler, E. (2005). Working with families. In F. R. Volkmar, R. Paul, A. Klin, & D. Cohen (Eds.), *Handbook of autism and pervasive developmental disorders: Vol. 2* (3rd ed., pp. 1055–1086). Hoboken, NJ: John Wiley & Sons, Inc.

McCubbin, H. I., & McCubbin, M. A. (1988). Typology of resilient families: Emerging roles of social class and ethnicity. *Family Relations, 37,* 247–254.

McCubbin, H. I., & Patterson, J. M. (1982). Family adaptation to crisis. In H. I. McCubbin, A. E. Cauble, & J. M. Patterson (Eds.), *Family stress, coping, and social support* (pp. 26–47). Springfield, IL: Charles C Thomas.

McCubbin, H. I., & Patterson, J. M. (1983a). The family stress process: The double ABCX model of adjustment and adaptation. In H. I. McCubbin, M. B. Sussman, & J. M. Patterson (Eds.), *Social stress and the family: Advances and developments in family stress theory and research* (pp. 7–37). New York: Haworth.

McCubbin, H. I., & Patterson, J. M. (1983b). The family stress process: The double ABCX model of family adjustment and adaptation. *Marriage and Family Review, 6,* 7–37.

McCubbin, M. A., & McCubbin, H. I. (1989). Theoretical orientations to family stress and coping. In C. R. Figley (Ed.), *Treating stress in families* (pp. 3–43). New York: Brunner/Mazel.

Minuchin, S. (1974). *Families and family therapy.* Cambridge, MA: Harvard University Press.

Minuchin, S., & Fishman, H. C. (1981). *Family therapy techniques.* Cambridge, MA: Harvard University Press.

Nichols, M. P. (1987). *The self in the system: Expanding the limits of family therapy.* New York: Brunner/Mazel.

Olson, D. H. (1997). Family stress and coping: A multisystem perspective. In S. Dreman (Ed.), *The family on the threshold of the 21st century: Trends and implications* (pp. 259–280). Mahwah, NJ: Lawrence Erlbaum.

Olson, D. H., Russell, C. S., & Sprenkle, D. H. (1979). Circumplex model of marital and family systems: Cohesion and adaptability dimensions, family types, and clinical applications. *Family Process, 18,* 3–28.

Olson, D. H., Russell, C. S., & Sprenkle, D. H. (1983). Circumplex model of marital and family systems: VI. Theoretical update. *Family Process, 22,* 69–81.

Patterson, J. M. (1988). Families experiencing stress: The family adjustment and adaptation response model. *Family Systems Medicine, 6,* 202–237.

Patterson, J. M. (2002). Integrating family resilience and family stress theory. *Journal of Marriage and Family, 64,* 349–360.

Patterson, J. M., & Garwick, A. W. (1994). Levels of meaning in family stress theory. *Family Process, 33,* 287–304.

Selvini Palazzoli, M., Boscolo, L., Cecchin, G., & Prata, G. (1978). *Paradox and counterparadox.* New York: Jason Aronson.

Steinglass, P. (1987). A systems view of family interaction and psychopathology. In T. Jacob (Ed.), *Family interaction and psychopathology* (pp. 25–65). New York: Plenum.

Stoddart, K. P. (1999). Adolescents with Asperger syndrome: Three case studies of individual and family therapy. *Autism, 3,* 255–271.

Walsh, F. (1998). *Strengthening family resilience.* New York: Guilford.

Watzlawick, P., Weakland, J. H., & Fisch, R. (1974). *Change: Principles of problem formation and problem resolution.* New York: W. W. Norton.

White, M., & Epston, D. (1990). *Narrative means to therapeutic ends.* New York: W. W. Norton.

Wierson, M., & Forehand, R. (1994). Parent behavioral training for child noncompliance: Rationale, concepts, and effectiveness. *Current Directions in Psychological Science, 3,* 146–150.

Author Index _____

Abbott, R. D., 143, 144, 154
Abel, E. K., 360
Aber, J. L., 123
Abidin, R. R., 26
Abraham, W. T., 196
Achterlonie, J. L., 387
Acierno, R., 151
Acitelli, L. K., 104, 107
Acock, A. C., 370
Acott, J. P., 142
Adalbjarnardottir, S., 151
Adams, J., 81
Adamsons, K., 237, 239, 240, 245, 250
Adler-Baeder, F., 245, 246, 253, 254
Afifi, T., 243
Agarwal, S., 190
Agigian, A., 270
Agnew, R., 129
Aguiar, L. J., 152
Aguilar-Gaxiola, S., 169
Ahrons, C. R., 213, 245, 248
Akutsu, P. D., 292, 303
Alati, R., 150
Aldana, S. I., 35, 200, 202
Aldaronodo, E., 125
Aldous, J. C., 10
Aldwin, C. M., 54, 55, 56, 57, 58, 59, 146, 153, 154
Alegria, M., 168, 169
Alfaro, E. C., 211
Alford, G. S., 153
Allegretto, S., 188, 190, 192
Allen, C. F., 269, 270, 276
Allen, J. P., 123
Allen, K. R., 369
Allen-Byrd, L., 148, 153
Allison, P., 75

Almeida, D. M., 55, 56, 358, 360, 361, 362, 363, 365, 366, 369, 372, 373
Almeida, R., 86
Alpert, A., 171
Alvarez, A. N., 304
Amato, P. R., 199, 213, 214, 215, 216, 219, 220, 221, 222, 239, 242, 251, 370
Ambert, A., 33, 34, 35
Amoroso, P. J., 387
Anderson, E. A., 333, 345
Anderson, K. G., 242
Anderson, L., 149
Anderson, R. N., 167
Anderson, S. A., 11
Anderson, S. C., 265
Anderson, W. G., 81
Ando, A., 199
Andrews, J., 171
Andrews, J. A., 149
Aneshensel, C. S., 60
Angell, R. C., vii
Angold, A., 173
Angus, D. C., 81
Anooshian, L. J., 341
Ansell, V. I., 175
Anthes, F., 350
Antoni, M., 75
Antonucci, T. C., 65
Appel, A. E., 133
Appleby, G., 274
Aquilino, W. S., 213
Arbunthnot, J., 224
Archer, J., 77, 78
Ardelt, M., 29, 197
Arendt, R. E., 142
Arias, E., 168
Aries, P., 74

Arnette, J. K., 66
Arnold, E., 294, 295
Arnold, J., 87
Arnold, R. M., 81
Aron, L. Y., 337, 339, 340
Arora, A. K., 304, 305
Assmann, S. F., 110
Astin, M. C., 126
Atiles, J. H., 289, 293, 294, 302
Attewell, P., 314
Attkisson, C. C., 168
Aubry, J., 58
Auchterlonie, J. L., 388
Austin, J. B., 132
Austria, A. M., 297, 303, 304
Avery, R. B., 193
Avitzuer, E., 387
Ayers, T. S., 88

Babcock, J. C., 133
Bachman, J. G., 142, 144, 154
Bacon, B. L., 224
Bacon, E. S., 177
Badgett, M. V. L., 273
Badr, H., 104, 107
Bailey, J. M., 274
Bailey, S. J., 26
Bakalian, A., 296
Baker, B. L., 27, 29, 33, 35
Baker, D. B., 35
Baker, J., 87, 88
Baker, J. R., 145
Baker, P., 266
Ballantyne, P., 59
Balling, K., 102, 103
Balsam, K. F., 266, 267, 269
Baltes, M. M., 64, 65
Baltes, P. B., 64, 65
Bandura, A., 127
Bandwater, E. A., 197
Banks, A., 266, 275, 276
Banyard, V. L., 340, 347
Barber, B. K., 30, 34, 37
Barber, B. L., 217, 220, 224
Barkley, R. A., 168
Barling, J., 126
Barnes, C. L., 109, 110
Barnes, G. M., 148
Barnes, V. A., 388
Barnett, O. W., 126
Barnett, R. C., 12
Barnow, S., 146
Barreira, P. J., 89

Barrowclough, C., 172
Bartle-Haring, S., 32
Bass, D., 110
Bassuk, E. L., 339, 341, 343, 345
Bates, J. E., 123
Bathurst, K., 34
Batt, R., 373, 374, 375
Baucom, D. H., 172, 410, 411, 412
Bauer, D., 147
Baum, A., 75
Baum, K., 120
Bauman, K. E., 148
Bauminger, N., 411
Baxter, L. A., 247
Beach, S. R. H., 104, 107, 214, 220
Beals, K. P., 265
Bean, F. D., 287
Beatty, A. L., 346, 347
Beauchaine, T. P., 266, 267
Beaudry, M., 254
Beaujot, R., 244
Beck, A., 240
Beck, C. J. A., 225
Beck, U., 25
Beck-Gernsheim, E., 25
Beckham, J. C., 387
Bédard, M., 109
Bedford, V. H., 51
Beldavs, Z. G., 254
Bell, N. S., 387
Belsky, J., 38, 128
Benda, B. B., 150
Bengtson, V. L., 61
Benight, C., 75
Bennett, D. A., 108
Berberich, D., 351
Berg, C. A., 104, 105
Berg-Cross, L., 410
Berge, J. M., 100, 102
Berger, R., 253
Berk, R. A., 132
Berk, S. F., 132
Bermas, B. L., 107
Bernstein, D. P., 149, 192
Bernstein, J., 188, 190
Berry, J. W., 32, 34, 287, 288
Bersani, B., 146, 148
Best, C. L., 151
Beutler, I. F., 196
Bhadha, B. R., 304
Bhattacharya, G., 289, 290, 293,
    294, 297
Bianchi, S. M., 214, 367

Foa, E. B., 392
Foley, D. L., 173
Folkman, S., 3, 4, 13, 63, 64, 110, 358, 359
Fong, R., 304
Fong, T. P., 41
Forehand, R., 171, 414, 415
Forgatch, M. S., 254, 414
Forgue, R. E., 200, 201
Forthum, L. F., 147
Foshee, V. A., 148
Foster, E. M., 197
Fox, G. L., 25, 186
Fox, J. J., 199
Fox, K., 107
Foy, D. W., 126
Foy, J. M., 269, 270, 276
Frampe, E., 320
Frankenhaeuser, M., 3
Franks, M. M., 110
Frauenglass, S., 150
Frazier, P. A., 9
Fredman, S. J., 172
Freud, S., 76
Friedman, R. M., 168
Friend, R., 107
Frierdich, S., 102, 103
Friesther, B., 235
Fristad, M. A., 173, 176
Frodi, A., 31
Fromer, J. E., 287, 288, 298, 299
Furstenberg, F. F., Jr., 237, 241, 243, 250
Futrell, J. A., 11, 17

Gable, S., 223
Gackstetter, G. D., 387
Galaif, E. R., 149
Gallelli, K., 101
Gammon, E. A., 325
Ganong, L. H., 99, 214, 217, 223, 235, 236, 241, 243, 245, 246, 247, 248, 250, 251, 252
Gans, D., 61, 65
Gao, Z., 152
Garbarino, J., 128, 129
Garber, T., 247
Garcia-Presto, N., 86
Gardner, K. A., 196
Garey, A. I., 218
Garman, E. T., 193, 200, 201
Garmezy, N., 17
Garner, S., 247

Garnets, L., 265
Garrett, J., 152, 153
Gartrell, N., 266, 275, 276
Gartstein, M. A., 100
Garwick, A. W., 102, 407
Gates, G., 269, 270, 273
Gavazzi, S. M., 11, 126, 173, 176, 178
Gaze, C., 27, 28, 29, 31, 36, 37, 38, 41
Ge, X., 236
Geasler, M. J., 223
Gelles, R. J., 122, 123, 124, 125, 126, 128, 130, 131, 133
Gemma, P. B., 87
Genalo, T., 223, 224
George, R. A., 30
Gerson, K., 374, 375
Gerstel, N., 218, 339, 349
Gewritz, A., 349
Gibbs, D. A., 388
Gibbs, R., 319
Gibofsky, A., 108
Gibson, D. M., 84
Gierveld, J. D. J., 55
Gilbert, K. R., 74, 78, 82, 85, 86
Gilbreth, J. G., 221
Gilcrist, K., 247
Gillman, S., 360, 363, 371
Given, B. A., 109, 110
Given, C. W., 109, 110
Giza, D., 89
Glynn, S., 387
Godsall, R. E., 149
Godwin, D. D., 199
Goetz, D., 104
Gold, D., 104
Goldberg, A. E., 268, 270, 271, 272, 274, 277, 278
Golden, J. C., 144
Golding, A. C., 277
Golding, J., 273
Goldman, M. S., 143
Golish, T., 243, 248, 254
Golombok, S., 273
Gomel, J. N., 190, 193
Gondolf, E. W., 133
Goodman, L., 339, 340, 345
Goodman, M. R., 217
Goodnow, J. J., 39, 40
Gordon, D. A., 224
Gore, S., 10, 12
Gotay, C. C., 107

Raj, A., 120
Raley, R. K., 237
Raley, S. B., 367
Ranck, K. H., vii
Rand, M., 120
Rando, T. A., 74, 76, 77, 81, 87
Rantala, R. R., 122, 125
Rapp, R., 315
Rasbash, J., 249
Rath, W. R., 341, 345
Ray, V., 276
Rayens, M. K., 102
Ready, R., 104, 107
Redd, W. H., 101
Reed, N., 266, 275
Rees, H., 7
Refior, S., 143, 144, 153
Regier, D. A., 166, 167
Reid, C., 177
Reidman, A., 311, 314, 315, 319
Reier, D. A., 165
Reifman, A., 148, 150
Reinharcit Pederson, C., 198
Reiss, D., 63, 236
Reker, G. T., 65
Relf, M. V., 122
Renner, A. D., 197
Rentz, E. D., 388
Repetti, R. L., 358, 360, 361, 362,
    363, 364, 370, 372
Resick, P. A., 392
Resnick, H. S., 151
Resnick, M. D., 151
Retzlaff, R., 103
Reuter, M. A., 171, 196, 199
Revenson, T. A., 108
Rhoden, L., 252, 253
Rice, C., 168
Richards, J. A., 277
Richards, L. N., 61
Richards, M. H., 368, 369
Rigg, A., 236
Riggs, D. S., 387, 388
Rime, B., 83
Rimmerman, A., 33
Roberto, K., 104
Roberts, R. E., 61, 168
Robie, C., 133
Robinson, J. P., 214, 367
Rodas, C., 266, 275.276
Rodger, M. L., 81
Rodgers, R. H., 10
Rodican, C., 89

Rodrigues, A. E., 215, 216
Rodriguez, J., 323, 324
Rodriguez, M., 75
Rodriquez, E., 126
Rofey, D., 351
Rog, D. J., 349
Rogan, D. P., 132
Rogers, S. J., 188, 199, 214, 215,
    216, 370
Rohrbaugh, M. J., 104, 106
Rohrbeck, C. A., 102
Rolland, J. S., 79, 97
Rollins, B. C., 38
Rollison, P. A., 337
Ron, P., 110
Rones, P. L., 57
Roper, S. O., 102
Rosaldo, R., 82
Rose, J. S., 148
Rose, K., 120
Rosen, E., 86
Rosen, K., 32, 40
Rosen, K. H., 104
Rosenberg, L., 339
Rosenberg, M., 122
Rosenblatt, A., 168
Rosenblatt, P. C., 75, 76, 77, 80,
    84, 87
Rosenthal, C. J., 60
Roskies, E., 14
Ross, G. J., 172
Ross, J. L., 316
Rossi, P. H., 344
Rossiter, L., 100
Rossman, R., 122
Rothbaum, B. O., 392
Rothblum, E. D., 266, 267, 269
Rothrauff, T. C., 251
Rounds-Bryant, J. L., 153
Routh, D. K., 150
Routhier, L., 100, 103
Rowe, C. L., 172
Roy, E., 100, 103
Roy, K., 25, 241, 320, 321
Rubin, K. H., 34, 35
Rubin, L., 339, 345
Rubin, S. S., 76
Rudy, T. E., 104, 107
Ruffin, V. M., 271
Ruggiero, K. J., 151
Rumbaut, R. G., 286
Russell, C. S., 10, 409
Russell, D. W., 196

Subject Index _____

ABC-X model, vii, 4, 6, 6 (figure)
  adaptation/family adaptability and,
      14–16
  coping mechanisms/processes and,
      13–14
  developmental perspective and,
      401–402
  double ABC-X configuration and,
      15–16, 15 (figure)
  events/perceptions, stress response
      and, 11–12
  family resiliency and, 17
  family systems perspective and,
      12, 14, 402–405
  resource availability and, 10–11
  stressor events and, 7–10, 8 (table)
  stress pileup and, 15–16
  See also Family stress intervention;
      Family stress theory; Parental
      stress; Social systems
      perspective
Abuse, 83, 119
  attachment theory and, 130
  child maltreatment, 120, 123, 128
  child protective interventions and,
      130–131
  childhood sexual abuse, 123, 127
  coping with, 123
  ecological theory and, 128
  elder abuse, 121
  homelessness in adulthood and,
      340–341
  homicide of children, 121, 124
  intergenerational transmission of,
      126–127
  intervention approaches, 130–133
  outcomes of, 122, 123
  partner abuse, 120–121
  psychopathological model of, 124
  social exchange theory and, 128

  social learning theory and, 127
  sociobiological theory and, 128–129
  witnessing family violence, 122, 126
  See also Family violence; Intimate
      relationships
Abusive relationships, 83
Accidents, viii, 2
Acculturative stress, 32, 34, 287–288,
      290, 292–293
Adaptation, vii
  aging family systems and, 57, 63–66
  childhood illness and, 102
  conflict/change and, 16
  coping process and, 13–14
  death/dying and, 78–79, 80–86
  divorce and, 213
  family adaptability, 14–16, 57, 409
  family system resources and, 10–11
  lesbian/gay closeted lives and, 265
  parental stress and, 41–42
  postcrisis/poststress factors and,
      15–16, 15 (figure)
  reciprocal relationships and, 14–15
  resiliency and, 17
  selective optimization with
      compensation principle and,
      64–65
  stress adaptations, 3
  See also Acculturative stress;
      Immigrant families;
      Vulnerability-stress-adaptation
      (VSA) model
Adjustment, vii, 15
Adoption process, 1, 129, 170
  closed adoptions, 271
  lesbian/gay couples and, 264, 269,
      270–272, 276
  open adoptions, 271
  transracial/transcultural adoptions,
      273, 274–275

443

About the Editors _____

Sharon J. Price is Professor Emerita and former Head of the Department of Child and Family Development at The University of Georgia. She has published extensively in professional journals and coauthored or coedited several books. She won several teaching awards including the Osborne Award, presented by the National Council on Family Relations, and the highest honor for teaching at The University of Georgia, the Josiah Meigs Award. She was active in several professional organizations, serving in many capacities, including President of the National Council on Family Relations, and is a Fellow in NCFR. She received her PhD from Iowa State University.

Christine A. Price is Associate Professor, Department of Family and Child Studies, at Montclair State University. She teaches family gerontology, and her scholarly interests emphasize the transitional adjustment and psychosocial experiences of retired women. Her work has been published in several scholarly journals including the *International Journal of Aging and Human Development, Journal of Women and Aging, Family Relations,* and *Journal of Ethnographic and Qualitative Research.* She is a Certified Family Life Educator in the National Council on Family Relations. She earned her PhD and a Graduate Certificate in Gerontology at The University of Georgia.

Patrick C. McKenry and Sharon J. Price worked together for almost three decades. He was Professor of Human Development and Family Science and African-American and African Studies at The Ohio State University. His work focused on family stress and coping with particular interest in gender, cultural, and lifestyle variations. In addition to books, he published numerous articles in professional journals. He received his PhD from the University of Tennessee in Child and Family Studies and was a postdoctoral Fellow at The University of Georgia in Child and Family Development. He died in 2004.

About the Contributors _

Suzanne Bartholomae teaches in the Department of Human Development and Family Science at The Ohio State University. Her research interests include financial stress and coping, the financial socialization process, and the efficacy of financial education programs. Her work has been published in several scholarly journals including *Family Relations*, the *Journal of Family Issues*, *Journal of Family and Economics Issues*, *Journal of Adolescent Health*, and *Journal of Consumer Affairs*. She earned her PhD from The Ohio State University.

Stephanie Bohon is Director of the Center for Social Justice and Associate Professor of Sociology at the University of Tennessee at Knoxville. Her research focuses on the growth and needs of Latino migrants in the South, Latino immigration policy, and the difference between Latino migrant adjustment in traditional and emerging gateways. Her work has been published in several scholarly journals including *Social Problems*, *Social Science Quarterly*, *Rural Sociology*, *Population Research and Policy Review*, and the *Journal of Latinos and Education*. She is the author of *Latinos in Ethnic Enclaves: Immigrant Workers and the Competition for Jobs*. She earned her PhD from Pennsylvania State University.

Kevin Ray Bush is Associate Professor in the Department of Family Studies and Social Work at Miami University in Oxford, Ohio. His research and scholarly interests focus on the role of culture in parent–child/adolescent relationships and child and adolescent development. He has conducted studies with U.S. and international samples of children, adolescents, and parents. His work has been published in several scholarly journals, including *Child Development*, the *Journal of Adolescent Research*, *Family Psychology*, *Journal of Marriage and Family*, and *Marriage and Family Review*. He earned his PhD from The Ohio State University.

David H. Demo is Professor and Director of Graduate Studies in the Department of Human Development and Family Studies at the University of North Carolina at Greensboro. His research focuses on divorce and family transitions, changes in family relationships accompanying divorce, and the consequences of family transitions. He has published in professional journals and has coauthored and coedited several books, including *Handbook of Family Diversity, Parents and Adolescents in Changing Families, Family Diversity and Well-Being*, and *Marriage and Family in Transition*. He currently serves as editor of the *Journal of Marriage and Family*. He earned his PhD from Cornell University.

Rachel Engler is a Doctoral Graduate Research Assistant in Human Development and Family Studies at Texas Tech University. She is interested in the impact that addiction has on families. She earned an MA from West Texas A&M University.

Mark Fine is Professor, Department of Human Development and Family Studies, at the University of Missouri, Columbia. His research interests include family transitions, early-intervention program evaluation, social cognition, and relationship stability. He has published numerous peer-reviewed journal articles and book chapters. He coauthored *Beyond the Average Divorce* and *Children of Divorce: Stories of Hope and Loss* and is coeditor of *Keepin' On: The Everyday Struggles of Young Families in Poverty* and the *Handbook of Divorce and Relationship Dissolution*. He served as editor of *Family Relations* and the *Journal of Social and Personal Relationships*. He is a Fellow in the National Council on Family Relations. He earned his PhD from The Ohio State University.

Judith Fischer is Professor of Human Development and Family Studies at Texas Tech University. Her research focuses on family problems, addictions, and adolescent problems. Her work has been published in *Alcoholism Treatment Quarterly*, the *Journal of Youth and Adolescence, Addictive Behaviors*, and *Journal of Personal and Social Relationships*. She is coeditor of *Familial Responses to Alcohol Problems* and serves on the editorial board of the *Journal of Marriage and Family*. She is past president of the Groves Conference on Marriage and Family and was the first holder of the C. R. & Virginia Hutcheson Professorship in Human Development and Family Studies at Texas Tech University. She earned her PhD from the University of Colorado.

Jonathan Fox is Associate Professor in the Department of Consumer Science at The Ohio State University. His research focuses on financial education and financial socialization. He has served as PI for several financial education evaluations, and his publications appear in journals such as *Financial Services Review, Financial Counseling and Planning*, the *Journal of Family Issues*, and *Journal of Consumer Affairs*. He teaches family financial management and methodology in family resources management. He received his PhD from the University of Maryland and won the Mid-Career Award from the American Council on Consumer Interests.

Lawrence H. Ganong, Professor of Nursing and Human Development and Family Studies at the University of Missouri, Columbia, has coauthored more than 175 articles and book chapters as well as several books, including *Stepfamily Relationships*, the *Handbook of Contemporary Families*, and *Family Life in 20th-Century America*. His primary research program has focused on stepfamilies, particularly addressing what stepfamily members do to develop satisfying, effective relationships. He serves on the boards of several journals and has served as associate editor of the *Journal of Social and Personal Relationships*. He earned his PhD from the University of Missouri.

Stephen M. Gavazzi is Professor of Human Development and Family Science at The Ohio State University and is Co-Director of the OSU Center for Family Research. His research identifies the impact of family dynamics on adolescent development, psychopathology, and problem behavior. He has been involved in the development and evaluation of a number of family-based programming efforts, including a family-based diversion initiative for use with juvenile offenders and their families. Currently, his efforts are directed toward the development of a Web-based instrument known as the Global Risk Assessment Device (GRAD), designed to measure potential threats to the developmental needs of adolescents. He earned his PhD at the University of Connecticut.

Richard J. Gelles holds The Joanne and Raymond Welsh Chair of Child Welfare and Family Violence and is Dean of the School of Social Policy and Practice at the University of Pennsylvania. He is the author or coauthor of 25 books and numerous articles and chapters on family violence. These include *The Violent Home, The Book of David: How Preserving Families Can Cost Children's Lives, Intimate Violence in Families*, and, most recently, *Current Controversies on Family Violence*. Former U.S. secretary of Health and Human Services Donna Shalala appointed him to the Kinship Care Advisory Panel of the Administration for Children, Youth, and Families. He is also a member of the National Academy of Science's Panel on "Assessing Family Violence Interventions." He received the Outstanding Contributions to Teaching Award from the American Sociological Association and has presented many lectures to policy-making and media groups. He earned his PhD from the University of New Hampshire.

Abbie E. Goldberg is Assistant Professor of Psychology at Clark University. Her research interests include family diversity, work–family issues, lesbian/gay parenthood, adoption, and gender. Her work has appeared in several scholarly journals including the *Journal of Marriage and Family, Family Relations, Journal of Social and Personal Relationships, Journal of Family Psychology, American Journal of Orthopsychiatry*, and *Adoption Quarterly*. She is the author of *Lesbian and Gay Parents and Their Children: Research on the Family Life Cycle*. She earned her PhD from the University of Massachusetts Amherst.

Heather M. Helms is Associate Professor, Department of Human Development and Family Studies, at the University of North Carolina at Greensboro, where she has been recognized with both Research and Teaching Excellence

Awards. Her research focuses on marital quality, parents' work, and family relationships. Her work has been published in numerous scholarly journals including the *Journal of Marriage and the Family, Journal of Family Psychology, Journal of Family Issues,* and *Family Relations.* She currently serves as the book review editor of the *Journal of Marriage and Family.* She earned her PhD from Pennsylvania State University.

Charles B. Hennon is Professor of Family Studies and Social Work and Associate Director of the Center for Human Development, Learning, and Technology, Miami University, in Oxford, Ohio. His areas of teaching and scholarly interests include family life education, religion and families, at-home workers, stress, divorce, and families in cross-cultural perspective. He has published in numerous scholarly journals and has edited, coedited, and coauthored several books including *Families in Rural America, Gender and Home Based Employment,* and *Lifestyles of the Elderly.* He was founding editor of the *Journal of Families and Economic Issues* and has served on the editorial boards of several professional journals. He is a certified Family Life Educator with the National Council on Family Relations. He earned his PhD from Case Western Reserve University.

Melissa J. Herzog is an Assistant Research Professor in Special Education and an Adjunct Faculty member in Human Development and Family Studies at the University of Missouri, Columbia. Her research interests focus on family relationship processes, perceptions of familial and social relationships, and children's psychological and social adjustment. She is currently directing a federal research project focused on improving the social competence of adolescents with Asperger's syndrome. Her work has been published in *Family Relations,* the *Journal of Abnormal Child Psychology,* and *Journal of Divorce & Remarriage.* She earned her PhD from Arizona State University.

Áine M. Humble is an Associate Professor in the Department of Family Studies and Gerontology at Mount Saint Vincent University in Halifax, Nova Scotia, Canada. Her research interests focus on family–work issues, retirement, gender, qualitative research methods, and feminist pedagogy. Her work has been published in several scholarly journals including *Family Relations* and the *Journal of Family Issues.* She is a certified Family Life Educator in the National Council on Family Relations. She earned her PhD, with a minor in Women's Studies, at Oregon State University.

Hyoun K. Kim is a Research Scientist at the Oregon Social Learning Center in Eugene. Her research interests include adolescent and young adult development, development of intimate relationships, marital transitions and psychological well-being, and Asian American adolescent development. Her work has been published in several scholarly journals, including *Developmental Psychology, Development and Psychopathology,* the *Journal of Family Psychology, Journal of Marriage and Family,* and *Criminology.* She earned her PhD from The Ohio State University and completed a postdoctoral fellowship at the Oregon Social Learning Center.

Terence R. Knox is a graduate assistant in the Department of Family Studies and Social Work, Miami University, in Oxford, Ohio. His research and scholarly interests include parental and adolescent stress, religion and family, at-risk youth, and families in the cross-cultural perspective.

Barbara L. Larsen is a doctoral student in the Interdisciplinary PhD Program in Social Psychology at the University of Nevada, Reno. Her research interests focus on the effects of traumatic stress. She is currently examining post-traumatic growth, PTSD and traumatic stress among veterans, and social influences on attitudes toward physician-assisted suicide. She earned an MA in social psychology from the University of Nevada, Reno.

Michelle Lee is Visiting Assistant Professor in the Department of Family and Child Sciences at Florida State University. Her academic training is in marriage and family therapy with a specialization in working with complicated families such as stepfamilies. Her focus has been on translating research-based information into effective practice. She earned her PhD from Michigan State University.

Elizabeth Lindsey, Professor and Chair, Department of Social Work at the University of North Carolina at Greensboro, studies homeless families and runaway youth. She has published in several journals including the *Journal of Social Work Education, School Social Work Journal, Journal of Youth Studies,* and *Child & Adolescent Social Work Journal.* She was funded to evaluate North Carolina's child welfare staff development program and served as Coordinator of the UNGC International Educational Exchange Program with the University of Strathclyde Department of Social Work and the Glasgow (Scotland) School of Social Work, and has received the UNCG School of Human Environmental Sciences Outstanding Teacher Award. She earned her PhD from The University of Georgia.

Kevin P. Lyness is Associate Professor, Associate Chair, and Director of the Marriage and Family Therapy Programs in the Department of Applied Psychology at Antioch University New England. His research focuses on adolescent development in the family context and clinical processes in couple and family therapy. He is a former assistant editor of the *Journal of Marital and Family Therapy* and serves on the editorial boards of the *Journal of Feminist Family Therapy* and *Journal of Couple and Relationship Therapy.* He earned his PhD from Purdue University.

James A. Martin is Professor in the Graduate School of Social Work and Social Research at Bryn Mawr College. He is a Licensed Independent Clinical Social Worker and a Board Certified Diplomate in Clinical Social Work. His focus is on behavioral health issues impacting individuals, families and communities, and military and veteran populations. He is a national leader in military family services and support and serves as a subject matter expert for the Department of Defense and other federal agencies. He is a retired Army Colonel with a 26-year career in the Army Medical Department where he served in clinical, research, and senior management and policy assignments. He earned his PhD from the University of Pittsburgh.

Shane Moulton is a doctoral student in the Interdisciplinary PhD Program in Social Psychology and a graduate research assistant with the Sanford Center for Aging at the University of Nevada, Reno. His research broadly focuses on the effects of stigma on social interaction. He is currently examining the effects of race and nonverbal reactions on perceptions of racial comedy. He earned an MA in social psychology from the University of Nevada, Reno.

Colleen I. Murray is Director of the Interdisciplinary PhD Program in Social Psychology, Professor of Sociology, and Adjunct Professor of Human Development and Family Studies and Women's Studies at the University of Nevada, Reno. Her research focuses on the social construction of meaning and culture, with particular emphasis on parent and sibling grief following sudden loss or mass tragedy, the intersection of posttraumatic growth and stress theories, and media portrayal of adolescents. She has published numerous articles and chapters on family relationships, grief, adolescents, gender, and culture. She is a Fellow in Thanatology with the Association for Death Education and Counseling. She earned her PhD from The Ohio State University.

Kay Pasley, Professor and Chair of the Department of Family and Child Sciences at Florida State University, has studied and written extensively about remarriage and stepfamilies since 1977, with an emphasis on marital quality and stability in remarriage and fathering after divorce and remarriage. She has coauthored *Remarriage* and coedited *Stepfamilies: Issues in Research, Theory, and Practice* and *Remarriage and Stepfamilies Today: Current Research and Theory*. She is a Fellow in the National Council on Family Relations, and served as Chair of the Research Committee and as a member of the Board of Directors of the Stepfamily Association of America. She is a member of the Scientific Advisory Board for the National Resource Center for Stepfamilies. She earned her EdD from Indiana University.

Gary W. Peterson is Professor and Chair of the Department of Family Studies and Social Work at Miami University in Oxford, Ohio. His areas of teaching and scholarly interest pertain to parent–child/adolescent relations, adolescent development, cross-cultural influences on adolescent development, and family theory. His research and scholarly articles have appeared in numerous academic journals and edited collections. He has edited and coedited books on fatherhood, cross-cultural parent–child relations, and family theory. He is coeditor of the *Handbook of Marriage and the Family* (2nd edition), past editor of the journal *Marriage and Family Review*, and was recently named a Fellow in the National Council on Family Relations. He earned his PhD from Brigham Young University.

Christina A. Sanchez, MSW, graduated from the Joint Master of Social Work Program, a collaboration between the University of North Carolina at Greensboro and the North Carolina A&T State University in May 2009. She has been a trainer in training with the Leadership and Empowerment Institute providing workshops on dismantling racism. She is currently working as a hospital social worker.

Angie M. Schock-Giordano is an Associate Professor in the Department of Family and Consumer Sciences at California State University, Northridge. She teaches in the areas of child/adolescent development, family theories, and family coping and resiliency. Her research interests focus on the father's role in the family and community, Latino fathers' influence on adolescents' self-esteem, the coparental relationship, and the manner in which ethnic families experience and cope with mental illness. Her work has been published in *Family Relations; Fathering: A Journal of Theory, Research, and Practice About Men as Fathers;* and the *Journal of Divorce & Remarriage.* She earned her PhD from The Ohio State University.

Michelle D. Sherman is a licensed clinical psychologist and Director of the Family Mental Health Program at the Oklahoma City Veterans Affairs Medical Center. She is a researcher with the South Central Mental Illness Research, Education and Clinical Center, and a clinical associate professor in the Department of Psychiatry and Behavioral Sciences at the University of Oklahoma Health Sciences Center. She has worked extensively with families dealing with traumatic experiences, including military combat, domestic violence, and sexual assault. She has published extensively in professional journals, primarily focusing on family issues surrounding trauma and mental illness. She is also the author of several books for teens whose parents have experienced mental illness or trauma. She earned her PhD from the University of Missouri, Columbia.

Pearl Stewart is an Associate Professor in the Department of Family and Child Studies at Montclair State University. Her research interests focus on African American families, specifically the importance of incorporating culture into work interventions for families and children and the needs and challenges of first-generation/or impoverished college students. Her work has been published in several scholarly journals including the *Journal of Human Behavior in the Social Environment, Families in Society, Journal of Family History,* and *Journal of Intergenerational Relationships.* She earned her PhD from the University of Delaware.

Katalin Toth is a graduate of the Interdisciplinary PhD Program in Social Psychology at the University of Nevada, Reno. Her research focuses on close relationships, commitment, and family interactions. She is currently examining divorce attitudes across the world and the relationship between division of domestic labor and marital satisfaction from a cultural perspective.

Jill K. Walls is a doctoral candidate in the Department of Human Development and Family Studies at the University of North Carolina at Greensboro. Her research focuses on intersections of work, family, and gender as they relate to maternal well-being, with consideration for how women's attitudes toward mothering shape their work and family experiences.

Jeremy B. Yorgason is Assistant Professor in the School of Family Life at Brigham Young University. His research interests pertain to later-life family relationships, with an emphasis on marriage and health, and daily health stressors caused by multiple chronic illnesses, with an emphasis on resilience. His work has been published in several professional journals including *Family Relations*, the *Journal of Marital and Family Therapy*, *Research on Aging*, *Journal of Aging Research*, and *Journal of Applied Gerontology*. He earned his PhD from Virginia Tech University and was a postdoctoral Fellow at the Gerontology Center of Pennsylvania State University.

Supporting researchers for more than 40 years

Research methods have always been at the core of SAGE's publishing program. Founder Sara Miller McCune published SAGE's first methods book, *Public Policy Evaluation*, in 1970. Soon after, she launched the *Quantitative Applications in the Social Sciences* series — affectionately known as the "little green books."

Always at the forefront of developing and supporting new approaches in methods, SAGE published early groundbreaking texts and journals in the fields of qualitative methods and evaluation.

Today, more than 40 years and two million little green books later, SAGE continues to push the boundaries with a growing list of more than 1,200 research methods books, journals, and reference works across the social, behavioral, and health sciences. Its imprints — Pine Forge Press, home of innovative textbooks in sociology, and Corwin, publisher of PreK–12 resources for teachers and administrators — broaden SAGE's range of offerings in methods. SAGE further extended its impact in 2008 when it acquired CQ Press and its best-selling and highly respected political science research methods list.

From qualitative, quantitative, and mixed methods to evaluation, SAGE is the essential resource for academics and practitioners looking for the latest methods by leading scholars.

For more information, visit **www.sagepub.com**.